Roger Audolott

Emmanuel Libra
Emmanuel S
Route 6
John

D1256498

A. M. Morris.

BS
647
.M67

15-3978

THE
PROPHECIES UNVEILED

OR

PROPHECY
A DIVINE SYSTEM

By

A. M. MORRIS

Author of "Evolution and Progression", "Lessons for the
Masses," and other Religious Works.

———

"Prove all things; hold fast that which is good."—*I Thess. 5:21*

———

1914
THE COURIER PRESS
Winfield, Kans.

INTRODUCTION

*T*HE WRITER of the Introduction to this edition of *Prophecies Unveiled* knew the author personally for a number of years, but he cannot pretend to an intimate friendship. However, he did know him well enough to appreciate him very much and to estimate him highly as a Christian gentleman, and a fine scholar. The first contact he had with this work was when he was just a young man starting out in the ministry of the Word. At that time Brother A. M. Morris lived in Kansas, and was a nationally known Bible student and preacher. He was famous for his general knowledge of the Bible covering the entire volume from Genesis to Revelations. Brother Morris for a long number of years taught the whole range of Scripture in protracted teaching schools that were designated "Bible Readings". They were an unique thing, now nearly discontinued, but in those days for half a century or more they were conducted by a number of able men; and among them none abler than Brother Morris. There was but little of study in these courses besides the Bible itself. For a number of years before this work was produced Brother Morris had covered the entire range of prophecy time and time again in these Bible Readings, and long and careful study besides was given to preparation of the course, of which prophecy was the heart.

For some years before he passed on Brother Morris was editor of *The People's Bible Advocate*. This periodical carried much of his fine thoughts for a wide range of admirers.

During his latter years, Brother Morris made his home at Long Beach, California. There he died and was laid to rest in the Inglewood, California, cemetery. The writer was present at that funeral. An old friend, W. P. Reedy, preached the funeral. J. J. Hogan, also a long time friend, participated in the funeral. On a gentle slope, under a shading evergreen, and amidst perpetual green his mortal remains was laid to rest.

This particular copy from which this edition is reproduced was given to this writer by Brother John Fretwell, then in his eightieth year, at Creswell, Wonskop, Nottinghamshire, England, in the year 1947, while the writer was on his second period of work among the churches in the British Isles. Some years before the writer had met Brother Fretwell's Brother, Godfrey, in New Zealand.

31169

It was rather odd that this particular copy had crossed the sea, and now has recrossed it to appear through lithography before you, gentle reader. But it is a book worthy to have made such a journey, and to have come down to you.

It is not to be taken for granted that the editor of the Old Paths Book Club necessarily endorses every turn of prophecy that is expressed in this work. Perhaps there is not a man in the world who will one hundred per cent endorse every statement made by any writer on the subject of prophecy. It is indeed a fertile field for critical research, and even brilliant turns of fancy, resting, as they should upon some little foundation of fact; and which may here have the wondrous outreaching that poets, having imbided the *divine afflatus*, use to scale the ladders of the sky and to vault into the eons of the unfulfilled years. In prophesy God the Eternal has seen fit to draw away a bit the vast curtains of the ages for mortal man to catch a glimpse of things which shall be. Great minds have striven to penetrate into the outreaching caverns of time. The Apostle Peter said that even angels had desired to look into some things that were spoken before the time of Christ. And of course great hearts, sanctified by the truth, have wished to know the things which God has in store for the sons of men. Among these great hearts and strong minds was Brother A. M. Morris.

It is a real pleasure to perpetuate the works of a Bible scholar, so that we may extend the influence of one who so quietly rests, in mortal frame, in a beautiful spot in sunny Southern California. "His works do follow after." Whether you agree with certain interpretations or not, you will be enriched by the careful persual of this volume, in which he set down, while in mortal life, the things that intrigued him; not with mere wanton fancy, but in sanctified devotion to the Judge of all men, and the One Who moves adown the years, unconscious of the passing of time while He adjusts the eternal spirits of men to a celestial paradise where He Himself dwells.

JOHN ALLEN HUDSON

HOLLYWOOD, CALIFORNIA
JULY 1952

Reproduced and Distributed by

THE OLD PATHS BOOK CLUB

BOX V
ROSEMEAD, CALIFORNIA
SPRING, 1952

PREFACE

The writer cannot remember the time when he did not love to read and meditate upon the Bible. Its prophecies, types and promises in the Old Testament are largely fulfuilled in history in the Two Testaments. Circumstances have made it possible for the author to devote almost his whole time, for the last quarter of a century, to the study and interpretation of the Bible from Genesis to Revelation. Large classes of students have been conducted through these sacred pages, year by year, and each chapter and each verse of prophecy have been passed under review many times. Our sole aim has been to acquire that very meaning in reading that the prophets gave in writing the prophecies. I acknowledge, first of all, the blessing of our Heavenly Father in all things. His marvellous goodness has attended us in all "our work of faith and labor of love;" and "blessed be his glorious name forever!" I express the highest degree of appreciation for the services of my faithful and uncomplaining Christian helpmeet, without whose loving services this volume could never have been written. And with feelings of gratitude to all generous friends I greet you with a new book.

But, you may wish to know my apology for writing a book on the prophecies, when there are so many already sown broadcast over the land. It is not difficult to explain the whole matter. There are the Jews; and there are the Millennialists. The Jews rest almost wholly upon a traditional interpretation of the ancient prophecies for their hope of the future as a nation. The Millennialists, especially Pre-Millennialists, do the same thing. It is this fact primarily that led me to write the following chapters. Having learned that prophecy is a divine system reaching from the garden of Eden to the eternal ages, and perceiving many years ago that neither the

Jews, who reject Christ, nor any class of Millenialists were governed by that system in interpretation, the writer was led to prepare a series of lectures on the chief items of the System of prophecy, showing how the prophecies are mutually related to that system or form component parts thereof. There has been a growing interest in the study of prophecy in the last few years, and many have become bewildered in the romancing methods of interpretation adopted by the Millennialists. We live in an Era of prophetic fulfillment and many are the theories set forth (all propfessedly founded in prophecy) concerning the immediate future.   Some tell us "It is the end of time; the Lord is at our doors and eternity will soon dawn upon the entire human family." A very large class of expositors are heralding the near approach of the "Son of man," to resurrect the martyred dead, and reign on earth one thousand years.   Millennial Dawnism gathers up the oft-exploded theory of Second Chanceism, and, by appealing to the imagination, weaves a theory of Millennial glory presided over by Christ and the New Testament saints as "sons" on earth in invisible spirit-bodies; and the Old Testament saints resurrected and reigning visibly as "servants" in the kingdom now being set up.   This system set forth by Mr. C. T| Russell receives ample notice in this volume.   When the manuscript was almost completed, my attention was directed to a series of articles in a religious Journal from the pen of Mr. A. J. Battenfield, and a brief review of these will be found at the close of this volume.   You will find this book is not a sensational document.   It treats the subjects set forth in the index with frankness and candor, and is a careful review of the great System of Prophecy, intended to be useful, not for a day, but permanently.   It considers Test-Prophecies, Type-Prophecies and Time-Prophecies, and by a liberal induction of Scripture proof, seeks to lead all lovers of truth who peruse its pages, into appreciation of the well-accredited fact that our God is in the history of nations.   The writer has had the "common people" in mind on every page, and has accommodated the teaching, both in matter and manner, to them, avoiding technical terms to the utmost. I have said, we live in an Era of prophetic fulfillment, and this deserves emphasis in this place.   Nearly all of

the schemes of interpretation, which either in our days or
in the past, have been sent forth to herald the near-
approach of Christ's second coming have been founded
on Time-Prophecies. The authors have assumed to cal-
culate that great event from some date in the past and
have blundered into the imagination that the end was
near even at the doors.   In this volume it is clearly
shown that the Time-Prophecies were not given to mark
the time when our Lord returns and that "no man knoweth the day nor the hour when the son of man cometh."
The very fact that Time-Prophecies were given, to measure off along the pathway of the ages, the great events
concerning nations and Empires, and the destiny of
God's people as related to those governments, proclaims
in no uncertain way that the Time-Prophecies were to
serve as cumulative proofs from age to age, of the inspiration of the Bible. They were to take the place of
living prophets and miracle workers, in the ages after
those ceased. Miracles could be seen by only a few at
any time; but fulfilled prophecy is a miracle of mind
that may be seen by all, as age after age adds that
measure of fulfillment then due; so that all the miraculous evidences of the divine authorship of the Bible will
not be given, until all its promises, types and prophecies
are fulfilled. It has been a growing conviction with the
author for many years, that the veil of tradition, cast
over the prophecies by the Jews, was being fastened
there by the method of literal interpretation given by
Millennialists to that portion of the Jewish prophecies
that foretold a restoration of the Israelites to the favor
of God. This veil is removed in the volume you now
hold in your hand. The treatment of that subject I
apprehend, will go far towards clearing up the mystery
that hangs over prophecy to the generality of man-kind.
The prophecies were written to be understood by both
Jews, and Gentiles; else why were they ever given to
the world? The great moral lessons are highly profitable, it is true, and a source of continual blessing to all
sincere inquirers after truth. But the predictions in the
main, especially those that relate to the present and to
the future fortunes of the Jews and the saints of God,
are enveloped in impenetrable obscurity to very many.
I have dared challenge the whole method of interpreta-

tion adopted generally in the interpretation of these predictions and have shown that the *types are legislated away
forever.* Fleshly Israel were a typical people. Their
land, tabernacle, priesthood, sacrifices, feasts, king, the
manna, the water from the smitten rock, their deliverance from Egypt, and the conquest and possession of
Canaan, were all typical. This whole system of types
ceased to be effective in that nation when the Gospel of
Christ went into effect. Hence, the primary question to
be determined is as to the nature, purpose, and duration
of these heavenly ordained types. Each type was, in an
important sense, a prophecy. It was not an end, but a
means to an end. When we have learned that these
types were local in nature and not universal; that is were
for the fleshly descendants of Abraham and only for a
given time, this limitation as to those who lawfully used
them and the time when they were to cease even for
them, prepares the way as nothing else can to understand the prophecies relating to the same time and people
and to their later history.

Is it not self-evident that if the types ceased with
the introduction of the gospel, that all prophecy must
and does harmonize with that controlling fact? my
position is that Israel has no authority from God to revive a single type given to them by Moses; and hence the
whole interpretation of Millennialists that predicates a
reign of Christ upon earth with his saints upon this tradition of the Jews, that they shall reign in a material
kingdom, is false in premise, argument and conclusion.
The veil must be removed from prophecy. Then the
Jews will come to Christ, neither desiring nor expecting
an earthly kingdom of glory such as once rose into dominion in the days of David and Solomon. I charge all
Millennialists with the far-reaching error of reading the
prophecies through Jewish tradition. If this point is
seen in its clearness, as illustrated by the lives and labors
of Christ and the apostles, who would not suffer Gentile
Christians to have Moses' law bound upon them, we
are then in a fair way to understand the prophets. I
request a patient reading of my message and diligent
comparison with the Sacred Text and think we may get
along admirably together. There is no flattery for speculators, nor unkind criticism, but an honest and earnest

effort to make this work useful to all. I believe it is greatly needed to head off the flood of speculations sweeping over the land, and cherish the fond hope that it may be the means, under God's blessing, of unveiling the prophecies, and showing them forth as a divine system, to the delight and profit of many sons and daughters of our wounded and dying race.

I will not be surprised if this production is criticised. It would be a marvel if it were not. I request three things of every reader. First, reserve a liberal margin for all mistakes and consider whether they are vital and fundamental errors or simply unavoidable errors in a human composition prepared piece-meal, and amidst many other duties and active labors. Second, wherein the document is criticised let it be in the fear of God. If the reader wishes to sustain the Literalists' position, and thinks I have not considered that method of interpretation, let him recall the fact that I have read the ablest authors and their masterpieces for a quarter of a century. Third, if you see clearly after the veil is removed which Jewish and Gentile speculators have thrown over these holy prophecies, then cooperate with the author of this volume in getting it before the largest possible number of Jews and Gentiles as a means of aiding the honest-hearted seekers after truth in finding the right way of the Lord.

"Prove all things; hold fast that which is good."

THE AUTHOR.

INDEX

THE

PROPHECIES UNVEILED

OR

PROPHECY

A DIVINE SYSTEM

CHAPTER I.

EVIDENCE AND PRECEPT.

"The entrance of thy words giveth light, it giveth understanding to the simple." (Ps. 119:130). "Faith cometh by hearing and hearing by the word of God" (Rom. 10:17). But this light, understanding and faith come to us by comparing spiritual things with spiritual. Promises and their fulfillment, types and their anti-types, prophecies and their fulfillment in the facts of history, constitute a vast three-fold system of divine testimony. "A three-fold cord is not easily broken." Nothing but truth can resist the tooth of time. The Bible is indestructible. Time only serves to develop the truth of the Bible especially in its evidences. This is notably true of its prophecies. In a world of change it is unchanged. There are two great systems in the Bible, one evidential, the other preceptive. One proves to us the divine origin and authority of the Bible; the other gives the principles and duties to be observed by God's people, enforced as they are by that divine authority. The chief demand of one system is faith, hence the evidences are numerous. The other system demands obedience to God. The two systems are as distinct as the Osseous, Venous, Muscular, Nervous and Cutaneous systems of our bodies, and, withal, as inseparable. As these all blend to form the human body, so do the evidential and preceptive systems unite to make the Bible.

There can be no acceptable faith without obedience, and no obedience without faith. The law of God in every age has consisted of belief and practice, faith and obedience. The Faith rests upon testimony, and obedience grows out of authority. "We speak that we do know and testify that we have seen" sums up the whole. The Book speaks with the authority of God. It draws the line between truth and error, right and wrong, vice and virtue, with courage and absolute plainness. In this volume we are considering chiefly the evidential system set forth in prophecy.

FOUNDATION PROPHECY.

In Genesis (Ch. I) is a grand summary of Creation. The inspired account of the origin of the heavens, earth, plants, animals, and grasses, is concisely given. To each species of animals, and plants, grasses and trees, as well as to man was given a law of propagation "after his kind." This implies a sort of double miracle in creation—the production of the initials of each species of plants, animals and man, with the inherent power of reproduction. We need not tarry here to consider Evolution but make a few suggestions.

1. There is no such thing known as Transmutation of Species, that is, one species never develops into another. The whole evolutional theory collapses at this point. We may improve species by domestication, either among plants or animals but cannot produce new species. There is in each species a perfect type (originally given in creation) back towards which plants or animals may be developed. This fact may be made evident to the agriculturist and horticulturist as well as to the breeder of stock. The wisdom of man in domestication improves the species, but never goes so far as to evolve a new species of plants or animals from a lower species.

2. The above is abundantly proved by the fact that Hybreds are sterile, and are thus a living refutation of the evolutional theory that plants and animals have been

developed from the simple to the complex, from the lower
to the higher organism, or from the rudimentary forms
to the highest known forms.

3.   The soul of man, or the human mind, must be
accounted for.   The generation of mind and spirit out
of matter is not conceivable.   The nature, not the degree, of mind in all humanity is the same, just as the
nature of their bodies is the same in all.   We can not
assume the gradual growth of the *spirit* of man, through
countless years, from ante-cedent substances or existences, and they *material* in their properties and nature.
The mind of man or spirit was evidently a creation, not
an evolution.

4.   Lastly we may observe that the theory of evolution supposes a continuous chain of animal organisms,
connected by ordinary generation, but ascending higher
age after age, and all related; and as species grow out
of the lower into the higher, by improvement, natural
selection and the survival of the fittest, they approach
nearer to man, until ultimately man is evolved as the
culmination of the process.   But at what stage in the
process of development the mind of man was evolved no
one attempts to tell us.   Whence came reason? imagination? reflection? combination of ideas? memory? discrimination between different ideas? and that marvellous conscience?   To such questions evolution gives no answer.
I see no similarity between the soul and body of man,
one being material, the other spiritual, and the methods
employed by the Almighty in the creation of the body
and soul of man were as different as the things created.
(Gen. 2:7; Zech. 12:1).   In case of the body "dust" is
mentioned, and we know our bodies are material.   But
the spirit is a distinct entity, (as we consider at some
length later), and capable of existence separate from
the body.

THE LAWS OF REPRODUCTION.

Every plant and herb of the vegetable kingdom, and
every animal, bird, fish and reptile of the animal kingdom, descended from their original parents which were
created.   The trees had seed within themselves, and the
animals had the power of propagation.   Everything was

to bring forth "after its kind." This meant an enormous reproduction. Then men existing in this generation are lineal descendants of the first generation or the created pair. We may see by this that birds are all related, the fish related, animals related, and men related respectively, to their kind, in all countries and in all ages, as we ascend from the present back to the creation tracing effect from cause.

It is reassuring to see that the Bible, written by some forty authors, the first and last of whom were some sixteen centuries apart, is all related. As there are demonstrative proofs that plant life, animal life, and even human life, are all joined to their primitive heads, just so each book and each chapter of the Bible are interrelated. This is notably true of the prophecies. They constitute a system. In Genesis the predictions are as follows:

1. The seed of the woman shall bruise the serpent's head, and his head shall bruise his heel." (See Gen. 3:14, 15). This is the germ prophecy. It includes all that follow. It is an epitome, a summary, of all the succeeding prophecies. The whole Bible is the outgrowth of this prediction.

NOAH'S PROPHECY.

This prophecy survived the flood in Noah and his family and received an enlargement, initial unfoldment in Noah's prediction (Gen. 9:25:27), Cursed be Canaan: A servant of servants shall he be unto his brethren. And he said "Blessed be the Lord God of Shem and Canaan shall be his servant, God shall enlarge Japheth, and he shall dwell in the tents of Shem; and Canaan shall be his servant." Here we have another summary of history. This is the first distinct national prophecy. Bishop Newton and others have clearly shown the correspondence of the facts of history and the plain prediction of the revered prophet of God and "preacher of righteousness," the venerable Noah.

"THE CURSE UPON CANAAN."

It may not be amiss to cite the fact that Cain and Canaan lived seventeen centuries apart. Noah and hence Canaan his grandson were not descendants of Cain, but of Seth. The curse upon Canaan was not a repetition of the mark placed upon Cain. If the mark placed upon Cain was turning him into a black man, then there should be no black men now for his descendants perished in the Flood. It is presumption pure and simple to say that Canaan and his descendants were turned into negroes by the curse upon Canaan. Whence came the red men? brown men? yellow men? Paul tell us (Acts 17:26) as well as the Bible throughout, they descended through modifications and changes wrought by nature and habits, climate and other powerful agencies, from the originals of the race, Adam and Eve.

The mark upon Cain was not necessarily physical or visible, but was probably like the mark of degeneracy and slavery to sin mentioned (Rev. 13:16:17, Rom. 16: 17) or as the word is used in (Ezek. 9:4), as a mark known to the prophets of God. It was like Paul's instructions (in II Thess. 3:14), "And if any man obey not our word by this epistle, note that man, and have no company with him, that he may be ashamed." In each instance God notes or marks men in their relation to him.

CALL OF ABRAHAM.

Some four centuries after the Flood God took up the thread of prophecy given at Eden, and enlarged upon to Noah, and gave several details concerning Shem to his descendant Abram, while he dwelt in Ur of the Chaldees. (Gen. 12:1-3).

1. He was to leave his father's house, his country, and people, and go into a land which God would show him, which proved to be Canaan's territory.

2. God would bless him, make his name great and he should be a blessing.

3. He would make of him a great nation.

4. God would "bless" or "curse" men according to their attitude towards this "Friend of God."

5. Lastly in him and his "seed" should all families or nations of the earth be blest.

This prophecy is clearly linked with Shem, who

survived the Flood, and with Eve the "mother of all
living." Abraham lived one hundred years in Canaan's
territory. This prophecy kept him in the land. It was
repeated to him from time to time during that century,
and once it was confirmed to him by an oath, after he
had offered Isaac. This last great trial of his faith served as an eminent type of the death and resurrection of
Christ. Sacrifice was evidently of divine origin, as the
cases of Abel (Gen. 4, Heb. II:3, Rom. 10:17), and the
instance of Job's sacrifices (Job 1:5), of his comforters
(Job 4:8,9) and Abram (Gen 15:9-21, Gen. 22:1-19),
clearly show. All these, but especialy Isaac, typified the
sacrificial nature of Christ's death as "the Lamb of God
which taketh away the sin of the world." This was a
form of prophecy whose nature appeals to the heart.

SACRIFICE OF ISAAC.

God worked out some marvellous details of this
prophecy in Abraham's time.

1. Promised him a son, heir, even Isaac.
2. Promised him a land, Canaan.
3. Promised him a remote son, Jesus, as seen in
(Gen. 12:1-3, Gal. 3:16). Abram offered Isaac as a type
of the latter son Jesus, as a blessing in sacrifice, by
sacrificing his promised son and heir Isaac. As these
prophetic types would serve to establish the mission of
Jesus, we may pause to consider this *human* sacrifice in
outline and note some correspondences between Isaac and
Jesus (Gen. 22).

1. Isaac was a child of promise.
2. He was Abraham's only and well beloved son.
3. Isaac heired the promises of God.
4. God's covenant was with Isaac.
5. Isaac was made an offering to God.
6. Isaac was raised from the dead in a figure.

1. Jesus was promised for ages.
2. Jesus was the only begotten and well-beloved son of God.
3. Jesus heired the promises of God.
4. God's new covenant was with Jesus.
5. Jesus was called upon to die as a sacrifice.
6. Jesus was raised from the dead in fact.

7. Isaac returned to his father's house and took a bride.

8. Isaac heired all his father had.

9. Abraham's flesh and blood sons, not children by promise, received presents only.

10. The land of Canaan was typical.

7. Jesus returned to his Father's house as a bridegroom.

8. Jesus heired the name and glories he now enjoys.

9. We must be sons of God to heir through Christ.

10. Heaven is the anti-typical Canaan.

The verbal prophecies given to Isaac and later to Jacob, added few details to the ground covered in Eden—the germ or foundation prophecy, as it had been developed to Noah, and later to Abraham. But it was repeated (Gen. 26:1-5; Gen. 28: 10-15; Gen. 49: 10). In the latter Jacob was informed "the scepter shall not depart from Judah nor a law-giver from between his feet until Shiloh come and unto him shall the gathering of the people be." Thus we pass through Genesis from the creation to the flood 1656 years; to the call of Abraham 427 years; to the death of Joseph 286 years; or 2369 years. This is more than half way from the creation to Christ. Genesis covers a longer period of history than all the rest of the Old Testament combined. All these prophecies are united. They all grew out of the condition of man as a sinner in need of a Savior. Hence the promised "Seed of the woman" the predicted blessing upon Shem after the Flood, and the oft repeated promises made to Abraham, Isaac and Jacob, that through their seed or descendant (Christ-Gal. 3:16) all the families of the earth should be blessed. As an unbroken genealogy runs down from Eve to Shem (Gen. 5); from Shem to Abram (Gen. 11) or for twenty generations and thereafter is preserved to Joseph, (Matt. 1) and to Mary (Luke 3), to identify the "seed of the woman" as Jesus of Nazareth, so the prophecies were given from time to time verbally as we have seen, and also typically in the sacrificial system as we have suggested.

In the succeeding chapters we may see that the original prophecy was never ignored, but grew and expanded, in the second two thousand years as it had done in the first two thousand years recorded in Genesis. It continued in Abrham's family and whole books were written concerning it. We hope to trace it down to David another thousand years, and thence to Daniel and the last prophets of the Old Testament. The fact that many nations spring up in our pathway as we make this mental pilgrimage of the ages, and some feature of the cumulative prophecy relates to them, increases our task, but the research abundantly rewards us, for we find "God in the history of our world." We may tnus see that prophecy is a majestic system, and a miracle of mind as much as raising the dead is a miracle of power.

CHAPTER II.

THE BLESSING AND THE CURSE.

In taking an extended view of the prophecies as a system we should observe the "blessing" and the "curse." In (Gen.3:14-15) it is said that enmity should be between the serpent and the woman, between his seed and her seed. Seed here refers to children. There is probably no question that the old serpent, the devil and Satan (and his children) are meant, in one member of this prophecy, and Jesus and his followers chiefly in the other. The enmity however is of early origin and manifestation. The children of the wicked one have ever and always been persecutors of God's children, even Abel being slain by his brother.

"Not as Cain who was of that wicked one and slew his brother. And wherefore slew he him, because his own works were evil and his brother's righteous." (1 Jno. 3:12).

Here we learn that Cain was of that wicked *One*. The same facts are in evidence in (John 8:44; Rev. 12:9; 20:2; II Cor. 11:3). Here we have the Liar, Murderer, the old Serpent, Deceiver, full of subtility, and Jesus charged the wicked Jews of being his children——the children of the devil.

ILLUSTRATIONS.

When we reached the days of Noah in studying the prophecies we saw that the blessing was very extensive, as given to Shem, and the curse rested upon Canaan, whose seven sons grew into seven tribes or nations in the land of Canaan or Palestine. Thus we see as nations advanced in their history, they could look back into any period of their origin (as the Canaanites in Moses' day, for instance could trace their history back to Canaan, the fourth son of Ham, the son of Noah). So the Bible can compare their history with the particular phophecy given to or concerning them. Just as the topmost twig of the tallest oak owes its life and origin to the little acorn hidden in the earth, or the mightiest river may be traced back to the little spring far away that is its source. In the latter instance, the fact that a multitude of creeks and rivulets feed the majestic river in its course to its destiny in the sea, but illustrates more beautifully the fact that often other prophets arose and poured the wealth of their inspired minds into the prophetic current, increasing the volume of the original prophecy, and marking out the channel through which the predicted nation was to pass to its final destiny.

You will see therefore the two-fold nature of these related prophecies as they each contain a *"blessing"* and a *"curse."*

BLESSING UPON ABRAHAM.

To Abram God said: "I will bless them that bless thee and curse him that curseth thee." (Gen. 12). This same language was repeated to Isaac and later to Jacob. (Gen. 26 and Gen 27:29).

We should observe that several hundred years later Balaam sought to curse Israel but blessed them on three occasions, and almost in these words. (Num. Chs. 22 to 24). In (Deut. Chs. 27 to 30) Moses sets forth this subject in one of the greatest warnings and entreaties to obey God, given in the entire Old Testament. He pronounces the blessings for obedience and the curses for dis-obedience, the greatest in number, ever spoken by man concerning the fortunes of any nation. He provided that these blessings should be spoken to assembled Israel, likewise the curses, the former from Mt. Gerizim, the latter from Mt. Ebal, twin mountains near the center of Palestine, and all the people should respond "Amen" to each of them. The prosperity or adversity of Israel, as a nation has conformed to these warnings and entreaties. From any period of their history their condition could be traced back to these blessings or curses.

As a general principle this rule of God is set forth by two prophets (Jer. 18 and Ezek. 18).

GOD IN HISTORY.

We shall study the history of a few of the ancient nations, in their relation to the provisions of this prophecy and thus direct the reader to a subject of primary import-ance in investigating the history of nations. They were each and all embraced in these prophecies. These things are in the Bible, both the prophecies and, in a large measure, their fulfillment. By what other method of in-quiry can we satisfy ourselves that we have the true facts of the case, but by a careful induction of the prophecies relative to a specified people, and the history that follows as a demonstration of the veracity of the prophet? It is a delightful task we set ourselves, to pass in review the nations as God's ancient prophets knew them, enter into sympathy with these prophets, read their clear predic-tions, and pass on down the centuries and read the ful-fillment of these predictions both in sacred and profane history.

We should not mistake that these nations were blessed as they blessed Abraham and cursed as they cursed him. Was this an arbitrary "blessing" or "curse"? In no wise, rather Abraham believed in and worshipped the true God. As peoples and nations were like-minded God consistently blessed them: and as they turned away from the worship of God to Idols he cursed them. *The same rule held true with Abraham's fleshly descendants, and their history is a mournful testimony to the fact that "righteousness exalts a nation but sin is a reproach unto any people."*

The attitude of the world towards God determined the prosperity or adversity of the nations. This fact is primary and should preface our examination of the "blessings" and "curses" attending the nations that are marshalled before us in the Bible, whose history in origin, continuance and often the end, are clearly set before us on the sacred pages, and is as plain as the history of our own country. God is and always has been in the history of nations, and the proof of this is reiterated in the Bible that we can make no mistake in refernece to this great fact. The purpose of the writer of this book is to show this fact to every reader.

MOABITES AND AMMONITES.

These people were the descendants of Lot and lived throughout their national history near neighbors to Israel. They went into idolatry very early and became a besotted people like the Sodomites from whose city Lot was delivered when it was overthrown for wickedness, (Gen. 19). They did not like to retain God in their knowledge and cast off the worship of the High and Holy One, who inhabits eternity, and worshipped idols. They were enemies of the Jews and the Jewish prophets denounced the righteous judgment of God against these nations. They consequently fell under the "curse" (Is. 17:2). "The cities of Aroer are forsaken: they shall be for flocks, which shall lie down, and none shall make them afraid.

"I have heard the *reproach* of Moab, and the *revilings* of the children of Ammon, *whereby they have reproached my people*, and magnified themselves against their border. *Therefore* as I live, saith the Lord of hosts, the God of Israel, surely Moab shall be as Sodom and the children of Ammon as Gomorrah, even the breeding of nettles, and saltpits, and a perpetual desolation: The residue of my people shall spoil them, and the remnant of my people shall possess them. This shall they have for their *pride*, because they have reproached and magnified themselves against the people of the Lord of hosts. The Lord will be terrible unto them: *for he will famish all the gods of the earth*: and men shall worship him, everyone from his place, even all the isles of the heathen." (Zeph. 2:8:11).

Ponder well these sacred utterances. Notice how Moab and Ammon, two nations bordering Israel were united in wickedness and inseparable in punishment.

"Though hand join in hand the wicked shall not be unpunished: but the seed of the righteous shall be delivered." Of Moab it was said, "For because thou hast trusted in thy works, and in thy treasures thou shalt also be taken, and Chemosh shall go forth into captivity, with his priests and his princes together, and the spoiler shall come upon every city and no city shall escape: the valley also shall perish, and the plain shall be destroyed, as the Lord hath spoken." "Make ye him drunken: for he *magnifieth himself against the Lord*: Moab also shall wallow in his vomit, and he also shall be in derision. For was not Israel a derision unto thee? was he found among thieves? For since thou speakest of him thou skippest for joy." "And Moab shall be destroyed from being a people, because he *magnifieth himself against the Lord,*" (Jer. 48:7, 8, 9, 10, 42).

I scarcely think it necessary to comment upon these plain prophecies. The " curse" was visited upon them for their wickedness *against the Lord and his people*. The cities of Moab are all gone down under the curse of God, as manifestly as did Sodom and Gomorrah. The whole territory is strewn with ruins of ancient cities and towns, Aroer, Dibon,, Eleale, Medaba, Meon, Heshbon, each of which flourished in the days of Moses and later, all show that the prophets which "spake as they were moved by the Holy Spirit" gave the ultimate judgment, and assigned the holy reason why these cities are now mouldering away. They nearly all wear their ancient names, and by imagination one can retrace the centuries and go back to the source of these calamities and find it in *their hatred of God and his people*, and learn the certainty of their doom was predicted by the prophets.

REFLECTIONS ON THE ABOVE.

If you have read the Bible as you would read any other book, from the beginning to the end, this will all be plain and convincing. It is God's argument. It cannot be duplicated by any merely human author. As God lived from Adam to Moses, from Moses to the prophets, from the prophets to Christ and onward, he could use men as he saw fit, some as prophets, others as historians. We follow the unfolding of his great purpose when we read his Book and learn that he saw the end from the beginning. If one attempts to unwind a ball of yarn by breaking threads he will fail; but if he will get hold of the right thread it will unwind easily. If one reads the Bible prophetically and historically it un-rolls before him in all its beauty and grandeur. He finds it to be a great system and he has only to study the *individual* prophecies in their connection with the whole system. You will observe that as time passed and new nations arose and came in contact with Israel, the people whom God had chosen that his name might dwell among them, these newly-risen nations were found to be sub-jects of prophecy, given ages before——the "blessing" and the "curse" awaited all nations. True the prophets of God, living in the particular time of these newly risen nations, were usually chosen of God to enlarge upon these ancient prophecies, unfold the meaning and give the true application of the provisions of the ancient proph-ets; but their warnings, exhortations and fervent appeals to fear God and obey him, were in harmony with the law of God as spoken and written by their predecessors. This lesson has been seen in the case of Ammon and Moab.

"Son of man, set thy face against the Ammonites and prophesy against them; and say unto the Ammonites, hear the word of the Lord God; because thou saidst Aha against my sanctuary when it was profaned; and against the land of Israel when it was desolate; and against the house of Judah when they went into captivity; behold, therefore I will deliver thee to the men of the East for a possession, and they shall set their palaces in thee, and make their dwellings in thee, they shall eat thy fruit and they shall drink thy milk.

And I will make Rabbah a stable for camels, and the Ammonites a couching place for flocks; and ye shall know that I am the Lord. For thus saith the Lord God; because thou hast clapped thy hands and stamped thy feet, and rejoiced in heart with all thy despite against the land of Israel: behold therefore, I will stretch out my hand against thee, and will deliver thee for a spoil to the heathen: and I will cut thee off from the people and I will cause thee to perish out of the countries: I will de-stroy thee, and thou shalt know that I am the Lord." (Ezek. 25:2-7).

I give this quotation in full that the reader may see *why the "curse"* came upon the *Ammonites.* (See also Ezek. 21:28-32).

FOREORDINATION.

These nations did not inherit either a blessing or a curse only as they voluntarily chose to live a certain life. They were not fore-doomed or predestinated to ruin as you see. Their doom was predicted to come on them when their sins deserved it. Before that time, while the curse had been pronounced in general against them, it had not been spoken directly either against Moab or Ammon, and whether they should be blessed or cursed remained to be determined by their attitude toward God and his rightful authority. In this fact we see the mercy of God, not dooming any nation to destruction only as they were in rebellion against him. The blessing was to induce them to follow the right, and the curse was to dissuade them from following the wrong, and this urged them to choose the right and live. The appalling fact that so many nations forsook God, adopted idolatry, and became the enemies of God does not in the least modify this statement. Israelites themselves were under the same rule, and probably the majority of that people from Joshua to the Babylonian captivity chose to be idolaters, and thus inherited the curse, forfeited their land inheritance in Palestine, and were finally driven from the land. Yet they were entreated by all the holy prophets God raised up from time to time, and had the authoritative predictions of Moses their law-giver, who gave them the conditions of blessings and of curses, as cited above, to hold them to the right way that they might inherit a blessing. All of which should speak to us in thunder tones, emphasizing the fact that God's favor can only be secured and maintained by those who love and obey him. But as the Jews come up for large notice in later chapters, it may suffice at this time to suggest to the reader that the grant to them of peaceful inheritance in Palestine during their continuance, as a national distinction as the people of God, was predicated upon their obedience to God. As other nations were to be blessed or cursed upon the conditions already specified, so, too, the fleshly descendants of Abraham were shut up to the alternative of giving up the land of promise or of obeying God. Nothing could be further from the facts than to say Canaan was the inalienable home of Abraham's posterity, regardless of their attitude towards God.

"See I have set before thee this day life and good, death and evil: in that I command thee this day to love the Lord thy God, to walk in his ways, to keep his statutes, and his commandments, and his judgments, that thou mayest live and multiply, and the Lord thy God *shall bless thee in the Land* whither thou goest to possess it.

But if thine heart turn away, so that thou wilt not hear, but shalt be drawn away and worship other gods and serve them: I denounce unto you this day that you shall surely perish, and that ye *shall not prolong your days upon the land* whither thou passest over Jordan to possess it. I call heaven and earth to record this day against you, that *I have set before you life and death, blessing and cursing.* Therefore chose life that thou and thy seed shall live. That thou mayest love the Lord thy God and that thou mayest obey his voice, and that thou mayest cleave unto him; for he is thy life and the length of thy days: *That thou mayest DWELL* in the land which the Lord sware unto thy fathers to Abraham, to Isaac, and to Jacob to give thee." (Deut. 30:15:20).

Here is the language of the law-giver Moses, to Israel on the borders of Canaan ready to go over Jordan to possess the land. Nothing could be plainer than the fact that a "blessing" for obedience, and a "curse" for disobedience accompanied Israel in their taking possession of Palestine. *By disobedience to God they would inherit the "curse", which entailed the forfeiture of the land,* as obedience would insure to them the land throughout their generations or while the typical age lasted.

CHAPTER III.

ISHMAEL

The first angelic visitation recorded in the Bible was to Hagar, Sarah's hand-maid. Her son was named Ishmael, before he was born, a distinction belonging to Isaac. Cyrus, John (the baptist) and Jesus our Lord. He was the subject of a distinct verbal prophecy at that time, and another made to his father Abraham, when he was thirteen years of age. The latter says,

"As for Ishmael, I have heard thee, behold I will *bless* him, and will make him fruitful, and will multiply him exceedingly; twelve princes shall he beget, and I will make him a great nation." (Gen. 17:20).

When Isaac was weaned, at the feast made by Abraham, Ishmael, born after the flesh, mocked Isaac, who was born after the spirit, the whole narrative of which Paul declares to be an allegory (Gal. 4:21-31). Hagar and Ishmael were sent away with bread and water because of this persecution, while Isaac heired all that his father had. This illustrates David's remark when praying to be delivered from the wicked, "Men of the world who have their portion in this life," as he was only expecting his satisfaction, "when I awake with thy likeness." (Ps. 17:14-15). The men of the world today have in their "lifetime their good things," but do not become "heirs of God and joint-heirs with Jesus Christ." There was a national blessing pronounced upon Ishmael because he was Abraham's son. But these blessings, when given after this manner, were modified and limited. For instance, Ishmael in no case would be permitted to take the rank of Isaac the son of a free woman—"In Isaac shall thy seed be called." This did not mean that Ishmael and all his descendants were lost, or that Isaac and all his descendants were saved. The election or ordination of Isaac and the rejection of Ishmael were not with reference to heaven and hell. But as one of Adam's sons must be selected to be the progenitor of Christ, related to him according to the flesh, Seth was chosen:

of Noah's three sons, Shem was chosen: of Terah's three sons Abram was chosen, of Abraham's two sons Isaac was chosen: of Isaac's twin sons Jacob was chosen: of Jacob's twelve sons Judah was chosen: of Jesse's eight sons David was chosen.   These all were chosen of God to transmit the promise in their own person that the "seed of the woman should bruise the serpent's head." The selection of a man to carry down this genealogy, did not certify that he would be a good man, and finally reach heaven.   Read the history of the kings of Judah and learn that most of them were far from being good men, and some of them were idolaters and violent persecutors of God's obedient ones, though all were ancestors of Christ.   The blessing upon these nations was in temporal things chiefly, and the curse was chiefly temporal. The lesson presented to us nevertheless is one of solemn import.   The history of Ishmael is an illustration in this group, and bears witness to the fact that Moses was a true prophet of God, in that he recorded these predictions concerning Ishmael, one given to his father when he was thirteen years of age.   Ishmael received circumcision the same day his aged father submitted to the rite, and was thus included in the terms of the covenant, noted above as temporal.   Many nations trace their history back to Abarham.

1.   The nation of Israel, his descendants through Isaac.

2.   The Ishmaelites, his descendants through Ishmael (Gen. 17:20).

3.   The Edomites, descendants of Abraham through his grandson, Esau (Gen. 36).

4.   The Midianites, his posterity through Midian. (Gen. 25:2).   The Samaritans were a mixed people. (2 Kings. 17:24).

6.   The Amelakites were probably descendants of Esau's son Amalek (Gen. 36:16).

To these might be added the Ammonites and the Moabites descendants of his nephew, Lot, and violent persecutors of Israel.

Here are eight nations, whose history was parallel from the early days after Abraham, all for more than a thousand years, some for nearly two thousand, while

Ishmael and Isaac are still in existence, both a circumcised people, and the Arabs still living in tents, and preserving, in a marked degree, their primitive mode of life. One becomes familiar with these nations in studying the Sacred Volume, and they prove that Abraham was the father of many nations:

"Neither shall thy name any more be called Abram, for a father of many nations have I made thee; and I will make thee exceeding fruitful, and I will make nations of thee and kings shall come out of thee." (Gen. 17:5, 6).

Suppose we were able to add all of these nations together and have a list of all their kings, the sum would be very great. These nations as recorded in history prove that God blessed Abram, as He gave him all these nations except one after he was ninety years old; and the history of these nations showed the blessing, and the curse in constant operation. Our citations and quotations are necessarily limited in number and extent, and intended to excite interest in the study of prophecy, rather than to detail prophecies and their marvellous fulfillments concerning all these nations. It is manifest that God dealt with the nations on principles of righteousness and justice, and this lesson is written in letters of light on the Biblical history; while human historians usually overlook God and his prophecies and attribute their success or failure in war wholly to strategy, heroism and military strength or to their absence. Pharoah counted God out; Sennecherib counted God out; and infidelity always counts Him out. But the nations passing in review before us demonstrate their folly. It is not the battle of a day we are considering, but the composite history of nations, stretching through ages, subject to the pleasure or displeasure of God, and illustrating his sovereign power and disposition to bless or curse them as he originally foretold in these prophecies.

THE PROPHECY OUTLINED.

In (Gen. 16 and 17 ch's) is given a prophecy concerning Ishmael. He was to be the father of twelve princes and become a great nation because he was the son of Abram. He would be a wild man, his hand against every man and every man's hand against him, and he should dwell in the presence of all his brethren (Gen. 16:13). The primary facts in the fulfillment of this prophecy are given (Gen. 25:12-18), as the names of the twelve sons of Ishmael are recorded by Moses. The

Ishmaelites are found as we progress in the history of Israel, sometimes under the name of Hagarines, named after Hagar. Joseph was sold to a band of Ishmaelites. Emphasize the word "Band" and you sound the keynote of their history. They were known as Nabatheans from his son Nebaioth; Itureans from his son Itur or Jetur, and are known in history as Saracens. They became a great nation, and like the Hebrews continue to this day. The Arabs are the descendants of Ishmael, and Mahomet, who figures in history as the founder of a religion that over-ran a large part of the world, and established an empire that is still one of the great powers of the world, professed to be the son of Abraham through Ishmael. As the descendants of Ishmael still exist, not only a distinct people, but exhibiting all the characteristics of the founders of the nation, thirty eight centuries ago, it is wise to search the only Book that has come down in history from that remote age and learn that God is in history. They dwell in the land of their fathers, and subsist largely by preying on others, or by robbery. They are in a territory inaccessible to other people, and as a whole, have never been conquered. The Israelites, Edomites, Moabites, and Ammonites, lived on the borders of Arabia, but could not wholly subdue them, "They dwelt in the presence of their brethren." The Egyptians, the Persians, the Greeks, and the Romans all failed to conquer the Ishmaelites. Their skill as horsemen and ability to endure the intense heat of the vast plains, their familiarity with the location of water and shrubbery (for there is little or no tillage), and their universal rule to unite against all peoples for pillage and plunder, constitute them the rulers of the desert. Among conquerors they take very high rank. They over-ran a large part of the old world and for ages were masters of most of the learning of the world.

REMARKS BY NEWTON.

Bishop Newton says, "Ishmael was circumcised when he was thirteen years old, so were the Arabs at the same age, according to Josephus. He was born of Hagar, who was a concubine; and they still indulge themselves in the use of mercenary wives and concubines. He lived in tents in the wilderness shifting from place to place; and so do his descendants, particularly those therefore called, Scenites formerly, and those called Bedouins at this day.

He was an archer in the wilderness; and so are they. He was the father of twelve tribes; and they live in clans or tribes to this day. He was a wild man and every man's hand against him; and they live in the same state of war, their hand against every man and every man's hand against them. This I say is somewhat wonderful, that the same people should retain the same dispositions for so many ages; but it is still more wonderful, that with these dispositions, and this enmity to the whole world, they should stil subsist in spite of the world an independent and free people."

CHAPTER IV.

THE EDOMITES.

I present an extended notice of Esau the twin brother of Jacob, as an illustration of the manner in which these prophecies may be verified in history, both Sacred and Profane. No student of prophecy should rest satisfied with anything less on the other nations mentioned, although our space will not permit us to follow Ammon, Moab, Amalek, Syria, Assyria, Egypt and other nations so closely.

Moses preserved the prophecy concerning Esau, Abraham's grandson with the facts of his birth and growth into a nation and thus gives us a good start in witnessing the fulfillment of the predictions. And other writers of the Bible bring the history down age after age, and thus help to make the great Bible, with its unique argument. The birth of Isaac's twin sons, Esau and Jacob, is recorded in (Gen. 25). He gives Isaac's age as sixty years at their birth. The angel said to Rebecca, their mother, before they were born, "And the Lord said unto her, two nations are in thy womb, and two manner of people shall be separated from thy bowels; and the one people shall be stronger than the other people: and the elder shall serve the younger." The facts predicted were many and very great—they reached so far into the future. She was to bear twin children; those children were to live to manhood; they were to found two nations; one nation was to rule the other and be stronger than they.

If we drop down to the time of Christ or eighteen centuries, there are the twin brothers, in the person of their descendants—Jesus of Jacob, and Herod of Esau! Think of the thousand chances, humanly speaking, of one or more of these items failing to be realized! Yet the children were born and named Jacob and Esau. They were different physically, mentally and morally. Esau was a hairy man, became an expert hunter, was profane, a fornicator, married two heathen wives, and later one of Ishmael''s daughters, but was withal his father's favorite. Jacob was a "plain man" and beloved of his mother. Esau sold his birthright to Jacob "for one morsel of meat."

JACOB'S DECEPTION.

Jacob executed a deception on his father that had been planned, and to which he was incited by his mother, thus showing that he was capable of acting a deceptive part in what was an otherwise sacred transaction. It is plain that he was afterwards deceived by Laban, his father-in-law and his life embittered for many years. Many times people practice deception on others without conscience, but the wickedness of the course awakens them to horror when others choose to practice it upon them. The Lord did not need the deception of Rebecca and Jacob to carry out his purpose, neither did he approve of it, but bestowed the blessing as He had promised before they were born. We should not apologize for any one in this transaction. They were human. The historian records their conduct impartially. Human biographers extol the virtues and suppress the vices of their heroes. God's Word records faithfully the weaknesses and failings of the best of men. In the Bible we have the portraiture of character as it is in heaven's sight. We may rest assured that the representations of God, of Christ, of the Holy Spirit, of the angels of God, of the being and character of the devil, of demons; as well as the descriptions of heaven and of hell, are true. The Bible neither over-draws nor under-draws its pictures, so we should not try to change them.

ESAU IN SACRED HISTORY.

To follow him even in outline throughout his history is a task we can not set ourselves at this time, as it is foreign to the plan of this book. He settled in Mt. Seir, south of Palestine, and his nation was known as the Edomites. His people are brought down by Moses to his day, (Gen. 36), and a list of their kings recorded. We see in the case of Esau and Jacob that these ancient prophecies relate more to nations than to individuals.

"And David put garrisons in Edom; throughout all Edom put he garrisons and all they of Edom became David's servants." (2 Sam'l 8:14). Thus after some seven centuries these nations existed side by side, the elder made servant to the younger by David the warrior-king. The rivalry and cruelty of Edom were not able to keep his stubborn neck from the yoke. In this condition, a century and a half more rolled by and they were governed by deputies from Israel, or the younger son, as it had been predicted by their father eight hundred and fifty years before, (Gen. 27:27-29). In the days of Jehoram, king of Judah, they revolted and "made a king over themselves," (2 Kings 8:20). Later Amaziah, king of Judah,

"Slew of Edom in the valley of salt ten thousand and took Selah by war, and called the name of it Joktheel to this day" (2 Ks. 14:7). "And other ten thousand did the children of Israel carry away captive, and brought them to the top of the rock, and cast them down from the top of the rock, that they were all broken in pieces." (2 Chron. 25:12).

The Edomites were frequently made subject to the Jews, and the Hebrews were never the servants of the Edomites. Thus the prophecy was fulfilled for thirteen centuries as the sacred history, supplemented by Maccabees and Josephus abundantly shows in great detail. We find many prophecies strewn along their historical path, (Ezek. 25: 12-14; Jer. 49:7-22; Joel 3:19; Amos 1:11,12; and Obadiah entire;) all of which one should read carefully.

ESAU IN PROFANE HISTORY.

All travellers to the scenes of Esau's ancient greatness, certify us the fact that the land is utterly waste and desolate. The ruins of thirty cities are within three days journey of the Red Sea. At the time of the destruction of Jerusalem by the Romans the Edomites were nearly as numerous as the Jews. There is one phase of the prophecy we should not pass without particular notice—"None shall pass through it forever and ever. I will cut off from Mount Seir him that passeth out and him that returneth." (Is. 34:10; Ezek. 35:7). The descendants of Esau have perished from the earth. One century after Christ they passed out of history. Volney, Burckhard, Stevens and many others, with no desire to connect the facts concerning the former existence of populous cities, and of great highways through Edom, and the modern desolations with the ancient predictions, have given a vast amount of credible testimony showing the fulfillment of the prophecies concerning Edom. Perhaps it may be said that no territory on earth to-day, once inhabited, is as impenetrable as Idumea. A variety of obstacles await the traveller. The whole land is forbidding, because of its desert wastes, scarcity of water and intense heat and exposure to the tropical sun in summer. The territory abounds with fierce and ravenous beasts. The Arabs guard it from invasion with a degree of hostility scarcely paralleled. One can neither bribe nor compel guides to enter that territory. The country has had the line of emptiness and confusion stretched upon it. Broken walls, heaps of stones, and vestiges of paved roads, numerous tombs, ancient sepulchers, mausoleums, fragments of paved streets, columns, ruins of palaces, abound in the heart of that land. The Jews are in all lands but there is no man remaining to the house of Esau in any land. Why the difference in these twin sons of Isaac? They lived side by side for eighteen centuries. Edom sleeps in the grave yard of centuries today, by the side of Moab, Ammon, Amalek and others that rose up against Israel. The solitude of the tomb reigns over the naked walls of her emporiums of trade, while her deserted temples echo to the cry of the wild beast, and her palaces and theaters are never disturbed by the footfall of a descendant of the founder of the nation. Moses, Isaiah, Jeremiah, Ezekiel, Obadiah, Amos, Joel, Malachi, in turn, foretold the destiny of Edom. In the awe-inspiring ruin of that country and people the united voices of the prophets find their fulfillment. They said "Thus it shall be;" and from the loftiest mountain to the deepest cavern, and from the rude lips of her buried glory, there rises the hundred voiced chorus, "thus it is."

Esau married two heathen wives and also the daughter of Ishmael later, and thus set the example and led the nation founded by him into the path of superstition and wickedness that swallowed them up. They cast off all pity and cherished a perpetual hatred against the Israel of God. As nations become like the gods they worship, and Esau worshipped idols, conceived in the lusts of the flesh, their hope of success was doomed from the start, and they were under the curse of God. Yet, be it observed, that Isaac blessed him with "the fatness of the earth, and of the dew of heaven from above." These facts are in keeping with Esau's history. I can see no divine reason for giving so minutely the circumstances of Isaac's marriage, a whole chapter; the fact of Rebecca's barrenness for twenty years; the prediction concerning the children; and the somewhat chequered history of both men; and especially *why* distinct mention is made of Esau or Edom, and their relative strength, location geographically, and their attitude towards Israel, unless it was to show God in their history. I see that Esau and his descendants, the Edomites, appear on the scene, as we read the story of the Bible, just often enough, and pictured in just such enmity to God and his people, as to deserve a "curse" rather than a blessing; and, hence, before he was born, this fatal choice and conduct were foreseen and fore-told. The fact that the prediction was fulfilled, does not lead us to think that he and his people were shut up to fate or necessity, or had to be cruel, idolatrous, profane and merit a "curse." If I should see a child approach a lion, or ready to fall over a precipice, I might rather certainly predict his death, but my *prediction* would not *cause* his death. The child was free to act, and chose the wrong course perhaps in this case unconscious of danger. Fire will burn, poison will kill, water will drown, whether the person burned, poisoned or drowned knows the fact or not. Just so sin will degrade men, rob them of purity, nobility of purpose, and grandeur of achievement. "Reuben—unstable as water—thou shalt not excel." Typhoid fever will kill whether any physician is present to notify the patient of it or not. As death follows disease of the body, whether known or not beforehand; just so God's dealings with men are charged with consequences. To live so as to merit the curse insures its being visited upon the nation that demands the proof. In what other way could God have shown us *in this life*, his approval of men for obedience and his rejection of them for dis-obedience? *These matters having been worked out on a national scale, AND RECORDED FOR OUR ADMONITION, should prove salutary warnings to mankind in all succeeding ages.*

For my sword shall be bathed in heaven; behold, it shall come down upon Idumea, *upon the people of my curse, to judgment.* * * * * * From generation to generation it shall lie waste; none shall pass through it for ever and ever, but the cormorant and bittern shall possess it, the owl also and the raven shall dwell in it: and he shall stretch out upon it the line of confusion and the stones of emptiness. They shall call the nobles thereof to the kingdom, but none shall be there and all her princes shall be nothing. And thorns shall come up in her palaces, nettles and brambles in the fortresses thereof; and it shall be a habitation of dragons, and a court for owls. The wild beasts of the desert shall also meet with the wild beasts of the island, and the satyr shall cry to his fellow: The screech owl shall rest there and find for herself a place of rest. There also shall the great owl make her nest, and lay and hatch, and gather under her shadow: there shall the vultures be gathered, everyone with her mate. Seek ye out the book of the Lord and read: no one of these shall fail none shall want her mate [fulfillment] for my mouth it hath commanded, and the spirit it hath gathered them. And he hath cast the lot for them, and his hand hath divided it unto them by line: they shall possess it forever: from generation to generation shall they dwell therein." (Is. 34).

In this land of death today and for ages past, the truth of the Word of God has been witnessed to by the exact fulfillment of the prophecies.

CITY OF PETRA.

Petra, the long lost capital of Edom is known both to sacred and profane writers as the City of Rock. This city was hewed and chiseled out of solid rock; eight successive kings and numerous dukes reigned there" before

any king ruled over Israel" (Gen. 36). Three hundred
years after Malachi closed the Old Testament, or about
one hundred years before Christ, the king of Arabia issued from his palace at Petra at the head of fifty thousand men, horse and foot and entered Jerusalem, uniting
with the Jews. They pressed the siege of the temple,
which was only raised by the advance of the Romans;
and in the beginning of the second century, though its
independence was lost, Petra was the capital of a Roman
province. After that time it rapidly declined, its history
became more and more obscure, and for more than a
thousand years, it was lost entirely to the civilized world,
until in 1812 Burckhardt discovered it, (except it was
known to the Bedouins)." *Stevens.* Think of it! From
the earliest ages of recorded time, from the day when
Esau separated from his brother Jacob, this was Esau's
land.

"And Esau took his wives, and his sons and his
daughters, and all the persons of his house, and his cattle,
and all his beasts, and all his substance which he had got
in the land of Canaan; and went into the country from
the face of his brother Jacob. For their riches were
more than that they might dwell together; and the land
wherein they were strangers could not bear them because of their cattle. Thus dwelt Esau in Mount Seir;
Esau is Edom." (Gen. 36:6-8).

From this remote past the prophecy hung over him.
And now his capital city rises up to testify to the truth
of heaven. A city of rock, its temples, theaters, grottoes,
palaces, triumphal arches, dwelling houses, aqueducts, all
as enduring as the masonry of God, because hewn out of
solid rock, presenting one of the greatest lessons in the
whole world. A vast amphitheater surrounded by
mountains on all sides, in their native grandeur, lifting
their summits five or six hundred feet high, the city of
rock, the capital of Edom, lies in desolation. The tombs
and mausoleums in number and greatness testify to the
fact that long ages ago kings ruled in that land. Where
are they now? Shall we believe Moses and the prophets,
when we see a city as imperishable as the rock-ribbed
hills, her monuments of greatness forsaken, not a foot of
man to tread her streets, worship in her temples, visit her
theaters or live in her palaces? This city so singular, so
remote in origin, so rich in historical associations, so

beautiful in desolation, stands forth as a colossal monument to the veracity of the prophets of God. Who could ascend Mount Seir and look over that wide stretch of barren waste, almost destitute of trees and verdure, the ancient highways deserted and buried beneath the accumulated sands of ages; the barren mountains lifting their summits like sentinels to the skies and the nation of Esau asleep in death at his feet, and doubt the voice of the prophets? I close in the words of Ezekiel, uttered six centuries before Christ, when Edom took rank with the surrounding nations, and pressed along the course of his national career, cursing and persecuting Israel, unmindful of the curse of God and the threatened doom awaiting him.

"Moreover the word of the Lord came unto me saying, son of man set thy face against Mount Seir, and prophesy against it, and say unto it, thus saith the Lord God, behold, O Mount Seir, I am against thee and I will stretch out mine hand against thee, and I will make thee most desolate. I will lay thy cities waste and thou shalt be desolate; and thou shalt know that I am the Lord. Because thou hast had a perpetual hatred and hast shed the blood of the children of Israel by the force of the sword in the time of their calamity, in the time that their iniquity had an end: therefore as I live, saith the Lord God, I will prepare unto thee blood, and blood shall pursue thee; since thou hast not hated blood, even blood shall pursue thee. Thus will I make Mount Seir most desolate, and cut off from it him that passeth out and him that returneth. And I will fill his mountains with his slain men; in thy hills and in thy valleys, and in all thy rivers shall they fall that are slain with the sword. I will make thee perpetual desolations, and thy cities shall not return; and ye shall know that I am the Lord. Because thou saidst, These two nations and these two countries shall be mine and we will possess it; whereas the Lord was there: therefore as I live saith the Lord God, I will even do according to thine anger and according to thine envy which thou hast used out of thy hatred against them; and I will make myself known among them, when I have judged thee. And thou shalt know that I am the Lord and that I have heard all thy blasphemies which thou hast spoken against the mountains of Israel, saying they are laid desolate, they are given us to consume. Thus with your mouth ye have boasted against me, and have multiplied your words against me; I have heard them. Thus saith the Lord God; when the whole earth rejoices, I will make thee

desolate. As thou didst rejoice at the inheritance of the
house of Israel because it was desolate, so will I do unto
thee, O Mount Seir and all Idumea, even all of it; and
they shall know that I am the Lord." (Ezek. 35).

CHAPTER V.

AMALEK.

The history of Amalek, as he came in touch with
Israel, extends from (Ex. 17 to the book of Esther) or
a thousand years. When Israel came up out of Egypt,
Amalek met him, smote the feeble and faint ones and
feared not God. "And the Lord said unto Moses, write
this for a memorial in a book, and rehearse it in the
ears of Joshua: for I will utterly put out the name of
Amalek from under heaven. And Moses built an altar,
and called the name of it Jehovah-Nissi [the Lord my
banner], for he said, because the Lord has sworn that
the Lord will have war with Amalek from generation to
generation." (Ex. 17:14-16). Some forty years later,
Moses recited briefly the facts of Amalek's unprovoked
assault upon Israel, and God's purpose concerning him,
summing up as follows:

"Therefore it shall be, when the Lord thy God hath
given thee rest from all thine enemies round about, in
the land which the Lord thy God giveth thee for an inheritance, thou shalt blot out the remembrance of Amalek from under heaven; thou shalt not forget it."
(Deut. 25:19).

This shows us that the first condemnation of Amalek by Moses was not in anger or a violent burst of pas-
sion. Amalek by *cursing Israel* and *Israel's God*, brought
himself under the "curse." His conduct, as a nation, determined his destiny as a nation. We have only to keep
close to Israel's history in the Bible, for the next thousand years, to see the exact fulfillment of this judgment
against Amalek.

BALAAM'S PREDICTION.

Mention has already been made of Balaam, who loved the wages of unrighteousness, seeking to curse Is rael for Balak, king of Moab. We have noted the doom of Moab, that he fell under the curse and perished, and it may be added that "Balaam also the son of Beor they slew with the sword," (Num. 31:8; Josh. 13:22). In closing his predictions on the occasion of Balak's attempt to curse Israel, Balaam said, "And when he looked upon Amalek, he took up his parable, and said, Amalek was the first of the nations [probably to fight with Israel, not the first in rank or origin]; but his latter end shall be that he perish forever," (Num. 24:20). Thus Balaam confirmed the prophecy of Moses.

GIDEON'S PART IN FULFILLMENT

In the time of the judges, (or two hundred years after this), Israel did evil in the sight of the Lord, and was delivered into the hand of Midian seven years. The Amalekites joined forces with Midian and destroyed the increase of the earth till thou come to Gaza or all southern Palestine, and "left no substance for Israel, neither sheep, nor ox, nor ass. For they came up with their cattle and their tents, and they came as grasshoppers for multitude, both they and their camels were without number: and they entered into the land to destroy it. And Israel was greatly impoverished because of the Midianites; and the children of Israel cried unto the Lord."

The Lord answered them by a prophet, reminded them of their great deliverance from bondage in Egypt, and from oppressors, frequently; that their land was given to them because the heathen had polluted it, and God drave them out, but Israel had not lived in obedience to God, but had served Idols. Gideon was chosen as their deliverer, a man whose family was poor in Manasseh and he least in his father's house. His faith in God was strengthened by a series of miracles, and he blew the trumpet of war and gathered about him thirty-two thousand men. Twenty-two thousand of these were fearful and afraid and were sent back. Out of the ten thousand remaining, God chose three hundred and the rest returned every man to his place. It is expressly stated that

the Lord chose to deliver Israel by a small number from
this great host "lest Israel vaunt themselves against me,
saying, mine own hand hath saved me." With these
three hundred men, Gideon gained a great victory over
the multitude of Midian and Amalek, and the land had
rest for forty years.   (Judges 6 to 8 chs.) . .

SAUL'S DISOBEDIENCE.

When Saul came to the throne of Israel and was
established, Samuel the prophet brought him a message
from God.

"Samuel also said unto Saul, the Lord sent me to
anoint thee to be King over his people, over Israel: now
therefore hearken unto the voice of the words of the
Lord.   Thus saith the Lord of hosts, *I remember that which
Amalek did to Israel*, how he laid wait for him in the way,
when he came up from Egypt.   Now go smite Amalek
and utterly destroy all that they have, and spare them
not; but slay both man and woman, infant and suckling,
ox and sheep, camel and ass."

With an army of two hundred ten thousand men,
Saul went against Amalek.   It should be observed that
the Kenites who dwelt among the Amalekites were urged
to depart and were not destroyed, *"because they showed
kindness to all the children of Israel, when they came out
of Egypt."*   So we see the operation of the "blessing" and
the "curse" in the case of these two peoples, and the
reason assigned in both cases.

"But Saul and the people spared Agag, and the best
of the sheep, and of the oxen, and would not utterly destroy them; but everything that was vile and refuse,
that they destroyed utterly."

For this act of disobedience largely Saul lost his
kingdom.   It was said to him, "Because thou hast rejected the word of the Lord, he hath also rejected thee
from being king."   The whole narrative shows the danger of rejecting or tampering with God's commandments.
Saul professed to have spared the choice of the flocks and
herds to sacrifice to God, in Gilgal.   But "to obey is better than sacrifice and to hearken than the fat of rams.
For rebellion is as the sin of witchcraft, and stubborn-
ness is as iniquity and idolatry."   (1 Sam'l 15).

Some critics think Saul was sent on a merciless mission in that he was to slay the infants and sucklings.   He,
however, did not disobey at that point, but rather spared

the king. There are many things worse than death, viewed in the light of eternity, and idolatry, with all its attendant debauchery, and corruption of mind and morals, is certainly one of these things. Infants were better off than to be raised to a life of iniquity. How frequently we hear parents say they would rather follow their children to the grave, than to see them grow up to be tools of Satan to accomplish the ruin not only of themselves but of all whom they can lure into vice and crime. God's mercy is often like fire, and purifies to save. It is the surgeon's knife, and smites in kindness. As you would prefer to see *your child* rescued even by *death* from a life of slavery in vice and pollution of mind and body, why not grant the same privilege to others. As God could have stricken with plague or pestilence this devoted people, sparing none, but chose rather to use one people to destroy another, that his hatred of sin might be known, and the certainty of Judgment against sin be impressed upon mankind, who art thou that thou repliest against God? The innocent in all of these sweeping judgments were delivered from the danger of becoming criminal in this world, and were not sinful so as to be condemned ultimately, so were dealt with after the wisdom and mercy of Him, who doeth all things well, and loves his creation and would bless them eternally.

THE BOOK OF ESTHER.

We pass by the experience of David in dealing with the Amalekites, and notice briefly that the book of Esther records, in a fascinating story, the final overthrow of this people. That book analyzed shows that Amalek could not have perpetual hatred against God and His people and escape the withering curse of heaven. "Whosoever exalts himself shall be abased and he that humbles himself shall be exalted," was illustrated in Haman and Mordecai.

RECHABITES WERE BLESSED.

It is with Amalek as with all other nations and cities of great antiquity that were chosen of God as the subjects of prophecy—their history fulfills the predictions. When Israel was declining and her national sun about to set in the days of Jeremiah, that faithful servant of God, and opponent of idolatry, base idolatry was ripening the chosen people for national judgment. Jeremiah cited the case of Rechab's sons who had obeyed their father, drank no wine, built no houses, nor had vineyards feed nor seed, but dwelt in tents and obeyed all their father had commanded. Then he denounced the Jews for their unfaithfulness to God, foretold their captivity in Babylon, which was soon thereafter fulfilled, and then pronounced these remarkable words against the Rechabites.

"Because ye have obeyed the commandment of Jonadab, your father, and kept all his precepts and done all according as he had commanded you; therefore thus saith the Lord of Hosts, the God of Israel; Jonathan the son of Rechab shall not want a man to stand before me forever." (Jer. 35).

In the neighborhood of Mecca, the very center of Mahometanism, these people live at present. They glory in their descent from Rechab, all speak Hebrew and verify this chapter of Jeremiah as the Word of God. If the ancient peoples are thus remembered, in this instance for twenty-five centuries, the Ishmaelites for thirty-eight centuries, and God's word is constantly fulfilling in their history before our eyes, how certain it is that all his promises and threatenings will be fulfilled ultimately to the whole of our race. Some sixty thousand Rechabites all clinging to Judaism as anciently and living in tents as did their father, and as he commanded them to do—make us to wonder what spell is over the professed sons of God in our day, as with ancient idolatrous Judah, that we are not, and at all times, as true to our heavenly Father as they are and always have been to their earthly father.

CHAPTER VI.

EGYPT IN PROPHECY.

The destiny of more than thirty great cities and nations is foretold in the Bible. One might conclude by reading Abraham's prophecy, or Balaam's "I will bless them that bless thee and curse him that curseth thee" that the judgment would be the same in each instance, but it was not. The prophecies might have been charged with vagueness if they had been in such declarations alone. But when we note that these were developed into details as applied to the various nations the vagueness disappears in the multitude of specific points foretold. No two of them are alike in particulars. It is as if one should foretell the destruction of thirty cities, one by fire, one by earthquake, another by dynamite, another by cyclone, and another by various other agencies and elements. The word destruction would vaguely foretell the ruin. But if one should descend to particulars of time and manner of each destruction, and specify which one should go down by earthquake, which by cyclone, and so on throughout, and whether the destruction would be sudden or gradual; whether the city would be revived or remain a ruin forever; whether it would be a pool of water or a desert waste; by multiplying particulars one would decrease the human probability of the predictions ever being fulfilled. The nations were not grouped together and condemned wholesale; but, rather, they were separated and condemned to a detailed overthrow. It is evident that the word "cursed" applied to the nations

31169

and cities overthrown although the predicted judgment against one city or nation would not apply to any other city or nation, whose destruction was predicted to be different and accomplished by different means. I might safely predict that thirty different men in Kansas would die in the twentieth century. But if I should venture the prediction that all of them will die within five years from today, and specify the manner of each man's death as follows: Smith will die in a sleeping car in a train collision; Jones will die of apoplexy at his breakfast table, two years, three months hence; Rogers will die of Typhoid one week before Ross dies in an automobile accident in front of his own house; Madison will die of blood poisoning, contracted from a bad tooth, three years after Richards falls from a tree and breaks his neck, and so on through the list, such predictions would demand more than human wisdom in their delivery. I would be a fool or a mad-man to hazard such predictions. If I should add that certain men would be exposed to the same perils and survive, one with the loss of his right eye, another with the loss of three fingers on his left hand, and so on specifying the mutilations of body in each instance, this would elevate my predictions into the same rank as Scripture prophecies. The Scriptures specify the nation, its crime, its punishment, and, in some instances, the time and manner of its infliction, and the nation or people that would inflict it.

This was not the sagacity or forecast of statesmen. These Seers were all among the Hebrew people. Babylon, Medo-Persia, Greece, Rome or Egypt, out of their countless priests and religious guides, could not give the world any such prophecies concerning themselves or other nations. Moreover the Hebrew prophets were as faithful in foretelling the ruin and overthrow, the captivity and dispersion, of their own people as they were in foretelling the destiny of other nations. This proves that it was not national pride or patriotism that induced them to foretell the decline and ruin of other nations. They spake the truth concerning all, themselves included. Truth is impartial. "They spake as they were moved by the Holy Spirit." There are seventeen books of prophecy, and seventeen books of history in the Old Testament. These books cannot be duplicated in the world.

GENTILE NATIONS.

The prophecies concerning Gentile nations are often in groups. Isaiah (ch's 13-27) illustrates this point. Here we have Babylon, Medo-Persia, Palestina (or Philistia), Moab, Ammon, Syria, Ethiopia, Egypt, the great city of Tyre, and the closing chapters were given to denunciation of sin and national wickedness, while universal victory of truth is also predicted. Jeremiah's prophecies are not put together according to the time of their delivery, but in (ch's 46 to 51) we have his predictions concerning the Gentiles. He saw concerning Egypt, Philistia, Moab, Ammon, Edom, Damascus, Kedar, Elam (or Persia) and the great Babylon.

Ezekiel prophesied against the Gentiles (ch's 25 to 32). The same nations were before him, in the main, Ammon, Moab, Edom, Philistia, Tyre, Egypt, and the wicked Assyria or Babylon, and finally Gog and Magog. It is not contended that all each prophet had to say concerning these nations is in these chapters. The historical books contain some prophecies just as the prophetic books give some history. But our inquiry is simplified by knowing these groups, laying them side by side for comparison, and mutual explanation, remembering that the prophets lived far apart in time as well as in space. When we go through all the books and study these groups, we are prepared to draw our conclusions, as we compare their statements with the facts of history, both sacred and profane.

EGYPT.

Egypt was among the oldest and greatest of all nations. Israel had much to do with them, and many prophecies were given concerning that nation. "And he said unto Abraham, know of a surety that thy seed shall be a stranger in a land that is not theirs, and shall serve them; and they shall afflict them four hundred years; and also that nation whom they shall serve will I judge: and afterward shall they come out with great substance, (Gen. 15:13-14). Abraham sojourned in

Egypt for a time. The fascinating story of Joseph, brings out the event of Abraham's descendants all going into Egypt some two hundred years later, and occupies thirteen chapters in the close of Genesis.

The book of Exodus relates how God judged and overthrew the Egyptians and delivered Israel on the day the prophecy was completed (Ex. 12:40-42). "Moses was learned in all the wisdom of the Egyptians, and was mighty in words and deeds, (Acts 7:22). "By faith Moses when he was come to years refused to be called the son of Pharaoh's daughter; choosing rather to suffer affliction with the people of God than to enjoy the pleasures of sin for a season; esteeming the reproach of Christ greater riches than all the treasures of Egypt; for he had respect to the recompense of the reward. (Heb. 11:24-26). "And God gave Soloman wisdom and understanding exceeding much like the sand that is on the sea-shore. And Solomon's wisdom excelled the wisdom of all the children of the east country, and all the wisdom of Egypt (I Ks. 4:29, 30). Thus Egypt is celebrated for wisdom and riches. Egypt contested with Assyria for ages the sovereignty of the then known world. Israel, situated between these two rival countries, was tempted to appeal, and often did appeal, to one or the other for assistance and protection. This contributed to Israel's national ruin, because they cast off faith in God, trusted in the arm of flesh, and looked more to the munitions of war and to fortified cities, and alliances with these heathen nations, than to the Most High. For all this the prophets rebuked them sharply.

EZEKIEL'S PREDICTIONS.

"It shall be the basest of kingdoms; neither shall it exalt itself any more among the nations; for I will diminish them that they shall no more rule over the nations. And it shall no more be the confidence of the house of Israel, which bring their iniquity to remembrance, when they shall look after them; but they shall know that I am the Lord in that day." (Ezek. 29:13-16).

This shows us the nation was to continue, but be a base kingdom, yea, the basest of kingdoms. Has it perished like Edom—none left to the house of Edom? Have

her cities entirely perished and become the jackal's den,
like Babylon? Nay, verily.   But Egypt has sunken down
to the lowest and basest kingdom of the world.

"Thus saith the Lord God; I will also destroy the
idols, and I will cause their images to cease out of Noph;
and there shall be no more a prince of the land of Egypt,
and I will put a fear in the land of Egypt.   And I will
make Pathros desolate, and will set fire in Zoan and will
execute judgments in No. ....   Thus will
I execute judgments in Egypt and they shall know that I
am the Lord." (Ezek. 30:13, 14:19).

ISAIAH'S PREDICTIONS.

"In that day shall five cities in the land of Egypt
speak the language of Canaan, and swear to the Lord
of Hosts; one shall be called the city of destruction.   In
that day shall there be an altar to the Lord in the midst
of Egypt and a pillar at the border thereof to the Lord.
And it shall be for a sign, and for a witness unto the
Lord of Hosts in the land of Egypt; for they shall cry
unto the Lord because of the oppressors, and he shall
send them a savior, and a great one, and he shall deliver
them.   And the Lord shall be known to Egypt, and the
Egyptians shall know the Lord in that day, and shall do
sacrifice and oblation, yea they shall vow a vow unto
the Lord and shall perform it; and the Lord shall smite
Egypt, he shall smite and heal it and they shall return
to the Lord, and he shall be entreated of them and
shall heal them." (Is. 19:18-22.   See also the whole
of chapters 19 and 20).

Alexander invaded Egypt in the glory of his conquests and they yielded to his rule peaceably.   He treated
them with generosity and kindness.   This was a little
more than three centuries before Christ.   The great Alexandria was planned and built and took its name from its
founder.   At one time it boasted of having the largest
library in the world.   The philosophers and learned class
came from all quarters to search the books in this center
of learning.   This huge collection of seven hunderd
thousand volumes was consigned to the flames by order
of Omar, a Mahometan ruler.   Thus perished the knowledge of many subjects and it might be supposed something concerning the Sphinx and wonderful Pyramids.

MONUMENTS OF EGYPT.

The catacombs of Egypt are very numerous and of

great antiquity, as many of them were excavated in the days of Pharaoh. The river Nile runs through Egypt. It has a fertile valley hemmed in on each side of the river by a range of mountains or hills. The width of the valley varies from a few rods to as many miles. The overflowing annually of this river makes the valley productive, and the grain of Egypt is raised chiefly in this valley. The temples and palaces, pyramids and other massive structures now remaining in Egypt are supposed to have been quarried from these hills. The Egyptians had a way of embalming the dead which has preserved mummies from thirty to thirty-five centuries. These mummies were deposited in sandstone chambers, carved out of solid rock, and these catacombs with their mummified inhabitants may be found at short intervals all along the mountain sides on both banks of the Nile for scores of miles, but are most extensive near the cities of Memphis and Thebes. Tombs of kings are described by an English writer.

CATACOMBS BRIEFLY DESCRIBED

"They stand on the edge of a vast funereal ground, extending from the cultivated alluvium to the sandstone mountain which bounds the plain, intersected by numerous dangerous paths among yawning mummy-pits and graves. Ranges of tombs, hewn in the mountain side above, some greater than those of the kings, penetrate far into the bowels of the mountain, chamber after chamber, passage after passage, whose walls as the light is applied to them, kindle into a vivid epitome of the light of the old Egyptian world—its religious solemnities, its familiar usages, its progress from the cradle to the grave, its scenes of daily domestic life, of high festivity and solemn funeral with the passage of the dead into the realms of futurity, the judgment and the mysterious transmigration of souls. Who could suspect that all this is revealed to us in these wonderful sepulchers, which externally appear but holes in the sandy rock? And how strange and sad it is to come forth to the light of day, after this long and absorbing converse in these dusky recesses with the past life of this great people and behold the wrecks of their proud city, wide spread over the empty, desolate plain." *Abridged from "Catacombs of Rome."*

The pyramids of Egypt are probably the oldest and greatest monuments in the world. The three great pyramids and their smaller companions, with the colossal Sphynx form a group of wonders testifying to the ancient wisdom and arstistic skill of the Egyptians.   Large and small they are standing in small groups, in an irregular line, down the west side of the Nile for sixty miles.   Six miles out from Cairo, the chief city of Egypt is the pyramid, Ghizeh.   This is the most ancient, and, perhaps the most wonderful work of man for monumental glory. Seven hundred sixty seven feet square, built of large blocks of stone, which form gigantic steps two hunderd in number, to the top, with a flat top some thirty feet square.   It is thus one hundred thirty six feet nine inches higher than St. Paul's, London, and forty-three feet nine inches higher than St. Peter's, Rome.   It covers thirteen acres of ground.   From its top you look in one direction upon the great desert, a wilderness of sterility and death.   Facing about, fertility, verdure, the great beauty of the Nile valley meets your gaze.   "Life and death are here side by side, and the line closely and abruptly drawn, for the Nile goes right up to the desert and deposits its rich soil right along side the sands. So close indeed that you might pull an apple from the tree of the Delta and cast it into the wilderness of the desert."   This shows us how necessary the water of the Nile is to Egypt.   I can only mention Pompey's Pillar in the center of the ancient city of Alexandria, and the temple of Karnak, the greatest ruin in the world.

CONCLUSION.

But the prophecy uttered twenty-five centuries ago has been fulfilled in detail.

1.   Idols ceased out of the land.

2.   A temple or pillar of testimony was built to God in the land.

3.   They worshipped God in sacrifices, ablutions and in fulfillment of vows in Egypt.

4.   Their native rulers ceased out of the land two thousand years ago.

5.   They are, and for ages have been, the basest of kingdoms.

6.   Great churches were established in Egypt. These corrupted the doctrine of Christ and thus destroyed the

only means of their preservation, and sank down in poverty, vice, ignorance and stagnation.

7. The monuments of her ancient greatness survive and thus declare her guilt, for in many ways they proclaim that she was a proud, idolatrous, cruel nation, and merited the humiliation and shame that overwhelmed her.

We must not forget the altar and witness built. Jeremiah and many Jews went to Egypt at the destruction of Jerusalem and the temple. Alexander the Great planted many of the Jews in Egypt, settling them in large numbers in Alexandria. The Old Testament was translated into Greek about (280 B. C.) Onias, a Jew of great distinction, obtained the privilege to build a temple in Egypt like that in Jerusalem. The temple was built in Heliopolis. The tribe of Levi ministered before the temple, performing the services there that were enjoined in the law of Moses, similar to the way they did in Jerusalem. It should be noted that Vespasian destroyed this Jewish temple after the temple at Jerusalem. Thus the language of Canaan was spoken in Egypt, and God was worshipped there. Under the gospel age many people in Egypt turned to the Lord. The church at Alexandria ranked with Jerusalem, Antioch, Constantinople and Rome. Idolatry has perished in Egypt. Who but One Infinite in wisdom and in power could have foretold and accomplished all these things? One by one they have been turned into history, as the prophets so faithfully predicted. "He spake and it was done; He commanded and it stood fast."

CHAPTER VII.

LITERALISM APPLIED TO ISRAEL.

It is asserted by the Literalist expositors that as Israel had a literal land given them by promise to Abraham; God drave out seven nations under Joshua to place them therein; and frequently subdued their enemies in the times of both the Judges and the Kings, giving them back their land even after the Babylonian Captivity, that they are yet to enjoy that land as a national home. A restoration of Israel to a spiritual inheritance under Christ, however, does not necessitate a restoration to their former temporal inheritance. The fact that Moab, Ammon, Amalek, Philistia, Edom, Tyre, Ninevah, Babylon and other pagan nations had the prophecies concerning them fulfilled literally, added to the fact that Israel, as a nation, had a multitude of prophecies concerning their land fulfilled literally, BEFORE CHRIST, does not under the gospel, logically demand a temporal restoration of Abraham's descendants to the former typical arrangement in order to fulfill the prophecies. There is a certain degree of plausibility only in this view of the Literalists, but no solid ground upon which to build such a carnal hope for Israel.

It promises under Christ, what was only promised under the law of Moses. It gives to converted Jews an earthly inheritance, where-as none is given to their brethren the Gentile Christians. The converted Jews in apostolic days suffered the loss of all things instead of being enriched, in temporal things, and Paul says, did so gladly.

1. Israel, from the days of Abraham till Christ, were the covenanted people of God. From the days of Moses they were living under a law very exclusively theirs. It bound them sacredly to maintain it in the land, (Deut. 4: 1, 2, 25, 26) and demanded, in many particulars, their residence in that land.

2. They had the Tabernacle or Temple in the center of the nation "which was a figure for the time then present, in which were offered both gifts and sacrifices, that could not make him that did the service perfect as pertaining to the conscience" (Heb. 9:9). While the Tabernacle was yet standing, (or its service acceptable to God), the way into the holiest of all was not yet made manifest.

In Jeremiah's prophecies, there is a section (ch's 21-31) spoken in the days of Zedekiah. Ezekiel also prophesied concerning the same "Profane, wicked prince" —that he should be the last one until Christ. The family of Abraham lost their *independence* in his reign, twenty-five hundred years ago. I style this a TEST PROPHECY. It may not have occurred to the reader that (Jer. 31:31-38) foretold that God would make a covenant with the house of Israel and with the house of Judah. It should be observed that this covenant was "not like the covenant that God made with their fathers in the day that he took them by the hand to bring them out of the land of Egypt; which my covenant they brake although I was an husband unto them, saith the Lord." The student needs no emphasis put upon the fact that the author of the Hebrews quotes this prophecy and applies it to the gospel covenant. My argument is as follows:

1. God rejected as temporal kings the house of David, after this manner:

"O earth, earth, earth, hear the word of the Lord. Thus saith the Lord, write ye this man childless, a man that shall not prosper in his days; for no man of his seed shall prosper, sitting upon the throne of David ruling any more in Judah." (Jer. 22:24-30).

Zedekiah his uncle reigned in his stead in Jerusalem for eleven years, but under oath to serve the king of Babylon. This Coniah, Jeconiah or Jehoiachin, as he had these three names, was taken captive to Babylon, and remained in prison thirty-seven years. Expositors have much trouble with him. First from the statement (1 Chron. 3:16); second, because Zerubbabel, his grandson was Governor in Judah on the return from Babylon (Ezra 3; Haggai 1:1, 13-15); also that Jeconiah is recorded by (Matt. 1:12) in the lineage of Christ. But we should note the fact that Zerubbabel did not sit upon the throne of David. He was viceroy of the king of Babylon. Zedekiah, Jeconiah's uncle was the very last king of Judah. This was predicted (Ezek. 21:25-27). Jeconiah was in prison in Babylon, when this was spoken to Zedekiah.

Jeremiah in the next chapter predicted a king, in the line of David who *should* reign and prosper, THE LORD OUR RIGHTEOUSNESS, and thus contrasted the two kings, (23:1-8).

3. In Zedekiah's days, IN THE SAME PREDICTION, HE FORETOLD THE NEW COVENANT Ch's 27-31). The kingly line failed, temporally, twenty-five centuries ago. The NEW KINGDOM began in Christ. The NEW COVENANT began in Christ. NO KING HAS ANY RIGHT TO DAVID'S EARTHLY DOMINION TO-DAY. THE NEW COVENANT HAS FOREVER SET ASIDE THE OLD COVENANT, AND JESUS SET ASIDE DAVID'S KINGLY LINE FOREVER. Jesus would not accept the temporal rule over Israel. It is here predicted by Jeremiah that it shall be occupied no more by the house of Coniah; and Zedekiah was to be the last king until Christ, according to Ezekiel; so as Jesus would not have the temporal rule, we see the temporal sovereignty in the line of David is vacated forever in the persons of Coniah and Zedekiah. This is true unless it can be shown that Jesus is yet to be an earthly ruler, which we hope to show is not predicted nor possible. The throne of David had been vacant five hundred eighty seven years at Jesus' birth, and six centuries and more at his baptism. The throne has been vacant nearly nineteen centuries more since then and is still vacant, in a *two-fold sense*. The new covenant was made with Israel and Judah. The Literalists treat this subject as though the new covenant was a provision for the Gentiles and not for the Jews. But Jesus came to his own nation, and was first sent only to "the lost sheep of the house of Israel." He was the long promised king. Matthew says he was king. The parables are illustrations of the nature of his kingdom. He said to Pilate "My kingdom is not of this world; if my kingdom were of this world, then would my servants fight, that I should not be delivered to the Jews; but now is my kingdom not from hence." (Jno. 18:

36). Daniel said Messiah would confirm the covenant with many for one week, and be cut off in the midst of the week (Dan'l 9). (Heb. Ch's 8 and 10), as well as the whole book, represents to Christians that the Old Covenant was done away, and that the New Covenant was established on better promises, sealed by better blood.

Now since God rejected the temporal kings in the line of David, six centuries before Christ: since he condemned the old covenant, and took it out of the way, what strange havoc men make of the prophecies who try to interpret them so that the temporal promises and provisions of the typical dispensation shall still be binding. What man among the Jews of our day is authorized to adminster the law of Moses? What Jewish Rabbi could offer a lamb on an altar that God would accept? The whole system has expired by limitation. It is to uphold Caiaphas and the Sanhedrin that crucified our Lord to defend the Jews in their disobedience. No soft words and eloquent sophistry can bridge the chasm between faith and infidelity. The apostles are the converted Jews to imitate, the men who accepted Christ as the end of the law for righteousness to EVERY ONE THAT BELIEVES. To follow the chief priests, elders and scribes is to reject him whom they crucified. There is no middle ground. Jesus said "He that is not with me is against me; and he that gathereth not with me scattereth." (Luke 11: 23). All the prophets in condemning Judah and Israel called them back to the observance of the Mosaic law. "Remember ye the law of my servant Moses, which I commanded him in Horeb, FOR ALL ISRAEL WITH THE STATUTES AND JUDGMENTS," Mal. 4:4). What Christian man will say this is the will of God today? This law with its statutes and judgments never was, and never will be, binding upon the Gentile, or the church. Moses predicted the prophet whom they were to hear in all things (Deut. 18:25); the apostle Peter and the martyr Stephen both say that he spake of Christ. (Acts 4:22-24; 7:37). There were a list of heirs-apparent to the throne of David from Jeconiah to Joseph, eleven names spanning the six centuries, but none of them prospered sitting on the throne of David. They simply carried the royal lineage down to Jesus that the promise of God should not fail. But since the destruction of Jerusalem by Titus, forty years after Christ, this line is lost, so that no man on earth today can prove that he is a lineal descendant of David. These facts ought by themselves to settle this question.

1.   David had a line of sons to Christ whom the apostles teach us was and is the King of the Jews.

2.   Since Jesus there is no one can show his descent from David, hence can ever aspire to sovereignty in Judah for there is no Judah or house of David remaining distinct from the rest of Abram's descendants

3.   Ezekiel said no descendants of Coniah should sit upon the throne of David, any more and prosper. Jesus has sat upon the throne of David, not temporally, but as the great anti-typical King, for nearly nineteen centuries. Ezekiel said no one should follow Zedekiah till he came whose right it was.   Jesus came after the throne had been vacant six centuries, was rejected and crucified as the King of the Jews.   He claimed to be the King, to make the covenant, as foretold, and it is as evident as noonday that he made that covenant with Israel and Judah, for the Gentiles were not called into the covenant until the apostles had preached to the descendants of Abraham for some years (most likely three and a half years).   The Jewish hope is in vain, and the Gentile interpretation that promises a temporal reign is erroneous. There is to be no other rule or covenant.   The strongest evidence that the ministry of Jesus lasted three years and a half is in Daniel's prophecy (9:27); this period is not clearly made out in the New Testament, only by counting (Jno. 5:1) a Passover, which it most likely was, but no one can say positively.

LITERAL AND FIGURATIVE.

There was a profound reason why those prophecies concerning Israel, which had their fulfillment before Christ, should have had a literal fulfillment; and those that were fulfilled in Christ and the gospel age should be fulfilled figuratively.   The nature of the mission of Moses and of Christ were as different as flesh and spirit, temporal and eternal.   Tons of Millennial literature

might have been spared if this distinction had been observed in writing as it is set forth in the inspired Volume.
The two covenants, one with fleshly Israel, concerning
Abraham's natural seed; and the new covenant with
spiritual Israel concerning Abraham's children by faith;
set forth two radically different states and conditions.
"Moses was faithful in all his house as a servant, for
a testimony of those things that were to be spoken
after." (Heb. 3:5). THE JEWS DID NOT AND DO NOT
REJECT CHRIST BECAUSE THEY BELIEVE MOSES. THEY DO
NOT UNDERSTAND EITHER MOSES OR THE PROPHETS ANY
BETTER THAN THEY UNDERSTAND CHRIST AND THE APOSTLES.
MOSES AND ALL THE PROPHETS BEAR TESTIMONY TO CHRIST.
The hope of fleshly Israel was and is false, and can never
be sanctioned by the people of God, who are true to our
great King.

The city of Jerusalem, yea the land, had a sacredness while it was occupied by the typical people of God.
They had a typical house, typical priesthood, typical
sacrifices, typical feasts and a kingly line in whose genealogy the Messiah was to come. The Jews naturally became attached to that land, and revered its very dust.
But millions of Christians who have lived and died under
our KING, HIGH-PRIEST, and PROPHET, have never
seen the land of types and shadows. It is sacred to them
also in the only true sense it can be sacred today. Not
that a prayer offered in Gethsemane would bring one
nearer to God than if offered in one's own closet; not
that Jordan has medicinal, cleansing virtue, that one
should be baptized therein; not that the water of Cana
would turn into wine on our wedding tables; and not that
fishing would be satisfactory in Lake Galilee; but we
revere the memory of the prophets and apostles of our
Lord, recorded in the Bible, and the Holy One of whom
Moses and the prophets did write. Of him we can say
with Peter.

"Whom having not seen ye love; in whom, though
now ye see him not, yet believing ye rejoice with a joy
unspeakable and full of glory, receiving the end of your
faith the salvation of your souls." (I Pet. 1:8, 9).

Under Christ and the new covenant no such sacredness as belonged to the land and city belongs to locality.
In fact, it could not. His religion is of universal appli-

cation; is for all nations. In every nation he that fears God and worketh righteousness is accepted with him, (Acts 10:35). Jesus' discourse at the well, to a Samaritan woman, shows us this consoling fact, and this was the subject of prophecy, (Jno. 4:21-25; Mal. 1:11). The Jews could all live in the land granted to Abraham, could all attend their feasts, give their tithes, support Levi and maintain their forty-eight cities, carry out the provisions of the law concerning war, laws concerning marriage, cities of refuge, offerings of first-fruits, consecration of the first-born, water of purification from leprosy of man, house or garment. But God's people under the New Covenant, established on better promises, are not required to live in the land where the types were worked out. We are now living under the reality.

A SOPHISM.

It is urged with confidence by some that the prophets Haggai, Zechariah and Malachi speak of the return of the Israelites to their land and Zechariah, especially, is very plain on the subject. He is no plainer than the other prophets who preceded the Babylonian captivity, though he lived afterwards. The fact that all the prophecies concerning the land, cities, and peoples, which we have considered, and all that are given in the Old Testament concerning Gentile nations, were fulfilled literally, and those concerning a "Remnant" of Israel returning from the Assyrian, Egyptian and Babylonian captivities, were fulfilled literally; these facts, I say, do not require that the remaining predictions concerning the fleshly posterity of Abraham shall have a like literal fulfillment. Are the conditions not as radically different as could be imagined? To interpret after this manner is not to distinguish things that differ. It is to mix the law and the gospel. It is to regard Israel today in rebellion against God and against the New Covenant as they were regarded and treated by the God of heaven while they were in covenant relationship with God. Indeed! Has nothing occurred to merit the disfavor of God? Will God condemn a Gentile for rejecting Jesus Christ, yet elevate a Jew to the highest heaven while doing the same thing? Be careful that you do not read the Old Testament with a veil on your heart too! It is to ignore the life and mission of Christ entirely, set him aside and allow the Old Covenant to continue in force from the day the Hebrews entered the land of Canaan under Joshua. Such blindness, to characterize it mildly, may be called sophistry. No one can go through the books of prophecy, consistently, with any such system of interpretation. It demands too much literalism, when, confessedly, the New Covenant is in force. Such interpretation is distinctly Jewish, I may say, both in origin and result. They adopt almost entirely the Jewish hope, and would convert the church into a great world-power, the fifth universal monarchy on earth, and this, too, IS NOW DUE BY THEIR SYSTEM OF DATES. The great "European war" now in progress, is an opportunity to test the merits of the respective systems of interpretation. Pre-mellinalists are sure we are nearing the end of the Gospel age. I, on the contrary, am trying to show, by the Word of God, that they can not be right.

TYPE-PROPHECIES.

How should we view those predictions that use the phraseology common to Israel in foretelling the fortunes of the Israel of God under the gospel? They may be called TYPE-PROPHECIES. The prophets who lived in the age of shadows, used the language current in their day, and convey to us the idea that is in the things foretold, by *symbols*. The prophets in the verbal predictions, foretold in *words* what the ceremonials foretold *typically*, (*by things*); the *things* were typical of *better* THINGS. Thus under the *literal names* they predicted for the gospel age, a greater David, Temple, Altar, Priest-hood, Sacrifices, Canaan and the like. The verbal prophecies were predictive of the same times and blessings. As the prophets took their illustrations, type-prophecies, from the then reigning order of things, we see why they used David, the temple, sacrifices and other types, to foretell the gospel. There is a definite idea in burnt-offering, sin-offering, peace-offering, and the like, and such language used, (typically), sets forth the literal antitype or fulfillment. It is manifest that the burnt-offerings, sin-offerings, and the like among the Jews were ordained as types to be observed till they were redeemed in their anti-types, but not later. We are now living in a house built for a habitation of God through the Spirit. Any other interpretation brings out opposite and contradictory results and can not be true.

The prophecies are preserved and can and should be examined calmly, and with patience. Is it possible to have two Davids, one in Jerusalem, reigning on earth, the other reigning in Jerusalem above? Jesus and the church or kingdom of which he is head, cannot be both a literal, temporal, earthly monarchy, like the four great monarchies that preceded it, and remain what it is, and has been since he instituted it. There is not to be a literal priesthood on earth, and the priesthood in Judah ministered by Christ in heaven. There is not a typical and anti-typical system of sacrifices to be in effect at the same time. Jesus abolished the typical forever. There is not to be the law on the one hand, restored and in full force in earthly Canaan, by the fleshly seed of Abraham, with circumcision, clean meats, appointed sacrifices, a magnificent temple, richly dressed priest-hood, gorgeous ritual, ancient Levites in full dress performing their ancient duties, and the nations going up in caravans to the annual feasts, and the antitypes of all these existing at the same time. It is not Jesus or Moses; but it is Jesus predicted and typified by Moses and the prophets, or Jesus rejected for a carnal tradition, with Moses and all the prophets upholding the claims of Jesus and rejecting and condemning the blind traditionists. The Jews read the prophets with a veil on their hearts, the veil of Tradition. We should not veil our hearts to the simplicity and beauty of the prophecies concerning Christ and his spiritual kingdom, for the rejected tradition of a temporal kingdom of Christ yet to be set up according to the Jewish hope.

THREE THEORIES.

There are three theories of these prophecies now being advocated:

1. That the present, or Gospel Age, is closing in

first, universal war; second, universal anarchy will follow; next the second coming of Christ to raise the righteous dead and reign over all the earth for a thousand years, all other governments being swept away.

2.   Millenial Dawnism teaches that Christ has come, the resurrected saints are all here in spirit bodies (whatever they are, the Bible says not one word about such bodies) ; the millennium is on, and this is the *cause* of the present wars and they will overthrow every organization of earth, founded by man, whether it be civil or religious, by the close of 1914.   There is a good deal of annihilation in these theories, especially the latter, and the attentive reader will see that they mutually annihilate each other; for Christ cannot be here with all the dead saints raised to life again, be making this war and getting ready to take over the governments of earth himself for a thousand-year reign, and not be here but carrying on the war getting ready to come!   Some body is wrong in every feature of his scheme, manifestly, and it is possible both are wrong.

3.   The writer will show that both systems are founded in the mutual error that the prophecies concerning the reign of Christ are wrested to mean a temporal rule, when we have the Lord himself and the inspired apostles rejecting that traditional view.   I will show the reason why the theories are false throughout.   The subject is one for careful thought and the reader should not permit the jingle of words to sway him, or prejudice him for this or that; but the undying truth of God must prevail.

CHAPTER VIII.

A TWO-FOLD ERROR.

There is a two-fold error quite prevalent in the interpretation of these prophecies. The Jews have made the mistake of interpreting these predictions in the time of Christ and since, as setting forth a temporal kingdom, for the Messiah, and were disappointed that Jesus would not become a temporal ruler. They have clung to that false interpretation ever since. This is mistake number one. Many systems of interpretation among the Gentiles have adopted the erroneous notions of the Jews, *in that they teach that Jesus has not yet set up his kingdom, but is soon to come and reign on the earth, giving a double portion of honor to the Jews in his temporal rule over all the nations of this earth. This theory is wrong from center to circumference.* The chief difference between the Gentile and Jewish interpretations is on the *time*. The Gentiles say that Jesus came the first time to *suffer*; he comes the next time to *reign* on earth. There are tons of literature being sown broadcast over the land today, in which are exact dates assigned for Jesus to come again, and begin this universal and glorious reign. These dates and their meanings will be examined later. But I merely state here that this pretentious array of dates only complicates the subject, and in no sense adds to the value of the exposition. If Jesus is not to reign as a temporal Ruler over the earth, with head-quarters in Jerusalem, as the Jews expected him to do, and as modern Jews expect someone else to do, whom they call their Messiah, then what advantage is it to array a complicated system of dates before the readers, setting forth the *time when*, as they undertake to show the *place where*, this great Millennial reign will begin? The Jew, in his wildest dreams, never surpassed the Gentiles in their fanciful and unfounded expositions of these prophecies. We hope to sift these twin errors to the bottom, in this work.

ISRAEL DIFFERENT FROM OTHERS.

The fact that the nation of Israel was a TYPICAL NATION, should never be overlooked in studying their history. Those expositors who are generally known as Literalists, because they apply the terms of prophecy used concerning Israel, in the gospel age, in a literal way, as they do the prophecies concerning Moab, Ammon, Amalek, Edom, Egypt, Tyre, Nineveh, and other Gentile cities. ignore that fact, if they ever observed it. Israel was in covenant relation with God. They were the great prophetic and *typical nation*. The grant of land to them was from the river of Egypt to the great river, Euphrates. They ruled over that territory less than one century out of thirty-eight centuries, since the grant was made to Abraham. If the Jews should forsake all lands, and, under impulse, return to that land and seek out their old boundaries and reign under Jesus our Lord for one thousand years, that would be only one-fifth the time from Abraham to the close of such residence there. David and Solomon are the only ones of Abraham's descendants that ever had the rule over the entire territory. But Israel lived at least two centuries, some say four, in Egypt. They spent nearly half a century in the wilderness. Ten tribes were taken to Assyria, and never returned. Later the remaining families were carried to Babylon for seventy years. In the days of Esther, they were living in all parts of the Persian Empire. They only had kings for five centuries out of thirty-eight. They were living, and had synagogues in, all parts of the Roman Empire in the days of Christ. They were driven out of Palestine, (70 A. D.) and are found in all countries today.

DESIGNATED PLACE TO WORSHIP.

The Tabernacle, and later the Temple, was *the place* where they were to bring all their offerings and sacrifices, and perform their vows. They had priests in the tribe of Levi only, and all the tribe of Levi was consecrated to minister for Aaron and the common priests and their successors. They had three annual feasts in Jerusalem and all the circumcised males were commanded to attend these and not appear empty before God. They had sacrifices daily, doubled on the Sabbath, and multiplied on stated occasions. They had a great day of Atonement, the tenth day of the seventh month. (Lev. 16). The providence of God was over them in basket and in store, in olive yards and vineyards, in the increase of their flocks and herds, in the health and wealth of the people. The land was the Lord's and by obedience to Him they inherited farms, houses, orchards, and vast stores. No one should desire their land, or invade their heritage, while the males were congregated at Jerusalem at their feasts. They had to let the land rest every seventh year. The Lord promised them a blessing upon the sixth year to carry them through this enjoined period. The rule applied to fields, orchards, vineyards and all products. They had a Jubilee the fiftieth year, when all debts were cancelled and every man returned to his possessions. They could not loan money to their brethren for interest.

These and a multitude of such like laws applied to typical Israel. They were living *wholly under the law of Moses*, given to them as a nation. They could not eat meats as other nations. Priests could not touch or defile themselves by dead bodies. They had laws concerning sowing mingled seed, muzzling oxen, women wearing that which pertaineth to men, plowing with different kinds of beasts yoked together, and various similar injunctions. None but the house of Aaron could be their priest. *All distinction as to tribes is now lost. Their registers were destroyed in the overthrow of the nation by Titus in* (A. D. 70).

WHAT COULD ISRAEL DO?

Is Israel to return to Palestine? Who is to be King? Will it be Jesus? If not how can Jesus be *our* Messiah? The Jews have lost their tribal distinctions— no one knows whether he is from Judah, Benjamin, Levi or Asher. The fact is, their whole system collapsed and fell into ruin, never to be revived on this earth. when they rejected Jesus Christ as their GREAT KING, PROPHET and HIGH-PRIEST. The law with its provisions concerning land, sabbaths, annual feasts, jubilees, Atonement, temple and sacrificial system conducted by Levi for the nation, can not be revived in that or any other land. "The law," says Paul, "was our schoolmaster to bring us unto Christ that we might be justified by faith. But after that faith is come, we are no longer under a schoolmaster." (Gal. 3:24, 25).

A FAR-REACHING ERROR.

I know of no more harmful error in interpretation of these ancient predictions than that which excuses the Jews for rejecting Jesus Christ. The Gentile expositors who promise the Jews a *blessing from God*, while they denounce and *curse his Son*, are inexcusable perverters of God's word. They, the Jews, crucify the Son of God afresh twelve million times a day, if there are so many of them. The error of teaching from these prophecies, (that foretold the return of Israel to their land, when the threat of heaven was about to be executed in driving them out of it for idolatry), that there is a return literal and yet future, is one ladened with many sad consequences.

1.   It encourages the Jew to continue in his rebellion against God, by despising his Son; "who is a liar but he that denieth that Jesus is the Christ, [Messiah]? He is an anti-Christ that denieth the Father and the Son. Whosoever denieth the Son hath not the Father." (I Jno. 2:22-23).

2.   It is injurious to the whole church of God to build up fine theories and awaken hope of a speedy Millennium with Jesus in person, and his resurrected saints, then living on earth to administer it, and in some vague, mystical, mysterious manner, reigning over a world of converted nations, the Jews pre-eminent in such a kingdom.

3.   It is the climax of absurdity to go back to the Mosaic law for the model of a prospective kingdom, and speak of a revived Judaism, elevated to the rank or above the rank of Solomon and David, in the fulness of their temporal riches and glory, with the *natural* seed of Abraham lifted above Gentile Christians in Millennial blessedness.   If Israel were to return to Palestine under

some powerful "Zionist" movement, this year, (and this year is supposed by some jugglers with dates and the vast system of Chronology, to be the year they return), it would either be to revive the law or to accept the gospel. Are they repentant? No. They cling to tradition where Caiaphas left them.

CASES OF REPENTANCE CITED.

When Israel sinned and lost the Ark to the Philistines, (I Sam'l 4:11), their priests, both Eli and his two sons, died, the Ark of God was taken and thirty thousand footmen fell, as God forsook Shiloh, (See Jer. 7:1-16; 26:1-7; Ps. 78:56-64). The Ark and Tabernacle were never united again. Samuel taught Israel saying,

"If you do return unto the Lord with all your hearts, then put away the strange gods and Ashtaroth from among you, and prepare your hearts unto the Lord, and serve him only, and he will deliver you out of the hand of the Philistines. Then the children of Israel did put away Baalam and Ashtaroth, and served the Lord only." (I Sam'l 7:3-4).

And Israel gained a great victory that day on the same battlefield and over the same people who defeated them there twenty years before. What is the history of the book of Judges and of Kings but a masterly presentation of the fact that Israel sinned and was punished; they repented, put away their idols, cried unto the Lord and served Him only, and he invariably healed them. Whether the captivity was long or short, it terminated WHEN ISRAEL REPENTED: When the seventy years captivity of Judah in Babylon ended, it found a *repentant* and *willing* people. The prayer and confession of Daniel (ch. 9) is very explicit on this point. The law of Moses did not provide for national favor to Israel only on this basis. *The gospel promises no favor without repentance.*

Solomon, in dedicating the temple, used this feature of the divine arrangement, with impressive clearness in his prayer, (I Ks. 8:44-53; which see on this point).

The same thought is brought out by Jeremiah, "At what instant I shall speak concerning a nation, and concerning a kingdom, to pluck up and to pull down and destroy it. If that nation against whom I have pronounced, turn from their evil, I will repent of the evil that I thought to do unto them. And at what instant I shall speak concerning a nation, and concerning a king-dom, to build and to plant it; if it do evil in my sight, that it obey not my voice, then, I will repent of the good wherewith I said I would benefit them." (Jer. 18:7-10).

This, as the reader sees, is the old doctrine of *blessings* and *curses* that runs through the entire Bible. The conditions of obtaining the *blessing*, or falling under the *curse*, were either expressed, or necessarily implied, in every case. *Israel can not run away from, or outlive, this law. When Israel repents, as of yore, God will bless them. For in Christ, all the families of the earth shall be "blessed."*

It is not a return to the deserted cities, and ancient dwellings, the untilled fields, the neglected vineyards, the lonely highways of Palestine, that will bless Israel. They might revere the memory of Abraham, and visit the tomb of David, with heart-felt lamentations. They might ascend the rocky eminences, and scan with delight the Promised Land, as did Moses from Pisgah. But while they revile the name of Jesus, the more illustrious Son of Abraham, and David's Lord, they can not scrip-turally hope to be *blessed* with *faithful* Abraham. The types are done away. They did not know the voice of their prophets or they would not have slain the Lord of Glory. The same veil is over their hearts this day in reading the Old Testament, and this refers especially to the destiny of their nation, and the claims of Christ upon them.

ISRAEL IN CAPTIVITY.

What is Israel's sin, today? It is the rejection of Jesus Christ, not as a national ruler, a temporal deliverer, and earthly savior. It is their rejection of Him as their HIGH-PRIEST, their PROPHET and KING. Every Is-raelite, when he comes to the years of responsibility, is a sinner, just as a Gentile is. They are all the servants of Satan. Peter told the Jews of his day, "This is the stone which the builders rejected, which has become the head of the corner. Neither is there salvation in any other; for there is none other name under heaven given among men, whereby we must be saved," (Acts 4:11-12). This is as true today as when spoken, and has been true every moment since Jesus "took the Law out of the way, nailing it to his cross." Jesus would not deliver the Jews from the Roman yoke, when here. The blinded Jews said,

"We be Abraham's seed, and were never in bondage to any man; how sayest thou, ye shall be made free? Jesus answered them, Verily, verily I say unto you, whosoever committeth sin is the *servant of sin.* And the *servant abideth not in the house forever*; but the Son abideth forever. If the Son, therefore shall make you free, ye shall be free indeed, I know that ye are Abraham's seed; but ye seek to kill me, because my word hath no place in you. I speak that which I have seen with my Father; and ye do that which ye have seen with your father.

They answered and said unto him, Abraham is our father. Jesus saith unto them, if ye were Abraham's children, ye would do the works of Abraham. Ye do the deeds of your father. Then said they unto him, we be not born of fornication; we have one Father, even God. Jesus said unto them, if God were your Father, ye would love me; for I proceeded forth and came from God; neither came I of myself, but he sent me." (John 8:33-42).

What is all this talk about "Zionist movement," in the light of this revelation? "Oh," you say, "a return of the Jews to Palestine!" Very well! A converted Jew wrote to all other converted Jews after this manner, "But ye are come *unto Mount Sion,* and unto *the city of the living God,* the heavenly Jerusalem, and to an innumerable company of angels," etc. Have these Jews, in this "Zionist Movement," done this? Do they contemplate reviving the old Phariseeism in the land of their fathers, and pray God's blessing upon the land, cities, restored temple, and worship, and to enjoy the fertility and ancient fruitfulness of the land and nation of Israel? Do we Gentiles sympathize with this blasphemous attempt to dethrone Jesus Christ our Lord, and give back in his stead the traditions of the Jewish Rabbis, whose envy, and hatred for Jesus, led them to "crucify the holy one and the Just"? The whole foundation of such an interpretation of the Jewish prophecies is false and pernicious. Any interpretation that uses the prophets to uphold the Jews, ancient or modern, in their contempt for Jesus Christ, arrays the prophets of the Old Testament against the Apostles, prophets and teachers of the New Testament, and is false to the facts. This whole theory of the revival under heavenly blessing of the Jews, in their

blind attachment to their *false shepherds,* and in rejection
of the *"good SHEPHERD,"* is logically, a repudiation of
Jesus Christ, and his inspired apostles and the church.

Is it because the Jews are out of Palestine, and can
no longer observe the sacrifices, feasts and holy days,
after the ancient manner, that they are condemned?
Nay, verily; It is because they are disobeying God, in rejecting his Son.   They are clinging to traditions and
have been led by their Targum and Talmud, rather than
by Moses.   Moses would lead them to Christ.   "If they
believed Moses' writings, they would believe Christ's
words, for he wrote of Him."   (Jno. 5:45-47).   Moses
accuses them to God.   So do all the prophets.   The
writers of the Bible are a unit in condemning Jews and
Gentiles who reject Christ.

"And this is the condemnation that light is come into
the world, and men loved darkness rather than light
because their deeds were evil. For every one that doeth
evil hateth the light, neither cometh to the light lest his
deeds should be reproved. But he that doeth truth
cometh to the light, that his deeds may be made manifest, that they are wrought in God," (Jno. 3:19-21).

THE JEWS ARE NOT IN BONDAGE TODAY,

As they were in Egypt or another Moses could lead
them out.   They are not in bondage in Moab, Ammon,
Amalek or Philistia, or the Judges could lead them out.
They are not in bondage to the Babylonians, or a Cyrus
could restore them to their land.   They can not recover
the favor of God by rebuilding their material temple so
long in ruins, or a new Zerubbabel and Jeshua, under
royal favor, could restore their holy house.   All the
kings on earth today, and the wealth of the Rothchilds,
supplemented by the treasures of all lands, *can not purchase back to them the favor of God.*   It is the precious blood
of Christ that was spilled for their redemption, and he
is the only rightful King over them.   His temple is already built (I Cor. 3:16-17; 19,20; I Tim. 3:15; I Peter
2:1-9).   This holy nation, holy temple, precious sacrifice
and compassionate High-Priest, have forever set aside the
temporal, typical, fleshly arrangement ordained by Moses,
(II Cor. 3), and it is inexcusable in us to contribute to
the blindness and obstinacy of the modern Jews in giving

an interpretation of their ancient books that tends to ease their minds, and allay their fears, when they treat with sovereign contempt the Son of God. I fail to see how any conscientious interpreter of God's word can sustain the Jew in his contention, or aid him in the Utopian dream, *that a restoration to Palestine would be a restoration to the favor of God, as it was while the law of Moses was in force.* The nature of this error will receive additional illustration in the next chapter, and recurs, in different connections, in later portions of this book.

CHAPTER IX.

THE TWO PROMISES.

The two-fold promise made to Abraham that God would make of him a great nation and in his seed should all the families of the earth be blessed, forms the basis of the entire Bible. Moses wrote his five books more than four centuries after these promises were made to Abraham, his ancestor. So, to understand the Bible, one must study the accomplishment of these two great promises. The Old Testament history is taken up directly with the origin, growth, maturity and experiences of the great nation; and, indirectly, with the history of other nations as they came in contact with this nation. Many people are in total ignorance of the prophecies; it is certain, therefore, that they are ignorant of the history contained in the Bible. Prophecy is history written beforehand. This was because God was making Himself known to that nation, and through them to all nations. The predictive features were among the least duties of the prophets, measured by the vast amount of revelation they were to make, of the attributes of God, the nature of sin and His hatred for, and the futility of it.

IDOLATRY.

We should know that all nations had cast off the

knowledge, worship and service of God, and the mighty
task of enlightening and rescuing them was assigned to
Abraham and his seed. How should this be done? This
is best answered by studying the history of how it was
done. This means that the Bible tells us in the history
of Israel. It was not done in a day or century, but it
has measurably been accomplished. These two promises
span the ages. What is the most ancient thing we know?
Is it the Mahometan religion? The Roman Catholic or
Greek Catholic church? These are young compared with
the Jewish race. They arose in the seventh century
after Christ; the Jewish race sprang from Abraham
twenty centuries before Christ. These churches and
governments are thirteen centuries old, but the Jewish
race has been here for nearly forty centuries. They have
outlived all the ancient nations, and have witnessed the
rise, growth, maturity and extinction of the four great
monarchies, Babylon, Medo-Persia, Greece and Rome,
excepting the fragments of the iron kingdom, last mentioned, as they still exist in Europe. Israel has been
compared to a great forest that stands for ages, and the
various governments that have risen, flourished and disappeared, to the successive crops of the fields, and the
illustration is true.

In (Gen. 11:26) we find Abraham, "THE FATHER
OF THE FAITHFUL," in Ur of the Chaldees.   In (Gen.
12) he is in Canaan, seventy-five years old, Sarah sixty-
five, and childless. Twenty five years later, Isaac is
born, and the first step towards the great nation has been
made. This was nineteen centuries before Christ. Sixty
years later Esau and Jacob were born to Isaac.   One
hundred and thirty years later Jacob, his twelve sons,
their wives and children went into Egypt to join Joseph
who had been exalted to be ruler over all the land of
Egypt. This finishes Genesis.

In Egypt these people grew into a great nation.   It
is not material, in our survey of the rise of this "GREAT
NATION," to decide whether their stay was two hundred
fifteen, or four hundred thirty years in Egypt. Moses
comes into the history now as deliverer, mediator and
lawgiver. He leads the nation out of Egypt, gives them
the law of God, educates them for forty years in the

wilderness, appoints Joshua as his successor, and dies. Thus we are led through one hundred twenty years (the lifetime of Moses) and have read Exodus, (the going out of Egypt); Leviticus, (as the ceremonials for Levi); Numbers, (the number of the nation in tribes and how they were governed in their encampments and marches); Deuteronomy, (or a repetition of parts of the law). They were growing into a nation, but had not yet obtained their land, but Moses had secured all east of Jordan for Reuben, Gad and the half tribe of Manasseh, leaving nine tribes and a half unprovided for at his death. Joshua took the nation across the Jordan, subdued the heathen nations, and got the people back to the promised land. They were now where Abraham lived the last century of his life; where Isaac spent the whole one hundred eighty years of his life; and where Jacob spent the larger part of his earthly pilgrimage. These patriarchs were all buried in a cave at Hebron some eighteen miles south of Jerusalem.

The nation was then settled in the land, with a divine law, a wonderful tabernacle, and a whole tribe consecrated to look after national worship. Then followed about four hundred and fifty years that the nation had no kings but occasional Judges. We read of the thrilling experiences of these men in the book of Judges and the first seven chapters of (I Samuel).

THE KINGS.

Saul of the tribe of Benjamin, was the first king, and reigned forty years. He was succeeded by David, who reigned forty years, and conquered or put under tribute the whole territory promised to Abraham, some sixty thousand square miles. David's reign was ever afterwards regarded as the ideal reign of the whole kingly line, and in our next chapter we shall note the great promise of an unending dynasty in his family.

Solomon, the wisest and richest king, but not the greatest from a moral standpoint, succeeded David, his father, and reigned forty years. His greatest achievement was the erection and dedication to the service of God of the greatest temple of history.

THE DIVISION.

In the next place, the historian records the division of Israel into two nations. Ten tribes went off after Jeroboam and were called Israel, and two tribes, Judah and Benjamin, later Levi and true servants of God from the other tribes, all wore the name of Judah. They, of course, had the capital, Jerusalem, also the temple, and could observe the sacrifices, feasts and fasts at the place where the Lord had recorded his name. This division of the nation took place about (B. C. 975). There were envy and strife between the two peoples, and necessarily confusion and every evil work. Israel was often called Ephraim, because the tribe of Ephraim, one of Joseph's sons, was the leading tribe; just as the tribes around Jerusalem were called Judah. There were no kings in Judah, however, except the descendants of David, while the ten tribes had no such rule to govern them. The ten tribes existed as a distinct nation for two hundred and fifty-four years and were carried out of their land into Assyria, which at that time was the leading heathen nation. Later their territory was re-occupied by peoples brought from various countries and they "FEARED GOD AND SERVED IDOLS." This mixed people (I choose the word "mixed" to picture to us the inter-marriages of descendants of Jacob with the heathen, and the adoption of many heathen rites and customs), were called Samaritans. They were quite numerous and occupied central Palestine during the earth-life of our Savior, as they had done since the days of their first settlement, (II Kings. 17).

The kingdom of Israel was overthrown in the sixth year of Hezekiah, the thirteenth king of Judah, (II Ks. 18:9-12). He reigned twenty-three years longer and was succeeded by his son Manasseh, who reigned fifty-five years, the longest reign in either nation. It was an eventful half century, for Manasseh led the nation to do more evil than the heathen nations whom God drove out in the days of Joshua, and he slew many of the faithful servants of God, and, SHED INNOCENT BLOOD VERY MUCH, TILL HE HAD FILLED JERUSALEM FROM ONE END TO ANOTHER." This was early in his reign. He was taken a captive to Babylon, but upon his repentance he was released, an sought to change the conduct of his nation to be according to the law of Moses, but it was not effected.

His son Amon succeeded him, at his death, but no acts are recorded of him except his wickedness, and he was followed by Josiah, one of the very best kings that ever reigned over the children of Abraham, David not excepted. His zeal and unwearied industry in behalf of Judah, however, only postponed, but could not save his nation from the national captivity in Babylon, so often threatened by the prophets. He reigned thirty-one years, and with his family the final overthrow came and by sword, famine and pestilence the nation was reduced till only a small remnant was left to be carried to Babylon.

A SUMMING UP.

The facts stated in this and in the preceding and succeeding chapters, are repeated, in different connections, as it is indispensible to any clear understanding of the Bible, that we do not lose the thread or golden line on which all the historical and prophetic facts, are strung. We are now considering the rise, growth, maturity and experiences of the "GREAT NATION" promised to Abraham. We see by this hasty survey that age after age witnessed new features in their form of government, but they were all of one original family, that of Abraham. To aid the memory I set before the reader the following facts:

1. Abraham received the promise that he should become a great nation, (Gen. 12:1-3), while he was in Ur of the Chaldees.

2. Isaac was born twenty-five years later, or when Abraham was one hundred years old, and dwelling in Palestine, the land promised him.

3. Isaac married Rebecca, and to them twin sons, Esau and Jacob, were born when Isaac was sixty, and Abraham one hundred and sixty, years old. Abraham died fifteen years later.

4. The little nation, numbering seventy-five souls, went into Egypt, when Jacob, the father of twelve sons,

whose families became the twelve tribes of Israel, was
one hundred and thirty years of age, (Gen. 47:9). Jacob
lived in Egypt seventeen years (Gen. 47:28) and after
blessing his two grand-sons by Joseph (ch. 48), and his
sons (ch. 49), died and was carried back to Canaan and
buried beside his wife, Leah, his father and mother
Isaac and Rebecca, and his illustrious grandfather and
grandmother, Abraham and Sarah, (Gen. 50), in the
cave at Hebron.

5.   The growth of the nation is briefly described in
the opening chapters of Exodus, and in (Numbers chs. 1
and 2).   When they came out of Egypt under Moses,
there were six hundred and three thousand five hundred
and fifty men above twenty years of age, exclusive of
Levi, who numbered twenty-two thousand two hundred
and seventy-three males, from a month old and upward,
(Num. 3:43).

6.   This vast company fell in the wilderness through
disobedience, except Caleb and Joshua.

In (Num. 26) we have the enumeration forty years
later than their entrance into the wilderness and they
have decreased eighteen hundred and twenty persons, in
the twelve tribes, but Levi has gained about one thousand persons.

7.   Joshua took the nation across the Jordan, and
conquered the land and settled the tribes in their possessions, after Moses' death.   The book of Joshua records
their great experiences, and the miraculous power that
aided the nation in taking possession of the land so long
promised to them.

8.   We have seen that Judges were raised up from
time to time to deliver the nation from heathen oppressors, who had been suffered to chastise Israel because
they adopted, in a measure, their idolatry.   This check-
ered history covers the next four centuries and a half
down to the time when the nation chose a king.

9.   Kings ruled over the nation for five centuries.
The first one hundred and twenty years Saul, David and
Solomon reigned forty years each, (not to consider Ish-
bosheth, Saul's son who contested the sovereignty with
David, and made a cleavage of the nation along about the
same tribal lines as came later under Jeroboam, II Sam'l.

2:8 to 4:1-12). Saul's history as King is given from (I Sam'l. 9 to ch. 31); also David's history is closely identified with his from the (16th ch.). David as active king is given the entire book of (II Sam'l and I Ks. 1), besides the parallel history in (I Chron. 11 to 29 ch's). A very large amount of space, indeed, for one man! To which we should add the Psalms chiefly written by this eminent poet-king.

10. Solomon's early reign was peaceful and very great, and he ranks above that of any other earthly king, living or dead, for wisdom and riches, (I Ks. 3:11-13). Ten chapters, (2 to 11) are devoted to him in First Kings, and he is very conspicuous in the last two chapters of (I Chron), and the first nine chapters of (II Chron), the parallel history.

11. *The rebellion and apostasy of the ten tribes comes next*, under Jereboam and his successors, for two hundred and fifty-four years. One may read this history from (I Ks. 12 to II Ks. 18).

12. The Kingdom of Judah survived the overthrow of the ten tribes one hundred thirty-four years, but these years have a history condensed into six and a half chapters, (II Ks. 18:13 to ch. 25) and in the parallel history (II Chron. 29 to 36). These chapters give one an insight into the lives, political and religious, of the kings.

13. Judah was in Babylon for seventy years, according to the definite period Jeremiah predicted, (Jer. 25:11-14 also 27:7-11). The prophet Daniel was in captivity in Babylon during the whole period, and prayed for Judah's restoration to their land, knowing by these prophecies that the time of their captivity was due to end, by studying this time prophecy, (Dan. 7). Ezra and Nehemiah tell us how Israel were delivered from this captivity and restored to their land in different companies about (B. C. 536).

14. They were cleansed from Idolatry, rebuilt their temple and multiplied again into a numerous and mighty nation, but never regained their independent rule, saving for a brief period in the time of the Maccabees. Five centuries after the return from Babylon they were very numerous and while they lived in Palestine in large

numbers, they were found then as now in "EVERY NATION UNDER HEAVEN."

CONCLUSION.

1. The nation was then *great in age*, some two thousand years old.

2. It was *great in numbers*—as innumerable as the sands of the sea or the stars of heaven.

3. It was *great in wealth*, and had one of the most productive countries in the world.

4. Its *chief greatness* however consisted in the fact of its *great mission in the world*. It has been the teacher of the knowledge of the true and living God, to the greatest nations of the world. To Egypt under Moses; to Canaan, Moab, Ammon, Edom, Assyria, Babylon, Medo-Persia, Greece and Rome in later centuries. They, like all other teachers, had to learn before they could teach; and they learned under that hard preceptor, experience. But they gave the world all the prophets, and these were strictly Monotheists, or believers in one God. In the synagogues throughout the Roman Empire this, now almost universal belief, was first made known to the benighted nations among whom they dwelt. Joseph in Egypt; David in Israel as royal-prophet; Daniel and the three Hebrew worthies in Babylon making known to the assembled dignitaries of the great empire, the power and majesty of God; and the leavening power of the Old Testament when translated into the Greek language, the common tongue of the masses about (B. C. 280), not to speak of the great temple service in the capital city, which for five centuries was teaching the folly and emptiness of idolatry and the glory and power of the one true and living God; all these things surely entitle Israel to be called a "GREAT NATION." Abraham's name ranks first among some two hundred millions of Mahometans, as the great father of the faithful. The Jews, throughout the ages, and the Christians since Christ, revere that great man. He was not a king, a statesman, a warrior, a sculptor, a painter, an orator or a millionaire philanthropist, but an humble servant of the one true and living God, and he and his little family became the custodians of "the promises." The fulfillment of these promises in-

volved the divine assistance for him and his seed for ages. Century after century rolled by and the knowledge of the one true and living God, deposited with Abraham, pervaded the world. It was the mission of Israel to learn there is but one God, and other nations were to learn this fundamental fact from them. *This is the one feature of Israel's history that forever distinguishes them above all other nations.* ✱This element made them great. The "BLESSING" and the "CURSE"were so inseparably connected with the doctrine that there is but one God, that nations rose or fell, prospered or were chastised, lived or died, owing to whether they respected it, on the one hand, or rejected it, on the other.✱ And, let it never be forgotten that, the nation of Israel *learned* this doctrine in victory and defeat, in prosperity and adversity, by being exalted above the nations or by being enslaved by them; by "BLESSINGS" for obedience and "CURSES" for disobedience, and through it all we learn not only the fact that God sees the end from the beginning, but we learn what God is in holiness. His character, if the word is a proper one, is revealed in his hatred of sin and love of holiness, manifested on a basis nation-wide by the unique and marvelous history of Abraham's seed. They became a "GREAT NATION;" not that they were right in conduct, or approved of heaven, generally speaking, for they were the reverse. But we learn as much by the mistakes of others as by their successes. Men often ignorantly criticise the life of Israel, assuming that God approved them in sin. A greater error could not easily be imagined. One says look here! This man was a liar, this one an adulterer, this one a murderer, and they were God's special people. Look at this covetous, bloodthirsty, idolatrous nation, for ages of their history, and they the *chosen* and peculiar *people of God*! Well, dear reader, *chosen for what*? Can you cite a single case of an individual, city, tribe or nation that God indorsed in disobedience? No, the reverse is true. "EVERY TRANSGRESSION AND DISOBEDIENCE RECEIVED A JUST RECOMPENSE OF REWARD, IN ISRAEL." They were not great because always pious, peaceable, honest, just, generous, merciful, prayerful and true to God. They were great because of their mission in the world as a nation. Because God used them as witnesses for Himself but much oftener testifying *against their sinful conduct*, than *for* themselves in holiness, because they were oftener wrong than right. But the fact remains that by choosing them, giving them a law, "BLESSING" them for obedience, "CURSING" them for disobedience, and by dealing through them with all surrounding nations after the same fixed rule, the great God, slowly but surely made that nation the recipients and dispensers of the knowledge that there is but one God, the God of Abraham, of Isaac and of Jacob, and idolatry was drven from the nations. This fundamental fact was made evident to Israel and through Israel to the Gentiles, before the gospel came by Abraham's seed—descendant, Christ, "FOR HE THAT COMETH TO GOD, MUST BELIEVE THAT HE IS, AND THAT HE IS A REWARDER OF THEM THAT DILIGENTLY SEEK HIM."

CHAPTER X.

THE SECOND PROMISE.

The promise that the "SEED OF THE WOMAN, SHOULD BRUISE THE SERPENT'S HEAD" was some two thousand years before the promise to Abraham that he should become a "GREAT NATION." This promise was revived, however, in these words, "AND IN THEE SHALL ALL FAMILIES OF THE EARTH BE BLESSED;" and later stated more fully, "AND IN THY SEED SHALL ALL NATIONS OF THE EARTH BE BLESSED; BECAUSE THOU HAST OBEYED MY VOICE," (Gen. 12:3 and 22:18). The nation could not perish while this promise was unfulfilled. In the reign of Athaliah the whole royal line of David was slain except a child—Joash. God often defended Jerusalem for his name's sake, and for David's sake, or because of this promise, when Judah went into Babylon it was not time for this Child of Abraham to bear rule. Isaac was born to Abraham twenty-five years after the promise to begin the nation; but Jesus did not come for some *two thousand* years after Abraham to fulfill the second promise. This is all matter of history, and shows us how the Bible is constructed. *It required centuries and ages to redeem its promises.* This is not a long, but a very short time for Him whose name is Eternal; but it seems long to us because our brief lives are lived in carrying out brief plans. God's plan spans all time and stretches into the endless ages. This promise was repeated to David.

JUDAH'S GIBRALTAR.

The tribe of Judah, from the days of David, had an abiding hope, (II Sam'l 7). David desired to build a temple and house the Ark of God, which had been separated from the Tabernacle Moses built, since the early days of Samuel, I Sam'l 4:11). Nathan endorsed David's project, but God did not. The Lord said to David through Nathan that David's son should build the house, and that God would build up David's house or dynasty forever. David's kingdom was to have no end. In David's prayer on the occasion, by implication and express statement, he mentions this feature six times, like the promise to Abraham that in his "SEED" all the families of the earth should be "BLESSED," specifying no one descendant by name through whom the blessing should come; so David's family is spoken of as a dynasty, or succession of sons, rather than as one son as they led up to Christ. It was made plain that evil kings should be chastened but the kingly line should be perpetual. This became the basis, as noted briefly hitherto, for many predictions. I have said it was a peculiar fact, not possible to any other tribe or nation on earth, and faith in this promise caused *Judah* to hope in the darkest hours of her national history. The *ten tribes* had no such basis for hope of continuance of their kings or nation and no other nation or family had such hope. IT WAS THE EXCLUSIVE PROMISE TO THE HOUSE OF DAVID. To this promise they clung in all their captivities and chastisements. Amos predicted the restoration of David's tabernacle.

"IN THAT DAY WILL I RAISE UP THE TABERNACLE OF DAVID THAT IS FALLEN, AND CLOSE UP

THE BREACHES THEREOF; AND I WILL RAISE UP HIS RUINS, AND I WILL BUILD IT AS IN THE DAYS OF OLD: THAT THEY MAY POSSESS THE REMNANT OF EDOM, AND ALL OF THE HEATHEN WHICH ARE CALLED BY MY NAME, SAITH THE LORD THAT DOETH THIS." (Amos 9:11, 12). The sheepfolds were sometimes made of stones built into rough walls, and a rude house for the shepherd. The shepherds moved their flocks to other parts for pasturage and water and returned and repaired the house with tented coverings at the winter season. So, the lost sheep of the house of Israel, would wander for ages, and the tabernacle of David would fall into ruin, but ultimately the great Shepherd, the owner of the sheep, would build up again the royal house of the king and lead and feed the long deserted flock. This house of David fell into ruin when Zedekiah the last king of Israel (B. C. 587) was taken to Babylon. The preceding verses in the prophecy show us how the walls of defense crumbled, and the house was deserted and torn down and the sheep were scattered.

X "BEHOLD THE EYES OF THE LORD GOD ARE UPON THE SINFUL KINGDOM, AND I WILL DESTROY IT FROM THE FACE OF THE EARTH; SAVING THAT I WILL NOT UTTERLY DESTROY THE HOUSE OF JACOB, SAITH THE LORD, FOR LO I WILL COMMAND, AND I WILL SIFT THE HOUSE OF ISRAEL AMONG ALL NATIONS, LIKE AS CORN IS SIFTED IN A SIEVE, YET SHALL NOT THE LEAST GRAIN FALL UPON THE EARTH. ALL THE SIN- NERS OF MY PEOPLE SHALL DIE BY THE SWORD, WHICH SAY, THE EVIL DAY SHALL NOT OVERTAKE NOR PREVENT US." (Vs. 8-10).

The evil day did overtake them. They fell by fam- ine, sword, and pestilence, and a small remnant were *fortunate enough, under this promise,* to go into captivity in Babylon for seventy years. But David's house was never rebuilt, or the rule and sovereignty restored. No king has sat upon David's throne in Mt. Zion from the Baby- lonian captivity till now—twenty-five centuries. Has the prediction failed, then? Or is it yet to be fulfilled? No, neither supposition is true, for the inspired apostles quoted and applied the prophecy to Christ and the Church.

"James answered saying, *men and brethren, hearken unto me: Simeon* [Simon Peter on the same occasion, Acts

15:7-11] *hath declared how God at the first did visit the Gentiles, to take out of them a people for His name.   And to this agree the words of the prophets* [though he cites but one]; *as it is written, after this I will return and will build again the tabernacle of David, which is fallen down; and I will build again the ruins thereof, and I will set it up: that the residue of men might seek after the Lord, and all the Gentiles upon whom my name is called, saith the Lord, who doeth all these things.   Known unto God are all His works from the beginning of the world."*   (Vs. 13-18).

This prophecy of Amos, linked with (Hosea 3:4, 5) is very beautiful.   *"For the children of Israel* [here Israel is used in its wide sense meaning the descendants of Israel] *shall abide many days without a king and without a prince, and without a sacrifice, and without an image, and without an Ephod, and without Teraphim.   AFTERWARD SHALL THE CHILDREN OF ISRAEL RETURN, AND SEEK THE LORD THEIR GOD, AND DAVID THEIR KING; AND SHALL FEAR THE LORD AND HIS GOODNESS IN THE LATTER DAYS."*

These two prophets lived and labored at the same time: Hosea worked chiefly among the ten tribes or Ephriam, and Amos, while of Tekoa, Judah, labored likewise chiefly among the ten tribes.   But the ten tribes became extinct as a nation.   Nothing can be affirmed of them as a people since the days of Esar-Haddon, (B. C. 678—2 Ks. 17:24).   Both of these prophecies show how these holy men looked forward in hope to the rebuilding of David's house.   The Gentiles were to be ruled over by him, in *all nations, all who called on God's name.*   It could not be that some temporal prince would meet the demands of these predictions.   The Spirit that inspired Amos to predict, inspired James to apply the prediction, and Luke to record it.   It is doing manifest violence to the text to claim it is unfulfilled.   It is to intrude a speculation, where James has settled the question by inspiration.   It is evident that the *"possession* of Edom and of all the heathen; who are called by my name saith the Lord that doeth this," referred not to the conquest of heathen territories, or the subduing of Gentiles to pay tribute, *but to their conversion to God.*   Christ rules over larger and more glorious possessions than David ever did.   He smites the nations with "THE SWORD OF THE SPIRIT."   James tells us in applying the prophecy that God did at the first, [the household of

Cornelius], visit the Gentiles to take out of them a people
for his name.   Not by partiality, for "GOD IS NO RE-
SPECTOR OF PERSONS," and "WHOSOEVER SHALL
CALL UPON THE NAME OF THE LORD SHALL BE
SAVED."   He was showing that David's house was rebuilt, the great and good Shepherd had built his sheep-
fold, and Jews and Gentiles, of the faith of Abraham,
were being led, fed and protected by him.   James could
have cited (Jno. 10) and certified that the prediction of
the good Shepherd, "AND OTHER SHEEP I HAVE,
WHICH ARE NOT OF THIS FOLD: THEM ALSO I
MUST BRING, AND THEY SHALL HEAR MY VOICE;
AND THERE SHALL BE ONE FOLD AND ONE SHEP-
HERD," was fulfilled in uniting the two peoples in the
endearing friendship of children of God, and Jews and
Gentiles were the sheep and Jesus the Shepherd.   It
was not a political rule that was foretold but a sacred
rule.   David was king for forty years, but he was not
an independent ruler, for God was above him and, strictly
speaking, the King of Israel.   For Israel to seek God and
David their king, therefore, is not for Israel who for
ages has been without a country, without a city, without
a king or prince, without a temple, sacrifice or ephod, to
restore these.   They are as much out of date, and out of
place under the gospel, as Noah's Ark.   One could as rea-
sonably hope to be saved from sin, by imitating Noah in
building and furnishing the Ark, as he could in building
the temple of Solomon or Zerubbabel, and reviving its
ritual.

JEREMIAH.

As the nation of Judah declined lower and lower,
after the ten tribes became extinct as a nation, the prophets spake with confidence concerning the preservation of
the *house of David*.   This one promise was the hope of the
nation.   Jeremiah lived and wrote in the last generation,
before the captivity of Judah by the Babylonians, and
was in Jerusalem when the last king was taken.   His
predictions were many and very plain.   He foretold the
"seventy years" captivity of Judah in Babylon, and their
return to their land.   He could not, therefore, have hoped
that the *royal house of David would rule continually*, and
predicted that Coniah was the last ruler by direct descent

from David, who should prosper sitting upon the throne of David. Zedekiah, his uncle, was of one generation earlier, and Coniah was thus the last ruler by lineal descent from David. But this did not mean that God's word to David should fail. The prophet had God's not man's view of the prophecy, and, in company with his inspired brethren, leaped over the dark and troublous centuries, and settled the question forever as to what particular Son of David should *rule forever*.

"BEHOLD, THE DAYS COME, SAITH THE LORD, THAT I WILL RAISE UNTO DAVID A RIGHTEOUS BRANCH, AND A KING SHALL REIGN AND PROSPER, AND SHALL EXECUTE JUDGMENT AND JUSTICE IN THE EARTH. IN HIS DAYS JUDAH SHALL BE SAVED AND ISRAEL SHALL DWELL SAFELY; AND THIS IS HIS NAME WHEREBY HE SHALL BE CALLED THE LORD OUR RIGHTEOUSNESS."

As this was God's will everything necessary to pre- serve a remnant of Judah, and especially the family of David, till he came, would be done.

"THEREFORE, BEHOLD THE DAYS COME, SAITH THE LORD, THAT THEY SHALL NO MORE SAY, THE LORD LIVETH WHO BROUGHT UP THE CHILDREN OF ISRAEL OUT OF THE LAND OF EGYPT, BUT THE LORD LIVETH, WHO BROUGT UP AND LED THE SEED OF THE HOUSE OF ISRAEL FROM THE NORTH COUNTRY, AND FROM ALL COUNTRIES WHITHER I HAD DRIVEN THEM; AND THEY SHALL DWELL IN THEIR OWN LAND," (Ver. 8).

As a captivity was foretold, he insists, it was not to exterminate the nation, as the Assyrian captivity did the ten tribes, for *God had a Ruler yet to come into the world, Christ the Son of David*, and the tribe of Judah, though chastised, though scattered in judgment among the nations, though possessing no son of David for six centuries, to sit upon his throne and prosper in Israel, yet should be preserved, and be in the land of their fathers when "THE LORD OUR RIGHTEOUSNESS," came to his own. You will find the same order of items predicted in (Jer. 33:14-18). But the prophet goes further and says, "FOR THUS SAITH THE LORD; DAVID SHALL NEVER WANT A MAN TO SIT UPON THE THRONE OF THE HOUSE OF ISRAEL; NEITHER SHALL THE PRIESTS, THE LEVITES, WANT A MAN

BEFORE ME TO OFFER BURNT OFFERINGS, AND TO
KINDLE MEAT OFFERINGS, AND TO DO SACRIFICE
CONTINUALLY." Here it was foretold that the Ruler,
Priest-hood and Sacrifices were to be continuous. Have
they been, in a temporal sense? Nay, verily. Daniel
said they were to cease, (Dan'l 9:27). Both were speaking for God. They are not contradictory. But no such
tribal distinctions have been maintained since Christ took
the law out of the way "nailing it to his cross."

"AND THE WORD OF THE LORD CAME UNTO JERE-
MIAH, SAYING, THUS SAITH THE LORD: IF YE CAN
BREAK MY COVENANT OF THE DAY, AND MY COVE-
NANT OF THE NIGHT, AND THAT THERE SHOULD NOT
BE DAY AND NIGHT IN THEIR SEASON, THEN ALSO MAY
MY COVENANT BE BROKEN WITH DAVID MY SERVANT,
THAT HE SHOULD NOT HAVE A SON TO REIGN UPON
HIS THRONE; AND WITH THE LEVITES THE PRIESTS,
MY MINISTERS. AS THE HOST OF HEAVEN CANNOT
BE NUMBERED, NEITHER THE SAND OF THE SEA
MEASURED; SO WILL I MULTIPLY THE SEED OF DAVID
MY SERVANT, AND THE LEVITES THAT MINISTER UNTO
ME. MOREOVER THE WORD OF THE LORD CAME TO
JEREMIAH SAYING, "CONSIDEREST THOU NOT WHAT
THIS PEOPLE HAVE SPOKEN SAYING, THE TWO FAM-
ILIES WHICH THE LORD HATH CHOSEN, HE HATH
EVEN CAST THEM OFF? THUS THEY HAVE DESPISED
MY PEOPLE, THAT THEY SHOULD BE NO MORE A NA-
TION BEFORE ME. THUS SAITH THE LORD: IF MY
COVENANT BE NOT WITH DAY AND NIGHT, AND IF I
HAVE NOT APPOINTED THE ORDINANCES OF HEAVEN
AND EARTH: THEN WILL I CAST AWAY THE SEED OF
JACOB, AND DAVID MY SERVANT, SO THAT I WILL NOT
TAKE ANY OF HIS SEED TO BE RULERS OVER
THE SEED OF ABRAHAM, ISAAC AND JACOB:
FOR I WILL CAUSE THEIR CAPTIVITY TO
RETURN AND WILL HAVE MERCY UPON THEM."
(Jer. 33:19-26).

The patient investigator will read the whole chapter.
He will learn that Jeremiah was in prison. The last
king, Zedekiah, a profane, wicked prince, was finishing
up his reign. The whole land was lying in ruins. The
capital was reduced to famine. Pestilence stalked abroad
at noonday. Yet Judah's hope had not perished. Captivity was inevitable, but justice should be tempered with
mercy. A "REMNANT" should return. The promise to

David was as certain to be fulfilled as that day should succeed night. What consolation this must have been to Judah in this midnight of her history! But what can the Literalists do here? Is the throne of David in Palestine to exist forever? No, it has been down for twenty-five centuries. Is Levi to continue to worship God at an earthly temple, with burnt offerings, meal offerings and sacrifices continually? This would demand an eternity for the temporal. This would necessitate,

1. That the children of Abraham should live on earth, and preserve their tribal distinctions *foreever*, as men in the flesh like David and Levi and offering animals as sacrifices forever.

2. It would demand that a tabernacle, or succession of tabernacles, should exist in Palestine through eternal ages.

3. It would call for the daily sacrifice of animals upon Jewish altars, by Aaron's descendants forever.

4. All this, in our day, would demand that Moses' provisions for typical ceremonies should be revived and continued through all succeeding ages, when Jesus has abrogated them, *"For the weakness and unprofitableness thereof."* But using these as TYPE-PROPHECIES, foretelling in the language of the types not the types themselves but greater realities, all is plain. "But they shall serve the Lord their God and David their king, whom I will raise up unto them," (Jer. 30:9). It is *this* David, [Christ] whom all must serve. No Literalist can possibly get through these manifold predictions on his principles, and not do the following:

1. Ignore the gospel age entirely and conjecture that the gospel age will end, and the Millennial age will be a return to literalism in temple, priesthood, Levites, sacrifices, and rulership, thus exchanging the gospel for the law. Or. 2. Have the types and the anti-types both in operation on earth at the same time. Or 3. Take the Jewish position that Jesus was an Impostor and when the *true* Messiah comes he will restore the lost genealogies, revive the tribal distinctions, rebuild the ancient wastes, erect the temple, and enact anew the fleshly sacrifice of brute beasts.

On gospel principles, where we have no such slavery

of the mind to the carnal appointments, we can read those texts as we do a similar text in

EZEKIEL.

Ezekiel denounced the Shepherd's of Israel, and then under the *figure* of the good Shepherd, Christ, said,

"AND I WILL SET UP ONE SHEPHERD OVER THEM AND HE SHALL FEED THEM, EVEN MY SERVANT DAVID; [David means beloved of the Lord], HE SHALL FEED THEM, AND HE SHALL BE THEIR SHEPHERD. AND I THE LORD WILL BE THEIR GOD, AND MY SERVANT DAVID A PRINCE AMONG THEM: I THE LORD HAVE SPOKEN IT.   AND I WILL MAKE WITH THEM A COVENANT OF PEACE, AND WILL CAUSE THE EVIL BEASTS TO CEASE OUT OF THE LAND; AND THEY SHALL DWELL SAFELY IN THE WILDERNESS, AND SLEEP IN THE WOODS."   (Ezek. 34:23-35).

Or again in that great prophecy in (Ch. 37); we see the two sticks of Judah and Ephraim, the two scepters, united in one, and an explanation of this action is then given.

"THUS SAITH THE LORD GOD: BEHOLD I WILL TAKE THE CHILDREN OF ISRAEL FROM AMONG THE HEATHEN WHITHER THEY BE GONE [they were now in captivity, both houses], AND WILL GATHER THEM ON EVERY SIDE, AND BRING THEM INTO THEIR OWN LAND: AND I WILL MAKE THEM ONE NATION IN THE LAND UPON THE MOUNTAINS OF ISRAEL: AND ONE KING SHALL BE KING TO THEM ALL; AND THEY SHALL BE NO MORE TWO NATIONS, NEITHER SHALL THEY BE DIVIDED INTO TWO KINGDOMS ANY MORE AT ALL, NEITHER SHALL THEY DEFILE THEMSELVES ANY-MORE WITH THEIR IDOLS, NOR WITH THEIR DETEST-ABLE THINGS, NOR WITH ANY OF THEIR TRANSGRES-SIONS: BUT I WILL SAVE THEM OUT OF ALL THEIR DWELLING PLACES, WHEREIN THEY HAVE SINNED AND WILL CLEANSE THEM: SO SHALL THEY BE MY PEOPLE, AND I WILL BE THEIR GOD.   AND DAVID MY SERVANT SHALL BE KING OVER THEM; AND THEY ALL SHALL HAVE ONE SHEPHERD: THEY SHALL ALSO WALK IN MY JUDGMENTS, AND OBSERVE MY STATUTES, AND DO THEM.   AND THEY SHALL DWELL IN THE LAND THAT I HAVE GIVEN UNTO JACOB MY SERVANT, WHEREIN YOUR FATHERS HAVE DWELT; AND THEY SHALL DWELL THEREIN, EVEN THEY AND THEIR

CHILDREN, AND THEIR CHILDREN'S CHILDREN FOR-
EVER: AND MY SERVANT DAVID SHALL BE THEIR
PRINCE FOREVER.

MOREVER I WILL MAKE A COVENANT OF PEACE
WITH THEM; IT SHALL BE AN EVERLASTING COVE-
NANT WITH THEM; AND I WILL PLACE THEM, AND
MULTIPLY THEM, AND WILL SET MY SANCTUARY IN
THE MIDST OF THEM FOREVERMORE.   MY TABER-
NACLE ALSO SHALL BE WITH THEM; YEA, I WILL BE
THEIR GOD, AND THEY SHALL BE MY PEOPLE.   AND
THE HEATHEN (GENTILES) SHALL KNOW THAT I THE
LORD DO SANCTIFY ISRAEL, WHEN MY SANCTUARY
SHALL BE IN THE MIDST OF THEM FOREVERMORE."
(Ezek. 37:20-28).

You observe the things that were to be eternal.

1.   They should dwell in the land forever.

2.   David should be their prince forever.

3.   The covenant of peace was an everlasting covenant.

4.   The sanctuary should be with them forever.
This last item is mentioned twice.   All of these facts are
so united as to make the conclusion inevitable that the
eternal things were all to be realized in the same place by
the same people.   It was not literal sheep, sleeping in the
woods, under the care of David!   It is necessarily figurative.

The whole family of Abraham were now in captivity.
Their last king had been blinded and carried to Babylon.
Next to the last king, Coniah, had been a prisoner in
Babylon many years.   Their fortified towns were destroyed.   Their capitol was in heaps.   Their *"Holy
House"* had been burned to the ground.   The nation had
wasted away until only a few people were left.   All the
riches, pomp and glory of the nation were swept away.
The vessels of the Lord's house were in a heathen temple
in Babylon.   Yet above the smouldering ruins of the
palace on Mount Zion, and above the sacred ashes of
the temple on Mount Moriah, and out of the graveyard
of the nation, the prophet saw a new Israel.   The promise of an eternal dynasty to David could not fail.   And the
terrors of fire and sword, famine and pestilence, captivity and national humiliation to the very dust of death,
could not frustrate the purpose of God.   When David

was reigning, in all the strength and riches of his match-less dominion, a prediction of perpetuity was strange and wonderful; but what shall we say of it when four hundred and fifty years had witnessed such ravages of the nation? The nation still clung to their one great promise, and out of death hoped to see the life of a new nation, stronger, purer, nobler and to outlast the conquerors as much as eternity exceeds the lifetime of man.

But who was this David who should *live so long?* Did the prophets know? Verily, no. What Covenant was that, and what its provisions, which should *continue forever?* How could Judah and Ephraim become *one nation,* and inhabit *one country,* or live in *one land, forever?* Who of them knew, or could wisely conjecture? Not one. (I Peter 1:10-12) shows us that these holy prophets did not comprehend the imperishable spiritual realities set forth in type and figure under their prophetic pens. But even in Babylon they could say, as given in the (89th Psalm all of which you should read).

"AND I WILL MAKE HIM MY FIRSTBORN, HIGHER THAN THE KINGS OF THE EARTH. MY MERCY WILL I KEEP FOR HIM, FOREVERMORE, AND MY COVENANT SHALL STAND FAST WITH HIM. HIS SEED ALSO WILL I MAKE ENDURE FOREVER, AND HIS THRONE AS THE DAYS OF HEAVEN. . . . . .

"MY COVENANT WILL I NOT BREAK, NOR ALTER THE THING THAT HAS GONE OUT OF MY LIPS. ONCE HAVE I SWORN BY MY HOLINESS THAT I WILL NOT LIE UNTO DAVID, HIS SEED SHALL ENDURE FOREVER, AND HIS THRONE AS THE SUN BEFORE ME. IT SHALL BE ESTABLISHED FOREVER AS THE MOON, AND AS A FAITHFUL WITNESS IN HEAVEN." (Ps. 89:27, 34-37).

Why this oath, and solemnity, this appeal to the ordinances of day and night, and awe-inspiring repetition? This points us to Jesus, the Son of David, and David's Lord, ruling in Zion, reducing the nations to his righteous scepter, and having everlasting ages in which to celebrate his victory over death and the grave. Let us sanctify the Lord God in our hearts, imbibe his spirit, obey his laws, worship in his temple, make all lands a Holy Land, and unite all the sons of men into one holy nation, and "having received a kingdom which cannot be moved, let us have grace, whereby we may serve God acceptably with reverence and Godly fear."

Dear Reader, the word *everlasting* or *eternal* in these texts sets aside the whole Millennial theory. It is true and consoling to say Jesus is eternal; heaven is eternal; the new covenant is everlasting, and the like. *But the very fact that these things are eternal, and that we already have them in fulfillment of these prophecies, forever excludes the literal interpretation* of them. *Jesus was not literally David.* So the chief member in *all* these predictions was confessedly figurative, and this compels us to interpret every other member of the predictions in harmony with it. The *everlasting covenant* evidently was the *Gospel* covenant with no land grant features in it, as far as this earth is concerned. The *sanctuary* is identified by the apostles as the Church of the living God, as we have already seen. Eternity is written over all these, Christ, his covenant, his sanctuary, and his inheritance. But no David will live forever in Palestine. The Levites for ages have mixed and mingled with the other tribes and become extinct as a tribe. Neither David nor Aaron, the King nor the priest, can declare his pedigree. Pedigrees are out of date. John the Baptist announced this fact in his ministry. Why should one persist in saying these prophecies cannot be fulfilled until Israel returns to the land of Canaan? That, I grant you, would be using the predictions literally, but the prophets did not so use them—David was not literal, the Sanctuary was not literal, the Levites and priests were not literal, the burnt offering, meal offering and continual offerings were not literal, and, we confidently conclude, the land was not literal. We must, to be honest and consistent, treat all as literal or all as figurative. We are compelled to adopt the figurative by the fact that the house of David who should rule forever, as long as the sun and moon, meant Jesus Christ our Lord. He did not begin his reign on an earthly throne, and should we conjecture that he will soon assume it, then be it remembered that it is unending, eternal, and that Levi is there; the priests are there; the burnt-offerings and all the Mosaic ritual are there; the tabernacle is there; and *their duration is as ceaseless as the days of heaven.* These and many other incontrovert-

ible facts necessitate us to reject the Literalist's interpretation and adopt the figurative upon which Christ and
the apostles built the Church and which has witnessed
the overthrow of the Jewish nation, so that they have
been,

"WANDERERS AMONG THE NATIONS," AND "ABID-
ING MANY DAYS WITHOUT KING, PRINCE, WITHOUT
SACRIFICE, IMAGE, EPHOD OR TERAPHIM."

Let us hope and labor that soon,

"THEY SHALL RETURN AND SEEK THE LORD
THEIR GOD AND DAVID THEIR KING, AND SHALL FEAR
THE LORD AND HIS GOODNESS IN THESE LATTER
DAYS."

CHAPTER XI.

DAVID AND CHRIST.

"Remember the days of old, consider the years of
many generations: ask thy father, and he will shew thee;
thy elders and they will tell thee.

"When the Most High divided to the nations, their
inheritance, when he separated the sons of Adam, he
set the bounds of the people according to the number
of the children of Israel." (Deut. 32:7-8).

It is reassuring to observe God's dealings with the
nations through Israel. Abram leftUr of the Chaldees,
one idolatrous country, and went out not knowing where
he went, but pitched his tent in Canaan, another idolatrous country, (Josh. 24:2-8); Gen. 12:1-9). In Canaan he built an altar unto the Lord. Abraham became
a circulating teacher of the knowledge of the one true
and living God. Study his life in connection with Pharaoh, Abimelech, the Sodomites and all others. Isaac,
his son, and Jacob, his grandson, were living exponents of
the same doctrine. "He is the Lord our God: *his judgments are in all the earth.* He hath remembered his covenant forever; the word which he commanded to a thousand generations. Which covenant he made with Abraham, and his oath unto Isaac: and confirmed the same

unto Jacob for a law, and to Israel for an everlasting covenant:

"Saying unto thee will I give the land of Canaan, the lot of your inheritance, when they were but a few men in number; yea, very few, and strangers in it.

"When they went from one nation to another, from one kingdom to another people; he suffered no man to do them wrong; yea, he reproved kings for their sakes; saying, touch not mine anointed and do my prophets no harm: Moreover he called for a famine upon the land; he brake the whole staff of bread. He sent a man before them, even Joseph, who was sold for a servant; whose feet they hurt with fetters; he was laid in iron; until the time that his word came; the word of the Lord tried him.

"The king sent and loosed him; even the ruler of the people, and let him go free.

"He made him lord of his house, and ruler of all his possessions, to bind his princes at his pleasure; and teach his senators wisdom." (Ps. 105:7-22).

JOSEPH.

The history of Abraham's family has its climaxes. The life-time of Joseph is one of these. In the mountain range of great and holy events, Joseph's life is a lofty peak. He was used of God to show the folly of magic and to teach Senators wisdom, religious wisdom. The greatest nation of the then known world—Egypt—was ruled over by an inspired man of God, and he a son of Abraham. The influence and power of this chaste statesman upon the bordering nations may never be known on earth. It was in impressing his religious hope upon his own people, however, a nation within a nation, that his mightiest work was accomplished. He died in faith, or the belief that,

"God will surely visit you and bring you out of this land, unto the land which he sware to Abraham, to Isaac and to Jacob. And Joseph took an oath of the children of Israel, saying, God will surely visit you ,and ye shall carry up my bones from hence. So Joseph died, being an hundred and ten years old; and they embalmed him, and he was put in a coffin in Egypt." (Gen. 50: 24-26).

This oath was faithfully kept by the Israelites, centuries later. (Ex. 13:19; Josh. 24:32).

MOSES.

Moses is the next great mountain peak, according to our illustration. What a teacher God made him! I speak especially of the work done against idolatry. Egypt fell, and the fall of it shook the world. The great plagues against Egypt filled the surrounding nations with fear ages after the events. Moses predicted this in a song, celebrating the victory, (Ex. 15:14-18). It was recalled by Rahab, when the two spies came to Jericho, (Josh. 2:9-11). The Philistines, nearly four centuries later, trembled in the presence of the Ark of God, when they recalled the great judgment against Egypt, under the leadership of Moses, (I Sam'l. 4:5-9). The victory was not only the basis for Hebrew poetry and national song, and enduring hope, but the nations far and near felt the tremendous shock given to idolatry, in Egypt, by Moses, and in Canaan by Joshua, and the elders that outlived Joshua. It seemed for a time that complete victory was gained over that foul doctrine in Egypt, Canaan and surrounding nations.

TYPICAL EVENTS.

It seems to have been ordained of God, not only from the time he called Abram, but ages before, to settle Israel in Palestine. We may discover the wisdom of this purpose in more than one particular. The relation of that land to other lands will be considered below. But the Lord worked out types of our great redemption in bringing Israel out of Egypt and into Canaan. I know of no other land where this could have been made so evident. 1. Pharaoh was a type of Satan. 2 . Moses was a type of Christ. 3. Israel in Egyptian bondage, was a type of our bondage in sin. 4. Israel left Egypt by way of the Red Sea—"were all baptized unto Moses in the cloud, and in the sea," as we leave the sinful world by way of the blood of Christ, are baptized into Christ. 5. They were then in a wilderness, entirely dependent upon God for guidance, food, clothing, protection, the remainder of their lives. We are dependent, spiritually upon Christ for manna, the robe of righteousness, and for our guidance and protection. 6. They ultimately crossed the Jordan, and entered, after conquering their enemies, into *houses they had not built.* We cross the Jordan of death, and after the last enemy is destroyed, shall enter into houses not made with hands, eternal in the heavens. The rough outline of our salvation from sin and salvation in heaven, was thus set forth, not only in the organization of Israel into a nation, but also the countries, sea. wilderness, river and promised land, were so situated as to illustrate our Journey to our promised inheritance. Too much may easily be claimed for types, but there is also danger of treating them too lightly. The types should be explained by the anti-types, not the anti-types by the types, (See I Cor. 10:1-11).

THE JUDGES.

The period of the Judges leads us into the valley of humiliation. Israel went into idolatry. Paul gives the period as "about the space of four hundred and fifty years," (Acts 13:20). The second chapter of Judges throws much light on the whole period. Deeds of valor, heroism, and faith were plentiful in that age, but were performed by the few. However, the land had rest under the Judges much longer than it suffered oppression under the enemies of Israel. It is manifest that the Israelites were their own worst enemies, during this long period, they did not understand their great mission to the bordering nations, as they copied the religion and vices of their neighbors, and brought many chastisements upon themselves. The oppressors only subdued parts of Israel's territory from time to time, but this was the reverse of what should have been, for they were charged with the mission of driving out the heathen and cleansing the land of idolatry.

Finally Israel reached the conclusion that they need-ed an earthly king, like the nations around them, and rejected the Lord that he should not rule over them. You remember that Saul, of the tribe of Benjamin, served in that capacity for forty years. The beginning of his reign was somewhat hopeful as he felt and exercised his dependence upon God. But soon he was disposed to fol-low his own judgment, lean upon his own understanding, and disregard the law of God. He even presumed to exercise the functions of a priest, (which he was not and could not be), and received a withering rebuke from

God's prophet Samuel ,(I Sam'l. 13:8-14). Later, as already considered in the chapter concerning Amalek, he forfeited his right to the kingdom by "rejecting the word of the Lord," (I Sam'l. 15). "But the Spirit of the Lord departed from Saul, and an evil spirit from the Lord troubled him." He grew violent, and implacable, and used his high office more to destroy the good than to promote the welfare of Israel. He slew the priests of the Lord, hunted David, his son-in-law, like a partridge upon the mountains, and spent his years in a cruel but fruitless effort to frustrate the purpose of God and destroy his chosen servant, David. In this unenviable record, we may see jealousy in its hideousness. His nation declined, year by year, and near the close of his miserable life, "And when Saul saw the host of the Philistines, he was afraid, and his heart greatly trembled. (I Sam'l. 28:5-6). In his fear and helplessness, forsaken of God, pursued by inveterate enemies, his disappointed life ended on the battle-field of Gilboa, (I Sam'l. 31).

DAVID.

It would be pleasant, had we space and time, to follow David from the Bethlehem sheep-cotes to the throne of Israel. His courage displayed in slaying a lion and a bear; his faith in God in accepting the challenge of Goliath and defeating him; his love for Jonathan, and kindness to Saul his bitterest and most persistent enemy; and his final triumph, furnish interesting and instructive chapters. But we can only review his work as King and Prophet of Israel. "David was thirty years old when he began to reign, and he reigned forty years. In Hebron he reigned over Judah, seven years and six months; and in Jerusalem he reigned thirty and three years over all Israel." (II Sam'l. 5:4-5).

The greatest glory of Israel as a nation was in the days of David and Solomon. David subdued the bordering nations and Solomon ruled over them. Their combined reigns covered a period of eighty years. The Philistines, Moabites, Ammonites, Edomites, Syrians and other peoples paid tribute to, or were governed by deputies from, Israel. David ranks high among the foremost leaders of all past ages. He was a great poet, a great musician, a great warrior, a great statesman. He reigned over all the territory given to Abraham, from the river of Egypt to the great river, Euphrates—-some sixty thousand square miles. We see in his times, Israel had become " a great nation." He and his chief men made provision to build the temple of God, and their gifts were astonishingly large, and given with a willing mind. The reader can find few chapters of more interest to him than (I Chron. 28, 29). The manner of selecting and appointing Solomon King on that state occasion, was truly grand. The piety, liberality and humility of David were beautiful and ennobling. The charge to Solomon was pathetic, and coming from an aged, but too indulgent parent; it can not but find a hearty approval in every pious heart, (I Chron. 28:1-10). Read those verses, and then follow the aged ruler to the throne of grace, (Ps. 72), and behold in this prayer how his soul was rapt in delight in the throne of Israel, and was filled with joy in forecasting the reign of Messiah. Having given the pattern of the temple to Solomon, the abundance of material, the solemn appointment of the pious young man to the rule over the greatest nation in western Asia, the king "died in a good old age, full of days, riches and honor," (I Chron. 29:28).

TEMPLE.

Solomon though young in years, was surrounded by faithful men, and under the blessing of God carried out the cherished wish of his father and erected and dedicated in Jerusalem to the God of heaven the most magnificent piece of work beneath the stars—The Holy Temple. When David desired to build this temple, Nathan the prophet said it was not God's will that he should do so. He recounted David's history; his rise from Shepherd boy to be ruler over God's people, to overcome his enemies and obtain a great name in the earth. But David had shed blood and could not build this house. But God promised to build David a house, to set up his seed after him upon the throne of Israel. His son should build an house for God's name, and he would establish the throne of his kingdom forever. "And thine house and thy kingdom shall be established forever before thee:

thy throne shall be established forever," (II Sam'l 7:16).

The promise made in Eden and enlarged upon to Abraham, is repeated to David. His son should sit upon the throne of Israel forever, (II Sam'l. 7). This is the highest peak in the mountain range of Old Testament prophecy. The outline is as follows:

1. The seed of the woman should bruise the serpent's head—this spoken in the Garden of Eden.(Gen. 3).

2. This "seed" was to be Abraham's descendant through Isaac, in whom all the families of the earth should be blessed. (Gen. 12).

3. This "seed" should be David's son, upon his throne forever. (II Sam'l. 7). To this it was added later that he should be High Priest. (Ps. 110).

Out of this cumulative prophecy grew all the marvellous descriptions of the universality, perpetuity and blessedness of the reign of Messiah. These are the prophecies the Jews misapplied to temporal sovereignty and the Millennialists do the same thing today. (Ps. 132: Ps. 89:28-38; Ps. 110; Ps. 22;23-24; Ps. 45; Ps. 72; Ps. 145; Ps. 16).

In the New Testament see (Luke 1:31-33; Acts 2: 25-31; Acts 13:35-36; Matt. 22:41-46). These show us the proper use of the ancient predictions.

We have reached to within one thousand years of Christ in tracing this great prophecy of the "seed of the woman."

I have space only to cite a list of references, giving the method employed by close students of the Bible in comparing the things "written in the law, in the prophets and in the Psalms," with the life and teaching of our Savior as recorded in the New Testament.

"Seed" of the woman, (Gen. 3:15; Gal. 4:4); of Abraham, (Gen. 17:7; 22:18; Gal. 3:16); of Isaac, (Gen. 21:12; Heb. 11:17-19); of David, (Ps. 132:11; Jer. 23:5-6; Acts 13:23; Rom. 1:3); The True Messiah was to come, (Gen. 49:10; Dan'l. 9:24, 25; Luke 2:1-52; Gal. 4:4).

Son of a Virgin, (Is. 7:14; Matt. 1:18; Luke 2:7).

His name given, (Is. 7:14; 9:6, 7; Jer. 23:5, 6; Zech. 6:12; Matt. 1:22, 23, etc, etc).

City of his birth, (Micah 5:2; Matt. 2:1; Luke 2:
4-6).

His forerunner, (Is. 40:3; Mal. 3:1; Matt. 3:1-3).

Anointed with Spirit, (Is. 11:2; 6:1; Matt. 3:16;
Acts 10:38).

Prophet like Moses, (Deut. 18:15-18; Acts 3:20-22).
Priest and King like Melchisedec, (Ps. 110:4; Heb. 5:
5; 6:10).

Coming to Temple, (Hag. 2:7-9; Mal. 3:1; Jno. 2:
13-16; Matt. 21:12).

The poverty of Jesus, (Is. 53:2; Luke 9:58).

Without guile, (Is. 53:3; I Pet. 2:22).

Teach by parables, (Ps. 78:2; Matt. 13).

Miracle worker, (Is. 35:5-6; Matt. 11:4-6).

The whole of Is. 53 diligently compared with Jesus'
life in Matt., Mark, Luke and John.

Stone of Stumbling, (Is. 8:14; Rom. 9:32; I Pet.
2:8).

Rulers combined against him, (Ps. 2; Luke 23;
12; Acts 4:27).

Betrayal in type-prophecy, (Ps. 41:9; 55:12-14;
John 13:18-21).

Forsaken by disciples, (Zech. 13:7; Matt. 26:56).

Sold for thirty pieces of silver, (Zech. 11:12-13;
Matt. 26:15; 27:7).

Crucifixion suggested as manner of Jesus' death,
(Ps. 22:16; Jno. 19:18).

Garments parted, (Ps. 22:18; Matt. 27:35).

Make intercession for transgressors, (Is. 53:12;
Luke 23:34).

His death, (Is. 53:12; Matt. 27:50).

Pierced, Zech. 12:10; Jno. 19:34-37).

Flesh not corrupt and resurrection, (Ps. 16:10;
Acts 2:31).

The Ascension, (Ps. 68:18; Luke 24:51; Acts 1:8).

Be a priest upon his throne forever, (Zech. 6:13;
Rom. 8:34).

Be a King in Zion, (Ps. 2:6; Luke 1:32; Jno. 18:
33-37); Couversion of Gentiles; (Is. 11;10; 42-1: Acts
10;45-47); Universal rule and authority; (Ps. 72;8: Daniel. 7;14: Phil. 2;9-11).

Everlasting kingdom, (Is. 9:7; Dan'l. 7:14; Luke 1: 32-33: 1 Cor. 15;24-28);

"To him give all the prophets witness," etc. (Acts 10:43). ABRIDGED FROM BIBLE LORE. (P. 185-8).

CHAPTER XII.

SOLOMON AND ISRAEL.

The Lord stirred up three powerful adversaries against Solomon, Hadad, an Edomite; Hadad-Ezar of Syria; and Jeroboam the son of Nebat, a great man in Israel. True to the prophecy, however, he retained the Kingdom all his days. Solomon had two daughters and one son, Rehoboam, the latter became King upon the death of his father. But Jeroboam who had fled to Egypt for fear of Solomon, returned at this time, and ten tribes revolted as had been predicted by Ahijah in a dramatic manner, (I Ks. 11::26-40), and founded a new capital, set up two idols, one at Dan on the extreme north of Palestine, the other at Bethel, just north of Jerusalem; he ordained a feast for the eighth month instead of the seventh, put the tribe of Levi out of the priesthood, probably confiscated their property, and made of the lowest of the people priests. This was by far the greatest national disaster that had ever befallen Israel. The nation was now divided, and ten tribes were with Jeroboam, Judah and Benjamin staying together. Levi later joined them, and so did many others out of the other tribes, from time to time.

The two nations were afterwards known as Israel (the ten tribes), and Judah (the two tribes), the latter retaining the temple and southern Palestine. *Judah had many advantages over Israel, chiefly the promise to David, that of his seed the Messiah should come.* They also held the tribe, city and temple where God recorded his name and promised to meet and bless the people. That the *place* was significant beyond description is seen by the whole of (Deut. ch. 12). These two rival nations continued to occupy the land granted to Abraham and his seed, for two centuries and a half, side by side, exercising mutual hatred and hostility towards each other. Israel had nineteen kings in that time, all of them idolaters without exception. Many of those kings were worse than the rulers of the nations cast out before them. The kingdom of Judah survived the nation of Israel about a century and a quarter, but during their national existence after Jeroboam's schism, they had the same number of kings and one queen, thus showing the longer reigns of the kings of Judah, and it should be added, that the last kings were suffered to reign but a short time owing to their wickedness. In the list of the kings of Judah we find some of the greatest and best men in history, also a few that may be classed among the worst. But Asa, Jehosaphat, Hezekiah, and Josiah are illustrious.

THE PROPHETS

After the division of the nation, when *Israel* virtually cast the law away, the prophets appeared upon the scene. I have found in teaching the Bible for the last twenty years, that *the prophets must be read in connection with the history of these two kingdoms to be understood.* And why so? The *two* nations were professedly the "great nation," God said he would make of Abraham.

THAT PERIOD OF THREE HUNDRED AND NINETY YEARS WAS THE PERIOD OF THE PROPHETS. ALL THE PROPHETS WHOSE WRITINGS WERE PRESERVED AS BOOKS, EXCEPTING DANIEL AND THE LAST THREE, (HAGGAI, ZECHARIAH AND MALACHI), LIVED AND LABORED IN THAT PERIOD OF THE NATION'S HISTORY. THE PROPHETS WERE TRUE TO GOD, IN A TIME OF GENERAL APOSTASY. THEY LIVED SIDE BY SIDE, SO TO SPEAK, WITH THE KINGS: OPPOSED THE COURSE OF THESE WICKED RULERS, AND IT IS TO ROB THEIR WRITINGS OF THE VERY KEY THAT UNLOCKS THEIR MEANING, TO SEPARATE THEM FROM THE HISTORY BEING ENACTED IN THEIR NATION, AGAINST WHICH THEY WROTE.

Who would think of separating the prophecies of Ahijah from the times of Jeroboam? Or Elijah from the times of Ahab and Jezebel? or Elisha from the

reigns of Hazael, king of Syria, and Jehu, king of Israel?
We find their lives and predictions in the books of the
kings, and necessarily read them in their connection.
But it can not have escaped the reader that the prophets
generally *date their predictions* and limit 'them to the
reigns of certain kings. Why this particularity if their
writings and that concerning the kings they mention,
were not mutually related, the one imperfect without the
other, as Ahab's life of idolatry in Israel would be imperfect in description without Elijah's history and prophecies connected therewith.

It is also pertinent to remark that the prophets
gave many predictions concerning individuals, on vital
matters, and these events, when fulfilled, make parts of
the same book. Ahijah predicts Jereboam's exaltation
to the throne of Israel, over ten tribes (I Ks. 11). This
was fulfilled and is recorded in the next chapter. An
anonymous prophet predicted the altar should be rent,
whereat Jeroboam was sacrilegiously offering in Bethel.
The fulfillment is recorded in the same connection. He
also predicted a king of Judah, Josiah by name, should
burn priests bones upon that altar. As one of his predictions was fulfilled *at once*: it became a miraculous
proof that he spake by inspiration concerning the other
matter which was not fulfilled till three hundred and
twenty-five years later, (II Ks. 23:13-18). The same
prophet that uttered this prophecy, died according to an·
other prophecy given concerning him by the old prophet
at Bethel, the same day. (I Ks. 13:21, 22, 29, 30). The
fact is these prophecies form a part of the warp and
woof of the narrative. The prophecies concerning kings
and queens, (such as could not be mistaken or misapplied), abound in these Sacred Oracles. "In the place
where dogs licked the blood of Naboth, shall dogs lick
thy blood even thine." (I Ks. 21:19). A fearful doom
was predicted for Jezebel and the fulfillment of both
predictions is recorded. (I Ks. 21:23; II Ks. 9:30-37).
This Jehu had a prediction that "thy children of the
fourth generation shall sit on the throne of Israel," (II
Ks. 10:30). The fulfillment is given, (II Ks. 13:1;
ver. 10; 14:23; and 15:8-12). Josiah was not only
foretold by name and some of his work of a peculiar

nature, three hundred fifty years before-hand; but Cyrus, the great conqueror was foretold by name, and also his work towards Judah by the prophet Isaiah, ((44:28; 45:1-4, 13); and most wonderfully realized by that nation nearly two centuries later, (Ezra 1). So the prophets did not hesitate to predict the rise or fall of individuals, cities, nations, and time had nothing to do with it—that is they would prophecy like Jeremiah, "Then said the prophet Jeremiah unto Hananiah the prophet, 'Hear now Hananiah, the Lord hath not sent thee; but thou makest this people to trust in a lie. Therefore thus saith the Lord; behold, I will cast thee from off the face of the earth; this year thou shalt die, because thou hast taught rebellion against the Lord. So Hananiah the prophet died the same year in the seventh month," (Jer. 28:15-17); or they would foretell that a repentant king should be delivered from the invasion of a heathen king; that he should recover from an otherwise fatal sickness, have his life prolonged fifteen years, and all this made sure to him by a miracle on the dial of Ahaz, (II Ks. 20). In the same chapter is recorded a prophecy by the same prophet to the same king, but on another occasion, which was later fulfilled in his descendants. Sufficient has been said on these isolated prophecies, if we may so style them, to show us the absolute necessity of acquainting ourselves with the history of the individual, city or nation concerning whom predictions were made, in order to appreciate the predictions and their fulfillment. The connection of some of these prophecies *with the great system of prophecy* reaching from Eden to Christ and on to the end of this world and into the endless ages, is not at first apparent. But most generally we can discover the connection by sufficient research. For instance, in the last case, Sennecherib, the heathen king, blasphemed the name of God, and sought to profane his temple and enslave his people; this would have operated powerfully against the many predictions concerning the prosperity of Israel *when obedient*, (Hezekiah had repented), and, at the same time, would have prospered the heathen king, who *had brought himself under the ancient curse pronounced so distinctly to Abraham*— "Cursed be he that curseth thee." This rule may be applied to the cases cited above, and it will be seen that "blessing" or "cursing" followed the conduct of the individuals, kings, queens, and prophets, as well as the cities and nations that came in contact with Israel. And we should not overlook the fact that these kings of Israel and of Judah were living under the same all-embracing rule of divine procedure. It is impossible to conceive of the operation of a law with more certainty or uniformity. It was as certain as the revolving seasons—the eclipse of the sun or moon, or the vicissitudes of day and night. To obey God gives light and blessing, to disobey him brings night and cursing. It is with this fact stated to Abraham when he was called out of Ur of the Chaldees, that we have been engaged in all our previous chapters. In them we studied the nations neighboring to Israel and found it true for thousands of years. We have returned to Israel and find the same facts emphasized in the almost countless instances recorded concerning that great people. It was true of Saul, of David and of Solomon. God set before them a blessing and a curse, and dealt with them accordingly. The history of the nineteen kings in Israel, and the twenty in Judah, through four centuries more, but pass before our eyes the scenes of these ages in harmony with this great prediction. The details are all but infinite. The prophets helped to make this marvellous and absolutely inimitable net-work of fulfilled prophecy. Because the prophecy is fulfilled by the history, and the history shows the accuracy of the prophecy in all its manifold applications, and the people wrest the prophecies out of their connections, and give them arbitrary and often contradictory applications, confusion reigns supreme, with the masses, concerning the prophecies. This comes from making Type-Prophecies to be predictions of Israel's future glory in Palestine as a nation, rather than humble servants of God in anti-types as the nature of types demand.

INEXCUSABLE BLUNDER.

Textuary preaching has led to much confusion. For one to take a text, regardless of its context, and press it into associations, and give it meanings that the writer never designed is to "Wrest the Scriptures." Our business as interpreters of the Bible is to get at the evident purpose and meaning of the writer. In no case should we ignore the speaker, person spoken to, the time, circumstances and evident purpose of the speaker or writer. To ignore the time when a prophecy was uttered and the other features just mentioned, gives flight to the imagination. Collect all the predictions, in all the prophets, on any given subject, then draw your deductions from all that was said. From the days of the division of Israel into two nations, till their final captivities, the prophets foretold these national overthrows. The *curse* was now falling upon Abraham's descendants as Moses had predicted, (Lev. 26: Deut. 27 to 32 ch.s). Yet the nation, in its two rival branches, seemed to be insensible of danger, especially idolatrous Israel. I do not see how the fact could have been made plainer than it was by the prophets, that both Israel and Judah were condemned for idolatry, and *were to go into captivity because they forsook the Lord and served Baal*. The story is the same, as we descend the line of kings, and read with the new kings the new prophets. The prophets have no *new remedies* to offer, but demanded a complete return to God in heart and life, obedience to the law of Moses and a complete rejection of heathenism.

THE PERSPECTIVE.

From the lofty summit of the era of David and Solomon, we look over the vast field to be traversed by Israel for the next thousand years, or till the Messiah should come. With a library of twelve prophetic books in our hands we are furnished with all necessary prevision. God could have made us all so that we can foresee the future as well as remember the past, but did not. This is a power that he, in mercy, has withheld from us. But these prophets or seers were gifted with this prevision that all the earth might know, that God knoweth the end from the beginning, and worketh all things according to his will. From Solomon, in all his glory, reigning over all Israel, the temple standing in unrivalled splendor in his rich capital, himself the most highly gifted son of Abraham and surpassing all men for wisdom and riches, there are only two centuries and a half till

ten tribes are carried from the land into Assyria, to return no more, as tribes, and to be swallowed up in heathenism. The largest part of the land conquered by David,
and ruled over by him and his son, was repeopled by
heathen nations. A century and a quarter after the ten
tribes were deported, the remaining tribe of Judah, increased by Benjamin, Levi and men who had joined them
out of all Israel, was taken from the land of their fathers
into what had by this time become the greatest empire
of the ancient world—Babylon. Why this universal calamity? Why should the highly fortified cities, the populous towns, the rich country, the covenant people, suffer this unparalleled disgrace? Why should they take
the fatal plunge "from the sublime to the ridiculous?"
Only three hundred ninety years from Solomon to Zedekiah! These four centuries witnessed the impoverish-
ment of the nation. It fell amid fire and sword, pestilence and famine, and the whole land became an Acelda-
ma or "field of blood." One word explains it all—
Idolatry.

The chosen nation was now to learn, in Babylon under divine judgments, what they would not consider in
Palestine, under divine blessings; "except the Lord build
the house, they labor in vain that build it: except the
Lord keep the city, the watchman waketh but in
vain," (Ps. 127:1). From the mountain height of
glory the city, temple and nation sank into the sea of
calamities that overwhelmed the nation for their apostasy
and entered into the seventy years of servitude.

The last king of the line of David actually to rule
over Israel till Christ, was Zedekiah. Among the manifold predictions by the faithful prophets, is this one.
"And thou profane wicked prince of Israel, whose day
is come, when iniquity shall have an end, thus saith the
Lord God; remove the diadem, and take off the crown;
this shall not be the same; exalt him that is low, and
abase him that is high. I will overturn, overturn, overturn, it: and it shall be no more, until he come whose
right it is: and I will give it him." (Ezek. 21:25-27).
We may properly call this a

TEST PROPHECY.

For be it noted that from the day of Zedekiah's fall,

and the captivity of Judah by the Babylonians twenty-five centuries ago, no prince of the house of David has swayed the scepter over that unhappy nation in a temporal rule. When Jesus came six centuries later he did not seek, nor would he accept, such sovereignty. And here I stake my all as a consistent interpreter of these prophecies in the statement that Israel, according to the flesh, lost in the person of Zedekiah their last temporal king. I am fully aware of what such a statement means to the vast body of writing and attempted exposition of this and its kindred predictions. Fortunately I am in possession of the writings of the greatest expositors of prophecy, ancient and modern. Confessing my indebtedness to them in many ways, having profited beyond expression by their historical research, and vast collections of facts illustrative of the fulfilled prophecies, I reluctantly antagonize any of them. But conviction of truth and sense of duty are stronger with me than respect for learning, eloquence, and candor, and stronger than the desire to be esteemed and praised of men. I would be false to my purpose to adhere strictly to the truth of heaven, if I should suffer myself to follow the beaten path of prophetic interpretation given by commentators and writers on prophecy, simply to avoid the odium of criticism, and the charge of being pedantic and ambitious. I crave from the reader the justice to himself and the writer of a patient examination of the arguments presented in succeeding chapters in defense of my position, and in refutation of the generally received ideas concerning the future of Israel as a nation, and especially that place which they must fill in the world in fulfillment of the prophecies, both of the Old and New Testaments.

For the present I can only remark that the prophets who lived from Solomon to Zedekiah, who gave us all that rich store-house of prophecy found in Isaiah, Jeremiah, Ezekiel, Hosea, Joel, Amos, Obadiah, Jonah, Micah, Nahum, Habakkuk and Zephaniah, uniformly predicted the return of Judah to the land of their fathers. It would be consistent and methodical for an interpreter to endeavor, as far as possible, to place himself mentally with the people who received these prophecies, enter into the plan and purpose of the prophets, one by one, as they arose among that obstinate and apostate people, rebuked, warned, entreated, and uttered predictions concerning them. Nothing is gained, but much is lost to the cause of truth, by exciting false religious hopes in any people. As to Israel, the messages of these prophets, during the four centuries from Solomon to Zedekiah, their last king, may be brought under five general heads, as follows:

1. The nations, Israel and Judah, were condemned to fall by sword, famine and pestilence and go forth from that land into captivity.

2. This national judgment would be discriminative, as the Lord would punish the proud, disobedient, corrupt, idolatrous portion, and effect a marvellous deliverance for his faithful servants. The latter are known as "the remnant" that would pass through the fire of the great ordeal and be purified from all idolatry.

3. This remnant should return to Canaan, rebuild the old wastes and enjoy the *blessing* of God in the land after it had enjoyed its sabbaths (or seventy years at rest).

4. Above all these great temporal designs concerning these people, the prophets enlarged upon the promise given to Mother Eve, repeated to Abraham and to David, concerning the promised "Seed." It is interesting to note how high, great and glorious this "ruler" was to be, as set forth by these prophets. The contrast between him and their kings, among whom the prophets lived, was very distinct. They were, for the most part, everything that he would not be, and nothing that he would be. As the nation sank lower and lower, and lost almost the last feature that would entitle them to be called the children of Abraham, and the national sun was about to set, these prophets saw the streakings of the dawn of a better day. They poured forth their inspired utterances concerning the king, his righteousness, the universality and unending nature of his kingdom, and exhausted the power of language to picture the blessedness of his work among men. Under these four divisions may be gathered the whole of the predictions given by these "holy men of God who spake as they were moved by the Holy Ghost."

5. These predictions are often given in Type-Prophecies, and especially after the nation began to decline from the worship and service of God. As certainly as the Types can never be revived, then the Type-Prophecies are fulfilled figuratively. The type-king, type-temple, type-priesthood, type-sacrifices, type-feasts, type-Jesrusalem, type-Zion, type-Levites, and type-nation were legislated away forever by Christ and the apostles, hence the prophets meant the same as the types meant, that their glorious anti-types would be given and last forever under the Lord Jesus Christ.

CHAPTER XIII.

THE WRITING PROPHETS.

The prophets who did not write books were before Jeroboam II, thirteenth king of Israel. The writing prophets began in the reign of Jeroboam II. So the latter began where the former left off. This enables us to associate the written prophecies with the Kings under whose reigns they were spoken and written. This is important, because prophecies always relate to the future, whether that be the future of Kings, priests, prophets, cities or nations. The predictions concerning all these, to be properly applied, must be connected with the individual, or city or nation, *after* the predictions are *given*, and *before* they are *fulfilled*. Thus they subserve a divine purpose. These remarks should apply with particular force to the prophets who lived after *Jeroboam II*, thirteenth King of Israel, and Uzziah, tenth King of Judah. Some of the prophets date their prophecies by the reign of certain Kings. We notice the nature and structure of a few of these books, and begin with the first in the list of the "minor prophets." While the rebukes given to traitorious kings, villainous priests and false prophets, as well as the condemnation of all sinners of every shade and grade, may be studied with a degree of profit without such strict regard for the time when they were spoken, yet the *predictions* were usually in the nature of *Judgments* sent upon the people for their sins. To know the sins therefore, enables one to see the degree of punishment threatened and inflicted for those sins, and thus to *learn the practical nature* of the predictions, that others might *fear to do the same things*. In this manner God wrote his imperishable record against sin, by using the prophets to photograph, so to speak, the sinners of all classes, predict for them *specific*, not general calamities and chastisements, and, when the judgments were visited, men might fear to sin and rebel against God. It is this great *moral teaching* that pervades the prophetic books, that should impress us all most profoundly. The prophecies, in other words, are not mere skeletons or outlines of future events; but they come to us warm and instinct with life. They reproduce for us the lives of men, whether rebellious or obedient to God, and preserve the imperishable record of their history, what God did and said concerning them, and these things are written to teach the lesson in (Is. 57:15); "For thus saith the high and lofty One that inhabiteth eternity, whose name is Holy; I dwell in the high and holy place, with him also that is of a contrite and humble spirit, to revive the spirit of the humble, and to revive the heart of the contrite ones."

HOSEA, CHAPTER I.

"The word of the Lord that came unto Hosea, the Son of Beeri, in the days of Uzziah, Jotham, Ahaz and Hezekiah, Kings of Judah, and in the days of Jeroboam the son of Joash, king of Israel," 1:1). This begins the prophecy, and tells us when the prophet wrote. Under the illustrations that follow, several in number, he pointedly rebuked the nation. The illustrations are,

1. An adulterous wife. Idolatry is spiritual adultery. So the prophet in taking a wife, in idolatrous Israel, married a "harlot." The wife in harlotry, represents Israel as unfaithful to God as a nation. This illustration is familiar to students of the prophets. It is applied in Revelation to the apostate church. She is a Harlot. I think it would aid our Literalist expositors to learn the meaning of these prophets, to study this fig-

ure in its every appearance in the Bible. Let me suggest one controlling point.

"But she that liveth in pleasure is dead, while she liveth (I Tim. 5:6. The CHURCH in Sardis was dead, but had a name to live, (Rev. 3:1). Just as the PRODIGAL SON was dead to his father, but made alive again, upon repentance. (Luke 15:24, 32). So a repentant son is considered AS RAISED FROM THE DEAD; a repetant WIFE, IS RAISED FROM THE DEAD; a repentant NATION IS RAISED FROM THE DEAD, (Ezek. 37); a repentant CHURCH IS RAISED FROM THE DEAD, (Eph. 5:14) from (Is. 60:1); and as the Harlot has to vacate for the true Bride, so the Beast, false prophet and dragon, under other symbols, vacate for those whom they persecuted. The whole is a figurative use of these striking symbols to illustrate the facts of religious life. The Beast was not literal but symbolic, so was the Harlot; so was the false prophet, and so on.

2. Their first son was called Jezreel, "For yet a little while and I will avenge the blood of Jezreel upon the house of Jehu, and will CAUSE TO CEASE THE KINGDOM OF THE HOUSE OF ISRAEL. And it shall come to pass at that day, that I will break the bow of Israel in the house of Jezreel," (Vers. 3-4). Jeroboam II was the third generation from the massacre at Jezreel of the two kings by Jehu, and his successor reigned only six months and was slain. The nation was thus drawn nearer to the time when it should "cease to be a nation."

3. The second child, a daughter, was called Lo-ru-ha-mah "for I will no more have mercy on the house of Israel; but I will utterly take them away," (Ver. 6). How many years after the birth of the first child this child was born and used as a sign, is not stated. "But I will have mercy upon the house of Judah, and will save them by the Lord their God, and will not save them by bow, nor by sword, nor by battle, by horses nor by horsemen," (Ver. 7) Judah's strength always was to trust in God as did David meeting Goliath, (Sam'l 17); Asa (II Chron. 15:9-15); Jehoshaphat (II Chron. 20); before Hoshea's day; and Hezekiah thereafter, (II Ks. 18:13-19).

Emmanuel Library
Emmanuel School of Religion
Route 6
Johnson City, Tennessee 37601

4. The third child was a son, named "Loammi, for ye are not my people and I will not be your God." This language could not be plainer on the subject of the rejection of *Israel*, as the *fleshly* descendants of Abraham. Paul applies the next verse to the calling of Gentiles, (Rom. 9:24-26). "Yet the number of the children of Israel shall be as the sand of the sea, which can not be measured nor numbered; and it shall come to pass that in the place where it was said unto them, ye are not my people, there it shall be said unto them, ye are the sons of the living God," (Ver. 10). When the Gentiles became sons of God through Christ, this prophecy began to be fulfilled, and has been fulfilling ever since. The next verse tells us, "Then shall the children of Judah and the children of Israel be gathered together, and appoint themselves one head, and they shall come up out of the land; for great shall be the day of Jezreel," (Ver. 11).

Though multitudes of fleshly Israel were cast off, yet the true Israel of God, composed of Jews and Gentiles converted to God, can not be numbered. "Ye are all the children of God, by faith in Christ Jesus. For as many of you as have been baptized into Christ have put on Christ. There is neither Jew nor Greek, bond nor free, there is neither male nor female; for ye are all one in Christ Jesus. *And if ye be Christ's*, then are ye Abraham's seed, and heirs according to the promise," (Gal. 3:26-29). Jezreel means "seed of God." Jesus was here considered as the head or ruler of both Judah and Israel, not in their old nationalities, nor yet as united again under the Old Covenant, but as the true Israel of God under Christ. This could be true as foretold, when God rejected the nations, as such, and saved all the true Israelites as individuals. Since Christ, the Jews have no nation, made up of tribes, with certain laws of priority or distinction, but spiritual Israel, under Christ, are "a chosen generation, a royal priesthood, an holy nation, a peculiar [purchased] people; that ye should show forth the praises of him who hoth called you out of darkness into his marvellous light. WHICH IN TIME PAST WERE NOT A PEOPLE, BUT ARE NOW THE PEOPLE

OF GOD, which had not obtained mercy, but now have obtained mercy, (I Peter 2:9-10).

II.

In the (2nd Ch.), under the same figure, the children were commanded to plead with their mother to return to her husband. The three children in chapter one illustrate:

1. Israel ceasing to be a nation, and disorganized, when carried from their land, under Shalmanezar, and Esar-Hadden.

2. Judah continuing as a nation, preserving the royal line of David down to Christ.

3. The third child represents, according to Paul and Peter the Gentiles converted to God.

In the study we should ignore the chapter divisions. Then we see that the children of God, who survived, were to take their father's side, God's side, against the mother. Paul's allegory in (Gal. 4) is very similar to this.

1. Hagar, a bond-woman, represented the Old Covenant.

2. Ishmael, Hagar's son, hence a servant, represented the Jews still clinging to their mother, the old covenant, and being cast off with their mother from their Father's house.

3. Sarah represented the gospel covenant.

4. Isaac represented the children of God, from among Jews and Gentiles, who cling to both their Father and Mother, remain in their Father's house, and inherit all that he has as Isaac did. In Hosea (3rd ch) we see why the husband was grieved,—because the wife was a harlot. Israel, was following after strange gods, hence must be punished. (Vers. 1-13). From (Vers. 14-22) is a prediction of her forsaking idols, and returning to God. The last verse shows us that we Gentiles were comprehended in the New Covenant, and should obtain mercy.

III.

"Then said the Lord unto me, go yet, love a woman beloved of her friend, yet an adulteress, according to the love of the Lord toward the children of Israel, who look to other gods, and love flagons of wine.

So I bought her to me for fifteen pieces of silver,

and for an homer of barley, and an half homer of barley; and I said unto her, thou shalt not play the harlot, and thou shalt not be for another man: so will I also be for thee."

This is the illustration. The mother and wife was still loved by her husband. This is the whole family of Abraham. But she had been unfaithful, must remain in obscurity, have scanty provision, not engage in questionable associations, for a long time, and ultimately return to her former husband. Then the verbal prediction applies this figurative prediction as follows:

"For the children of Israel shall abide many days without a king, and without a prince, and without a sacrifice, and without an image, and without an ephod, and without a terraphim. AFTERWARD SHALL THE CHILDREN OF ISRAEL RETURN. AND SEEK THE LORD THEIR GOD, AND DAVID THEIR KING: and shall FEAR THE LORD and his GOODNESS in the LATTER days."

1. Let it be distinctly noted that this was to be Israel's condition *after the calling of the Gentiles*, (2:23). They rejected their lawful king and sacrifice, and have continued in widowhood since the rejection of David (their promised Messiah) or Christ.

2. They have had no temple, no priesthood, and no sacrifice for the same length of time. Paul says there is none, (Heb. 10:26).

3. They have stood aloof from idolatry, for ages, even from images, such as Jeroboam gave and the other kings adopted.

4. They have had no ephod. The breast-plate of the High-priest was attached to the Ephod, and contained the Urim and Thummim, by which the priests received direction from God. This power has also been taken from Israel, and like Saul, they receive no answer from God "neither by dreams, nor by Urim, nor by prophets."

5. *"Afterward* shall the children of Israel return, and seek the Lord their God and *David* their *King*: and shall fear the Lord and his goodness in the latter days."

The reader will notice that ISRAEL does the RE-TURNING, not DAVID. The Jews rebelled against Jesus, (David), and they must return to him, and seek him. JESUS IS NOT TO RETURN TO EARTH TO SEEK THEM, BUT THEY ARE TO SEEK GOD AND

THEIR KING DAVID, IN THE LATTER DAYS. How plain! David had been dead for twelve generations, when Hosea made this remarkable prediction; hence, it was not fleshly David, the son of Jesse, but spiritual David, the Son of God, who is meant.

This prophecy gives the outline of events as they have transpired from that day to this as follows:

1. The ten tribes ceased to be a nation. This was Jezreel, and fulfilled (Is. 7:8).

2. The house of Judah should continue, not by their own strength or power, but by God's providence, Lo-ru-ha-mah!

3. The Gentiles should find mercy and be called the people of God, after the numberless seed of Jacob turned away from their own mercy. Lo-am-mi!

4. The children begged the mother to repent, or the children of God, from among Jews and Gentiles, seek the confession and restoration of Israel to the favor of God.

5. Israel should continue for a long time, many days, like a desolate and rejected widow, her Husband longing for her repentance, and finally should seek God and *their* King in the latter days.—The name David used to identify him. This outline of the events concerning the children of Israel, fleshly and spiritual, embraces all the ages since Hosea. It is not contradicted by Hosea, by fortelling any other ORDER OF EVENTS, this would be suicidal. It is not CONTRADICTED BY ANY OTHER PROPHET, this would be inconsistent. This prophet, and the succeeding prophets, may enlarge upon one or all of these items, but the ORDER OF THE EVENTS IS NOT MOLESTED, BUT CONFIRMED. Thus, what awaits Israel is *not* a return to Mosaism, Judaism, heathenism or a mixture, of these; it is not the return of DAVID TO ISRAEL; but is a RETURN OF ISRAEL TO GOD AND TO DAVID THEIR KING IN THESE LATTER DAYS, or plainly conversion to God under Christ the great King.

IV to VIII.

These chapters are strong rebukes of Israel and Judah,
"because there was no truth, nor mercy, nor know-

ledge of God in the land. By swearing, and lying, and killing and stealing and committing adultery, they break out, and blood toucheth blood," "My people are destroyed for lack of knowledge; because thou hast rejected knowledge, I will also reject thee, that thou shalt be no priest to me; seeing *thou hast forgotten the law of thy God*, I will also forget thy children," (4:1-2,6).

Ephraim was the leading tribe of the ten, as Judah was of the two. So the ten tribes are often addressed as Ephraim, and the two tribes as Judah. Ephraim never included Judah and Judah never included Ephraim. Sometimes, however, Israel included all the house of Jacob, called Israel.

The prophets, priests and kings also are specified as leaders in sin and meriting severe chastisment. The fatal trend of the whole nation of the ten tribes is apparent, in all these chapters, and God's determination to end the nation in the Assyrian captivity, is fully revealed. "Ephraim is joined to his idols; let him alone," (4:17). Ephraim shall be desolate in the day of rebuke; among the tribes of Israel, I have made known that which shall surely be," (5:9). "Ephraim also is like a silly dove without heart; they call to Egypt they go to Assyria," (7:11). Thus they put confidence in *Human* covenants, fortified towns and military strength. "For Israel hath forgotten his maker, and buildeth temples and Judah hath multiplied fenced cities; but I will send a fire upon his cities, and it shall devour the palaces thereof," (8:14). Their whole defense should be taken away. So of all now who have a false confidence.

IX to X.

In chapter nine the prophet foretold the Assyrian captivity (9:3), which was completed in installments beginning with Menahem (II Ks. 15:20; 1 Chron. 5:25,26) to Hoshea (II Ks. 18) and Esar-Haddan (II Ks. 17:24).

"All their wickedness is in Gilgal; for there I hated them; for the wickedness of their doings I will drive them out of mine house. I will love them no more; all their princes are revolters. Ephraim is smitten, their root is dried up, they shall bear no fruit; yea though they bring forth, yet will I slay even the beloved fruit of their womb. *My God will cast them away, because they did not hearken unto him*; and they shall be wanderers among the nations," (9:15-17).

The whole ninth chapter shows us it was the prophets like those slain by Elijah, and by Jehu, that were destroying the nation. The tenth chapter continues in the same mournful strain. The King is sorely condemned, as the ruler in wickedness and should be "cut off as the foam upon the water." Their palaces and temples should be destroyed and the idols carried away to the Assyrian King. (10:2,3,5,6-8, 13-15). All of these items were fulfilled in the captivity of the ten tribes as predicted.

XI to XIV.

The eleventh chapter represents the goodness of God to Israel from the days of Moses and how he delivered them from bondage, but they were ungrateful and forsook God and now "He shall not return into the land of Egypt, but the Assyrian shall be his king, because they refused to return to the Lord. And the sword shall abide on his cities, and shall consume his branches, and devour them, because of their own counsels. When we recall that Assyria and Egypt were each aspiring to universal rule, this prophecy deepens in meaning, for the prophet had to discriminate in *favor of Assyria* and predict its *supremacy*.

The twelfth chapter is a masterly analysis of the condition of Ephraim and Judah. They were making alliances with the heathen nations of Egypt, on the south and Assyria on the north. These nations were exploiting them and deriving much revenue from them. The change in Jacob's life, at Peniel is used as an exhortation. When he humbled himself and wrestled with the angel, "wept and made supplication unto him; he found Him in Bethel and there he spake with us; even the Lord God of hosts; the Lord is his memorial. Therefore *turn thou* to thy God; keep mercy and judgment, and wait on thy God continually," (12:4-6).

He shows them the necessity of being humble and observing the teaching of the prophets of God. "And Jacob fled into the country of Syria, and Israel served for a wife, and for a wife he kept sheep. And by a prophet the Lord brought Israel out of Egypt, and by a prophet was he preserved," (vers. 12-13). Then surely God can raise up a great nation from very humble sur-

roundings, as in the case of the herdsman Jacob; and deliver a great nation by simple means, as evidenced by the
prophet Moses; and preserve a great nation, as the whole
history of Israel's days of prosperity verify the observation of Hosea, "and by a prophet was he preserved."

The humility of Ephraim secured God's *blessing*; his
pride and self-sufficiency offended God and he died.
"When Ephraim spake trembling, he exalted himself in
Israel; but when he offended in Baal, he died. And now
they sin more and more, and have made the molten
images of their silver, and idols according to their own
understanding, all of it the work of the craftsmen; they
say of them, let the men kiss the calves.

Therefore they shall be as the morning cloud, and
as the early dew that passeth away, as the chaff that is
driven with the whirlwind out of the floor and as the
smoke out of the chimney," (13:1-3). Before honor is
humility. The four fleeting things mentioned should
show us how little good one gets out of the tinselry and
show of this world.

Again he says,

"O, Israel thou hast destroyed thyself; but in me is
thy help, I will be thy King; where is any other that
may save thee in all thy cities? and thy judges of whom
thou saidst, give me a king and princes? I gave thee a
king in mine anger, and took him away in my wrath,"
(Vers. 9-11).

This recalls the fatal day when Israel demanded a
King in the days of Samuel, (who lived in another age
of moral apathy and national wickedness), and the people rejected the Lord that he should not rule over them.
Samuel had spent a life-time in humble devotion to his
people.

But see how the kings had corrupted them and disappointed their worldly hearts. The fifteen or more
kings of Israel "were cut off like foam upon the waters."
Saul was a suicide. His son was murdered. David died
full of days, riches and honor. Solomon brought the
nation to the verge of ruin. Jeroboam divided the nation and largely corrupted it. He died in ignominy.
Nadab reigned two years and was slain by Baasha. The
latter reigned twenty-four years and died as the murderer of his predecessor and all his brethren. Elah, his

son, reigned two years and was slain and all his family
by Zimri, who reigned one week, and when near capture,
suicided. Omri died a natural death after reigning
twelve years. Ahab reigned twenty-two years, and died
from a wound received in battle. Ahaziah reigned two
years and died under the curse of God. Jehoram was
killed by Jehu. Jehu reigned twenty-eight years and
died a natural death. Jehoahaz reigned seventeen years
in wickedness, and died a natural death. Joash reigned
one year less than his father, but maintained the reputa-
tion for wickedness, and died a natural death. Jeroboam
II reigned forty-one years, and died a natural death.
Zechariah was slain by Shallum after a reign of six
months. Menahem slew Shallum after he had reigned
one month. Menahem died a natural death after a ten
years' reign. Pek-a-hi-ah reigned two years and was
slain by his captain Pekah. Pekah reigned twenty
years and was slain by Hoshea. Hoshea reigned nine
years and was carried away captive with his degenerate
family and princes by Shalmanezar, King of Assyria.

Thus the Kings of Israel by cowardly suicide, by
assassination or in battle, went to their doom. Many of
them were denied burial. The priests were revolters, the
Judges grafters, the false prophets foolish and the spiritual men mad, and the whole nation plunged to ruin.
Judah was coming after them, like a leprous sister, in-
curably diseased with idolatry. Yet God promised them
he would be their King, if they would repent and serve
him as King, and He would "Ransom them from the
power of *Sheol*, and redeem them from death. O death,
I will be thy plagues; O *Sheol*, I will be thy destruction;
repentance shall be hid from mine eyes." Paul says this
prophecy will be fulfilled at the resurrection of the
righteous. (I Cor. 15:54-55). THIS ONE TEXT
FOREVER DISPROVES MILLENNIALISM. When the
righteous are IMMORTALIZED, death is swallowed up
in victory, and *Sheol* is destroyed. *Sheol* and *Hades* are
names for the same place. *Hades* is Greek, *Sheol* is Hebrew. *Hades* is *not* destroyed at the FIRST *resurrection*,
but at the LAST *resurrection*, (Rev. 20:13-14); therefore
the saints are *not* raised to IMMORTALITY and INCOR-
RUPTABILITY at the FIRST resurrection. This is positive

proof that the first resurrection is a figurative use of resurrection. *When* this mortal shall have put on immortality, and this corruptible shall have put on incorruption,
then (not a thousand years plus a little season later),
shall be brought to pass this saying, as well as the one in
(Is. 25:8), "He will swallow up death in victory; and
the Lord God will wipe away tears from all faces; and
the rebuke of his people shall he take away from off the
earth; for the Lord hath spoken it." I do not fear to
take my stand right here, and affirm, with all confidence
that this removes forever any consistent interpretation of
(Rev.20:4-6) as a literal resurrection of the saints of
God in immortal, incorruptible bodies; for John joins
both Isaiah, Hosea and Paul and predicts the destruction of *Hades* after this, a *thousand* years *plus* the *little
season*. We are compelled to interpret any and all other
uses of resurrection, predicted to precede this one and
only literal resurrection awaiting the entire human family, (that shall have died), as figurative only of the
actual resurrection at the end of time. But the degenerate nation was so far gone in infidelity, graft, lewdness,
covetousness, cruelty and pride, that God's faithful warnings, through his prophets, failed to move them to repentance. The prophet lifted his eyes to the future, dark
and dismal concerning the nation, but radiant and full of
blessing for the obedient "Remnant," and closed his marvellous predictions.

"Who is wise and he shall understand these things?
Prudent and he shall know them? For the ways of the
Lord are right, and the just shall walk in them; but the
transgressors shall fall therein.".

CHAPTER XIV.

MICAH.

The prophets Amos, Micah, Hosea and Isaiah, lived at the same time. See the first verse in each book. So ninety-six chapters of prophecy were given in the reigns of four kings. Micah foretold the Babylonian captivity. But he outlined the future in the same order as Hosea. They parallel each other as we shall see. His great systematic prophecy is given (ch. 3:1 to 6:9).

1. Zion should be plowed as a field; Jerusalem should become heaps; and the mountain of the house as the high places of the desert. Those three things were fulfilled. Rome destroyed the city and Temple (A. D. 70), and Rufus plowed up the hill of Zion seeking treasure.

2. The prophets looked forward to the building of another house—the Royal-Priest (Christ) was to build it.

Micah says "the mountain of the house of the Lord shall be established in the top of the mountains, and it shall be exalted above the hills."

As the capitols were usually built on high hills and strongly fortified, it was common with the prophets to speak of the governments under the name of the mountains where they were situated. To say Mount Seir, mountains of Samaria, Mount Zion, and the like, was the same as saying the Edomites, Samaritans and Judah. This eminent mountain which was predicted as established *above the mountains*, represents the kingdom established far above all rule, authority and power; and "exalted above the hills," is not to call attention to some physical mountain raised to a lofty height by either human or divine power, but the supremacy of the government of God, in the latter days.

3. "And people shall flow unto it. And *many nations* shall come and say, Come, and let us go up to the *mountain of the Lord*, and to the *house* of the God of Jacob; and he will *teach* us of his ways, and we will walk in his

paths; for the law shall go forth of Zion, and the word
of the Lord from Jerusalem."

Who does not know that "the law of the spirit of
life, that makes us free from the law of sin and death,"
the gospel, or "perfect law of liberty," was proclaimed in
Jerusalem on the day of Pentecost? A temple was built
also according to prediction and type. It is called the
"Temple of God," (I. Cor. 3:16-17; Eph. 2:11-22; II
Cor. 6:16); the *house* of God," (I Tim. 3:15; Heb. 3:6; I
Pet. 2:3-9).

The imagery would not be complete without the
mountain, so (Heb. 12:22) says, "But ye are come unto
Mount Zion, and unto the city of the living God, the
heavenly Jerusalem," etc. John saw this "holy Jerusalem, descending out of heaven from God," (Rev. 21:
10). If Christians have come to Mt. Zion and it is not
rock and dirt, is not the rest of their land just like their
mountain? You can not build any other palace for our
King. Going up to the mountain of the Lord, to the
house of the God of Jacob is not making up caravans for
Jerusalem, and travelling by yards and miles toward a
material house; but when we come to Mt. Zion as
Paul did, and go to the spiritual house of worship, "the
tabernacle which the Lord pitched and not man."

Now, nothing is plainer than the fact that the
temple of God, his house, was not made out of material
stones or erected on a material mountain. Yet it is the
predicted house, the exalted temple, and is high above all
other governments. These plain passages of scripture
tell us it is the church. The church, temple or house
here foretold, also in (Is. 2 and Zech. 6:9-15), could not
be built together and form a material house. It would
be impossible to build the Corinthian church or temple
of God, for instance, on Mount Moriah, where Solomon,
and later Zerubbabel, built Jewish temples. The sacredness of *place* has been transferred from a *material* house
on Moriah to the hearts of the people of God.   God
dwells in this "holy temple of the Lord," by his Spirit.
This prophecy is fulfilled and fulfilling, as the temple
grows, and there can be no earthly, material mountain or
temple contemplated in the prophecy.

4.   "And he shall judge among many people, and

rebuke strong nations afar off; and they shall beat their swords into plowshares, and their spears into pruning hooks; nation shall not lift up a sword against nation, neither shall they learn war any more." (4:3).

Is it not the law of the Lord, the law of justice, of mercy, of brotherhood and unselfish devotion to the weak, that is hastening, in our day, the ultimate realization of this member of the prediction? Is it not Jesus who rebukes the avarice, greed, plunder, rapine, tyranny and oppression of strong nations? Is it not the diffusive power of the gospel of the Prince of Peace that makes possible The Hague, and leads strong nations to the serious consideration of disarmament? It is not the doctrine of Mahomet, for he was a temporal prince. This war in Europe is against the protest of millions of crushed and bleeding hearts. I can scarcely believe that such cruelty and slaughter will ever again be repeated. Jesus came not to kill but to make alive. These nations were the upholders of tyranny and despotism, from their inception. The war is at root the murderous element of desoptism. The name of God has been blasphemed for ages by kings claiming to rule by "divine right." It is not the end of the world; or the end of the Gospel age, that is reached in this era of prophetic fulfillment; but it is the overthrow of despotic rule. Universal peace, though apparently far away, is at our doors. The very exhaustion of nations must hasten it. I believe God's prophets. Despotism is doomed to eternal defeat. The vision of the Prince of Peace is too great and glorious to fail to win the hearts of men. Those nations called "Christendom" are not Christian. There are Christians there, but all the enginery of war that mows down armies and nations disproves the assumption that they are Christian nations. They know not what spirit they are of, and wars come from the lusts that war against the soul. It is the corrupt church in unholy union with the state that is being rebuked and overthrown in this titanic struggle.

The financial burdens of the modern scientific enginery of war are intolerable. There is no greater question before the governments of earth today than that of disarmament of the nations. It is sure to come soon.

The nations have signified a desire for universal peace. The truth of heaven will be vindicated. Since society grew into nations, the sun has never risen on a world of peace. War has incardined the ages. The Pharaohs, the Kings of Babylon, Medo-Persia, Greece and Rome, and rulers in all the lesser states, rode to their seats of dominion in a deluge of blood. Who has not been appalled at the universality of this greatest scourge of the ages? Think of the myriads slain on the battle-field. Visit the war fleets, sailing out over the mighty seas, to pour volleys of death into the strongholds of neighboring nations. Follow the marching armies in the fatigue and exhaustion of the march, and visit the battle-field strewn with dead and dying brethren. Move with solemn tread through the ranks of the shattered and maimed in the hospitals, and look narrowly into the prisons of torture. Stand speechless before the barbarism and savagery, the dangers and horrors of massacres. Think of the vices that demoralize, the diseases and pestilence that mow down their rich harvest in death. Follow in the path of war and see the debris of pillaged towns, burned cities, ruined crops, and universal desolation. Listen to the loud cries of the helpless women and orphaned children, when their husbands and fathers perish in the brutalities and cruelties of war.

Shall all this cease? Shall the whole war-system be discarded? Yes, verily. How shall the fulfillment be brought about, you say, by the coming of Christ? No. There is no need, neither is there promise, of miraculous aid. But the gospel of peace is so revolutionizing the sentiments of men, and nations, as to cause them to revolt at war. Christ will put an end to slavery. It is the gospel working through the governments of earth, enlightening them, that cultivates a national or international protest against war. Temperance is a doctrine of Christ, and it educates men to such a hatred of rum and its consequences as to be formulated into statewide, and we confidently hope, nation-wide, prohibition of the entire liquor traffic. The gospel is the law that went forth from Zion as the divine remedy to cleanse and exalt the nations, and it begins with individuals, works out through families into society, the state, the nation and the world.

The whole fabric of despotism in church and state is doomed to complete overthrow and this without a miracle or the enlisting personally on earth of Jesus and his glorified saints, in its accomplishment. The kingdom of heaven is the agent, and the gospel the means, which Jesus uses to overthrow the beastly nature of man and elevate human governments to the plane where they are the almoners of peace. The voice of public opinion today is loud in its demands for "Arbitration of international disputes, rather than War." Our President and his Secretary of State, Mr. Wilson and Mr. Bryan, have expressed themselves with clearness upon this point, and are seeking to enlist the foremost nations of the world in the adoption of Arbitration as the humane method of settling these international difficulties. I hail with unspeakable delight, the generous gift of Andrew Carnegie to the world's Peace Movement, and had I a million dollars to give for the *world's* good, could think of no better investment. We are learning that rulers can reach settlements of their differences, without involving whole nations in war, butchery, debt, widowhood, orphanage, demoralization and ruin, and we demand relief from such burdens. The highest interests of the human race demand it. The millions of idle men in standing armies parading the frontiers, or living in indolent ease out of the national treasury, and the billions of dollars expended in dreadnaughts and scientific machinery serviceable for but one thing under heaven, the *destruction of men and cities*, bring the nations to the door of bankruptcy. I am full of assurance that our own nation is destined to rank among the leading nations, if not the first, in restoring to men their long-lost liberties, and we must needs teach against the horrors and atrocities of war. We may do signal service to the yet misguided and misgoverned of earth, and hasten the dawn of universal peace, when soldiers shall be returned to the arts and helpful industries of life. Let the swords and cannon, the armor and retinue of war be locked up in the bottom of the deep, blue sea. Let martial music that has charmed the millions living and dead, be forgotten in one song of peace, and our sons be trained to the courage of fighting the good fight of faith, and let them be panoplied

in the armor of the living God. Let the millions of men
and billions of money now necessary to national defense,
be turned into the development of mankind in all that
goes to uplift and ennoble the race. "They shall beat
their swords into plowshares, and their spears into pruning hooks; nation shall not lift up a sword against nation
neither shall they learn war any more." Let it be done
speedily. Israel owned their land, and Ahab was "cursed" because he sought to alienate Naboth from his inheritance by force and murder. Men owned houses,
lands, and property as individuals. That was under the
Jewish law. The same was true under Christ and the
law of liberty.

4. Micah (like Is. 2) says that men shall have
peaceful possessions, after war ceases, and *individual
ownership*, every man under *his own vine and fig tree*, and
none shall make them afraid. His predictions have been
fulfilled so faithfully that we may confidently expect this
latter feature in its due order.

5. In those times, the "Remnant" shall become a
strong nation; and the Lord shall reign over them in
Mount Zion from henceforth even forever." What sort
of a "nation"? Evidently such as is described in (I Pet.
2:9). We have already seen the prohet did not foretell
a literal Zion, hence the consistency of the prophecy must
be maintained. The mountains have lost their sacredness, even as Jewish altars, Ark of the Covenant, tabernacle, priesthood and the like have been set aside forever. This "Remnant" or remaining part of the Jewish
nation, converted to God, can go to Mount Zion, and
ascend the mount of the Lord's house, visit the temple
and worship therein, and never see Palestine. The typical age is a closed chapter. They must worship God according to the law that went forth from Zion, the gospel,
for there is no other, and is to be no other. The curse
of God rests upon the man that preaches any other gospel.
(Gal. 1:8-9).

6. Judah was the only tribe that ever reigned in
Zion, in David and his successors, so Judah reigns now
in the person of Jesus, over all the true Israel of God.
The first dominion, or supreme rule, is in the hands of
the great Shepherd of the flock, Christ, (ch. 4:8).

Then the prophet encouraged his countrymen that they would be brought safely through their then perilous condition. He can not mean a carnal warfare in (ver. 13) for the reason that such warfare was forbidden under Christ our King. Any interpretation that makes Jesus and the saints ministers of war, in the carnal sense, is erroneous. It is this spirit that united Church and State under Constantine and has filled the world with crime and sorrow in the sacred name of Jesus, for fifteen centuries.

7. Next the town whence this great ruler would come is given. It was Bethlehem-Judah. (5:1-2). Jesus was born in Bethlehem, when David's tabernacle was down. There had not been a king on the throne of Israel or Judah, since Zedekiah, (B. C. 587). The word was made flesh. The eternal nature of the Ruler is mentioned, "whose goings forth have been from of old, from the days of eternity." As a Shepherd he feeds his flock "in the strength of the Lord, in the majesty of the name of the Lord his God; and they shall abide; for now shall he be great unto the ends of the earth." This great "Ruler in Israel" being thus promised, *it was necessary for the fulfillment, that Judah should not be destroyed till he came.* Hence this man was their peace when the Assyrians invaded the land, plundered the palaces and would have destroyed that nation as he did others. They could marshall against him seven shepherds, (a perfect number), hence enough, or eight principal men, more than enough for their deliverance.

8. The' Remnant," (not all of Israel, but the faithful ones) should be as dew and rain are to grass, on the one hand, or a "blessing"; and like a lion in his destruction of sheep, on the other hand, or a "curse."

It was not their horses, chariots, fortified cities and strongholds, their witchcraft, soothsayers and graven images that would protect them. The "Remnant" were to instill into the minds and hearts of the nations the knowledge of the one true and living God, and thus "bless' them, and the judgments of God against the nations that would oppress this "Remnant" might be compared to the ravages of a lion or the "curse." So the true Israel had nothing to fear, and the history of Daniel, of the three Hebrew children in the fiery furnace, and of Mordecai and his brethren, are but illustrative of these principles. As the dew and rain give necessary moisture to the grass and cause it to ripen into harvest, so the true Israel of God among the nations, were a continual blessing to those nations, and "no weapon that was fashioned against them prospered."

The attentive reader should now read (Micah 3 and 6:1-16). These chapters do not so much predict the future of Israel, as they unfold the nature of their sinful course. They gave heed to false prophets, sought to suppress the true prophets; used injustice, violence and oppression; maintained the formal acts of worship, but denied the power thereof. The corresponding prophecy in (Isaiah 2) is set among the historic revelations of crimes, individual, social and national, and unitedly these prophets denounce their rulers, priests and prophets and foretell the great gospel dispensation, *under the new David.* The order of the events here as in Hosea is plain. There is no place or demand for the second coming of Christ and the resurrection of the righteous dead to be associated with him in an earthly rule over the nations, in the predictions. The prophets all teach the same doctrine and all foretell the great events in the same order, when they mention them. Moses and his law have had their day—or age. The Jewish age has passed away never to be revived by Jews or Gentiles. The gospel age reaches to the nd of the world. It is impossible to blend Judaism and Christianity by divine authority. We go up to the mountain of the Lord's house, his temple, today, just as the apostles and converted Jews went up. No Christian grieves at the base of Mt. Zion, or Mt. Moriah, that David's palace is not on the first, or Solomon's temple on the latter. We have lost nothing by their removal; the Jews have lost nothing. If the Jews would be children of God, and be ruled from heaven by David, the Bethlehem King, (Jesus, our Lord), let them abandon their carnal views of the kingdom of Messiah, and return to God and "David their King" and go up with the nations in obedience to (Is. 2:5), "O house of Jacob, come ye, and let us walk in the light of the Lord."

CHAPTER XV.

HAGGAI—ZECHARIAH—MALACHI.

It is assumed by many that we are living in the last days near the end of the Christian age. What is to fol-- low this age they are not agreed upon. Some tell us it is a Millennium or a thousand years of almost sinless perfection. They predicate this belief chiefly on (Rev. 20:1-7). The Millennialists are divided, and sub-divided. This being the only passage in the Bible that speaks of the church in connection with a thousand years, of course, we find the many theories built around it. The Millennium by most advocates of the theory, is said to be at our doors. Many are in daily expectation of the second advent of Christ, the resurrection of the righteous dead, or, as s me affirm, the martyred dead, and that he, and they, will reign on earth a thousand years. I will, first of all, in addition to our preceding arguments, show how loosely and unwarrantably they handle the prophets. In order to set the matter clearly before the reader, let us read in

HAGGAI.

"For thus saith the Lord of hosts; yet once, it is a little while, and I will shake the heavens and the earth, and the sea and the dry land; and I will shake all nations, and the desire of all nations shall come, and I will fill this house with glory, saith the Lord of hosts. The silver is mine and the gold is mine, saith the Lord of hosts. The glory of this latter house shall be greater than of the former, saith the Lord of hosts; and in this place will I give peace, saith the Lord of hosts." (Haggai 2:6-9).

ZECHARIAH.

"And the word of the Lord came unto me, saying, Take of them of the captivity, even of Heldai ,of Tobijah and of Jedaiah, which are come from Babylon, and come thou the same day, and go into the house of Josiah, the son of Zephaniah. Then take silver and gold, and make crowns, and set them upon the head of Jeshua the son of Josedech, the high priests; and speak unto him, saying, thus speaketh the Lord of hosts, saying, behold the man whose name is The Branch; and he shall grow up out of his place, and he shall build the temple of the Lord, Even he shall build the temple of the Lord; and he shall bear the glory, and shall sit and rule upon his throne; and the counsel of peace shall be between them both.

And the crowns shall be to Helem, and to Tobijah, and to Jedaiah, and to Hen, the son Zephaniah, for a memorial in the temple of the Lord. And they that are far off shall come and build in the temple of the Lord, and ye shall know that the Lord of hosts hath sent me unto you. And this shall come to pass, if ye will diligently obey the voice of the Lord your God.   (Zech. 6: 9-15).

MALACHI.

"Behold, I will send my messenger, and he shall prepare the way before me; and the *Lord*, whom ye seek, shall suddenly come to his temple, even the messenger of the covenant, whom ye delight in, behold he shall come saith the Lord of hosts. But who may abide the day of his coming? And who shall stand when he appeareth? For he is like a refiner's fire, and like fuller's soap. And he shall sit as a refiner and purifier of silver; and he shall purify the sons of Levi and purge them as gold and silver, that they may offer unto the Lord an offering in righteousness. Then shall the offering of Judah and Jerusalem be pleasant unto the Lord, as in the days of old, and as in former years.

And I will come near to you to judgment, and I will be a swift witness against the sorcerers, and against the adulterers, and against false swearers, and against those that oppress the hireling in his wages, the widow, and the fatherless, and that turn aside the stranger from his right, and fear not me, saith the Lord of hosts. For I am the Lord, I change not; therefore ye sons of Jacob are not consumed." (Mal. 3:1-6). "Behold, I will send you Elijah, the prophet, before the coming of the great and dreadful day of the Lord; and he shall turn the heart of the fathers to the children, and the heart of the children to their fathers, lest I come and smite the earth with a curse." (Ch. 4:5-6).

These three prophets lived after the Jews returned from Babylon. The first two were raised up to encourage Judah in building the temple. Cyrus, who overthrew the Babylonian Empire, authorized them to build. (Ezra 1). This had been predicted of Cyrus by Isaiah. (Is. 44:26 to 45:19). Zerubbabel, a descendant of David, was the governor, and Jeshua, a descendant of Aaron, the highpriest in the days of these two prophets. The books of Ezra, and Nehemiah take up the thread of Israel's national history, at the close of the predicted seventy years of Babylonian captivity, and carry it down to the close of the Old Testament narrative.   The Babylonian Empire was succeeded by the Medo-Persian, as had been foretold, both in the symbolic prophecies of the metallic man, and the four wild beasts (Dan. chs. 2 and 7), and in the verbal predictions of Isaiah (13:17-22; 21:2) and (Jer. 51:11-28).   Daniel lived to see these great prophecies fulfilled.   (Dan'l 1:21; 6:23). After the death of Cyrus, the building of the temple was interrupted for some eighteen years, and Israel had grown careless and indifferent concerning it.   These two prophets were sent to the nation to stir up the people and to have the work carried forward to success, which was done. (Ezra 5:1-2).   What we are to consider especially is whether or not their predictions, quoted above, have been fulfilled.   According to Haggai's prediction, the following points should stand forth prominently in the life of Christ.

1.   There was to be a general shaking of heaven, earth, sea, and dry land, before Christ came.   The desire of all nations should come.

2.   The glory, not material, but spiritual, of the second temple should be greater than that of the first. Materially it was far inferior to it, and the elderly people who had seen the first house wept when they saw the foundation of the latter house.   (Ezra 3:12-13).

3.   And in that place, God would give peace.   Jesus met all these requirements.   He was the only One, whose coming and mission could meet the desires of the whole human family, for mercy and pardon and eternal happiness.   As the true *glory of God*, when he visited this temple five centuries later, it had a greater glory from God, than ever belonged to Solomon's temple.   As the silver and gold all belonged to God, he could have built it of gold, but the Desire of all nations would not redeem men on golden altars, nor purchase their peace with God with gold and silver.   He is our peace.   He is the Prince of peace.   He gives us peace with God, and makes peace between Jew and Gentile.   All these luminous

facts testify to Him as the one who redeemed this prophecy.

In (Zech. 6) is another marvellous Type-Prophecy.
Some men came from Babylon with gold and silver for
the temple being erected. By making two crowns, one
to represent the king and another to represent the High-
Priest, and putting them both on the head of the high-
priest, Joshua, he made another type-prophecy; (both a
type-prophecy, and a verbal prophecy).

1.   The man whose name is The Branch was typified
as a Royal-Priest. He should combine the two offices in
his person. These two offices could not be united in
one person, under the Mosaic law. Melchisedec, before
the Mosaic law was given, was priest and king, and thus
an eminent type of Christ. DAVID FORESAW THAT
HIS DESCENDANT, CHRIST, WOULD REVIVE THAT
ORDER, AND FORETOLD IT.   (Ps. 110:4); BUT THIS
COULD NEVER APPLY TO ANY KING OR PRIEST
RULING AND SERVING UNDER THE LAW OF MOSES.
This was, in effect, to foretell that the law, with all its
rites and ceremonies, should cease.   For without the
Aaronic priesthood the temple worship could not be conducted. For no king could act as priest under the law
of Moses. King Saul tried it and it was so great a sin
as to demand the surrender of his kingdom.   (I Sam'l
13:8-14). However he reigned for some time thereafter.
Jeroboam tried to act as royal-priest and was severely.
rebuked by a prophet of God, (I Ks. 13).   Uzziah was a
great and good king of Judah, but became a leper, lived
and died such, because he presumed to act the part of a
priest, (II Chron. 27:16-21). So when Zechariah predicted that "The branch" shall sit and rule upon his
throne, and he shall be a priest upon his throne, and the
counsel of peace shall be between them both," he was
predicting an event beyond the continuance of the Mosaic
law. Paul tells us in (Heb. chs. 5 to 7) all about this
new ruler-priest, Christ.   He says,

"For the priest-hood being changed, [from the tribe
of Levi to the tribe of Judah], there is made of necessity
a change also of the law. For he of whom these things
are spoken pertaineth to another tribe of which *no man
gave attendance at the altar*. For it is evident that our
Lord sprang out of Judah, of which tribe Moses spake

nothing concerning priest-hood." (Heb. 7:12-14).
Again:

"For if he were *on earth*, he should not be a priest, seeing that there are priests that offer gifts according to the law, who serve unto the example and shadow of heavenly things, as Moses was admonished when he was about to make the tabernacle; for, see, saith he, that thou make all things according to the pattern shewed to thee in the mount. But now hath he obtained a more excellent ministry, by how much also he is the mediator of a better covenant, which was established on better promises." (Heb. 8:4-6).

Now, nothing could possibly be made plainer by the apostle than that Jesus Christ was the Priest foretold by David and typified by Melchisedec. He speaks of Him as the Son of God, and of the tribe of Judah. He calls Him our Fore-runner who has entered within the veil, and that our hope of entering there is sure and steadfast, founded upon the oath-bound promise of God, and the redeeming power of our great High-Priest. It is self-evident that the Royal-High Priest in Zechariah's prophecy is the same person typified by Melchisedec, and foretold by David, and the Hebrew letter tells us this was Christ.

2. Moreover, he should build the temple of the Lord. This thought is doubled by the prophet, apparently for emphasis, for this was the great work of this King-Priest. The "counsel of peace" was to be maintained between the King and Priest, no rivalry or contention exist under the law as when these offices were coveted and became subject to barter and bribery. The Kings and priests of Judah often united in wickedness, but sometimes the king was loyal and the priest corupt, and, *rice-versa*. But under the double rule of "The Branch." entire harmony should exist between the two offices for they would be united in one person and he should" build the temple of the Lord." As Jesus was the Royal-Priest, it is beyond question that the *church* is *his temple.*

3. And they that are far off shall come and build *in the temple* of the Lord and ye shall know that the Lord of Hosts hath sent me unto you. And this shall come to pass, if ye will diligently obey the voice of the Lord your God. (Zech. 6:15).

Does not the whole of Ephesians (ch. 2) show how Jews that were nigh, and Gentiles afar off, were builded together for a habitation of God, through the Spirit? The apostle says the house was "*a holy temple in the Lord.*" SO THE WHOLE OF THE PROPHECY HAS BEEN GLORIOUSLY FULFILLED.

ELIJAH.

We need not tarry long with Malachi. John the Baptist was the Elijah that was for to come. (Matt. 17:10-13), "For all the prophets and the law prophesied until John. And if ye will receive it, this is the Elias which was for to come. HE THAT HATH EARS TO HEAR LET HIM HEAR." (Matt. 11:13-15).

THIS IS A KEY TO UNLOCK THE TYPE-PROPH-ECIES. Nothing could have been plainer than the prediction that Elijah was to come before the destruction of the Jewish nation, and labor with them in the way he did with apostate Israel in the days of Ahab and Jezebel. But John the Baptist was the man. He came in the "*spirit* and *power* of Elijah," to turn the hearts of the people back to God. Literalists make no progress here. No system of interpretation is correct that will not harmonize all the facts, both prophetic and historic. I have shown that the prophets, when foretelling the gospel age, used the language that Literalists demand shall have a literal fulfillment, to describe, in type-prophecy, under the name of *the type*, the higher reality under the gospel. Let us note that Malachi speaks of Jesus, as the messenger of the covenant. He is to cleanse the *house of Levi*, that *they* may *offer unto the Lord* an *offering in righteousness*. Consider the following facts.

1. Jesus is foretold as *David* in the list of prophecies already cited on that great fact. Well, if the *king* was predicted under the *name* of Judah's ideal king, by Hosea (3:5); by Jeremiah (30:9); by Isaiah (53:3-5); by Ezekiel (34:23; 37:24); what could the Spirit in these prophets mean but that Jesus was to be David's Son and Lord, the beloved of the Lord, and reign over the true Israel of God? Jesus was *not* David, even by name, and no looseness in handling these scriptures AS THOUGH THEY WERE NOT ALREADY FULFILLED, will ever bring one to the truth. They are fulfilled. How were they fulfilled, literally or figuratively?

2. We have just seen that *John the Baptist* was the *Elijah* that was to come. He positively denied that he was Elijah (Jno. 1) and he was not, either in PERSON or in NAME: yet Jesus said, "And if ye will receive it, this is Elias, WHICH WAS FOR TO COME. HE THAT HATH EARS TO HEAR, LET HIM HEAR." Jesus would open our ears to hear the meaning of this prophecy, for after one as plain as this, where Elijah's name was used, was not literal, but a type-prophecy, others of the SAME KIND MUST BE INTERPRETED IN THE SAME WAY. These prophecies are *representative* of the whole. King, temple, priesthood, sacrifices and feasts are predicted. Everything must be settled right here. Is David, (the David who was dead when these prophets wrote), to rise from the dead and reign over Israel forever? Is literal Elijah to precede his coming? Is Levi to return to his station as national priest of Israel and minister forever? You must decide these questions. Everything gravitates to this common center. If you answer "Yes" then you are a Literalist. If "No" you are a Figuratist. If you decide "Yes" you will be good material to work up into a Millennialist. If "No" you will not mix Judaism with Christianity, but will be able to separate type from anti-type, the shadow from the substance, and will have no use for the speculative theories and vague assumptions of men who seek to fuse the law of Moses with the law of Christ. Let us consider again (Jer. 33:15-18) and identify "The Branch."

"In those days, and at that time, will I cause The Branch of righteousness to grow up unto David; and he shall execute Judgment and righteousness in the land. In those days shall Judah be saved, and Jerusalem shall dwell safely; and this is the name wherewith he shall be called, THE LORD OUR RIGHTEOUSNESS. For thus saith the Lord; David shall never want a man to sit upon the throne of the house of Israel. Neither shall the priests, the Levites, want a man before me to offer burnt-offerings, and to kindle meat offerings and to do sacrifice continually."

The original of this prophecy of The Branch is in Isaiah, as in (Is. 9:8 to 10:4) is predicted the overthrow of the ten tribes of Israel. Next (10:5 to the close of 12th ch.) is the great prophecy of the staff, or rod. I analyze as follows:

1. The Assyrians would be used of God to overthrow the nation for their sins. Yet the Assyrian was simply carrying out his ambition, and everything seemed to be moving along with him in overthrowing Israel as in other countries. He did not discover or recognize God in the transaction, but said, "By the strength of my arm have I done it, and by my wisdom; for I am prudent; and I have removed the bonds of the people, and have robbed their treasures, and I have put down the inhabitants like a valiant man." Yet he was God's *ax* to hew down the forest, and his *rod* and *staff* by which He chastised His people, and then rejected them.

2. Under the figure of a great forest, the prophet showed how the nations would come down. Israel should fall before the ax, yet a "remnant" should be spared. After describing the general desolation of Judah, the overthrow of her king, princes, and great ones, to which he compares the prostration of the mighty Lebanon forest, (that is the stately trees in the Lebanon mountains just north of Palestine) one would think the hope of Judah was perished. But not so. "And there shall come forth a rod out of the stem of Jesse, and a branch shall grow out of his roots. And the Spirit of the Lord shall rest upon him the spirit of wisdom and understanding, the spirit of counsel and might, the spirit of knowledge and of the fear of the Lord." (Ch. 11:1-2). This prophecy is universally applied to Christ, and could be appropriated by no one else. I will consider it later, at some length, but here only as to "The Branch." The kingly tree was down, the dynasty of David fell in the person of Zedekiah, last temporal ruler of Judah (B. C. 587). This Stem, or Branch, grew, not out of the tree, but out of his roots. Royalty was down as far as David's family was concerned, when Jesus was born. He was not born in a palace on Mount Zion, but in a stable in Bethlehem, the home of Jesse. He was as a stalk out of dry ground. The Branch then, was a Son of Jesse, and as Jeremiah said, grew up to David, and he executed Judgment and righteousness in the land.

3. HE ASCENDED THE THRONE OF ISRAEL, FOR ISRAEL HAD TWO THRONES, ONE VISIBLE ON MOUNT ZION, THE OTHER INVISIBLE IN HEAVEN.

IT SEEMS TO THE WRITER AS VERY PUERILE TO
SAY THAT JESUS HAD TO REIGN, OR DOES YET
HAVE TO REBUILD, A PALACE AND THRONE IN,
EARTHLY JERUSALEM, AND OCCUPY THEM, TO RE-
DEEM THESE PROPHECIES.

He is reigning in Jerusalem, but it is above, and is
free, which is the mother of us all.   He is on the throne
of Israel, but not the earthly throne, for he is divine, and
his throne is high and lifted up.

4.   In those days shall Judah be saved and Jerusalem shall dwell safely, and this is the name whereby he
shall be called THE LORD OUR RIGHTEOUSNESS.

Salvation, not temporal, but spiritual and eternal
was brought to Judah by "THE LORD OUR RIGHTEOUS-
NESS," and certainly Jerusalem is well fortified and
safe from all assault, human or Satanic.

"In that day shall this song be sung in the land of
Judah; we have a strong *city*; *salvation* will God appoint
for *walls* and *bulwarks*.   Open ye the *gates*, that the
righteous nation which keepeth the truth may enter in.
Thou wilt keep him in perfect peace, whose mind is
stayed on thee; because he trusteth in thee.   Trust ye in
the Lord forever: for in the Lord Jehovah is everlasting
strength."   (Is. 26:1-4).   "Violence shall no more be
heard in thy land, wasting nor destruction within thy
borders; but thou shalt call thy *walls* Salvation, and thy
gates, Praise.   The sun shall no more be thy light by
day; neither for brightness shall the *moon* give *light* unto
thee: but the Lord shall be unto thee an everlasting
light, and thy God thy glory."   Surely this is spiritual
light for *spiritual* Israel.

4.   It was as strongly affirmed that the priests, the
Levites, should continue forever, and offer burnt-offerings, meat-offerings, and do sacrifices continually, as the
continuance of David's dynasty was predicted.   Here are
more items of the Jewish system, as it then existed,
WHICH WAS NEVER TO CEASE.   IN THE LITERAL
SENSE THEY HAVE ALL CEASED, AND THAT BY
DIVINE AUTHORITY, AGES AGO.   But the worship
of God has not ceased, in the reality of which these are
types, and shall not cease.

So we have David on the throne in Jerusalem above,

which is free and the mother of us all. He is our merciful and faithful High-priest upon the throne of Israel, for The Branch of (Is. 11; Jer. 33 and Zech. 6) is the Lord our Righteousness. He built the true tabernacle, and was the only Priest that could make atonement for us therein. He is on Mount Zion (Ps. 2) and has the heathen for his inheritance and the uttermost part of the earth for his possession. Instead of reigning like earthly David over a few of Abraham's descendants, he reigns over the true Israel of God, from the rising to the setting sun. His dominion is an everlasting dominion, and his kingdom shall have no end.

FIGURATIVE INTERPRETATION PROVED

We have the most direct scripture proof.

1. That *David* was used in the type-prophecies to *foretell* Christ.

2. *Elijah* was used by *name* and *labor* to *foretell* John the Baptist.

3. The *temple* was used to *foretell* the *church* or *spiritual* house of God.

4. The *Levites* and *priests* were used not ony as *types*, but by *name* to *foretell* the true servants of God under the *spiritual* rule of THE LORD OUR RIGHTEOUSNESS.

5. The *sacrifices*, specified by *name*, were used to *predict* "spiritual sacrifices, acceptable to God through Jesus Christ."

What more could we ask? What more could we have? This comprehends the entire Jewish arrangement. As *these* prophecies have this meaning, and have not now and never had any other meaning, they determine the *rule* by which all kindred predictions must be interpreted. This rule will bring the Jews to Christ; it will exclude all use of *types* in the so-called Millennium; and it will maintain the gospel to the end of time. "But now the righteousness of God *without the law* is *manifested*, being *witnessed* by the *law* and the *prophets*." These types, as *written witnesses* continue while time lasts, but are never to be reproduced. Suppose there were no Gentile believers in God, and the Jews wished to serve God, would they be acceptable to God in rejecting Christ and the New Covenant? Do you not see that this would do away with Christ and the church entirely? They were "broken off through unbelief"; and Gentiles were grafted in "by faith." The portion of the Jews who accept God's covenant that he made with Judah and Israel in Christ, are saved, and those who do not are blind and in bondage to tradition. The fact that Israel was once a typical people, and were acceptable to God, in the typical age, through a typical temple, priesthood and sacrifices, does not justify one in siding with that part of the nation who followed Caiaphas and rejected Jesus Christ. The apostles and primitive church for some years were in the New Covenant and were blessed of God in Christ before the Gentiles obtained this spiritual blessing. The fact that the Gentiles are blessed in Christ today and the Jews refuse to be blessed in the same manner and are waiting for another Messiah, should be made plain to the humblest understanding, as the crime of the ages. It can not be explained away, and should not be encouraged by the Literalists among the Gentiles who hope to see the literalities of the law, or in other words, the types revived. These men need to learn the nature, use and time of continuance given to the types of the Old Testament, and that they ceased with Christ and the gospel; then they will be in a fair way to give a correct interpretation to the Type-Prophecies, and will know that their whole theory of the Millennium that demands the presence and use of these ancient but fulfilled types is erroneous.

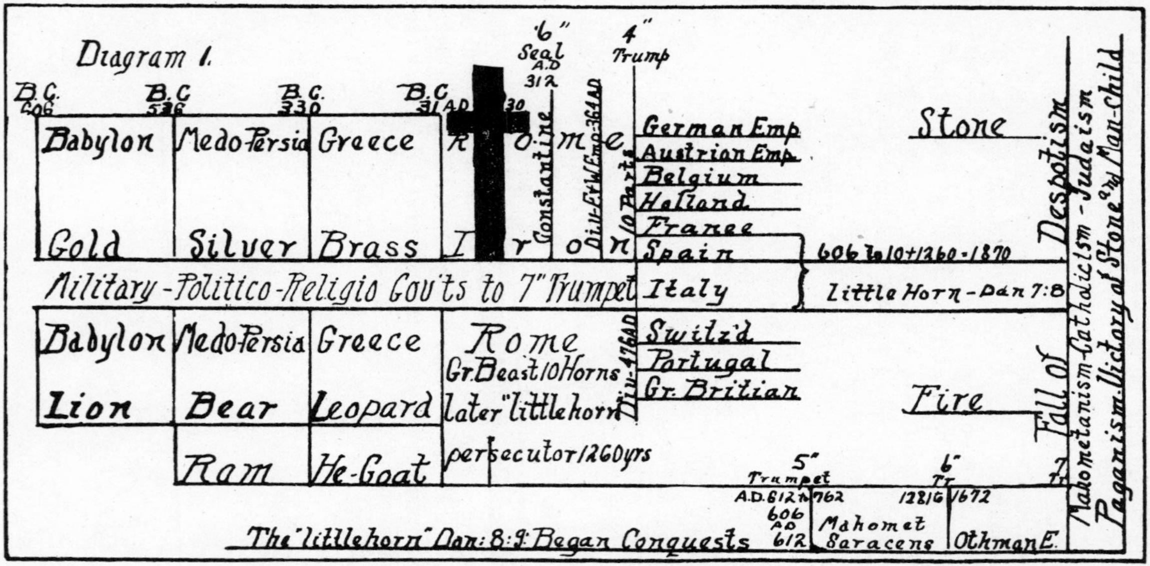

Diagram 1.

Babylon | Medo-Persia | Greece | Rome
B.C. 606 | B.C. 538 | B.C. 330 | B.C. 30 A.D.

Gold | Silver | Brass | Iron

Military – Politico – Religio Gov'ts to 7" Trumpet

Babylon | Medo-Persia | Greece | Rome
Gr.Beast 10 Horns | later "littlehorn" | persecutor 1260 yrs

Lion | Bear | Leopard | He-Goat
Ram

The "littlehorn" Dan: 8:9 Began Conquests

Constantine | German Emp. | Austrian Emp. | Belgium | Holland | France | M.Spain | Switz'd | Portugal | Gr.Britian

Div-Em 476 A.D.

"6" Seal A.D. 31? | "4" Trump | Italy | 606 In 10+ 1260 - 1870 | Little Horn – Dan 7:8

Despotism
Paganism-Catholicism-Judaism

Stone

Fall of

Fire

Fall of Turkey

"5" Trumpet | A.D. 612 | 762 | 606 A.D. | 6/12 Mahomet Saracens
"6" Tr. | 1281 | 612 | 1672 Othman E.

DIAGRAM I, PAGE I.

The gold, silver brass, iron and iron and clay parallel the lion, bear, leopard and beast great and terrible; and the toes of the man and ten horns of the fourth beast are parallels. Babylon, Medo-Persia, Greece, and Rome are symbolized. As a man has but one spirit, the military, Politico-Religious despotisms were essentially one; this is true even of the ten toes, and ten horns, and of the "little horn" of the papacy, and the "little horn" of Mamometanism.

The Ram and He-Goat present Persia and Greece again and show the rise of Mahomet. Revelation is joined in the diagram first at the "sixth seal" (Constantine) or (A. D. 312); the "fourth trumpet" or tenfold division of the W. Roman Emp. (A. D. 476). Next the fifth trumpet is the date for Catholicism and Mahometanism (606 to 612) and the latter system was victorious for the predicted five months or (150) years as the Saracens, and the "sixth trumpet", signalized the Ottoman Empire (itself Mahometan) and a cruel, aggressive power for (391) years. The "seventh trumpet," when it begins to sound brings the fall of despotism. This trumpet is sounding in our days. You see the "stone" is grinding the metallic man from feet to head to dust, the entire image; and the fire is consuming the fourth beast, horns and all. What the symbols were in agents, actions and results are the divine suggestions as to agents, actions and results in the governments symbolized. The issue is not doubtful. Despotism is doomed in all the territory once covered by the governments symbolized by the Man and the Beast. The "Stone" in its destructive and constructive work, effaces them from the earth, and gives us the government symbolized by the man-child in (Rev. 12).

CHAPTER XVI.

THE GIANT MAN.

As the books of Daniel and Revelation are closely related and are largely made up of Symbols, we should study them together. The unity of prophecy till the days of Daniel has been shown in the preceeding chapters. The giant image in (Daniel 2) shows us prophecy is a system. The image, composed of five materials, was in the form of a man. The unity of the man, and, hence, the unity of the prophecy, demands an unbroken history to redeem the prophecy. The gold, silver, brass, iron, and iron mixed with miry clay, are so compactly joined together as to leave no space between them, and thus show that the events predicted by these symbols are consecutive in order. The image has been called the calendar of prophecy. As one descends from the head to the feet, he is following the course of prophecy, from the days of Nebuchadnezzar to the ultimate fulfillment of the great prophecy. The stone smote the image on his *feet*, not in his breast or head, thus indicating the *time* when the *things symbolized* by the image would be swept away. The four great heathen monarchies, foretold by these symbols, are all identified in the Bible; the first three by name, making identification easy. Israel was now beginning their seventy years' captivity in Babylon, hence these additional prophecies concerning the heathen nations.

THE GOVERNMENTS SYMBOLIZED.

In (Daniel 2:36-43; Jer. 51:7) these Kingdoms are mentioned, and Daniel said to Nebuchadnezzar, "Thou art this head of gold"; not personally, however, as he added "And after thee shall arise *another kingdom*, [not king], inferior to thee and another third *kingdom of brass,* which shall bear rule over all the earth," (verses 38-39). This shows us that the great Babylonian kingdom was meant as the head of Goid. Medo-Persia succeeded the Babylonian government, (ch. 5:28-31). The Babylonian

Empire had lasted seventy years, according to the prediction of Jeremiah, (Jer. 25:10-14; 27:6-11). The
Medo-Persian government lasted two hundred years, and
brings us down in history to the Brass in the image, or to
the Greek Empire. (Daniel 11:2-3) aids in giving an
inspired application of this part of the composite symbol:
Alexander the Great established this third universal Empire. His rule was short, some ten years, but his government was divided into four parts under his generals, and
continued till overthrown by the Romans. The last kingdom receives more notice in the prophecy than all the
others combined. Our inquiries lead us to give much
space also to this kingdom.

STONE.

On what did the vision terminate? A stone. The
stone is represented as both *destructive* and *constructive*.
It was a stone in the beginning; a mountain world-wide
in the end. The stone represents agency, and the metaphor of a mountain, its increase and prevalency. As the
image crumbles, it is by the agency of the stone, which
grows and enlarges. The growth of the stone comes by
the relaxing of the sway of the idolatrous man. It will
appear, as we proceed to examine the other prophecies
relative to this subject, that the governments symbolized
by the "Giant Man," four in number, were obstacles in
the path of the stone, and were destroyed to give full
scope and power to the stone, or the government symbolized by it. Hence, I have said it was destructive, for
it destroys them; and it was constructive, for it becomes a great mountain, and fills the whole earth.

AN ERROR EXPOSED.

The disposition to separate this prophecy from its
parallel prophecies in (Daniel 7 and in Rev.) has led
some expositors to view the CHURCH AS ALL THAT
WAS SYMBOLIZED BY THE STONE. But the stone is
composite. It is generic, rather, and like the foundation
prophecy of which it is a *partial* development, "The seed
of the woman shall bruise the serpent's head," it comprehends much in little. As a symbol it could not do
otherwise. But we may learn as we proceed to examine

it in the light of its parallels, that the stone in its *matur-ity*, in its world wide governmental features, neither represents Christ in person, nor his church, exclusively. The kingdom of heaven destroys the four despotic, idolatrous governments, evidently; but it does so by reducing them to their lawful functions. The kingdom of heaven does not displace wholly all earthly governments.

THE FOUR WILD BEASTS, (Ch. 7).

In this vision of the four wild beasts, Daniel saw nearly half a century later than the king had the dream of the Image and Stone, more symbols of the, same historic period. But you observe that the last beast was not named. He was great and terrible, having many peculiarities. Some one has said that the symbol of the colossal image was very beautiful to Nebuchadnezzer, a man of cruelty and ambitious to rule the whole earth; but to Daniel the kingdoms were symbolized by wild, ferocious beasts. And it does seem that there was adaptation to the men, even in the choice of symbols. But we do not tarry to moralize on this subject.

1. The source of the beasts was out of the sea, lashed to fury by the winds of heaven. They did not all come up together but one after the other. The troubled sea represents the commotions among men, it seems, the warring elements producing these monsters to symbolize the cruel, despotic, idolatrous governments, four in number ,that were to hold sway on earth.

2. You notice as Israel was connected with goevrnments, these governments became subjects of prophecy. This was true of Amalek, Moab, Ammon, Edom, Nineveh, and now of Babylon, Medo-Persia, Greece and Rome, both in her unity and in her division and subdivisions. THUS GOD ENABLED HIS PROPHETS TO FORECAST THE DESTINY OF ALL THESE NATIONS, WHOSE TYRANNY AND CRUELTY, SYMBOLIZED BY THE IMAGE (idolatry), AND THE WILD BEASTS (cruelty) WERE TO CRUSH AND PERSECUTE THE PEOPLE OF GOD FOR AGES. Both sets of symbols cover the same ground down to the division of the Roman Empire into ten parts.

BABYLON.

.1   The lion is known as the king of beasts.   He is proud and lordly. So Babylon was the glory of the Chaldees' excellency.

2.   With power to crush and destroy, he rules through terror. So Babylon crushed and terrorized the nations.

3.   The lordly beast had two wings, the wings of an eagle, king of birds. This suggests the rapidity of conquest, by the Babylonian government, symbolized by the lion. Nebuchadnezzar's conquests were very great.

4.   The wings plucked, suggested there would be no more conquests: and with Nebuchadnezzar they ceased, the nation declined in power and passed out of history in Belshazzar's heathen feast. (Daniel 5).

5.   The beast was given the heart of a man, and the history of Nebuchadnezzar's lunacy and its results, is included at least, in the mighty change that passed over that government.   Daniel passes to the Bear or Symbol of the Medes and Persians. The governments arose and flourished in the order set forth in these symbols. See the Chart.

MEDO-PERSIA.

Medo-Persia was set forth as a Bear, and as the second government.

1.   It raised itself upon one side, or Medo-Persia is represented here as in (ch. 8) where the ram with two horns which were high, with one higher than the other, and the higher coming up last, shows the *order* in which the Bear, or government symbolized, rose into power. This Medo-Persian Empire, came after the Babylonian, subverted it and was founded by Cyrus, who united the *two governments* of Media and Persia into *one*.   The ancient name of Persia was Elam, named after Elam, the second son of Shem. Thus *two* states, *acting* as *one*, under the governing power, Cyrus, accomplished the prophecies relating to the overthrow of Babylon.   The Bear was lifted up upon one side or into *one dominion* as the text suggests.

2.   It had three ribs in its mouth and the command to it was, "Arise, devour much flesh." Egypt, Lydia

and Babylon are usually regarded as the ribs crushed by this Bear. The Persians are noted in history for their cruelty. Herodotus, "the father of heathen historians," says: "Wherever Cyrus marched through the earth, it was impossible for nations to escape him." Xenophon said :"He ruled the Medes, subverted the Syrians, the Assyrians, the Arabians, the Cappadocians, the Phrygians, the Lydians, the Carians, the Babylonians, the Phoenicians, the Greeks, in Asia, the Cyprians, the Egyptians and struck all with such dread and terror that none ventured to assail him. He subdued from his throne, east, west, north and south." Cyrus was foretold by name and what he would do for God's people. (Is. 44:26-28; 45:1-7). Cyrus said, "The Lord God of heaven hath given me all kingdoms of the earth; and he hath charged me to build him an house at Jerusalem, which is in Jud-- ah." (Ezra 1:2). Thus we find several of earth's greatest rulers mentioned by name in the Bible, as they fulfilled some prediction that had been made; in this case, Cyrus was foretold by name (200) years before.

GREECE.

The reader, if versed in Ancient History, knows what the Leopard symbolized,—the Grecian Empire. The Leopard is a small animal, strong, active and all but irresistible. It is among the swiftest of the beasts, and, like the cat, quick and sure in leaping upon its prey. The four wings intensify its power and speed. The four heads, show the kingdom divided into four parts, after Alexander the Great. These symbols receive some light from chapter eight, where the Ram with two horns (the kings of Media and Persia, (verses 20) was assailed by the rough goat (king of Grecia); and the great horn between his eyes is the first king, (Alexander). "Now that being broken, whereas four stood up for it, four kingdoms shall stand up out of the nation, but not in his power." (Dan. 8:22). I have a copy of Herodotus' history before me, and several other great histories, but think the fundamental facts are admitted, and that every High School pupil knows that the next universal kingdom was that of the Greeks. I will, therefore, not cumber these pages to establish points so universally known. It must be conceded, however, that the prophecy was fulfilled in the kingdom of Brass. The "Brazen Coated Greeks" is a name that the great warriors of Greece wear in history. About (334-330 B. C.) Alexander, the mighty military genius, turned the Medo-Persian Empire into his dominion. Lust of conquest and earthly glory led Alexander to overthrow the Medo-Persian Empire, as ambition had led Cyrus, two centuries before, to overthrow the Babylonian Empire; and as love of eminence and power had led the great Nebuchadnezzar, seventy years before Cyrus to found the great Babylonian Empire. Thus as we come down the pathway of history we find it lined on each side by the pathway of the symbols of prophecy, or the history parallels the prophecy.

ROMAN EMPIRE.

The Roman Empire came next, and the symbols concerning it are not all fulfilled to this day. The animal is not named this time, but in (Rev. 13th ch.) when he reappeared, he was like a *leopard*, and his feet were as the feet of a *bear*, and his mouth as the mouth of a *lion*. So we see he partook of the nature of the other three. He was compounded of three beasts, just as the Roman government was, in some of its most striking characteristics, like the three great empires that preceded it—they were all related. The re-appearance of this leopard-bearlion beast in Revelation, so unites even the symbols of the otherwise distinct animals, as to demand a continuous history in fulfillment of the wild beast symbols, in harmony with the gold, silver, brass, iron and clay symbols, which constitute *one* "Giant Man." The features of this beast are very prominent as follows: (Dan. 7).

1. Diverse from all the others. So the Roman Government was. It passed through seven forms of government as we shall see later.

2. He was exceeding dreadful, with iron teeth and brazen nails and he brake in pieces, and stamped the residue with his feet. Gibbon says

"The arms of the republic, sometimes vanquished in battle, always victorious in war, advanced with rapid steps to the Euphrates, the Danube, the Rhine and the Ocean; and the images of *gold*, or *silver*, or *brass*, that might serve to represent the nations and their kings,

were successively broken by the iron monarchy of Rome."
(Vol. 3, p. 634, Millman's E'd).

Rome was founded (753 B. C.) as a city and state.
The prophet said that the "beast is the fourth kingdom
upon earth, which shall be diverse from all kingdoms, and
shall devour the whole earth, and shall tread it down
and break it in pieces." (Ch. 7:23).

3. The Beast has ten horns, representing the ten-
fold division of the Western Roman Empire. There has
never been any nation on earth except Rome that meets
the requirements of this prophecy. There is no speculation in fitting these four governments to the double line
of prophecy that foretold them as shown in the accom-
paning diagram.

Verses 11-12.

"I beheld then because of the voice of the great
words which the horn spake: I beheld even till the beast
was slain and his body destroyed and given to the burning flame. As concerning the rest of the beasts, they
had their dominion taken away: yet their lives were prolonged for a season and time."

This peculiarity should not escape our notice. In
the case of Babylon, Medo-Persia and Greece, their
power to rule was taken from them, but the governments
simply changed masters, and continued to be the same
tyrannous, idolatrous countries as before. But the symbols show us that when the last beast is slain, the power
does not continue, as heretofore, to be wielded by men of
like principles. The revolution is radically different, as
the beast is slain and his body given to the burning
flame. The cruel, despotic, idolatrous rule, propagated
from Babylon through Medo-Persia, Greece and Rome,
and in the latter through its ten-fold division, and its
"little horn" as well, is consumed. Just as the stone destroyed the image in the DAYS OF THE FEET AND TOES,
and thence became the great world-mountain, so here
the fire consumes this beast of horrid features, and awful
history, and the time has then come that "the saints of
the most High shall take the kingdom and possess the
kingdom forever, even forever and ver," (verse 18).

The two prophecies are a unit, although expressed in
different symbols. You notice that in the image the
ten-fold division was indicated by the toes, but the *elev-*

enth toe is not there. The image is normal, and evidently has ten toes. This is a necessary inference, just as if one should say a neighbor had his eyes put out, or his hands ground off, or his ears frozen, or his feet crushed, in each instance we would have no hesitancy in saying how many members were involved. So in two instances the language speaks of the toes of the image, and as the composite symbol is a man, the necessary conclusion is that his toes were ten in number. But in the case of the fourth beast, the number of horns is specified, and the "little horn" which came up last, or the eleventh horn, had to be described. Thus the prophecy is cumulative, and shows us that the Roman Empire would have one government to come up later than its division in (A. D. 476). The horns, be it strictly noted, are parts of the beast. They grew out of the head of the beast. This fact makes it necessary to interpret the ten horns as parts of the Roman Empire, and the little horn also as a member of that family of nations and united to the government as the horn of a beast is a part of the beast. This shows us the government symbolized by the "little horn," grows up out of the fourth kingdom, later than the ten-fold division of that government as the symbols plainly foretold, also the verbal prophecy. This is indicated in the Diagram. It is evident that as the "Giant Man" is joined together, so the governments are joined together, which fact once proved is proved forever. Hence the symbols of gold, silver, brass and iron foretold four successive governments; and the toes the state of the last one predicted (or Rome) in its second stage of history, or divided form and the wild beasts and verbal prophecies, though not connected so closely. and plainly in symbol can not be separated to *contradict* the symbols that form the man. All of the symbols are demanded, and in the exact order given to form the "Giant Man" and these forever settle the number and order of the governments.

NATURE OF THIS WORK.

The mere outlines of ancient history are all that my subject demands. Daniel foretold that four universal heathen monarchies should exist in historic succession.

All of our Ancient Histories present the rise, progress, and overthrow of these four governments, thus verifying the prediction. It is interesting and instructive, indeed, necessary, to familiarize one's self with these great pages of history, if one would lay any just claim to being an educated person. But the credibility of the Bible, its prophetic accuracy, does not depend upon a detailed account of the arts, sciences, philosophies, and architectural skill of the people who constituted these governments. The prophet said there would be four idolatrous, cruel governments of universal dominion, in the then known world, and no more. The historians say there have been four, and no more, and abundantly redeem every feature predicted concerning these governments. With this we are satisfied as students of the prophets, but as historians we love to ponder the magnitude and glory, the riches and splendor of these ancient empires. But for exegetical purposes, we need not consider the lofty height and thickness of the walls of Nineveh or Babylon; whether the latter city was fifteen miles square, had streets one hundred fifty feet wide, and had mammoth brazen gates at their entrances, the height of her towers, the beauty of her palaces, hanging gardens, temple of Belus, famous bridges, aqueducts, sun-dried brick, fertility of soil, provisions for twenty years siege, and the like, all only circumstantials. We wish to know that Babylon fell as the prophets predicted; her broad walls came down; her overthrow was by the Medes and Persians; Cyrus was the conqueror; that the captivity lasted the predicted seventy years; that Babylon became a pool of water; that wild beasts and owls dwell there; and the whole territory is desolate and waste. Such facts were *predicted*, and very unlikely of fulfillment; but each was fulfilled and thus Scripture prophecy is redeemed in history. (Is. 13: 19-22; 14:4-28; Hab. 2:1-14; Jer. 25:8-14; 27:5-22; 51st and 52nd chs) and many other predictions.

CHAPTER XVII.

THE 'FOUR WILD BEASTS.

(Daniel 7:7-14).

The interpretation of these symbols, will go far to-wards the proper unfolding of the meaning of all the symbolic prophecies, bearing on the same period of time. We cannot therefore, exercise too much pains in our study of the symbols before us.

1. These four beasts never had a real existence. The lion with eagle wings, the Bear with three ribs in his mouth, the four-winged Leopard, and the unnamed animal with eleven horns, were not real, living animals. The purpose of foretelling the future down to a certain period was.evident in the *dream* of the rich and powerful, heathen monarch, of that mammoth, strangely composite man, and the action and consequences of the stone smit-ing him. The *time* of destroying him was shown by the stone smiting him on the *feet* and *toes*, the symbols farth-est removed *from the head*, and thus the most remote per-iod foretold by the composite symbol of the man. The things symoblized by the image disappear *at the time*, and *in the manner*, pictured by the symbols. But the stone sym-bol *outlasts* the man symbol, and grows wonderfully after that is ground to pieces, becomes as chaff and is swept away. This imports that the *things* symbolized by the stone are to continue and grow into their *greatest power* and *universality* after the *governments* symbolized by the man are *swept away*.

2. The symbols in the (7th ch.) are given down to the (14*th verse*) *inclusive*. Daniel's inspired interpreta-tion, REPRODUCES SOME OF THESE SYMBOLS. (Vers-es 19-22). We greatly err, and are led into hopeless con-fusion, by failing to treat symbols as *symbols*, and if we treat as an *interpretation*, what the prophet used as a *sym-bol*. Now, applying this observation to the chapter before us, we discover the following symbols:

1. A fourth beast, great and terrible, and strong exceedingly.

2. It devoured, break in pieces, and stamped the residue with the feet of it.

3. It was diverse from all the beasts that went before it.

4. And it had ten horns.

All this is symbolic, for not a word of interpretation has thus far been given by the prophet as to what these symbols mean. The prophet's attention was next given to a consideration of the horns, which were ten in number. These all symbolized some REALITY OF THE FUTURE, which was to receive definite prediction.

5. He saw another symbol, "a little horn," and three horns fell before him, or were plucked up by the roots. This foretells the exploits, in a measure, of something pictured to Daniel by this horn. The nature of the horn is next described. He had eyes like the eyes of a man, and a mouth speaking great things. What was seen was a menagerie of wild beasts, but not actual, living animals, like one sees in cages at a show, or in their native haunts, but beasts made up for predictive purposes, with just such appearances, as would best picture the governments and dynasties to arise. I wish the reader's whole thought on this discrimination. THE WHOLE SCENE WAS SYMBOLIC; and not the animals, four in succession, the ten horns, later another horn, then his plucking up three horns all symbolic as universally interpreted; AFTER THIS ALL LITERAL: that is, thrones cast down, son of man coming in the clouds of heaven " a little horn" judged, Beast condemned, his body burned, and son of man and his saints possess the kingdom. The first part is not symbolic, and the last part a literal return of Christ to earth to judge popery, destroy despotism and reign on earth. This is the *false method of interpretation* followed by the Literalists. If Christ is not coming to earth in this passage to reign, he is in none, in the entire range of prophecy. I ask your whole attention at this vital point. The scene is a PICTURE in SYMBOLS of what? So far all is symbolic beyond question, and no interpretation of even one symbol is given.

But the panorama had not all passed before the prophet yet, and more symbols are given him.

6. I beheld till the thrones were cast down, and the Ancient of days did sit. This is symbolic of God's Judgment, (not the final Judgment of all mankind, of course) but the Judgment of this *Beast* and his *horns*. No symbols can adequately picture God, so we are told his *garment* was white as snow, and the *hair* of his *head* like the pure wool; his *throne* was like the fiery flame, and his *wheels* as burning fire. "A fiery stream issued and came forth, from before him: thousand thousands ministered unto him, and ten thousand times ten thousand stood before him: the Judgment was set and the books were opened." Whose trial is this? Whose life and character are to be examined? Is this history? or is it prophecy in symbol, the same as the preceding? It is the latter, and is a local Judgment. The Beast was weighed in the balances and found wanting," as the next verse represents in symbol.

7. "I beheld then because of the voice of the great words which the *horn* spake: I beheld even till the *Beast was slain*, and HIS *body destroyed* and given to the burning flame." Next we are told that the other Beasts, when they lost their dominion, did not cease to exist; but this fourth Beast shall cease to exist. So I remarked previously on this verse. The symbols, and the prophet's comment, demand that the government in such form and ruling with such cruelty, shall pass away. With the field now cleared of the Beast, like the field cleared of the "Giant Man " there is room for something better. In that symbolism, the stone rolled on and became a great mountain and filled the whole earth; so here, we might expect the prophecies to harmonize in symbol, and they do.

8. "I saw in the night visions, and behold, one like the Son of Man came with the clouds of heaven, and came to the Ancient of days, and they brought him near before him.

And there was given him dominion, and glory, and a Kingdom, that all people, nations, and languages, should serve him: his dominion is an everlasting dominion, which SHALL NOT PASS AWAY, and his Kingdom that which shall not be destroyed.

THE INTERPRETATION.

It has surprised me for some years to see the confusion of interpreters at this point. THE LITERALISTS HAVE QUITE GENERALLY MADE THESE LAST VERSES REFER TO A PRE-MILLENNIAL ADVENT OF CHRIST TO THIS EARTH TO SET UP HIS KINGDOM. This point once fixed in their system all other predictions are twisted to sustain it. This is the fulcrum upon which they place their lever to hoist the whole millennial theory into being. I unhesitatingly remove the fulcrum. The reader should study the issue here with all sincerity and openness of mind. Like the Literalists or Futurists interpretation of David, the Temple, the priesthood and the sacrifices, *this* is a *point of cleavage*. We may misinterpret symbols or verbal predictions, but cannot *make the events* to sustain our erroneous views. Hence we should calmly study the symbols, in harmony with the verbal prophecy, to get at their exact meaning. I suggest a few points on this celebrated prophecy.

1. I have said, from the first, that these prophecies are all related, they are a complete system. Just as the parables and the literal teaching of Christ are a unit, so the symbols and verbal predictions teach the same things. This is not the place to discuss that question, even if it needed any illustration. I assume that the reader is too well versed in the Scriptures to think that the figurative language contains another meaning than that given in the unfigurative language.

2. The giant man, and Daniel's interpretation of the symbolic meaning of each metal, the final destructive action of the stone against the idol, and the marvellous growth of that stone, show us that the God of heaven shall set up a Kingdom, IN THE DAYS OF THESE KINGDOMS, *it* shall break in pieces and destroy *these* Kingdoms, and IT SHALL STAND FOREVER. The God of heaven made known what SHALL COME TO PASS HEREAFTER.

3. The same prophet that interpreted that *dream*, of the image and stone, interpreted this *vision* of the four wild beasts; the last with ten horns; the little horn; the Judgment against this horn; the destruction of the beast; and the triumph of the Kingdom of God. Consistency

demands, and the interpretation of the prophecy furnishes harmony in the symbols of the Dream and of the vision. I may add, that like harmony necessarily exists between our Savior's great prophecy in (Matt. 24 and 25) and John's visions given in Revelation. They are all parts of one systematic order of things foreseen and foretold in the ages past, of the fortunes and destinies of governments, and especially of the Kingdom of God as related to these governments. The old doctrine was still to be maintained, "Blessed be he that blesseth thee, and cursed be he that curseth thee." The mammoth governments never grew too large for the God of heaven to punish them for their sacrilege and persecution of his people, as we hope to remember throughout this entire investigation.

"Horn" sometimes means, king, sometimes a dynasty. The angel said, "Ten kings shall arise" and this means what? The whole Protestant system is at stake here. It evidently means ten kingdoms. Why? THE WORD IS SO USED AND APPLIED BY THE ANGEL TO THE FOUR GREAT MONARCHIES, Babylon, Medo-Persia, Greece and Rome, (ch. 7:17). THE PROPHECY IS CONTINUOUS as the metallic man shows; and the wild beast in (Rev. 13) was a composite of Lion, Bear and Leopard, showing that the fourth government was made up out of the three that preceded it; and, moreover, this is history. The "Little horn" in (Rev. 17) is the eighth head, and as the seven forms of Government that preceded it in Rome are symbolized by heads, the *eighth* head had to mean what each of the seven heads meant,—a dynasty. To recite history; there were seven kings ruled for about two hundred years; next consuls, tribunes, decemvirs and dictators ruled for some five hundred years; sixty-five emperors ruled in Rome for five centuries; the Exarchs of Ravenna ruled more than a century; these are seven heads; but finally, the "little horn," popery, ruled for thirteen centuries. This is historical fulfillment. Thus anti-christ arose on the fall of the Roman Empire. EIGHT POINTS OF IDENTITY.

1. Eighth head of the Roman Beast.
2. "Little horn," small, temporal possessions.
3. "Came up *after* them," this reads like history.

4.   Be a persecuting power against the saints.

5.   Self-exaltation for definite period.

6.   His dominion should be taken away, and

7.   The people of the saints possess the ruling power under the whole heaven.

8.   This King lives forever and rules over all the people of God eternally.

"And he shall subdue three Kings. And he shall speak great words against the most High, and shall wear out the saints of the most High, and think to change times and laws: and they shall be given into his hand until "a time, times and the dividing of time."

The three horns, (that is three of the *ten*), plucked up were, according to Sir Isaac Newton, the exarchate of Ravenna, the Kingdom of the Lombards, and the State of Rome. The popes wear a triple crown. All this was revelation pure and simple. The rise, character, progress and time of continuance of *one* government, that should grow up like a horn, after the government symbolized by the Beast had been divided into ten, necessarily smaller governments, are brought out in detail, making identification easy. The expositor has only to learn which was the FOURTH universal government; WHEN it was divided into ten lesser governments; and, finally, when a *little* government, IN THE SAME TERRITORY OF THE FOURTH GOVERNMENT, (like the eleventh horn in the head of the Beast) arose; study its hideous characteristics, and learn the meaning of the figurative language limiting the time of its power to prevail against the saints, and he has both the *symbols* and the *literal* prophecy, side by side, to compare with the *historic reality*.

6.   Next the writer explains the symbols of the Judgment, MARK YOU WELL, NOT OF ALL NATIONS, NOT OF THE DEAD AND OF THE LIVING, BUT A LOCAL JUDGMENT OF THE GOVERNMENT OF THE HORN. The expositor who makes this to mean the END OF THE GOSPEL AGE, the Judgment of ALL NATIONS, as set forth in (Matt. 25:31 etc) ignores all the symbolism, and the inspired interpretation of the same, not only here, in (Daniel 2) and in (Matt. 25), but also in Revelation, where the Judgment of THE GREAT HAR-

LOT IS CONSIDERED AT LENGTH. (Rev. 17). "But the Judgment shall sit, and they shall take away his dominion, to consume and to destroy it unto the end." If these ten toes represent the ten kingdoms of Europe into which the Western Roman Empire was divided in (A. D. 476) and the "little horn" represents, in symbol, the papal dominion, then we may see in prophecy the overthrow of this system of government, which continued for "a time, times and the dividing of time," (or 1260 years). We next inquire as to what shall survive it. "And the kingdom and dominion and the greatness of the Kingdom under the whole heaven, shall be given to the people of the saints of the most High, whose kingdom is an everlasting kingdom, and all dominions shall serve and obey him."

VERBAL PROPHECY.

The explanation or *interpretation* of these symbols should be read in order, LEAVING OUT THE SYMBOLS AND MAKING SIMPLY A VERBAL PROPHECY. This is done as follows: "These great beasts, which are four, are four kings, [kingdoms,] which shall arise out of the earth. But the saints of the most High, shall take the kingdom, and possess the kingdom forever, even forever and ever," (verses 17-18). This is the interpretation as to *all the Beasts*, and what the *saints* shall ultimately accomplish. Then Daniel would descend to particulars concerning the last Beast, with ten horns, and the peculiar little horn, how *long* he should war with and prevail against the saints, and the transfer of sovereignty to the saints, and so the interpretation is given.

1. "The fourth beast shall be the fourth kingdom upon the earth, shall be diverse from all kingdoms, and shall devour the whole earth, and shall tread it down, and break it in pieces."

This is beyond any reasonable doubt the vast Roman Empire, which held the universal dominion as the fourth great idolatrous empire. It was held together for five centuries, after obtaining the mastery over such vast territory. It was divided into the Eastern and Western Empires in (A. D. 364). The Western Empire or Latin speaking portion, with headquarters in Rome, "The eternal city," becomes the subject of the remaining portion of this prophecy. (It will be shown in due time why the ten toes of the image, and the ten horns of the beast, are held as symbols applying to this territory and not to the whole Roman Empire).

2. "And the ten horns out of this kingdom are ten kings [kingdoms] that shall arise." The Western Roman Empire was divided into ten kingdoms in (A. D. 476). This date is as celebrated as any in history. Allison begins his history at this date. Dr. Leonhard Schmitz divides the history of the Middle Ages into two periods—"the first extending from the downfall of the Western Empire to the Crusades (A. D. 476-1096); and the second from the beginning of the Crusades to the Protestant Reformation (1096-1517). The fall of the Western Empire (A. D. 476) forms an era in the history of Europe and of the world. It will be seen when we consider the *time prophecies* that it was not only foretold by the toes of the image, and by the ten horns of the fourth beast, but the *time* of it was predicted as well. All we care to note here is the fact that all our standard historians of these ages, sustain the prophecy at this point.

"And another shall arise after them; and he shall be diverse from the first, and he shall subdue three kings.

And he shall speak great words against the most High, and shall wear out the saints of the most High, and think to change times and laws; and they shall be given into his hand for a time, and times and the dividing of time."

Here is a distinct prophecy, and no obscurity, except it be on the length of time this kingdom shall have dominion, and this point receives abundant illustration in other uses of the statement, and other terms of expressing the length of time set forth. But there was to be: 1. Another kingdom. 2. It was to come after the Empire was broken up into ten parts, hence after (A. D. 476). 3. It was to be different from the ten kingdoms. 4. It was to subdue *three* of the *ten* kingdoms. 5. He shall blaspheme the name of God. 6. He shall be a violent, successful persecutor of the saints; (New Testament Saints for it is all after A. D. 476). 7. He shall think to change times and laws, or be as Paul styles him, a "lawless one." 8. The saints shall be given into his hand for a "time, times and the dividing of time."

The great Protestant world has with great uniformity, applied this prophecy to that power which arose in the seventh century and dominated Europe for thirteen centuries, the *Roman* Catholic power. It united civil and religious power, or church and state. The chief ruler in the church claimed to be heaven's appointed ruler in the state as well. He was a law unto himself. His disposition and power to persecute the saints, or all who resisted his pretentions, instituted and perpetuated a long reign of terror.

"But the judgment shall sit, and they shall take away his dominion, to consume and to destroy it unto the end." As noted above, this *judgment* was *local, not* universal. It was an arraignment and condemnation of this government for the high crimes and misdemeanors of which it was notoriously guilty, and which are classified here as against God and man. The judgment is like that against Moab, Ammon, Amalek, Nineveh, Babylon, Tyre, Ishmael and Egypt. This government merited the "curse," as did they, and forfeited all right to exist. But her overthrow is not at a stroke, or suddenly. There is nothing miraculous about the overthrow. The catholic power rose gradually, and required ages to mature her plans and attain sufficient power to elevate a pope to the head of the state and rule both in church and state. Her decline is by natural means, and likewise gradual. Since (A. D. 1870) the power to rule the state has not been in the hands of the catholic church. The temporal possessions were taken from the Pope in Italy and he was reduced to an ecclesiastic or religious ruler, and the text says his dominion (rule) will be consumed or destroyed to the end. Forty-four years have rolled by, nearly a half century, and this arrogant power is still prostrate in the dust ,as a state, and the terms of the prediction confirm the forceful symbols "the beast was slain, and his body destroyed, and given to the burning flame." Just so. This power to sit as head of church and state, tyrannize over men civilly and religiously, has received its mortal wound, and while the colossal tyrant is desperate and struggling like an expiring giant, the subject nations, too, like a blind, imprisoned Samson, are feeling for the pillars of the idolatrous temple, and mean, under God, to destroy forever that hideous structure. It requires no miracle to accomplish it. The Bible is the dynamic force. when faithfully applied to uplift the very roots of the mountains of tyranny and oppression. Free speech, free press, free schools are the triple alliance that shall free the world. By their means the beast with deadly horns and adulterous eyes and blasphemous mouth is having the fagots of long slumbering justice heaped around him, and is consumed as a righteous judgment for his course of tyranny in church and state, that filled the world with grief for thirteen centuries.

"And the Kingdom and the dominion and the greatness of the Kingdom under the whole heaven, shall be given to the people of the saints of the most High, whose Kingdom is an everlasting Kingdom, and all dominions shall serve and obey him. Hitherto is the end of the matter."

You notice it is "the people of the saints," not the Lord Jesus in person, neither his saints, exclusively, that finally possess the Kingdom, or rule. The Ruler, Christ, overthrows the usurper, the Pope, but not by miracles. It is not that he leaves heaven to break down despotic rule on earth, either in church or state. His rule over the church directly began on Pentecost (Acts 2); and his right to rule over the state, (indirectly) no faithful subject of his can question. His presence on earth is neither needed nor promised for either. As shown at length in preceding chapters, Israel's unfounded hope of a temporal Ruler in the Messiah, was overthrown. It will be seen in succeeding pages, that the views now being industriously circulated, and emphasized by tongue and pen, that Jesus is to return to earth in person to inaugurate a Millennium, are as unfounded as were the Jewish dreams of temporal dominion and glory under the Messiah.

A SUMMARY.

1. The eternal *God* is *Judge* in these prophetic *symbols* not the *Son* as in (Matt. 25:31); hence not the same Judgment.

2. The *Roman Empire*, and especially the *last phase of it* and the *"little horn"* are condemned in these books— prophecies and the records of their blasphemies and sins.

3. When the fourth beast loses his power, is consumed, it will be by Judgment of such a nature, as to be a *blessing* to the people, but an all-consuming *curse* upon idolatrous,. persecuting power.

4. One like the Son of man was evidently our Lord advancing to the thrones vacated by the Beasts, especially, that of the fourth Beast. He was not COMING TO EARTH, however, AWAY FROM THE FATHER IN HEAVEN: but was brought NEAR BEFORE HIM. The symbol demands that he GO TO God, rather than that he COME FROM God. It is a pictorial representation of his assumption, by God's just decree, of the rule over men, which the Beast had usurped for ages. He is not coming in the clouds FROM heaven TO earth, as in (Matt. 25: 31 and elsewhere) to raise the dead, and judge all nations, every man; but he is ascending TO GOD to exercise the grant of "all authority in HEAVEN and in EARTH."

5. Jesus has had this authority since he went up and a cloud received him out of the sight of his apostles. With the sword of the Spirit in this great battle-field he has smitten down his enemies, and cast down their strongholds, and will ultimately attain the mastery over the nations, not personally like David, but in the person of his faithful followers.

6. The duration and severity of this unique persecuting power were foreseen, and perhaps have never been equalled in any other government since the foundation of the world. The length of this period is given repeatedly. (Ch. 12:5-9: Rev. 11: 1-6; 12:3-6, 14; 13:5-10). From the decree of Phocas (A. D. 606) declaring the Bishop of Rome, UNIVERSAL BISHOP AND SUPREME HEAD OF THE CHURCH to (A. D. 1866) or the predicted period, this mystical Babylon had the saints in his hands, could change times and laws at his pleasure among men; but at that period the word of God was fulfilled in that his dominoin was taken away, as it was first given by the state, and the system, as such, has been consuming, like a beast in the fire, ever since.

7. The parallel of the Dream (ch. 2) and of the consequences of the stone destroying the image and after this becoming a great mountain and filling the whole

earth, is duplicated by the sovereignty of the long oppressed saints, who claim and exercise their rights as
sons of God, and write into the constitutions and laws of
the governments such principles and restrictions of rule
as insure to them their inalienable rights, and forever
repudiate the interference of despotic ecclesiastics in
state or nation. This all-pervasive and all-regulative
principle, so long trampled under the feet of Kings and
Emperors, priests and bishops, and wholly ignored by this
"little horn" for more than a thousand years, is sweeping
like fire in dry stubble across governments and empires
today, and is destined to consume the arrogant claims
of tyrants in state and church, and recover to the downtrodden and oppressed, the misguided and misgoverned,
inhabitants of our world, the blessings and privileges
granted to them by God in Christ. This is the vindication of truth, and a proof of the veracity of the prophets,
and, at the same time, a demonstration on a basis world-
wide, of the original decree——"Blessed be he that blesseth
thee, and cursed be he that curseth thee." It seems to
me that this lesson is most salutary at this time. We
should read of the mighty revolutions in, and overthrow
of, tyrannous governments in our day in the light of these
prophecies. The fulfillments on a national scale, of
these prophecies, make our generation especially fortunate in the marvellous proofs, given in prophetic fulfillment all about us. It is, I doubt not, the group of prophecies, (both symbolic, verbal and time-prophecies, now fulfilling in the overthrow of the "little horn" and of Mahometanism and despotism, that bewilders many, who
think the end of these things is the end of the world, or
end of the gospel age. But this is taking things back-
wards. It is the end of organized tyranny that is due
and the advancement of civil and religious liberty in its
place.

CHAPTER XVIII.

TIMES OF THE GENTILES.

The Gentiles kept Israel in Babylon seventy years because of their sins. They have been persecuted, despised, oppressed, desolated now for some eighteen centuries. It seems to me that the *time-prophecies* are about fulfilled concerning them. The literalists say, "Yes they are to return to their land, revive their ancient capital, Jesus is to reign over them personally,'" etc, etc. No. They are not a nation in temporal bondage, and, can not be delivered from temporal bondage. This is shown above. They are not *Israelites* but *Ishmaelites* viewed from the gospel. Ishmael was a servant, was in bondage, and was cast out. *As servants* the Jews are cast out, and can only heir *as sons*, and they only become sons of God through Christ. The Jews are to be received *from* the dead—*not as dead, or while dead.* They are dead as a nation to God. *Their* hope is lost, is perished. The Gentiles as persecuating powers are nearing their end. The "little horn" was to continue (1260 years). The *time-prophecies* converge to one point at the end of Gentile dominion—the Metallic man is ground to dust; the wild beast, representative of the fourth monarchy, is burned; the "little horn," of the He-goat (Dan'l 8:9) comes to his end). All despotism is grouped together and goes down. Thereafter the "little stone" becomes a great mountain and fills the whole earth. All governments have been gravitating towards this end. The "Holy Roman Empire" is dissolving. Germany, Austria, and Italy were pledged each to each to maintain the assumption that this beast still lives. But Austria early received the fatal wound that paralyzed her defiant sons; Italy shrank from the contest, and the "war lord of Europe" wheeled into the war the whole strength of his empire. But one text of Scripture is stronger than all the hosts of men, fighting upon land, sea, under the sea, and mid-heaven. The orgy of blood will pass, and we may learn that this was a war against war. The nations of earth may federate to

keep the beastiality and horrors of war from again destroying their fair domains. We know the world sentiment is today, as never before, against war. This war
is more destructive only as war machinery is more efficient. The spirit of Christ forbids it all. Austro-Hungary is the largest state, save Russia, in Europe. The
Empire has half as many inhabitants as the United
States, some fifty millions, nearly all Catholic. The government is a hereditary Monarchy. The whole strength
and power of Austria has been wielded for seven centuries in upholding Catholicism. The various alliances
and wars of that country have led to the spilling of the
blood of millions. The "thirty years War" cost Europe
fifteen millions of men alone, and this in a vain attempt
to restore Catholicism in the Protestant countries of
Europe. It has been her cherished hope to rule over all
the Balkan States. With her crushing defeat in this
war the hope of Catholicism in central Europe dies amid
the defeaning roar of this Titanic struggle.

We students of the prophetic era should discern
the clerical party in all Europe, animated by the hope of
uniting the Catholic forces under the leadership of the
powerful Austro-Hungary Empire and sweeping the field
for the recovery of sovereignty for the pontiffs. The
assassination of Arch-duge Francis Ferdinand formed the
occasion only for testing out the deep laid plans of Aus-
trian statesmen, both civil and religious. The European
war is the result. Germany, hemmed in on all sides and
desiring to take "her place in the sun" lined up with
Austria; Russia, the largest country of Europe, awoke
her sleeping millions and swept down through Austria,
while Great Britain and her dependencies, shoulder to shoulder with France, fronted the millions of Germany's war-clad men, and the world
stands aghast at the spectacle. But the "beast,"
now lingering in Austria-Hungary and Germany,
as the *invisible power* back of all this "war of the ages,"
is popery. It is this power, above all others, that is having the sword of war to strip her of her riches. It is not
difficult to see that when nations sunken into bankruptcy,
and driven by the masterful voice of authority that roars
like the deep-toned sea, because humanity is outraged,

impoverished, mangled, and dying, the inevitable must come and universal peace prevail. With the nations in inter-national agreement to preserve the world-peace, "The Hague" will stand forth like a colossal pillar of fire; and Peace Societies enlightened and energized by the holy teachings of the prophets of God, shall have won the throne for the Prince of Peace. Henceforth all mankind shall sit under their own vine and fig-tree and no Militarism and huge equipments for slaughter shall make one wish for death to deliver him and his from the barbarism and brutalities of war. This is predicted and is at our doors. The world is now in the throes of war, and you will note that it is the territory of the four wild beasts in (Daniel 7); and what befell the symbols, *signifies* what shall befall these *governments*. They are doomed to overthrow. As I understand the symbols, out of the mighty desolation, Judaism, goes down and the Israelites, converted to God, are to be grafted into their true olive tree. They are to be received as from the dead. This would give the mightiest impulse to the gospel since apostolic days. The Reformation in the 16th century and since has been mighty in church and mighty in the state; but state churches, and human authority and traditions hold the largest portion of the followers of Christ in bondage. The Jewish traditions have blinded the nation. They are not likely to exchange these for Catholic or Protestant traditions. What the church needs today, the converted Jews can give it. They can cut loose from all human authority in religion that erects walls and barriers between the professed servants of God, and rally humanity around the standard of divine truth. They can, and upon Paul's prediction, I believe they will, be the great reserve army of God to bring in the greatest victory for truth the world has ever witnessed. We are now in a transition era. Old governments that have stood as sentinels for ages are falling on every hand. Judaism is a belief. It is untenable. The foremost Jews are tired of it. The tide of Jewish thought and endeavor needs only to be turned towards Christ and the gopsel to effect the mightiest religious revolution in the history of our race. My confidence is in the victory of truth, both in state and church. Out of this great war in Europe may come first, death; then life. Death to despotism; to tyranny; to oppression; a quickening into life of all the elements of civil and religious liberty. The governments may, so to speak, have a new birth, and the iron hand of tyrrany give place to the scepter of love, of equal privilege, of equality before the law, of unfettered intellect, of the assertion of conscience enlightened by the Word of God, and the peoples of the earth, after the tempest has past, may walk in the light and adopt the principles of the divine Book more than ever before in earth's long history. Foremost among these forces of righteousness should be that exclusive race, whose mission in the world was first to teach the Gentiles that there is but one God; and in this age may prove from the same divine source, that Jesus Christ is His Son, the Author of the New Testament and the great Head of the Church.

Do I think the Zionist movement is divine? First answer me, Who are chiefly advocating and advancing it? Is it that portion of the Hebrew people, largely, who are the Higher Critics, the disbelievers in miracles, the rejectors not only of our Lord, but of inspiration, as the word is generally known? As well ask me if the Higher Critics in the church are the safe leaders of the church. The destructive critics are the scoffers and infidels who pit their genius against the wisdom of God. They are the class who ridicule miracles, explain away all prophecies, belittle the Revelation of God, and would reduce it to the level of a human composition, and that essentially made up by men in an ignorant age of the world. No, I do not attach much importance to any movement propogated by that class, only as an effort to defeat the evident purpose of all divine revelation. There are few, if any, hopeful signs from that quarter. But for Israel there is hope. The common people heard our Savior gladly. I hope to see the persecuting power of Russia, of Spain, of the unspeakable Turks, and of all other nations, destroyed. And in the new-born days of civil and religious liberty that are coming on the wheels of light by day, and on the wheels of darkness by night, the Jewish people, turned away from ungodliness; turned away from tradition; begotten again to a living hope, may step to the front rank of the peoples of the earth; not in Davidic and Solomonic earthly splendor, with millions to invest in an earthly temple, and the wealth of an empire to erect walls and fortifications about earthly Jerusalem but to say:

> Triumphant Zion lift thy head,
> From dust and darkness and the dead;
> Though humbled long awake at length,
> And gird thee with thy Savior's strength.

> Put all thy beauteous garments on,
> And let thy excellence be known;
> Decked in thy robes of righteousness,
> The world, thy glories shall confess.

> No more shall foes unclean invade,
> And fill thy hallowed walls with dread;
> No more shall hell's insulting host,
> Their victory and thy sorrows boast.

> God from on high, has heard thy prayer;
> His hand thy ruins shall repair;
> Nor will thy watchful Monarch cease,
> To guard thee in eternal peace.

Thenceforth as the tame olive tree, they should thrive and prosper as the tree of the Lord's planting, and teach the world the lesson in humility, in self-denial, in obedience to Christ in missionary zeal, in serving God as priest in the temple of the living God, or church, which their types demand and their prophecies predict. As the Isaacs, Jacobs, Elijahs, Pauls, and Jerusalem church they may say, "God be merciful to us and bless us; and cause his face to shine upon us, that thy way may be known among the nations. Let the people praise thee, O God; let all the people praise thee. O let the nations be glad and sing for joy; for thou shalt judge the people righteously, and govern the nations upon earth. Let the people praise thee O God; let all the people praise thee. Then shall the earth yield her increase, and God, even our God, shall bless us. God shall bless us; and all the ends of the earth shall fear him." (Ps. 67).

The times of the Gentiles are fulfilled when the time-prophecies concerning their persecuting powers are fulfilled. The children of Abraham may then return to God. The Jews are not converted to Christ. The Millennialists say they are to figure prominently in the Millennial age. Paul says, "What shall the receiving of them be but life from the dead?" This is such a resurrection as Ezekiel predicted for them—a figurative resurrection. They are working against their own interests, against their spiritual destiny. They expect literal Elijah; they look for a Messiah; they are looking for a temporal deliverer; they hope to worship God in a new temple with the old order of things. But as they are blind, in unbelief, in bondage, and many of their brethren who forsook Judaism, for Christ and the gospel, were no longer blind, or in unbelief, or in bondage, I think it conclusive that the gap of centuries between the time when they were "broken off" through unbelief and when they shall be grafted in again, is the period of death, and the grafting in is because "they continue not in unbelief," and they have "life from the dead." Hence, I hope for Jewish conversion from, not reversion to, the types and shadows. I think the Gentiles with this Millennial theory are doing the Jews a great injury. They do not need Christ to come to them, they need to come to Christ for sight, for faith, for deliverance from bondage, and for the eternal inheritance.

The Gentiles interpret the prophecies as these blinded Jews, when they interpret them literally concerning Elijah, David, Levi, the temple, the sacrifices and Feasts, SINCE THOSE TYPES WERE DISPLACED BY THE ANTI-TYPES OF THE GOSPEL. The Jews expect to have all these things without Christ, or the gospel, or church, and that God will bless them while they treat Christ as an impostor, his church as of human origin, and the worship of the church as idolatry. The Millennialists aid them, though unconsciously, by conceding that they are right in expecting a personal Messiah, to revive David's throne and reign in Mount Zion for (1000) years over fleshly Israel (converted to God, of course) yet with all the elements of their ancient national greatness intensified and multiplied. Israel is looking forward to material greatness, earthly glory, temporal salvation. Their hearts are with David and Solomon, in their hope for restoration. Millennialists strengthen them in their estrangement from Christ. It is IMPOSSIBLE TO CONVERT THEM TO CHRIST BY ADOPTING AND TEACHING JUDAISM. Instead therefore, of turning them to the gospel, Gentiles, turn back to the old Jewish tradition, and are Judaizers, when they adopt this Jewish interpretation instead of the interpretation Christ and the apostles put on the prophecies, which exists today as the inspired, yea divine, interpretation, never to be repealed or reversed. Who was right, Caiaphas the High Priest, or Paul the apostle? They first condemned Jesus to death as an impostor. The Jews are led by him and his class. If you say Paul was right, then be consistent. I do not mean to speak harshly or roughly, but if our Jewish friends are blind, in unbelief, in bondage, then they would be so with the finest temple that ever graced the earth, and the sacrificial system in full operation on the ancient sacred site of Solomon's temple. A greater than Solomon has built the true tabernacle, which the Lord pitched, and not man. All this literalism that reproduces Jewish types (for necessity it is the Jews that would reproduce them, headed by Christ and all the righteous dead and changed living saints) is Judaism, and when Gentiles teach it they not only set aside the antitypes for the types and thus advance by going backward, but help to keep the Jews in blindness and unbelief. My sincere prayer and humble hope in writing this volume is to aid the anxious students of prophecy, both Gentiles and Jews, to understand the same. When the literalist's theory is seen to be false, as advocated by the Jew first and also by the Gentile, I pray that misguided souls shall turn to Jesus Christ our Lord as the true David; his sacrifice as the last one to be made for fallen man; his Priesthood as eternal and unchanging; his temple, the church as sanctified once for all for both Jews and Gentiles; and our country to which we are all hastening that heavenly country; and the Jerusalem we hold sacred, the New Jerusalem, which is free and is the mother of us all.

The Jew, blinded by the god of this world, conjures

up a future glory for his nation it can never realize.   He would turn backward to the law and its shadows.   He reads the Old Testament with a veil upon his heart.   He would literalize these prophecies, if possible.   Then we would see the following:

1.   Jerusalem rebuilt as God's earthly capital as in the days of David.

2.   The earthly house rebuilt after the same typical appointments and pattern as in the days of Solomon.

3.   A descendant of David reigning in oriental luxury, with a retinue of princes, and celebrities sharing with him the riches and honors of office.

4.   A horde of Levitical priests ministering daily, as of yore, insulting God and Christ by spilling the blood of bulls and of goats upon their altars, "counting the blood of Christ unholy."

5.   Observing their annual feasts and fasts, even the great day of atonement.

6.   Tithing the land to support Levi and the priesthood.

7.   Circumcising the Gentile world to proselyte them and make them worthy to participate in the rights, privileges and immunities of the old covenant, which has been vacated for nearly two thousand years.

This is the legitimate result of literalism.   For, mark you well! we have no alternative.   If the literal interpretation is correct, these prophecies are Jewish, and nothing short of a literal reproduction of their veritable men and sacrifices, will answer.   We can not make them literal where it suits us, and figurative where we may elect; but if we arrive at the truth, we must follow Christ and the apostles.   Now, I can see how a Jew, blind and prejudiced, can cling to the forlorn hope of his nation, and give such a pleasing turn to these already fulfilled prophecies.   But the mystery to me is, how can Gentiles who profess to believe in Christ, in the new covenant, the new Jerusalem, the holy Zion, the church as the temple of the living God, sanction, for a moment, the wild, fanciful, speculative, theory of a Millennium of earthly glory for the church, made up from these carnalities.   I cherish the hope that as we travel together through the remainder of the volume, we may learn the unspeakable vanity of such interpretation of the sacred Volume, and shall "continue in the faith, grounded and settled, and be not moved away from the hope of the gospel, which ye have heard, and which was preached to every creature which is under heaven." (Col. 1:23).

It can not be true that these prophecies have a two-fold meaning, one applied to Christ, and the spiritual Israel; the other yet unfulfilled but to be applied to fleshly Israel after Christ has come. If they ever had such meaning, (which is to me, very doubtful), the application would have been *first* to *fleshly* Israel, as a *typical* people, and *secondly* to *spiritual* Israel, types come *first*, then *anti-types.* But the assumption that they *now* have a secondary meaning and that they will be fulfilled in a Millennium, is impossible of proof, and would unhinge the entire gospel age, and go back to the law of Moses for THE HIGHEST EXPRESSION OF SPIRITUAL WOR-SHIP and SERVICE THROUGH CARNAL ORDINANCES. This is the very acme of absurdity of interpretation, and seems to me to need no further refutation.

THE WHOLE MILLENNIAL THEORY IS PREDI-CATED ON THE ERRONEOUS VIEW OF THE PROPH-ECIES THAT CAUSED THE JEWS TO REJECT AND CRUCIFY THE LORD OF GLORY, PERSECUTE THE TRUE ISRAEL OF GOD, AND DESPISE THEIR OWN MERCY. To rescue the Bible from the imputation cast upon it, that Christ and the apostles were right; and the blind, prejudiced, traditionized Jews of our day are right also in expecting a return of God's favor to them, while they refuse to obey David (Christ their King-Priest) is the desire of the writer. The Millennialists contribute to the obstinacy of the Jews, by holding up before them golden visions of approaching glory for their nation, *while the curse of God* is resting upon them in their rebellion against their predicted King, Sacrifice, Priest, Temple and Covenant of peace. (Gal. 3:8-14).

CHAPTER XIX.

DANIEL'S SEVENTY WEEKS.

You will find in (Dan. 9) the prediction of the "Seventy Weeks." Daniel read and pondered (Jer. 25: 11-12; 29:10) and other prophecies. He knew the time-prophecy of seventy years of the Babylonian Captivity was almost run out. He received another prophecy, a time-prophecy of the coming of Christ. It was not by dream or vision but by the angel, Gabriel. The number seven figures very prominently in the prediction.

1. A seventy years captivity was closing, but it would not bring the Messiah. It had to be multiplied by seven (70x7 equals 490) years.

2. It was divided into three periods. (7 plus 62 plus 1 equals 70) weeks.

3. He uses the word *weeks* in a *typical* sense, for there were "weeks of years," as well as weeks of days.

BEGINNING OF SEVENTY WEEKS.

"From the going forth of the commandment to restore and to build Jerusalem unto Messiah the Prince shall be seven weeks, and three score and two weeks: the street shall be built again and the wall, even in troublous times." There were four commandments given by the Persian rulers, favoring Jerusalem.

1. The first given by Cyrus, King of Persia. (Ezra I).

2. The second given by Darius. (Ezra VI).

3. The third in the seventh year of Artaxerxes. (Ezra VII).

4. The fourth in the twentieth year of the same King. (Neh. 2).

The third of these decrees is usually counted from, but we shall see that the last two are both beginning dates. Dean Prideaux and Faber locate the date of the third decree at (B. C. 458); Horne and a host of chronologists at (B. C. 457). As we are not able to decide

the exact date of the decree, I request the reader to observe that after exhaustive treatment of the question
there is a difference of two years only, this is because
we do not know whether Artaxerxes' reign began at his
father's death, or one year earlier.

All who begin the count at (B. C. 458) seek to have
it end at the death of Christ, and include the ministry of
John the Baptist in the last week, and date the kingdom
of heaven from the beginning of John's ministry. They
locate the beginning of Jesus' ministry three
and one--half years after the beginning of his
fore - runner's ministry (A. D. 30); and the crucifixion three and a half years later, or (A. D
34). According to this arrangement, Jesus *began* his
ministry when John had *ended* his, and was thirty-six
years of age at his crucifixion. The coming of the Messiah was not his birth, but evidently his anointing and
death; the first at his baptism, the latter at his crucifixion. I regard it as necessary to remember that in the
midst of the week "he shall cause the sacrifice and the
oblation to cease," and this puts the crucifixion in the
middle of the last week, ($69\frac{1}{2}$ weeks, or $486\frac{1}{2}$ years),
and not at the full close of the prophetic period. John
said: "And I knew him not: but that he should be
made manifest to Israel, therefore am I come baptizing
with water." (John 1:31). Jesus said a short time
after this: "The time is fulfilled and the kingdom of God
is at hand: repent ye, and believe the Gospel." (Mark
1:15). We know that Jesus and his disciples were baptizing *before* John's ministry ceased (Jno. 3:22), and if
his ministry began after his forty days temptation, which
it did, (Luke 4:1-14), he was about thirty years of age.
(Luke 3:23). The three-fold division of the prophecy
was as follows:

1. Seven weeks (7 times 7 equals 49 years) from
the decree of Artaxerxes (B. C. 457 less 49 equals 408
B. C.) to the rebuilding of the walls of the city, under
Nehemiah (Neh. 2, 3, 4, 5, 6, chs.) These seven weeks
of years witnessed the completion of the Reformations
under Nehemiah, and the close of the Old Testament.

2. Sixty-two weeks (7 times 62 equals 434 years)
from this period takes us down to the baptism of Jesus,

called "anointing the most Holy," and the beginning of his great ministry. Add (434 years to B. C. 408) and you have (A. D. 26) and Jesus was born four to six years before our received Calendar begins, making him about thirty years of age.

3. This takes us down to the time when according to Peter "God anointed Jesus of Nazareth with the Holy Spirit and with power: who went about doing good, and healing all that were oppressed of the devil; for God was with him," (Acts 10:38).

In the middle of this week, (3½ years later) he was crucified, caused "the sacrifice and the oblation to cease," so far as divine arrangement was concerned, by making the great Atonement, which gave virtue to all preceding typical sacrifices, not only under the law of Moses, but also under the preceding Patriarchal age.

MESSIAH THE PRINCE.

There were two princes in this verbal prophecy, one Messiah the Prince. He was anointed (or Christed) at his baptism, to begin his ministry among the "lost sheep of the house of Israel." Israel's age as the great nation, the typical people, was determined. The people, and the holy city, had their measure of time:

"Seventy weeks are determined upon thy people and upon thy holy city, to finish the transgression, and to make an end of sins, and to make reconciliation for iniquity, and to bring in everlasting righteousness, and to seal up the vision and the prophecy, and to anoint the most Holy."

The great Messiah, the Prince, certainly sealed up the vision and prophecy, fulfilling them in all their details, and no pretender can even make a respectable beginning at fulfillment. Look at the many points that meet in Jesus Christ our Lord, that no impostor could duplicate.

1. He was of the lineage of David, and David's family is now merged and lost in the other tribes of Israel.

2. Jesus was baptized by John, a heaven-sent prophet, and was declared to be the well beloved Son of God. Jesus, John, the Holy Spirit and the Heavenly Father all bore direct testimony to him at his baptism.

3. Jesus died as a sacrificial offering in the middle

of the last week (486½ years) after the decree as the prophecy said he would. This shameful death did not prevent him from confirming the covenant with many for one week, for some of the greatest miracles of recorded time, followed his death; namely, his resurrection, his forty days with the disciples, changing their carnal views of the nature of his kingdom, his ascension to heaven in their sight, and descent of the Holy Spirit upon these hitherto timid and worldly minded men, filling them with courage and power. Out of these marvels grew the church, that institution of heaven that embraces every virtue and every grace, and properly interpreted and actualized by the sons and daughters of men, moulds and shapes their characters into the likeness of its Founder and Head.

5. At the end of the seventy weeks (490 years) the door of faith was opened to the Gentiles, at the house of Cornelius, (Acts 10), and the great transforming power of the cross began among the heathen world.

6. The sacrifices and oblations ceased, at Jesus' death, resurrection, ascension, and the out-pouring of the power and blessing of heaven on Pentecost, which we have noted fulfilled the set of types in the Passover, First Sheaf and Feast of Weeks, or the death and resurrection of Christ, and the birthday of the church. No impostor can duplicate any of the events and they were all necessary for the true Messiah, all of which argues that the Lord Jesus Christ, was the Jewish Messiah. These things are in the Jewish Scriptures, and like the song of Moses (Deut. 32) testify against the carnal Jews of our day. Their hope for their kind of a Messiah, such as they looked for in harmony with their traditions, and still vainly hope to see in Palestine, does not exist in fact, and is not contemplated in the Old Testament, as shown by the exact fulfillment by our Savior, as recorded in the New Testament.

THE DESTRUCTIVE PRINCE.

Daniel was informed that a destructive prince (evidently Titus the Roman) would destroy their city and nation. He did not say when the destruction would begin or end. But it began after the true Messiah came and the capital city fell, (A. D. 70). The desolation was universal and complete, and when Jesus said, "Behold your house is left unto you desolate," he left that city and temple, nationally to the flame and the plow share. Josephus, the Jewish priest, general in the war, and historian, survived the slaughter, and wrote with harrowing details, the war, the final siege, the famine, pestilence and general massacres that reduced that nation to helplessness, and defeat. Out of all this group of desolating forces a little "Remnant" only, escaped, as the condemned witnesses to the veracity and justice of God. The proof is incontestible that desolation of the city and temple were predicted to follow the rejection of the true Messiah, (ver 26) and some forty years after his rejection and crucifixion this desolation was visited upon them "by the people of the prince that should come." (Titus and the Roman Army).

OBSERVATIONS.

Whence did Daniel acquire all this wisdom?

1. The captivity was to end after seventy years.

2. The city and temple were to be rebuilt and the walls in troublous times, and seven weeks, (49 years) would cover these events.

3. It would be sixty-two weeks more (434 years) to Messiah, the Prince. On his coming the greatest spiritual blessings were to be bestowed.

4. This final week was to stand out by itself, not only from all the rest in the seventy, but above all the weeks of earth's eventful history, for the greatness of its events. Messiah was to be anointed at its beginning, cut off in the midst of the week, cause the sacrifice and the oblation to cease, make reconciliation (atonement), seal up the vision and the prophecy, and bring in everlasting righteousness.

5. After this a prince and people should destroy Jerusalem and the temple, with protracted desolation.

It was the angel, Gabriel, not a man simply, who revealed these things. "O Daniel, I am now come forth, and I am come to shew thee: for thou art greatly beloved: therefore understand the matter, and consider the vision." It was this Gabriel who announced the birth of Jesus to Mary, five hundred years later.   (Luke 1:26-35).   Thus these great events are linked in history and prophecy.   The same angel that predicted the Messiah to Daniel, five centuries before, here predicted his miraculous conception and birth and; "He shall be great, and shall be called the Son of the Highest: and the Lord shall give unto him the throne of his father David: and he shall REIGN OVER THE HOUSE OF JACOB FOREVER: and of his kingdom there shall be no end." This, you will see, links this person with the second member of the promise made to Abraham, and enlarged upon to David, when he desired to build the temple. This prophecy and its fulfillment settles several very important matters.

1.   It proves that Jesus Christ our Lord is the true and only Messiah of the prophets.

2.   It demonstrates that Daniel was a true prophet of God.   He was ranked with Noah and Job by Ezekiel. (14:14-20), and was spoken of as Daniel the prophet, by our Savior.

3.   This prophecy is a key to the explanation of the time-prophecies in Daniel, and elsewhere, that are revealed in figurative language, "Time and times and the dividing of time" for we see this prophecy was fulfilled on the year-day calculation, that is every *day* in the prediction represented a *year*.   This was first intimated as the method to be used in the figurative numbers by Moses, (Num. 14:33-34); later was employed by Ezekiel, who lived in the early days of Daniel's labors, (Ezek. 4:1-6).   No less important is the fact that both Solar (365), and Lunar (354), days are used in the time-prophecies.   I call attention to the latter important fact, especially, as we shall have occasion to notice it in several counts later.

THE COUNT.

The Solar year consists of (365) days; the Lunar of (354); and the Calendar (360) days.   You observe the long count, has eleven more days than the short or Lunar count, and five more than the Calendar.   In (490) Lunar years, there are but (375) solar, as you learn by multiplying the number of years and dividing the result by the number of days in a Solar year as follows:

(354 times 490 is 173,460, divided by 365 is 475).
This is a simple calculation, but, of course, has to be
made each time we determine the number of Solar years
in a specified number of Lunar years. There are several of the most important points in the earth-life of
Christ, and the rejection of the Jewish people, that are
determined accurately by this method.

1. From Artaxerxes to the nativity of Christ was
seventy weeks (490 Lunar or 475 Solar years).

2. From Ezra's commission to the calling of the
Gentiles was seventy weeks, the last week taken up with
the baptism and crucifixion of Christ and the confirming
of the covenant with many, as shown at length above.
(B. C. 457 plus 483 equals A. D. 26), Jesus' baptism;
(3½) years later his crucifixion; (3½) years later the
call of the Gentiles.

3. (B. C. 444 plus 490) Lunar years gives the
same results. Thus the Baptism and Crucifixion are
doubly foretold, the long count from Ezra (ch. 7) and
the shorter count from Nehemiah, commissioned thirteen
years later. So both Ezra and Nehemiah or the two
decrees of Artaxerxes are beginning points in the Seventy
Weeks of years.

4. From the close of Ezra's reformation to the
desolating war of the Romans against the city and temple,
was (490 Lunar years) that is (B. C. 408 plus 475 equals
A. D. 67-8).

5. From the last prophet of the Old Testament, to
the last prophet of the New Ttestament, Malachi and
John, was (490 Solar years). That is we have Seventy
weeks from the close of the Old to the close of the New
Testament.   (B. C. 395 plus 490 equals A. D. 95).

It is not necessary for us to know the exact year
when Jesus was born, when he was baptized, and when
he was crucified: or when the Gentiles were called by
miracles at the household of Cornelius, nor yet when
the Roman war prostrated the nation, and in what year
John was banished to the Isle of Patmos. I have an
abiding hope that my readers will see the overwhelming
proof that the seventy weeks of Daniel were redeemed in
the life and ministry of our Lord. All this was predicted
five centuries and more before it took place, and has

been history for nineteen centuries; or twenty-five centuries ago, Daniel foretold these greatest events in universal history. There they are in the Jewish prophets; and their fulfillment is recorded in the New Testament, and in Josephus and Tacitus, and thus Jesus is upheld by the imperishable proof of the fulfilled Scriptures as "The Lord our Righteousness."

WE SEE THAT THIS TIME-PROPHECY WAS GIVEN TO LIMIT THE OTHER PROPHECIES OF A MESSIAH TO JESUS OF NAZARETH, SO THAT NO AMOUNT OF GARBLING OR WRESTING THE SCRIPTURES COULD EVER WREST THIS FACT FROM ITS ETERNAL BASE—HE HAD TO COME WITHIN (490 years) FROM THE COMMANDMENT TO RESTORE AND REBUILD JERUSALEM, AT THE EXPIRATION OF THE SEVENTY YEARS BABYLONIAN CAPTIVITY, AND THE PERSIAN DECREES ARE RECORDED IN THE BIBLE, FOUR IN NUMBER AND NO MORE, AND PROFANE HISTORY FIXES THEIR DATES.

It is impossible to evade the conclusion that Jesus was the "Messiah the Prince." In closing let me urge upon you the reflection that Jesus has not only fulfilled the prophecy as *to dates*, but as *to the character of his work*. "What can the man do that cometh after the king?" Who could perform greater prophecies, inspire greater faith, zeal, hope, love, joy and righteousness? What is left for any later Messiah? Is it to do more than Jesus promises—raise the dead, change our vile bodies, and give us eternal blessedness with all the redeemed of the ages? The Jews are held captive by the traditions, and when this veil is removed they shall exultingly shout "Blessed be he that cometh in the name of the Lord."

CHAPTER XX.

THE FEASTS AND PARABLES.

There were three annual feasts of the Jews. They were governed by the number seven. They all came each year in the first seven months, and they were regulated by seven days. I call your attention to these feasts in the Old Testament to show that none of them typified a Millennium, and incidently dig up this feature of Millennialism by the tap root. It will appear also that our Lord gave his parables to illustrate his Kingdom and they reach, not to a Millennium, but to the end of time. Under the Jewish law, the number seven was prominent as it is under the gospel. There were weeks of days and weeks of years. Every seventh year the land rested, but this was one seventh of the time to Jubilee, or a New Era; so after seven sabbaths complete, "sabbaths of years," was Jubilee, (Lev. 25:8-10); when all debts were cancelled, all slaves set free, every man went to his possessions, and from which all land values were determined, beginning always on the day of Atonement, (Lev. 25:9).

It followed the seven sabbaths of *years*, just as Pentecost followed the seven sabbaths of *days*. The only differnce is Pentecost was the fiftieth day, while Jubilee was the fiftieth year. Pentecost typified the beginning of the gospel harvest. (Acts 2); Jubilee day, (I say *day* because Atonement day was the beginning) typified the final Atonement of all Israel, when the *trumpet* shall "proclaim liberty throughout all the land unto all the inhabitants thereof." The last bondage will have passed. "Because the creature itself also shall be delivered from the bondage of corruption into the glorious liberty of the children of God," (Rom. 8:20). This corruption shall have put on incorruption, and this mortal shall have put on immortality, and "Death is swallowed up in victory." *That day was a sabbath*. It was the greatest sabbath in Israel's history.

1. They did no work. 2. They were assembled in their capital city. 3. They afflicted their souls, and turned from all their sins. 4. The High Priest appeared in the presence of God for them, with blood and incense. 5. All debts were forgiven. 6. All servants were set free. 7. Every man went to his own possessions. Was not this the climax? There is nothing else like it in the Jewish law, wherein the love of God and the love of man, forgiveness human and divine, and liberty, were so conspicuous. Did this apply to all Israelites? No. These blessings were conditional. "For whatsoever soul it be that shall not be afflicted in that same day, he shall be cut off from among his people." (Lev. 23:29-30). The priest's atonement only reached those who complied with the conditions, otherwise they forfeited all rights among the nation, and this mark you! in the great day of atonement, yearly, and, hence, on the Jubilee day. It was no Jubilee to the impenitent. The application to the gospel age is easy, and serves a double notice on us, a typical and verbal, that obedience precedes the favor and blessing of God through our great atoning, High Priest. He is now in the Holiest of all, but when he returns to be admired in all them that believe, and sound the "Jubilee Trumpet" over all the land, we shall *congregate in Jerusalem* (the heavenly, as they did the earthly), all debts forgiven spiritual Israel, as they have forgiven one another, and we shall heir our inheritance incorruptible, and enjoy the peaceful sabbath that remains for the people of God. This day was the annual climax for fleshly Israel; and certainly typifies the greatest blessings promised to man, under the gospel, as follows:

1. Jesus in heaven, with atoning blood and intercession.

2. Jesus returning to bless his people.

3. The people all forgiven and reconciled to God.

4. The entire company dwelling peacefully together in Jerusalem, all sorrows, labors, debts cancelled.

5. All bondage into which sin had plunged them removed.

6. Their titles to "Mansions in our Father's house," were critically examined and given to them for whom

they were prepared: And "we may inherit the kingdom prepared for us from the foundation of the world." The. temporal foretold the spiritual, types, on the fleshly plane typified anti-types on the spiritual plane. Land, and houses and debts forgiven did not typify themselves to be *reproduced in Christ's reign.*

VALUES REGULATED BY JUBILEE.

It is no wonder that all values were regulated by the year of Jubilee, (Lev. 25:23, 25-34, 50-55). Just so everything earthly is *regulated in value by its relation to the great eternal day.* We should value our fields, houses, factories, and the lives and labors of men, in view of eternity. We should make all our temporal interests to aid us in our higher spiritual interests and regulate time by eternity.

A COMPARISON.

I.   In counting for the Feast of Weeks or Pentecost, they began on the first day of the week and counted seven sabbaths complete, (7 times 7 equals 49 days), and the *next day* was Pentecost, always on the first day of the week, (Lev. 23:15).

II.   In the Jubilee, they counted "seven sabbaths of years" complete (7 times 7 equals 49 years) and the *next year* was Jubilee.

III.   In the Seventy Weeks of Daniel, there were *ten* so-called *Jubilees* to Christ (49 times 10 equals 490 years. You note the *forty-nine* in each count. It was followed in the first by Pentecost; in the second by Jubilee; in the third by the manifestation and anointing of Christ at his baptism at the *opening* of the week, and everlasting righteousness began to be preached to the Gentiles at *its close.* The reader will see that the Pentecost and Jubilee in the first two followed (7 times 7 equals 49 days and years respectively). They each contradict the millennial theory. To fit the millennial theory, Pentecost should have been at the opening of the seventh week, (6 times 7 equals 42 days) *if six days typify the time till Christ comes,* then the Millennium. Thus Pentecost would have been the *forty-third* day instead of the *fiftieth.* So the theorists are seven days short. It fits what it was made to fit, but will not tolerate the Jewish tradition, ancient or modern. In the second, the same observation applies, (7x7 equals 49 years), the Jubilee, and gives no opening for a Millennium until the beginning of the *eighth week of years.* You will see there was no intention to lay a foundation for Millennialism in these ordained sevens.

In the (70x7 equals 490 years) to Messiah, we saw that the last week was predictive of our Savior's great work in behalf of the Jewish nation before the call was extended to the Gentiles. The last week (7 years) is separated from the (70 weeks or 490 years). But as these weeks were simply prophetic weeks and *not typical like feasts,* when Jesus came at the close he ended the prophecy. So we learn that great events were connected with these feasts and the sacred sevens, but in no case was there an intimation that the last seven, or the final seven of seven sevens, was predictive of a Millennium. The Millennium is supposed to be one thousand years long, so the seven days, or seven years, do not fit either as typical or predictive numbers. The tradition breaks down in every point, when the Bible, and not imagination, controls. Mr. Russell's guess is that each creative day was (7000 years) long; Adam was created at the close of (42,000 years) that six thousand years from his creation ended about (Oct. 10, 1874), and Jesus came again. This was at the end of (48,000 years) just *one thousand years too soon;* for if he wished the Millennium to fit the Jubilee, it will have to begin on the *fiftieth thousand years,* (the opening of the *eighth* seven thousand year day), whereas he begins it at the opening of the *forty-ninth thousand.* Concerning his "Photo-Drama of Creation" the advertiser says, "The originals of the pictures of the Photo-Drama of Creation complete, cost millions of money. * * * Pastor Russell's fifty years of Bible study are behind the concise lectures delivered at these entertainments and printed in the Scenario." Then I approach the subject with all the more confidence. If Pastor Russell has spent half a century trying to determine the length of creative days, what was done on each day, and has decided that (6000 years) of the last creative day are past and there is but (1000 years) of that day remaining, and, that is to be the Millennium, beginning (A. D. 1874), I remind the reader that the "Pastor's search has been fruitless, for he has his Millennium staged in the Photo-Drama for (1000 years) too early! If he would tell his gaping auditors that he is just imagining what will be one thousand years from now, as he imagined what was in the first forty-two thousand years, we would tolerate him as a wealthy artist, working on the world's love of the sensational and spectacular. But when he gravely appeals to the Bible, and professes superior light from that infallible Document, I cheerfully meet him and expose his dreams.

THE BIBLE AND RUSSELL CONTRASTED.

I hereby expose the oft-recurring thousand year tradition of a Millennium by contrasting the two fifty day and fifty year counts with Mr. Russell's lectures in the Scenario.

PENTECOST.

1. Seven sabbaths of days complete were *followed* by Pentecost. (Lev. 23), which lasted one day.

(7x7 equals 49 plus 1 equals 50 days) or Pentecost, the opening of the *eighth* week of days.

JUBILEE.

Seven sabbaths of years complete were *followed* by Jubilee—one year, which always began on the day of Atonement.

(7x7 is 49 plus 1 is 50 years) or Jubilee, the opening of the *eighth* week of years.

PASTOR RUSSELL AND SCENARIO.

Creative days (7000 years) long, with last (1000 years) of seventh day a Millennium.

(7000x6 are 42,000 years plus 6000 are 48,000 plus 1000 are 49,000) or END OF THE MILLENNIUM AT THE TIME IT SHOULD BEGIN, TO FIT EITHER PENTECOST OR JUBILEE.

He has Adam created at the close of (42,000 years); Six thousand years since to (A. D. 1874); making (48,-000 years); Millennium began at (49,000 thousandth year), *one thousand years too soon*! This uproots Russell's scheme by showing that neither Pentecost nor Jubilee were types of his Millennium and it is wresting the Scriptures to use them thus, because they do not fit the theory.

ANOTHER COUNT.

Israel was in Babylon seventy years. He tells us each year was prophetic and that seventy Jubilees had to pass over the land from the time Joshua crossed the Jordan till the second coming of Christ. This is reducing types to absurdity. It makes God to punish Israel (19) years for imperfect observances of (19) Jubilee years, and (51) years for Jubilees yet to come. He thus accuses God of punishing Israel *three times as long* for sins they had *not* committed as he did for sins *they had committed*, in order to make the Babylonian captivity prophetic. Poor logic and worse ethics! The simple fact is plain to one not blinded by a theory, that God punished Israel for seventy Sabbatic years they *had violated* (Lev.26:34, 35-43; II Chron. 36:21). The land had sabbath every seventh year, and the *guilt* of Israel was at *this point* as the whole history shows; they had desecrated these sabbatic years, seventy of them, and were punished for what they *had* done, and not (19) years for what they had done, and (51) years for what they *had not done*.

But conceding, for argument's sake, that the seventy years' captivity were prophetic of seventy Jubilee periods to pass from Joshua's entrance into Canaan to Christ and the Millennium, Mr. Russell is wrong in staging the events for (Oct. 10, 1874). He is *fifty years* too early.

The count began after crossing Jordan. Fifty years later, (10th) day of the seventh month was Jubilee one; one hundred years later was Jubilee two; one hundred and fifty years later was Jubilee three; and counting off (70) Jubilees, the seventieth is due the (3500th year) or (A. D. 1925). Mr. Russell first *assumed* there should be *seventy*, the Millennium the *seventieth*; then he switched off and did not follow his own assumption, but begins his Millennium with the *sixty-ninth* (Oct. 10, 1874); The figures are as follows:

From crossing Jordan to Babylonian Captivity 969 years
Captivity lasted 70   "
Captivity ended .... B. C. 536   "
From (A. D. 1 to 1875), 69th Jubilee 1874   "

Total 3449   "

Surely (3449) years are not (70) Jubilees!

Mr. Russell assumes that to square the Jubilees (50x50 equaling 2500) years will settle the time predicted (?) by the (70) years captivity. There were (19) Jubilees *before* the Babylonian captivity; he then uses (50) more; and the *fiftieth* after they went into captivity is the *sixty-ninth* after entering Canaan under Joshua. So he is one Jubilee short!

He made the Millennium (1000) years too early on his assumption that (70) years' captivity prophesied (70) Jubilees.

The reason he is (1000) years too early in one count and (50) years too early in the other, is because a *day* is (1000) years, and a Jubilee period is (50) years, (in his count), and he is a typical *day* short in one, and a typical *Jubilee cycle* short in the other. I have repeatedly stated that the Bible does not give time-prophecies of the second coming of Christ, and of a Millennium to be instituted by him at his second coming. I am confident that he is a day short, thousand-year day, and one Jubilee cycle (50) years short, so he is *short one Millennium*. He seemed to feel afraid to send forth his figures, conscious they were (50) years short, and that he accounted for (69) Jubilee years only and he had said the Millennium was to be the (70th) so he makes another table. This time he counts (49) years for each Jubilee, *since* the captivity, and (50) years for each one *before* the captivity and lands again at (Oct. 10, 1874), as follows:

(19x50 is 950), and (51x49 is 2499); (950 plus 2499 is 3449) years. So he gets only (3449) years for *seventy Jubilees*, the same as he had before for SIXTY-NINE JUBILEES. It is safe to say if the Lord predicted *seventy* he will not begin the Millennium on the SIXTY-NINTH, all of Mr. Russell's crass assumptions to the contrary notwithstanding. So, if the Lord did not intend to begin the Millennium till the seventieth Jubilee

year and that is (3500) years from the time Joshua
entered Canaan, the event is not due till (1925). Then
Jesus did not come (Oct. 10, 1874); Restitution back to
Edenic conditions did not begin there; the Harvest did
not end after (40) years or in (Oct. 10, 1914) in the
destruction of all earthly governments; and the Kingdom
of Christ, ruled over by resurrected saints, is not to begin at the latter date. IN FACT THERE IS NOT A
SINGLE POINT TRUE, CONCERNING THE MILLEN-
NIAL ERA AS ADVOCATED BY DAWNISTS RELATIVE
TO (A. D. 1874). His own *theory* demands that Christ
shall come (1000) years *after* (1874) or the fiftieth *day*
(Pentecost) and fiftieth *year* (Jubilee) ARE NOT TYPI-
CAL OF THE EVENT. But to discard that count and
make the seventy years captivity in Babylon, typical or
prophetic of (70) Jubilees from the entrance into Canaan till Christ's second coming, demands (3500) years,
and this lands him (A. D. 1925), fifty years later than
(Oct. 10, 1874) where the whole transaction begins—
coming of Christ, Restitution, Millennium and so on.

IF HE IS CORRECT ON PENTECOST AND JUBILEE
BEING TYPES, HE IS (1000) YEARS TOO EARLY; IF
WRONG ON THIS, BUT RIGHT ABOUT THE (70) JUBI-
LEES, THEN HE IS (50) YEARS TOO EARLY; BUT IN
EITHER CASE JESUS AND THE SAINTS ARE NOT HERE,
NOT DUE TO BE HERE, AND THE MILLENNIUM IS NOT
GOING ON.

I now proceed to show that the Parables of our
Lord are written as though one chief purpose was behind
them—and that was to show there is no second coming of
Christ to begin a Millennium, (A. D. 1874) or at any
future date and remove this dependence of Millennialists
as we do on the Type-Prophecies and the Feasts.

THE PARABLES.

How many of our Lord's parables end at the Mil-
lennium? *Not one.* YET THEY ALL END AT HIS
SECOND COMING, HENCE HIS SECOND COMING IS
NOT THE OPENING OF THE MILLENNIUM. I only
cite the parables, do not analyze them, for want of space.
They all end alike at the Lord's return.

1. THE SOWER. As long as the seed of the King-

dom is the Word of God; different classes of hearers are in evidence, and the devil can steal the word out of the heart, this parable will be in force. But if the time should come that all should be righteous, the devil bound and could not deceive men, the parable would not fit the conditions.

2. THE TARES. Both grow together until the harvest; then every tare is burned, and nothing but wheat put in the granary. When a man has his wheat all harvested, the tares all burned, harvest is over. The wheat and tares only grow together *until* harvest, not during the Millennium, or as Mr. Russell says, (1914) ends the harvest, and devotes (120 pages) in "Thy Kingdom Come" to this subject. The Harvest is the end of the world, or age. All agree that it is at the *end of the Gospel Age*. But Dawnists and others would not allow that this is the end of the world, or end of time; but it introduces the Millennium, Christ coming in Person to carry on the work. I have showed Pastor Russell is one thousand years too early with his dates, but now call attention to the fact that all these parables *end when Christ comes*. Now notice Pastor Russell's theory dissolve. 1. The Harvest lasts forty years, (1874 to 1914), when all human governments, churches and worldly organizations cease. 2. In (1914-15) Jesus takes the Kingdom. 3. The wicked are to have their (1000 years) chance for eternal life. To fit the parable, not a tare will be left when *Harvest ends*, in 1914. The *wheat* has all been harvested. Now where do all the church members that died as backsliders, hypocrites, formalists, and corrupt, with all the countless wicked dead get in for the second chance? They may truly say after (1914), "The harvest is passed, the summer is ended and we are not saved." No tares become wheat, no wheat tares, after harvest, and harvest ends (1914). I take it that Jesus used his illustration normally, and men gather tares *before* harvest; Jesus said, "Gather ye *first* the tares, and bind them in bundles to burn them." The parable fits the end of time, but does not fit a period imagined as the end of the gospel age, midway between the first and the final coming of Christ.

THE FISH-NET. *They were done fishing.* They gathered the good into vessels, but threw the bad away. "So shall it be at the end of the world; the angels shall come forth and sever the wicked from among the just, and shall cast them into the furnace of fire; there shall be weeping and gnashing of teeth." Are there two ends of the world? If not, these and all the other parables are positively against Christ's coming at the opening of a Millennium.

4. THE MUSTARD SEED. There is one mustard seed, that grows into one herb. To fit Dawnism, there will have to be a new mustard seed planted in (1914) to illustrate a new kingdom. The seed Jesus used illustrates the kingdom of heaven in all its earthly history. If *this* is not the kingdom which is to be, but the age and kingdom end, and a new age and kingdom begin, we must have a new parable, for the doctrine is not in this one.

5. THE LEAVEN. The woman took the leaven and hid it in three measures of meal until the whole was leavened. Shem, Ham and Japheth must all experience the quickening power of the gospel. The leaven works from within and pervades the whole frame-work of society. I dare say it is the diffusive power of the gospel that is moving the masses of humanity today, an revolutionizing nations in many ways. What we call national and civic righteousness; the loud demands for reform in business methods, in social inequalities; the curse of rum, the perils of white slavery, gigantic graft, the adulteration of food, the blight of child labor, the infamies of priest-craft and king-craft, the bane of despotism hoary with age, and all things human, demanding remedial measures, may be seen in the light of the quickening process of the gospel of Christ, the leaven in the meal. We can not throw away the leaven and get more. and retain the parable. It works till the whole is leavened, and this can mean nothing else, than that the means Jesus Christ and the apostles used are adequate to accomplish the work, without the miracles so confidently expected by Dawnists. How shall we arrest the progress of the leaven, and put in a new lump? That would spoil the bread! I fear bread would fall as flat as this theory does when the light of the gospel shines

on it. The leaven was put in once, not twice, and it works to the end. (All these in Matt. 13).

6. THE TEN VIRGINS. When the bridegroom came, the five wise virgins went in to the marriage, the five foolish were without and the *door was shut*. This is final. The whole lesson is ended WHEN THE BRIDE-GROOM COMES. Not a foolish virgin ever gets in after the door is shut. There is no second probation there. It does not look like Mr. Russell's Millennium for them! The parable has peculiar solemnity, because Jesus was answering the question as to the time and manner of his second coming. The foolish virgins represent all the foolish, unprepared church members to the end of time; the wise virgins, all the prepared ones till the same time. The parable *ends* when the Lord comes—the lesson is plain that destiny is fixed by our conduct now. (Matt. 25:1-13).

7. THE TALENTS. (vs. 14-30), together with the Pounds, (Luke 19:12-27), may be considered as one lesson although spoken on different occasions. The Nobleman went into a far country to receive a kingdom and to return. He intrusted the pounds to his servants saying "Occupy till I come." After a long time he returns and reckons with his servants. When Jesus ascended to heaven, "Angels and authorities and powers were made subject unto him." (I Peter 3:22). He is Ruler over Hades, (has the key, or power), is David's Ruler, (Matt. 22:41-46; Rev. 1:18), for all live unto God, (Luke 20:38). He is head over all things to the church. (Eph. 1:22-23; Col. 1:18). If you submit to Jesus' rule now, he will rule over you till death; after death in Hades; after the resurrection and reckoning, He will rule over you in the everlasting kingdom. The wicked servants were cast out into outer darkness, where there is "weeping and gnashing of teeth." Why do they weep? Because they have a second chance, under more favorable conditions?

8. MARRIAGE OF THE KING'S SON. Here at the close is a guest without the wedding garment. This, too, when the king came in to see the guests. This is the sad ending of this representative man. When the king had him bound hand and foot and taken away into

outer darkness, there was "weeping and gnashing of teeth," (Matt. 22). Thus Jesus taught * * * Remember these are all *human* transactions, chosen by our Lord to picture *divine* realities. *The Harvest* ends the parable of the wheat and tares; the wheat saved, the tares destroyed; the fishing ended with one net full, the good put in vessels, the bad cast away; the leaven was used once and the process was one and uninterrupted from the time the leaven was put in till the meal was all leavened; the mustard seed was a vital unit, and needed no other, just as the Sower went over his field but once, and when the field is sowed, the different results follow at harvest, not afterwards; the five virgins were shut out from the earthly wedding, and no ingenuity can get them in; the man with the abused talent, and the man with the one pound, were rejected, and severely punished, and the last ever heard of them is punishment; while the faithful in both instances were suitably rewarded; the man without the "wedding garment" joins his class in all other sacred illustrations, is suffering punishment, while the wedding is in progress. In (Matt. 25:31 to close) the same division is made between sheep and goats, and those on the left hand go into everlasting punishment, but the righteous into life eternal.

Jesus promised to be with his apostles always even unto the end of the world, "consummation of the age," (Matt. 28:20). That can not mean until the Millennium. These visionaries all stop at that half way place. I do not believe Jesus was so full of a Millennium that he framed all his parables to end there! The parables end where apostolic authority ends, at the end of the world. NOW, BE SURE OF THIS ONE THING, WHENEVER THESE PARABLES END, PROBATION ENDS. Not a *tare* was spared after harvest; not a *bad* fish ever got in with the good fish after the separation; not one FOOLISH virgin ever got in to the wedding after the door was shut; the men who were *rejected* for not using their talents, remained in outer darkness and grief; the man without the wedding garment made a mistake that could not be corrected; and the goats joined the devil and his angels in everlasting punishment. Each and all of these parables, like the feasts, are in whole and in part against the second coming of Christ to inaugurate a Millennium, before probation ends. Probation ends when he comes with rewards for faithfulness and punishment for unfaithfulness. I have thus briefly touched upon the *closing features* of several of these parables, that the careful student of the Bible can see that Pastor Russell promises life where Jesus threatens *death*; he promises *probation* in its fulness to begin, where Jesus leaves the sinner bound hand and foot; he promises *light*, where Jesus leaves them in *"outer darkness"*; he promises a *second chance* to foolish virgins, where Jesus leaves them *shut out*. Whom shall we believe? I know that the parables teach just what the literal parts of the Bible teach; the parables are prophetic and harmonize with both the figurative and unfigurative parts of the Bible; for the whole Volume is a system. Prophecy is a system, and the "blessing" or "curse" of God is predicated on our conduct both as nations and individuals. The parables end when Christ comes and give no intimation of any second chance after he comes. Thus I show by the Feasts that according to the theory that the fiftieth day typified a Millennium, Mr. Russell staged it (1000) years too early; according to the theory that the (70) years Babylonian Captivity typified (70) Jubilees from Joshua to the second coming of Christ, he was *fifty years* too early in (1874) granting him the privilege of supplying the two "missing links" of time in the Old Testament history (which no ingenuity of man has ever determined); and the Parables of our Lord dig up the whole system by the roots, by showing that probation ends with the close of every parable concerning the kingdom; men are not then put *on* trial, but trial *ends* and Judgment is rendered *for work done*.

If the "First Resurrection" is literal it comes in where these parables end. Ten virgins from one generation represent the whole church of all generations. So with the Talents, the Pounds, and the Fishnet, illustrations. Each illustration is complete in itself as though no other generation lived; but, manifestly, the servants that received the Talents and Pounds who were to "Occupy till I come" were not the disciples then living only; but, rather, all disciples in all generations are illustrated. To view the Parables otherwise would limit them to the apostolic age. So the application is continuous, age after age, and to the last age of the church as well as the first. No one of the Parables admits of the coming of Christ and the resurrected saints a thousand years before it closes. ALL END THE PROBATION OF MAN. All end in judgment; and (Matt. 25:31-46) shows this separation is eternal. Dead men have to live before they can have even a "little season," and no dead men come back to earth at the close of these parables for (1000) years probation, or for the "little season" that follows the (1000) years; but all the events predicted in any part of the Bible connected *with time*, end at the second coming of Christ, and that is (Rev. 20:11), the general reckoning, separation of wheat and tares, good fish and bad fish, wise virgins and foolish virgins, the rewards for the men faithful in the use of their talents and pounds, and the punishment of the unfaithful, and not a single gleam of hope of second chanceism is found in one of our Lord's parables, but on the contrary the accoount of the rich man and Lazarus seems to have been given expressly to show:

1. Death does not destroy conscious existence.

2. Death ends probation.

3. The word of God whether accepted or rejected determines eternal destiny.

The Parables are true to nature. As you study them you observe their simplicity. No one would ever dream that Jesus meant to teach that the *foolish* virgins at *that* wedding recovered from their mistake; or that the *bad* fish were ever changed; or the man with the *one talent* ever *rectified* his mistake; or the man with *one pound* had not made a breach of trust that could not be remedied; or that the man without the wedding garment, ever enjoyed the favor of the king. These *human* affairs are simple and very plain. They each and all teach finality. There is not a ray of light for them beyond the reckoning. Not one of them was told that he was still in favor and could try it all over again under more favorable circumstances. His probation was ended and rewards and punishments were meted out to all. Remember. Jesus gave these Parables to illustrate his kingdom and that we are *now on trial* and he reckons with all *at his coming*.

CHAPTER XXI.

EZEKIEL'S VISION OF GOD'S GLORY.

Ezekiel was a priest. He was carried captive with
Jehoiachin, the last king of Judah but one, and dated his
predictions, generally, from this captivity (See 1:2; 8:
1; 20:1; 24:1; 29:1; 31:1; 32:1; 29:17; 40:1).
These verses show the respective dates of his prophecies
and cover some twenty-two years. Thus while Jeremiah
was in Jerusalem warning, and admonishing the "Remnant" of the nation, Ezekiel was with the captives in
Babylon. Daniel was also in Babylon. Ezekiel spake
very highly of Daniel, associating him with Noah and Job.
(ch. 14:14, 16, 18, 20). Ezekiel uses many illustrations,
but usually explains them, and if one understands the
history of his nation and times, one can read his marvellous volume with great interest and profit. The first
eleven chapters form a section, which we shall examine in
this chapter. Another section is found in the latter part
of the book, and is very closely related to the one we
are now to consider. It is difficult to present the argument in the first eleven chapters in a condensed form,
and, I crave the most careful consideration of the following exposition. The reader should have his Bible before
him in reading, as I have before me in writing, and thus
he can verify the Scripture citations and quotations. It
is no light task to quote sufficiently to impress the full
sense of any of these passages on the mind, and it will be
highly beneficial to all readers of these pages to read the
whole connection in which the Scriptures cited or quoted
are found.

EZEKIEL'S GREAT VISIONS.

Ezekiel, as priest, doubtless, held the same views
as many of his countrymen that he could not be a priest
to God, because removed so far away from the temple at
Jerusalem. The Jews regarded the temple superstitous-
ly, as though it could and would save them (Jer. 7).

Their crimes, idolatries, thefts, adulteries, and cruelties were not considered by them as effacing the terms of the covenant; just as many today think — "belonging to church" will save them, although they are "reprobate to every good work." Ezekiel, though a holy man, must have shared, in a measure, the views of his countrymen, that their captivity was a calamity, instead of a blessing, to the true Israel of God. THIS VISION IS DISCRIMINATIVE. It showed him, and through him his countrymen either then captives like himself, or soon to be captives, that God's covenant was not forgotten, because this chastisement must visit the nation; but that his true people would be loved, and protected, while the sinners were being destroyed. To Abraham it was said that the children of Israel should return, (from Egyptian bondage), in the fourth generation, and it was fulfilled in the person of Caleb and Joshua, two witnesses to the veracity of God. So it was predicted that Israel should never cease to be a nation; yet the tribe of Benjamin was almost exterminated as recorded in (Judges 19 to 21); the ten tribes had then been out of their land for a century and a quarter; and now Judah was partly in captivity, and it was *evident to the prophets* that her ENTIRE CAPTIVITY was CLOSE AT HAND. These appalling scenes and experiences needed the light of heaven thrown upon them to make it manifest to all that it was the UNFAITHFULNESS OF THE PEOPLE, (not of God), that demanded these chastisements; and that a "remnant" would escape; be preserved and blessed; return to their land; restore the ancient worship; and, ultimately, introduce the greater David, greater covenant, greater sanctuary, and everlasting blessing, so long and so frequently, foretold by the prophets.

I. SYMBOLS OF GLORY.

1. Chapter one is to us full of mystery, was perhaps so to the enraptured prophet. It was like God's appearance to Abraham, (Acts 7:2); to Moses (Ex. 3:2); to Isaiah, (Is. 6); and to John (Rev. 4 and 5). "The glory of the Lord" was in the Tabernacle and later in the Temple, and was a symbol of God's presence. There was no arrangement for light in the inner room of

the temple, but the Shekinah, or glory of God, did give light. The scenery in (ch. 1) recalls the temple. There are the throne, the cherubim, the one seated upon the throne, and the great light. The whole scenery however is *movable*, not confined to *one place* as was the temple. Ezekiel saw a GREATER GLORY OF GOD IN BABYLON than the priests could have seen *in Jerusalem*!

2.   The living ones had four faces each, a man, a lion, an ox and an eagle.   We may gather from these compound symbols, that the intelligence of man, the courage of the lion, the patient industry of the ox, and the swiftness of the eagle, characterized these servants of God. They also went straight forward, as all obedient ones are said to do, neither turning to the right hand nor to the left. The wheel within a wheel seems to import that God's providence encircles everything; and, let man go where he would, if faithful to Him, (as Ezekiel and a few others were), that God's encircling power, goodness and mercy were about him.   The governments of men are enclosed in a greater rule, or that of God.   The closing part of the chapter, however, seems to me to be a great climax. There was the *appearance* of the *likeness* of a *throne*—that is, sovereignty, ABOVE ALL ELSE, and the *appearance* of the *likeness* of a man ON THE THRONE.   Now, observe this vision came and went.   The living creatures, by the wheels full of eyes (or wisdom), had a crystal firmament *above them*; the *throne* was *above* the *firmament*, and the man *above* upon the *throne*.   Above it all was the rain-bow, the token of mercy showing that God is a merciful, covenant keeping God.   To reduce these figures to the terms of literal prophecy requires in us much caution, and we may not discover all their meanings. But this much is clear.

3.   The King in Jerusalem, Zedekiah, soon to be taken captive as the *last king* of *fleshly* Israel, would not destroy the glory and dominion of THIS MAN.   If you see it as I do, the whole imagery is briefly summed up as follows:

a.   Their "holy house," so called, was to be *deserted*, as was the TABERNACLE IN SHILOH, (Jer. 7:1-16; I Sam'l 4:10, 11; Ps. 78; 60; Jer. 26: 1-7).   Jeremiah predicted this in *literal language*.   But this would not destroy GOD'S PRESENCE with Israel, for He was meeting with his priest, Ezekiel *in Babylon*, and showing him the GLORY OF GOD. (So it was not confined to Jerusalem).

(b). The intelligent, courageous, faithful, patient people of God, swift to hear and obey his spirit, as shown by the living ones, would be enclosed in his great and immeasurable counsel, (wheels), for his purpose was one throughout and would accompany them wherever they were directed by his wisdom, (eyes) to go.

(c.) The subverted earthly thrones of Israel and of Judah, would not affect the rule and government of the true King of Israel, for His throne was over all, and his love, mercy, justice and holiness were as transparent as the clear crystal, and his covenant was sure as shown by the rainbow. This man, upon the throne, this greater Son of David and David's Lord, who was predicted in verbal statements by both Ezekiel and Jeremiah as well as by Hosea and others, (as we have seen), could not fail, or be discouraged, but would rule all events to the honor and glory of God. These facts seem to me to redeem this imagery from hopeless obscurity, and enable us to see here, in Judah's darkest hours of national histoy, in this *unexplained vision*, what afterwards was revealed in *plain language*.

II. IMPUDENT NATION.

In (ch. 2) the prophet is informed that the house of Israel was a rebellious nation, impudent and stiff-hearted; and was warned against them; to beware as one would be of briars, thorns and scorpions; and not to be dismayed by either their words or looks. The prophets were not esteemed by the rebellious, who somehow associated the prophets with the calamities predicted by them, as though to predict a thing was to produce it. They regarded the predicted calamities as under the control of the prophets, much as believers in witches blamed them with their troubles of various sorts. So, added to the unpleasantness of the message itself, was the additional fact just stated, that the ignorant and vicious thought the prophets were responsible for the judgments coming upon the nation. "And thou shalt speak my

words unto them, whether they will hear, or whether they
will forbear: for they are most rebellious." (ver 7).
Then he was instructed to eat the roll of the book, written
within and without; and there was written therein "lamentations, and mourning and woe."

III.   THE LITTLE BOOK.

The third chapter continues the figure of eating and
digesting a book, in prepartion of the prophet to receive
into his heart the message of God, that he might go to
them of the captivity as God's representative, "whether
they will hear, or whether they will forbear."

(Verses 12-14).

In these verses we are told WHY THE VISION WAS
GIVEN. Then the spirit took me up, and I heard behind
me a voice of a great rushing, saying BLESSED BE THE
GLORY OF THE LORD FROM THIS PLACE."   He
heard the noise of the *living creatures, of the wheels, and of
the great rushing.* "So the spirit lifted me up, and took
me away, and I went in bitterness, in the heat of my spirit; but the hand of the Lord was strong upon me." This
seems to have completed the first vision with its great
lessons, and would be plainer to us if we ignored the
division into chapters and read from the beginning of the
book down to (ch. 3:1-3).

THE PROPHET'S CHARGE.

(3:15-21).

After this the prophet began his mission to them of
the captivity at Telabib, among whom he sat in astonishment seven days, when the necessity came of prophesying against his sinful people.   When God said the wicked
should surely die the prophet had to warn him, and if
he turned from his wickedness, he should live and the
prophet had delivered his own soul.   If he did not warn
him, he should die in his iniquity, and his blood should
be required at the prophet's hand.   If he warned him
and he did not repent, the wicked should die in his iniquity, but the prophet delivered his own soul.   The
same rules should govern him in dealing with the righteous who turned away to iniquity and perished in his
wickedness.   This left the prophet no choice in the matter; but he should "speak as the oracles of God speak."

The PRINCIPLE evidently is the same with the teaching and services of professed teachers of God in our day. (vs. 22-27).

He was commanded to go to another place. "Then I arose and went forth into the plain; and, behold, THE GLORY OF THE LORD STOOD THERE, as the glory which I saw by the river of Chebar: and I fell upon my face."

You have doubtless observed that no revelations were made *by* the prophet, and all were made *to* him, in the first three chapters. He is sent to his house in the deep-seated consciousness of his duty to Israel, of what and when and to whom he should speak, and when keep silent; but thus far he had not begun to reveal to the captives the "lamentations, mournings and woe" of the little book; nor to show them how the judgment was necessary to cleanse the land of Judah of Idolatry; and that the sinners, who were chief in authority as King, princes, judges, false prophets, mercenary priests, and a blinded, foul multitude following them, must be purged out of the nation, but that this would not extirminate the nation, for the man on the throne—the David of the future, under a new covenant and a new sanctuary, would dwell with them forevermore.

IV. THE YEAR DAY RULE.

Here, properly, the revelations to the people begin, in a group of figures, which the prophet first gives, then explains, one after the other.

1. A picture of Jerusalem was drawn on a tile. Ezekiel was eloquent in the use of figures. All would know their capital city and lament its condition. He represented it as besieged by an army. He then placed an iron pan between himself and the city, representing the wall about it or fortifications. Ezekiel set his face against it, showing the siege by the Chaldeans. The prophet was to lie on his left side (390) days, representing, (by a day for a year) that it would be (390) years from the division of the nation by Jeroboam to the final overthrow of the city of Jerusalem. Next he was to lie on his right side (40) days, each day prophetic of a year, representing that forty years from some definite period

would also terminate at the same time in the overthrow
of Judah.   This was most likely to be counted from the
eighteenth year of Josiah when the people covenanted to
serve God, but afterwards violated it.   The coarse food,
the limited quantity granted him daily, the manner of
cooking it, as well as the scarcity of water, all set forth
the famine that should prevail.   When one thinks of this
transaction repeated daily for three hundred ninety, plu;
forty days, by the prophet, it shows us his faith, day by
day, in the predictions which follow:

"Moreover he said unto me, Son of Man, behold, I
will break the staff of bread *in Jerusalem*; and *they* shall
eat bread by weight and with care; and *they* shall drink
water by measure, and with astonishment; that they may
want bread and water, and be astonished one with another, and CONSUME AWAY FOR THEIR INIQUITY.

V.-VI.-VII.   BARBER'S RAZOR.

2.   The next illustration was drawn from the bar-
ber's trade.   With a razor he shaved off his hair and
beard, weighed, and disposed of it, so as to represent
the destruction coming upon the inhabitants of Jerusalem AT THE TERMINATION OF THE SIEGE.   One
third was burned in the fire in the *midst* of the city; a
third part was smitten around with a knife; a third part
was scattered in the wind.   This is explained (ver. 12).
A third of the inhabitants of Jerusalem should die by
pestilence and famine; a third part should fall by the
sword; and a third part should be scattered and the
sword pursue them.   A small number was to be first
bound up in his skirts, then brought forth and burned.
This was the "little remnant" to be spared.   The prophet
then gives the reason why all these calamities were coming on the nation, from (ver 5 to 17).   Remember, dear
reader, this was all real experience of Israel, set forth
by the prophet under these figures.   The sixth chapter is
a part of this great prophecy, and is in literal language,
setting forth with clearness and power the sins, and the
punishment to be inflicted for them upon Israel.   As the
ten tribes had been gone for more than a century, the
prophet speaks of the remaining seed of Abraham as
"Israel."   (See vs. 8-10).   The seventh chapter con-

tinues the doleful strain.   At (ver 20) he sets forth the reason the temple should fall.   At (ver. 23) he predicts captivity by a chain, showing all along the meaning of his appropriate figures.   The last verse shows how the King, Zedekiah, and the princes should mourn and be desolate, and the people in trouble.   All ranks and classes should be distressed without remedy, except the little "remnant" who served God.

Ezekiel addresses the mountains, hills, rivers, and valleys, and predicts the destruction of the idols and the children of Israel together.   In all your dwelling places the cities shall be laid waste, and the high places shall be desolate, that your idols may be broken and cease, and your images may be cut down, and your works may be abolished.   And the slain shall fall in the midst of thee and ye shall know that I am the Lord.   (vs. 6, 7).   The "Remnant" to escape these calamities were brought in for timely comfort in the next verses.   In the seventh chapter the prophet showed.

"An end, the end is come upon the four corners of the land.   Now is the end come upon thee, and I will send mine anger upon thee and will judge thee according to thy ways, and will recompense upon thee all thine abominations."   (vs. 2, 3).   "But they that escape of them shall escape, and shall be upon the mountains like doves of the valley, all of them mourning, every one for his iniquity."

He predicted that the "Secret place" or "Holy of Holies" should be plundered.   Then under the figure of a chain he pictures the approaching captivity, the enemies take their lands, houses, and holy places.   Did not all this take place twenty-five centuries ago?

3.   He saw the "Image of Jealousy" or the idolatry before the temple, probably the image of Baal.

4.   THE GLORY OF THE GOD OF ISRAEL WAS THERE ACCORDING TO THE VISION I SAW IN THE PLAIN.   This represented God's presence, and, (as it leaves), God leaving the city and temple to be destroyed; while the remnant preserved showed that God at that time had not forsaken Israel.

He was next instructed to dig in the wall, and, found a door and entered in, or discovered the secret idolatry practiced by the seventy men—the great men of the nation. Thus the prophet saw, (in vision), the actual state of idolatry practiced either openly or secretly by Israel.

6. Next he saw the women near the temple weeping in their devotions to Tammuz.

7. Next some twenty-five men, evidently priests, were seen between the porch of the temple and the altar, with their backs towards the temple and their faces towards the east as they worshipped the sun, or Baal.

In (ch. 9) a slaughter is pictured. Seven men, (a perfect number, for the judgment was exact), appeared. Six of them had slaughter weapons, and one was clothed in linen with a writer's ink-horn by his side. This man selected the true Israel of God, the "remnant," at God's command. The executioners then went forth through the city and slew all except those who had God's mark in their foreheads, or minds. The execution began at the "house of God," as it did, six centuries later, in apostolic days. (I Pet. 4:17). The very courts, defiled by idolatry as shown in (ch. 8), were profaned and would be polluted with dead bodies. This was all in vision, not real transactions. The attentive reader will consult (9:3; 10:1-5) and observe that THE GLORY OF THE GOD OF ISRAEL, seen in (ch. 1), in Babylon, later (8:4) (in vision in his house, as though he was at Jerusalem), WAS FORSAKING THE CITY. The progress of this work in (ch. 10) shows us that God would not dwell among such profane, idolatrous people, and was forsaking Jerusalem and the temple as he forsook Shiloh in the days of Samuel and Eli, (I Sam'l 4:11). Read the whole tenth chapter of Ezekiel, noting (vs. 15-18) and see that the *glory of God*, was ready to leave Jerusalem. THE WHOLE WAS A THRILLING VISION OF GOD LEAVING ISRAEL.

In (Ch. 11) the five and twenty men, seen as gross idolaters (8:16), received judgment. While he prophesied, Pelatiah, evidently a great man, died. This impressed the prophet profoundly, and caused him to exclaim, "Ah, Lord God! wilt thou make a full end of the remnant of Israel?" The Lord vindicated his justice by picturing anew the iniquity of Israel, and how they thought the land was given them to possess. They pre-

sumed that Canaan was theirs in everlasting possession.
They had not studied the "curse," which was now due
upon the land. It was shown by the prophet that Israel
had life and death, a "blessing" and a "curse," set before
them, and their iniquities had ripened them for the curse,
which would surely come upon the nation; "yet will I
be to them a little sanctuary in the countries where they
shall come." Then he foretold that they would cast off
their idols and detestable things and they would return
to God in heart and life; "That they may walk in my
statutes, and keep my ordinances, and do them; and *they*
shall be *my* people, and I will be *their* God. But as for
them whose hearts walketh after the heart of their detestable things and their abominations, I will recompense
their way upon their own heads, saith the Lord God,"
(vs. 20-21). Then in (vs. 22, 23) THE GLORY OF THE
GOD OF ISRAEL, left the TEMPLE and the CITY, went
to the MOUNT OF OLIVES, and DISAPPEARED. This
closed the VISION; and it only remained that the prophet should RETURN IN VISION to his brethren in Captivity, and make the revelation to them.

JESUS' ASCENSION TYPIFIED.

Jesus entered Jerusalem and rebuked the chief
priests, scribes and elders, and was rejected by them as
their king. In (Matt| 23) he pronounced his woes upon
them, and their city, and lamented its ruin; but upon
leaving the temple said, "Behold, your house is left unto
you desolate. For I say unto you, ye shall not see me
henceforth, till ye shall say, blessed is he that cometh in
the name of the Lord." This last expression was used by
the multitude when Jesus entered the city (Matt. 21:9),
and is the attitude of mind to which Israel must come as
foretold in (Ps. 118:22-26). Then Jesus foretold the
destruction of the Jewish nation and temple, and his own
great mission to the church, and his second coming, at
which time he would Judge all nations. (Matt. 24-25).
He was rejected and crucified, and after his resurrection
on the third day, was with his disciples for forty days,
speaking to them of *the things pertaining to the Kingdom of
God*, and ascended to heaven from MOUNT OLIVET.
(Acts 1). His course or pathway was that of the GLORY

OF GOD in the vision of Ezekiel; and he, as the TRUE GLORY, THE MAN, WHO SAT UPON THE TRUE THRONE OF ISRAEL, FIRST IN THIS VISION, AND IN THE VERBAL PROPHECIES, AS DAVID, FULFILL-ED THE TYPE-PROPHECY IN HIS PERSON. Ezekiel foretold these things as applicable to his nation in his own days and they were fulfilled in the destruction of Jerusalem by Nebuchadnezzar. But six centuries later, the glory of God, Jesus, forsook the fleshly seed of Abra-ham, gave them up to the Roman sword, and their forti-fied cities, their capital and temple were burned to the ground. Simeon said, while holding the infant Jesus in his arms, "Lord, now let thou thy servant depart in peace, according to thy word, for mine eyes have seen thy salvation, which thou hast prepared before the face of all people, a light to lighten the Gentiles, and *the glory of thy people Israel.*" (Luke 2:29-32). *This* glory left the *nation* when Jesus FORSOOK THEM and LEFT THEIR HOUSE DESOLATE. The glory that left Israel in "Ezekiel's day was but a type of the true glory of God, Christ, who forsook Israel six centuries later: one as type, foretold the other.

The glory that left Israel in Ezekiel's vision, was rep-resentative of God's favor, but was shown in Israel's national history by a glorious light. For this light to de-part was for God's favor, of which it was the visible sign, to leave the people. For Jesus, the glory of Israel, to leave them desolate, was for the *spiritual light* to leave them. "But if our gospel be hid, it is hid to them that are lost; in whom the God of this world hath blinded the minds of them which believe not, lest the light of the glorious gospel of Christ, who is the image of God, should shine unto them." (II Cor. 4:3, 4). Idolatry blinded the Jews in Ezekiel's day to the knowledge and service of God, and they lost their king, their prophets, their priests, their land, their temple, their sacrifices, and, as at Shlioh, Ichabod, "the glory has departed" was an ap-propriate name for them. The god of this world, (not the God of heaven), blinded all but a "remnant" of Israel in Jesus' day, and they clung to their traditions and sacrificed the favor of God. We should learn how-ever, that the favor of God, his glory, RETURNED TO

ISRAEL, IN TYPE, ON THEIR REPENTANCE, AND
WHEN THEY REBUILT THE TEMPLE; so NOW, the
favor of God is promised to Israel WHEN THEY RE-
PENT AND COME TO THE TEMPLE OF GOD, in which
the *true* king of Israel, High Priest, and Prophet, dwells,
by his spirit. The two glories are contrasted at length
in (II Cor. 3).

1. The law was written on tables of stone; the
gospel on fleshly tables of the heart.

2. The law was the letter, the gospel, the spirit;
or one the husk, the other the kernel.

3. The law killeth, condemns to death; the spirit
quickens or makes alive the sinner, dead in trespasses
and in sins.

4. Moses had to veil his face when he approached
the children of Israel, after his forty days' communion
with God. This was a great glory for a man, a servant of
God. But that glory soon left his face. The gospel
was ministered by the Holy Spirit and was more glorious.

5. If the law, now done away, was glorious, much
more is the gospel, which remains. (II Cor. 3:11).

6. As the veil was on Moses' face, that the glory
might not shine out, so Paul says, the glory of the gospel
was hidden from the Jews, (read on into the next chap.)
because THERE WAS A VEIL ON THEIR HEARTS—
the veil of traditions, carnality, and worldly pride. He
said, however, that "when it shall turn to the Lord, the
veil shall be taken away." When Moses turned and went
into the tabernacle to talk to God alone, he removed the
veil. Paul used that fact to show that Israel did not
read the Old Testament aright, nor see Christ in the
types and prophecies; but when their hearts get right,
"when it [the heart] turns to the Lord," all blindness
disappears, and they read the Old Testament as he was
doing (vs. 14-16).

This shows us that the Word of God is clear and
plain, all-sufficient, and that no miracles are promised
or should be expected to convert Israel in these latter
days. What they need is to throw away their traditions
and return and seek God and David their King, the
Lord our Righteousness. "Now the Lord is that Spirit;
and where the spirit of the Lord is, there is liberty. But

we all with open face, beholding as in a glass the glory of the Lord, are changed into the same image, from glory to glory, even as by the Spirit of the Lord." (vs. 15-18). The glory of Moses' face was not communicated to Israel; but the Glory of Christ is transferred in a measure, from him to us. *While we behold him,* in his life, we are purified, changed into his image, receive of his glory, and this is done by his Spirit, through his Word, and power. THIS LESSON TEACHES US THAT THE GLORY OF GOD THAT ISRAEL REJECTED IN THE DAYS OF CHRIST WILL RETURN TO THEM, WHEN THEY TURN TO THE LORD JESUS CHRIST. I said the glory of God left Israel and returned when they rebuilt their temple, meaning that it was seen returning in Ezekiel's vision of the Temple (43:1-6). These visions were concerning fleshly Israel; but as that temple, and every other, was but a type, so all the services were but shadows of good things to come. As the manna, the water from the smitten rock and other sacred things pointed forward to Christ, the miraculous Light that guided Israel was not that " true Light, which lighteth every man that cometh into the world." It would be just as plausible that God would feed Israel forty years on "angel's food" or manna, and quench their thirst with a miraculous supply of water, as that a miraculous light should shine in a Jewish Temple as evidence of God's presence and blessing. Christ is the true Bread which came down from heaven; he is the Fountain of living Water; and he is the "Light of the world," the anti-type of these Jewish types. The Jews can have no manna, no water of life, and no spiritual light away from Christ. The king, priests, princes and false prophets had polluted Jerusalem and the Temple so that God would no longer dwell in that place; hence the vision of "The Glory of God" leaving them. Six centuries later, Christ, (the glory of Israel), left the nation, according to this figure, and thus the desolate house or temple was given over to the heathen to be destroyed. But the "Glory of God" now dwells in the spiritual temple, or church, and when the Jews repent and come to God in Christ, LED BY THAT ANTI-TYPICAL LIGHT, God's favor will rest upon them.

VIII.-IX.-X.-XI. THE REMNANT.

These four chapters showed that Judah's idolatry was deep-seated. Yet depraved as Judah was the prophet should not despair for there was a "Remnant." The "Glory of God" had not departed from all Israel. The prophet was brought in visions of God to Jerusalem, and by inspiration was made to see the incurable idolatry of high and low, rich and poor, even the chief religious guides, as formerly Hophni and Phinehas were corrupt, when God forsook Shiloh as he was now about to depart from Jerusalem. The prophecy of God forsaking Jerusalem was given by Jeremiah (ch's 7:1-20; 26:1-7) as verbal prophecy; and by Ezekiel in symbols. In both places it was the glory of God leaving the house. Jeremiah exhorted to repentance. Ezekiel pictured the "Remnant" of the men "who sigh and that cry for all the abominations that be done in the midst thereof," (6:4); these were spared like Lot in Sodom or Noah at the Flood. In (8:1) is the throne and the command given to cast coals of fire into the city. This was the execution, (in vision), of the judgment then hastening; and the "Glory of the Lord", step by step, left the Holy of Holies, the temple, the city, and was last seen on the Mount of Olives. No more wonderful vision is recorded in the Old Testament. Ezekiel, far away, beheld the stages of decline in his sinful nation still in Jerusalem and Judea, and saw, (in vision), the withdrawal of "The Glory of the Lord" from the temple. This lesson was the foundation for the awe-inspiring series of denunciations, the "Lamentations, mourning and woe" from the (12 to 24 chs.) From (chs 8:1 to 20:1), as you will see, were given in eleven months.

Jesus, the anti-typical glory of God, left the temple, city, people and Mosaic arrangement as empty and worthless, as desolate and condemned, as the typical glory left them in Ezekiel's day. The return of God's favor to Israel was predicted to meet them in the new temple, the church, and, upon Pentecost, the glory and blessing of God came upon converted Israel. When the nation leaves Babylon and returns to the place where God has recorded his name, (or to Christ) then the veil is removed and they shall be filled with the glory of the Lord. (II Cor. 3:13-18).

CHAPTER XXII.

EZEKIEL'S PREDICTIONS OF WOE.

From the (12th to 24th ch's) Ezekiel used various illustrations and made many predictions of the overthrow of the nation. We can not follow him fully, and I deem it unnecessary to the purpose of this work. He seems to have acted out his prophecies, then explained his actions, making them predictive of similar things being enacted in his nation, far away at Jerusalem. He acted out the captivity of Judah and the King—Zedekiah —by digging through a wall, carrying forth his household stuff in the twilight, with his face covered that he should not see the ground. Explaining this type-prophecy, he said the king would leave Jerusalem in that manner would be *brought to Babylon, and die there*, though he should not see it. (12:13). Jeremiah predicted about the same time (Jer. 34:1-3), the same desperation, and that Nebuchadnezzar would burn the city of Jerusalem; the king should surely be taken; "thine eyes shall behold the eyes of the King of Babylon, and he shall speak with thee, mouth to mouth, and thou shalt go to Babylon." Furthermore, he predicted that Zedekiah should not die by the sword, but should die in peace, and have honorable burial. When we turn to (II Ks. 25:7) we learn that they slew the *sons* of Zedekiah before his eyes, *put his eyes out*, and bound him with fetters of brass, and carried him to Babylon. So both prophets were correct, were literally fulfilled. He remembered the "Remnant," gave them hope, but foretold famine of bread and water for the masses. Closing the chapter he insisted that these predictions were soon to be fulfilled, that he was not predicting distant events, but calamities at hand. Any attempt to make this language to be a prediction of our days is to be regretted; for did not Zedekiah's captivity form one of the chief items of Ezekiel's, as well as Jeremiah's prophecies, seeing that they lived at the very time of the captivity? Is the Lamentations of Jeremiah a historical book? We all know it records the punctual fulfillment of many of these predictions of the overthrow of the nation. It is to ignore the history of the downfall of the nation, as well as the seventy years captivity in Babylon, during which the nation was cleansed by judgment from their tendency to idolatry, to assume that Ezekiel's "Vision that he seeth is for many days to come, and he prophesieth of the times that are far off." He denounced that sentiment in the people in his day; and if it was not true then it is not true now. (Ch. 12:21-28).

When we pass through the next three chapters we are instructed that Israel has become cross; and a long catalogue of crimes is charged up against the murderous princes, the irreverent children, the oppressors of strangers, the lewd, the bribe-giver and the bribe-taker. The false prophets were like lion roaring for prey, devouring souls, taking treasure and precious things, making many widows by their conspiracies and murders.

"Her priests have violated my law, and have profaned my holy things; they have put no difference between the holy and the profane, neither have they showed difference between the unclean and the clean, and have hid their eyes from my sabbaths, and I am profaned among them. Her princes in the midst thereof are like wolves ravening for the prey, to shed blood, and to destroy souls, to get dishonest gain." (22:25-27).

Such and such like, was heaven's indictment against Israel in her last days, before the Babylonian captivity.

XV.-XVI. FRUITLESS VINE AND UNWORTHY BRIDE.

Judea was a country of vineyards, so the true people of God were often compared to the fruitful vine, and the disobedient to a wild vine. Ezekiel is not peculiar in his use of the vine to set forth the fact that the people of Israel were a choice and well cultivated vine, and the Lord would justly demand good fruit or cut down the vine that it cumber not the ground. (Isa. 5; Jno. 15) might be consulted to impress the lesson so easily grasped.

His next illustration was of an infant, deserted and helpless, adopted and cared for by a generous man, who reared to womanhood and married her and after he had lavished overy attention upon her, she was untrue to her vows and turned against her benefactor.   This was Israel's history.   By such faithful and solemn portrayal of their own faithlessness to God the prophets sought to awaken concern for their condition in the hearts of his countrymen.   All of his illustrations were used to set forth the sinfulness of his nation at that time and earlier in their history and thus vindicate the justice of God in punishing them.

XVII. THE TWO EAGLES.

Two great events are given in this chapter, leading up to the final captivity.   The two eagles(king of birds) represent the king of Babylon and the king of Egypt, as the prophet explained.   The king of Babylon took Jehoiachin the king of Judah and many of his subjects to Babylon, (Ezekiel among the number); he took an oath of Zedekiah that he would be his servant.   But Zedekiah leaned for strength toward the Egyptian king, and by alliance with him hoped to free himself from Nebuchadnezzar.   The tree is Judah.   As Lebanon, north of Palestine, grew lofty trees, the prophet predicts that God will be the husbandman, prune the trees, and plant one great tree "In the mountain of the height of Israel."   This is not Nebuchadnezzar's tree but God's tree.   Jesus Christ is the loftiest tree and the Monarch of this great forest.

XVIII.-XIX. SOUR GRAPES—THE LIONESS AND WHELPS.

In this chapter the lesson is brought out that God deals with individuals, and holds them responsible for their own deeds, not rewarding or punishing them for their ancestors' conduct.   He shows that wicked parents may have good children, or good parents may be brought to shame by the evil conduct of their children.   In all cases men must answer to God for themselves.   The statement, "the soul that sinneth it shall die," is not a proof that souls become extinct.   It should be examined in the light of its context.   It evidently means that the son or the father pollutes his own soul, and not that sin is hereditary. This is apparent in the expression "the fathers have eaten sour grapes and the children's teeth are set on edge." This is his text, the sentiment of which he denies; and what he says about sin is to show that man cannot hide his guilt and shield himself behind some-one else. The soul sins and dies in this world in the very act of disobedience; (Eph. 2:1). Hence these people were exhorted to turn to God and live. The next chapter shows how earnestly the prophet applied his exhortation to the princes. Their mother is a lionness, they are whelps. One after another grew up to devour and rule and was destroyed. Jehoahaz, who ruled Judah (3 mo,) was taken to Egypt (ver. 3, 4). Jehoiakim ruled eleven years, incurred the displeasure of the king of Babylon and perished. Jehoiachin reigned three months and was carried to Babylon, and Ezekiel's prophecies are generally dated from this captivity, as he was one of the illustrious captives. He closes the chapter by illustrating how the kings had degenerated, and the nation had sunken in sin, since the glorious days of David and Solomon, and how feeble was Zedekiah's rule as compared to theirs. The whole chapter shows how Josiah's family had apostatized from God, and forsaken the pious example of that great and good father and worthy king, illustrating and enforcing the lesson in (chapters 18 and 19).

XX.   ELDERS CONDEMNED.

Here is a rebuke of the elders, as the preceding chapter had been of the kings, in which the history of Israel from the days of Egyptian bondage is reviewed. This furnished one of those great groupings of events, causing to pass before the mental eye the history of God's continued but despised mercies, until the sum total was appalling, and demanded the doom, then big with terror, ready to burst upon the sinful nation. The long chapter closes with another parable of the trees, and the people complain of his manner of addressing them in parables.

XXI.-XXIV.   ISRAEL'S LAST EARTHLY KING.

These three chapters close his prophecies before Jerusalem was besieged. He showed that the whole land of Judah was to fall before Nebuchadnezzar. In (vs.

18-24) he shows that the invading king was undecided
whether to invest with his army the capital of the Ammonites or the capital of the Israelites; but he would
decide against Jerusalem because Zedekiah had violated
his oath of allegiance to him. (vs. 18-24). In (vs. 28-
32) he showed that the Ammonites shall fall after the
Israelites because they gloried against Israel. But the
chief prophecy, the one not to be overlooked, is in (vs.
25-27), which I have given before in this volume, and
now repeat for clearness, for we should all understand
it. This is the *last* prophecy against the *last king* of
Judah, given by Ezekiel before the Babylonian Captivity.
It is pathetic and sublime. You see the Christ in the
distance. This is Israel's very last earthly king, rejected
of God, and given into the hands of the heathen.

　　"And thou profane wicked prince of Israel, whose
day is come, *when iniquity* shall have *an end*, thus saith
the Lord God: Remove the diadem, and take off the
crown: this shall not be the same: exalt him that is low
and abase him that is high. I will overturn, overturn,
overturn it: and it shall be no more, until he come whose
right it is: and I will give it him." The end, the end
had come.

　　For six hundred years there were no more kings in
Israel. Zedekiah was carried to Babylon and died there,
having been blinded by the king, showing that the tender mercies of the wicked are cruel. "Now, did Ezekiel
mean,, "It shall be no more, until he come," (the second
time), "whose right it is," to rule Israel: "and I will
give it him" at the Millennium? Surely not; but that
the temporal rulers should cease forever in Israel, and
that the Messiah, or man upon the throne, in the vision
of the first chapters, would come to his long predicted
and typified rule over the true Israel of God and rule
forever. This was an old prophecy, simply repeated, by
Ezekiel. It dates from the garden of Eden. It was
NOT DUE TO BE FULFILLED, and the prophet showed
that the nation was to be punished in Babylon not
blessed, (as if faithful they would have been) in their
land. The captivity in Babylon was the burden of his
message, in a series of predictions for four and one-half

years of "lamentations, mourning and woe," then due
for past sins.

XXII. JERUSALEM'S PHOTOGRAPH.

The twenty-second chapter is a catalogue of crimes
charged against the prophets, priests, princes and people
of Jerusalem, appaling in its nature. It is an arraignment of the nation similar to that divine condemnation,
pronounced six centuries later by our Savior against "the
scribes, pharisees and hypocrites" in Jerusalem, (Matt.
23) revealing the justice of God about to be vindicated
in their overthrow.

XXIII. AHOLAH AND AHOLIBAH.

The twenty-third chapter of Ezekiel is the climax.
Jerusalem is seen as dedicated to greed ,lust and violence.
Jerusalem and Samaria were reduced to the lowest level
of humanity, and pictured as two harlots revelling in all
the baseness of their depraved lusts. Their profligacy
merited and was about to receive the retribution that was
meet. The high and low were guilty of idolatry. Aholah
and Aholibah were two sisters, the first Samaria, the
latter Jerusalem, or Israel and Judah. Through forty-
nine verses the prophet poured forth the contempt and
scorn that were due for the treachery, ingratitude, filthiness, and pollution of these two nations. This was his
final message before the terrible crisis set forth in the
next chapter, and which demanded this fearful, national
judgment. In the (24 ch.) by the typical actions of the
prophet and in verbal prediction, HE ANNOUNCED
THAT THE SIEGE OF JERUSALEM BEGAN THAT
DAY, and that it would end in all that was choice and
valuable being consumed. The city should be cleansed
of her scum, and filthiness by this judgment. The sanc-
tity of his home is exposed to view and the desire of his
eyes is taken from him in the death of his wife. But he
was forbidden to mourn. Explaining these last actions
to the people, like Jesus on the way to crucifixion, he
said in substance, "Weep not for me, but weep for yourselves and for your children," and predicted that the
sanctuary would be profaned, and their sons and daughters, (remaining in the stricken land,) should fall by

the sword.   From that day forth he ceased to predict the future of Israel, because the calamity was upon them; and he was dumb to Israel, as a prophet, for nearly three years, or all the while the siege lasted, and until word was brought that "The city is smitten," as noted previously.   Compare (24:25-27 with 33:21, 22).

During this time he seems to have levelled his denunciations against the Gentile nations (chs. 25 to 32). These have received brief notice in the early chapters of this work.   I may add, that Ammon, Moab, Edom and Philistia rejoiced in the downfall of Judah hoping to profit thereby.   Their chief offense however, was in reviling God, as though the God of Israel was not able to resist the gods of Assyria.   Tyre received a merited rebuke and faithful forecast of her impending doom as did Egypt.   Nebuchadnezzar was the chosen rod that the Lord used to chastise these nations.   "He that is glad at calamities shall not be unpunished."   How appropriate that these predictions should follow the downfall of the chosen people, showing that God would punish sin, and that while judgment began at the house of God, the ungodly and the sinner merited even worse punishment, and this was predicted!

A GREAT CHANCE.

One can scarcely realize the greatness of the change that had taken place in Israel's condition between the last prophecy given by Ezekiel at the beginning of the siege of Jerusalem by the Babylonians (ch. 24) and the time when he uttered his next predictions to Israel after word was brought that the city was smitten, (ch. 33).   The first twenty verses of this chapter seem to have been spoken by the prophet the evening before the news of the fall of the city reached them. These verses are strikingly in harmony with the manner in which he was instructed to act, when he was first called and commissioned (ch. 3:15-21).   Please to compare them.   See how faithful the prophet had been as a watchman for the nation!

Some would like to see a prophecy in the actions of the prophet, which are not explained, as well as those which are explained.   This is dangerous.   The period of time from his first vision (chs. 1:1-2 to 33:21) is SEVEN YEARS AND SIX MONTHS. To make his silence in (3:16) for SEVEN DAYS predictive of so many *years*, it is seen that his message to the stubborn and rebellious house was plain enough when fulfilled. After the frightful destruction of rich and poor, king and nobles, priests and false prophets, and the desolation of the land and destruction of the temple, in their great distress (the sorrowful message of the prophet having been wrought out in its soul-sickening details,) they were ready to hear him. Those of you who are disposed to make an analysis of this book will turn and read (3:15-21 and 33:1-20) and see how one great period of his prophetic life was passed. Over the ashes of their capital and temple, the voice of this priest was now their comfort and stay. His prophecies up to and including the greatest national judgment against the land, cities, king, nobles, and idolatrous people, was fulfilled and fulfilling before them, thus enabling the prophet to renew his message to a people broken and crushed for their iniquities, as he had predicted. Hence his commission is renewed in this chapter, and his book naturally falls into these two divisions—his first prophecies to the nation full of "LAMENTATION, MOURNING AND WOE," largely fulfilled in these seven years and six months, and from (33:21 to 48) the HOPE held forth to the TRUE CHILDREN OF ABRAHAM, "the remnant," who, like Ezekiel, SAW THE GLORY OF GOD and that Israel was the real sanctuary, EVEN IN BABYLON. I do not regard the seven days' amazement of the prophet as typical but the division in the book follows the profound judgment of God against the nation.

CHAPTER XXIII.

HOPE FOR THE REMNANT.

But, not to lose sight of the structure of the book, let us now consider the king proposition. Their last *king* was then in captivity. The *sheep* were scattered. The *cities* of Judah were in ruin, the *capital* was lying waste; the *temple* had been plundered and burned to the ground; while thousands of the golden *vessels* of the house of the Lord were in a heathen temple in Babylon. War with all its savagery had laid waste their heritage. The prophet could not now predict "lamentation, mourning and woe," for that was the portion of all classes and conditions of his people. Let us note the great earthquake that separated the people in the *succeeding* chapters, from those in the *preceding*. I am sure that you will appreciate the condition of desolation then prevailing, and will keep distinctly in mind that from (ch. 33:21) to the close of the book the prophet was speaking to the nation as CAPTIVES IN BABYLON. With this much premised, what does he say about the future of the nation?

XXXIV. THE SHEPHERDS.

Here the shepherds are denounced in the most unsparing way. The Shepherds were the great men of the nation, the Kings, princes, judges, priests and false prophets. This whole chapter showed there was one great and good Shepherd yet to come.

"And I will set up one shepherd over them, and he shall feed them, and he shall be their shepherd. And I, the Lord, will be their God, and my servant David a prince among them; I the Lord have spoken it. And I will make with them a covenant of peace, and will cause the evil beasts to cease out of the land: and they shall dwell safely in the wilderness, and sleep in the woods. And I will make them and the places round about my hill a blessing: and I will cause the showers to come down in his season; there shall be showers of blessing." (vs. 23-36).

This can mean no other than Jesus, the Son of

David, and Son of God. In (Jno. 10) Jesus delivers us a discourse claiming to be the good Shepherd. He gives to his sheep pasture, and ultimately, eternal life. He was sent to the lost sheep of the house of Israel, (Matt. 15:24). Under the figure of sheep, wilderness, woods, waters, and fruit the prophet predicted the blessing of God, through Christ, the David of the text, then to come to Israel. He was the plant of renown to be raised up to them, and they were to "be no more consumed with hunger, in the land, neither bear the shame of the heathen any more. Thus shall they know that I, the Lord their God am with them, and that they, even the house of Israel, are my people, saith the Lord God. And ye my flock, the flock of my pasture, are men, and I am your God, saith the Lord." (vs. 29-31).

So, in the very chapter where he rejects the shepherds of Israel, he predicted the true Shepherd, or King David, and this mark ye well, AS THE FIRST PREDICTION CONCERNING THE KING, SINCE THE PREDICTION HE MADE CONCERNING ZEDEKIAH, THAT THE THRONE SHOULD EXIST NO MORE TILL HE CAME WHOSE RIGHT IT WAS, AND HE WOULD GIVE IT HIM, as quoted above. One was (ch. 21:25-27) concerning their last king, under the Law of Moses; the other was spoken after the city was smitten, the last earthly king blinded; his sons, and thus his heirs, dead, and it was concerning the King of the spiritual Kingdom, and Jesus Christ alone can be the person contemplated. THE OLD ORDER OF KINGS WAS NOW DONE AWAY NEVER TO BE REVIVED, and the vision of the new order is given with clearness and beauty to the prophet. As the first section of his prophecies showed that the glory of the Lord was not confined to the land, and temple; and the destruction of the temple and captivity of the priests verified it; and God gave visions of his glory in a far away land to his faithful priest, Ezekiel; so this revelation concerning their FUTURE KING, (when understood), teaches that although the earthly kingdom was in ruin, David (our Savior) could and would raise up the rule over the true Israel into a higher, holier and more enduring sovereignty than had just passed away.

THE REMNANT.

In all the sad experiences of Judah's apostasy and overthrow, three points tower above all the rest. First, there was a *"Remnant"* of the nation would survive, as worthy of reward, and fit subjects for mercy and preservation. This fact should be read and pondered in the following Scriptures. (Ezek. 5:10-12; 6:8-10; 9:4; 10:7-16; 11:16-21; 12:21-28), and the references. This fact is of two-fold meaning: it teaches that the judgment against the nation was discriminative, including the wicked and excluding the righteous, and was thus a proof, on a national scale, that "God will by no means clear the guilty;" and another fact, of equal importance, was that the national judgment *was then due.* Second it was shown that the fulfillment of all the visions of Israel's overthrow, numerous and plain, (though their execution had been deferred), *was then due.*

"And the word of the Lord came unto me, saying, Son of Man, what is that proverb that ye have in the land of Israel, saying, The days are prolonged, and every vision faileth? Tell them therefore, thus saith the Lord God: I will make this proverb to cease, and they shall no more use it as a proverb in Israel; but say unto them, the days are at hand and the effect of every vision. For there shall be no more any vain vision nor flattering divination within the house of Israel. For I am the Lord. I will speak and the word that I shall speak shall come to pass; it shall be no more prolonged: *for in your days,* O rebellious house, will I say the word, and will perform it, saith the Lord God. Again the word of the Lord came to me, saying, Son of Man, behold, they of the house of Israel say, The vision that he seeth is for many days to come, and he prophesieth of the times that are far off. Therefore say unto them, Thus saith the Lord God; there shall none of my words be prolonged any more, but the word which I have spoken shall be done, saith the Lord God." (12:21-28).

It is evident that these predictions of "lamentations and mourning and woe" against Judah were soon to be fulfilled, when this was declared to the nation. If his prophecies are all dated, then this one was given between the dates (8:1 and 20:1), or, at most, less than four years before the Babylonians besieged Jerusalem; hence this warning of its near approach. To say this prophecy related to the second overthrow of the whole

nation by the Romans, six centuries later, is to contradict
the central thought of this prophecy. To say that "The
vision that he seeth is for many days to come, and he
prophesieth of the times that are far off" EVEN TWEN-
TY-FIVE CENTURIES REACHING TO OUR TIMES, is
to negative his statements. The whole series of visions
relating to the Jewish people in the first half of his
book, were manifestly included in these statements. As
"a remnant" were to be spared and brought through the
trial of faith and devotion, in order that Jesus our Lord
might come of the seed of David, the third great fact of
these predictions of Ezekiel was that David should come
to that remnant. This feature of his predictions however, was in the symbols of the first eleven chapters
("the *likeness* of a throne, as the appearance of a sapphire stone; and upon the *likeness* of the throne was the
likeness as the appearance of a man above upon it") ; and,
as the then future Ruler of Israel, he appears in the verbal predictions under the name of David. THUS HE
WAS FORETOLD IN SYMBOL AND IN TYPE-PROPHE-
CY IN THIS BOOK, AT THE TIME THE NATION WAS
RIPE FOR JUDGMENT. It behooves us to notice this
all-controlling fact in all of these prophecies, as they are
"as a light shining in a dark place."

JESUS NOT JEHOVAH IN THE TEXT.

Another fact not to be forgotten is, "And I the Lord
will be their God, and MY SERVANT David a prince
among them": also "David MY SERVANT shall be king
over them; and they all shall have one shepherd; they
shall also walk in my judgments, and observe my statutes,
and do them." These and similar texts show conclusively that the DAVID of these predictions IS NOT JE-
HOVAH; *but* THE SERVANT OF *Jehovah*. This distinction is vital, and shows us that, as David had been dead
for many generations, the prophet could not have meant
that royal-prophet; but his more illustrious Son, Jesus,
as Ezekiel was nearly midway between them. Some
would have Jesus to be the Jehovah who appeared from
Genesis to Malachi, on occasion, to the prophets. I do
not so understand the history. This would make Jesus
a type of himself, in a few instances, at least, and would

introduce confusion into all such plain texts as these. (See Ps. 2): The King in this prediction is the Son, and must be, therefore, in every other where the Gospel Age is the subject as in (Ezek. 37:22). The virtue of Christ's death reaches back to Adam, but there is a plain distinction in the New Testament we should not forget, (Heb. 1:1, 2; 2:1-4; 12:25), not to multiply quotations, show that the speaker and revealer in the gospel is not the same person "who spake unto the Fathers." The Old Dispensation was ministered by angels, but the New Covenant by the Son.

THE FINAL PROPHECIES.

We may observe that Ezekiel's "mouth was opened and he was no more dumb" after the news was received that "The city is smitten." "Son of Man, they that inhabit those wastes of the land of Israel speak, saying, Abraham was one, and he inherited the land: but we are many; the land is given us for inheritance," (33:22-24). It is not the number of Israel that counts. There were but eight souls in the Ark, but the promise that the seed of the woman should bruise the serpent's head, was preserved in the person of Shem. There were but two men out of six hundred three thousand five hundred and fifty, who were numbered of Israel at Mt. Sinai, that reached Canaan; but they were of the "fourth generation" as predicted, and thus redeemed the promise. There were but few men, comparatively speaking, in any generation of Israel, who took God at his word, but they were "blessed" while the disobedient were "cursed." From (ch. 40) in Isaiah to the close, this distinction is sharp and clear. The evidence is overwhelming that Jesus is the "Servant" who was so faithful to God, in all those chapters. I think we should also study the "mountain" in these predictions. The literalists would confine the "mountain of the Lord's house" to Moriah, and "Zion" to the hill where David's palace stood. But there is a Zion where Jesus rules. There is a mountain, (or government), on whose glorious summit is the church, or true tabernacle, which the Lord pitched, and not man. The Holy Mountain in (Is. 11:9) is the kingdom of heaven. It has been exalted above the hills," and the Lamb and wolf, the leopard and

kid, the calf, the young lion and the fatling are all companions, and a *child leads them*. This is a *result* pictured by
the change made in beasts. There is nothing to hurt or
to destroy in all *"God's* holy mountain," or government,
ruled over by Christ. It describes but *one* government,
the Governor, and his tamed, docile, teachable, and harm-
less subjects, led, (in disposition) by a little child. This
holy mount reappears in numerous places, (Is. 27:12, 13;
2:1-5; Mic. 4; Dan. 2:35; Is. 40). John the Baptist
LEVELLED the *hills*, exalted the *valleys* and *prepared* a
highway for our God. In (Is. 35) there is "The highway
of holiness," the unclean shall not pass over it, neither
the lion nor any ravenous beast. Waters shall break out
in the wilderness and streams in the desert. "This
mountain of the Lord's house," *exalted* above the hills,
established in the *top* of the *mountains, all nations* flowing
unto this house, to be *taught* the Lord's ways, to *walk* in
his paths, are ideals, not literal hills, and houses. The
law to go forth from *Zion*, and word of the Lord from
Jerusalem, were gospel promises, redeemed by Christ.
In the last chapter of Joel there is Zion, Jerusalem,
mountains, an earthquake, then God dwelling in Zion,
his holy mountain, and no strangers passing through.
There is a *fountain* comes forth from the *house of the
Lord*: Edom and Judah, enemies of Israel, shall be desolate, but Judah shall dwell forever, and Jerusalem from
generation to generation.

In (Zech. 14), the *mountains* are *levelled*, the *valleys
exalted* "the mountain of the Lord's house" the highest
point, all the rest a *plain*. The living waters flow as
rivers towards the seas, both in summer and in winter.
"And the Lord shall be king over all the earth: in that
day shall there be one Lord, and his name one." In
(Ezek. 47) the waters flow from the *house of the Lord*,
from under the *altar*, growing deeper, wider, healing the
land, quickening the dead sea (of humanity). On its
banks are trees that nourish and heal the nations. In
(Ps. 2) it is the same "holy hill of Zion," Jesus as ruler,
the Gentiles his inheritance. In (Ps. 72) the king rules
from sea to sea and from the rivers to the ends of the
earth.

He shall judge thy people with righteousness, and

thy poor with Judgment. The *mountains shall bring peace to the people*, and the *little hills* by righteousness. He shall judge the poor of the people, he shall save the children of the needy, and shall break in pieces the oppressor. They shall fear thee as long as the sun and moon endure, throughout all generations. He shall come down *like rain* upon the mown grass; as showers that water the earth."

"His name shall endure forever; his name shall be continued as long as the sun; and men shall be blessed in him; all nations shall call him blessed. Blessed be the Lord God, the God of Israel, who only doeth wondrous things. And blessed be his glorious name forever; and let the whole earth be filled with his glory; Amen and Amen. The prayers of David the son of Jesse are ended."

Thus all the prophets close their life's work, and their predictions, with glowing accounts of the future of the ransomed of the Lord. It robs these matchless prophecies of their beauty and power to confine them to a narrow literalism, and make mountains, rivers, seas, deserts, temples, sacrifices an the like to be the things in mind. The arguments submitted in this volume are an humble contribution to the end of enlightening the earnest students of the Bible on the nature of Israel ancient and modern, or typical and anti-typical, and to draw the lines between the former inheritance and the latter. This has been considered vital to the removal of the speculating, romancing method of the Millennialists, who would reproduce Judaism, enlarged, and have the law of Moses and the gospel of Christ in operation at the same time. This is to subvert the hearer. The gospel has superseded the law, and the ceremonies of the typical age are now *recorded* types only. The reader should do himself the justice to note this fact. As the *types* were once *realities, in operation in fleshly Israel*; that is the King, the army of priests, the holy house, the animal sacrifices, the feasts, the occupancy of the land, with miracles to maintain Israel's stay therein, and to *bless* them temporally for obedience, and to *curse* them for disobedience, and all these *things* passed away when the gospel was proclaimed to Israel, you know they were *legislated away forever*. But they were *types* in *action* until Christ took them out of the way. Since then they are *written* types only. This fact understood, we are com-

pelled to interpret the *prophecies* in HARMONY WITH
THESE FACTS, to be consistent. Hence the prophecies
that foretold gospel blessings under the *names of these
types* were Type-Prophecies, that is using the types as
prophecies, (which every type was by its very nature and
use). To ignore this fact and assume that the prophecies are to be fulfilled *literally* is to assume that the *types*
were *not types*, but to be realities under the gospel age,
the same as under the law of Moses. This contradicts
the whole history of the use Christ and the apostles made
of them, and encourages the Jews, (who are in rebellion
against God, because in enmity against Christ), to hope
to see this old system revived. All of which is strictly
contrary to revelation. There can be no such carnal,
fleshly Millennium, as these romancers picture, without
the types; and as the types are set aside forever by the
gospel, the sooner the professed people of God discard
the Jewish traditions and Jewish hope, and unitedly exalt
Christ as King; his church as the temple; his people as
the holy nation; Jerusalem above as our great Capital;
the Zion upon which he sits as the majestic government
of God; and his rule co-extensive with the whole earth
and all time, the better for the sin-sick millions of our
race. As the fleshly King, material temple, animal sacrifices, annual feasts, and the whole system of Jewish ordinances, were never anything but types, even in Moses'
day, and during the continuance of their lawful observance by fleshly Israel, to us they are now *written types.*
To assume, as the Jews do, that they are to be *revived* and
the gospel *ignored* is blindness and perverseness. To
grant the Jew that the gospel is ever to cease, while time
lasts, and the world stands, and that these TYPICAL
things shall be RESTORED by CHRIST and the *resurrected martyrs for* (1000) *years* is to read the prophecies
and types with a veil over our hearts. But this veil is
done away in Christ. In him we have the reality, which
all the types foretold as types, and the prophecies foretold in Type-Prophecies. As certainly as the types are
never to be restored, just that confident we should be
that all the Type-Prophecies are to be interpreted figuratively; as it is impossible to interpret them literally

and not assume that the types are to be revived and continue forever.

CONSOLATION AND HOPE.

In (Chs. 33 to 48) Israel has hope. The judgments of God were vindicated against the sinful nations, and now the prophet directs their attention to the future. The *doctrine* had not changed. God would deal with the *Remnant* as he had with their fathers. A whole nation may be swept away as were the children of Israel, but God's holiness and justice demanded of their children *obedience* if they were to enjoy his favor. The prophet's mission, therefore, was still to *warn against sin*. Compare the third chapter where he was sent to the rebellious house of Israel before the captivity, with the thirty-third chapter where his mouth was opened again to Israel seven years later, when his first series of predictions had been turned into lamentable history.

I repeat, if the seven days' dumbness had any prophetic meaning it was now fulfilled, for seven years had rolled by, and surely the little book, containing "lamentation, mourning and woe" had been fulfilled in the frightful history of those seven years. To pass this by and make these illustrations to foretell the history of Israel for (2520) years is so unwarranted as to method of interpretation, and takes such daring liberties with the language of the prophet, as to be unworthy of confidence for a moment.

Chapter 35 shows Edom in perpetual desolation for their enmity against Israel, that is against God, as shown in the chapter on the Edomites.

In (Ch. 36) Israel was contrasted with Edom and all the enemies of God who had joined hand in hand against her, and the mountains of Israel were to be reoccupied, the land tilled and sown, and the nation rejoice in their ancient possessions, all of which they did after the seventy years' captivity.

RESURRECTION FIGURE.

Chapter 37 pictured a "valley of dry bones." Under the thrilling picture of a resurrection of bones, very many and very dry, the revival of the nation is set forth. The next predicted event for Judah and Israel was to make the nation over again. They were to be united in an undying fellowship, under a new king. Ephraim and Judah as two sticks, were to become one stick, one people, under David. He was to make a new covenant with them, a covenant of peace, and be their prince forever. He was to build a sanctuary in their midst, and God would dwell with them forevermore. I think no Christian can doubt that all this was accomplished in Christ when he came to earth and sought out the lost sheep of the house of Israel. The twelve tribes were blended with the Gentiles into one harmonious family. No tribe of Israel was discriminated against, and even we sinful Gentiles were gathered into the Fold of Christ, and there was one fold and one Shepherd. Not all the decendants of Abraham accepted the gospel call, but it was extended to all; all Gentiles were eligible also, but not all accept of the proffered mercy. The Lord has done his part. The way is provided. And all may come to him as the "great Shepherd of the Sheep, through the blood of the everlasting covenant." In (chs. 38 to 39) there is an obscure prediction, evidently relating to the future, and not sufficiently fulfilled to be identified in history. The (40th to 48th chs) give us *the vision* of a *city* and *temple*. When we recall that Jerusalem and the temple were then in ruins, but destined to be rebuilt, we may consider the vision helpful at that time to fleshly Israel. The fact that the "Glory of God" returned to this city and temple (43:1-7) shows that God's favor would return to Israel upon repentance and restoration to their land and city and when their temple was rebuilt. As *in vision* God was seen *leaving* the *temple* and *city* in the *first chapters*. He is seen, *in vision*, *returning* in this chapter. These things have a figurative meaning, and are therefore helpful to spiritual Israel, in showing us the *high mountain*, the *temple* of God, the *enlarged* capital, the *fountain* of living water emanating from the altar, (or cross of Christ), and, as all types are now done away, we love to drink of this pellucid stream, whose soul renovating waters grow deeper and wider as the ages roll by. On the banks of the dead sea of humanity we love to cast the gospel net and be "fishers of men," who have been quickened, and to drink freely of the water of life. In the morning of life one may think the stream is only ankle deep. In young manhood, as mentality expands, one learns the stream is knee deep. In mature manhood he has sunken deeper in its clear flowing depths, even to the waist. In old age, as one looks out over the broad expanse, it is one all-compassing river, wide and deep as the sea of God's love and mercy that can not be measured nor fathomed, and over whose ample surface no human mind can pass. O that we may ever have the exhaustless blessings of God! I think the Psalmist had the picture of this city and river in mind when he said,

"God is our refuge and strength, a very present help in trouble. Therefore will we not fear, though the earth be removed, and though the mountains be carried into the depths of the sea: though the waters thereof roar and be troubled, though the mountains shake with the swelling thereof. There is a river, the streams whereof shall make glad the city of God, the holy place of the tabernacle of the most High. God is in the midst of her; she shall not be moved; God shall help her and that right early." (Ps. 46:1-5). And John in closing the final message to us in (Rev. 21 and 22 ch's) pictures forth the joys and enduring blessedness of that city which hath foundations, whose builder and maker is God. If you desire an interest in that home of the soul, read those chapters, and open your heart to receive their holy message, and let us cultivate that soul hunger and thirst after righteousness which heaven alone can satisfy.

CHAPTER XXIV.

SYMBOLS IN REVELATION.

The book of Revelation is a book of prophecy expressed mostly in symbols. Jesus SIGNIFIED these things to John. This fundamental fact should not be lost sight of in reading the volume; for, as it is written in these signs, if we do not study the symbols we will not get the meaning of the writer. The types of the Tabernacle; the solar system; the animal kingdom; the vegetable kingdom; as well as the numbers used in the book are generally used in the Sign Language. One of each of the groups or families of symbols is defined in the Bible, and many of them by John. The candlestick is a symbol of the church, and stars symbols of great men and rulers (1:20). This is an inspired definition, and we should give them no other meaning in the symbolic portions of the book. The sun, moon and stars are associated together in nature, and are associated together in symbolism; hence when one member of the group is defined, we should use all the members of the group in harmony with it. The candlestick is simply one member of a family of types, and as it is used in the book as a symbol of something else (the church); then the temple, altar, censers, incense, fire from the altar, and the furniture throughout are symbolic in harmony with it. The wild beasts are symbols, and literalism shocks our common sense here. The seven-horned and two-horned lambs are symbols, and SIGNIFY not themselves, but realities to be discovered. As none of these beasts ever had any existence as real animals, we are to identify the governments they signify. This is easy in Revelation as Daniel had taught us the only proper use to be made of them. Revelation is largely an inspired commentary on Daniel. The numbers, associated with the beasts, are used in the same figurative manner in this volume; are, indeed, the same numbers, in the long count that Daniel gave us. (1260) days for a government are too short a time; as (1260) years for a beast is too long a life; so the beast signifies a government; the days signify its lifetime: (this on the year day rule as given by Ezekiel (4: 4-6). The time is expressed as "time, times and the dividing of time"; or as "forty and two months"; as "a thousand two hundred and three score days"; and as "an hour, a day, a month and a year"; all of which indicate that the writer was not expressing time in literal language, but used figurative numbers to correspond to his figurative beasts and symbols.

For instance, James says, "It rained not on the earth for three years and six months." (Jas. 5:17). David reigned seven years and six months. This is the Scriptural manner of expressing *literal* time.

The vegetable kingdom is used symbolically all through the Bible. Men are trees, good or bad; they grow on the river bank, or in the desert; bring forth fruit or are dead and plucked up by the roots. The great tree in (Dan'l. 4) is used by the historic expositors to determine the time of the Gentiles, (2520) years; that is, it pictured the seven years of Nebuchadnezzar's insanity, (or 2520 days); he was then restored to his throne and kingdom; this is used as God's chosen type of Gentile dominion (2520 years), enlarging the days by the year day rule used by Ezekiel in his Type-Prophecy. (Ezek. 4:4-6).

Pharaoh's two dreams of famine under two sets of symbols, are good illustrations. Fat cattle is a good symbol of plenty; lean cattle of famine; good ears are clear symbols of plenty, and blasted ears of famine; but seven ears of corn *eating* seven ears of corn, and seven lean cattle *devouring* seven fat cattle, could only be used as symbols for predictive purposes: never as historic realities. So a woman clothed with the sun, having the moon under her feet, crowned with twelve stars, is beautiful symbolism: but could never be a literal transaction. A scarlet clad woman, seated on a seven-headed ten-horned beast, a cup in her hand, all nations drinking and drunken from the wine in her cup, symbolized a reality: but was not a reality. The death and revival of the beast, and death and resurrection of the two witnesses, were similar transactions. A government may die and be revived so one can think of a mortally wounded beast revived to picture the transactions. Death and resurrection can be predicated of men, and so the witnesses die and are alive again. As the beast represented a government, and the witnesses represented a government, each was *signified* in symbols appropriate to their nature and work. Beasts are never resurrected but men are: so the beast was wounded unto death and lived: the witnesses died and were raised from the dead. Each symbol was appropriate; one a beast, (used throughout for a cruel, persecuting government); the witnesses used to represent a persecuted people. Witnesses are martyrs and can appropriately rise from the dead, literally; and hence, figuratively. John had to be in the Spirit to see and hear the symbols. He saw candlesticks, stars, horses, riders, bows, swords, thrones, crowns, mountains, seas, rivers, beasts, dragon, kings, priests, censers, incense, fire, temple, courts, altars, books, seals, smoke, pits, locusts, chains, resurrections and the like, and heard thunder, trumpets, and voices.

I purposely mix the symbols. To bring order out of confusion group them naturally, placing the Holy City, temple, priesthood, sacrifices and all the types of this group in one class: then set the solar system, vegetable kingdom, animal kingdom, and the numbers in their respective groups, the women clothed in *white* or clothed in *scarlet* in their group: the mountains, seas and rivers in their group: and begin your analysis by locating the inspired definition of one member of each group, and you will be edified and gratified. The candlestick and stars are defined (1:20); the waters are defined (17:15). The temple was no more when John wrote; but it had been a type of the church: so he had to use the names of the type OR ELSE NOT WRITE IN SIGNS. If he had been writing like he did in his letters he would have used literal language: but as he was using SIGNS we ought not to think he was using them to mean beast, scorpions, furnaces, smoke, horses, swords, temple, censers and so on throughout; but he defined the symbols by giving us the meaning of one member of each group; and, as one member of the group was figurative, the others have to harmonize with it. This reduces his imagery to its simplest form; as consistency in interpretation demands that we do not deviate from his definitions.

Thus we see that a literal interpretation of Revelation is impossible without violating all the rules of symbolism. If we have learned our lesson, then Type-Prophecies are plain to us; and we will not try to have the literal temple, priesthood, and the like in Revelation; as literal stars falling into literal rivers, or burning mountains falling into seas of literal water; or a literal woman clothed with the sun, crowned with twelve stars, and standing on the moon; nor a literal marriage of this same woman later; nor a literal death and resurrection of this same woman. We will not think of a literal seven headed, seven-horned beast persecuting her. In a word we will escape the crudities and ambiguities of a literal interpretation; will not make John's rules of interpretation of no effect; but will allow the symbols of this book to harmonize with the same and similar symbols in the prophecies of the Old Testament.

It may be seen that we are face to face with the strangest assortment of awe-inspiring miracles, monster beasts, and monstrosities among trees, women, horses, swords, and all the imagery mentioned; or else all these things are symbols. John says these things SIGNIFY other things. So I am content to go through with the whole group of monsters, viewing them all as symbols. The Solar system is a family of signs; the vegetable kingdom is a family of signs; the animal kingdom contributes its group; and the "numbers" are expressed in figurative manner to correspond therewith. The types were used by the Old Testament prophets; and as they are all fulfilled in their anti-types in the New Testament, and can never be revived, they can only appear in Revelation as signs of higher realities.

In other words, we must interpret these Signs as we do the Type-Prophecies; for, it is self-evident that, the types are no more predicted in John's writing than they are in any other book of prophecy, relating to the gospel age. Revelation is not a new system; but a development of an old system of prophecy, and necessarily conforms to the rules of interpreting symbols that were in use before his day. Revelation is not a plea for a material temple, Aaronic priesthood, animal sacrifices and the like; but is the last use in the Bible of the well-established rule of the prophets in *signifying* the spiritual realities of the gospel in the name of the types of the former age, or as Type-Prophecies.

John did not look down the ages and see a mountain fall into the sea in Europe, Asia, Africa or America. He did not witness a literal star leave its orbit, and fall upon literal rivers and fountains of waters and embitter them, as that would make him contradict his inspired definition of the symbolic use of rivers, seas and stars. There has been no such literal disturbances among the mountains, seas, rivers and stars, and such physical convulsions are not contemplated in his well chosen symbolism. If one cares to indulge the fancy, and revel in the imaginative, very wild, wierd, and grotesque physical displacements may be conjured up to appall the reader. But you will observe that the stars fell to the earth; the heavens were removed as a scroll; and every mountain and island were moved out of their places; under the *sixth seal* (ch. 6: 14). But John goes right on with his predictions of the things under the *seventh seal*, and you notice the mountains, seas, rivers, stars are still intact under this seal for (ch. 8) was under the seventh seal. Any literalist will find it difficult to understand how the stars and heavens, mountains and islands could all be removed, and still be here; and mountains and stars still falling into seas and rivers, as before. If you will take heed to John when he tells you these things only *signify* other things, or observe caution not to make a literal transaction out of a symoblic action, you will save yourself the humiliation of contradicting the prophet; and the embarrassment of making him contradict the former prophets; will avoid the dreamland and mysticism of the speculator; and will arrive at the truth concerning the things *signified* as they are turned into *history*. HE TELLS US WHAT STARS AND WATERS MEAN IN HIS SIGN LANGUAGE. DO WE BELIEVE HE KNEW?

NAME "SYMBOL" JUSTIFIED.

Some critics object to the use of the word "symbol,"

because it is not in the Bible. The laws of figurative language are given in a work before me. It gives an enumeration and definition of the figures—comparison, metaphor, metonomy, synecdoche, hyperbole, hypocatastasis, apostrophe, personation, allegory or parable—nine figures. Some of these are *named*, all of them are *used* by the sacred writers. The fact that the writers used them, is sufficient. They did not teach grammar, or rhetoric, but they employed both. Any student of the Bible has to know figurative language or be confused, rather than edified, by its use, as all the figures of speech abound therein, especially in the prophecies. It is as necessary to understand the Scripture use of symbols, as it is to understand the use of parables and allegories. "This is my body," is an illustration. "I am the vine, ye are the branches; Jehovah is my rock, and my fortress and my deliverer." The agents, actions and results attributed to symbols, illustrate agents, actions and results in the things symbolized. The prophecy is thus inseparable from the symbols.

TO ILLUSTRATE SOME PROPHECIES.

1. Pharaoh's dream. (Gen. 41). Seven fat kine were eaten by seven lean kine and the lean kine were as ill-favored as before. Seven thin ears devoured seven good ears. Here are agents, actions and results shown in symbols. Seven fat kine and seven good ears *signify* seven plenteous years. Seven lean kine, and seven blasted ears, eating up the fat kine and good ears, respectively symbolize the seven years of famine—"and the famine shall consume the land. And the plenty shall not be known in the land by reason of that famine following; for it shall be very grievous." Here corresponding agents, actions and results fulfilled the prophecy in the symbols.

2. Nebuchadnezzar's dream. Here was a composite metallic man, with artificial division into golden head, silver breast and arms, brazen body, legs of iron, feet part of iron, part of clay. This image was smitten on his feet by a stone. Result; the whole image ground to pieces and swept away, and the stone became a great mountain and filled the whole earth. The image and

stone were lifeless. But they were symbols only. Despotic, cruel, idolatrous governments, dashed to pieces and swept away by the action of the things symbolized by the stone and wind, followed by a new form of the stone, or a government set up by the Almighty, never to be destroyed, were SIGNIFIED. WE SHOULD KNOW, HOWEVER, THAT A HEATHEN, DESPOTIC GOVERNMENT CAN BE DESTROYED BY SUPPLANTING ITS IDOLATRY AND MISRULE WITH PURE PRINCIPLES IN CHURCH AND STATE. Not a vestige of the image was left; but the *people* were *not* destroyed. What heathenism needs, and what despotism in church and state needs, *are in the stone.* The symbols indicate, and the inspired writer promises, annihilation for despotism, and the substitution of righteous rule. (Dan. 2).

3. The four wild beasts, the fourth with ten horns, followed by another little horn, which plucks up three of the ten horns, has eyes and a mouth, are plain symbols. We see Babylon, Medo-Persia, Greece and Rome, as governments, come up in history in the order of time suggested. The fourth kingdom was divided into ten parts. The eleventh horn, the papacy, plucked up three of the ten governments *into which* the Western Roman Empire was divided. The papacy had eyes, (wisdom), a mouth, (assumed authority human and divine); and was a persecuting power. The fire consumed the beast. So the corresponding results must follow the Roman Empire in its ten fold division, and the little government that succeeded then as well. (Dan. 7). The agents, actions, and results, in symbols, demand corresponding agents, actions and results, in the governments symbolized.

The symbol of the stone destroying the image by smiting it ON THE FEET, and the symbol of fire destroying the beast with eleven horns, AFTER the exploits of the little horn, demand that despotism, symbolized in both cases, be overthrown AFTER THE GOVERNMENT OF ROME has run its course through the *ten* kingdoms and the *little* kingdom (politically) and be FOLLOWED by the RULE OF THE PEOPLE OF THE SAINTS. The agents, actions and results set forth in symbol are prophetic of agents, actions and results in the things symbolized.

4.   The candlestick is a great light-bearer, physically, and the church is a great light-bearer spiritually; hence it is a beautiful symbol of the church.

5.   Stars are great dispensers of light, while night broods over the earth, and are symbols of the light of great men in church or state; while the sun is the ruler of the day, and the moon the ruler of the night. The symbols used in Revelation can be better understood by considering them in the chapters in which they occur. It is no part of my design to write a commentary on the whole book, hence I have made this extended notice of the use we should make of the symbols, for it applies with equal force to all parts where they occur, whether in the sections we notice or elsewhere. Be it known, however, that the groups of symbols which pass under review in this volume, are those which set forth the prophecy of the rise, growth, maturity, decline and overthrow of the great apostasy. This fact established and we have little need to contend over what is not reviewed, for it has no direct bearing on the subjects before us. Ever remember that the symbols, and the things symbolized, each have an existence independent of the other. The church would have had the same experiences, it has had, if it had never been foretold either literally or symbolically; just as a person may exist if he never had his picture taken.

CHAPTER XXV.

THE OPENING MESSAGE.

When a symbol is used, the first duty of the expositor is to learn the meaning of the symbol, heaven's inspired meaning, for one can not take the first step as an expositor, and adhere to the truth, without he knows the definition of the symbol. This is true of all the symbolic prophecies, and especially so of Revelation, which is composed almost wholly of symbols. The symbol is not the thing signified any more than the pattern of the tabernacle was the tabernacle; or the pattern of the temple, given to David, was the literal temple built by Solomon. Even the tabernacle and temple when built were not the THINGS TYPIFIED. The Jews clung to the types and overlooked the realities. A map of a country is not the country; a geography is not the earth; and the blue-print of a house is not the house. The star seen through a telescope is just as much a star without a telescope, although invisibile. The things predicted in symbol were real, but the symbols were only pictures of them. The beasts, horns, eyes, and the like, were not the kingdoms they were used to describe; but signified or symbolized them. A naturalist has no use for the four wild beasts in Daniel's vision (Dan'l 7) nor for the beasts in Revelation. A physiologist or anatomist would find nothing in harmony with his study of the giant, metallic man in (Dan'l 2). It would be a baseless assumption to treat the composite beasts in Revelation as realities either ancient or modern, and would lead one far from the truth. The realities are set forth by the use of symbols. To get at the truth one must read the definition of the symbol into the interpretation. The following exposition of the prophecy is governed throughout on this principle.

"The Revelation of Jesus Christ which God gave unto him, to show unto his servants things which must shortly come to pass; and he sent and SIGNIFIED it by his angel unto his servant John.   Who bore record of the word of God, and of the testimony of Jesus Christ, and of all things that he saw. Blessed is he that readeth and they that hear the words of this prophecy, and keep those things which are written therein, for the time is at hand.'' (1:1-3).

Here are mentioned God, Christ, his angel, his servant John, other servants and all who read and obey the requirements of the King.   The book begins as it ends, showing us how to obtain the "Blessing" in Jesus Christ, (22:14).   One should read (Matt. 5:16; Acts. 3:25, 26) and learn how Jesus proposes to "bless' everyone in turning him away from his iniquities.   Can he "bless" them in iniquity?   John limits the "blessing" to the obedient; Peter limits it to the obedient; and so does our Saviour.

VERSES 4-8.

In these verses are mentioned seven Asiatic churches, the Everlasting Being, the seven Spirits before his throne and the Lord Jesus Christ.   There is but one spirit of God (Eph. 4:4) hence perfection is *signified* here by the numeral seven.   Jesus is described as the faithful witness, just as he spake of himself (Jno. 18:37); and Paul spake of him (II Tim. 2:11-13; I Tim. 6:13).   He is the first begotten from the dead, the Prince of the Kings of the earth.   In his blood, John and the churches he addressed, had been washed from their sins. THEY WERE MADE A KINGDOM AND PRIESTS UNTO GOD, but the Glory and the dominion belong unto him forever and ever. This thought of the kingdom is fundamental in this prophecy as it was in the Old Testament prophecies. When we reach John's times "David" had come and set up, in the hearts and lives of his disciples, his kingdom or rule. Daniel (2:44) was then fulfilled, as to the establishment of the kingdom, although its perpetuity is endless.   Mr. C. T. Russell and his class deny that the kingdom was set up by Christ or his apostles.   He "proclaims" that Jesus came back to earth in a spirit-body (A. D. 1874); raised up the saints in (A. D. 1878); and is setting up the Millennial kingdom now.   "Thy Kingdom Come. pp. 302-6."

I read of some, "Who concerning the truth have erred saying that the resurerction is past already; and overthrow the faith of some." (II Tim. 2:18). Paul styles this a gangrene; mortification is eating up any man's faith who accepts this teaching. Mr. Russell set the time for Christ's return in Octotber, (1874), but the Lord ignored his almanac, (as he always does when men set the time for him), and did not come or even send a Lazarus back to warn men. They have Moses, the prophets and apostles, let them hear them, not pervert them. Mr. Russell says, O yes! he came secretly, so did all the saints three and one half years later; they are here and the Millennium has been running full blast for thirty-six years. The Savior said,

"For there shall arise *false* Christs and *false* prophets, and shall show great signs and wonders; so as to lead astray if posibile even the elect. BEHOLD I HAVE TOLD YOU BEFORE. If therefore they say unto you, Behold he is in the inner chambers; believe it not. For as the lightning cometh out of the east, and shineth even unto the west; so shall be the coming of the Son of Man." (Matt. 24:24-27).

This one statement from Jesus Christ is enough to destroy the whole Millennial theory. The lightning comes on no *secret* errand. IT CAN NOT BE HID. Neither does it *halt* and *hesitate* for forty years. It is visibile and immediate in manifestation. O yes; but Jesus is visible to the mental eye, they tell us. Well, I observe that the Charles C. Cook literature, being sowed broadcast, holds to the idea that, 1. Christ comes FOR his saints, raises the dead, changes the living saints and they meet him in the air, for an indefinte stay (probably *seven years*, Daniel's seventieth week); then he comes WITH the saints, and his feet stand on Mt. Olive. These Literalists are about the strongest religious opponents Mr. Russell has, and their literature denounces his system radically. I heard once that a pot called a kettle black. They both teach that Jesus comes *secretly* (as a thief) *for* his saints; Mr. Russell has the events passed forty years (Oct 10, 1914); the Futurists are expecting him any minute. Jesus says *false* prophets will say he COMES SECRETLY. So I group the whole bunch under the phrase *false prophets*. If Rome, in "forbidding to marry and commanding to obstain from meats," is proven to be the *apostate church*, are not the Dawnists and Futurists

proven to be the *false prophets* when they teach either
that Jesus has been here secretly for forty years, or that
he is to come secretly any day soon? My mental eyes
do not see Him, and I have no acquaintance with any
one WHO EXPECTS TO SEE HIM MENTALLY ONLY,
when he comes (except a few Dawnists and Futurists who
are blinded by a theory, or an old Jewish tradition). My
Book says he will come as he went away (Acts 1:11).
That was *visibly* TO THE PHYSICAL EYES OF MEN, they
GAZED after HIM, WATCHED HIM, as HE went up.
Read that text and be convinced that it was an *ascent*
visible to men; and his coming is to be *like* it, and will be
a *visible descent*. Did a single disciple ever talk to him,
see him, gaze on him, watch him in the clouds of heaven,
in (A. D. 1874)? "Pastor Russell" says, he is now
invisible, men in the flesh could not see his spirit-body.
When did he become invisible, when *near to* or on *earth*?
He was not invisible to Stephen (Acts 7); nor to Saul
of Tarsus, (Acts 9). The trouble with Mr. Russell is
his MENTAL VISION IS DEFLECTED, and he is trying
to see Jesus, when he is NOT HERE. His "Divine Plan
of the Ages" should be called "Human and Erroneous
Plan of the Ages." If Jesus went away visibly and returned invisibly, then he did not come as he went. But
he said *false prophets* will say I am here secretly, believe
them not. Behold I have told you before. So Mr. Russell's theory is false. And to be paying him money and
supporting him in deceiving the people, is, on this showing, to be aiding a false prophet, when Jesus tells you
thus plainly not to believe him. The same remark justly
applies to all who tell you that Jesus ever did or ever will
come to earth *secretly*. If the lesson was good for the
disciples at the destruction of Jerusalem, it is none the
less saving at all other times. It is immaterial how many
"Signs of the Times" are produced; how many wars, famines, pestilences or earthquakes occur; how profane the
world, or how ungodly the churches; or how energetic
the advocates of Jesus' invisible presence; each and all
are misapplied when given by *false prophets as evidence* of
Jesus' secret presence on earth. All the holy angels will
be with him(Matt. 25:31); and all the saints, (I
Thess. 3:13). Mr. Russell says this is all now turned

into history. Then it was a very quiet affair! No
human eye has seen Jesus, the angels or the saints
Many saw Jesus when he went away; and he will save
you from Pastor Russell's *false* prophecies, also the
false prophecies of the Futurists, who say his *Parousia*
is to be secret, if you will take heed to what he told you
before—do not believe I am returned secrety.

VERSES 9-18.

In these verses, John tells the churches first, who
he is, and, second, what he saw and heard in the Isle or
(Island) of Patmos, on a certain Lord's day. He was
their brother, and companion in the tribulation and kingdom and patience which are in Christ Jesus (not which
shall be in Christ Jesus, when the Millennium begins in
(A. D. 1878). He, like Paul, experienced tribulation in
the kingdom (Acts 14:22); "And, he [Jesus] said to
them all, if any man will come after me, let him deny
himself and take up his cross daily and follow me."
(Luke 9:23). This required patience, for the godly people suffered great persecution from both Jews and Gentiles in the apostolic age. Moreover John was writing
a prophecy of the greatest and most protracted persecutions against the people of God, or the kingdom of heaven,
both by pagan Rome, and Papal Rome, Mahometanism
and other Anti-christian powers; and he was an exile at
the time of the vision, "for the word of God and the
testimony of Jesus. The Lord's day was evidently the
first day of the week, just as the "Lord's table" (I
Cor. 10:21), and "Lord's Supper" (I Cor. 11:20) refer
to the table and the supper that memorialize our Lord's
death for us. His sacrifice gave virtue to the ordinance
of the ("Lord's Supper") and sacredness to the "Lord's
day", the day on which he arose from the dead. He
was in the Spirit, or wrapt in vision, and made acquainted
with the things that follow. It was not simply the normal working of his mind, but he was in the Spirit of
revelation. He heard the great voice as of a trumpet,
(the voice of authority), directing him to write what he
saw, and to send it to the Asiatic churches. Not what he saw
naturally and daily all about him on the rocky island;
but what he saw supernaturally on that Lord's day. So

he turned to see the voice that spake with him,

"And saw seven golden candlesticks, and in the midst of the candlesticks one like unto a son of man, clothed with a garment down to the feet, and girt about the paps with a golden girdle. And his head and his hair were white as white wool, white as snow; and his eyes were as a flame of fire; and his feet like unto burnished brass, as if it had been refined in a furnace; and his voice as the voice of many waters. And he had in his right hand seven stars; and out of his mouth proceeded a sharp two- edged sword; and his countenance was as the sun shining in his strength. And when I saw him I fell at his feet as one dead. And he laid his right hand upon me, saying, fear not; I am the first and the last, and the Living one; and I was dead, and behold I am alive forevermore, and I have the keys of death and Hades."

This is a description of what John saw—seven *golden* candlesticks, a robed and girdled man in their midst, with pure, white hair; his feet beautiful as refined brass; his voice tremendous in depth and power as the ocean's roar; and his eyes bright as flames of fire. Evidently those *eyes* can see in darkness, not only of night, but into the darkest recesses of the heart; and that *voice* can awaken the dead to earth's remotest bounds. That *sword* is the Word of God (Heb. 4:12; Eph. 4:17). There is warmth and life to the saints in his *countenance*. As Aaron said, "The Lord bless thee, and keep thee; the Lord make His face to shine upon thee, and be gracious unto thee; the Lord lift up His COUNTENANCE UPON THEE, AND GIVE THEE PEACE. And they shall put my name upon the children of Israel, and I will bless them." (Num. 6:24-27), "Make thy face to shine upon thy servant; save me for thy mercy's sake." (Ps. 31: 16). "God be merciful unto us, and bless us and cause his face to shine upon us, that thy way may be known upon earth, thy saving health among the nations." (Ps. 67:1-2). "For we preach not ourselves, but Jesus as Lord, and ourselves as your serpent for Jesus' sake. Seeing it is God that said, light shall shine out of darkness, who shined in our hearts, TO GIVE THE LIGHT OF THE KNOWLEDGE OF THE GLORY OF GOD IN THE FACE OF JESUS CHRIST." (II Cor. 4:5, 6).

Next John tells us how overwhelming was the sight, and that the *right hand* of the Living one was laid upon him, while he proclaimed to him his victory over death, not only in his own person, but, prospectively, over all mankind. Keys were used by the apostles. The keys, sword, stars, and candlesticks were all used symbolically. There is a Type-prophecy in the services of Eliakiam (Is. 22:20-25), referring to this power to open and shut, here claimed by our Savior. The word "keys" is used in the sense of power (Matt. 16:19), when Jesus spake to Peter, directly, and to the other apostles, indirectly, of giving them power to open the kingdom of heaven—not some mystical, invisible kingdom; or a kingdom to be set up in the Millennium, but the kingdom which was then "at hand" and, when John wrote, was in being. Jesus had power over *death*, (this affects the body); and Hades, (the place of departed spirits). Jesus is the proven Master of both having raised his body from the sleep of death, and delivered his spirit from Hades.

(VERSE 19.)

"Write therefore the things which thou sawest, and the things which are, and the things which shall come to pass hereafter."

The things which he had seen were not prophetic, necessarily, (that is if we confine the statement to the person whom he had seen;) but, otherwise, the symbols of stars, keys sword, and candlestick have in them elements of prophecy, as they represent or signify persons, actions or effects, to be considered later. However, the verse seems to classify the writing into past, present and future. In this view of the case his first chapter describes what he had seen in preparation for his task of writing. The things "which are" probably meant a divine analysis of the conduct and standing of the seven churches addressed. "And the things which shall come to pass hereafter ,(in any view of the case), were to be the great prophecy which he was thus solemnly, and miraculously, commissioned to write.

VERSE 20.

"The mystery of the seven stars which thou sawest

in my right hand, and the seven golden sandle-sticks. The seven stars are the angels of the seven churches; and the seven candlesticks are seven churches."

Here is an inspired explanation of two of the symbols, candlesticks and stars. Both *signify* men. The candlestick, the congregation; the angel, the rulers or shepherds of the flock. Some have assumed that because but one messenger, or angel, is addressed, in each congregation, that they had but one shepherd or pastor. Ephesus is the first congregation mentioned each time and we know that Ephesus had a plurality of elders. (Acts 20:17-28). The fact that Ephesus had but one angel, the same as the rest of the seven, sets aside the theory, that the pastor was addressed in any of them. Evidently there were elders in every congregation, for this was the apostolic rule. "For this cause left I thee in Crete, that thou shouldest set in order the things that were wanting, and appoint elders in every city as I gave thee charge." (Titus 1:5).

SYMBOLS OF CHRIST.

The reader will see in (Dan'l 7:9) that the God of heaven was described as "the Ancient of days, whose garment was white as snow, and the hair of his head like the pure wool. In (Rev. 1) Jesus is *signified*. As on the Mount of Transfiguration, his *face*, (not an apparition, but his face), did shine as the sun, and his raiment was white as the light," (Matt. 17:2); so here, Jesus appeared in the garb of Prophet, Priest and King. The "sharp two-edged sword" represents his prophetic office, as do the "stars in his right hand"; as a Priest, he walked " in the midst of the seven golden candlesticks;" his robe of royalty, and golden girdle, from which were suspended "the keys of death and hades," picture his kingly power. But when we attempt to literalize these significant symbols, darkness envelopes us thus:

1. There are seven literal candlesticks.

2. There is the literal person of Christ; a literal two-edged sword comes out of his mouth; he holds seven literal heavenly bodies, stars, in his right hand; and has literal keys to death and hades, attached to a literal girdle. He laid that same right hand upon John also. Now in the (20th ver) he calls the seven stars and seven candle

sticks "mystery," and UNFOLDS the "mystery" by saying, "The seven stars are the angels of the seven churches; and the seven candlesticks which thou sawest are
the seven churches." You do not think, for a moment,
that Jesus held the seven messengers in one hand, and
walked up and down among seven Asiatic Churches!
But as churches were the great Spiritual light-bearers
for our Prophet, Priest and King, and the rulers, (under
shepherds), were under the direction and protection
of Christ, they were pictured to John as *stars* in his
hand, contrasted with the *sun* of his *countenance.* This
last verse furnishes the key to the interpretation. Jesus
gave to Peter and the apostles the keys of the Kingdom of
heaven," yet no wooden or metallic keys figured in the
transaction. He gave them power—"But ye shall receive power, when the Holy Spirit is come upon you; and
ye shall be my witnesses both in Jerusalem, and in all
Judea, and Samaria, and unto the utmost parts of the
earth." (Acts 1:8); yet the apostles did not wear literal
keys even as symbols, like the pope of Rome. Jesus
condemned the Jewish lawyers for taking away the "Key
of Knowledge." (Luke 11:52).

Jesus is described symbolically in (ch| 5:5-6) as
"the Lion of the tribe of Judah", and as a Lamb standing,
as if "having been slain, having seven horns and seven
eyes." He is symoblized again (ch. 6:2). "And I saw,
and behold a white horse, and he who sat on him having
a bow; and a crown was given to him; and he went forth
conquering and to conquer." Again in (ch. 19:11-16)
this rider reappears with many crowns, etc. It is Jesus,
"The word of God."

All these instances *signify* much; but they were not
written to give us a mental conception of the personal,
bodily appearance of Christ. He is not literally walking
among candlesticks, stars in his right hand, keys at his
girdle; or standing as a seven-horned, seven-eyed lamb;
or riding a white horse in heaven, a two-edged sword
coming out of his mouth. But each of these descriptions
signify qualities and functions justly applicable to our
Savior. No writer of the New Testament ever gave us
a desription of the body of Christ. We do not know
whether he was tall or short, handsome or homely, or

whether his eyes were dark or blue, gray or brown. The fact that his face shone, in this revelation and when he appeared to Saul of Tarsus, argues nothing as to his bodily presence, for his face shone as the sun in his strength at his Transfiguration before his death. To assume that John described his actual appearance: and that he was literally present to his natural vision, on any of the occasions in Revelation, is to assume that he wore a robe, had a girdle with literal keys attached, carried stars in his hand, had a sword coming out of his mouth; or that he was a Lion; next a peculiar looking lamb with seven horns and seven eyes; or that he was changed back into a man, wore a bloody garment, had on his head many crowns, and some writing on his garment and on his thigh. Moreover he is followed *in heaven* by *saints* on white horses and clothed in spotless white. These things are pictures, it is true, but symbolic pictures, and not what one would expect to see as the literal revelation how Jesus looks. The meaning is deeper than that. The great Prophet, Priest and King lives and rules by his Word, has all power in heaven and in earth, over the living, the dead, and the spirits in hades, and is the atoning Lamb, and the Conquering Lion. He is just as real though unseen (I Peter 1:8) as when on earth. The battles of the church are his. He is among the churches, seeing their labors, witnessing their persecutions, consoling and blessing them, and is head over all things to the church, though he is in heaven. The heavenly Father and the Holy Spirit are interested in the congregations, the called out people; and Jesus has been invested with all rule and authority, all atoning functions, and is able to bring his people out of death and hades and associate them with himself in dominion and glory. All of which are plainly set forth in this imagery, as we find it in the literal teaching of the holy Volume.

CHAPTER XXVI.

THE THRONE SCENE.

The Tabernacle that Moses built and the Temple built by Solomon serve to illustrate many of the great truths of our redemption. A Christian is supposed to be familiar with the typical meaning of the tabernacle, and the use made of it in this book is very instructive. In this chapter are the throne and its Occupant; a rainbow; twenty-four thornes, occupied by twenty-four elders, clad in white raiment, wearing crowns; lightnings, thunderings and voices; seven lamps of fire before the throne; also a sea of glass like crystal; four living creatures full of eyes, with faces borrowed from the human and brute creation, (the wisdom, courage, patience and swiftness of obedience); each living creature having six wings, (Rev. 4).

John saw and heard these symbols. It is evident that in reality there are no thunder-storms, and rainbows in heaven. The living creatures with the face of a lion, a calf, an ox, and a man, full of eyes within and without, and with six wings each, were strange looking creatures. I think the first eleven chapters of Ezekiel give us a fuller view of these creatures. They are also in Isaiah (ch. 6). The chief point to decide in reading this and succeeding chapters is how to interpret the symbols, properly. The VISIONS are ALL PAST, as much so as Ezekiel's lying on his side; or Jeremiah's yokes; or Nebuchadnezzar's dream of the Metallic Man; or Daniel's vision of the four Beasts; or the vision of the Ram and He Goat. These are not reality, but *signify*, or symbolize the reality. The chapter, built up from Tabernacle types largely, shows us God in the Most Holy Place, or (heaven), upon his throne, (The Ark of the Covenant symbolized his throne in Israel).

2. A rainbow, signifying a covenant of peace and mercy, arches the throne.

3. Twenty-four elders are crowned and upon

thrones, clothed in white. Israel had twenty-four courses of priests, who officially drew near to God. They had twelve princes, and the church has twelve apostles; these are Israel's rulers.

The seven lamps signify the Holy Spirit or seven Spirits of God, (seven being the sacred number of perfection). There are not seven Gods, or seven Saviors, or seven Holy Spirits, (Eph. 4:4-6). But the lamb, (ch. 5) has seven eyes, (perfect wisdom); and seven horns (perfect power); and in symbol the spirit is spoken of as seven, as neither God, Christ, the Spirit, nor the people are mentioned by name in the symbols. (I Cor. 12) tells us there are different manifestations, but the same Spirit.

5. Next mention is made of a sea of glass, and the temple sea comes before us as a cleansing type.

6. Israel, in the grand encampment had four standards, and hence there are four living creatures full of eyes, and with six wings and odd faces, or composite creatures; man, lion, ox, and eagle constitute a creature (Ezek. 1); with eyes without and within, and the same qualities are signified here.

EXPOSITION.

Moses desired to see God, "And he said thou canst not see my face: for there shall no man see me, and live," (Ezek. 33:20). John wrote ,"No man hath seen God at any time; the only begotten Son who is in the bosom of the Father, he hath declared him." (Jno. 1: 18). As John survived this vision, and many others, we conclude he did not see God, personally, but only such symbols of his relationship to the people of God as were best calculated to set forth in illustration the reality. We can not assume that John enjoyed a higher degree of intercourse with, and vision of, God than the other apostles. He was "in the Spirit" and saw these things, not that he might draw a pen picture of what he saw, (that we should conclude that these things are really thus and so); but that we should interpret his inspired symbols by other inspired symbols and thus acquired the sense of what was signified. We should not think Jesus looks like a lion, and that he looks like a seven-horned, seven-eyed sheep; this would be to ignore the symbol entirely. Neither should we think the symbolic, living creatures are such monstrosities as a literal interpretation would make them. The visions are all past. They were prophetic. When John saw the lamb with seven horns and seven eyes, no one, I infer, thinks he saw Jesus Christ. He was a lamb while on earth, (in an *anti-typical* sense, Jno. 1:29), yet did not look like a Lion or a Lamb. He was only these for purposes of revelation. He was not standing for his Photograph to show us his outward appearance; but rather was making a revelation of his personality and relationship to the church. To "signify" is to shew by signs, symbols, and not by the reality. The first verse of the book says these things are SIGNS. The realities to be perceived are clothed in the symbols before us. The absurdities of a literal interpretation are manifest, when one thinks seriously. Has there ever been a Beast with seven heads, ten horns, and ten crowns on his horns? Has there ever been a scarlet clad Woman riding such a Beast, with a cup in her hand, out of which all nations drank to drunkenness? Historically, such a Beast and such a Woman exist in John's visions, but only as inspired SIGNS OF REALITIES to follow his day. Hence we are not to labor to picture to ourselves the curious symbols as accurate pictures, but as *elements of prophecy*, revealing attributes and characteristics of the persons or things signified; and all becomes plain. David said: "The Lord is my rock, and my fortress, and my strength, in whom I trust; my buckler, and the horn of my salvation, and my high tower." (Ps. 18:2).

Jesus is our Rock, our Manna, our true Vine, our Paschal Lamb, our Shepherd, our David, our Lion, and our Lamb. In this figurative way we behold him as our all in all.

1. There was a throne, symbol of sovereignty, and One seated thereon. This images forth the uncreated and Holy One who inhabits eternity and presides in high authority over all things. Ezekiel saw, "the *likeness* of a throne, as the appearance of a sapphire stone, and upon the likeness of the throne was the likeness as the appear-

ance of a man above it." (Ezek. 1:26). All *likeness* and *appearance*!

Israel was represented by twelve stones in the breast-plate of the High-Priest. Jasper was the twelfth; and Reuben, Jacob's first-born son, had his name thereon Sardius was the first stone, with Benjamin, the youngest son's name thereon. So the tribes of Israel, represented by gems, are here. And the people of God were thus represented before God formerly. The first stone, (Sardius), was the sixth foundation stone; and Jasper the first in the foundation of the New Jerusalem. (Rev. 21: 19-20), also (Ex. 28:17-20). So this sovereignty is represented as over Israel.

2. And there was a rainbow round about the throne in sight like unto an emerald." The rainbow is the well known token of the covenant of peace and mercy made with Noah. It is composed of the seven primary colors, green predominating. Emerald was Judah's color; and our Ruler, Christ, came of that tribe; so all the merc! and peace arching this throne come from that tribe. The *sign* is just right for all Israel, (spiritual Israel), from the eldest to the youngest to approach God's throne under the covenant of peace in the tribe of Judah, through Christ, our Priest and King.

3. There were twenty-four thrones before the great throne. These were occupied also. The occupants are called "elders" all through the book. The Lord dealt with us through the apostles. They are our rulers, in the sense that they are Ambassadors, have the words of reconciliation and he that is of God heareth them. (II Cor. 5:19-20 and I Jno. 4:6). Jesus gave them authority to "bind" and "loose" on earth and it would be ratified in heaven. The crown is a portable symbol, while the throne is stationary. (Matt. 19:28) is a text in point. We live in the gospel age, the regenerative period. There are just enough thrones, (twelve) for the apostles. You hear much in these days of a "Bride Class' a "Little Flock" as though these thrones were in reserve for them. Who rules the church or Kingdom of God on earth today? God, Christ and the apostles guided by the Holy Spirit. Loose thinking leads to loose practice and many who think they are soon to be elevated into rulers, not only

over the wicked world, but over saints of God in the Millennial Age, are not even loyal *subjects* of our King.

A few plain questions ought to set one right here.

1. Is the regeneration now going? "Not by works of righteousness which we have done, but according to his *mercy he* saved us, by the WASHING OF REGENERA- TION and the renewing of the Holy Spirit, which he shed, (not will shed), on us abundantly through Jesus Christ our Savior; that being justified by his grace, we should be made heirs according to the hope of eternal life." (Titus 3:5-7). The apostles are dead physically, but reigning officially. Their gospel is regenerative and saving, is the power of God unto salvation to every one that believes." They will not abdicate at some imagin- ary date known as a Millennial Era. According to these Speculators who say the resurrection is past, and the Mil- lennium has been in progress (36 years), the "Bride Class" ought to be on their thrones right now.

2. How do the Dawnists know that Jesus came in (A. D. 1874)? How do they know the saints were raised from the dead, as spirit-beings, in(1878)? How do they know the regeneration began in (A. D. 1878)? How do they know they are not a deluded class of visionaries? How do they know that Jesus is present with them, and not in heaven? They know nothing, absolutely nothing, on any of these subjects. It all hinges on interpretation. If they are safe interpreters, let them explain the follow- ing:

How do they know that each creative day was seven thousand years long, no more and no less? Who told them so? How do they know that Adam was created forty-two thousand years after the opening of the first day? How do they know that this world had existed just six thousand years since Adam's creation? God rested on the seventh day; did he rest seven thousand years? If so, he is still resting. Who knows that an- gelic beings ever cohabited with women? Who knows that such contradiction of Jesus Christ who said, (by necessary inference), the angels neither marry nor are given in marriage, makes even decent pictures for a Photo-Drama? Who is it that does not know that Noah took of clean animals by sevens into the Ark? The Photo-Drama says by twos, only. The Photo-Drama has Noah closing the door; the Bible says, God shut him in. The fact is that the Bible doctrine of regeneration has been set aside to make room for some grotesque, imaginary pictures of some imaginary periods or Epochs, before the creation of man and of an imagined Millennium now going on. A greater perversion of the Scriptures has never been written or pictured; and were it not on subjects the most sacred known to humanity would merit caricature and scorn. I question neither the motives nor abilities of the men who advertise themselves as the "International Bible Students Association"; but demand of them a few things occasionally in this work to set honest minds to sober thinking.

4.   There were lightnings and thunderings and voices. In nature these usher in a storm. As the rainbow is symbolic of peace, these signify trouble, for those against whom they are given, (shown later in the book). At Mt. Sinai, they preceded the revelation of the law, with statutes and judgments.

5.   The Holy Spirit was symbolized by seven lamps, and it is the spirit whose seven-fold or perfect spiritual light controls the judgments and mercies proceeding from the throne. God's dealings with mankind are in the broad light of revelation—nothing in the dark.

6.   The sea of glass comes up later in the book also, and signifies the purity of those who stand upon it, as in the type the priests washed at the sacred sea before the temple.

7.   The four living animals represent all Israel in their near approach to God. "Nearest the throne and first in song, man shall his halleluiahs raise, while wondering angels round him throng to swell the chorus of his praise." The four standards of the camp of Israel, included the whole army of the Lord. As the imagery is that of fleshly Israel, evidently the four living creatures are representative of the entire host of redeemed men. They are not angels for (5:8, 9) proclaims that they were redeemed from every tribe, and tongue and people. The four living creatures, and the twenty - four elders, worship God as Creater. "Thou art worthy, O Lord, to receive glory and

honour and power: for thou hast created all things, and for thy pleasure they are and were created." They acknowledge God as Creator and cry thrice holy unto Him day and night. They are, therefore, the intelligent creation of God, who recognize his creation as bespeaking the glory and honour of the Holy One, and they are thankful to Him for their being, realized that man is his crowning creative work, and that he gives to all life and breath and all things.

THE LAMB OF GOD.

In (ch. 5) is pictured the helplessness of men and angels, and the worthiness of Christ to open the seven-sealed book. After Jesus took the book he was worshipped by men and angels in a perfect manner.

1. The book was written within and on the back-side, (outside). Some things are known by nature; and some by revelation. God, as Creator, was known in his works, and was worshipped as Creator in (ch. 4). The invisible things of God, even his eternal power and godhead, are seen in nature. Astronomy, Botany, Geology, Physiology, Chemistry, Mathematics, Natural History and Mental Philosophy all proclaim "the hand that made us is divine." These open pages all testify in hundred-voiced chorus the wisdom and power of the Founder of this universe. Cause and effect, adaptation and design show us that wisdom made and upholds all things. The infinite wisdom and infinite power necessary to make the sun, moon, stars, mountains, seas, and rivers, beasts and man; to adapt light, heat and moisture to the earth; and to make the laws of nature, are neccessities in any consistent view as to why these things are here.

1. There was a sealed book or roll. Each seal represented a period of time, for John saw only so much under each seal, but could not tell what was contained under the next seal till it was loosed. Like the locks of a canal take one through space, so a seal broken, exhibited all under that seal, but nothing that was under the next one, only as they overlapped. For instance, what he saw under the fifth seal was followed appropriately by what he saw under the sixth seal; but we can not reverse them.

2. This book was in the right hand of Him, who sat upon the throne; and, down to (ver. 5), there was no one found able to open the book or look thereon. It was a sealed mystery. The inability and unworthiness of men and angels is first made manifest. There are no inspired prophecies outside the Bible. The magicians were silenced before Joseph and before Moses in Egypt. The Magicians were silent before Nebuchadnezzar and Daniel; and before Belshazzar and Daniel. Sorcery, Witchcraft, spiritualism, Necromancy, and all the wisdom of man can not reveal the future. The good Book says: "Ye know not what shall be on the morrow." The wise will act on this principle and not consult fortune tellers to learn,—they will live many years, succeed in business, marry and live happily, and such like.

3. The Lion of the tribe of Judah, the Root of David, prevailed to open the book, and to loose the seven seals thereof. This is a fulfillment of Moses; and Isaiah's prophecies concerning Christ.

4. Next comes this person for special notice. He is a slain, but revived lamb, typified by the two goats on the day of atonement (Rev. 16), one slain, the other preserved alive. He has seven horns, symbols of perfect, or infinite power. (I Sam'l 2:1; Ps. 18:2). He has seven eyes symbols of wisdom, especially of wise government and direction. (Num. 10:31). Here the eyes of this lamb are seven as he is unto us "wisdom, righteousness, sanctification and redemption." He is both the knowledge of God and the wisdom of God, and had the Spirit of God without measure. Jesus was not like an inspired man who knew in a measure, or in part; but he spake that he knew and testified that he had seen.

THE WHOLE SCENE.

1. God is upon the throne.
2. The Lamb is next to God.
3. The living creatures, are next in order.
4. The next are the twenty-four elders.
5. These were representative of the vast congregation of every kindred, tongue, people and nation that constitute the kingdom and priests, and reign with Jesus on earth.

6. And back of these are the myriads of angels saying with a loud voice "Worthy is the Lamb that was slain to receive power, and riches, and wisdom, and strength, and honor, and glory, and blessing"; seven things, or perfect worship. "And again, when he bringeth the first begotten into the world he saith, and let all the angels of God worship him." (Heb. 1:6). The loud-voiced chorus of heaven and earth cried—"Blessing, and honour, and glory and power, be unto him that sitteth upon the throne and to the Lamb forever and ever." The living creatures, representing the whole host of God redeemed by Christ, said Amen. And the twenty-four elders fell down and worshipped him that liveth forever and ever.

You notice the beginning of this universal honor to Christ as our Redeemer began in (ver. 8), when he took the book. Vials full of incense is interpreted to mean "the prayers of the saints;" just as the candlesticks were the churches; and the stars were the angels of the chruches. (See Ps. 141:2). It was the prayers of God's people and their praises in song, (for harps evidently symbolized the new song, as incense symbolized the prayers). The figures are well known as they were used in the Jewish temple worship, and a TYPE NEVER TYPI-FIES ITSELF. Incense did not typify incense, and harps did not typify harps, and the lambs did not typify literal lambs. But, in Revelation, the realities are spoken of in the NAMES OF THE TYPES, but always under the rule given (ch. 1:1, and interpreted 1:20) that they are *signs*.

So we have,

1. A sacrificed lamb *signified* Christ.
2. Incense *signified* prayers.
3. Harps *signified* songs of praise.
4. Stars *signified* prominent men.
5. Sharp two-edged sword *signified* the word of God.
6. Candlestick *signified* the church.
7. Seven eyes of the Lamb *signified* perfect wisdom.
8. Seven horns of the Lamb *signified* perfect power.
9. Keys of Hades and of death *signified* authority over them.
10. The Lion *signified* the Ruler in Judah.

Reduce the symbols to literal characteristics of the persons, places or things predicted by them and the document yields its great teaching, to the reverent hearts of God's people. Some times the signs are explained; and, in other instances, they are made plain by the events themselves. See how the song, begun by the church, was taken up, IN PARTS by the angels, and was re-echoed BY THE WHOLE CREATION.

"And madest them to be unto our God a kingdom and priests; and they reign upon the earth." (Ver. 10). If the American Revision is correct, this *class* were reigning at the opening of the Revelation, as well as in (Rev. 20th ch). Not they SHALL reign after the first resurrection! You observe they were a kingdom and priests, just what reappears(11:17; 2:26-27; 3:21; 20:4-6; I Cor. 6:2-3).

"Now, therefore, if ye will obey my voice indeed, and keep my covenant, then ye shall be a peculiar treasure unto me above all people; for all the earth is mine. And ye shall be a kingdom of priests, and an holy nation. These are the words which thou shalt speak unto the children of Israel." (Ex. 19; 5-6). This was God's Kingdom, and he was ever its INVISIBLE Ruler. Jesus is NOW King over the Kingdom of grace and is INVISIBLE. We have positive assurance that this was a "new song." Under the Old Covenant they worshipped God, but not Christ. After the Lamb was slain, raised from the dead, exalted to the right hand of the Father, and by the ministry of the word of reconciliation gathered near to God the cleansed sinners, and ruled over them as his kingdom, their prayers were acceptable to God, and their praises of him day and night were such as God accepted through the power and worthiness of Christ. In the former chapter, God was worshipped as Creator; in this chapter, the holy Redeemer represented by the slain Lamb, drew near to God for us, and gathered from all nations adoring multitudes, which evoked from myriads of angels such a song of praise as was never known before that time. "I say unto you, that likewise, joy shall be in heaven over one sinner that repenteth, more than over ninety and nine just persons, who need no repentance." (Luke 15:17).

The living creatures, full of eyes within and without, were qualified to examine themselves internally and
externally. They looked beneath the exterior, or mere
profession. They were enabled to watch their thoughts,
desires, purposes and affections. They did not draw
nigh to God, (as they symbolically do), while their
HEARTS WERE FAR FROM HIM. They did not make
clean the outside of the cup and the platter and leave
the extortion and excess within. They did not outwardly
appear righteous unto men, but inwardly remain full of
hypocrisy and iniquity. Their introspection was as necessary as their external vision, and thus we learn how
they got the victory and were Overcomers.

CHAPTER XXVII.

TEST PROPHECIES AND SEVEN SEALS.

1.   As I showed from Amos, (Ch. 9), from Hosea,
(3:5,5) Jeremiah (23:5, 6; 33:15-18 also 30:9); Ezek.
(34:23-25; 37:20-28; Ps. 89), to which should be added
Zech. (14:16-21) that the prophets predicted that:

1.   David would occupy the throne of Israel forever.

2.   He would rebuild the tabernacle of David which
was fallen down.

3.   God would place his sanctuary among the Israelites *forever*.

4.   He would make with them an *everlasting* covenant, even the sure mercies of David.

5.   Levi should *exist forever* and serve in the Priesthood.   (See Is. 66:21).

6.   The Burnt offerings, meal offerings and continual offerings shall be made upon God's altar forever.

7.   The Feast of Tabernacles shall be observed annually in Jerusalem *by all nations*.

*These seven items are predicted as belonging to the
gospe*l *age.* The literalist says, of course, they belong
to the Millennium. It is evident that not one of the

seven items has been in existence on the earth for nearly nineteen centuries, now and the whole matter to be decided is this—do the prophets foretell the *endless* use of these former *types*? One says, "You treated that subject in your examination of the Old Testament Prophecies." True, but the temple and its furniture reappear in Revelation, so we need to stay close to our subject, in both books.

1. The strong presumption is that the prophets did not predict eternal literalism for David, the temple, tribe of Levi, Aaronic priesthood, burnt offerings and other offerings and the Jewish Feasts, for each and all of them ceased nearly nineteen centuries ago.

2. They all ceased by divine limitation, that is, because they were supplanted by their anti-types. (Gal. 3:23-29).

3. Was the Jewish system in its meridan glory a *higher, better, system than the gospel*? Or was it lower and inferior? Evidently the latter, (Heb. 10:1). Paul says "the priesthood being changed there is made of necessity a change also of the law," (Heb. 7:12). The priesthood is not simply driven out of Palestine, or Jerusalem by the arms of the Romans and others, but GOD HAS CHANGED THE PRIESTHOOD FROM AARON TO CHRIST, FROM LEVI TO JUDAH, AND THE LAW IS CHANGED, FROM THE LAW OF MOSES TO THE GOSPEL OF CHRIST. MOSES SPAKE NOTHING CONCERNING JUDAH'S PRIESTHOOD.

Now all this Millennial literalism must of necessity change this law back again from the higher to the lower, from the anti-type to the type. They picture the Millennial age as a purer, better, more spiritual age than the gospel age.

4. The last prophecy of the Old Testament said, "Behold I will send you Elijah the prophet before the coming of the great and dreadful day of the Lord, and he shall turn the hearts of the fathers to the children and the heart of the children to the fathers, lest I come and smite the earth with a curse," (Mal. 4:4, 5). Did Elijah come back and preach? No. Is his prophecy unfulfilled? No. Jesus said of John the Baptist, And if ye will receive it, this is Elias, which was for to come.

He that hath ears to hear, let him hear," (Matt. 11:13-15).

Thus the last prophet and last prediction of the Old Testament foretold John the Baptist. He was not literally Elijah any more than Jesus was literally David. Jesus our Lord emphasized the point, as much as to say, "Here is a rule of interpretation for these Type-Prophecies. Study it well. It will govern your interpretation on other prophecies just as plain and will lead you into the truth." "He that hath ears to hear, let him hear," *John was predicted* under the *name* of *Elijah.*

5. If the prophets of the Old Testament, in predicting the higher realities and blessings of the gospel, can not be interpreted literally, because *Jesus* is *not David, John* the *Baptist* is *not Elijah,* and Jesus has built his *temple,* changed the *priesthood* and the *sacrifices;* on what a sandy foundation does the whole Millennial theory rest!

These literalists would like for us to give them an opening for the KING TO ENTER and they will insist on his fixing the Millennium after he gets here, BY MAKING A NEW REVELATION. But we are satisfied with the Book we already have. Nothing is plainer than the fact that a temporal ruler, temporal Levi, temporal tabernacle, temporal sacrifices, temporal covenant, temporal feasts, and temporal everything, came in together. An eternal Ruler, eternal temple, ministered in by an eternal Priest, who made one sacrifice of eternal virtue, in an eternal covenant, have supplanted the typical arrangement, *and it has been laid aside by divine authority, forever.*

6. Jesus was not literal David when here and would not be if he were to return this year. He did not build a material temple and would not should he return, for he already has his temple, the church. So there is absolutely no means of interpreting these prophecies literally. They cover the whole group. I think it is high time some of our would-be expositors forsake Judaism and recognize that "ye are complete in him who is the head of all principality and power." (Col. 2:10).

REVELATION AGAIN.

I have produced these vital points concerning the type-prophecies of the Old Testament, because in Revelation the temple and its furniture reappear. The Jewish temple, priesthood, sacrifices, feasts, covenants, fasts, and king were DOUBLY DONE AWAY, when John wrote.

First, God had put them all away, as far as accept-ableness was concerned, and had given in their stead, the better King, Priesthood, sacrifice, Temple, Covenant and feasts of the gospel. Secondly, they were put away lit-erally by the fire, and sword of the Romans. There was no temple standing in Jerusalem when John wrote, and of necessity, the whole Mosaic economy was literally abolished by man, as well as rejected of God.

The question confronting the reader is, who will revive any feature of that obsolete system? and for what purpose? Will the Lord Jesus Christ? Then why was it abolished at the opening of the Christian age? When I say "abolished," I do not mean overthrown by the Ro-mans in the frightful desolations of war; but I mean, why did God reject the earthly temple, Aaronic priest-hood, animal sacrifices and carnal ordinances? It seems to me that a superficial study of Hebrews would enable any one to see that He rejected them because they were types and shadows and were only imposed on THEM until the times of reformation. As these types were imposed ON THE JEWS, (never on the Gentiles), when the times of reformation or fulfillment came THEY PASSED AWAY. The Jewish ritual is no more binding on the Jews, now, than upon the Gentiles; that is, the Gentiles were never under that law, the Jews were until the gospel came, when it ceased and they are free to be married to another," (Rom. 7:1-3). They had served their day, and were set aside "for the weakness and unprofitable-ness thereof." Has there ever existed, or does there now exist, any reason to revive them? Would Aaron, Levi, the temple, the sacrifices, the feasts and fasts add any spirituality to the gospel? Is the type better than the anti-type?

Nay, verily, to both questions.

1. I have drawn the irresistible conclusion that if the leading characters in the Type-Prophecies were simply types, of, but not the real persons predicted, then all such prophecies are necessarily figurative, because a lit-eral temple demands a literal priesthood; and a temporal king a temporal kingdom and *vice versa*. We can not

mix the two. All are literal, or all are figurative; and we proved the latter to be true, because Jesus is the David foretold, and Hebrews says he is the High-Priest and Sacrifice, has a better covenant and better tabernacle, "which the Lord pitched and not man."

2. It is also clear as a sunbeam that if Jesus and his gospel set aside the law with its temple, priesthood and sacrificial system, that when John uses them in Revelation, (which was written after the DOUBLE rejection of them spoken of above, the divine followed by the human), he uses them as *symbols* or *illustrations* and not as *realities* that *would* exist in the future. In other words he foretold or SIGNIFIED things pertaining to the church under the names of those typical things of the Jewish age. As I have shown, (I hope clearly,) that the OLD TESTAMENT PROPHETS DID THIS, we make an easy transition to our great prophetic guide in the Revelation, and find him following the well-beaten path of his predecessors.

3. We may note in conclusion that John had already shut us up to the symbolic use of the tabernacle and its furniture by defining the candlestick to *signify* a church; but we feel doubly strong, WHEN WE LEARN THAT THE THEN FULFILLED PROPHECIES OF THE SAME NATURE, WERE APPLIED BY OUR SAVIOR AND THE APOSTLES IN THAT MANNER. Indeed, it seems to me that, after we have thoroughly examined the predictions at the head of this chapter, and learned that they are necessarily figurative from the King and priests clear down, we would not think for a moment of literalism when we find the temple in Revelation. We have the whole ritual spiritualized, so to speak, in the gospel. The letter to the Hebrews, unfolds to us our Ruler in all his glory, and it would be beneath the dignity of sober exegesis to think that John in Revelation deviated from the apostolic precedents. John could have written Hebrews—it was his doctrine. He believed and adopted it all. Then, manifestly, he could not construct a book reviving any feature of the Mosaic types. All of which should teach us that it is the church and its fortunes that are *signified* when the Jewish group of symbols or any of them is used; and he is not even remotely considering

the restoration to the Jews of their once typical arrangement, which was done away in Christ. I would as soon
expect to meet the veritable dragon, with seven heads,
and ten horns in visiting the ten kingdoms of Western
Europe, as to expect to see the literal temple, priesthood
restored and the temporal age as the Literalists are compelled to conclude is the meaning of these symbolic and
Type-Prophecies.

The only law of God by which Jew or Gentile can
approach to God, is the gospel of Christ; and this was
predicted in *Type-Prophecies*. If the spiritual King, Priest,
Sacrifices, temple and servants of God were not complete,
one might expect a few types to be added to complete
them. But the law, as a typical system, has passed
away, forever; and only the followers of Caiaphas could
feel any need of it, and they do so because they reject
Him "who is able to save to the uttermost all that come
to God through him." These are Test-Prophecies because they *test the theory*. If there is to be literal Elijah,
literal David, the literal temple, in the literal Jerusalem,
with Levi offering literal sacrifices and the nation observing the law of Moses and attending the literal annual
feasts, or being cursed if they do not, and the Gentiles
cursed for not doing so, then that settles the interpretation for all similar prophecies. We will then have to interpret these prophecies as though we never heard of
Jesus Christ, his temple, sacrifice, priesthood and anti-
typical service. We will then have David, to mean
David; Elijah, to mean Elijah; Levi, to mean Levi; and
so on. It is nonsense to talk of both the literal and
figurative meanings being correct. While the law lasted
the ANTI-TYPES had no existence; when the anti-types
came, BY DIVINE AUTHORITY, there were no more
TYPES. The Test-Prophecies demand:

1.   Jesus is David. (Jer. 33:17; 30:9; Ezek. 34:
23; 23:25; 37: 26-28).

2.   John the Baptist is Elijah, (Mal. 4:5, 6).

3.   Christians are Levites. (Is. 66:21).

4.   The church is the temple predicted.   (I Cor.
3:16; Ezek. 37:27-28).

5.   Our royal-priesthood set aside the Aaronic priest
hood (I Pet. 2:5, 9).

6. Spiritual sacrifices set aside animal sacrifices. (Same verses, also Heb. 13:15).

So we find by testing the prophecies that, as every feature of Judaism has been set aside for the higher realities of the gospel, Jesus is predicted under the *name* of David; John the Baptist under the *name* of Elijah; and the royal priesthood under the *name* of Levi, (Is. 66:21; Jer. 33:18). If the rule is established by one set of Test-Prophecies, then it applies to all of that nature. For this reason, I do not feel the need of reviewing all that the prophets say, but samples, tests, or some of their plainest, strongest Type-Prophecies or predictions, where we know they used the name of types to predict persons, offices or realities to be under the gospel, AFTER THE TYPES WERE LEGISLATED AWAY FOREVER.

VI.-VII. THE SEVEN SEALS.

The seven seals include all the events predicted from (ch. 6 to 20). Six of the seals are opened in (ch. 6). The first *five* seals occupy eleven verses; the *sixth* twenty-three verses. The seventh seal stands out by itself (ch. 8:1). It contained seven trumpets; the seventh trumpet is signalized by seven vials. The long protracted controversy between the "beast," „dragon" and "false prophet," the church, and the church's ultimate victory, were symbolized.

The first six seals relate to the period before and including the overthrow of Paganism by Constantine, (A. D. 312). This is known as the "Historic Fulfillment," (and as I am not writing a commentary, it will only be necessary to say there is substantial harmony, though minor differences, of interpretation, as to the events covered by the first six seals, but uniform agreement, among the historic expositors, as to the end—the momentous overthrow of Pagan rule in the Roman Empire in the beginning of the fourth century, by Constantine the Great).

However the Rider on the white horse and the events of the fifth seal should be closely identified. The Rider on the white horse had a crown, (sovereignty), and a bow, (war instrument), and came forth "conquering", (was doing so in that very time), "and to conquer," evi-dently throughout the entire period predicted. He had conquered *death* and *hades*; had overthrown Judaism; and was thus, as king in Zion, wearing his crown. "And to conquer," looked to the future contests, pictured more definitely later in the book, when he would meet and overthrow the combined forces of Anti-Christ. There was a definite prediction connected with the Rider as well as a statement of what he was doing—"conqeuring and to conquer."

2. We see by reference to (ch. 19:11-21) that this same horse and Rider reappear after the battle, which we shall study in their connection. Thus at the opening of the First seal, the Rider on the white horse comes forth crowned—King in Zion; at the closing up of the last seal, he rides forth crowned with many crowns, and described at length as our all-glorious Captain and Deliverer.

THE MARTYR SCENE

There is a similar connection between the martyrs of the fifth seal, and crowned martyrs in (ch. 20). They cried for Judgment against their persecutors on earth (6:9-10); and obtained the judgment and victory in (ch. 20). What is described in both chapters John *saw* eighteen centuries ago, in symbol. What did these things signify? There were ten bloody persecutions before Constantine, recorded in history as follows:

1. Nero (A. D. 64). Paul and Peter were slain among a host of others. This was confined chiefly to the Capital, Rome.

2. Domitian (A. D. 95). John was banished to Patmos.

3. Trojan. (A. D. 106).

4. Marcus Aurelius. (A. D. 166). Polycarp, a disciple of John, was burned at the stake.

5. Severus, (A. D. 202).

6. Maximin. (A .D. 235).

7. Decius. (A. D. 250).

8. Valerian, (A. D. 258).

9. Aurelian (A. D. 272).

10. Dioclesian, (A. D. 303).

Dioclesian began to reign about (A. D. 284). In the latter part of his reign was this bloodiest of all the persecutions known as the "Era of the Martyrs." Eusebius, who baptized Constantine in (A. D. 337) shortly before his death, gives a large account of the history of the two centuries covered by the first six seals, and leading up to Constantine and his successors—especially of the persecutions. Dioclesian and Maximian resigned as Emperors and retired to private life, being driven there-to by Galerius. Constantine upon the death of his father, came to the rule of his part of the Empire. Galerius was smitten with a very loathsome disease, insupportably tormented, and often tried to commit suicide. He had his physicians slain because they did not cure him. Finally he thought of the Christians, and, by public edict, put an end to their persecutions and requested them to pray for his recovery; but died soon thereafter, about (A. D. 311).

One should judge Constantine in the history of his times. Early in his reign he followed heathen cruelties and had multitudes slain by wild beasts. He had his wife and son Crispus executed, and was slow to learn and adopt the subduing principles of the gospel of Christ. His reign was a great turning point in history. He dealt with armies of men whose cruelties were unbounded. He was cruel and revengeful, and it is difficult to say how far he was governed by policy of state in his espousal of the Christian religion. But we are not his judge, and can study only the effects of his too carnal policy in making the offices of the church places to be sought by the covetous and ambitious, thus paving the way to install an army of mercenary priests and bishops in the churches and drive out the pious and humble followers of Christ. By making Christianity a state religion, he misinterepreted the nature of the kingdom of heaven, and, virtually, removed every barrier to the final exaltation of the Pope in temporal as well as religious authority over the then known world. Constantine, through the influence of his mother, Helena, was favorable to Christianity. He removed his residence to Byzantium, which from this time, was called Constantinople. He fortified the city with walls and towers, and erected great palaces, church buildings, race grounds and pleasure grounds. He revolutionized the government of the

Roman Empire, made the Emperor sole ruler, and surrounded himself with a brilliant court of chamberlains, ministers, officials and servants, and established a galling system of taxation.   He divided the government into four lieutenancies, and each of these he subdivided into districts, (dioceses), and these into states.   This was perhaps the mightiest revolution in the history of the world, up to that time.   From the days of Nebuchadnezzar the four great Empires, symbolized by the giant metallic man and the four wild beasts, had been ruled over by heathen princes.   The closing scenes of the fifth seal, when martyrdom was universal, was a fitting close of the ages of tyranny and oppression, revealing the spirit of cruelty and bloodthirstiness that reigned supreme in Paganism.   Constantine was baptized late in his life.

"He founded many churches, and endowed them with landed estates.   He granted to the clergy, an immunity from taxes, and other privileges, and allowed legacies to the Church.   From this time forward, the constitution of the church was changed.   From this time the priesthood were separated from the people and were known respectively as the clergy and the people the laity. He introduced degrees of rank among the clergy, modeled after those of the state.   The Bishops, in the principal cities, were over those of the smaller cities and were called Metropolitans; and these lower Bishops controlled the priests.   The church services lost their simplicity of reading the Bible, prayer and singing, and were embellished by art and worldly pomp."

The overthrow of Paganism and establishment of Christianity, as the state religion of the vast Roman Empire, was a mighty achievement; and is justly celebrated in history, as one of the greatest revolutions, civilly and religiously, of all time.   But the unlawful interference of Constantine and his successors with the government of the church, paved the way for the ultimate apostasy, and the Dark Ages.   The downfall of Paganism is plainly set forth under the sixth seal.   The consternation of the whole army of rulers and beneficiaries is graphically pictured by a great earthquake, the blackened the sun, the moon turned to blood; the stars falling from heaven to earth; the heavens themselves, and also mountains and islands removed.   The sublimity of this appalling picture is enhanced by the commotion among the kings, princes, chief captains, the rich, the strong, the bond, the free, in their desperation calling to mountains and rocks to fall upon them to hide them from the wrath of him that sitteth upon the throne and from the wrath of the Lamb. For the great day of his wrath is come: and who is able to stand."

It is easy to see how some would conclude this was the end of the world. All nature seems to be dissolved. But, as previously noted, when the *seventh seal is opened*, the earth is still there, with sea, mountains and rivers as before. The fact is these pictures of dissolving nature are energetic portrayals of civil and religious earthquakes and revolutions. If the whole fabric of nature had to be dissolved to redeem these symbolic prophecies, then nature would have perished many times.

1. At the overthrow of Babylon. (Is. 13.6-22).

2. At the overthrow of Egypt. (Ezek. 32:1-10).

3. The wrath of God against the Idumeans is set forth in similar language. (Is. 34:3-10).

4. The overthrow of Jerusalem was thus predicted by Joel. (ch. 2:31; 3: 15-17).

It is demontrably true that the stars have never fallen from heaven to earth, nor any of the physical phenomena taken place as mentioned in these chapters. But granting that these are symbolic prophecies, the complete subversion of the governments admirably redeems the imagery.

We must accept the language under the sixth seal as symbolic for the following reasons:

1. It is the sixth seal among a group of seven, and we know the first four were symbolic, also the seventh, and I think the fifth likewise, as I shall show.

2. The literality of the removal of the heavens and earth under the sixth seal, would make the seventh an impossibility, for there would have been universal chaos, nothing physical remaining.

3. John defines stars to mean men in (1:20); and they *signify* men in all the prophetic imagery, or there is no rule given for the interpretation.

4. We know the fact of the overthrow of the Pagan Roman Empire fulfilled this prophecy IN THE SAME MANNER as the overthrow of Babylon, of Egypt, of

Idumea and of Jerusalem, fulfilled the same sort of pre-dictions. If it be granted that the Babylonian govern-ment, Egyptian government, Idumean government, and Jewish government, were meant in the first instances, then, evidently, the Roman government was meant here And if these prophecies were not fulfilled when Babylon, Egypt, Idumea and Jerusalem were overthrown, then what prospect is there that they will ever be fulfilled? These governments have passed away, except it may be the Jewish people—but they were denationalized, and hence completely overthrown politically, by the Romans.

5. The Pagan Roman Government was destroyed under Constantine, who reigned thirty years. He was succeeded by Constantius the Second, who reigned twen-ty-four years. The wonderful Julian, (known in history as the Apostate because he openly renounced Christian-ity and embraced Paganism) came to the throne (A. D. 361). Julian was mortally wounded in a battle with the Persians. Jovian succeeded him (A. D. 363) and restored Christianity as the state religion. After his death the empire was divided under Valens (A. D. 364) into the Eastern and Western Roman Empire.

HERESIES.

The religious student is interested in watching the gradual development of "the mystery of iniquity" that was at work in Paul's day. In Mosheim's history of the first three centuries of the Christian Era one may read this history. Many other works are profitable, and one should study these things a century at a time in Milman's History of Christianity, Ruter's Church History and others, especially Eusebius. In these works one learns, by patient investigation, that the apostasy that finally seated the pope in supreme authority over the entire church was a growth of centuries. It requires volumes to set forth these facts in their order. The nature of this work forbids that the subject should be developed historically in these pages. But if our analysis and ap-plication of the seals is correct, the student can read the pages of Eusebius and can see the outlines of the sym-bolic prophecy of the first six seals abundantly verified. Especially am I impressed with the facts of martyrdom

predicted for the period of the fifth seal, and the overthrow of Paganism in the Roman empire under the
SIXTH.

CHAPTER VII.

It is a question of much importance as to what becomes of the dead? The symbols of the fifth seal represent the souls as alive after martyrdom. This is the
universal teaching of the Bible. "And be not afraid of
them that kill the body, but are not able to kill the
soul; but rather fear him who is able to destroy both
soul and body in hell," [Gehenna] (Matt. 10:28).
One declaration of this sort is sufficient to show, from
him who knew, that the death of the soul is not accomplished when martyrdom is visited upon mankind; and,
per consequence, at any other time, when one dies.
There must be *two lives*, or *one* death would destroy the
man. But as one death can be secured by man, (the
death of the body), and the soul can not be killed by
man, it follows that man has a two-fold life. Another
matter of kindred importance is, where is the soul between death and resurrection? Many assume that the
soul or inner man, at death, is immediately glorified in
heaven, if righteous, or consigned to Gehenna, if wicked.
I think this erroneous. The place called *Sheol* in Hebrew,
and *Hades* in Greek is the place of departed spirits. It
is impossible to prove, from the Bible, that any human
being is in heaven or Gehenna. John saw four angels
at the four corners of the earth, holding the four winds
of the earth, that no wind should blow on the earth,
or on the sea, or upon any trees. From this I learn,

1.   That earth, sea and trees were still in existence,
and that, therefore, his description in (ch. 6) was figurative.

2.   Restraining the winds produced a great calm
in nature, so evidently there was a political and religious
state of things corresponding to this. A religious tolera-
tion, favorable to Christianity followed Constantine, for
this is a part of that seal. As the first part was convul-
sive, this is quiet. The first set of symbols swept away
Pagan rule; and this permitted the cultivation of gospel
principles under the protection of the ruling class. The

elements were favorable to the multitudes, (the sea, 17:13), and also to the individuals, (the trees).

3.   Another angel ascended from the east and sealed the servants of God in their foreheads. The forehead is the proper place to seal men, the seat of the intellect. They were not branded, like cattle, but they "set to their seal that God was true." (Jno. 3:33). Their understandings were enlightened and the truth convinced them that an idol was nothing. See (Ezek. 9) for a similar illustration of separating between the children of God, and idolaters. The seal is used to denote the property of another. The Ephesians were sealed with the Holy Spirit of promise (Eph. 1:13, 14; 4:30). "Having this seal, the Lord knoweth them that are his." (II Tim. 2:19). Also Paul said the Corinthians were the seal of his apostleship in the Lord. (I Cor. 9:2).

There were one hundred and forty-four thousand sealed. This is the twelve tribes of Israel squared and multiplied by one thousand. As ancient Israel was numbered, so now spiritual Israel. There were exactly twelve thousand from each tribe mentioned, a very exact square, like the Grand Encampment and the Holy City. Judah is first, as Jesus has pre-eminence in all things. Dan is left out entirely, probably because he introduced idolatry in fleshly Israel (Judges 18). Joseph takes the place of Ephraim and Manasseh. Ephraim was the great leader in apostasy in the ten tribes of Israel, and is ignored here. Levi comes in for an honorable place. One can not literalize these texts for the following reasons.

1.   It is a part of the sixth seal. The earthquake and upheaval in nature, and disappearance of stars, heavens, mountains and islands were symbols of the overthrow of Paganism.

2.   The four angels holding the winds that they might not blow on the earth, sea or trees, till certain religious work was done, were certainly to *signify* something as belonging to the same seal. What connection is there between the wind blowing literally on sea or land and men preaching? or what literalist would assume that angels of God demanded a physical calm while they performed the physical miracle of putting a mark in

the forehead of one hundred and forty-four thousand descendants of Abraham? The thing took place in symbol in John's vision; was redeemed in the facts of history under the period of the sixth seal. Evidently it was not a literal transaction in either case, among mankind.

3. The sealing was discriminative —"They were not all Israel, who are of Israel." Not the whole baptized multitude, were "called and true and faithful;" but a multitude were, or God would not have sealed them as "the servants of our God on their foreheads." They were sealed by the truth in their minds and hearts; and were not moved about with every wind of doctrine; and they passed through the trying period of the union of church and state, when multitudes were engulfed in the sea, (that is forsook the simplicity of the gospel for the pomp and earthly glory of office and preferment granted by Constantine and his son and other emperors). They would rather suffer affliction with the people of God than to enjoy the pleasures of sin for a season. They esteemed the reproach of Christ more than all the treasure of the Roman Empire, held out to the politician and the time-server.

LAST SCENE UNDER SIXTH SEAL.

The last scene under the sixth seal was one of great honor conferred on the people of God in the presence of God and the Lamb and the holy angels.

1. There was an innumerable multitude out of all nations, tribes, peoples, and tongues, standing before the throne and before the Lamb. The imagery is still the same as in (chs. 4 and 5); throne, Lamb, four living creatures, the elders, the angels, (as the symbols have not CHANGED, AND DO NOT CHANGE IN ALL THE VISIONS), something great is *signified* by this multitude arrayed in *white robes* and *palms* in their hands. What are the white robes? They were washed and made white in the blood of the Lamb. In other words they were redeemed sinners. Their palms represent victory. In (verse 10) they ascribe their salvation to God and Christ. In (ver 12) seven-fold praise is given to God.

Their identity is pointed out in (ver. 14) as the people of God enjoying the peaceful presence of God.

They had exchanged the tribulation of earth for the enduring bliss of the heavenly temple. Death does not destroy the church or temple of God. "Unto him be the glory in the church, and in Christ Jesus, unto all generations forever and ever. Amen." (Eph. 3:21). Their perfect freedom from hunger and thirst, and sun and heat, and from tears, is assured to them. The Lamb shall lead them to living fountains of waters and God shall dwell with them.

This sublime and sanctifying picture of the soul's release from tribulation and tears, must be interpreted in harmony with the plain, literal portions of Scripture, where the symbols are not used, in order to derive that spiritual uplift from it which faith in the promise of Christ brings to us.

CHAPTER XXVIII.

THE SEVEN TRUMPETS

1. In Chapters (8 and 9) are the trumpets. The design of this work does not permit me to pause for much comment on parts of this symbolism. Silence rivets attention to the mighty acts for which preparation of mind and heart were necessary. (Vers. 2-4) Altar of incense, High Priest, Golden Censer, Smoke of Incense, with prayers of the saints, show us the humbling truth that no man can come to God but by Christ. (Ver. 5). Voices, thunderings and lightnings recall Mt. Sinai and suggest further révelations are to be made, in the nature of Judgments, as earthquake is revolution, civil or religious, sometimes both, in symbol. (Ver. 6-9). Trees and grass are in symbol people in high and low degree respectively.

The Roman Empire, in its two-fold division into Eastern and Western, was the subject of the trumpets. We may see the first four fulfilled in the Western part; the fifth and sixth in the Eastern. The first four relate to Catholicism and its connection with the ten governments; the next two relate to Mahometanism. Under the first four, the Goths, Scythians, Huns and northern warriors invade, like a desolating flood, the Western Roman Empire, and overthrow it under Momylus, the last Emperor, named in derision Augustulus, (Diminutive) in (A. D. 476).

With fire and sword they utterly destroyed cities towns, temples, priests, princes, the old and the young of both sexes. The sea here is as defined (17:15). A mountain is a symbol of earthly power, civil or religious (Jer. 51:25; Zech. 4:7; Ps. 48:2). The waters turned to blood and the fish died, was literal history in (Ex. 7:21); but symbolic prophecy here. (See Ezek. 29:1-7); the same is explained (vs. 8-12) and there the *dragon* was Pharaoh, and the fish were his people, dependent upon him. The evident design of these trumpets was to picture the destruction of the Empire, (the iron kingdom in the Metallic man symbol, the fourth wild beast in Daniel's vision).

(Vers. 10-11). The great star was some eminent man who fell, corrupting the minds and hearts of the people, for they are the rivers and fountains of water; when we drop the symbol).

(Vers. 12-13). The luminaries of heaven are darkened, fall, are removed; and earth, sea and rivers are correspondingly effected. (See Is. 13:1-10) on Babylon; (Ezek. 32:7-8) on Egypt; remembering that these things *signify* something,—the corruption of the rulers and great men in the church, at this period, when the five churches —Jerusalem, Constantinople, Antioch, Alexandria and Rome,—were each trying to reach universal rulership. The papacy was maturing. The decretal letter of Justinian the Emperor, (A. D. 533) made the Bishop of Rome "head of all the holy churches and of all the holy priests of God." Many commence the count of the (1260 years) at this date, as it was a focal date in the rise of popery. Gregory the great, in (A. D. 590), stands forth on the pages of history as the most notable character of his century, and set the cause forward marvellously for the Roman Bishop.

Most expositors, however, choose to count the (1260 years) predicted for the "little horn" from (A. D. 606-

10), in which period, Phocas, a usurper of the crown of empire installed Boniface III as lord over all the churches, including the one in the capital, Constantinople. The death of Phocas was in (A. D. 610). Boniface III was made pope three or four years earlier. Phocas had slain the emperor and all his family. So from (A. D. 606) the Roman bishop has ever been regarded as the Pope, as Phocas decreed the title should be restricted to him. It will appear in the sequel that (A. D. 606) was a focal date; but popery did not begin there. *"Rome* was not built in a day"; neither was *Romanism.* The rise of the system was gradual, marked by stages; its downfall likewise is gradual, marked by corresponding stages. The captivities of the children of Judah, by Nebuchadnezzar, covered nineteen years. The predicted seventy years, which counted from these various captivity dates, are remarkably verified by corresponding dates marking the return of Judah to their land. The same points are evident in the application of the (1260 years). They are counted from an era of captivity, covering at least seventy-five years; and they must have a corresponding closing Era. The church went into captivity in modern "Babylon" without miracle; and she comes out without miracle. These TIME-PROPHECIES do not foretell the end of the world.

THE TRUMPETS.

The trumpets are divided into three periods. They are all under the seventh seal.

First, the angel stood with the golden censer and much incense at the golden altar before the throne. Prayers of saints are in this world. The efficacy of prayer is in the intercession of Christ in heaven. (Eph. 5:20; Col. 3:17; Rom. 8:26). The prayers of the church on earth lead up to and prepare the way for these judgments.

The same censer and fire are used again. You recall that Nadab and Abihu lost their lives for offering strange fire. (Lev. 10). We offer strange fire when we do the right act in the wrong spirit in the worship and service of God. Jesus made a distinction in (Matt. 6:1-18). Almsgiving, prayer and fasting were used as illustrations.

The right thing done from the wrong motive, "to be seen of men," brings an earthly but not heavenly reward. (I Cor. 13) develops this thought at length. Neither ambition, love of vain glory, nor strife, is the true fire, consecrated of heaven, to use in worship. Sermons, prayers, songs and charity must have the fire of love to make them acceptable to God; and not the ambition to excel, to display our eloquence, to win applause, or fame or riches, or carnal ends of any sort. These four trumpets sounded the alarm against the Western Roman Empire. The sixth seal brought us down to the overthrow of the government in its pagan form, (A. D. 312); and it was divided into the Eastern and Western Empire, in (A. D. 364). But the division of the kingdom under the fourth trumpet was more than a century later, or (A. D. 476); and this was the division called for under the symbol of the *toes* of the image and the *horns* of Daniel's fourth beast, as well as the fourth trumpet. See Diagram I.

Why do expositors generally say that the toes and horns represent the ten-fold division of the Western Roman world, and not the whole of it, including the Eastern part that split off in (A. D. 364)? Because each empire from Babylon down, had its original territory which it governed. The successive Empires ruled for a time over the whole territory, then "their dominion was taken away, yet their lives were prolonged for a season and a time."

"The nations of Chaldea and Assyria are still the first beast. Those of Media and Persia are still the second beast. Those of Macedon, Greece and Thrace, Asia Minor, Syria, and Egypt are still the third. And those of Europe on this side of Greece, are still the fourth. Seeing therefore the body of the third beast is confined to the nations on this side of the river Euphrates, and the body of the fourth beast is confined to the nations on this side of Greece; we are to look for all the four heads of the third beast, among the nations on this side the rived Euphrates; and for all the eleven horns of the fourth beast, among the nations on this side of Greece. And, therefore, at the breaking of the Great empire into the four kingdoms of the Greeks, we include no part of the Chaldeans, Medes and Persians, in those kingdoms, because they belonged to the bodies of the two first beasts. Nor do we reckon the Greek empire, seated at Constantinople, among the horns of the fourth beast, because it belonged to the body of the third. For the same reason, neither can the Saracen or the Turk be the little horn or Anti-Christ, as some have imagined them to be; and neither do they come up to the character in other respects."—Bishop Newton.

We have the correctness of this interpretation verified in the fact also that the Western Roman empire WAS DIVIDED into TEN lesser governments, and FULFILLED THE PROPHECY. And out of this division popery arose and was established. As Daniel said: "These great beasts, are four *kings*, which shall arise out of the earth (7:17); then in (ver. 23) the fourth beast shall be the FOURTH KINGDOM upon earth," etc. We not only have the last beast representing a *kingdom*, but, by *necessary* inference the three that preceded it, and the ten kings that followed were KINGDOMS. That it was not individual kings, but dynasties, is made even plainer if possible in Daniel's interpretation of the Image. Speaking to Nebuchadnezzar he said, 'Thou art this head of gold. And after thee shall arise another KINGDOM inferior to thee, and another third KINGDOM of brass, which shall bear rule over all the earth. And the fourth KINGDOM shall be as strong as iron," etc. (Dan'l 2:38-40). The next *king* after Nebuchadnezzar was not signified by the silver, but the next *kingdom*. Even so the toes of the image and the horns of the beast signified kingdoms. I repeat, for emphasis, that the ten governments, sometimes fewer, sometimes more, but generally ten, that have existed in Western Europe, since the breaking up of the Empire in (A. D. 476), prove that GOVERNMENTS, not KINGS, as INDIVIDUALS, were meant. I need only to add that, no one POPE was signified by the "little horn" that came up last. As each beast in succession signified a kingdom in the symbols; and the ten horns represented ten kingdoms, as history shows; then, unquestionably, the horn that came up last, and ruled for (1260 years), meant a kingdom, not an individual king. History has stamped its identity on these symbols; and the historic fulfillment, is not only a *good* interpretation, but the only interpretation that meets the large demands of the prophecy. Cardinal Manning said:

"To the least discerning mind it must be manifest that God had some purpose of his divine wisdom in the migration of Constantine and the empire from Rome to Byzantium. What could be more improbable than that an emperor should forsake an imperial city of a thousand years? The Byzantine emperors ceased to be proprietors of Italy and of Rome. Now the abandonment of Rome was the liberation of the pontiffs. Whatsover claims to obedience the emperors may have made, and whatsover compliance the pontiffs may have yielded, the whole previous relation—anomalous, and annulled again and again, was finally dissolved."

"The providence of God permitted a succession of irruptions, Gothic, Lombard, and Hungarian, to desolate Italy, and to efface from it *every remnant of the empire.* The pontiffs found themselves alone, the sole fountains of order, peace, law and safety, and from the hour of this providential liberation, * * the chains fell off from the hands of the successor of St. Peter, as once before from his own. *No sovereign has ever reigned in Rome since, except the vicar of Jesus Christ."* "Temporal Power." Preface p. 42.

"The throne of sovereignty was vacant by the visitation of God. A power had grown up in Rome, far more imperial over the reason and will of man than the iron despotism of the Roman empire. This interior and supernatural power, of direction and government over the actions and hearts of men, flowed from one center, and was embodied in one person, the bishop of Rome."

"THE FLOODS WHICH SWEPT ALL THE OTHER AUTHORITIES AWAY, THREW OUT INTO BOLDER RELIEF AND MORE CONSPICUOUS PROMINENCE THE SUPREME PASTORAL AUTHORITY OF THE VICAR OF JESUS CHRIST.

To whom else should the people go? They alone had not only the words of eternal life, but the sole and supreme moral power to support and to recognize the shattered society of Rome."

"THE POSSESSION OF THE PONTIFFS COMMENCES WITH THE ABANDONMENT OF ROME BY THE EMPERORS. The rebellion against the vicar of Jesus Christ is in the same order as the rejection of the Master. God has instituted his kingdom on earth, and fixed the head and center of it in Rome, as of old in Jerusalem. I showed you how, by an indirect but divine providence, our Lord liberated his vicar on earth, in the plentitude of his spiritual sovereignty, from all evil subjection— first, by the translation of the seat of empire to the East, and then BY THE EVENTUAL EXTINCTION OF THE ROMAN EMPIRE IN ITALY. The world has been waiting at least for twelve hundred years for the fall of the civil sovereignty of Rome, to see if the text of Gamaliel would have effect. "If this counsel be of man, it will come to naught." pp. 182-245.

"The conversion of the empire to Christianity, and then its removal into the far East, freed the Vicar of Christ from temporal *subjection*; and then, by the action of the same providence, he was clothed. with the PRE-ROGATIVES OF A TRUE AND PROPER LEGAL SOV-EREIGNTY, FOR THAT STATE, AND TERRITORY AND PEOPLE WAS COMMITTED TO HIS CHARGE. From that hour, which I might say was fifteen hundred years ago, or to speak within limits, I WILL SAY WAS TWELVE HUNDRED, THE SUPREME PONTIFF HAS BEEN A TRUE AND PROPER SOVEREIGN, EXERCISING THE PREROGATIVES OF ROYALTY COMMIT-TED TO HIM BY THE WILL OF GOD OVER THE PEOPLE, TO WHOM HE IS FATHER IN ALL THINGS, BOTH SPIRIT-UAL AND TEMPORAL. IN THE PERSON OF PIUS IX JESUS REIGNS ON EARTH, AND HE MUST REIGN TILL HE HATH PUT ALL ENEMIES UNDER HIS FEET." p. 245.

Paul said: "For the mystery of iniquity doth already work; only he who now letteth [hindereth] will let [hinder] until he be taken out of the way. And then shall that wicked be revealed, whom the Lord shall consume with the spirit of his mouth and shall destroy with the brightness of his coming." (II Thess. 2:7-8). WHILE THERE WERE ROMAN EMPERORS EXERCISING UNIVERSAL POWER, OF COURSE A POPE COULD NOT DO SO. The *first* had to be *taken out of the way*, which was done when the last emperor, (Romulus Augustulus), fell. Machiavelli gives the original division into ten parts as follows: Lombards, the Franks, the Burgundians, the Ostrogoths, the Visigoths, the Vandals, the Heruli, the Sueves, the Huns, and the Saxons. The Cardinal has plainly shown us that the power of the pope, his final elevation to civil power, *followed this division*. That is what the prophecy said would follow. The prophecy was fulfilled.

1. In the rise of the ten governments, and that is what these four trumpets include.

2. In the exaltation of the "man of sin" of Paul; the "little horn" of Daniel's fourth beast; we interpert these to refer to the system of power, known as popery, and the eminent catholic we quote shows, at length, that all these temporal vicissitudes prepared the way for the great reign of the popes.

3. These ten nations, or the territory originally covered by them, (sometimes more, sometimes fewer, but generally ten), were to persecute the saints; and Manning says that for twelve centuries the supreme pontiff has been in authority in Rome, in spirituals and temporals. I hasten to say, however, that Cardinal Manning's appeal to Gamaliel's sage remark, is fatal to his contention, for since writing his book the pope has lost his temporal sovereignty. And the present ten states of Europe have hated the religious despot and thrown down his dominion with supreme contempt. England, Germany, Italy, France, Holland, Belgium, Austria, Switzerland, Portugal and Spain cover the territory today, and are each and all free from the one-time temporal despot in Rome, whom Manning honored as vicar of Christ. These ten governments, by giving their power to the beast, maintained his supremacy till the word of God was fulfilled, then took away his dominion to consume and to destroy it unto the end. As there is general agreement in the broad outlines of these trumpet events, I make another liberal quotation from Cardinal Manning, (with compliments to "Light for the Last Days, by H. Grattan Guinness"), in preference to submitting an historical review of the invasion of the Roman Empire by the northern invaders that dismembered it.

"When the church went out into the world, it found there a vast empire, which covered it with a perfect organization, social and political. In the time of Christ and the apostles, it had one chief city reigning over the whole world; it had one emperor whose will was the fountain of all law, one senate, one legislature, one code of laws. It had one political organization, uniting all nations, and one vast military system, holding all people in subjection. It had one great chart, and one center, the *Milliarium Aureum*, the golden milestone, which stood by the arch of Severus, upon which were marked all the distances throughout the world-wide empire of Rome. It was ruled by the most perfect and minute legislation which had ever governed the natural order of the world.

Perhaps you may think that it was this organization of which the church took possession. No; before the church assumed its *civil mission to create modern Europe*, the seven vials of heaven were poured out upon that empire, and the seven trumpets blew, and the four winds of heaven were let loose, and the great angel cast that mighty stone into the sea, and said: Babylon the Great

is fallen; for that great empire was ravaged and desolated, and pillaged by the invasion of barbarians, by
hordes from every quarter, until there remained of all
its structures, scarcely anything but mutilated ruins of
its greatness, its aqueducts, it military roads, the Flavian
amphitheater, and the Pantheon. Before Almighty God
sent his Church out into the world on its civil mission,
the whole of that vast empire was burnt up as by fire,
and deluged by blood. Italy became a desolation and
Africa was abandoned to itself, and Britain was cast off,
and Spain was forgotten; *for the empire departed to Constantinople*; the Byzantine emperors were feeble and helpless; they were harassed by the assaults of the oriental
tribes; and Italy they were no longer able even to protect. *This is what all historians tell us.* There was a time
when even Rome itself is said to have been without a
living inhabitant, when foxes ran over the Palatine hill,
and their bark alone was heard in the golden house of
the Caesars. Such was Rome, this mighty Rome, which
once had some two millions of inhabitants, and twelve
miles of diameter, stretching from the Mediterranean sea
to the Sabine hills; it had gone to desolation. And for
centuries after this it was ever and again the object of
attack. It was besieged; it was ruined again and again.
*All its civil power had departed, and its sovereignty existed
no more.* It was into such a world as this that the
Church was sent forth to do its work. Christian Europe
is not the remains of the old Roman Empire; it is a new
creation. Manning, "Temporal power," pp. 37-38.

The well-marked era of the end of the Roman empire and beginning of the new government, the ten kingdoms, is now sufficiently before us. I need not elaborate
further, at this point, because the end of Ancient and
the opening of Medieval History was (A. D. 476). Allison's great history begins with that date. It would serve
no good purpose to cite facts corroborative of this great
overthrow of the empire, because all historians, covering
the period, dwell upon it. It is as celebrated a date in
Roman history as (A. D. 1776) is in American history.
Our chief point is that upon the downfall of the empire
ten kingdoms, in the same territory were to succeed
it, and still another later, and the last was to have a life-
time of (1260 years). Does not the learned Cardinal
admit these facts? Read his words carefully and see
that he contends it was providential and a blessing to
the world for Rome to be reduced to her abject condition,
that the Pope might enjoy the sovereignty over Europe,

and *erect a new empire.* The reader will decide whether papalism was a blessing or a curse; the European states have deprived the pope of his temporal dominion in testimony of the fact that they were tired of him; but, mark you well, that the cardinal says he rose into temporal power after the empire was divided, when it was in a *weak* state, the iron and miry clay period; and that this new empire has lasted *more than twelve centuries,* just what the terms of the prophecy demand, and all histories covering the period, attest.

The next chapter presents the great Abyss opened, and it has been contended, (with some reason), that Boniface III, the first pope, was the fallen star that opened the pit. There may be room for diversity in unity of opinion as to the particular person *signified* by this *fallen star.*

So *many* great men figure in the opening of these colossal systems of error, that to be dogmatic is uncharitable, and betrays a conceit inconsistent with the humility necessary in the expositor of these symbols. I disclaim any disposition to dogmatize on any obscure point of Revelation; and on all these great prophecies, am giving my mature judgment, subject to revision, and only that I may serve my generation, with clear conscience, in presenting the fruits of a long and patient study of these subjects, aided by the best that has been said in the learned and critical expositions of both Pre-Millennial and Post-Millennial advocates. Dogmatism on such a point is unnecessary, and, in any view of the symbols, consistent with the large field of vision passed over by the prophet, there is liable to be an element of truth. As the symbols relate to events, composite in nature, it is more than probable that agencies were employed opening the pit, which under the symbols of star, key, smoke, locusts, etc, have a composite meaning.

CHAPTER XXIX.

MAHOMETANISM.

In examining the two trumpets in (ch. 9) we are led to consider the great usurper, Mahomet, a false prophet. The symbols signify much. The twin evils, Popery in the West, and Mahometanism in the East, parallel each other from the early part of the seventh century. To give a few suggestions.

LITERALISM IMPOSSIBLE HERE.

It was not a literal angel, nor literal star, fallen from heaven to earth, for *he* had the key to the abyss. *He* opened the bottomless pit, like uncapping a volcano. Smoke arose like the smoke of a great furnace. The light of the sun was obscured (certainly not by the actual smoke of hell!) There would not come literal locusts out of the literal smoke of hell! They had power as the scorpions of earth. They were not to hurt grass, green things, nor trees, (contrary to their nature); but *men* only; and, of these, only such as have not God's seal in their foreheads. They were not to kill them but torment them five months. Literalism would reduce this whole scene to a local affair, not lasting half a year, like a grasshopper year. Men seek death, and do not find it. The locusts were shaped like horses prepared for battle; wore crown *like unto* gold; and their faces were *like men*. These locusts had *hair* like women, and *teeth*, like the teeth of *lions*. They had breast-plates *like* iron, wings, (battalions in motion) *like* the sound of chariots and many horses rushing to battle. The tails gave the sting like scorpions. The *five* months is repeated ,(vs. 5, 10). Their king is supreme in the Bottomless pit. His name is Destroyer.

I think the symbols are faithfully interpreted as follows:

1. Sergius——a Nestorian Monk, who wrote the

Koran, opened the pit.   Angel is a great *man* in the symbols.   (1:20).

2.   Key is power; Koran was the book the king ruled with.

3.   The pit was hell.   Smoke was the confused state of things religiously or doctrinally.

4.   This power comes from the same pit the beast does in (11:7).   Catholicism and Mahometanism rose up together out of the obscurity of vision, belonging to the times.   The pope assumed absolute spiritual and temporal control over all Christians; Mahomet assumed the same.   Both were impostors; but the track of Mahometanism was in the *wake* of *Arianism*—Arius denied the divinity of Christ.   It was easy for Mahomet, a mere man, to destroy nominal Christians; they did not have the seal of God in their foreheads or the belief of Jesus Christ as the Son of God.   Popery could destroy those who did not have this seal also, for they would accept him as their ruler and high-priest.   Mahometans came from Arabia, where Ishmael lived; and the nativity of locusts in vast armies.   Wicked, impenitent men, agressive and cruel, are called locusts by Ezekiel (2:6).   Five months, (the life of a locust), when converted into prophetic times, is as follows: five months are one hundred fifty days, and a day for a year would signify one hundred fifty years.   From (A. D. 612) when Mahomet began his conquests to (762) when Bagdad was built as a "city of peace" was the prophetic five months, and this was the period of Saracenic conquest, as to origin, continuance and end.   They overran Syria, Persia, India, Egypt and Spain.   So, Western Asia, South Europe, and Northern Africa were swept by the locusts.   Their chief strength was in their cavalry, the Arabs being the world's best trained horsemen, and the owners of some of the handsomest, fleetest animals ever ridden by man.   The turbaned riders, or else the ceaseless victories of their arms, are pictured in the crowns.

The stings were in their tails,   "Therefore, the Lord will cut off from Israel head and tail, branch and rush, in one day.   The ancient and honorable, he is the head; *and the prophet that speaketh lies, he is the tail.*   For the leaders of this people cause them to err; and they that are led of them are destroyed."   (Is. 9:13-15).

If there ever was a prophet who spake lies it was. Mahomet. He and his successors instilled the deadly virus of his doctrine into the minds and hearts of the untold millions whom they conquered—all who had not the seal of God in their foreheads. King Abaddon, the Destroyer; what a name and Mission! Jesus was and is the *Savior*, this vile ruler a *Destroyer*. This is beyond question the great Eastern Anti-Christ, which arose at the same time as the Western Anti-christ. From the opening of the (7th) century, for thirteen centuries, these great powers were reigning over the vast territory where the gospel had previously spread, and the life of the true church was all but destroyed from the earth.

MAHOMET

Arabia was a country some eighteen hundred by nine hundred miles. Many churches were established in Arabia. Paul was in that country three years. The churches were corrupted later by images and Arianism. Mahomet was an orphan. He began trading at thirteen years of age in overland traffic in a caravan. He could neither read nor write. The nobility of England and other countries are put in the same illiterate class by many writers. The Caaba or Temple was located at Mecca. The Arabs claim that Adam built it, and it was rebuilt by Abraham and Ishmael. Mahomet married Kadijah, a rich widow. He was sixteen years a merchant, met Jews, Christians, Greeks, Romans, Arians, Trinitarians, and all classes. His father was the custodian of the Caaba. Mahomet succeeded him. In (A. D. 606), (the same year Boniface III became pope), Mahomet retired to a cave three miles from Mecca. He professed to talk to Gabriel. His Koran ADOPTED THE TRUTH that there is but one God and this was agreeable to Christians and Jews; he ADDED "And Mahomet is his prophet:" this does not follow, as he is not mentioned in the Bible, and his blasphemous pretentions knew no bounds. I need not relate his history further than to say he taught and practiced polygamy; promised his soldiers a carnal heaven; and took the carnal weapons which Jesus rejected by which to found his empire. His first convert was his wife; the second his servant, Zeid;

Ali, his cousin next; Beer, a man of talents and energy came next, (and Mahomet married his seven year old daughter). He began his public work in (A. D. 612). He was run out of Mecca to Medina ten years later, (July A. D. 622), which is known as the Hegira or Flight. Mahometans count time by lunar measure (354 days to the year), from (A. D. 622). In (A. D. 625) he fought with three thousand men and finally won the victory, although he was pelted with stones, cut in the face, had two front teeth knocked out, and was badly used up personally. He gave one-fifth to propagate the faith, the rest of the spoils of war to his soldiers. He died in (A. D. 632) in the sixty-third year of his age.

His conquests and the spread of his imposture went on. Beer took Damascus (A. D. 635). After Beer died Jerusalem was taken by Omar (A. D. 637) in April. From which date it has been under Mahometan control, practically the whole time. Omar built a Mosque on the ancient site of Solomon's temple, and there is one there today. They took Tyre, Cesarea, Memphis, Alexandria, and all of Egypt. Mahomet's sword followed the path of Arianism. The last victory of the Mahometans in conquest was (A. D. 1672), but as this was under the next trumpet, I subjoin an outline of sixteen points of identity of the great Ottoman Empire that arose from (A. D. 1281 to 1672) or the next *Time-Prophecy,* covering (391 years). This was a later phase of Mahometan rule, in which the entire Eastern Roman Empire fell.

SIXTEEN POINTS OF IDENTITY.

1. Four agencies. 2. Bound or restrained for a time. 3. These coalesce into one mighty power. 4. The purpose was conquest, havoc, bloodshed. 5. Located in the valley of the Euphrates. 6. Advance and prosper three hundred ninety-one years. 7. Destruction against the Empire. 8. Armies immensely numerous. 9. The forces consist largely of horsemen. 10. Must use gunpowder. 11. Military equipment, red, blue and yellow. 12. Cavalry very ferocious. 13. Influence Saracenic, hence Mahometan. 14. Empire addicted to demonology. 15. People sunken in idolatry and image worship. 16. People degraded exceedingly morally.

Many great events have signalized the Euphrates river. It is supposed that it was the "cradle" of the human family. The first martyr, Abel, was slain in that locality. Noah began the race anew in the mountains of Armenia. The first colonies after the flood migrated from the Euphrates. Despotism began there under Nimrod. It has been the Mahometan center for ages. The entire chapter, in my judgment, is devoted to Mahometan conquest and imposture. It is immaterial to the understanding of the prophecy, (in the main), whether Sergius, the Monk, who is reputed to have written the Koran, (that is the Mahometan Bible), was the star of (ver 1) or whether it was Boniface III the pope who was elevated to the head of the church in (A. D. 606); or whether it was Mahomet himself, as a fallen king in his own country, (because he was of the Koreish tribe and this tribe was in supreme control of the Caaba or temple); or, to be more charitable to the honest judgment of others, let it be established that hell opened on earth, in the opening of the pit, in the rise of the deadly doctrnes, Popery and Mahometanism, and we shall have no controversy over the angel who opened the pit. All of these characters darkened the air, obscured the Sun of Righteousness, and destroyed the church over a large part of the world; the pope in arrogating to himself the offices of Christ as ruler and high-priest in the church on earth; Mahomet, by exalting himself to supreme power over his subjects. He inculcated two deadly principles—one is generally known as fatalism, or predestination; the other was a promise of sensual delights in heaven. For (150) years the sword of the Saracens laid waste the territory since held by them, (A. D. 612 to A. D. 762), when their conquests ceased. The Christians, (believers in Christ) were styled infidels and dogs, insulted and oppressed shamefully. The cry was "Ye Christian dogs, ye know your option — the Koran, the tribute or the sword." The bitter contempt and hatred flowing out from the Moslem faith toward them could not but be felt perpetually. It was marked in the very terms of appellation—Christian dogs and infidels. The enactments of the capitulations granted them were then every-day remembrances of it. Deprived of the use of arms, like

the Helots of old, and with tribute enforced as their annual life-redemption tax, with a different dress enjoined
them from their masters and a more humble mode of
riding—an obligation to rise up deferentially in the presence of the meanest Moslem, and to receive and grat-
uitously entertain for a certain time, whosoever of the
Moslems, when on a journey, might require it—such were
the marks of personal degredation ordained in the capitulations. And then, in token of the degredation of their
religion, that to which, notwithstanding all their superstitions, they clung with fond attachment, there was the
prohibition to build new churches, or to chime the bells
in those retained by them, or to refuse the admission of
the scoffing Moslem into them, though they regarded
his presence as a defilement. Add to this the induce-
ments to apostasy to Mahommedanism, operating to an
incalculable extent on the young, and thoughtless in
families more especially, *and then the penalty of death*
against those returning to the Christian faith—the in-
sults, moreover, to Christian females, and a thousand
indefinable injuries and oppressions; and how could it
be but that the bitterness of their lot should be felt, and
the poison rankle within them, even as it was in other
days with the Jewish captives in Babylon? "And in
those days shall men seek death, and shall not find it,
and shall desire to die, and death shall flee from them;
as it is said of the Jews, (Jer. 8:3) "and death shall be
chosen rather than life, by all the residue of them that
remain of this evil family, which remain in all the places
whither I have driven them." When we remember that
in the short space of ten years, from (A. D. 634 to 644)
the Saracens captured (3060) cities, destroyed (4000)
church edifices, and erected (1400) mosques, we hear
faintly the thunder of these trumpets.

OTHMAN EMPIRE.

I deem it unnecessary to dwell on the story of the
Ottoman Empire. The division is made in this instance
not only by the trumpets, but the woes (ver. 12), showing us there is more to follow later. And the rise of
the Othman empire and Turkish power, from (A .D.
1281 to A. D. 1672) the predicted (391 years), answers

the demands of the prediction. The three woe trumpets take in the whole period from the rise of Mahometanism to its overthrow; and, while no *time*-prophecy is added, the description of the Saracenic locusts and their conquests at the opening covering (150) years; and the Euphratean horsemen" requiring (391) years at the close, both of which dates are by historians shown to be the important dates of conquest by Mahometans. The Mahometans *possessed the country all the time* although a period of five hundred years lies between the last conquest of the Saracens (A. D. 762) and the first by the Turks (A. D. 1281). This fact illustrates the nature of the work, as there are two sets of symbols representing warfare; and they abundantly show that the conquests of the first set were not to be continued to the close; but the symbols of the Turks and Ottomans, a new set of symbols, different from, and yet akin to, the first, and with a longer period of conquest, signified further conquests by the same imposture.

In (A. D. 1453) Constantinople fell and thus the Eastern Empire went down. The Crescent, (or new moon), supplanted the cross and Mahometanism was supreme in the city, rebuilt by Constantine the Great and made the capital of his vast domain. Adrianople had been the capital for nearly a century of the Ottoman power, and was embellished with some of the finest mosques in the world. When the Sultan was seated in Constantinople his power against the followers of Christ, was at its height. It is said that gunpowder was first used in reducing this great city (A. D. 1453). "St. Sophia" one of the finest church buildings in the world was converted into a Mahometan mosque, and so stands to this day. It has been reported by correspondents recently that, a million manuscripts have been preserved in the basement and hidden in this great church edifice. Since the new Turks came into power, these are being discovered and promise a rich harvest to the antiquarian. Constantine's palace has been unearthed and many other great monuments of the past. As Mahometanism is doomed to overthrow and is closely linked with Catholicism in time of origin, continuance and end; and as they are now practically driven from Europe, we may confidently expect every great uprising against them in these times to be hastening their end. I need not tarry here, to identify the "little horn" (Dan'l 8:9) with this semi-heathen government. I feel that the work is unnecessary in our day, when all the arguments possible on the subject have been given by so many expositors. The Mahometans are waning as a nation, as a religious force, and stagnation broods over their entire domain, except as the modernists break away from their old environments and are seeking to keep step with the revolutionary movements in all despotisms, and to secure constitutional governments. The Mahometan people are learning that they are a deceived and misguided people, and are throwing off the iron yoke of tyranny; may we hope, to become wise in the life and mission of the true Prophet, who loved, and gave himself for them? The great European war is destined to destroy more than men, cities and fleets; it is destroying systems of tyranny and despotic rule. The world can not long remain half despotic and half free. We can not have mid-night and mid-noon at the same time. THE ERA PREDICTED IS HERE AND LIBERTY IS AT THE DOORS. The multitudes of men slain in the rise, progress and reign of the forces of darkness herein symbolized are all but incredible. A hundred thousand, or two hundred thousand, men falling on the battle-fields, during an aggressive campaign was not considered. But we notice that (A. D. 1453) when Constantine fell to the terrible Turks was near the Reformation in Germany, when in (1517) Luther nailed his ninety-five Latin theses to the Wurtemburg door, thus sounding the great trumpet blast for Reformation. It is plain, however, that impenitence reigned over the world in general as the close of this chapter shows.

Mahomet combined some Christianity and some Judaism in his Koran, with eastern maxims and customs. He claimed to receive communications from Gabriel. His blasphemy reached its most terrible climax in his claim that he was the Holy Ghost. Mecca where he was born and died, (for he compelled them to recognize him some years after his flight) and Medina, are regarded by Moslems (a name of his followers) as sacred cities; and Pilgrimages are made to them. I have alluded to the fact that Mahomet's followers early marched into the Christian cities of Damascus, Antioch and Jerusalem. They hold that country to this day. They took the city of Alexandria in Egypt and destroyed the great library consisting of seven hundred thousand volumes. You will notice that Constantinople fell in (A. D. 1453) to the Turks, and thus the Greek empire passed away. Luther's Reformation began in (A. D. 1517) some (64) years afterward); the Turks extended their conquests to (1672), the end of the (391) years, when the wasting process began.

NATURE OF THE PROTEST.

Let it not be thought for a moment that the protest that convulsed Europe was religious, but not civil. The cry of the oppressed was smothered by church and state. And the revolt was against this double tyranny. The reformers were not restrained by the bishop of Rome, but by the rulers who upheld the pope. America was discovered in (1492). A grouping of elements, revolutionary in nature, and destined to destroy the last vestige of despotic rule, whether in the person of the Sultan of Turkey, the pope of Rome, or the crowned heads of governments hoary with age, all concentrate at this point. In the fourteenth and fifteenth centuries, the fore-runners of the Reformation from the darkness of the middle ages, were multiplied. Flavis Cioja, an Italian, prepared a compass, using the magnetic needle, and revolutionized navigation. John Gutenburg of Mayence gave the world the art of printing, and thus unshackled the human mind, and books, which had been the property of the rich, were available to a large number. But the Mariner's compass and the art of printing led the way into the untried paths of destiny. Bold navigators sailed the seas in search of wealth. A passage to the East Indies was discovered, which changed the commercial tide of Europe. The bold Genoese, Christopher Columbus, discovered America. Here opened a New Era in the history of mankind. It is from this time that the great discoveries began to be made. The Reformers discovered that popery was the Man of Sin, and electrified Europe with their message. The thunderbolts of the enraged

masses were hurled with titanic fury against the throne
of popery, and the united elements of destruction overthrew his *despotic power over the church*. But they did
not know, in full, the road that leads back to Christ.
Out of a dismembered papal despotism *they erected a group
of* STATE CHURCHES, (daughters of Rome), contrary
to the gospel of Christ. Like Jehu of old, they threw
off idolatry; but did not forsake the sins of Jeroboam.
They could not see the full-orbed light of heaven's truth,
and *secure their civil liberties*. Ascending this Pike's Peak
of civil and religious liberty, the clouds of superstition
that darkened the heavens above them, obscured the
summit. They lodged at the "Half-way house," and
were content. They erected protestant churches; but
their protests were not the final word against earthly lordship and priest-craft in *church* and *nation*. But more and
more students of God's word advanced; and higher and
still higher they ascended, until from the summit of the
loftiest peak of the mountains of prophecy, they look back
over the long road travelled. Today there is a political
and social earthquake, rocking down the thrones of despotism, and tumbling the crowns of autocrats in hopeless
confusion at the feet of the masses. The loud thunders
of war, echo and re-echo over the oligarchies of Europe
and the world. Revolutions follow each other like the billows of the sea. And we live in the momentous period,
when the vision is becoming clear. We are nearing the
summit from whence we may see the glorious fulfillment
of the prediction, of the angel who stood majestically
upon the sea and upon the earth, with uplifted hand, and
making oath by him that liveth forever and ever, who
created heaven, earth, sea, and all that dwell therein,
"that there shall be delay no longer; but in the days of
the voice of the seventh angel, when he is about to
sound, then is finished the mystery of God, according to
the good tidings which he declared to his servants the
prophets." (Ch. 10:5-7).

This brings us to the end *of the mystery*, not to the
END OF THE WORLD. It brings us in the overthrow
of Mahometanism to where the (7th) trumpet brings us
in the overthrow of Popery next (ch. 11:15). It belongs

to the period of the *Second Woe Trumpet*, but the end is
with the *third woe Trumpet.*

ANOTHER PARALLEL.

The reader should carefully compare the concluding
verses (10:8-11) with the concluding verses (11:15-18).
In those verses the victory is clearly referable to *the truth
preached* and made all-powerful in the earth. The victory
is always ascribed to THE GOSPEL in the various visions
by John covering this age of which we are now speaking.
And, (doubly corroborative of this fact), Daniel and John
are united in the fact that the sanctuary is to be cleansed,
that the power symbolized by the "little horn" of the
rough he-goat, "shall be broken without hand." This
is the logical place to show the decay and wasting away
of Turkish rule. But as the chapters are long, and the
identity of the power has been our chief point, and the
destiny of Mahometanism is closely allied to that of the
papacy, the two "little horns," in Daniel, chapters (7 and
8). I forbear except to say, The destruction of this
great Empire is predicted to be at the sounding of the
third woe trumpet (11:14). The whole territory once held
by this people in Europe, so vast in extent, is now taken
from the Turks, and the Balkan War was but a measure
of the woe due to fall upon this Anti-Christian power
and destroy it from the earth. The critical "Far Eastern" situation is and has been for some length of time
greatly embarrassed by the Sultan of Turkey. He is
propped up and allowed to continue on European territory, *not* because of his *own* power; but the states of
Europe need him. The yearly multiplication of battle-
ships, and the vast increase in the appropriations for war
purposes, as well as increasing demands for more soldiers, are destroying the nations. Despotism is dying
hard. This Colossus of the ages would fain continue
throughout the history of the world. But the doom of
Babylon is written upon every palace wall; and the doctrine that kings rule by "divine right," (and this right
coming through the office of the clergy), is exploded, in
almost all nations in our days.

THE TIME PROPHECY.

The (2300 days) may be considered briefly. (Dan'l.

9:14). There were four edicts made by the Persian Kings in behalf of Israel. We may try the (2300) prophetic days, (2300) years, on these.

Cyrus, B. C., 536plus 2300 equals A. D. 1764.

Darius, B. C. 518 plus 2300 equals A. D. 1782.

7th year of Artaxerxes, B. C. 457 plus 2300 equals 1843.

20th year of Artaxerxes B. C. 444 plus 2300 equals 1856.

The prophets used both Solar and Lunar counts; these are Solar, and to give the Lunar would double the number of dates, but no *second coming of Christ*, to cleanse the sanctuary is foretold in them. A fact not usually even *noticed* by Millennialists, but which is fatal to their theory is, there is a discrepancy of two hundred years in this text. The Septuagint manuscript reads (2400); Jerome gave it (2200); while the authorized version reads (2300). Most Millennialists have Daniel's Seventy Weeks, (490) years, "cut out" of this prophecy; their fulfillment a "seal" to the vision and the prophecy, so (A. D. 1843) is their terminal date. A few have hazarded other conjectures. Mr. Russell follows William Miller, M. Habershon, Cunninghame and others and has the cleansing to begin in the autumn of (A. D. 1846). The (2300) years cover the entire period until the doctrine of the Mahometan Impostor is swept away, by stages as it came up. I think the *Time*-Prophecies are waymarks of history. They reach certain great eras. In our days it is the overthrow of despotism; by the breaking up of the Metallic Man; and consumption of Daniel's fourth Beast, are the symbols. My mature judgment of the whole matter is that as dates for rise, continuance and overthrow of the Beast and the horns, are symbolized, that these dates are to be used to show the fulfillment of the prophecies in coming generations. Just as we look back to Noah and the Flood; the Exodus from Egypt; the forty years in the wilderness; the seventy years in Babylon; the previous dates of Ezekiel (ch. 4); of Israel's and Judah's possession of Canaan; or the sixty-five years of (Is. 7); or the (490) years to Messiah. As time advances, students of the Bible will look back and see that Popery and Mahometanism, and the ten horns of the

Beast, and ten toes of the Image came, acted their great
parts and were swept away. This, it seems to me, is the
very purpose of the dates. All the dates except the
thousand years of (Rev. 20) end with the OVERTHROW
OF THESE SYMBOLS. As the second coming of Christ
is not in the symbols, but still beyond the "little season"
that follows the thousand years, this grouping of dates
at this Era is significant. This is possibly the SIGN
OF THE SON OF MAN IN HEAVEN. (Matt. 24:30).
Fufilled prophecy is a sign, (Deut. 13:1-2). The "Tribulation" of the Jews was predicted to last a long time
(Luke 21:24; Daniel 9:27). The overthrow of the
great lights, like dissolving the whole fabric of nature,
is followed by this *sign*. They are the standing miracle
of history. *Immediately* after the long "tribulation,"
the sun is darkened, the moon fails to give *her light*, and
the stars fall from heaven, *then the sign*, and the mourning
of all the tribes of the earth. Similar language was used
concerning the overthrow of *literal* Babylon (Is. 13:10-
11); concerning pagan Rome, (Rev. 6:12-14); and, consistency of interpretation would demand that, when the
nations that worked this "tribulation" on Israel for ages
have ended it, their lights are extinguished, and so the
lines of prophecy focus on the Era, and become a divine
sign—or signify that Jesus rules in heaven. It may not
be amiss to notice that an event, and the SIGN of it, are
not the same. The SIGN of the woman, or the dragon
and the like (Rev. 12) illustrate this. Jesus coming to
earth is not a SIGN, but a *fact of literal prophecy*. There
is a predicted *sign*, and it is most likely the conversion
of the Jews—the receiving of them from their state of
death, to be grafted into their own olive tree, and to
say, "Blessed be he that cometh in the name of the Lord.
I think virtually all the expositors regard the conversion
of the Jews as the greatest event of their history. I
regard it as the fulfillment of a vast number of so-called
Millennial predictions, and as the certain goal towards
which time is bringing them; otherwise, I see no reason
for the preservation of the race, when all others are
swept away. The most marvellous events are impending,
as the time-prophecies are all but expired; but as I have
insisted on the inherent power of the gospel of Christ.

1. To overthrow the pagan Roman Empire.
2. To overthrow the papal dominion.
3. To overthrow Mahometanism.

I naturally look for the downfall of Judaism as the greatest victory for the King in Zion, this side of his ascension, the fruits of which will be unprecedented in earth's history, and will advance his truth by leaps and bounds to the ends of the earth.   Thus through ordained, all-sufficient means he gains the conquest of the nations. The Lord has always had the right men, at the right time, and right place, and his eternal purpose will unfold as time advances.   I am neither doubtful nor impatient of the results.   The Literalists tell us it is (2520) years from Judah's downfall as a nation; that the long week of "The Times of the Gentiles" is ended, and hence, it is time for Judah to reinhabit Palestine and restore the ancient wastes.   The "long week' is measured (Diagram III) in this volume; but does not indicate material, temporal restoration for Israel.   The receiving of Israel back to the favor of God must be through Christ and the gospel.   They were not rejected *the last time* for disobeying the Law of Moses, as they were while it was in force; and it is to shut our eyes to the revealed facts of the gospel to assume that, if the Jews would observe that law in Palestine perfectly, as Moses gave it, they would be approved of God.   It would not save them.   They need our Savior, for he is not a Gentile Redeemer; but the descendant of David, and his church is a Jewish church, (so to speak), as all its commands, ordinances, promises and threatenings were given first by THE AUTHORITY OF GOD, through converted Jews, to Jews exclusively.   The same things are spoken to them today, after we sinful Gentiles have been grafted into the covenant that God made WITH THE HOUSE OF ISRAEL AND WITH THE HOUSE OF JUDAH.   If the Jews are right in rejecting Christ, as the Messiah promised by the prophets, and in following Caiaphas, then the apostles were wrong in accepting him, and we would be wrong in obeying him as divine.   The Jews are strangers to their own mercy and fighting against God, Christ, the apostles of the New, and Moses and the prophets of the Old Testament.

CHAPTER XXX.

THE TEMPLE AND TWO WITNESSES.

The middle of the book of Revelation has one feature not belonging to the preceding part, the time is given when the prophecy begins, how long it continues and thus when it ends. There is room for some latitude of opinion, possibly, as to when each of the first six seals began, for no date is given. The history of the period covered by the fifth seal, ("Era of the Martyrs,") and the sixth seal, (the entire overthrow of the Pagan Roman Empire under Constantine), is, however, very plain, and sufficiently rescues this period from obscurity, that the greatest uniformity of exposition is found among those who follow the historic interpretation. There is general unity in diversity in the interpretation of the six trumpets in chapters (8 and 9). The first four lead down in history to the complete division of the Western Empire into the ten kingdoms, signified by the ten toes of the metallic man, and the ten horns of the fourth beast. Thus the way was opened for the complete development of the apostasy. Accordingly, the fifth trumpet sounds the alarm concerning the rise and progress of Mahomet, his religion and his Empire. The sixth carries the history on down to the close of these conquests, but under the Turks, as we have seen. This is the persecution of the church in the east.

FIVE-FOLD PICTURE.

Now, in the eleventh, twelfth and thirteenth chapters is given a five-fold picture of the fortunes of the church in the west. The bases of operations was Constantinople in the east and Rome in the west. As Rome was the Capital of the whole Empire and gave name to it; and as the church in the west exalted a bishop to be chief ruler in church and state throughout the world, and he was to rule from that ancient capital for the long period predicted, the symbols are used in this five-fold prophecy to picture the nature of the rise, progress and exploits of this great politico-religious power.

1. The Temple period covers 42 months. (11:1-2).

2. The period of the witnesses is the same length, expressed differently, "a thousand two hundred and three-score days" (11:3).

3. The dragon persecuted the woman "a thousand and two hundred and three-score days," and she was nourished in the wilderness "a time, and times and half a time," (12:6-14).

4. The beast which came up out of the sea had authority to continue 42 months (13:5). This time element holds these Symbols together as belonging to the same period. Another fact not to be ignored, (which ties these symbols together), is that the beast that comes out of the bottomless pit (11:7) slays the two witnesses; so we know that the ten-horned beast, the Western Roman Empire, in some phase of its rule not described in this chapter, is meant. It is,

1. The beast that comes out of the bottomless pit (11:7).

2. A great red dragon with seven heads and ten horns and on his heads seven crowns (or diadems) in (12:3).

3. It is a beast coming up out of the sea having ten horns, and seven heads, and on his horns ten diadems, and upon his heads names of blasphemy, in (13:1).

4. "And he carried me away in the Spirit into a wilderness; and I saw a woman sitting upon a scarlet colored beast, full of names of blasphemy, having seven heads and ten horns" is the description of the wild beast in (17:3).

5. The two horned lamb is the fifth set of symbols covering the period (ch. 13:11); but as we consider him later, we do not tarry here to describe him.

This is the cumulative evidence that identifies the beast in these chapters, when a full photograph is taken of him in (17:7-17). This is appropriate, for with this description *in full*, one can identify the cruel tyrant wherever he is mentioned from (11:7 to 20th ch).

ANOTHER POINT OF IDENTITY.

Daniel had used the same symbol (Dan'l 7) and

identified him as the *fourth* KINGDOM upon earth, which shall be diverse from all KINGDOMS, and shall devour the whole earth and shall tread it down, and break it in pieces. And the ten horns *out of this* KINGDOM are ten kings that SHALL ARISE; and *another* shall RISE AFTER them; and he shall be diverse from the first and he shall subdue three kings. Then he is a GOVERN-MENT that persecuted the saints of God and has dominion over them, "until a time and times and the dividing of time," when this government is overthrown, and in three stages goes to pieces?

1.   They take away his dominion.   (A. D. 1870).

2.   They consume it.

3.   It is destroyed unto the end.

The "little horn" is consumed at the close of the period. The attentive reader sees that the TIME fea-ture is the same as that given in (Rev. 11:2-3; 12:6-14; 13:5); and but one government could redeem the many features of this symbolic prophecy; that is, it must

1.   Be the *fourth* universal government in two sets of symbols which only allowed of *four* governments, and they in succession, as shown in the Metallic Man and the *four* beasts.

2.   The *fourth* government was to be divided into ten parts, each exercising sovereignty; and they were to give their support to one member of their family, the "little horn," and outlast him, because when the word of God was fulfilled, THEY would DESTROY him.   (Rev. 17:16-18).

3.   This "little horn" was to be of the beast, but come up *after* the other ten, later in history, and HIS TIME OF CONTINUANCE IS THE ONLY ONE FORE-TOLD and limits ALL these TIME-Prophecies, (Rev. 11, 12, 13) to that period of history covered by the "little horn."

4.   He was to "wear out the saints of the Most High," and they were to be given into his hand for the "time, times and the dividing of time."

5.   They were to take away HIS dominion to con-sume and to destroy it unto the end."

A CLOSER VIEW.

If you have the identity of the beast clearly in mind,

then you are prepared to study the "litle horn." Daniel represented the fourth beast, first, strong as iron; second, as weak, because of the mixture of iron and clay in the *feet*, and ultimately the toes. The mixture of iron and clay is thought by many to be the inter-marriage in Europe among the nobility. The following list will show how closely related are the titled class; and the war now raging will show how antagonistic are the elements united in these ambitious states.

"TIES THAT BIND" RULERS OF WARRING NATIONS.

King George V of Great Britain and Ireland, everybody's cousin.

Czarina of Russia, first cousin of King George and of Emperor William.

Emperor William of Germany, grandson of Queen Victoria.

Queen Sophia of Greece, sister of Emperor William.

Queen Victoria of Spain, first cousin of Emperor William, of King George and the Czarina of Russia.

Nicholas II, of Russia, first cousin of King George V.

Queen Helena, of Italy, daughter of King Nicholas of Montenegro.

King Albert of Belgium, cousin of King George V of Great Britain and Ireland.

Crown Princess Militza of Montenegro, cousin of King George.

King Haakon of Norway, first cousin and brother-in-law of King George and first cousin of the Czar of Russia.

Crown Princess Margaret of Sweden, granddaughter of Queen Victoria.

The system of government known in history as Papalism would have been impossible in any other period of Rome's history, even as it is impossible now. While the Roman government was strong such a ruler as the Pope was impossible. Daniel represents this power coming up after the strength of the empire had decreased, its unity was broken, and ten governments, each of which partook of the same weakness, had arisen. Out of this *political* situation it was made easy for a leader who assumed universal *religious* rule to demand and to secure recognition as universal civil ruler, and to crown or depose kings at his pleasure. His tremendous power and

influence over the conduct and consciences of his Myriads of followers in those governments, made it impossible for any one ruler to resist his autocratic power. If
ever there was absolutism this "little horn" exercised it.

His identity is preserved under different symbols,
introducing variety, but not contrariety, in the New Testament.

THE TEMPLE.

In (Rev. 11:1-2) there are the temple, altar, and
them that worship therein, subject to the measuring rod;
while the court and the holy city were profaned, forty-
two months. There was but one temple of God on earth
when John wrote, and has never been any other from his
day till now, to whom this language would justly apply.
Paul said, "The man of sin" should sit in the temple of
God. A meeting house was not the temple of God with
Paul; but the church or temple was composed of living
members, (I Cor. 3:16; 6;19; also Eph. 2:21), in all
of which the church is the temple. I have showed at
length the typical nature of Judaism, and need not but
to remind the reader that no revived Judaism could be
meant in this or any other passage of Scripture descrip-
tive of true worship in the gospel age. The description
is brief but comprehensive and covers practically the same
grounds as Paul in his announcement of the apostasy as
shown later. Here we may notice a few points only.
The reed was to measure:

1. THE TEMPLE. The word of God was the rule
by which the identity of the church, its name, organization and services must be tried. It was true or false
owing to whether or not it measured up to the righteous
standard of the great Temple-Builder, Christ. Whether
it was gold, silver, precious stones, wood, hay or stubble,
must decide.

2. THE ALTAR. I think one of the greatests tests
at this point was whether we need more than Christ's one
true sacrifice made on Calvary to redeem our souls.
Here we might see the mass, the mediators, especially the
Virgin, Mary, and the purgatorial fires, as supplemental
to this one altar on which "Christ was once offered to
bear the sins of many; and unto them that look for him

shall he appear the second time without sin unto salvation." (Heb. 9:28).

3. The worshippers. The forms and ceremonies, fasts, feasts, holy days, the observance of the seven sacraments, and things of that sort, do not come up to the measure. "God is a spirit and they that worship him must worship him in spirit and in truth."

In these verses one may learn that the church that boasted of her power and universality and measured up fully to the demands of carnal men, would be measured, by a perfect standard, also her altar (priesthood and his sacrifice of the mass) and the worshippers. The fact that the court was rejected and the holy city trodden under foot by the nations, suggests that Zion, the city of our solemnities, was disgraced during this age, as frequently under the Jewish age, the Gentiles defiled the literal temple. This condition lasted for (42) months. As the nominal church was the catholic church, the symbol of a temple here as in (II Thess. 2) where the man of sin presided so disastrously for a long time, shows this prophecy to be of the "little horn" under the symbols of (11:1-2) or the church considered during the (42) months, as a temple, altar and worshippers.

THE WITNESSES.

Next follows an account of two witnesses and they prophesy "a thousand two hundred and three-score days." We are told these are the two olive trees, and the two candlesticks standing before the God of the earth. It is useless to cite the theories advanced concerning these symbols. I prefer to go back to the original symbol (Zech. 4). The situation then was this: The children of Israel had returned from Babylon under an edict of Cyrus, king of Persia to rebuild their temple. They began the work but their enemies opposed them bitterly, and used their influence at the court of Persia, with successors of Cyrus and secured adverse decrees, and exultingly returned to Judah and forbade the erection of the temple. Haggai and Zechariah, two prophets, were raised up to encourage Israel to prosecute the work, which they did with success, but under bitter and protracted hostility from the envious bordering nations.

(You should read the entire fourth chapter of Zechariah before examining my suggestions further). To analyze his symbolism:

1. The candlestick represented the temple. It had but one bowl on the top of it for the reception of oil that fed it constantly.

2. It had seven lamps, signifying the perfect light, just as the seven candlesticks of (Rev. 1:20) while dividing the church into seven congregations, comprehended the entire church.

3. There were seven pipes from this bowl conveying severally oil to each lamp.

4. There were *two* olive trees, one on the right side, the other on the left side of the bowl. These trees, signifying men, furnished oil continually for the perfect seven-fold light. (vs. 3-6). Inspired men, (one a PRIEST, the other a GOVERNOR), representative of the two forms of government in Israel, one administered by Zerubbabel, the other by Jeshua, would build that temple. "Not by might, nor by power, but by my spirit, saith the Lord of hosts." These were the two anointed ones, representative of priesthood and royalty, united under God for the erection of that temple. (vs. 11-14). In transfering this imagery to (Rev. 11) it necessarily carries with it the same thoughts and suggestions.

In (Zech. 6:9-15) is a prophecy (already commented upon), in which the Royal-Priesthood of Christ is predicted. The pope united the kingly and High-priestly functions in himself, a thing forbidden under the Mosaic law, and belonging only to Christ under the gospel age. The two olive trees are expressly stated by John to be the two witnesses; and the two functions of government *in type* were signified by them according to Zechariah's inspired interpretation. If the two functions of government, (royalty and priesthood), were used by Zechariah in this manner, in the typical dispensation, we have an inspired rule to govern the interpretation of the symbols. Moreover, Zechariah foretold that Christ would be a Priest upon his Throne. David said:

"The Lord said unto my Lord, sit thou at my right hand until I make thine enemies thy footstool. The Lord shall send *the rod of thy strength* out of *Zion*: rule thou in the midst of thine enemies. Thy people shall be a willing people in the day of thy power, in the beauties of holiness from the womb of the morning: thou hast the dew of thy youth. The Lord hath sworn and will not repent thou are a priest forever after the order of Melchisedec. The Lord at thy right hand, shall strike through kings in the *day* of his wrath. He shall judge among the heathen, he shall fill the places with the dead bodies: he shall wound the heads over many countries. He shall drink of the brook in the way: therefore shall he lift up the head." (Ps. 110).

Our Savior asked the Jews about this wonderful passage, how the Messiah could be David's son and David's Lord? (Matt. 22:41-6). They could not answer because they did not recognize his divinity and that he was to be at *God's right hand* as Ruler, and not in an *earthly* government. Paul devotes three chapters in Hebrews, to explaining the priesthood of Christ, "after the order of Melchisedek," that is that he was a priest on his throne. The Millennialists would have us divide these offices, and have Jesus as a Priest for two thousand years in heaven; and then come back to earth and *reign one thousand years*, their Millennial day, personally. Thus they make him Priest some two thousand years before they make him king, (only as some Mediatorial king), with them he has not taken to him his "great power."

Babylon for the predicted period of (42 months) united church and state. The "little horn" assumed both offices, Lord and Priest. Both of these two offices of Christ, for which he was anointed of God, WERE PROFANED FOR THAT PERIOD. The two lamps burned dimly; the two branches of government were humiliated and dishonored. Such a rule and assumed authority over the nations, was a disgrace to the name of Lord, and such a High-Priest was a counterfeit. As the Popes advanced and revelled in the carnal security of assumed temporal rule as the so-called Representatives of Christ, and so managed the Priest-hood as to scandalize the office of Christ, the church whose light was fed and made brilliant by the law of Christ relative to his own Lord-ship and Priesthood became dark and desolate.

The fire coming out of their mouth devouring enemies, and killing them AFTER THAT MANNER, is evidently borrowed from Jeremiah, "I will make my words fire in thy mouth and this people wood, and it shall destroy them," (Jer. 5:14). The word of God would destroy these usurpers even as it did, under the former dispensation. Next were associated Elijah and Moses; Elijah shut up heaven that it rained not for (42 literal months). So there was a famine. In the (42 Prophetic months) of this prophecy, a moral and spiritual dearth prevailed, which was far worse. "Behold the days come, saith the Lord God, that I will send a famine in the land; not a famine of bread, nor a thirst for water, but of hearing the words of the Lord. And they shall wander from sea to sea, and from the north even to the east, they shall run to and fro to seek the word of the Lord, and shall not find it." Amos (8:11). I do not quote this as a direct prophecy of this famine and darkness, but as illustrative of it. The language of Amos was fulfilled when they had completely rejected the true prophets of God, and their false prophets alone were left. Then darkness covered the earth and gross darkness the people. And when anti-typical Israel rejected the Word of God, and allowed the two great lamps to go out for want of oil, the two olive trees to be destroyed, (the supreme authority of Christ, as KING in Zion, and his PERFECT PRIESTHOOD), then came on the DARK AGES. The Lamps were out. Gibbon says, "The Christians of the sixth century had insensibly relapsed into a semblance of paganism. The *throne* of the Almighty was darkened by a cloud of Martyrs, saints and angels, the objects of popular veneration." Gregory the Great, writing about (A. D. 590) said, "All things which were predicted are taking place. *The King of Pride is at hand,* and what is unlawful to utter, an army of priests is prepared for him. At this time true religion, weighed down by a heap of insane superstition, was unable to raise its head. The early Christians were wont to worship God and his Son only; but in this age (sixth century) they who were called Christians, worshipped the wooden cross, the images of saints, and the bones of men."

ITEMS OF APOSTASY.

The great Pantheon in Rome where all the heathen deities were collected, was converted into a Temple, and it is said that two of the idols, Venus and Jupiter, were christened under the names of the Virgin Mary and Peter! (It had as well be Jupiter and Venus as any others, for all image worship was forbidden even the Jewish people; and every image erected and venerated in any place, adopted from heathenism or manufactured for the occasion, is a violation of Christ's authority as King). It is to change times and laws. To crown a man with a triple crown, while he occupies a throne, and beneath his feet is the Lord's table, is to degrade the witnesses. The keys were placed in the hands of Jupiter, and he is still known as Saint Peter, and regarded with supreme veneration and respect; and many objects of adoration among the heathen first, were adopted under other names as the statues of saints. Prayers were offered to saints that they would intercede for them. Buildings were dedicated to saints. Purgatory began to be taught. The nature of the corruptions which had crept into the church, led the masses, more and more, into idolatry. The church buildings were named after Mary, Peter, John, Paul and other saints. The sixth century was prolific in the development of those fasts, feasts, processions and other "voluntary" acts, which cling to the apostasy to this day. Carrying the picture of the Virgin Mary in processions; burning of candles and tapers before altars, in the daytime, (before idolatrous altars,) should be noticed.

"If in the beginning of the fitfh century, Tertullian, or Lactantius, had been suddenly raised from the dead, to assist in the festival of some popular saint or martyr, they would have gazed with astonishment and indignation on the profane spectacle which had succeeded to the pure and spiritual worship of a Christian congregation. As soon as the doors of the church were thrown open, they must have been offended by the smoke of incense, the perfume of flowers, and the glare of lamps and tapers which diffused at noonday, a gaudy, and, in their opinion, a sacrilegious light; if they approached the balustrade of the altar, they made their way through the prostrate crowd, consisting for the most part, of strangers, and pilgrims who resorted to the city at the vigil of the feast, and who already felt the strong intoxication of fanaticism and perhaps of wine; their devout kisses were imprinted on the walls and pavement of the sacred edifice, and their fervent prayers were directed, whatever might be the language of their church, to the bones and blood or ashes of the saints, which were usually concealed by a linen or silken veil from the eyes of the vulgar.

The Christians frequented the tombs of the marytrs in hope of obtaining from their powerful intercession every sort of spiritual, but more especially of temporal, blessings. The walls were hung round with symbols of favours, which they, the pilgrim offerers, had received. Eyes, hands, and feet of gold and silver, and edifying pictures, which could not long escape the abuse of indiscreet or idolatrous devotion, represented the image, the attributes and the miracles of the titular Saint," Thus deposes Gibbon.

Thus through the centuries, the mystery of iniquity grew, until the Pope was ultimately seated in the Papal throne, and exalted himself above all that is called God or is worshipped, and sat in the temple of God(nominal church), saying he is God."

KING AND PRIEST.

The assumption of absolute power in church and state was used to persecute the witnesses. As in the parable of the Tares, "The good seed are the children of the kingdom, but the tares are the children of the wicked one," that is, represent them, so here the great offices of Christ were the Ruling and High Priestly functions IN THE CHURCH. I SEE NOTHING IN THE SYMBOLS REFERRING TO EARTHLY RULE, OR CIVIL RULE. The pope was all these—Lord of the church; High-priest of the church; and supreme head of all temporal authority. This is the historical fact. But this set of symbols refers to his *religious* supremacy, while chapter twelve symbolizes his fight against the civil rule, which the Man-Child lawfully exercises. The Man of Sin (the lawless one) opposed the man-child (the lawful one) produced by the church. The false church produced the false government, or "man of sin." The true church gave birth to the man-child who is to rule all nations, all men with a rod of iron—or shepherdize the nations. Both men are governments; one the unlawful combination of church, and state, the other claiming and exercising only the true functions of government, and protecting the church in her holy mission, a government that God can own and bless. The Pope was a religious usurper, BEFORE HE ADDED TEMPORAL RULE to his authority. When the sword of the civil magistrate was his, it merely backed up and made effective his blasphemous assumption of spiritual authority to rule the church and act as High Priest on earth. This, I take it, made the claims of Christ, upheld along the ages, by those who denounced the pope, an exceedingly hazardous business. This caused the persecution and lit the fires of martyrdom. To repudiate him in either office was a mortal sin.

"And when they shall have finished their testimony, the beast that cometh up out of the abyss shall make war with them, and overcome them, and kill them. And their dead bodies lie in the street of the great city, which spiritually is called Sodom and Egypt, where also their Lord was crucified. And from among the people and tribes and tongues and nations do men look upon their dead bodies three days and a half, and suffer not their dead bodies to be laid in a tomb. And they that dwell on the earth rejoice over them, and make merry; and they shall send gifts, one to another; because these two prophets tormented them that dwell on the earth. And after three days and a half the breath of life from God entered into them, and they stood upon their feet; and great fear fell upon them that beheld them. And they heard a great voice from heaven saying unto them, Come up hither. And they went up into heaven in the cloud; and their enemies beheld them. And in that hour there was a great earthquake, and the tenth part of the city fell; and there were killed in the earthquake, seven thousand persons; and the rest were affrighted and gave glory to God. The second woe is past; behold the third woe cometh quickly."

The fact that the Beast ascendeth out of the Abyss and slays these witnesses is strong evidence that *they* are not real persons, for *he* is only a *symbol* of *government*. The further fact that these witnesses bear testimony (1260 years), shows the same. The language concerning the fire coming out of their mouths, and their power to turn rivers into blood, and control the plagues, is an evident allusion to Moses and Aaron in Egypt, where fleshly Israel were in bondage. These actual miracles were performed there, in defense of the authority of God as Ruler over Israel. But the rivers in these symbols are people. It makes little difference to one, which people may be selected, (by historic expositors), say, Waldenses and Albigenses, (as these are commonly cited), they could not do *literally* what Moses and Aaron did in Egypt, or what Elijah did in Israel. It is a question of making

these symbols a group of the most awe-inspiring miracles, strewn along the pathway of popery, for more than
a thousand years, and closing with the death, resurrection
and ascension of these witnesses visible to their enemies,
none of which is veritable history; or of allowing them to
be impersonations before the prophet to be used as symbols of events in the history of the church, covering "a
thousand two hundred and three-score days." My knowledge of history would not permit me to say that one man,
or one sect, ever lived to be that old; ever existed, in
fact, during the reign of the "little horn," and wrought
as stupendous miracles as Moses and Elijah, whenever
they desired. I believe, rather, that true miracles ceased,
necessarily, when the last men died who received this
power from the apostles. Furthermore there is no promise that they shall ever be revived. We are necessarily
shut up to the facts of history in the church for the fulfillment of these symbolic forecasts. Discarding as I do
any exposition that makes these witnesses to work miracles in fact on nature, and holding the consoling view
that as Jeremiah and others were God's mouth pieces,
so "the testimony of Jesus is the spirit of prophecy,"
and it was the authority of Christ, his Lordship and High-
Priestly functions, being upheld by faithful followers
through the centuries, that turned the rivers into blood
and brought plagues upon apostate Christendom. "Christ
came to send not peace upon earth, but a sword,"—the
sword of the Spirit. Whenever that sword was unsheath-
ed in behalf of the sole right of Jesus to rule in religion,
it tormented the enemies of that heavenly doctrine, and
provoked persecution.

Men were not suffered to preach his authority as
King and Priest. While they lived they were boycotted,
persecuted and slain; when they were dead, they were
treated with indignity and not permitted burial in
consecrated (?) ground. All efforts were made to destroy *them* from the earth; but *the fight* was really against
Christ. Our Savior told Saul, "I am Jesus whom thou
persecutest." So, for twelve centuries, Jesus was persecuted, crucified afresh, in the martyrdom of his saints;
but the witnesses would continue to denounce the Popes
as usurpers of the titles and dominion of Christ. The

Lateran Council (May 5, 1514), declared the "heretics" all dead. They had been summoned to appear before that august tribunal, but none went. With exultation and festival, they celebrated the death of protest against the Pope. The representatives of the nations, princes in the church, held high jubilee and the people sent presents to one another, thinking that after many ages their object was at last attained and no protesting voice would any more be raised against the Pope. At the same council they refused burial rites to any dissenter from the faith, as if determined to fasten the odium of this arrogant assumption upon themselves at the very time the prophecy foretold. And what reader of these lines does not know that this is a law in the church (which professes that she never changes), to this day?

But (Oct. 31st, 1517,) Luther nailed his ninety-five theses on the door of the Wittenburg church, and from that day, we begin the Reformation. From (May 5, 1514 to Oct. 31, 1517) are just three years and a half. The slumbereing, suppressed witnesses, with the Spirit of life from God in them, (the inspired words of the Bible) stood on their feet. A religious earthquake convulsed the world. With the authority of the Pope as King and High-Priest, ruling in Christ's stead, rejected and despised, seven thousand men fell. A perfect number; and evidently a definite for an indefinte number, of Cardinals, Arch-bishops, bishops, priests, friars, nuns, and all the list of saints in the category fell with the groundless assupmtion of the Head. One of his chief governmental supports for ages, old England, fell away in Protest. Jesus was restored by a "cloud of Witnesses" as Lord of all, and High Priest over the house of God. And the long period of woe, made up of false teaching and infamous methods of holding the people as slaves to the religious despot on the Tiber, was passed.

The reader will notice that in the next period to follow according to (10:7 and 11:15) the mystery of God is finished, and the SOVEREIGNTY of the world is given to CHRIST, after thus being WRESTED FROM THE POPE. However this is developed in a new set of symbols, beginning with the last verse of this chapter and continuing through (ch. 12). While this (11th ch.)

pictures the (1260) years of Papal supremacy from the standpoint of his assuming to be universal bishop, and Lord of the conscience, the Vicar of Christ, the next chapter considers his temporal rule. He was a Nebu-chadnezzar, Cyrus, Alexander, Caesar style of ruler, in that he ruled in church and state. The "little horn," you remember, grew out of the head of the fourth or Roman Beast; and was, therefore, distinctly Roman. But it was a Roman Government for ages, a civil government, as well as a Roman church. It is as a government we stndy this power in the next set of symbols.

CHAPTER XXXI.

THE WOMAN AND MAN-CHILD.

1. A common figure to represent God's people is a woman. (Ezek. 16; 23) and references; (Eph. 5:25; Ps. 45; Rev. 21:2, 9, 11 and ch. 19).

2. She could not *signify* the Jewish Nation for two reasons: the *fulfillment* was under the *seventh* seal, (and the Jews were not God's people at that time), and they were not laboring under persecution from the Dragon to bring forth any power justly called the Man Child.

3. The Dragon had seven heads and ten horns and persecuted the woman (1260 years) and she was in the wilderness, "time, times and half a time." This defines the Western Roman Empire *after* it was divided into ten governments (A. D. 476), how *long* afterwards is not stated, but was the oft-repeated period of Daniel and Revelation, the reign of persecution under the little horn, whether that horn is regarded as beginning (A. D. 533 or A. D. 606). The fact that such a division had taken place before signified by the ten horns, sufficiently iden-tifies the time.

4. The woman could not have been Mary even if the imagery had been used before the birth of Christ, for several reasons. Mary was a literal woman; she was never in heaven, never had the sun for her clothing, never

stood on the moon, never wore a crown, did not flee into a wilderness after the birth of her child, and no serpent ever attempted to drown her.

5. Finally, Jesus' birth, life, death, resurrection, ascension, coronation, establishment of his kingdom or church, and her persecutions in apostolic days, are all matters of record in the inspired history of the New Testament. There would be nothing revealed, NOTHING SIGNIFIED in the chapter, if it were the Jewish Nation or the Virgin Mary. It would, in that case, only be an obscure allusion to the *past*, and not a revelation of what was to be under the *seventh* seal. Where then would have been the GREAT SIGN? The attempt therefore to signify *the past* is to frustrate the design of *prophecy*, and add no item of knowledge concerning Christ or his Church not already given in the plainest matters of fact written by the apostles and evangelists of the New Testament. How could the stars be on the head of Mary before the birth of the Man Child or at any other time? If they signify the apostles then Jesus was not the Man Child. I will not consider Constantine for he was under the sixth seal and fits the symbol in no point whatever.

CONSIDERED FIGURATIVELY.

1. Great Sign. This is in harmony with (ch. 1:1), and signifies something; the stars are men (1:20) and the woman, sun, moon and twelve stars and the greater lights must be used in harmony with the symbols of their group. The second verse, of course, *not literal*; then, of necessity, none of the rest is literal.

The second *sign* (not animal) appears in heaven. Dragon, great, red, has seven heads, ten horns and seven crowns (dynasties) or forms of government such as Roman Empire had. As no literal woman has ever been literally in heaven, in such literal condition, it is certain that no literal dragon has ever persecuted her there. Women belong to earth, dragons to earth, literally, so the facts *signified* evidently belong to earth.

No dragon's tail is long enough to reach the stars and drag them down to earth. The stars are a long distance from earth! The woman fled from the seven-headed ten-horned, seven-crowned dragon into the wilderness—not a literal woman pursued by a literal dragon either in heaven or on earth. The days are prophetic days or sign days, a day for a year, and *signs* of the 1260 years. There was war in heaven. The contending forces are Michael and his angels and the dragon and his angels; and the dragon and his angels were defeated and cast out of heaven. Yes, John saw that in *sign* or *symbolic* prophecy. Milton, with poetic license, could grow eloquent here. But the results seem to forbid the notion of heavenly battle, and to be representative only of what was actually TO BE DONE BY MEN IN THE FLESH, in the period then future to John, and these men were under the Captain of our salvation on one side and the leader of the forces of darkness on the other. Why so? The victory was celebrated in these terms "Now is come (a) the salvation (b) and the power (c) and the kingdom of our God (d) and the authority of his Christ; (e) for the accuser of our brethren is cast down ,who accuseth them before our God day and night."

How was, the victory obtained? Not with celestial swords or perfected machine guns of heaven or catapaults of heavenly manufacture, or with powder and bullets, nitro-glycerine and the peerless, invincible charges of Jesus Christ and his angels. But (a) by the blood of the Lamb; (b) by the word of their testimony ; (c) and they loved not their life even unto death." We are commanded to overcome with this equipment of spiritual weapons, for this is not a carnal warfare. Then follows joy to one class; woe to the other class. The reappearance of the "blessing" and the "curse."

The dragon was cast into the earth (after the battle and victory over him) and persecuted the woman that brought forth the Man Child. The woman is given two great wings of an eagle, makes flight into the wilderness (into her place) alluded to again as the place where she was nourished the three and a half times or twelve hundred and sixty years. It should be noted that Elijah spent three and a half years in seclusion while the life of ancient Israel hung in the balance. When he returned, after this period, it was to defeat idolaters in his own person and that of successors. He was probably not a type but an example easily enlarged upon for predictive purposes in this and the preceding chapter. The serpent cast *out of his mouth the flood,* or water as a river to drown the woman. See the many uses of earth, (chs. 4, 9, 12, 13, 16). Here it helped the woman and frustrated the dragon. When did the woman and her seed get back to earth on the literalist's theory?

The dragon was with the woman, whoever she is, and went to make *war* with the remnant of her seed. Who are they? Heavenly or earthly residents? Evidently earthly (" who keep the commandments of God and have the testimony of Jesus"). These are practical duties for Christians, here and now, hence Christians "fight the good fight of faith and lay hold on eternal life." These remarks must suffice to show that this great chapter is figurative throughout. It was not written as actual history of realities in heaven, neither as predictive of angelic and satanic warfare in heaven at the time signified. This chapter has been verified in the history of the church on earth.

EXPOSITION.

I know of no exposition of this chapter, called by many the "Crux" of Revelation, (or most difficult part) that does not overlook the chief point in it—THE FACT THAT IT IS THE MAN CHILD WHO RULES THE WORLD AND NOT THE MOTHER. It is not true, according to these symbols, that the church shall ever grow into a world-power. It is not predicted that the church in its Millennial day will be the sole government on earth. The fifth monarchy expositors, and largely, all Millennialists, have Jesus to return to earth, sweep away all temporal rule, establish his kingdom, not only as supreme in temporal affairs, but as the sole government on earth. I emphasize this fact for it is vital to every scheme of the Personal Reign of Christ on earth for a thousand years. Any exposition of these symbols that makes the church, the sole ruler of the nations is visionary and untrue to the prediction. Not claiming infallibility, nor hoping to develop fully the sublimities of this chapter, I undertake the task of showing that the system of prophecy set forth in the *Metallic* Man and the four wild Beasts is not antagonized, but beautifully illustrated, in

some of its features, in this chapter.   My notes on parts
of it shall be brief.

1.   Woman.   The church of Christ.

2.   Her head.   Christ.   (Eph. 1:22; 4:15; Col.
1:18).

3.   Clothed with the sun, or Christ's glory. Mal. 4:2.

4.Crown of twelve stars.   Apostles.   Not one, as
Peter, but the twelve men associated doctrinally and as
rulers with Christ.   (Rev. 1:20; Mal. 3:17).

5.   Moon.   Typical dispensation, which like the
moon shines only from borrowed light from the sun or
Christ and had no glory by reason of the glory that ex-
celleth.   (II Cor. 3).

6.   *The woman brought forth after her kind*, CHURCH
(ekklesia) IS A GOVERNMENT, A KINGDOM, AND
BRINGS FORTH A GOVERNMENT.   There is no literal
birth of a child in the symbols; but the symbolic woman
bears a man-child.

7.   Dragon.   A particular government, actuated by
the devil, (as the church is by Christ) is defined by seven
heads and ten horns (or the Western Roman government that passed through seven forms of rule) is pictured as to its division into ten parts (A. D. 476).

The dragon's tail drew down stars; or eminent men
of the church were carnalized and they scandalized the
church either by upholding the union of church and state,
or by being drawn away from their spiritual vocation to
temporal or both.   The dragon (pagan government), or
government that persecuted the church, was not akin to
her but her mortal enemy.   This despotic government,
both in its pagan and papal form, was the bitter and
relentless foe of civil and religious liberty.   The church
had in her the elements of government, which after
gestation, would grow into a robust government in harmony with the church, his mother, and be her protector,
and together they would destroy the dragon form of
government.   That is Jesus would, through the church,
give rise, (birth, if you please), to a government antagonistic to despotism, in church and state; and the ultimate victory of this government(man child), in dashing
to pieces all antagonistic government, was assured.   Let
it be distinctly remembered that John showed us the

assumption by the papacy of the Lordship and Priesthood of the church. The two offices were obscured, or
the witnesses prophesied in sackcloth and ashes. Otherwise stated, these disciples of Jesus contended for these
two offices of Christ against the pope who arrogated to
himself these sacred titles. It was this spiritual rule in
question in (ch. 11).

It is the same church during the same period contending chiefly against the same power in (ch. 12); but
the contention is over another sort of ruler-ship. In
this chapter the civil rule or temporal lordship is in
question. I need only remind the reader that popery
claimed to rule in the state as well as in the church and
the pope wears a triple crown in testimony of the fact
that he rules in earth, heaven and Hades. The church
can not rule alone. She can not prosper under despotism. One of earth's greatest questions is and long has
been, what form of government is in harmony with the
rule of Christ! The long history of the struggle of the
church in contending with earthly rulers that tyrannized
over her, especially popery, is set forth in the symbols of
this chapter.

The government was given to Jesus (Ps. 2); to the
saints, (Daniel 7; Rev. 2:26-27). But it is not Jesus in
person, nor his church, directly that obtains the universal
sovereignty. It is not the *church*, because the church
gave birth to it. Mark well the continued identity of the
woman and her *son*. They do not change places in the
prophecy and are therefore separate in *fulfillment*. She
brought forth the man child and he, not she, is to rule.
The church preserves her individuality, is free to continue her appointed spiritual work and the son does the
work of an outside nature, or political work, rules the
nations with a rod of iron. Birth is not maturity. The
birth, infancy and manhood periods of a manchild are
clearly apparent in every man. So governments, begotten by the word of God, nourished and fostered by the
church, as a mother presides over her son, grow into all
the elements of strength and character belonging to this
ordinance of God. Civil government is not the child of
the devil, but of God. (Rom. 13:1-4). Every argument
that would do away with civil government because it has

been corrupted and made an agency of the devil would do away with the church on the same principles, for it, too, became a curse to untold millions when ruled from beneath. But evermore give thanks to God through Christ that both *church* and *state* are being set free from tyranny. And, later, I will show that, not only the church has had her partial restoration to her long lost liberties; but the state, as well, and both at the *same time*, the result of the same gospel. Despotism in the state brought forth despotism in the church. The seven-headed ten-horned dragon PRODUCED THE APOSTASY, for you can not have forgotten that the "little horn" grew out of the head of the beast, was therefore an essential part of it. By necessary sequence the apostasy of the church, or the little government of the papacy, (small as to territory), was a part of the Roman Empire out of which it grew. Like produces like. Just so the church after throwing down the throne of the pope in the church, overturns the thrones in the governments after which papacy was modeled. If the people have a free church they must have a free government. State churches are out of date. Kings ruling by "divine right" and priests ruling by "divine right" are survivals of heathenism. A despot in church or state is a monstrosity. The two could live together, and the Harlot woman could ride the scarlet colored beast with propriety of symbols, for they were both bent on the same mission; but she can not ride a free government.

CHAPTER XXXII.

TWO BEASTS AND TWO LAMBS.

CHAPTERS 13 AND 14.

The prophecy concerning the apostasy, known generally as Babylon, is given in eight parts; twice in Daniel (chs. 2 and 7), once in (II Thess. 2) and five times in Revelation (chs. 11 to 15). The remainder of this last book of the Bible down to (20:6) is devoted to a detailed account of the ultimate victory of the church or kingdom of God, over the combined foes known as Babylon. Most expositors have a temporal kingdom of Christ in mind and overlook the discriminations made in these seven prophecies. They degrade the symbols by making them predict a visible earthly reign of Christ and the resurrected saints on earth. The Pre-Millennialists make it easy for Dawnists. The fact is Mr. C. T. Russell could never get a hearing for his vagaries if it were not that the thousand year Tradition is advocated by all who hold to the Personal advent of Christ to reign on earth.

These inspired writers go over the same period seven times; but each time they give a new revelation. In order to show the various departments of the work, they went over the same period; but, while thus chaining the prophecies together, they kept them separate in a very important sense.

1. In Daniel the first set of symbols cover the whole period; but the Giant Man symbol does not show the apostate church. He describes the ultimate overthrow of Despotism, and the triumph of the Stone. But we learn later that this "stone" comprehends more than at first appears. It is composite, or destructive and constructive; but one errs grievously to think it is the church, as such, attaining to universal rule, with all other governments destroyed. (Dan'l 2).

2. The four beasts carry us over the same period; but when we get to the time of the horns of the fourth

beast, and see that the ten horns correspond to the ten toes of the Image, we are informed that a "little horn" has to be reckoned with also; and right there this pre- diction, (while continuing with the other), enlarges upon the subject, and thus introduces a *government* that con- tinues "time, times and half a time," and is a terrible force in the world. The horn or power grows up among the ten, out of the head of the *same* beast, but *later*; de- stroys three of those governments, and comes to his end by the power of the saints. (Dan'l. 7). This is the "two-horned Lamb," or "Image" of the Roman Empire.

3. John who lived some six centuries later, when three of these metals and the three first beasts had been turned into history; and the fourth metal and the fourth beast were then fulfilled in the *united* Roman Empire, NATURALLY DROPPED THOSE SYMBOLS, and en- larged upon the period covered by the TOES of the image, and the HORNS of the Beast. So his symbols, (that re- late to the same subject), were chosen to throw a flood of light on the fortunes and destiny of the church, and to explain that "little horn." His first symbols on this subject are in (ch. 11:1-2). The church, under the symbols of temple altar and worshippers, was to exist during the period of the "little horn," or the "time, times and the dividing of time," but subject to divine inspec- tion and measurement. The "court" was "cast out," not considered at all, but was to belong to the nations, (hea- then). The church in name, organization, work and wor ship would have a heavenly measure applied. Now, no one denies that the church, (using that word in its broad sense, including all professors of the Christian religion), has existed since Pentecost (Acts 2). It soon numbered millions of adherents, and spread like leaven into all nations. The Greek Catholic, Roman Catholic, Armenian, Albigenses, Waldenses or Vaudois and sects before and since these arose, have as manifestly proved that the church has never ceased, as the history of the Jews from Abraham to Christ proves that Abraham's posterity never ceased. But the corruption and apostasy of ancient Israel was a type of the corruption and apos- tasy of spiritual Israel. And, while we can not read the history since Christ without finding much concerning

the church, yet we see in (Rev. 11:1, 2) that the mere existence of a church was no proof that it met God's favor; but that it was to be measured by a divine rule. The altar, (whereon Christ made the great sacrifice, the atonement), was to be measured also; and the worshippers, as well. The nominal professors, who only came into the court, were accounted as heathen. This is an important distinction John makes in passing through this period of the (42 months), and teaches us that God did not endorse everything known as a church; and, especially, those who denied the virtue of Christ's atonement, and multiplied heresies around that altar. Neither did he endorse every church member; but, "righteousness he will lay to the line and justice to the plummet."

THE WITNESSES.

4. He passes over the *same period again*, but this time illustrating *another feature* of the apostasy, that wherein the Pope assumed to be LORD OVER THE CHURCH (not over the world, that is, it was his religious, not his civil, rule); and also to be the High-Priest. These two separate functions of *religious government* he sought to unite in himself. By this means he changed the ordinances, (or substituted others for them), ordained all the fasts, feasts, holy days, officers, services in general and in particular in his church and sat in the temple of God as God. As High-Priest he withheld official grace and blessing from some, and claimed to create and sacrifice the Lord daily in "the mass;" to remit or to retain sins; and in a word, to take the place of the great High-Priest on earth. *These assumptions* further corrupted the church. There is no intimation of TEMPORAL LORDSHIP in this set of symbols. He was ruler and priest IN THE CHURCH before, while, and since, he was temporal ruler. This power was acquired gradually, and is to be consumed gradually. You see after the death, resurrection, and ascension of the witnesses, the earthquake, or mighty upheaval in religious affairs, and the seven thousand men were killed,—the rest gave glory to the God of heaven—rather than to "Lord God, the Pope," as they did for more than twelve centuries. When the two witnesses were slain, the supreme Lord-

ship and High-Priestly functions of Christ, were entirely
dead in that city, spiritually, (not literally), called "Sodom and Egypt.' The children of God were in bondage
and their cause was dead in that wicked city. When
they arose it was by the repudiation of the pope as Lord
and High-Priest in the church; and the vindication of,
the kingly and High-Priestly, functions as belonging exclusively to our Lord Jesus Christ.

These seven thousand men were killed by the *words*
that came out of the mouth of the witnesses (11:5). It
was not a carnal warfare on the part of the witnesses—
Jesus would not vindicate himself in his kingly and
Priestly offices that way while here, neither did he
authorize the disciples to vindicate his claims, by the use
of carnal weapons. After the resurrection and ascension
of the witnesses to the heavens where they belong, and
the "cleansing of the sanctuary" of this foul usurper,
who had been so long the curse of the church, it was said,
"The second woe is past." But Babylon still existed and
exercised political power extensively; however, the third
woe, that would exterminte *her political*, as the second woe
had laid bare her *religious assumptions* would follow quickly; and it did, for this temporal supremacy of the Pope
began to fall in the wars of Napoleon at the opening of
the nineteenth century, and Victor Immanuel, half a
century later, swept away the last vestige of the political
or civil dominion. They have had no temporal dominion
since (A. D. 1870).

5. But having mentioned the civil rule, which was
such an important factor in the apostasy, and so wrapped
up in the symbolism of the horns, next in (ch. 12, as we
have seen) HE TAKES US OVER THE (1260 YEARS)
OF BABYLON, (confusion) AGAIN, this time to show
how the EARTHLY *sovereignty*, was worked out. He pictures the old despotism of Rome, (reappearing in the ten
kingdoms into which this last government was divided),
continued as unchanged in spirit under professed Christian rule as under Pagan rule, and these ten civil governments persecuted the woman for the (1260 years).
The fact that these ten governments were adherents of
the pope for a thousand years, and his religion was their
religion, his persecutions their persecutions, forever links

them with, the apostasy. The expositors of the Old World do not see, or, at best, do not develop, this symbolism. EVERY STATE CHURCH IS, IN THE LANGUAGE OF REVELATION, A HARLOT. The Roman Catholic was supreme, the mother; they are daughters. It is not enough to protest against the pope. As long as Kings and Emperors are considered as earthly heads of the church, popery, in its essential features, exists. The transfer of power from Rome to England, under Henry VIII, was not a return to the Bible. That was the turn Nebuchadnezzar took in the case of the three Hebrews. He would burn alive all who did not worship his image — that was popery. He was the *head* of CHURCH and STATE in *literal* Babylon.

His second decree was to slay any and all who spake against the God of the Hebrews. This was popery again. We do not wish the state to regulate our worship. This is not the province of the state: it can only protect men from the fury of the king and fanaticism of the vicious and superstitious. Let the church be free to serve God and have no earthly Lord either pope, king, council, synod or ecclesiastical board; and she in turn will render to the state devoted services in sowing the principles of righteousness that exalt a nation.

The fact that the ten governments of Western Europe upheld popery, and have been equal in guilt with her in her *whole history* of (42 months), makes us look suspiciously at them when they exalt leaders in the state to be the heads of state churches. This whole fabric of despotism is wrong and is doomed in these symbols. "What! Christian people persecute the church as did Pagans?" Yes, they hated what the WOMAN WAS TO BRING FORTH,—A MAN-CHILD. This man-child is the contrasted power over against the "man of sin, son of perdition." The man-child is a son of the church, and rules so as to gain the sovereignty of the world for Christ and his church, the woman. Not that the church seeks or will ever exercise universal rule directly, for the symbol would then have been single, whereas it is double. The woman gives birth to the man-child and he, not she in person, subdues this tyrannous form of government, INHERITED from the HEATHEN. There would have been no man-child without the woman, and her long period of suffering; but her functions are strictly religious, not civil, and during the (1260 years) of misrule and civil domination over her of the ten toes, she was as it were, in solitude, (in a wilderness)—a spiritual Sahara; or, like ancient Israel, that found no sustenance in the wilderness, but were nourished by manna and the water from the smitten rock, all food furnished by miracles; so this woman was nourished by the true Bread that came down from heaven and the Water of Life, which were furnished miraculously. That is the true Bread from heaven, and the Water of Life were given to us in this wilderness world by miracle. It is not gratifying to the pride of man to call this world a desert; but, morally and spiritually, when you take the Bible from the people as was effectually done during the "Dark Ages," you bring on spiritual famine. When literal bread is withheld from people they starve bodily; and when the Word of God is withheld they starve spiritually. This was the condition in which the woman was placed, except that she was nourished. The few copies of the Bible, guarded and treasured above rubies, fed her hungry soul, in the wilderness where the monster dragon sought to slay her. Today, I fear, when her board is spread with the rich repast of the unadulterated Word of God, and provided with the fountain of living waters, she eats and drinks too sparingly, and without regard to the great work she is called upon to do in this and all other lands. For this reason many are weak and sick and many sleep at their post of duty. Milk is for babes. But solid food is for full-grown men, even those who by reason of use have their senses exercised to discern good and evil. (Heb. 5:14).

It should be evident to all that in the (17th ch.) the "Woman" that actually rode this "Beast of ten horns" was the Harlot. She is in contrast with this woman in (ch. 12). The *apostate* church was upheld by the ten governments of Western Europe, while the *true* church was hated and pursued malignantly and watched because of her maternal condition, because her son would uphold her, and overthrow the Beast with ten horns *upon* which the Harlot rode. The Woman in one chapter, and the Harlot in the other, represent the two churches; while the Man-Child in one, and the Beast in the other, with ten horns, represent the civil governments, respectively, in harmony with their principles. We should not mix the symbols; and they picture to us the fortunes of the church under various adverse elements.

5. Next in (chs. 13 and 14) we come to the last set of symbols covering the same period in which the (1260 years) are considered. Here the old despotisms of Babylon, Medo-Persia, Greece and Rome are first represented by the *composite* Beast that came up out of *the sea*. The Leopard body, mouth of the Lion, and paw of the Bear, show us his savage, cruel nature has not changed. He is Daniel's fourth Beast, or plainly, the Roman Government, divided into ten parts and persecuting the true church. The ten governments of the Western Roman Empire fulfill these symbols. The history of Rome is given in the whole list of symbols as follows:

1. In its Unity as the iron legs of the Man and the body of the Beast.

2. In its divided state, by the toes of the Image part of iron, part of clay; and by the ten horns of the fourth Beast.

3. By the "little horn" or *last form* of the Roman Government. In Revelation (13:1-10) is the divided Roman Empire; (vs. 1:1-18) an Image of the Beast, a second form of it, existing at the same time but as a two-horned Lamb.

The whole period is covered by these symbols. Now, these ten horns crowned, (or wearing diadems), and persecuting the woman the (42 months), show us that these *ten governments exist* along with the "little horn." And is not this plain history today? Did not the Roman Empire exist in these *ten parts* all the while that *Popery* existed? Moreover, did not their religion degenerate until they, in strict propriety of speech, were the persecuting *agents* of the popes throughout the (42) prophetic months? How could the Roman church have carried out her policies only through these ten governments? She plucked up three of them; but the remainder were just as loyal and obedient to the popes. I wish the reader to see this.

Germany, France, Italy, Spain, England, and these faith-ful catholic supporters, were equal in guilt with the leader. This set of symbols shows that the principles of one were the principles of the other during the world's midnight. Later, the scarlet clad woman is pictured as riding the beast (these ten governments), and this brands them as united in purpose and effort.

PLAIN PARALLELS OF OVERTHROW.

1.   The God of heaven sets up a kingdom that shall never be destroyed, (Dan'l 2:44), in the days of the apostles.

2.   "And the kingdom and dominion, and great-ness of the kingdom under the whole heaven, shall be given to the people of the saints of the most High, whose kingdom is an everlasting kingdom, and all dominions shall serve and obey him." (Dan'l 7:27); they were saints, before they won this signal victory.

3.   "And the seventh angel sounded; and there fol-lowed great voices in heaven, and they said. The king-dom of the world is become the kingdom of the Lord and of his Christ; and he shall reign forever and ever," (Rev. 11:15).

4.   "Now is come the salvation and the power, and the kingdom of our God and the authority of his Christ; for the accuser of our brethren is cast down, who ac-cuseth them before God day and night." (Rev. 12:10).

The six trumpets were not miraculous, then why the seventh? Jesus' reign *forever* is *not temporal*; but he rules in the *church* forever; and the acquisition of the rule *in earthly affairs* is *incidental to* a very *limited part* of *that* rule. The pope did not come up as a "little horn" by miracles; neither does he go down by miracles. The ten toes of the image, and ten horns of the beast, were a *growth*. The horns GREW out of the head of a beast. Jesus had entered upon his *eternal* rule *before* the *time* set forth by the *ten horns*; he was reigning in heaven, over Hades and in his loyal disciples as their High-Priest and King, all the time Anti-christ reigned. The rule of Christ continues until there is no pope, no ten toes of the Beast, aye, no Beast. He overthrows them all by his almighty Word.

TWO PHOTOGRAPHS.

The two wild beasts held millions in their power. The Lamb of God is contrasted with the counterfeit lamb.

1. Ten horned beast; or beastly rule of the ten kingdoms.

2. Came up out of the sea; or had an earthly origin.

3. Mouth of Blasphemy against God's name, authority:

His church, true laws— Ordinances; and

His people, the true saints.

4. Overcame the saints and had power over the nations.

5. All worship him except one class; a plain distinction and honor for the true people of God.

6. Killeth with the sword to establish such a kingdom as Jesus rejected, and by the means he repected; hence he repeats here what was *said to Peter* there. (Jno. 18:11).

7. The measure of guilt demands a like measure of punishment.

1. The holy Lamb of God. The Lamb with seven eyes and seven horns.

2. Stood on sacred Mt. Zion. (Ps. 2; Is. 2; Micah 4) or from heaven.

3. (144,000) obtained the victory here as a like number did against pagan Rome. (ch. 7). Victory is proclaimed in both instances over Rome. In (ch. 7) it is over ten-horned Beast; in (ch. 14) it is over the two-horned Lamb, with dragon mouth, or the Image of the first Beast, ruling at the same time.

4. Victors sang a new song—the first fruits to God,—the first to die at the hands of professed Christians.

5. The sealed ones had God's name in *their* foreheads, and they were many.

6. Overcame as virgins; follow the Lamb; redeemed; in their mouths no guile; true overcomers of sin in themselves.

7. They followed the Lamb; preached his word and knew the *Time*-Prophecies were being fulfilled in the overthrow of Babylon.

NEXT AN IMITATION LAMB.

1. Two horns, or powers, i. e., Civil rule; and Religious rule.

2. Wrought signs and lying wonders. (II Thess. 2). These deceived the world as to his *spiritual* authority.

3. Made an image of the mortally wounded but revived beast. He would not let the Empire die, but revived it in all its persecuting power, and was its virtual head.

4. This usurper claimed to succeed the apostle Peter and to be appointed supreme earthly high-priest and Lord in the church; one horn. He assumed to rule the world temporally. And these absurd claims were backed up by the ten-horned beast, or the ten European governments for forty-two months.

5. The whole world received his mark and either upheld popery as subjects of his temporal states; or

1. The followers of the Lamb preached the everlasting gospel.

2. Jesus warned his disciples against false prophets in sheep's clothing. (Matt. 7:15). How timely against this dragon-sheep!

3. These holy ones called upon men to worship God who made the sea and fountains of water—all nations of men; this in holy contrast to those who bowed the knee in idolatrous worship under the rule of the dragon-lamb with two horns —civil and religious rule.

4. These protested against the Priesthood and Lordship of the whole group of popes. They opposed the system of popery, which claimed the civil rule of the popes should be supreme, *because* his religious rule was supreme. The faithful saints who followed Christ as Lord and upheld him as High-Priest, regarded both claims as blasphemous; the government of the popes as an Image of the Roman Empire, while the Roman Empire was standing in the ten-fold form and upholding popery.

5. The faithful adherents to Christ are clothed in white and follow the true Lamb at all times. Their

as citizens of the ten governments.

clothing indicates righteousness, and following the seven-horned Lamb and not receiving the mark of the Beast or Image shows they did not believe in nor sanction the state religion of the Empire.

6. This law had death, banishment, confiscation of property or a universal boycott to enforce it.

6. Babylon goes down by the preaching of the everlasting gospel not by the teaching of science, falsely so called.

7. She made the nations drunk. She terrorized them; and they drank of the wine of the *wrath* of her fornication. She was angry if they would not mix the sacred and profane, be friends with the world. (Jas. 4:4).

7. The wrath of an offended God is *contrasted* with the wrath of this Beast. Thus a faithful exposure of the counterfeit Lamb caused the dragon to speak and act out his true character. These two groups of symbols contrast the true and false religions of the period.

TEMPORAL AND SPIRITUAL BABYLON

As Babylon of old went down in a sacriligious feast, (at the *time* announced before the people of God were taken captive by her), so does spiritual Babylon. There, again is found the vessels of the Lord's house, his commandments, ordinances and laws; and, (as shown on (ch. 11), blasphemous power raised to the highest degree of enmity and contempt against God. The language of the overthrow of Babylon is largely drawn from the Old Testament prophets, which was given concerning *literal* Babylon. (Jer. chs. 50; 51). *That* was not at the first coming of Christ; neither is *this* at his SECOND coming. From Babylon the people went back and restored the old temple and revived the true worship of God. So, here, the cry for a return to the Bible and to rebuild the church is much in evidence. There, they only rebuilt the Altar, and neglected the temple until famine almost consumed them. Here, the true church has been neglected, the altar of prayer is the most prominent piece of the Temple revived, and the famine in spiritual things, among warring sects, is deplorable. They need to rebuild the apostolic church in theory and practice in all things. "And I heard a voice from heaven saying, write, blessed are the dead who die in the Lord from henceforth, yea, saith the spirit, that they may rest from their labors; for their works follow with them." (14:13).

No more purgatory! No more bequests of money to priests to get saints out of that place! How appropriate the time and place to mention this! The structure of the book shows this was at the Reformation, a time of the most cruel and protracted persecutions. It was the early teaching of reformers, in the sixteenth century, that Purgatory was an invention of men. And they taught the consoling belief that when they died in the Lord, they were at rest, not subject to the tardy masses of the priests; but their works accompanied and commended them in death as they had done in life. This consoling doctrine spread rapidly among the masses; and that gold-mine was closed against the priest among the first. Out of that superstition, and the doctrine of the works of merit that accompanied it, the nations were impoverished. If the priest had the power over this dread prison of the soul, and only masses would open the doors, how eagerly and faithfully would the living subscribe for the comfort of the dead. But the doctrine of the *true Lord of the Church* and her great High-Priest said, the dead in the Lord are blessed (happy—not miserable!) and I will let the Lord be true though every man a liar, especially that usurper of the power and dignity of Christ as Lord and high-priest. He is a counterfeit; and thought to change times and laws and arrogate to himself the keys of Hades and of death, when Jesus alone possesed that power.

MAN OF SIN.

I. In (II Thess. 2), is Paul's prediction of the man of sin. The "mystery of iniquity" contrasts with the "mystery of godliness." The main features are,

1. The mystery was at work eighteen centuries ago.

2. Some power hindered its development. Ireneus, disciple of Polycarp, who was a disciple of John, said it was the Roman Emperor ; and as there could not be two universal rulers in Rome, this is accepted generally as the all but self-evident meaning.

3. He was to come up soon after the Roman Empire fell, and he did. The Empire was divided into ten parts (A. D. 476). Popery arose (A. D. 533 to 606).

4. He came by *signs* and "lying wonders with all deceivableness of unrighteousness." And it would require a whole library to set forth the all but inconceivable catalogue of pretended miracles, and unrighteous conduct of this now historic government.

5. He exalted himself and opposeth all Gods, and is, therefore, anti-christ.

6. He sits in the temple of God, (or church), the only temple under the gospel. He could not be Mahomet for he never was a ruler *in the church.*

7. The Lord is to consume him by the spirit of his mouth. The Bible is the fire that burns up all false teaching, and, in all lands, where there is an open Bible, the "Man of Sin" is rejected and wastes away. Since the Reformation he is being consumed piece-meal, state after state falling away from him, until now he has no temporal rule; his life, as a temporal prince, is ended, we trust, forever.

8. The *ultimate* Judgment and *destruction* of this wicked one is when all other persecutors are to be destroyed, at our Lord's second coming, (II Thess. 1:7-12). We can consume the system by a free use of the gospel; but the Lord will sit in judgment on the individual members, in the great day.

This "man of sin" who usurped the supreme rule, spiritually and temporally, is doomed in these verses as the "little horn," and "two horned lamb," the "Harlot" and "false prophet" are in Daniel and Revelation.

John gives the name of "a man" in (Rev. 13:18); and it spells out (666). I will not introduce the Greek spelling, but sugest that *Lateinos* spells the name—"Latin man." The letters added together give us the numerals. L is 30; a is 1, t is 300, e is 5, i is 10, n is 50, o is 70, s is 200, equals 666.

Latin prayers; Latin Missal; Latin canons; Latin decrees; Latin breviary; Latin bulls; blessings Latin; curses in Latin; worship in Latin. The Latin church, reads the Scriptures in Latin. One point does not prove the identity of this apostasy. *Romiith* is the Hebrew name for the Roman Kingdom, and it likewise contains the fatal (666). But the *combined evidence* of this *group of prophecies* can scarcely fail to convince one that the tyrannous, idolatrous power predicted was the Roman Catholic Church; and her *daughters* are the *state churches* that are modeled after her more than after the apostolic church of God.

CHAPTER XXXIII.

AGE OF THE HUMAN RACE.

Septuagint Computation 5586
Septuagint Alexandrinus 5508
Septuagint Vatican 5270
Samaritan Computation 4427
Samaritan Text 4305
Hebrew Text 4161
English Bible 4004

JEWISH COMPUTATIONS.

Josephus
　　　　　　　Playfair 5555
　　　　　　　Jackson 5481
　　　　　　　Hales 5402
　　　　　　　Universal History 4698
Talmudists 5344
Seder Olam Sutha 4359
Jewish Computation.......................... 4220
Idem 4184
Chinese Jews 4079
Some Talmudists............................. 3761
Vulgar Jewish Computation 3760
Seder Olam Rabba, great chronicle of the world

A. D. 130 3751
Rabbi Lipman 3616

CHRISTIAN DIVINES.

Celement Alexandrinus 5624
Hales, Rev. Dr. 5411
Origen A. D. 230 4830
Kennedy, Bedford Ferguson 4007
Usher, Lloyd, Calmet 4004
Helvetius Marsham 4000
Melancthon 3964
Luther 3961
Scaliger 3950

ON THE DELUGE.

Septuagint Version 3246
Samaritan Text 2998
English Bible 2348
Hebrew Text 2288
Josephus 3146
Vulgar Jewish Computation 2104
Hales 3155
Usher 2348
Calmet 2344

ON THE EXODUS.

Josephus and Hales 1648
Usher and English Bible 1491
Calmet 1487
Vulgar Jewish Chronology 1312

If the Millennium begins the seven thousandth year of the world, then which one of the above dates is the beginning point? Is there a man living who can tell? No, for there are two whole links gone out of the chain of events in the Old Testament, and we do not know their length, and several other links are badly twisted and battered. No one can tell how long a time it was from Moses to Christ, as the above table abundantly shows. Now the Millennialists have to *know* the age of the world.

I need not speak again of Bengel and Charles Wesley, with the A. D. 1836 date; Wm. Miller, Cunninghame and M. Habershon, with their A. D. 1843 Calendar; Joseph Wolff with A. D. 1847; R. C. Shimeall with his scholarly and laborious researches settling on A. D. 1868.

But C. T. Russell is still with us and in "The Time Is AT HAND" he devotes about one hundred pages to get the *Time set* for Christ to come, at the end of 6000 years, from Adam's creation. He follows the old Jewish tradition of the thousand years and decides that A. D. 1874 was the date for Christ to come, in the fall! So we may give his effort more notice.

1.   He *assumes* that each day of creation was seven thousand years long. This should be welcome news to scientists who have speculated so much on the length of these days, without learning anything definite. It is disappointing to students of the Bible, because the author of the theory, who seeks to revolutionze religious thought on all subjects relative to earth, heaven and Hades, gives neither scientific nor Biblical proof of his assertion.

2.   He bluntly informs us that the six thousandth year of the world ended (A. D. 1873). But, inasmuch as the world's greatest chronologers and Biblical scholars, men *who do* know Greek, Latin, Hebrew, and who "searched diligently what or what manner of time" was meant in many prophecies; what space of time was represented by two missing links, failed to get to A. D. 1873 as the great date, we must set Mr. Russell down as an asserter without proof. He does not even deign to suggest the proof, or any clue to finding it, for his creative days being 7000 years long. As these were not, with him, *some* of that length and some a century different, more or less, but all exactly alike, one is curious to know who kept the Calendar for the first forty-two thousand years, and where one might go to consult it.

"THE TIME IS AT HAND."

3.   The first 100 pages are given to laying the basis for what is to follow. He first had to decide when the 6000 years ended. I have contended that Evolution can not be established because of the "Missing Link" between man and monkey. But this thousand year Millennial theory can not be maintained, because *two links* are out of it, and we do not know their length. Mr. Russell gives the full measure of Gentile times from (B. C. 606 plus 2520 equals A. D. 1914).

I have already given six dates when Israel and Judah went into captivity as follows:

ISRAEL.

Shalmanezer	(II Ks. 17)	B. C. 723
Sennecherib	B. C. 713	to 708
Esar-Haddan		B. C. 676

JUDAH.

Nebuchadnezzar	B. C. 606
Nebuchadnezzar	B. C. 602
Nebuchadnezzar	B. C. 587

These dates are, some, at least, of the beginnings for the measures of the whole week and the half-week, (2520) years and (1260) years, respectively. But inasmuch as Israel went into captivity in stages some (136) years elapsing between the first and the last captivities, so the terminal dates necessarily exhibit the same margin. It was also pointed out that at least three dates are set by historians for the rise of popery:

Justinian Decree	A. D. 533
Gregory the Great	A. D. 590
Boniface III	A. D. 606

The end of the (1260) years also marks important stages in the downfall of popery; and, as Mahometanism was associated with it in prophecy, the dates have to be considered also.

Mahomet receiving Koran	A. D. 606
His Flight to Mecca	A. D. 622
Capture of Jerusalem	A. D. 637

The downfall has corresponding stages, and both in rise and fall, these persecuting powers are without miracle or miraculous opposition.

Mr. Russell (The Time Is at Hand, P. 49) tells us the nineteen periods in Judges "are disconnected, broken, lapped and tangled so much that we could arrive at no definite conclusion from them, and should be obliged to conclude as others have done, that nothing positive could be known on the subject, were it not that the New Testament supplies the deficiency. Paul states that after God divided their land to them by lot 'He gave unto them Judges about (during) the space of four hundred and fifty years, until Samuel the Prophet. Afterward they desired a King, and God gave unto them Saul.'" (Acts 13:19-21).

How does Mr. Russell connect the "disconnected"? unite the "broken"? unlap the "lapped"? untangle the "tangled", chronology?

1. He makes Paul say *during* four hundred and fifty years, when he said *about*.

2. He throws out (I Ks. 6:1) entirely because it spoils his system. He substitutes 580 for 480 years in this text, *because he is tangled*. He says the Bible is tangled in Judges!

3. He accuses Bishop Usher of being *"misled* by the evident error" of (I Ks. 6:1).

Usher, who made the chronology in use among us, (as found in the margin of our Bibles), retains the text; Russell rejects it. He settles on 1873 and Usher on 1996, as the end of the 6000 years.

4. Mr. Russell *ignores* the fact that Caleb received his inheritance when eighty-five years old, during the early conquests in Palestine, IN THE LIFETIME OF JOSHUA, and links the 450 years of Judges to that date; whereas (Joshua 18) shows that *seven tribes* were allotted their possessions some time *after* this.

Again. The people went every man to his inheritance. They served the Lord all the days of Joshua. And all the days of the elders that outlived Joshua. Do we know how much time these two statements cover? No. Can we find out? No: for we have not reached the *Judges* yet. There arose another generation that knew not the Lord, forsook him, did evil in his sight, and served Baalim. How much time does that include? Paul, (even revised by Mr. Russell), does not say, because he only speaks of the time of the Judges, in the common version (which Mr. Russell doctors.) So here is a "missing link," from the eighty-fifth year of Caleb to that time after Joshua and his whole generation, and somewhere in the next generation, when they forsook the Lord, served idols, were delivered to their enemies and the first Judge was raised up to deliver them. (Judges 2:6-12). Mr. Russell has no trouble with this, he just throws the troublesome number away (I Ks.6:1); changes Paul's translation to be exact where it is indefinite; ignores the facts chronicled in (Judges 2); links the Judges up to Caleb when he was (85) years of age; and pro-

ceeds confidently to *criticise Usher for preserving the text*
that stands in his way. How simple and easy!

Once more: Many chronologers make (I Ks. 6:1)
to mean (591) or (592) years instead of Mr. Russell's
(580). Why not leave it (480) as it is, and as Usher
uses it in his elaborate system? You see if Usher is
right, (and he is if I Ks. 6:1 is correct), then the vaunted
Millennium cannot possibly be due for another century.
I do not like Mr. Russell's method of "untangling." Do
you? But a man who does not *attempt to prove* the days
of creation were seven thousand years long, can easily
manufacture Scripture away over in the "disconnected,"
"tangled" parts of the Old Testament; throw out a date
that is there, put one in, that is not there, then tell us
Jesus was due (A. D. 1874). Now if it had been predicted,

1. That Christ should come into the world the first
time, at the end of the *fourth* thousand years after the
creation, then no one could have told when the event
was due. But when (Dan'l 9) said he should come at
the opening of the seventieth "week" from the command
to restore and rebuild Jerusalem, after the Babylonian
captivity, it was ascertainable.

2. Or if his second coming had been connected with
the opening of the *seventh* thousand years from creation,
that event might have been a subject for legitimate in-
quiry as to when he would be due. We might then feel
much concern over the twenty-eight guesses, and learned
contradictions, set forth by these celebrated chronologers. *But the event is not so predicted.* Hence, we may
leave the logomachy, without scruple.

Mr. Russell professes to get his dates *all* in the Bible
as follows:

From the creation of Adam,

To the end of the Flood	1656	years
Thence to the covenant with Abraham	427	"
Thence to the Exodus and giving of Law	430	"
Thence to the division of Canaan	46	"
The period of the Judges	450	"
The period of the Kings	513	"
The period of the Desolation	70	"

Thence to A. D. 1 536   "
Thence to A. D. 1873 1872   "

Total 6000   "

One hour's study in the Bible will show that he is confident but in error.

1.   There has been a controversy for ages as to whether the descendants of Abraham were in Egypt (430), or only (215) years. Plain as some passages seem to be for one count, others seem to favor the other. If (430), he is (215) years short. This makes the calculation doubtful at best.

The purpose I have in citing this table is to show the sincere inquirer after the truth, that second Adventists by settling upon *one* of these dates to the EXCLUSION OF THE OTHERS ARE IN A TRI-LEMMA.

1.   The twenty-eight dates conflict so, that if they choose one, there are twenty-seven against them.

2.   The Lord, his apostles, nor any of the prophets said Jesus would come at the end of six thousand years, according to any table.

3.   They have to make the six thosarnd years end with the (2520) years of "Gentile dominion." How can one make a date that *is* given, harmonize with one that is *not* given?

Now, Mr. Russell, with a confidence that is bewildering to the unread and unstable, multiplies assertions without proof so fast that he carries one away from his difficulty. I believe, therefore, that you would do well to notice the following points, all of which are so related and inter-related, THAT HE HAS TO PROVE THAT JESUS CAME A. D. 1874, OR FAIL IN HIS WHOLE SCHEME. So he assumes without proof:

1.   Each creative day was six thousand years long.

2.   That Adam was created at the close of six epochs, or forty-two thousand years, from the opening of creation.

3.   That this world had stood six thousand years from the creation of Adam, (A. D. 1873).

4.   That the second coming of Christ was associated with the last thousand of this seven thousand year day.

Now, frankly! Is there a syllable in the Bible, or

out of it, in proof of any of the four assumptions? Not one.

Again; I have shown on the Jewish feasts, that Pentecost came *after* the count of seven sabbaths *complete* or on the *fiftieth* day. That feast can not be the basis for this groundless theory, for it was connected with the *first* coming of our Savior; and it would positively deny the Second Advent theory because if Pentecost typified the Millennium it would have to come *after* the *sevens* were all in. AND MR. RUSSELL IS 1000 YEARS TOO EARLY!

I showed that the Jubilee year was similarly calculated. Every seventh year the land had rest, but *not* Jubilee, until *after* "seven sabbaths of years" or 49 years and Jubilee was on the fiftieth year. If. Mr. Russell wishes to imagine that each of the years of this count represented 1000 years, then he is 1000 *years too early* for the second coming of Christ and the Millennium, for if Jubilee typified Millennium, and was on the fiftieth year, then the Millennium, will be the *fiftieth* thousand years after creation, and not the *forty-ninth* as he is so industriously striving to show. The same is true of all the feasts. Moreover, I thus show that the theory is false that makes the *seventh* thousand years a Millennium as well as the *forty-ninth* thousand. The number eight is in the Feast of Tabernacles, and Israel had to dwell in their booths and the *eighth* day was "an holy convocation" not the SEVENTH DAY AT ALL (Lev. 23:36).

5. But when Mr. Russell has assumed without proof, (and contrary to the Bible), that Jesus did not raise his body from the grave.

6. That the Kingdom was not set up by Christ and the apostles.

7. That the king has to come for us to have the kingdom *predicted for Christ* by the Old Testament prophets.

8. That the New birth, the birth of water, and the Spirit of which Jesus spake to Nicodemus takes place at the "First Resurrection."

9. That all the righteous dead experienced this "so-called" new birth by their souls that had ceased to exist, (some of them for thousands of years), being re-

stored to the functions of life in spirit-bodies in (1878).

10.   That "the harvest" lasts forty years and ends in 1914, when all human governments are to be dissolved; or, briefly, the Fall, (October, 1874) was Jesus' second Advent; The Spring of (1878) was the resurrection of the righteous dead.   Three and one half years later, what?

"SO WE RECOGNIZE A. D. 1881 AS MARKING THE CLOSE OF THE SPECIAL FAVOR TO THE GENTILES— THE CLOSE OF THE HIGH-CALLING, OR INVITATION TO THE BLESSINGS PECULIAR TO THIS AGE—TO BECOME JOINT-HEIRS WITH CHRIST AND PARTAKERS OF THE DIVINE NATURE."

So the theory runs;

1.   Jesus came to Israel at first Advent.   He came to Spiritual Israel, the second time, by returning to earth in Spirit-body (1874).

2.   Three and one half years after Pentecost, he rejected the Jewish nation.   This is *false*.   He rejected the *nation*, and they rejected him, at HIS DEATH.   No *sacrifice* was acceptable to God on Jewish altars after the law was nailed to the cross.   But Mr. Russell would have all church members constituting an *imaginary* Bride Class distinct from others, arise in an *imagined* spirit-body, (1878).   Then the door of hope is closed to *that class* (1881).   Thus a distinction between disciples is made not according to *their works*, but according to whether they lived before (1881) or not.   I am far from believing that C. T. Russell ever was mouth-piece for God either before or since (1878); or that to believe his heresies elevates one to the "divine nature" and constitutes one ruler in an imaginary kingdom of Christ to be set up this fall over all the earth.   I regard him as *assuming* the vital points to be proved in every instance, especially that (1874), (1878), (1881) and (1914) were to be freighted with the eternal realities he asserts.   Any one who studies the question knows his table of dates is not reliable, and therefore his whole theory, resting upon it, is doomed to be discarded by *all* as it is now by *most* of the religious world.   So all churches, as such, are rejected, (were spewed out by the Lord, (1881).   Since which time, they are in no degree recognized by him.   Next come the earthly governments, which must all be overturned by

(1914). As (1844) was just (30) years before (1874), Mr. Russell would have Wm. Miller, and his company to be right in expecting Jesus, as the Jews were at his birth thirty years before his manifestation to Israel at his baptism. and (70) years before the overthrow of their nation by Titus.

Indeed! Did Jesus come to earth *literally* in (1844) as he did when *literally born of the Virgin*? Were there prophecies to raise hopes of his coming when he did not intend to come at all? When he did come literally, and when he did not come at all, are analogous! (1914) is seventy years after (1844), it is true; but (A. D. 70) was some *seventy-four* to *seventy-six years* after Jesus birth, not just (70). No analogy here either! He *came* in one instance—did not come in the latter; so there can be no sort of analogy. Furthermore there is just as much evidence that Jesus came in (1844), seventy years before (1914), as there is that he came in (1874), forty years before (1914). As Jesus literally came in the first instance, and did not come at all in (1844), then there is nothing but crass assumption in the declaration that he came in (1874). He had not said he would—it is Mr. Russell's almanac, not the Bible that says Jesus is here, and all the righteous dead are here since (1878); can one join the bride class since (1881); the churches ceased to be God's in any degree then, and all human earthly governments are to be overthrown by our Lord in (1914) as the Jewish nation was overthrown in (A. D. 70).

Again. If you should take Mr. Russell seriously, consider that Bishop Usher, Calmet and Lloyd tell us the (6000) years end (A. D. 1996). So the invisible presence would be due then; the resurrection Dawnists talk about four years later; the bride class complete (A. D. 2004), the rejection of the nations, (2036) etc."

In order to give plausibility to the theory that the kingdom will be set up at Christ's second coming, they have to make all of Jesus' parables concerning the kingdom that reach to the end of time, reach only to his second coming; and all the promises of resurrection and glorification at the second coming, they have to fit to a material, earthly state of being at the opening of the Millennium.

Thus they pervert the Old Testament prophecies in opposition to Christ and the apostles; they wrest all the parables and apply them to an event more than (1000) years this side of where Jesus ended them; and grossly misapply every promise of the resurrection of the Just in immortal bodies to the Millennium, leaving neither parables nor promises of resurrection for the Just to apply, more than (1000) years later, where Jesus applied both.

Dawnists have to prove the resurrection in (Rev. 20:4) is unquestionably literal; (for if questionable it leaves the theory uncertain, and unsafe to build one's hope of eternity upon). They *assume* that it was fulfilled in (1878); applied only to souls, and that bodies, (the mortal part of the saints), will never rise. They *assume* that God forsook the churches in (1881) as he did the Israel that crucified Christ, and rejected him as an impostor. They have to *assume* that Jesus could convert men better, by being invisibly present on earth than invisibly absent in heaven. (Does Jesus have to be here to bless?). They mistake the nature of man, given him by his Cheator and respected as the work of God, by his Redeemer. Salvation is a moral and spiritual work, and the gospel is a moral and spiritual means adapted to that work. If the gospel, up to the year (1878) would make men to be partakers of the divine nature, the Christ, (on their theory), so that the whole reigning class will be Christ, along with our Savior, why can not the same gospel elevate others to the same divine nature, while living under his "more favorable conditions" in the Millennium?

This distinction is not in the Bible, and is manufactured for the occasion. Every thing changes at the Millennium with them.

1.   The Jewish feasts are fulfilled then.

2.   The Parables end then.

3.   The Gospel, with all its ordinances, ends then.

4.   All human governments end then.

5.   The Bride Class have a "baptism of the Spirit" and become divine, the *rulers*, the Sons.

6.   Old Testament saints become immortal, but servants only, the rulers of earthly governments.

They assume that death has one uniform meaning

in the Bible; that is, "cease to be." This makes Jesus to have been annihilated at his death. "Bible studies, vol. 5, p. 362." "Our Lord's being or soul, was non-existent during the period of death."

"The man Jesus, is dead,—forever dead." Vol. 5, p. 454.

Are you ready to follow such teaching in order to uphold a vague notion of a Millennium?

THE BIBLE DISSECTED.

The Russell theory begins its deadly work after the assumptions above. The Bible is dissected piece-meal; it is destroyed.

1. The Judgment day is (1000) years long.

2. The wicked and every man who has ever lived, who has not been exalted to the bride class is resurrected, literally of course, and put on trial for eternal life, or else wholly created, body and spirit

3. Annihilation is the end of all who do not serve God *without sin*, during the (1000) years, while the saints reign with Christ.

Now, I do not think that Charles T. Russell can disprove the literal resurrection of our Lord's body from the grave. He manufactures a spirit-body, the Bible says nothing about. He does away with Jesus' humanity entirely; and with the humanity of the Bride Class at their Spirit birth from the grave, so that they are henceforth *wholly divine.*

He makes the saints, converted thereafter, *wholly human* beings to all eternity, a distinction between saints of God, not hinted at in the entire revelation, and contrary to the necessary inference that God will immortalize and glorify all his saints alike.

1. That Jesus did not raise his *body* in which he died. He can not prove that Jesus created seven different bodies, or even one to materialize in.

2. He makes much of Jesus coming again *as* he went away, assuming that the angel meant secretly, silently, and unseen by the world.

But did not *all* his disciples *see* him? Was he not *visible* even till he went into heaven? Did not Peter say that he appeared to witnesses chosen before-hand? (Acts 10).

Has he *appeared* to the "Little Flock" in any sense?
His going away, was not *so* secretly that he was wholly
invisible to everybody; his so-called return was, and continues to be. Again. His manifestation to the mental
eye, (to the eyes of the understanding), does not meet the
requirements of the promise. For it all depends on
Arithmetic, not Bible. Has Mr. Russell got the right
date even assuming that Jesus is to come at the end of
six thousand years? Usher says, "No." Dr. Hales says,
"No." A multitude of Millennialists of different centuries say, "No." The Table at the head of this article
proclaims in a twenty-eight voiced chorus, "No."

3. As Mr. Russell is wrong about Christ's coming,
he is wrong about the forty years of harvest to begin
the Millennium; wrong about the saints all returning to
earth (1878); wrong about the door of hope being shut
against saints becoming partakers of the divine nature
since (1881); wrong about the Millennium beginning
with Christ' and the saints' coming; wrong about their
sitting on thrones on earth for (1000) years; and he is
as certainly wrong on his whole theory of second-chanceism, as that John is right. John said "BUT THE REST
OF THE DEAD LIVED NOT AGAIN TILL THE THOU-
SAND YEARS WERE FINISHED." (Rev. 20).

The wicked are as numerous as the sand of the
sea, and opposing the church after his (1000) years of
the elements of truth and righteousness exhibited in the
life of Christ and all the saints.

CHAPTER XXXIV.

THE HEBREW PEOPLE.

(Gal. 4:21-37).

There are three points clearly made out in the New Testament concerning the Jews that hold to the Mosaic law and reject Christ.

1. They are blind.
2. They are in unbelief.
3. They are in bondage.

Paul, a representative freeman in Christ, makes these points plain, as I proceed to show. And first on this Allegory. He and thousands of other Jewish converts were neither blind, in unbelief, nor in bonage. In this allegory he shows that the two families of Abraham, one through Hagar, a Bond-woman, the other through Sarah, the free yoman, illustrated the condition of the descendants of Abraham, UNDER THE GOSPEL, AND THAT IS NOW AS WELL AS THEN. Whatever was bound on earth, by the apostles, was bound in heaven; whatever was loosed on earth was loosed in heaven." (Matt. 16:19). This fact ought to settle this whole question with us all. Why so? Plainly, if the Jews were not blind, not in unbelief, not in bondage to a traditional and sinful view of the law, and its purpose, and time of continuance, THEY WOULD GIVE UP THE TYPES AND SHADOWS AS PAUL DID. They would believe the Hebrew letter, the Roman letter, and the Galatian letter. They would not seek to be under the law. Then, like the apostles and primitive Jewish converts to Christ, they would unite with Gentiles, on equal terms and conditions in the worship of God through Christ, and give up Jewish exclusiveness. Contrast the difference between Paul, building up the church, and a modern Jewish Rabbi! Why the difference? The latter is blind, in unbelief, in bondage to tradition; the other saw the truth, believed in Christ and was made free. There can be no compromise.

Jesus is, or is not, divine. He is, or is not, the Jewish Messiah of the prophets. As certainly as he is the Messiah, Paul is right, the Rabbi is wrong, and has no Millennium before him on his principies! If God would bless the Jews in that rebellion it would discredit the mission of Christ and the apostles. If the Jews were all like Paul they would not expect the literalities of the law to be reproduced for they would not need the temple, priesthood, sacrifices or feasts; and this would take away the whole Gentile argument for a Davidic, Solomonic Kingdom for Christ in this world.

The bond-woman bore a son, but he was a slave, necessarily, and Sarah bore a son, and, (she being the lawful wife of Abraham), Isaac, her son was a freeman. The bond-woman and her son persecuted the free woman and her son, and were cast out of the home, the territory promised to Abraham, and settled in Arabia, *a different country* altogether; they went away with bread and water, and only received presents but did not heir under Abraham. The argument was thus final that fleshly descendants of Abraham in Paul's day, and later, do not heir under Christ, *because* of that fact. Isaac, the son of the free-woman, heired all his father had, remained in the land, and was the child of promise, illustrative and typical of the converted Israelites in the gospel age, who heir heavenly Canaan because they are children of God. The same arguments Paul used here, or elsewhere, concrning the Jews of *his day*, apply NOW. Having shown the distinction between Hagar and Sarah, Ishmael and Isaac, the ones cast off, and the ones retained, the application was simple and easy, but far-reaching in consequences. So the two women are the two covenants (or represent them, of course)—that is, the covenant God made with fleshly Israel at Mt. Sinai, when he gave the law through Moses. (And of what use was it after the New Covenant was *made with Israel* in Jerusalem, by Christ fifteen centuries later)? To hold to it was to be in bondage to types, to ceremonials, to carnal ordinances, that could not free them from sin. So it is now. Have you lost faith in the gospel?

After Isaac was born, Ishmael persecuted him, and both Hagar and Ishmael were cast out. After the gospel of Christ was given, both the old covenant (the bond-mother in the allegory) and the people who clung to it were cast out. So they are out today on that basis, just as Ishmael was out under the Old Covenant. Paul made the distinction between the Jews who *believed in Christ* and those that *believed not*, that Abraham made *between* his *two* sons *Isaac* and *Ishmael*. That distinction is just as much in *effect now* as it was WHEN PAUL WROTE IT. It is just as *sinful* to uphold the Jews who denounced and crucified Christ as it ever was. So the DISTINCTION MADE BY THE HOLY SPIRIT THROUGH PAUL, between the JEWISH BELIEVERS on the one hand, (like himself and all the apostles, prophets, and disciples of Christ), and the BLIND, UNBELIEVING PORTION of the nation who rejected God's testimony in behalf of Christ, STILL EXISTS IN ALL ITS FORCE. It is not simply to reject Christ and the apostles, (as though they could be separated from the rest of the Bible); but whosoever rejects Christ, rejects Moses, and all the prophets for they wrote of him. You say, "No, the Jews hold to Moses!" How can they believe Moses, Isaiah, Ezekiel, Daniel or the prophets and reject Christ? That is to side with the sinful, unbelieving portion of the Jewish nation against Christ and the believing portion, and is to destroy the very foundation of the church. You assume that they believe in God because they would return to Palestine, revive the temple, the Priesthood and the sacrifices. What did the temple, priesthood, and sacrifices point forward to? What did they typify? Did they not point forward to the church and its Founder, Christ?

You have seen it was Ishmael and not Isaac, (the children of the old covenant and not of the new covenant), that went down under war, famine, fire and sword in (A. D. 70). What went down that had a right to exist? Can you think of a single thing that belongs to free men in Christ, such as Paul and the church were that should be revived? As well talk of rebuilding Noah's Ark to house the church of the living God today! Noah and his salvation were a type, never to be repeated. The Mosaic covenant with temporal tabernacle, priesthood, sacrifices and feasts, holy days, new moons and sabbaths, were divine pictures and figures of good things to come. But as the fierce, consuming fire of war raged through that "holy house"; and mountains of smoke hovered above it, these infatuated Jews, blinded to the nature of that house, unbelievers in the higher revelations of the gospel of Christ, and in bondage to the law, witnessed the disappearance from earth, literally, of that house which had been left unto them deserted of God, when Jesus erected the true temple the church of the liiving God. That house is not to arise again to mock the agonies of the Son of God, and discredit the salvation wrought out for us on Calvary by the sacrifice of himself. The apostle says, "For this Agar is Mount Sinai in Arabia, and answereth to the JERUSALEM THAT NOW IS, and is in BONDAGE WITH HER CHILDREN." They were not in bondage, when he wrote, as they once were in Egypt; and later in Babylon. But they were in bondage. What was the NATURE OF JEWISH BONDAGE?

He argued the point at length in Galatians, in Hebrews, and in all his great ministry—they were in bondage to the law, to types and shadows. In this connection he said: "Stand fast therefore in the liberty wherewith Christ hath made us free and be not entangled again with the yoke of bondage." Did Christ set the (Jewish) Christians free *from bondage to conquering nations*? Did he free them like Moses did? Like Cyrus did? Of course not. "Then said Jesus *to those Jews* which believed on him, if ye continue in my word, then are ye my disciples indeed; and ye shall know the truth and the truth shall make you free. They answered him, we be Abraham's seed, and were never in *bondage* to any man; how sayest thou ye shall be made free? Jesus answered them, verily, verily, I say unto you, whosoever committeth sin is the servant of sin. And the servant abideth not in the house forever; but the Son abideth ever." (John 8:31-35).

Ishmael did not abide in the house, but Isaac *did*. FLESHLY ISRAEL was to be CAST OFF like the SERVANT; but the DISCIPLES of Christ, AS SONS, made free from sin, were to ABIDE FOREVER. "If the SON therefore shall MAKE YOU FREE ye shall be FREE indeed." (Ver. 36). This applies to all Israel right now.

It is not the land, the city, the temple, that are in bondage; it is the fleshly children of Abraham. They are trodden down, cast out, rejected as Ishmael was, and are to continue so as long as they are blind in unbelief and in bondage to the old covenant made at Mount Sinai in Arabia. "Till the times of the Gentiles be fulfilled," is explained (Romans 11:25-26). "For I would not, brethren that ye should be ignorant of this mystery, lest ye should be wise in your own conceits; that blindness in part is happened to Israel, until the fulness of the Gentiles be come in. And so all Israel shall be saved; as it is written, there shall come out of Zion the Deliverer, and shall turn away ungodliness from Jacob, for this is my covenant unto them when I SHALL TAKE AWAY THEIR SINS." In (Rom. 9;10; 11 chs) Paul explains this matter. (Read the whole section). Observe:

1. THEY ARE NOT ALL ISRAEL WHO ARE OF ISRAEL (or descendants of Jacob). SO ALL THESE ARE NOT SAVED.

2 Neither because they are the seed of Abraham are they all children; but in Isaac shall thy seed be called. Then he shows this in history. Ishmael was *rejected* although Abraham's son. Esau was rejected although Isaac's son.

3. So as distinction was made by *Abraham* and by *Isaac*, between *their* sons, (and in the latter case between *twin* sons) a distinction that was later made between ISRAELITES TRUE TO THE COVENANT and those that were FALSE, (so that in the days of Elijah there were but seven thousand of the former in Israel), the argument is conclusive that, during all the history of the Jews under the old covenant there was an *election* or *selection* going on; and, usually the elect were a *small number contrasted* with those who were *disobedient*. This showed concerning the descendants of Abraham the very point at issue, that the PROMISES WERE NOT MADE TO ALL DESCENDANTS of Abraham or Isaac or Jacob. This point established as it was and is by the apostle citing the history, he is ready to make his application. Hence, when the gospel was preached to the Jews, some *accepted*

it, many *rejected* it, those who *accepted* it were the Isaacs, the Jacobs, the Elijah element, the remnant; while those who *rejected* it were the Ishmaels, the Esaus, the Ahabs of their day. WHAT ARE' THEY NOW? "They that are the children of the flesh, THESE ARE NOT THE CHILDREN OF GOD; but the children of the promise are counted for the seed."

The Old Testament closed with a prophecy; so did the lives of many of the saints. The New Testament closed with a prophecy; so did the personal ministry of our Savior, and the life-time labors of the apostles Paul, Peter and John. Many run into confusion by ignoring the order of events in the Bible. We have history and prophecy, combined. First, well digested truth, then parables, types and prophecy should be our course of study. Prophecy, when uttered, is no proof; when fulfilled, it is a demonstration. Its chief function is to produce faith and thus obedience. Some one said: Prophecies flow from divine understanding; miracles from divine power; the excellency of the doctrine from divine goodness; and moral purity from divine purity. Thus the Bible rests upon the four pillars—the understanding, the power, the goodness and purity of God.

(Deut. 28:48-58) specifies ten particulras in the overthrow of Israel. 1 Their enemies were from a far country. 2. The army should come as an eagle to its prey. 3. Speak a language unknown to the Jews. 4. Fierce and cruel people and not respect age, sex or conditions. 5. Station themselves among them, then devour them. 6. Besiege them in all their high-walled towns and fortresses. 7. Reduce them to such distress and famine they would eat their own children. 8. The nearest relatives should be evil affected towards each other. 9. The most delicate and tender ladies should devour their own children. 10. They should perpetrate these awful deeds in secret in fear of being robbed of their repast.

MATTHEW (CHS. 23 TO 25).

The condemnation of the nation is given by our Lord in the (23ch.) The first twelve verses were addressed to the disciples. Then follows a woe for every blessing given in the sermon on the mount. In these

DESTRUCTION OF JERUSALEM

	MATT. 24 Ch. Ver.	MARK Ch. 13 Ver.	LUKE 21 Ch. Ver.
1. The disciples showed Jesus the stones of the Temple			
2. Prophecy that all should be thrown down		2	6
3. Sat on the Mt. of Olives	3	3	
4. Matt. and Luke say disciples; Mark says four	3	3	7
5. Question three fold in Matt., two-fold in others	3	4	7
6. Jesus (1st) Warning against deception	4	5	8
(a) False Christs and their success	5	6	8
(b) Wars and rumors of wars, but the "end not yet"	6	7	9
(c) Nation against nation, kingdom against kingdom	7	8	10-11
(d) Famines, pestilences and earthquakes			
(e) Beginning of sorrows	8	8	
7. CONDITION OF THE DISCIPLES	9-12	9	12
8. Endure to the end to be saved	13	13	18-19
9. Gospel preached for a witness to all nations	14	10	
10. Disciples not to pre-meditate speech		11	14-15
Abomination spoken of by Daniel (Ch 9)	15	14	20
Directions. (a) If Judea	16	14	21
(b) On the house-top	17	15	Ch17;33-36
(c) In the field	18	16	" 19:41-44
(d) Woe to mothers	19	17	23
(e) Winter time, or Sabbath *day*	20	18	
11. Frightful nature of the calamity	21	19	22
12. Days shortened for the elect	22	20	
13. (2nd) Warning against false Christs and prophets	23-26	21-23	Ch17:21-23
14. Coming of true Christ in contrast	27		
15. The carcass and the eagles	28		Ch. 17:37
16. Tribulation for a long time	29	24-25	24
(a) Sun, moon and stars; Joel 2;3:14, 15 These are all SIGNS. See the earthly conditions, and the *time* in Luke			25-26
17. Signagain—tribes mourning	30		
18. See the Son of Man coming	27-30	26	27
19. Angels and great Trumpet sounds	31	27	
20. Parable of the fig tree	32-33	28-29	
21. Nearness of the redemption	33	29	28-31
22. Generation not pass away	34	30	32
Heaven and earth shall pass away	35	31	33
23. Practical (a) None know the time	36	32-33	34
(b) Noah cited as an example	37-39		Ch17:26-30
(c) Two in the field	40		
(d) Two grinding at the mill	41		
(e) See on the word "Watch"	42	35-37	36
	MATT. ONLY		
(f) Parable of the Ten Virgins	25;1-12		
(g) Parable of the Talents	14-30		
(h) Parable of the Sheep and Goats	31-46		

two sermons are the conditions of "blessing" and "cursing" given first to the Jew, but also to the Gentile. The lamentation of Christ over Jerusalem is given in the close of the chapter. The helpless, defenseless brood of chicken run under the outspread wings of a mother, who would die for them. She shields them from every foe. But the Jews here addressed ran away from their Protector to their death.

I have given a Harmony of Matthew, Mark and Luke on the events and the order of them predicted by our Savior. The house of Israel (not only the material house, but the nation) was left desolate when Jesus rejected it. This foretold certain doom. The Tabernacle was deserted at Shiloh (I Sam'l. 4:10, 11, Jer. 7). The overthrow of this house was like the overthrow of the Temple at the Babylonian Captivity; and, again, wholly unlike it. The unlikeness should be studied more than the likeness. Jesus made a New Covenant with the *house* of Israel, and with the *house* of Judah. He built a new *temple*; gave them a new *Priest*, consecrated forevermore. He made one *sacrifice* which can never be repeated or supplemented. He testified to the poverty of all the types by taking them out of the way, "for the weakness and unprofitableness thereof." And he testified, "Ye shall not see me henceforth until ye shall say blessed be he that cometh in that name of the Lord."

DECEIVERS FORETOLD.

Three times in this discourse Jesus warned against false prophets. They killed the true prophets and murdered the true Messiah; ever since their rejection of Christ and his apostles they have followed false prophets and have looked for a different Messiah. Pretenders have arisen as in Jeremiah's days. (Jer. 23:16; Ezek. 13). Josephus speaks of the false Messiahs in his day. Barchobas, "son of a star," was the most successful in deception, and should be called Bar-cosba, "son of a lie." False miracles or signs are usually given by all impostors. (Deut. 13:1, 2, 3; II Thess. 2:9).

WARS PREDICTED.

The world was at peace when Jesus made this prediction. The temple of Janus was closed. But Josephus,

Book of Wars is a splendid commentary on the "wars and rumors of war;" also as to the famines, pestilences, earthquakes, and general distress of his times. The reader should observe carefully that this was fleshly Israel as a nation that was overthrown. The last generation filled their cup of iniquity full, as did the Amorites. Hence all the righteous blood from Abel to Barachias (the last *recorded* martyr among the prophets) was *required*, (as he had prayed his blood should be required), of that generation. Wars among the Romans were frequent, and four emperors, (Nero, Galba, Otho and Vitellus) suffered violent deaths within the space of (18 months).

THE TRIBULATION.

The tribulation of Israel was predicted to be severe and protracted. It is expressed in (Matt. 24:29; Mark 13:24; Luke 21:24), and the latter verse is the key to the whole situation. It covers the history of the Jews from then till the present. This "harmony" of verses may be seen by opening three Testaments at the chapters and verses given in Matthew, Mark and Luke. This aids one greatly in studying the prophecy.

THE SIGNS.

You notice the disciples asked for signs of different events and the Savior gave them,

1. Signs before the destruction of Jerusalem (Luke 21:11). Josephus gives quite a list (Book 6, Ch. 5, Par 2, 3). *Before* THESE signs the disciples were to be persecuted. The whole history in Acts shows this fulfillment, and many references in the epistles as well. As Luke says the persecution and martyrdom were to be *before* the *signs*, in this instance, and wrote the Acts, he gave us the prediction and its fulfillment.

2. The second mention of these signs was by (Matt. 24:24); and, right here, (for the moment), he passed over the intervening history to the end and warned against all false Christ's in all ages, showing (ver 27) that, when the true Christ returns, He will be visible to all mankind. This is the *first sign* he gives that a doctrine of his coming is *false*; if it claims a SECRET COMING OF THE LORD. There can be no secret, invisible

coming of the Lord, while time lasts. Heaven and earth shall pass away, but his words shall not pass away. Mark gives this same *sign* by which to detect false teaching concerning the second coming of Christ. (13:21, 23).

3. *After the tribulation*, the long period of desolation, (Luke 21:24), there shall be *signs* in the sun, moon, stars, on the earth and in the distress of nations (Luke 21:25, 26); (Matt 24:29; Mark 13:24, 25). This is at the same point where catholicism, Mahometanism, Judaism, and Despotism go down. A "sign" is used variously. 1. A miracle (Ex. 4:17). 2. An evidence or example. (Ex. 3:12). 3. Anything strange or wonderful (Is. 19:18-20). 4. A type or prophecy, (Ex. 4:3; 14:18) If the *sign* come to pass it is a credential of authority. (Deut. 13:2; 28:46; Is. 55:13).

In (Matt. 24:30) "And then shall appear the *sign* of the Son of man in heaven." Not the sign of the Son of man in *Jerusalem*; or in the *desert*; or in the *secret presence*; but proof, not hitherto possible, (because his predictions had not come to pass), *that he is in heaven.* He gives no sign that he is in the earth, or has returned secretly to mankind.

When the Jews surrender their tradition of an earthly Messiah yet to come; when they return and seek God and David their king in the latter days, a vast collection of prophecies, grouped around this event, will be fulfilled. This group of prophecies fulfilled, becomes a great SIGN. As fulfilled Types are signs, and fulfilled prophecies are signs, so the one remaining sign of our times is the conversion to God of the Jews. When they have the veil removed from their hearts, abandon their ideas of a material, temporal kingdom, discard their bundle of false traditions, and led by Moses, David, and all the true prophets of God, they are grafted in again to the tame olive tree, Jesus shall have won the victory. The great sound of the gospel trumpet may then be heard throughout the earth.

I am aware of the fact that many will dissent, (as the commentators dissent) from this view. But Jesus did *not* come at the destruction of Jerusalem. The *sign* of the *Son of man in heaven* was not *due* till *after the tribulation*; Luke said the tribulation was "till the times of the

Gentiles are fulfilled." He was Paul's travelling companion, and Paul associates the final conversion of the Jews with the "Fulness of the Gentiles," (Rom. 11:25). The receiving of the Jews, their return, as it were, from death (Rom. 11:15) is at that time. As I have showed that they have to give up the literal, material types for the anti-types, so, when they do this, the Bible will not only be a new Book to them, but to the masses of the Gentiles, I say it with sorrow! the masses of Gentiles are full of tradition. It will possibly take the conversion of the Jews to explode this millennial notion with many. They will have to see the Jews give up the types as Paul did and the true Israel of God, then they will have no lingering excuse to hold to such a theory. When the Jews acknowledge Jesus as King in heaven over all the Israel of God, the last sign of that nature is manifested.

You notice that the second coming of Christ was mentioned by our Savior not fewer than ten times in the prophetic discourse. Turn and read (Matt. 24:27, 30, 42, 44, 50; 25:13, 9, 31). It is plain that each of these refers to ONE coming. I have showed on the three parables, The Virgins, The Talents, and the Sheep and Goats, that it is at the end of the world. This I need not repeat. However, this aids one in seeing that (24:27, and 30) neither refer to a Millennial coming, to unhinge the whole plan of salvation. When one reads the ten verses as I have given them, this is manifest. It is not, when the Son of Man comes, one time he will do *one* thing, when he comes another time he will do *another* thing; but the parables all lead us to the one and only coming in the end of all probation. The parable of the Fig Tree; the days of Noah and the Flood; the unexpected coming of a thief; the parable of the servants; the parable of ten virgins; the parable of the Talents; and the Parable of the Sheep and Goats, furnish us the Lord's grouping of seven events to illustrate his second coming. Consummation is stricken through and through them all.

The word "generation" indicates as much, "Verily, I say unto you, this generation, [race] shall not pass away until all these things shall be fulfilled." The Jewish race is still here, and their history in rejection of Christ and defeat in their carnal life, verifies our Lord's words.

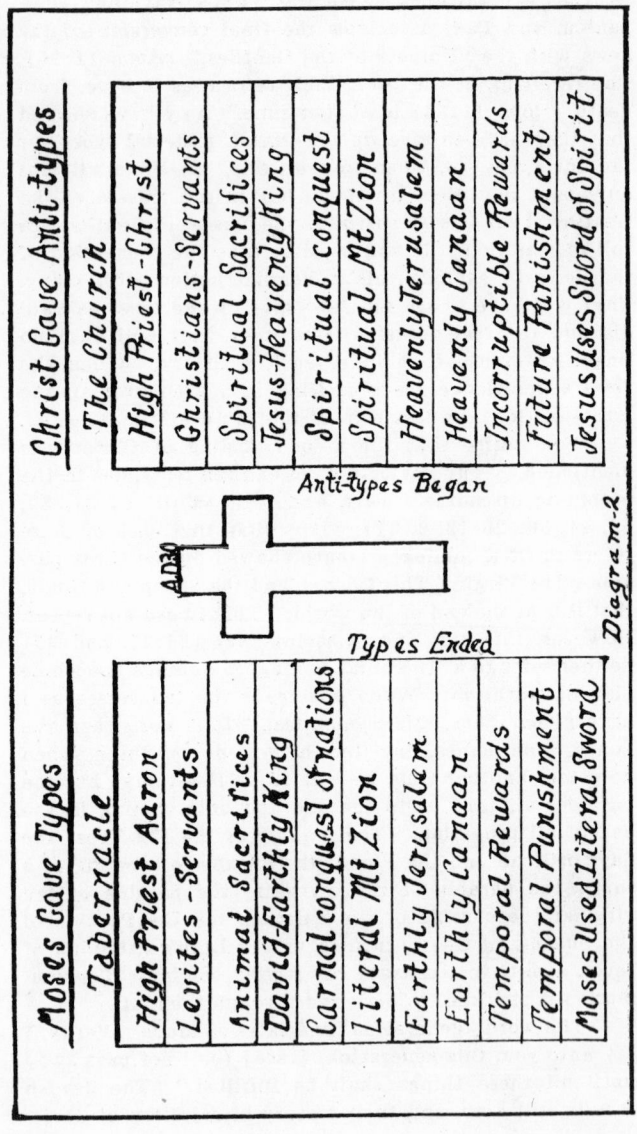

Moses Gave Types

Tabernacle

| High Priest Aaron |
| Levites – Servants |
| Animal Sacrifices |
| David–Earthly King |
| Carnal conquest of nations |
| Literal Mt Zion |
| Earthly Jerusalem |
| Earthly Canaan |
| Temporal Rewards |
| Temporal Punishment |
| Moses Used Literal Sword |

Types Ended

AD30

Anti-types Began

Christ Gave Anti-Types

The Church

| High Priest–Christ |
| Christians–Servants |
| Spiritual Sacrifices |
| Jesus–Heavenly King |
| Spiritual conquest |
| Spiritual Mt Zion |
| Heavenly Jerusalem |
| Heavenly Canaan |
| Incorruptible Rewards |
| Future Punishment |
| Jesus Uses Sword of Spirit |

Diagram 2.

DIAGRAM II.

Diagram two is self-explanatory. Moses gave the Jewish law some fifteen or more centuries before Christ. There were a large number of types connected with it, as a part of the system. I have cited the leading items in the diagram. These were, in their nature and use predictive of higher realities to be given later, under the gospel. They were merely shadows or dim outlines of the gospel, (Heb. 10:1). Moses, Aaron, Levi, the Temple, animal sacrifices, Jerusalem, Mt. Zion, Caanan, and all temporal arrangements, were of necessity but types. These types were consistent with the nation and kingdom then in being; but each and all are inconsistent with the nature of the kingdom they all typified under which we live. There can be no Millennium as set forth by these word artists, without these types. The whole theory rests upon them as its foundation. If David is not an eternal, earthly ruler in Caanan; if the sanctuary is not to be there eternally; if animals are not to be sacrificed by divine command on Jewish altars forever; if the annual Jewish feasts are not to be observed forever; if the temporal was a type of the spiritual; then we should drop the types and be satisfied with the anti-types. The fact that the Jews have been preserved as a race does not import that they are preserved that they may later revive their types. Cain was singled out as a man to be spared, and whosoever slew him would have vengeance taken on him sevenfold. Yet he was of that wicked one and slew his brother, as did the Jews. To tell a Christian, on any ordinary occasion, that the types are done away does not startle him, for he knows it is true, and that they can not be revived under the gospel; but when some romancer tells him the Millennial kingdom will have them, he is entranced. That expression "Millennial Kingdom," "Millennial age," is so fascinating! People know nothing about it; and, by mixing law and gospel, types and anti-types, they know they destroy the church, do away with the gospel, and introduce an age where everything is miraculous; but, in a very ectasy and transport of joy, they hail the theory of a Millennial kingdom.

The words race, nation, or generation are correct uses of this word; but the most likely meaning in this *proph-ecy*, covering *long time* (Luke 21, 24) is this "race" or "people." One can not gather the whole facts concerning this marvellous prophecy in a small compass. I have not quoted from Josephus or Tacitus. The appalling nature of the desolation of Israel is dimly perceived by everybody who lives under the sound of the gospel. They lived so as to inherit the "curse." They are to yield to God and his dear Son. This will be "as life from the dead," both to them and to the Gentile world. I think Catholicism and partyism aids in blinding them to the truth. I hope to see them converted to Christ and accept the Bible. They do not believe the Apocraphal writings, are inspired; but they hold to the false and ruinous Targum and Talmud. The Millennialists are blinding instead of enlightening them to the meaning of the inspired Scriptures. May we all speedily come to a knowledge of the truth in our Lord Jesus Christ.

The Jew, on his fleshly basis, would have *all of Abraham's descendants*, or Isaac's or Jacob's, to inherit the promise to temporal Israel. Paul showed that was unscriptural by citing the rejection of Ishmael, Esau and the Ahab following in the days of Elijah. Then he settles the sorrowful truth down upon the Ishmaels, Esaus and blind, unbelieving portion of his nation, in bondage to the law, and shows that, (on the same principle) they wert cut off THROUGH UNBELIEF IN CHRIST. Hence, the two olive trees, illustrate this matter. As not all the fleshly descendants of Abraham could inherit under the first covenant, it was all but self-evident that not all Abraham's fleshly descendants could heir under Christ; yea, not one of them, without obedience to Christ. The Jews with their low, fleshly, carnal views of the Messiah and his kingdom, (derived from tradition and contradictory of the Bible), fell in unbelief. The remnant who obeyed the gospel were not a handful chosen by the Lord after an arbitrary manner, but were all who believed Christ. IT WAS THE DUTY AND PRIVILEGE OF THE WHOLE NATION TO DO SO. "He came unto his own and his own received him not; but AS MANY as received him, to them gave he power, (privilege), to become the sons of God, even to them that believe on his name, who were born not of blood, nor of the will of the flesh, nor of the will of man but of God." (John 1:11-13). THAT PRIVILEGE HAS NEVER BEEN WITHDRAWN. The Jews are gospel subjects today, as they were then. The promise was to them and to their children, and to all that were afar off, even as many as the Lord our God shall call. The times have not changed. The Lord is the same; the covenant the same; the kingdom of heaven the same, as when given. And it is just as sinful to reject Christ for the law and types now as it was then, and WILL BE TO THE END OF TIME.

It all depends on their rejection or acceptance of Jesus Christ. Now, then, we see from his argument what destroys Israel. Jerusalem is in bondage with her children. They are blinded by tradition. Moses accuses them to the Father. Jesus and the apostles have the true interpretation of Moses and the prophets. THE BELIEVING JEWS came into the enjoyment of all that was promised, or the inheritance in Christ. The UNBELIEVING, BLINDED JEWS forfeited it all, like Ishmael, Esau, Ahab and the hosts of sinners under the law and thus they could not inherit these blessings promised in Christ.

"For if the casting away of them be the reconciling of the world, what shall the receiving of them be but life from the dead?" (Rom. 11:15).

The casting away of them on their principles, with their carnal views, the blindness that is on their hearts in reading the Old Testament, their opposition to Christ, their unbelief in the entire New Testament, was necessary to reconcile men to God; the law was out of date. They had a zeal of God but not according to knowledge. It was according to tradition. The one all-consuming tradition was their carnal view of the kingdom of heaven. That all had to be swept away forever. They had to be wanderers among the nations. Out of the desolation and havoc of the fiery pathway that swept away the Ishmaels, the Esaus, the Ahabs of their nation, together with their temple, priesthood, sacrifices and types and left them like the woods through whose branches had swept the roaring forest fire and burned it to the ground, would arise the Isaacs, Jacobs, Elijahs of the gospel. Yes men of faith, who could read the Old Testament without a veil, could understand the riches of the gospel are too great, too enduring, too spiritual, to be confined to any nationality.

"Whosoever shall call upon the name of the Lord shall be saved." So, (after this manner,) all Israel shall be saved, THE TRUE ISRAEL MADE UP OF FAITHFUL SONS AND DAUGHTERS OF GOD FROM AMONG BOTH JEWS AND GENTILES. "For ye are all the *children of God* by faith in Christ Jesus. For as many of you as have been baptized into Christ have put on Christ. There is neither Jew nor Greek, there is neither bond nor free, there is neither male nor female; for ye are all one in Christ Jesus. And if ye be Christ's then ye are Abraham's seed and heirs according to the promise." (Gal. 3:26-29). There is no national distinction determining one's acceptance with God now. It is all on the basis of faith and obedience of faith.

CHAPTER XXXV.

TIME-PROPHECIES.

There are but few Time-Prophecies in the Bible. These however, are connected with some of the greatest events in history. There are two great difficulties connected with chronology.

1. There are two periods the length of which are not known. Compare (I Ks. 6:1; Acts 13:17-22) or the interval from the Exodus of Israel to the fourth year of Solomon. The period from the death of Joshua to the first servitude, is not given, and the times of anarchy under the Judges.

"Israel served the Lord all the days of Joshua, and all the days of the elders that outlived Joshua, which had known all the works of the Lord that he had done for Israel." Of course that was a short link, between the death of Joshua, and that of the elders, but it is a link

gone. Also the time that Eli and Samuel judged Israel
is not given. These difficulties, solved variously by
Usher, Dean Prideaux, Dr. Hales and others, show us the
complicated nature of this section of chronology to mention no others. The nature of this difficulty is such as
to preclude the possibility of determining the exact
length of time from creation to Christ; and, consequently,
the exact age of the world at any time this side of Joshua.
While this is true of the long count, it happily does not
affect the shorter counts in the least, and the Time-
Prophecies are left unmolested. It should be noted, however, that the age of the world FROM ADAM is not DE-
FINITELY KNOWN, so that ALL THEORIES OF THE
END OF THE WORLD COMING, AT THE CLOSE OF
SIX THOUSAND YEARS, ARE NECESSARILY CRIP-
PLED IN THEIR VITAL POINT, BECAUSE THAT THIS
IS NOT, AND CANNOT BE KNOWN. The *one* point, the great
essential point, to make their theories even *plausible* from
the stand-point of *dates,* is not discoverable. This de-
cides, beforehand, the fate of their theories founded on
chronologic prophecy.

2. The dates that are given, the times the prophecies were to run, are not connected with the second
coming of Christ. If one should say we can determine
the beginnings, and endings of the great week (2520
years) and its bisections, the (1260 years), and *this* will
determine the time of the second coming of Christ! I
remind him that the *tradition* of the seventh thousand
years of the world being the Millennium, is the FATHER
of the THEORY; that the expositors link ALL their
systems with CREATION dates, or the SUPPOSED EX-
ACT age of the world, and would feel discredited, and humiliated, not to bring their systems out exactly with the
end of the six thousand years, the impossible thing; and,
cite the further fact that, the end of despotism is not at
the second coming, and this great week and its bisection
has to do with the downfall of despotism. To pile up
dates from Adam to Christ's first coming; and from there
to his second coming, may appear to be conclusive; but
"no chain is stronger than its weakest link"; and as two
gaps are in the one hundred and fifteen recorded links,
(periods) in the Old Testament, and we do not have a

reliable method of deciding the width of the gaps, how can we decide the length of the chain from Adam till now? "And he said unto them, It is not for you to know the times or seasons which the Father hath set within his own authority." (Acts 1:7).

"But concerning the times and the seasons, brethren, ye have no need that aught be written unto you. For yourselves know perfectly that the day of the Lord so cometh as a thief in the night." (I Thess. 5:1-2). THE SIX THOUSANDTH YEAR OF THE WORLD CANNOT BE DETERMINED. SO THE THEORY IS SPOILED FOREVER. The "little season" of Satan's release *after* the thousand years is not defined, in years, so *that* season is not known, hence we cannot know the day nor hour, the time or season, of his coming; and ALL THESE Pre-Millennialists, both on the year-day and literal interpretation theories, are unable to tell. This show us,

1. How preposterous is Mr. Russell's theory, that Christ came (Oct. 10, A. D. 1874) at the end of 6000 years! <How empty of proof! >

2. How futile are the efforts of all expositors to determine what God hath hidden!

The second difficulty is not so formidable. There are four ways of measuring the time-prophecies.

1. The Solar year consists of 365 days.

2. The Lunar year consists of 354 days.

3. The calendar year consists of 360 days.

We do not know whether to use one, two, or all three counts on a Time-Prophecy.

The Jews regulated their feasts by Lunar months; and their religious Calendar had (354) days, the same as the Mahometan now has. IT IS GRATIFYING TO KNOW, HOWEVER, THAT FROM THE DAYS OF EZRA, THERE ARE NO LINKS OUT OF THE CHAIN, AND THE GREAT TIME-PROPHECIES ARE ON A SOLID BASIS; for leaving out the (6000 years) theory, all the other Time-Prophecies are in periods not affected; and this applies particularly to Daniel and Revelation, both of which were given after the links were lost, and since their time, the Gentile records corroborate the dates of the Bible, or they mutually illustrate each other.

4. The fourth difficulty in counting is whether

to use the numbers mystically or literally. This difficulty is so great, that it naturally develops two classes
of interpreters.

Those who use the numbers literally. They regard the "days" as literal "days;" "months" as literal
"months;" and narrow down the prophecies accordingly.
On this theory there is no prophecy in (Dan'l 7) or in
Revelation concerning the rise, growth, exploits and
doom of a historic beast or government. But they interpret the whole of the imagery in Revelation as a
short period (forty-two months) yet to be. They are,
strictly speaking, Literalists; and have the resurrection
of the dead, Millennium, and so on, virtually the same as
other Pre-Millennialists. J. A. Seiss, D. D., in modern
times, has written extensively in defense of this theory,
as many others, whose literature is being liberally distributed by Mr. Charles C. Cook, New York. I have
neither time nor disposition to speak of the fatal errors
of this system, relying as I do upon the facts enlarged
upon hitherto, to nullify the whole argument concerning
the Personal, visible reign of Christ and his saints on
earth, for (1000) years. In making this contribution
to the subject of Millennialism, I had before me the various schools of Second Adventists, and saw that my work
should be confined mainly to the refutation of their chief
dogma—the literal, personal reign of Christ, because I
am not concerned especially in their differences. I will
not detain you long to defend the year day theory. This
however, I hold as shown concerning Daniel's Seventy
Weeks. I think that one fulfilled prophecy on the year-
day theory is a Scripture justification of its use, both by
Solar and Lunar count. I have nothing new to offer
on the subject different from what my readers already
know.

1. The twelve spies, representative of their nation,
searched the land forty days. The Lord condemned the
nation to wander in the wilderness forty years, a day for
a year. The smaller measure was made prophetic of the
larger. (Num. 14.33, 34).

2. Ezekiel, lying upon his side, representing the
humiliation of his nation, made the days prophetic of
years, by divine direction. (Ezek. 4:6).

3.   Daniel foretold the coming of Christ, in mystical numbers, "Seventy Weeks," and history shows that he used a day for a year.   (Dan'l. 9).

4.   The prophecy of the apostasy was defined, (not in literal years,) but was described as follows: twice as "time, times, and dividing of time"; once as "time, times, and a half"; twice as "a thousand two hundred and three score days"; and twice as "forty and two months"; not to speak of the thousand two hundred and ninety days, and the thirteen hundred and thirty-five days, so colsely connected with the period and expressed after the same manner as are the twenty-three hundred days, (Dan. 7:-14).   When the sacred writers used literal days, they said, "And it rained not on the earth for the space of three years and six months," Jas. 5:17).   "In Hebron, David reigned over Judah "Seven years and six months." "And the time that Solomon reigned in Jerusalem over all Israel, was forty years."

5.   It seems to me that the single fact that these mystical *numbers* are connected with mystical *beasts*, determines their figurative nature.   The numbers corresponding to the beasts are symbolic, (one thing signifying another;) and, secondly, the beast is a MINIATURE. As the beasts *signify* GOVERNMENTS, so the numbers *signify* larger NUMBERS, corresponding to the lifetime of such governments.   We find no such Lions, Bears, Leopards, Rams, He-Goats, and Nondescript animals, anywhere else in the Bible; and we find time, (as associated with some of these), nowhere else expressed in such a strange manner as "time, times and the dividing of time"; or "an hour, a day, a month and a year."

6.   Why should John in Revelation adopt the *very same expression as Daniel*, unless his meaning was as obscure as the symbol he used, and both the government symbolized and the time of its duration would both fall under the same laws of interpretation.

But as said above, I think the most conclusive evidence in favor of the year-day theory, is the fact that the first coming of Christ was predicted on that theory.   I believe the Bible is largely self-interpretive.   What I say in my opening remarks on symbols, applies here. GIVEN THE SCRIPTURE DEFINITION OF ONE SYM-

BOL OF A GROUP, ALL THE SYMBOLS OF THAT GROUP HAVE TO BE INTERPRETED IN HARMONY WITH IT TO PRESERVE CONSISTENCY. The Seventy Weeks are virtually so interpreted. Jesus said, "The *time* is fulfilled, and the kingdom of God is at hand; repent ye, and believe the gospel." (Mk. 1:15). What time could that have been but the opening of the last or *seventieth week* as he had just been baptized? (Gal. 4:4).

Now "days," "weeks," and "months," belong to the same family; and if weeks are used not as ordinary but as extraordinary, when associated with the greatest event in history, the coming of our Savior; and "days" are specified by two prophets, (Moses and Ezekiel), as prophetic of so many years, in each instance as referred to the continued humiliation of Israel, it is more than probable, and almost certain, that the symbolic beasts have symbolic numbers connected with them; and government *symbolized* has the life-time *signified* by the prophetic days enlarged into years. Moreover, this will reduce the prophetic periods into a harmonious systems as follows:

1. Israel's wandering in the wilderness forty years, (Numbers 14).

2. The three hundred and ninety years from Jeroboam's defection till Judah's overthrow.

3. The forty years from Judah's covenant under Josiah till their captivity, (Ezek. 4).

4. The Seventy Weeks, or 490 years, from Ezra's commission to Messiah. (Dan. 9; Ezra 7).

These four prophecies are divinely interpreted on that rule. Other Time-Prophecies are:

5. The dominion of the "little horn." (Dan 7).

6. The desolated sanctuary. (Dan. 8:9).

7. "Time, times and the dividing of time," and this supplemented by (1290) *days*, and (1335) *days*, that is the overplus is added to the (1260).

IN REVELATION.

8. There are the prophetic scorpions—five months. (Rev. 9:5).

9. The Cavalry-men let loose for an "hour," and a "day" and a "month" and a "year." (9:15).

How strange this sounds! It is figurative or prophetic counting.

10. The Holy City is trodden down forty and two months.

11. The two witnesses prophesy "a thousand two hundred and three score days." (11:3).

12. They lie unburied "three days and a half" (11:9).

13. The woman is nourished in the wilderness "a thousand two hundred and three score days," (12:6); also "for a time, times and half a time," (12:14).

14. The persecuting ten-horned beast continues "forty and two months." (13:5).

The argument briefly stated is this: The first four of these prophecies are fulfilled on the Year-day theory. They belong to a family group; therefore each member of the group must be so interpreted. Or stated otherwise: the history of Israel and the church was foretold from Daniel's day to the present on the Year-day theory; on the small count of 42 MONTHS NOTHING WAS FORETOLD OF THESE TWENTY-FIVE CENTURIES, AND ALL IS STILL FUTURE, AND WILL ONLY OCCUPY A PERIOD OF THREE AND A HALF YEARS, WHEN THEY BEGIN TO BE FULFILLED. The fact that Popery and Mahometanism have filled out the symbols as governments, so that a child can trace them in history, makes it morally certain that the numbers were intended to measure the life-time of the governments. Finally, I submit that, it is demonstrably true that Popery is the "little horn" (Dan'l 7) and Mahometanism the "little horn" (Dan'l 8:9), Futurists can not give a single evidence of even a beginning of fulfillment of their theory now after the whole is practically fulfilled; (and as certainly as my contention is sound as to the second coming of Christ, Elijah, all the saints and the literal personal reign) THEIR THEORY NEVER WILL HAVE EVEN A BEGINNING. This latter statement I most solemnly believe to be the overwhelming truth.

THE TRUE SITUATION.

I believe then that the Year-day theory is correct. That AS A MEASURE it is correctly used by the most of the Second Adventists. I acknowledge with thankfulness the great help I have received from Faber, Lord, Elliott,

Habershon, Shimeall, Brooks, the Newtons, and many others. But they are wrong, wholly wrong, on the EVENTS PREDICTED TO CLOSE THESE TIME-PRO-PHECIES. Babylon goes down; Mahometanism goes down; Judaism goes down; Paganism goes down; but all by *natural means*. I hold that no miracles are scheduled till near the end of the world, AND ONLY AS THE FUL-FILLMENT OF PROPHECY GIVES US CONSTANTLY MIRACLES OF MIND, ARE THERE MIRACLES NOW. The last statement could be enlarged upon into a volume. The miracles of creation were not seen by men. The mir-acles of Moses were seen by those who needed them. The miracles of Christ and his followers, ceased at the con-firmation of the gospel. We walk by faith. Prophetic testimony is cumulative, grows from age to age. *The fulfillment Era is upon us.* Let us rejoice that our God has not left himself without witness, but that the sure word of prophecy is being fulfilled on a national and world-wide scale, and the voice of the prophets can be heard above the roar of artillery on land and sea, making known unto us that the Metallic Man must be ground to dust and swept away; that the ferocious, symbolic Beasts are being consumed by fire; and the "little horn" de-stroyed; but at no point in the momentous programme do the countless hosts of martyrs, the sleeping saints, apostles, prophets, the holy angels and the Lord Jesus Christ appear on the scene to shock the world with the insufferable glory of their abiding presence, envelop the earth in the splendors of Eden, and reproduce the halle-luiahs of heaven in a veritable temple in Jerusalem on the rocky eminence of Mount Moriah.

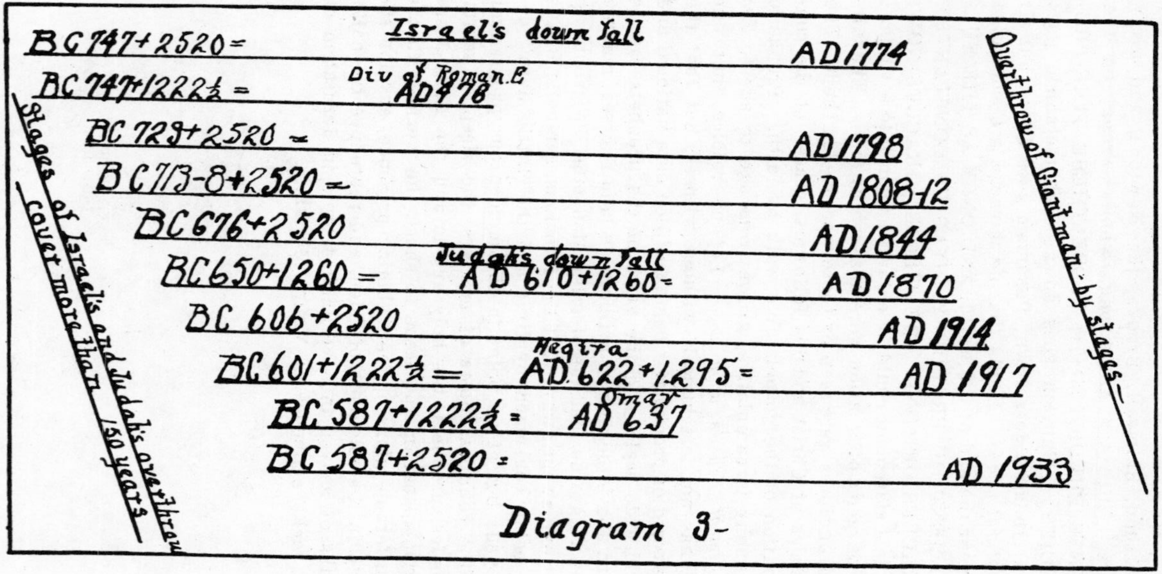

Overthrow of Giant-man - by stages -

Israel's down fall

BC 747+2520 =   AD 1774

BC 747+1224¾ =   Div of Roman.E
                              AD 478

BC 728+2520 =   AD 1792

BC 713-8+2520 =   AD 1808-12

BC 676+2520 =   AD 1844

BC 650+1260 = Judah's down fall
                AD 610+1260 =   AD 1870

BC 606+2520 =   AD 1914

BC 601+1224¾ =   Hegira
                AD 622+1295 =   AD 1917
BC 587+1224¾ =   AD 637
BC 587+2520 =   AD 1933

Diagram 3 -

Stages of Israel's and Judah's overthrow
cover more than 150 years

DIAGRAM III.

I select a few measures of the long week (2520) years; and of the half week, (1260) years. As the Lunar week of (2520) years would only make (2445) Solar years; and the half week of (1260) years only makes (1222½) Solar years, (as there are (11) more days in every year and this cuts off that many years in such a long time), I have used enough of these to enable the reader to see how to make the counts; and also to see that the time should be measured by both counts. It seems especially appropriate that Jewish and Mahometan time should be Lunar, as that is where we get Lunar time. Mr. Habershon and Mr. Guinness, (two Millennialists), saw that the captivities of Israel and Judah had more than one beginning date; and, hence, more than one fulfillment date. They were thus on the right track; but their visions of a Millennium led them to add another group each of prospective dates for the second coming of Christ, the beginning of the Millennial kingdom, and thus the end of the present order of things. This all called for the same group of miracles, usually given in these theories, to close the gospel age and introduce the Millennial kingdom. Their principle of measuring is to be commended; and I hope that we may all learn that any man who seeks to determine the day when the martyrs will arise; the day when Christ shall come back to earth either to end the world or to begin a Millennium; and that any one who counts the age of the world to a day or year is a visionary and unreliable expositor. Such facts are not set forth in Time-Prophecies; and, as no dates are given for them, it is time and labor worse than thrown away to seek to determine such matters. When we shall all learn the nature and use of Old Testament types, then these wild dreams of temporal plenty, and material greatness, will give way to the cultivation of a higher and holier life here in preparation, (not for a thousand year reign with Christ on earth among the revived types of an abrogated system), but to "Be forever with the Lord."

CHAPTER XXXVI.

THE JEWS AND TIME PROPHECIES.

1. Noah predicted the Flood for (120) years. (Gen. 6:3).

2. Abraham foretold the affliction, wanderings, captivity in Egypt and release of his posterity, covering (400) years. (Gen. 15). Fulfillment is given (Ex. 12 and Gal. 3).

3. Joseph arose to eminence as a "seer" by foretelling (7) years of plenty followed by (7) years of famine in Egypt, all of which was connected with the fulfillment of Abraham's prophecy, (Gen. 41).

4. Moses predicted the (40) years wandering in the wilderness, and used a day for a year. (Num. 14).

5. Isaiah predicted the ten tribes of Israel should cease to be a nation, within (65) years. Fulfillment is recorded (II Ks. 17:24; Ezra 4:2).

6. Jeremiah foretold the (70) years' Babylonian Captivity, (Jer. 25:11-14; 29:5-14).

7. Daniel foretold the first coming of Christ after "Seventy Weeks," (Dan'l 9).

It should be observed that these Time-Prophecies usually ended in deliverance and joy for God's faithful servants; but their enemies were overthrown and destroyed, because they had afflicted them. We should study this fact in all of these cases. The events were on a large scale, nation-wide or world-wide. These tremendous realities of history, (recorded for our admonition), teach the great lesson that, God sees the end from the beginning, and is faithful to reward his servants and to punish his enemies. The Flood was cited as a historical judgment of God against sinners by our Savior, (Luke 17:26, 27); by Paul, (Heb. 11:7); by Peter in both of his letters (I Pet. 3:19, 20; II Pet. 2:5 and ch. 3); and by Jude. Also the national judgment against Egypt, and later against Israel, is cited frequently by inspired writers, always as a warning from heaven against impenitence. Thus these Time-Prophecies come down to us charged with manifold warnings against sin.

THE GREAT PROPHETIC WEEK.

In Daniel (ch. 4) is the Giant Tree, and Nebuchadnezzar's insanity. The tree represented the king, victorious in war, grown into a mighty ruler. Or, possibly (as in the symbol of the Giant Image, where it was said, "Thou art this head of Gold," the meaning was that the Babylonian government was the head, so here) the tree stood for the government, and the king as the embodiment of its principles. The tree was cut down, but had a band of brass and iron around the stump of the roots thereof. Nebuchadnezzar was given the heart of a beast, and ate with the beasts of the earth, till "seven times" passed over him, when his dominion was restored to him. But he had learned his lesson well—he knew that the "Most High ruleth in the kingdom of men, and giveth it to whomsoever he will." See how often that thought is repeated. I observe on the whole lesson:

1. Nebuchadnezzar's *dominion* was objected to or his refusal to acknowledge God was condemned.

2. Earthly government was not a curse, as such; but the stately tree was cut down, with only the roots left. They were watered with the dews of heaven—the blessings from heaven. Out of the roots of government rises another government, more in harmony with the rule of heaven.

3. Viewed from any stand-point, human government was not destroyed, wholly; but was secured by the iron and brass band around the stump of the roots.

4. "Seven times" passed over the King, and those seven times ended in deliverance for him and the principles of righteousness in his government, and condemnation for the tyrannous, idolatrous government administered by him hitherto.

5. It is nowhere said the "seven times" were seven years. But as Nebuchadnezzar and the history of the tree are inseparable, and he was ruler over the whole earth, the change wrought in him during the "seven times" was the change wrought in human government. The fact that "time, times and half a time," are a bisec-

tion of a week, and this period is applied to the last half
of the period from the days of Nebuchadnezzar till the
overthrow of the Metallic Man, and the four Wild beasts,
is strong presumptive evidence that this whole transaction was prophetic. It was like Ezekiel lying on his left
and right sides (390) days and (40) days respectively, a
day for a year. So Nebuchadnezzar was to have seven
times pass over him, or (2520 days). That is a time is
a year—(360 days); seven times were 360 times 7 equal
2520 days). That was prophetic of the whole period of
Gentile dominion,—"the times of the Gentiles,"—so their
time will be fulfilled at the end of that period. Let it
be distinctly noted however, that governments do not
cease, but grow *anew out of the roots of the tree.* (Read
the chapter). Neither is it the church that rules directly
or solely; but it is the blessing of God upon the roots of
the tree, that preserves it. We are living in the days
answering to Nebuchadnezzar's restoration, (the fulfillment of the (2520) days being now about finished in
(2520) years that have passed, or the whole week). The
last half of the week is that which we have been considering, that is the (1260) years; but this half demands
a first half, and this we have extending back from the
beginning of the (1260 years) to the days of Nebuchadnezzar and the captivities of fleshly Israel. I proceed to
show how the week and half week are applied to the
governments of earth, and you will understand why the
Millennialists are expecting the restoration of Israel to
their land and the second coming of Christ. The time
prophecies are rapidly fulfilling. But as the captivities
of fleshly Israel covered several years, and thus the
periods had a two-fold and even three-fold beginning, so
they have a corresponding two-fold and three-fold ending. The same is true of the bi-section of the week as
applied to the gradual rise and gradual decline and fall
of the predicted apostasy. I cite a number of dates for
the students of these time-prophecies and show how easy
it is for one to be deceived into the belief that the end will
come at certain dates. This will teach us to be careful
in two points: 1. To know what events are predicted in
time-prophecies; 2. To know that the prophecies often
have double beginnings and double endings. To illus-

trate. The seventy years' captivity began in stages and
was fulfilled in stages. The primary commencement was
under Jehoiakim, the king, (II Chron. 36:6-7), (B. C.
606).   It terminated seventy years later under Cyrus'
edict (B. C. 536).   Cyrus was predicted to grant his royal
favor to the Jews.   (Is. 44:28; 45:1-13; IIChron. 36:
22-23; Ezra. 1:2).

But Jerusalem was destroyed after the final captivity of Judah about (587 or 588 B. C.), when Zedekiah
was taken, the temple burned and the whole land made
desolate.   Seventy years later or (518 B. C.), by decree
of Darius, King of Persia, the temple was rebuilt.

A GROUP OF MEASURES.

I give a group of measures of the "long week" and
of the half week, showing the gradual captivity of both
Israel and Judah indicate a gradual downfall for Despotism, including Catholicism and Mahometanism.

B. C. 747 DATE.

According to Ptolmey's Canon this year began the
Babylonian government, which finally captured Judah,
and became a type of spiritual Babylon. It was within
five years of the founding of Rome which has lasted for
more than (25) centuries, and for two thousand years
persecuted fleshly and spiritual Israel.   Consult Diagram
III and note the whole week measured from this date led
down to (1774) the French Revolution, (so disastrous to
Popery); and the half week ended with the period indicated by the ten toes of the Man, the ten horns of the
Beast, and the fourth Trumpet in Revelation, or the overthrow of the Western Roman Empire. (A. D. 476).

Between the rise of Babylon and its fall (B. C.
747-587) were (160) years.   This includes the period of
all the prophets from Isaiah to Haggai and Zechariah, (or
all the writing prophets except Malachi).   This was,
therefore, the prophetic period.   The prophets are grouped in those years.   It was also the period of the captivities of the two nations, Israel and Judah.   The Diagram
gives the approximate dates of Israel's captivities and
the (2520) year's measure therefrom. It is self-evident, to
any student of the history, that all the dates given were

the most important in both Israel's and Judah's downfall; and the long week, measured from these, ended
with important dates in the downfall of despotism. (A.
D. 1774) was the period of the French Revolution in the
Old World, and the transition of the American colonies
into the United States. (A. D. 1798 to 1812) was the
period of Napoleon, the greatest warrior of modern
times, who rebuked popery and reduced the pontiffs from
civil rulers to religious orders. The system never recovered from the shock he gave it; but lived a precarious
life until ultimately destroyed by Victor Immanuel (A.
D. 1870), another measure of the long week. I would
have you observe that, the half week (1260) years,
(measured by Solar time), indicated the rise of popery
(A. D. 606 to 610); and the last half of the week (1260)
years, led to the overthrow of the temporal power (A.
D. 1870). Likewise the Lunar half week, (suitable to
Mahometan measurement, as they use it,) measured from
the gradual decline of fleshly Israel, ended in two important dates affecting Mahometanism; that is (A. D.
622), the year their empire began; and (A. D. 637) the
year Omar captured Jerusalem and erected the Mosque
on the ancient site of Solomon's temple.

B. C. 587 DATE.

The last king of Judah was taken captive to Babylon at this date. It was final. The Lunar half week,
(as said above), measured from this date, ends with Omar
and the mosque; and the whole week, long count ends
with (A. D. 1933). This, being the last measure of the
(2520) years, leads many to think it predicts the end of
time, or the Millennium. It is not possible to determine when
Christ will come, nor is such a Millennium as many picture to us revealed to begin at any date imaginable. But
these measures which I have submitted may suffice to
show that it is speculation, pure and simple, to select one
of these captivity dates and make it the starting point
from which to measure. I decline to burden these pages
with a lengthy calculation on any of these measures.
Any one with the leisure and a disposition to do so, can
satisfy himself with these and all other dates submitted.
They are easily verified. Ever remember, the age of the
human race can not be determined exactly; and the time

from Adam to Christ is not known, within *several years.* How evident it must be, therefore, that ALL ATTEMPTS to make the measure of the long week end with (6000) years are FRUITLESS. IT CAN NOT BE DONE. This fact forever destroys the tradition that the Millennium is the (7000th) year of the world, and that it is connected with Time-Prophecy. As the age of the world is not revealed; (or no living man knows how many days, months and years have passed since Adam's creation), it is impossible to learn, from any source, when the (6000) years end. As God revealed many things in time prophecy, but left this one out, it would seem about time to quit locating it in order to spring a new theory of the Millennium! It is puerile and childish! See (ch. 33) on "Age of the Human Race," in this volume to verify these statements, and thus guard against that plausible but untrue assumption.

THINGS DEMONSTRATED.

1. We do not know when the (6000) years end.

2. We know the Feast of Passover, waving of the first sheaf, and Pentecost, typified Christ's death, resurrection and the establishment of his church and kingdom in the capital of the Jewish nation fifty days later. Neither of them could be used as types of the *end,* for they were types of the *beginning,* of the gospel age.

3. The year of Jubilee can not be a type of the Millennium for it would make it the (50) thousandth year of the world, not the (7) thousandth.

4. The Parables of our Lord ended all probation for every one on trial in the various illustrations he gave, and can, by no ingenuity of the human mind, be made to teach that the terms and conditions of probation were extended and increased to the ofenders.

5. The Types are each and all legislated away forever. It is to give up the entire New Testament to return to the observance of the Types of the Mosaic law; and this leaves the Millennial theory of interpretation of the prophecy without an inch of ground to stand on. It is as morally impossible to revive the types, as it is intellectually impossible to determine the age of the world. As neither one can be done, the Millennial theory that

demands both shall be accomplished, is doomed to eternal defeat.

6. I show in closing chapters that second chance-ism is impossible, and that the whole human race will be raised from the dead, judged and enter upon their eternal destiny at the same time.   All of these facts demonstrate that the Millennial theory is impossible of realization now or hereafter, and is sustained by mixing the law and the gospel, and rests upon assumption and imagination.

CHAPTER XXXVII.

FORMER MILLENARIANS.

There were many Millennarians at the opening of the Reformation in Germany, in the morning of the (16th) century.   This is not strange, as ignorance of the Bible and general superstition prevailed.   The mighty up-heaval in society seemed to portend something, and many confidently asserted it was the Millennium.   We look back over the four centuries and see that it was a giant stroke against "the Man of Sin."   This Millennial theory is like a stimulant, or an intoxication, which leaves the subject dejected and melancholy.   It is like reading any other romance, it excites the imagination.   The novel reader, generally speaking, has little use for sober, mat-ter of fact, literature.   The rebound from this Millennial theory is towards skepticism and infidelity.   After ima-gining one is soon to be rich and happy, a king and priest, to be aroused to the knowledge of the fact that it was all a dream, a romance, one blames the Bible, the church, the preachers, the Almighty, everybody and every-thing, and tries to screen himself.   Why not admit he was led away by a delusion and give up the romance?

MARTIN LUTHER.

At one time this great reformer thought the end of the world was not twenty years off.   Near the time of his death, he said, "God forbid that the world should last fifty years longer. Let him cut matters short with his last judgment." And to his last days he thought the coming of Christ was at hand. Table Talk, Michelet, p. 216.

MELANCTHON.

He thought the end of the world was at hand. He adopted the old Jewish tradition that six thousand years would end it.

"The words of the prophet, Elias should be marked by every one, and inscribed upon our walls, and upon the entrances of our houses. Six thousand years shall this world stand, and after that be destroyed; two thousand years without the law; two thousand years under the law of Moses; two thousand years under the Messiah; and if any of these years are not fulfilled, they will be shortened (a shortening intimated by Christ also) on account of our sins."

Elijah's words are not in the Bible if he ever made any such declaration. Again, the world stood twenty-five hundred years without the law, some fifteen hundred years under the law, and we have now reached approximately nineteen centuries of the gospel. So he was wrong in this also. This tradition came from an Elias, who lived after the prophets were all dead, and before the gospel was given. He belonged to the age when the Apocrapha was written, and men were guided by philosophy rather than by the Word of God. Why do not these expositors cite us to one text *in* the Bible, instead of citing us to this otherwise unheard of Elias? They have no text to cite, on this tradition.

JAMES ALBERT BENGEL.

He was born in Wurtenburg, Germany, June 24th, 1687, and ranks high as a writer on Revelation. He wrote on the subject in (A.D. 1740). He set the appearing of the Lord for (June 18, 1836). He said, "Should the year (1836) pass away without any such remarkable change in public affairs as I have anticipated some fundamental mistake in the arrangement of my system must be sought after." Think he was right as to the fundamental mistake! But he has a number of disappointed brethren to keep him company with their fundamental mistakes.

JOHN WESLEY.

He published his notes on the New Testament, following Bengel's mystical and erroneous system, and naturally fell into the same errors. He had "the time, times and half a time" from (A. D. 1058 to 1836), when Christ should come.

WILLIAM MILLER.

I have in my library a little volume of nineteen lectures of Miller's on the second coming of Christ. Most of my readers know that he set the time for (A. D. 1843). I think the reader will agree with me that he, like all his predecessors, was mistaken as to the world's greatest event—the coming of our Savior.

JOSEPH WOLFF.

This learned Jew, converted to belief in Christ as the Jewish Messiah, was sent as a missionary to the Jews at Jerusalem early in the 19th century. He wrote from "Mount Calvary Jerusalem, April 20, 1820, to the church of Christ in Great Britain and Ireland,

"In short I proclaimed for two months, to the Jews, this great truth.   1.   *That Jesus of Nazareth* came once on earth despised and rejected of men, to die for poor sinners: and 2ndly, *that he will come again with glory and majesty*, and glorious in his apparel, and travelling in the greatness of his strength: *He will come* The Son of Man, in the year *eighteen hundred and forty-seven*, in the clouds of Heaven, and will gather all the tribes of Israel, and govern in person as Man and as God, in the literal city of Jerusalem, with his saints, and be adored in the temple which will be rebuilt, and thus he shall govern 1000 years. And I, Joseph Wolff shall see with my own eyes, Abraham, Isaac and Jacob in their glorified bodies, and I shall see Elijah and Isaiah, David and Jeremiah, whose songs have guided me to Jesus of Nazareth. I shall meet them all here at Jerusalem, where I now write these lines." Millennial Tidings. (pp. 38-9).

A woman named H. Livermore took up the song in our country, and wrote and preached extensively, professing to be a "witness for Jesus," on the same great mission.   The Asiatic Cholera in this country in (A .D. 1832) gave her a fruitful theme with which to terrorize the muddled brains of her followers. You notice that Miller, Wolff, Harriett Livermore, Bengel, and John Wesley were within about ten years of each other in their time set for the coming of Christ. William Cunninghame, a scholar and man of leisure in England, wrote an elaborate treatise and reached the same dates with Miller. There were many other English expositors of the same notion. M. Habershon wrote,

"In this conclusion I am happy in agreeing with Mr. Cunninghame, who says, I am not aware of any more probable era which can be selected for the commencement of the (2300) years than that which has been chosen by some recent writers, who supposed this period to have begun at the same time with the seventy weeks of Daniel, or in the year B. C. 457, and consequently that it will terminate in the year (1843).

Mosheim tells of a great excitement at the time of Luther's Reformation; and the Anabaptists began the New Jerusalem. Luther's notion that the second coming of Christ was at hand aided them, as such notions, by the sects, aid Mr Russell.

(REV.) R. C. SHIMEALL.

This learned Presbyter of the Protestant Episcopal Church, in the Diocese of New York, published in A. D. 1842 his "Age of the World." He marked out (1847) as a critical year. And set (1868) as the end of the world.

"IN A. D. 1848 THE LORD JEHOVAH WILL APPEAR FOR THE RESTORATION AND REESTABLISHMENT IN PALESTINE OF THE SEED OF ABRAHAM, WHICH HE SWARE UNTO THEIR FATHERS."

This great man failed to establish his "golden chain." Jesus did not come in A. D. 1868 in the 'complete overthrow of Popery, Mahometanism, Infidelity and every opposing Kingdom." "This is the time of trouble, such as never was, since there was a nation to this time: no, nor ever shall be. Heaven prepare us for, and preserve us during our exposure to the days of calamity that awaits us."

"The Self-Determining Test, Sacred and Profane, Historic and Prophetic of the World's Chronology," marshalled about all the facts and arguments extant on the Jewish Tradition that the Millennium is the seventh thousand years of the world's history. Below is his summing up of 183 pages.

"We have at length reached the end proposed in this volume—that of furnishing the evidence on the basis of the corrected Hebrew version of the Holy Scriptures, that the current year A. D. 1859, is the year A. M. 5991: and that hence, the year A. D. 1868, completes the 6000th year of the world's history, from the creation and fall of man. If these several points have been sustained, then he would appeal to all to reflect, that in *Nine years* from the current year of our Lord 1859, the present Christian dispensation, as forming the larger portion of the period called, *the times of the Gentiles, will have closed upon the Church and the world forever.* What then? In reply, let it at present suffice that we say not the end of *time,* for only *six days* of the great anti-typical week will have passed away. The *seventh* must ensue. Not the destruction of our earth or world (Kosmos) by a universal conflagration; so far from this, it is to be, *"the time of restitution of all things,* which God hath spoken by the mouth of all his holy prophets, since the world began. In a word, the year A. M. 6001, will be the ushering in of the Great Millennial Sabbatism spoken of in Rev. 20: 1-6. This period of blessedness, however, will be preceded by that season of *unparalleled tribulation"* predicted by our Lord: such as was not from the beginning of the creation which God created unto this time, neither shall be; the days of vengeance (against the apostate Church and the ungodly, infidel world,); that all things that are written may be fulfilled."

THE SHAKERS..

"Mother Ann Lee" founder of a "Millennial Church" claimed that she was the female Jesus Christ, returned to earth to inaugurate the Millennium, (A .D. 1770). True her husband lost confidence in the source of her inspiration and left her, but she found enough followers to make a little sect. I have the history of her life and the origin of her sect and can compare some of her teaching with more modern teaching, touching the same subjects. They are enough alike to be one original and the other appropriated, but I do not say that this is true. She could neither read nor write, and was thus quite an illiterate "Christ"!

"Pastor Russell' is too late in announcing the coming of Christ in (A. D. 1874); "Mother Ann Lee' said he came, and her Biographer says he came, (A. D. 1770). My judgment is, it was she who came in (1770) and not Christ. It was a case of mistaken identity! You observe she was about one century ahead of "Pastor Russell," and instead of saying Jesus was *invisibly* present, claimed *she* was *Christ.*

Mr. Russell says,

"The sword of truth already sharpened, is to smite every evil system and custom—civil, social and eclesiastical. Nay, more, we can see that the smiting has commenced; freedom of thought, and human rights, civil and religious, long lost sight of under kings and emperors, popes, synods, councils, traditions and creeds, are being appreciated and asserted as never before. The internal conflict is already fermenting; it will ere long break forth as a consuming fire, and human systems, and errors, which for centuries have fettered truth, and oppressed the groaning creation, must melt before it. Yes, truth and wide-spread and increasing knowledge of it is the sword which is perplexing and wounding the heads over many nations." (Ps. 110:6).

I am glad the author of "The Time is at Hand" (p. 101), got down to the facts. It is the truth of heaven that is doing the great work, wide-spread and far reaching in its consequences. What single feature of it demands the presence of Christ? The whole theory is false in premise, argument and conclusion, that demands the literal but invisible presence of Christ, all the holy angels, and the righteous dead, to do the work now being done by men in the flesh.

RECAPITULATION.

I show in one concise view the erroneous dates set for Christ's second coming as cited in this chapter.

Bengel and Charles Wesley .... A. D. 1836
Luther, Melancthon, and others said it was
    near at hand in the sixteenth century.
Anabaptists began the New Jerusalem .... A. D. 1521
William Miller in America .... A. D. 1843
Cunninghame, M. Habershon and others in
    England .... A. D. 1843
Joseph Wolff, a converted Jew and mission-
    ary to Palestine .... A. D. 1847
R. C. Shimeall, New York .... A. D. 1868
C. T. Russell, now of Brooklyn, New York .. A. D. 1874

Now if the transactions were secret, invisible, both the coming in 1874; the resurrection of the saints in 1878; the withdrawal of God's favor from the churches in 1881; and the beginning of the Harvest at Christ's coming, what evidence has Mr. Russell that Jesus did not come earlier—at one of the other dates? A little reflection should enable one to see that his whole chain of events depends on one assertion—that Jesus came in (Oct. 1874).

If he *did not come*, then what follows?

1. The world's forty years' harvest to end (Oct. 1914) did not begin in (1874).

2. The saints were not resurrected three and one-half years later, in the spring of (1878).

3. The governments do not all go down in (1914).

4. The Old Testament saints are not on earth as servants, and the New Testament saints as sons of God in invisible spirit-bodies.

5. The Times of Restitution did not begin in either (1874) or (1878).

6. A thousand year judgment day did not begin with the resurrection of the Just, to be closed with the resurrection of the unjust.

7. The wicked have no promise of a resurrection to a thousand years chance or probation for eternal life.

8. The Jubilee to last one thousand years has not begun.

9. The Parables, ordinances and teachings of Christ in the New Testament are not ended.

10. The bride class have not had a "birth of the spirit" from death; the great trumpet has not sounded; no eye or understanding has seen Jesus; and his presence is not apprehended.

11. The Jews are not returning to God because they are returning to Palestine and are not to be ruled over by Abraham, Isaac, Jacob and the resurrected saints of the Old Testament, living among them on earth, in bodies nourished by earthly food, and conducting civil governments.

12. Mr. Russell is not the servant of (Matt. 24:25) whom God hath raised up to give the people their "meat in due season."

These twelve cardinal errors may suffice. They sweep away, the whole air-castle. If Jesus did not come in (Oct. 1874) at the close of (6000) years, Mr. Russell is wrong on every event that depends on that prior event, for it stands related to all the rest as cause to effect. I have taken some pains to show that he differs from the world's greatest chronologers; he differs (100 years) from (I Ks. 6); he makes the anti-type of Pentecost to be the FORTY-NINTH instead of the FIFTIETH day; he makes Jubilee to come on the forty-ninth instead of the fiftieth thousand years, and to get this *he* MANUFACTURES FORTY-TWO THOUSAND YEARS AND CALMLY HEADS THE LIST WITH THEM; he denies the continued existence of Christ at death, and denies his bodily resurrection; and his whole theory depends on the second coming of Christ in (A. D. 1874), as much as the spokes of a wheel depend on the hub. Remove the hub and the wheel collapses. I remove his central, fundamental assumption and his theory falls to pieces. There is absolutely nothing left to the theory when the colossal assumption is removed that Jesus is invisibly present and has been on earth forty years (Oct. 10 A. D. 1914). "If the blind lead the blind, both shall fall into the ditch." Can you see the ditch? Then save yourself from your blind leaders!

CHAPTER XXXVIII.

RESTITUTION.

Perhaps no text has been more frequently quoted and more blindly, than (Acts 3:19) on restitution. It was originally spoken to sustain the opposite of what it is quoted by Dawnists to uphold. It was shortly after Pentecost. Peter knew the Jewish hope of a temporal Messiah, how they believed he abideth ever. He had shaken loose from the old traditionary Jews, but recently, and spoke directly to the point. It was *ignorance* that prompted the people and rulers to slay Christ. Yet, it had been foretold by the prophets, and thus Jesus was rather proven divine by their fulfillment than disgraced as the rulers had hoped. He was now in heaven, from whence he came; and, furthermore, heaven must retain him till all things were restored, that the prophecies contemplate, then he comes again. The restitution, whatever it comprehends, must be accomplished while heaven retains him. If there should be a restitution to sinlessness as in Eden, it must be accomplished with Jesus in heaven. This was the opposite of Jewish expectations of national glory; and the same is true of Millennialists.

1. God may restore Israel to favor, if they continue not in unbelief, (Rom. 11); but not with a temporal Messiah.

2. He may restore spiritual Israel from Babylon, as many prophets have spoken; but heaven retains Christ.

3. He may restore countless hosts of souls from sin through the gospel; but not by his personal presence, for heaven retains him.

4. He may restore the religion of Christ to those countries that forsook it for Mahometanism; but not in person.

5. He may restore the Bible to the world in all its enlightening, convicting, converting power, and have the knowledge of God to cover the earth, as the waters cover the channel of the great deep; but he remains in heaven.

6. He may restore woman to be the help-meet of man, sharer of his joys, divider of his sorrows, his faithful companion, and help-meet, instead of his drudge and slave, or the object of foul and debasing lust. She may be elevated from polygamy and bigamy, or from enforced celibacy, and the harems of corruption. But the gospel is the cleansing, uplifting power.

7. He may restore slaves to freedom all round the globe; and exalt the downtrodden of earth into the front ranks of civilization and Christianity; indirectly and not personally.

8. He may restore the ignorant races to be the intelligent, commercial, educational, moral and spiritual rulers of men. "For there is one God, and one mediator between God and man, the man Christ Jesus, who gave himself as the redemption price for all—a fact testified to at its own appointed time." Weymuth's Translation. (I Tim. 2:5, 6). This is Mr. Russell's Gibraltar. He rallies his theory around this as the spokes of a wheel are grouped around an axle. The text, however, simply

declares that Jesus died for all and this fact was testified in due time. Certainly it was not testified to the Patriarchs or Prophets. It was a mystery hid from ages and from generations. But in due time Christ died for all, the just for the unjust. But even Mr. Russell, with his vivid imagination, can not get much out of the text. Why? Because the incorrigibly wicked have to be punished; and there are such multitudes of them after the Millennium closes, that it would seem that testifying to them had been useless. His theory does not save them. So of what use is the theory? Jesus knows the dead. Would he annihilate wicked men once; then bring them back to earth again knowing even a hundred year chance would end in the second annihilation? Knowing that he would have to annihilate a host, (the only revealed characteristic of whom, was their enmity to and war against the camp of the saints and the beloved city); the multitude of whom came up over the breadth of the earth, "the number of whom was as the sand of the sea"? (I believe that Jesus will leave all that class of wicked men in company with the rich man until the resurrection).

Is it possible to conceive that Jesus needs to resurrect the Sodomites to give them a chance to believe and obey the gospel? Do all generations have to obey the gospel? Then Moses and Noah, Enoch and Elijah, Abel and Malachi will have to obey it. The simple fact that every generation will be judged does not imply that Jesus will save or condemn them on the basis of baptism and communion or THE GOSPEL COMMANDS. Has God never given any but GOSPEL COMMANDS? Can not the Lord judge men to whom he never gave the gospel? Can not the people who lived in the first twenty-five centuries be judged without raising them from the dead to live a thousand years to try them? Can not the people who lived for the next fifteen centuries do the same? Where is the necessity for Abraham to render gospel obedience? or Noah? Where is the necessity for David and Isaiah to obey the gospel? Did not the virtue of Christ's death apply from Adam to the cross? Has it not applied from the cross to this holy hour? Will God reject the obedience to his law that was in force, because the obedient ones did not obey a law that was not in force? Will he make the PATRIARCHS and faithful JEWS SERVANTS FOREVER because they did not obey the gospel when there WAS NO GOSPEL? "Sin is the transgression of the law." (I John 3:4). "For until the law, sin was in the world, but sin is not imputed when there is no law." (Rom. 5:13). Is there a single candidate for eternal joys, who came to the years of discretion, who was not pardoned? No, not one. If God forgave the patriarchs under one law, and treated disobedience thereto as sin; those under the law of Moses by that law, and treated its violators as sinners; and now saves all gospel subjects on the conditions of the gospel, and ranks all as sinners who reject it, (and evidently all this is true), then do not be too inquisitive as to HOW GOD WILL JUDGE THE WORLD. That is not your work, but His, and he certainly is able for it. It will not decrease your responsibility to consider that Jesus saved David as a Jew and Abraham as a patriarch. It will not lessen your obligations to Christ if you know all mysteries and all knowledge, for without love, *you* will be nothing. You may never know just how many heathen will be saved; neither do you know what proportion of the professed followers of Christ will be approved by their Master. But you may know your individual duty and "make your calling and election sure."

Dawnists start out to bless *individuals*, irrespective of their lives while here, that is second-chanceism. Jesus is a blessing to *all* NATIONS; that is his blessings are as freely offered to Gentiles as to Jews, there is no respect of persons with God. But to be *individually* blessed, we must *obey* as *individuals*. Dawnists have as many lost at the end of their system as there are now—as "numberless as the sand of the sea." Then why quote the texts "bless all nations"; "Jesus gave himself a ransom for all to be testified in due time?" Does that do away with the necessity of obedience in order to salvation? Of what benefit to humanity is the second chance? DOES IT SAVE ALL? Does it end in "blessing" for all? Are there not to be a host of wicked after the thousand years? After the "little season"? And are they not to be judged out of the books and punished?

You can readily see that such writers are wresting the Scriptures when they picture to you that because Christ's blessing is FOR ALL NATIONS; and that he died for all; that, therefore, all nations are to be saved, and every individual is to be blessed, eternally. The Millennium would be fine for sinful men if heaven was to be gained that way. But "strait is the gate and narrow is the way that leadeth unto life and few there be that find it." There is nothing to hinder you from finding it, but your own stubborn will and refusal. You see universalism breaks down right where Dawnists need it—at the end of their pictured Millennium. The Restitution word has been filled with Eden restored, all the wicked restored to Adam's sinless perfection, as though they had never sinned, and a lot of things they wish to have; but, when you get to the close of the period, you see they have filled the word with a meaning the inspired writers never gave it.

RESTITUTION, OR ACCOMPLISHMENT, IS GOING ON EVERY MOMENT AND HAS BEEN SINCE PETER PREACHED THE SERMON, AND WILL CONTINUE TO THE END OF TIME; OR TILL ALL IS FULFILLED; HEAVEN RETAINS JESUS TILL THE END; AND THE WORLD IS WICKED, THE NATIONS OPPOSE GOD, AND ALL ARE JUDGED.

The sooner you see that the dead, from Adam to the present hour, have finished their course and are awaiting the judgment of the great day, and that you will soon be through with your probation, the better for you. God will judge you and them. No amount of twisting and wresting Scripture on earth will change their destiny, although it may determine yours or mine. Remember that if the *nations* are still here, the wicked still innumerable at the close of time, the Restitution CAN NOT mean the RESTORATION OF EDEN, (not as a Garden but as a world); and *blessing* all nations CAN NOT mean *saving* all nations; and the whole Millennial theory leaves the wicked to be *judged* and *punished*. You are not able to solve all the infinite depths of wisdom, and may try to help God to think out a plan of salvation for the heathen, only to find after half a century of labor that the wicked dead, at the final resurrection and Judgment, are still on hands, numerous as the sand of the sea, (as Mr. Russell has done as well as all who were before him speculating as to what God ought to do!)

SPECULATIONS DANGEROUS.

Of course men who seek to be wise above what is writen, try to frame up systems by which they think the billions of dead can have a *chance* which *they* think they *need*. He knows us all from the high forehead Greek professor, to the jabbering wild man of the woods. He knows our loves and hates, our aims and plans, our mental, moral and physical limitations. He sounds all the depths of human woe, and scales all the heights of sinful folly. From his all-seeing eye darkness flees like a shadow, and the deepest recesses of the soul are naked and open before Him. His sleepless eye takes in at a glance all motion, all life, all the puny struggles of men. The Judge of all the earth will do right. He will by no means clear the guilty. The righteous shall in no wise lose his reward. But our business is urgent. Our duty is plain. We could not judge a single human creature. But God who has known all perfectly; the law under which they lived; their abilities and corresponding responsibilities, will settle all accounts. Paul said: "For I know nothing against myself; yet am I not hereby justified; but he that judgeth me is the Lord. Wherefore judge nothing before the time, *until the Lord comes*, who will both bring to light the hidden things of darkness, and make manifest the counsels of the hearts; and then shall each man have his praise from God." (I Cor. 4: 4-5).

Dawnists would have the wicked dead to come back to earth as sinless and spotless as Adam in Eden to be on trial for eternal life. This is to ignore the sins of all the ages. It is to make a restoration or restitution, the prophets have not foretold. It is to encourage the wicked in rebellion and alienation from God. "His sins [in such a theory,] WILL NOT FIND HIM OUT." The indifferent church members will fail to be in the bride class, to be divine; but that is all. They can have eternal life, will have a hundred years for trial, and, if they make progress, will get (1000) years. All this is strengthening the hands of sinners. Not a breath of it is in the Bible! The sinner, either in the church, or out of it, is not promised a moment of second chanceism. He must appear before the Judgment seat of Christ that *each* may *receive* the things done in his body, according to what he hath done, whether it be good or bad." (II Cor. 5:10). According to Dawnists the murderer, libertine, liar, adulterer, and darkest, foulest, characters on earth, die—or cease to be. There is no Hades, no Gehenna, no Paradise. Not a spirit that ever dwelt in human body now exists. Beyond death is, what? Nothing. All is blank. Emptiness is everywhere. They all ceased to be at death. This, of course, they say, was the condition from Adam till (1878). Since then, what? The saints arose. How? In spirit-bodies and are all here now though invisible. So there is no future punishment! The wicked shall soon rise, but how? Holy as Adam—perfect human beings, to be *on trial* for eternal life!

This is the religious counterfeit that is encouraging men to sin, for they CAN NOT SUFFER BETWEEN DEATH AND RESURRECTION; they are not raised to be JUDGED, but to have an Edenic home like Adam, only world-wide; to have all the holy dead of all past ages as their companions on such a sinless earth; and the "bride class" ruling invisibly for (1000) years. If they fail this time—there is no pain, no suffering, no shame and everlasting contempt; they simply die again—cease to exist the second time, and they have no resurrection. Great theory of restitution is it not? Sin is a light affair in such a theory, and wicked men grow worse and worse deceiving and being deceived. Such restitution is only in the dreams of visionaries. It has no truth of heaven to support it. The Bible doctrine is—"Be not deceived; God is not mocked; for whatsoever a man soweth, that shall he also reap." (Gal. 6).

DEATH CONSIDERED.

Vegetables live and vegetables die; animals live and animals die; but vegetables and animals live but one life and die but one death. They can not be said to be "dead" while they live, nor "alive" when they are dead.

Men live and die; and men die while they live, and are alive while they are dead. Man is a moral, sentient being, and lives one life and dies one death in this world not possible to vegetables or animals. In (Gen. 2:17 and 3:17) death of man is mentioned; but death is used in the moral or spiritual sense in the first, and the death of the body or "physical" death in the last. This distinction runs through the entire Bible, necessarily, for sin began in Eden. One may be dead in trespasses and in sins, (Eph. 2:1; Rom. 6; Col. 3:1-3) while dwelling on earth. Death does not have a uniform meaning, therefore, when applied to men; death has a uniform meaning when applied to vegetables and animals, because they have but one life, and can die but one death. Vegetables and animals do not go to hades, tartarus, paradise or gehenna. They may die their kind of death and be buried! but they do not experience comfort or sorrow thereafter.

Hades occurs eleven times in the New Testament (Matt. 11:25; 16:18; Luke 10:15; 16:23; Acts 2:27-31; I Cor. 15:55; Rev. 1:18; 6:8; 20:13, 14). This is the Greek name for the place of the dead, as *Sheol* is the word used by the Hebrews. *Tartarus* is used once in the New Testament (II Pet. 2:4) as the place where sinning angels were cast—it certainly was not the graveyard. The whole theory of soul-sleeping ignores the figurative meaning of death. Jesus represented the Rich man and Lazarus as alive while their bodies were dead. Moses and Elijah were both alive and in glory, (Matt. 17) while the first had been dead some fifteen centuries; the latter had been out of the world half that long. Moses was sixteen hundred and Elijah eight hundred years old, counted in an earthly Calendar. Jesus said, "For he is not a God of the dead, but of the living; *for all live* unto him." (Luke 20:38). There is a use for Hades, Tartarus and Gehenna, but not while we live in the flesh. Let us be sure we die *to* sin, and are not dead *in* sin. As the Bible throughout considers *men dead* in a different sense from that which vegetables and animals suffer, (dead while they live), we know that animal death is not contemplated. Every sinner is dead and alive; every Christian is dead and alive; but while their animal lives are the same their deaths are as different as being "dead in sin" and "dead to sin." Adam died the day, the very moment, in which he disobeyed God; and yet he lived for centuries. A Christian "was dead and is alive again; was lost but is found." The Savior's teaching in (John chs. 6; 8 and 11) showing that he that *liveth* and *be-lieveth* in him shall *never* die, is all illustrative of the fact that the life and death he had in mind were spiritual. All of his disciples die; but none of his disciples die, according to that promise. How can that be? Well, death of the body does not include the soul (Matt. 10: 28). Jesus pictured the rich man dead and buried and existing in Hades; Lazarus dead and yet alive in Abraham's bosom (Luke 16). He said unto the dying thief, "Verily I say unto thee, Today shalt thou be with me in Paradise," (Luke 23:43). Paul had a desire to depart and to be with Christ (Phil. 1:20-25). He professed, "But though our outward man perish, yet the inward man is renewed day by day (II Cor. 4:16). These moral and spiritual realities can not be truly spoken of vegetables or beasts; but they belong to man, redeemed by Christ. The Psalmist predicted the soul of Jesus should not be left in Hades nor his body see corruption (Ps. 16); and the apostles affirmed that his history fulfilled it.

A good reading (in the American Revised) of all the places where *Sheol* is given in the Old Testament Hebrew, and *Hades* its Greek equivalent is given in the New Testament, will show one that the grave receives the animal part of man only; and *Hades* is the place where the spirit goes, when it returns to God who gave it. Millennial Dawnism has but one meaning for death as applied to man, i. e., cease to be; become extinct. That is not true even of the body. Houses are made of dead trees; and Mummified bodies exist for ages. As the gospel is not for beasts, but is for men; as animals feel no compunctions of conscience, and could neither obey nor disobey; but the gospel is for man, he has compunction of conscience, and can obey or disobey the gospel, he is in a higher order of beings. Therefore, to speak of the death of the body as the extinction of the man is to treat him as wholly animal, which he is not. The whole Bible is written to warn man against diosobedience to the law of God.

The same observations, substantially, apply to the condition of man, as expressed by a group of words of frequent occurrence in the Bible. He is lost or found; sick or in health, saved or destroyed; alive or dead. Destroyed, perish, consumed, burned up, ruined and the like are certainly not stronger words than death; and they are often used concerning man. The earth being overflowed with water perished, yet exists today. Jesus died for men, (but did not cease to be), that they should not perish, but have eternal life. David said the wicked are like the chaff which the WIND driveth away (Ps. 1); John the Baptist compared them to the chaff which he will burn up with unquenchable FIRE (Matt. 3). Jesus compared our lives to houses built on rock or sand *tested* by WIND and RAIN. (Matt. 7:24-28); Paul compared us to a house made of wood, hay, stubble; gold, silver and precious stones, and this building *tested* by FIRE. Such illustrations are clear and plain, when considered as illustrations; but we should not press figurative language too far. Jesus is a door, a Shepherd, a vine, bread, water, captain, a lamb, a lion, a bride-groom and the like. Literally he is none of these. Literally we are not precious stones, wheat or a house; we are neither chaff, nor dead trees plucked up by the roots; raging waves of the sea; wandering stars, neither wood, hay nor stubble. Jesus is thus *pictured* to us in some phase of his relationship to men by these parables and metaphors. But one is really not a sheep, a soldier, and does not eat Christ; neither are we to consider him as either a Lion or a Lamb. As we learn that the sword will not slay, poison kill, water drown, or fire consume man's soul in *this* world; but that the body dies, and the soul lives, we are prepared to interpret death as predicated of man. The souls of the martyrs were pictured as crying to God, (Rev. 6:9). There is more of man to live, hence more of him to die, than there is of a plant or animal. He dies while he lives; they do not. After death we live, "for all live unto God." At the resurrection the body, made deathless, by divine wisdom, power and love, we shall be like our Savior, "for we shall see him as he is." (Phil. 3:21).

CHAPTER XXXIX.

SECOND CHANCEISM.

Because there is a resurrection "both of the just and of the unjust" Millennialists try to separate them by a thousand years. No one can deny that both may occur at the same moment and yet be distinct in their nature. They make the hour in (Jno. 5:28-29) one thousand years long. You will recall that the resurrection of the Just, took place in the spring of (1878) by Mr. Russell's Calendar.

"But the rest of the dead lived not again until the thousand years were finished." (Rev. 20:5). Millennial Dawnism drops dead here! Mr. Russell's theory demands a thousand years in which the one hundred and forty-two billions of dead shall have a chance for eternal life. He has the wicked all raised during the Millennium to have a chance for one hundred years, and if they improve it, they will advance unto absolute holiness during the (1000) years. Mr. Russell would get rid of the force of this statement by telling his followers it is spurious. Every translation and all the editors of the Greek retain it. It is not safe to build your hope of a second chance on any theory. You will never see a version with that statement left out by any scholar on earth. But I will couple with it the companion verse so that it will not help Mr. Russell to deny one and retain the other. "And when the thousand years are expired, Satan shall be loosed out of his prison, and shall go out to deceive the nations which are in the four quarters of the earth, Gog and Magog, to gath r them together to battle; THE NUMBER OF WHOM IS AS THE SAND OF THE SEA."

THREE POINTS DESTROYED.

These verses destroy three pillars under the Dawnist temple.

1. The wicked dead do not resurrect the first,

second, third, fourth, fifth, sixth, seventh, eighth, ninth,
or tenth hundred years; BUT WHEN THEY ARE EX-
PIRED. So all his laborious efforts to get these people
back to earth for a second chance, under his much vaunted better conditions, fail. Not a man is raised till after
the thousand years end; AFTER THE MILLENNIUM IS
OVER.

2. Then that the Old Testament saints shall be
here as servants, carrying on the temporal affairs of
earth, yet in immortal bodies, supported by earthly food;
and the New Testament saints, or the bride-class, exalted
to the divine nature and reigning invisibly on earth with
Christ in spirit bodies, is not worth the paper he wrote it
on. The whole gross theory dwarfs into the latitude and
longitude of the point of a cambric needle, in the presence of the true Word of God. For the wicked do not
live till the thousand years, (not till 999), but the thousand years, have expired.

3. The third point I make is that at the EXPIRA-
TION OF THE THOUSAND YEARS THE WICKED ARE
AS NUMBERLESS AS THE SAND OF THE SEA.

Now, manifestly, on any theory of the Millennium,
the wicked that can not be numbered, are still UNCON-
VERTED AT THE END OF THE MILLENNIUM.

I am simply emphasizing the *revealed facts* in this
celebrated text. I dare say there never was palmed off
on the world a more clumsy and untenable theory than
Millennial Dawnism. These three points rob it of all
hope for the sinner during the (1000) years, IN THE
VERY PASSAGE THAT SHOULD BE PLAIN IN PRO-
MISE OF CONVERSION. IT FLATLY CONTRADICTS
IT.

Now, what shall we say concerning chapter after
chapter of his theorizing concerning Restitution back to
Edenic conditions? That is:

The bride class made up of all the saintly dead in
Christ coming to earth in invisible spirit bodies in (A.
D. 1878); Jesus having preceded them (3½ years);
about the resurrection of Abraham, Moses, Noah, David,
Daniel and all the holy dead of preceding dispensations,
at the same date (1878); of the immediate prospect of
the resurrection of one hundred and forty-two billions or

more to be on trial during the thousand years, or at least, for one hundred years, for eternal life? What shall we say as to the Judgment being (1000) years long, a day of *trial under more favorable conditions* for all the wicked dead, when practically all shall be saved? What about all that universalism woven around the texts "In thee and thy seed shall all the families of the earth be blessed;" and "For there is one God and one Mediator between God and men, the man Christ Jesus; who gave himself a ransom for all to be testified in due time"?

I would write at the close of every chapter that Mr. Russell ever wrote on any of these or kindred subjects: "BUT THE REST OF THE DEAD LIVED NOT AGAIN UNTIL THE THOUSAND YEARS WERE FINISHED."

If they do not live there are no conversions, no trial, no restitution to Edenic conditions; no saints reigning visibly as servants; others invisibly as sons, or as *divine beings*; the Lord is not here; the imaginary harvest is not closing, and the whole theory is wrong in premise, argument and conclusion.

The fact that nations are here, are in the four quarters of the earth, at the close of the Millennium, denies his theory. The nations are to be destroyed in (1914) on his theory. The fact that sinners are as numerous as the sand of the sea at the close of the (1000) years explodes his universalism. The Bible refutes the theory forever. John dismembers it and spreads the skeleton out in the valley of humiliation to be picked to atoms by all the birds of heaven.

Dawnism says the wicked will have the second chance during the Millennium; John replies they do not live.

Dawnism says the wicked must all be resurrected to be blessed during the thousand years; John says, "but the rest of the dead lived not again until the thousand years were finished." Which is true?

THREE CLASSES OF MEN.

The various theories of Millennialism mix three classes of men on earth during the thousand years by imagining that the First resurrection is literal.

1. All the holy dead are raised at the opening of the Millennium,, not as Lazurus or Tabitha were raised,

but in immortal bodies, suited to all the undying glories of heaven.

2.   The living saints are all changed and in celestial bodies and can not die any more.

3.   The unconverted billion and a half of sinners are here in diseased, dying bodies.

I do not detain you long to show the folly of this mixture of heavenly and divine beings, in association on earth. I might show that it is a carnal view throughout. But why uncover the absurdity of having every soul leave paradise, and all the holy angels leave heaven to come to this sinful world in glory, to conduct civil government?   Every *one* of them a king; every one a priest, in the most literal sense.

Now that class who have neither been resurrected nor changed, but are sinners when the saints are all re-surrected or changed, but multitudes of whom are to be converted, are left without a single promise of either resurrection or change, because the whole list of these texts is fulfilled *when the Lord comes*, which, on this theory, will be a *past event in every generation of the thousand years*; and ,at its close, the *unjust only, are raised.*   Surely it will not be contended that conversion of hardnered sinners will give them deathless bodies at once!   Into such crud-ities and false teaching does this theory of a literal resur-rection at the opening of the (1000) years lead.   No wonder Job tells us man shall not arise nor awake out of sleep until the heavens be no more.   It would mix things unsuited to each other and introduce confusion on earth, empty paradise of every departed saint, heaven of all the holy angels and the Lord Jesus Christ, while sinners are still on earth in vast numbers, and living as they do now.

MR. RUSSELL'S GUESS.

"Pastor Russell" varies the theory as follows:

1.   Jesus has been here in an invisible spirit-body since (Oct. 1874).

2.   The saints have been here in invisible spirit-bodies since (1878).

Then he divides the righteous dead into two classes, the sons and the servants.

The sons are the New Testament saints; the servants

are the Old Testament saints. The sons partake of the divine nature, become divine like Jesus; the servants are perfect human beings immortal, but human. All these are rulers. The servants look after the temporal kingdoms of earth; live with mankind, eat, drink, are men, indeed, but deathless; the sons are all here but invisible, during the (1000) years as they are now.

3. The one hundred and forty-two billions who constitute the dead sinners (according to his figures) are to be raised during the Millennium for their second chance. He thinks that alone can vindicate the mercy and love of God, and claims all but universal blessedness for these, thinking, possibly, a few incorrigible sinners may have to die the "second death."

Now, plainly, the whole theory is as false as falsity itself. Why so? "BUT THE REST OF THE DEAD LIVED NOT AGAIN UNTIL THE THOUSAND YEARS WERE FINISHED; AND AT THE CLOSE OF THE MILLENNIUM THE SINNERS ARE AS NUMBERLESS AS THE SAND OF THE SEA. I purposely bring this theory to the guillotine of truth and behead it with the Word of God, the Sword of the Spirit. Mr. Russell's whole theory is as helpless as Dagon before the ark of God. The student of prophecy will see here that he has to get his one hundred and forty-two billions of dead sinners back to earth and convert these masses, these inconceivably great numbers of the now extinct, non-existent dead, or his theory is gone. I say these two texts of Scripture behead his unscriptural theory. One says the wicked dead are not raised till the Millennium ends; the other says the wicked can no more be numbered at the close of time, beyond even the "little season" of Satan's release, than one can number the sand of the sea. Here I stand. I believe the inspired apostles and reject the Millennial Dawn theory as the vain assumptions of a false prophet.

These speculators teach that Jesus is not trying to convert the world, but is only making up the bride class, and the true work of conversion of the world begins when the resurrected dead reign. They even insult high heaven by telling us what a miserable failure God's arrangement is if he sent it to convert the world!

If it would be a reproach to the angencies of heaven,

(the gospel and the church) not to convert them all *now*, by what multiple shall we intensify that reproach when God, Christ, the resurrected saints of all ages, and the restitution period in all its pictured glories are brought to bear on the sinners, resurrected to a second chance, under more favorable conditions; the devil serving his sentence in the Pit; all misrule in government and state ended; the knowledge of the Lord universal; the ransom testified *to every man in due time* by the Lord himself and his holy associates numberless, and as illustrious as the stars of heaven; and all this fails on a multitude as numerous as the sand of the sea, and they in the four quarters of the earth. The simple fact is that The International Bible Students Association, and all other theorists who set the time for Christ and his saints to reign *personally on this earth* are mistaken visionaries. Their whole theory demands not only the improbable, but the impossible, (which I think is being made manifest in this book). For the preesnt let me impress it upon you that the more they *magnify* the agencies to be employed in the Millennium for the conversion of the world, and *minify* those ordained of heaven and now in use, the more hopelessly do they defeat their own purpose, for in this *one* and *only* passage in the Bible that gives the length of their traditional Millennium, a thousand years, instead of ending with universal, or all but universal conversion quarters of the earth? The simple fact is that The Inand world-wide peace, holiness and happiness, it ends with rebellion against God by a host of sinners.

ANGELS MARRIED.

Mr. Russell tells us that when "the sons of God saw the daughters of men that they were fair; and they took them wives of all whom they chose." (Gen. 6:3).— *"Thus the angels* became the FATHERS of a NEW RACE DISTINCT FROM ADAM'S." Mr. Russell can conjure up a new race, or nature, whenever he needs one in his mistakenly called "Divine Plan of the Ages."

"The disloyal course of the angels apparently continued for centuries without any outward manifestation of God's ability to check them. Thus all the holy angels were tested, and all who chose "were disobedient in the days of Noah" (I Pet. 3:20). "Noah's family was singled out as exceptional, in the statement, Now Noah was *per-*

fect in his generation—of pure Adamic stock. (Gen. 6:9).
Noah's family, therefore, included all the uncontaminated
—only eight persons."

"The account of the fall of the angels from being
sons of God to be demons, helps us to understand why
God decreed the Deluge to wipe out all of the human race
except Noah and his family. We perceive that God from
the first intended to deal only with Adam and his family.
The giant sons of the fallen angels (Nephilim) came into
being contrary to the Divine Will; hence, properly, no
provision was to be made for them. *They* never had a
right to life, nor will *they* have a resurrection. On the
other hand, all of *Adam's posterity*, redeemed by Jesus'
death, must be recovered *from death*, with *full opportunity*
to secure everlasting life."

PHOTO DRAMA OF CREATION.

I could quote more, but sicken of the whole salacious
mess. Only four women of this world that did not co-
habit with angels—"Sons of God"! Were not men
called sons of God then as well as now? Seth's family
and Cain's family intermarried. Much like Christians
marry infidels and are led into skepticism and infidelity
now, they did then. As Israel intermarried with idolaters and were led into idolatry. No, Mr. Russell must
contradict the Bible, and get a new race. as Jesus said,

"The children of this world marry, and are given in
marriage; but they which shall be accounted worthy to
obtain that world, and the resurrection from the dead,
neither marry nor are given in marriage; neither can
they die any more; for they are equal unto the angels;
and are the children of God, being the children of the
resurrection." (Luke 20:34-36).

"Pastor Russell," in imagination, creates a race of
demigods before the Flood; and, in the great Deluge,
they all became extinct. But, on his theory, all humanity, good and bad, before the Deluge and since, are extinct. They are as though they never had been, and you
and I are about to that place—death.

He exhibited the Pictures of the Demigods in his
Photo-Drama; also the picture of *Hades*, a grave-yard
with tombstones! So he creates and annihilates a race,
and gravely informs us *they* are never to be reusrrected.

No wonder a man who is competent to father such
a licentious doctrine concerning angels from heaven co-
habiting with women; can imagine that all the New Tes-

tament saints are exalted to become *divine* beings up to
(A. D. 1881); and that Old Testament saints are resurrected to immortality, but forever to remain human beings and conduct earthly affairs living here again as
literally, and sitting upon thrones as literally, as before
David passed away. All the wicked dead are to come
back for the second chance, (that is they wake up right
where they left off when they died, for they do not now
exist).

"BUT THE REST OF THE DEAD LIVED NOT
AGAIN UNTIL THE THOUSAND YEARS WERE FIN-
ISHED." If they do NOT LIVE, then Moses, David,
Daniel and all the Old Testament saints are *not to rule
over them as servants*; and Jesus and the New Testament
saints, the bride class, are not here now, and will not be
during the (1000) years in invisible spirit bodies, reigning as divine beings. This would elevate the bride class,
the little flock, above David and Isaiah, Moses and Daniel.
Such fantastic and unreal existences and conditions are
imagined to get rid of Hades, and Gehenna. Mr. Russell
makes all beyond death a blank, until resurrection. But
resurrection with him is a farce, for the spirits do not
exist after death, and the bodies are not raised, or any
part of them. The Lord himself ceased to be at death!
He has to utter such blasphemy to get rid of Hades.
For if even Jesus' spirit had any existence between death
and the resurrection, then there is a Hades besides the
graveyard, where the spirits of the departed go till their
resurrection, (which is the plain teaching of the Bible).
But Mr. Russell imagines a race of Hybreds, (half angels
and half men), who *never existed*, and annihilates them at
the Flood. He annihilates Hades where all departed
spirits *do exist*; destroys, (in imagination), Jesus Christ
during his absence from the body; he *creates* a new,
divine race out of the bride class in (1878); *resurrects* one
hundred and forty-two billions of *now extinct, non-existent*
sinners to have the (1000) year trial for eternal life
during the Millennium, and if they do not live perfectly
sanctified, sinless lives they are to die, become extinct
again, this time forever, or the second death); and he
grows half-way eloquent on the Restitution of earth back
to Edenic conditions, and all mankind to original purit~

except here and there a specimen who remains incorrigible, (and he blots out these when they are 100 years old). He even exhibits a *picture* of a flower garden, representative of Paradise restored, to make it realistic, all to have his dream dissipated at the end by two statements of the inspired apostle. If John wrote of this Millennium, he knew what would be and he says: "BUT THE REST OF THE DEAD LIVED NOT AGAIN UNTIL THE THOUSAND YEARS WERE FINISHED."

And after the whole period is finished, the Millennium *ended*, all probation *closed*, the *nations* still exist in the *four quarters* of the earth, they are very wicked, and "THE NUMBER OF WHOM IS AS THE SAND OF THE SEA."

Thus his whole theory of second chanceism is absurdly false. And if it were not for this feature of his Human Plan of the Ages, presumptuously called "The Divine Plan of the Ages," it would not be considered for a moment. It is what he unblushingly teaches as the truth of heaven, (that the wicked shall have the second chance, that probation does not end at death), that makes his infamous theory palatable to sinners. It all leads up to the First Resurrection (1878); when restitution back to Edenic conditions was scheduled to begin; all the churches were rejected in (1881); all the governments of earth are to be destroyed in (1914); the kingdom of God, (Millennial kingdom), is the only kingdom left; Old Testament saints reigning visibly on earth; New Testament saints, Christ at their head, reigning invisibly, but present in spirit bodies; and the one hundred and forty-two billions of resurrected sinners have their chance for eternal life for (1000) years under these more favorable conditions. John's testimony, as to who will not live till the close of the Millennium ends, stamps ICHABOD on every feature of this wild, weird, grotesque assortment of impossible, unscriptural notions. "BUT THE REST OF THE DEAD LIVED NOT AGAIN UNTIL THE THOUSAND YEARS WERE FINISHED." There it is, as imperishable as the truth of God, and as plain as simplicity itself, so that a little child may see that Mr. Russell's one hundred and forty-two billions of extinct sinners will not be here for his imaginary Restitution, nor for a "second chance," under more favorable conditions.

So where is all this second chanceism—everybody blessed—every man to have the ransom testified to him in due time? If the Millennium is the *due time*, and the gospel age is not, then, why the failure? The reason is, the theory is not in the Bible. The Bible says: "Today is the day of salvation; today if ye will hear his voice harden not your hearts." All such groundless theories harden men's hearts in sin, by promising them what the Bible does not promise, so that they put far away from them the evil day.

But reflect soberly that, Russell's chief reliance is upon this second-chanceism for the salvation of practically all men. You see the Bible has no respect for his theory; but the inspired man who wrote the vision of what Mr. R., and others have wrested and twisted into a prophecy of a thousand years of all but sinless perfection; Eden restored to the whole earth, Jesus and all the saints living here in glorious spirit bodies; devil chained; and heaven on earth, CLOSES THE PERIOD with a population on earth of sinners as numberless as the sand of the sea!!

CHAPTER XL.

RESPONSIBILITY.

"Repent ye therefore and turn again, that your sins may be blotted out, that so there may come seasons of refreshing from the presence of the Lord; and that he may send the Christ who hath been appointed for you, even Jesus; whom the heaven must receive until the times of the restoration of all things whereof God spake by the mouth of his holy prophets that have been from of old." (Acts 3:19-21).

Jesus came that we might have life and have it more abundantly. Eternal life is eternal well-being not simply eternal existence. Jesus said: "Verily, verily, I say unto you, except ye eat the flesh of the Son of man and drink his blood, you have no life in you." (Jno. 6:53).

He was not teaching Cannibalism either. The very acts of eating and drinking are evidences or life. A corpse can do neither, surely, and yet one may be alive and do neither, and thus in the sense Jesus meant, *be dead.* A cow or sheep could neither eat the flesh nor drink the blood of the Son of Man. It is spiritual eating and drinking that supports spiritual life, as physical eating and drinking nourish physical life. The theory ignores entirely this divine reality, which runs through the entire Bible, and so it misleads the people by giving a uniform meaning to death. But if one can *live* his three-score years and ten, and all that time BE DEAD IN TRESPASSES AND IN SINS, HAVE NO LIFE IN HIM; he may live, exist, indefinitely, in the same condemned state of sin. The body is mortal, but even it is to become immortal or deathless. (I Cor. 15).

We seek for glory, honor, immortality, and eternal life. The immortality accrues to our mortal part; and the expression "eternal life" is not a repetition, a redundancy, but sets before us the eternal well-being awaiting the sons of God. Now the Dawnist's theory demands, that all men who have died be recreated. Russell's theory is they are *extinct.* There is no Hades for departed spirits good or bad in his theory. The dead *bodies* do not rise at all. To hold to the *resurrection* of *extinct* spirits is to nullify every element of resurrection. Ezekiel, even figuratively, resurrected only a nation that *existed.* To raise *the dead,* is not to create a man that has no existence as God created Adam. But the theory demands even more. Even Jesus was not resurrected on this theory. He was, say they, only a perfect man, when he died; and he became *extinct* as every other man does at death. All this, to uphold soul-sleeping! The theory demands the very extinction of the being Jesus Christ, for how long? *Forever.*

This is evident from their denial.

1. That *Hades* exists as the place of departed spirits.

2. That one exists from death to resurrection;

3. That the body of Jesus ever arose from the grave any more than the body of a dead beast. That he created bodies every time he appeared to the disciples, and clothing also, and dissolved them both when he disappeared.

"That which is born of the Spirit is spirit; Jesus, therefore, at and after his resurrection, was a spirit—a spirit being, and no longer a human being in any sense." Dawnism.

"This change of nature from *human to divine* is given as a *reward* to those who within the Gospel Age, like Jesus did, sacrifice the *human nature*, with all *its* interests, hopes and aims, present and future—even unto death. In the resurrection such will awake, not to share with the rest of mankind in the *blessed restitution to human* perfection and all its accompanying blessings, but to share the likeness, and glory, and joy of the Lord, as partakers with him of the *divine* nature." (Rom. 8:17; II Tim. 2:12). "The birth of the new creature is in the resurrection; and the resurrection of *this class* is termed the *first* resurrection. (Rev. 20:5). This will be the first resurrection in the sense of being first or chief in importance, though it will also be first in point of time. It should be remembered that we are not actually spirit beings until the resurrection, though from the time we receive the spirit of adoption, we are reckoned *as* such. (Rom. 8:23-25; Eph. 1:13-14; Rom. 6:10-11). When we become spirit beings actually, when we are born of the Spirit, we will no longer be fleshly beings in any sense; for that which is born of the Spirit is Spirit." Millennial Dawn.   Vol. I, pp. 192-193).

There you have it. The new birth did not take place in apostolic days—no one had the new birth but Christ. It will be for the "Bride Class' only, the "Little Flock," to change their human spirits to divine Spirits, you notice he spells, human spirit with a capital, as it will then be divine. They have been extinct, non-existent for hundreds of years, but at the first resurrection they are born again. This is false in every item. The new birth will be at the second coming of Christ. It will be for the "Bride Class' only, the "Little

1. He *limits* the divine nature to the class raised in the first resurrection, which took place in (A. D. 1878). Hence all that will ever partake of the divine nature have already done so. The forty years harvest ending this year is imaginary, just as is his coming of Christ in a Spirit body in (1874) is, unless he could *demonstrate* that Jesus came on that date his Harvest has no foundation, and it is ideal anyway for no sacred writer ever gave a type of it, or prophecy concerning it. He makes the new birth which Jesus announced to Nicodemus, (Jno. 3) to *apply to but one portion of the church*,

and while he *includes* all that have part in the first resurrection, and the changed living saints, he *excludes* all
the saints of former dispensations.

His theory demands that the Ransom applies to all
and must be testified *to all in due time*; and that due time
is during the one thousand years. The apostle instead
of saying this, said *nothing* about it ever being testified
to all, in the thousand years or at any other time. The
thing Russell most needs, PAUL OMITTED ENTIRELY,
the "TO ALL' part of his theory. Sodom and her sisters
in sin are to be raised from the dead to hear the gospel
and have a chance for eternal life, according to this
theory. Dawnists conjure up great and dire results for
Sodom, Capernaum, Israel, and all the countless hosts
of sin, unless they are resurrected to have a chance for
eternal life under Christ and the saints ruling for a
thousand years in Spirit bodies. The very heart and
core of the theory is found here. Countless millions have
died without ever having heard of Christ and the gospel.
According to Dawnists they are now extinct; but have to be
raised from the dead, (not their bodies, of course, but a
new spirit created), to have the Ransom testified to
them in due season. We see thus how foolish and empty
of Scripture warrant the theory is.

"Then began he to upbraid the cities wherein most
of his mighty works were done, because they repented
not. Woe unto thee Chorazin! Woe unto thee, Bethsaida! for if the mighty works had been done in Tyre and
Sidon, which were done in you, they would have repented long ago in sackcloth and ashes. But I say unto
you, it shall be more tolerable for Tyre and Sidon in the
day of Judgment than for you. And thou Capernaum,
shalt thou be exalted unto heaven? Thou shalt go down
unto Hades; for if the mighty works had been done in
Sodom which were done in thee, it would have remained
until this day. But I say unto you that it shall be more
tolerable for the land of Sodom in the day of Judgment,
than for thee." (Matt. 11:29-24).

"The men of Nineveh shall stand up in the Judgment
with this generation, and shall condemn it; for they repented at the preaching of Jonah; and behold a greater
than Jonah is here. The queen of the south shall rise
up in the judgment with this generation, and shall condemn it; for she came from the ends of the earth to hear
the wisdom of Solomon; and behold, a greater than
Solomon is here." (Matt. 12:41-42).

1. They show that Sodom, Nineveh, Tyre, Sidon, Capernaum, Bethsaida, and that generation, would stand up in the day of Judgment, and also the unrepentant Jews to whom Jesus preached.

2. It is likewise plain that they will not condemn them to a second chance. For if all were resurrected back to the sinless perfection of Adam, how could it be more tolerable for one than another? Dawnists have them all sleep till the resurrection; then all resurrected, (not their bodies) but sinless beings to be on trial for eternal life.

The whole mischievous theory is based on colossal assumptions. It is assumed that:

1. Jesus as a spirit being, invisible but present has been here since A. D. 1874).

"OUR BELIEF that the Kingdom began to be *set up*, or brought into power, in April, 1878, BE IT OBSERVED, RESTS ON EXACTLY THE SAME FOUNDATION AS OUR BELIEF THAT THE LORD BECAME PRESENT IN OCTOBER 1874, AND THAT THE HARVEST BEGAN AT THAT TIME."
Thy Kingdom Come, p. 235.

"And since the resurrection of the Church must occur sometime during this "end" or "harvest" period. (Rev. 11:18) we hold that it is a *most Reasonable Inference*, and one in perfect harmony with all the Lord's plan, that in the spring of 1878 all the holy apostles, and other "overcomers" of the Gospel age, who slept in Jesus, were raised spirit beings like unto their Lord and Master. And while we, therefore, conclude that the resurrection is now an accomplished fact, and hence that they as well as the Lord are present in the earth, the fact that we do not see them is no obstacle to faith when we remember that, like their Lord, they are now spirit beings, and, like him, invisible. The facts that they are invisible, that tombs were not found opened and empty, and that none were seen going from cemeteries, are not objections to such as have learned what to expect—to such as realize that our risen Lord left no hole in the walls of the room which he entered and left while the doors were shut; who remember that none saw the risen Redeemer except the few, to whom he specially and miraculously *showed* himself, that they might be witnesses of his resurrection; who remember that he appeared in various forms of flesh or that any of the forms they saw was his glorious, "spirit body." Same connection.

If you can adopt the inferences, and opinions of a man as full of vagaries and spiritualism as these lines show this man to be, then no further reasoning is necessary. Swendenborgians, and Shakers maintain the resurrection and judgment take place at death; Dawnists that it takes place at the *first* resurrection. Into such uncertainty does a false theory degrade the subject. With both it is a soul resurrection. With Dawnists the soul is extinct from death till,—what? I was about to say the resurrection, but there is no resurrection, as you see what he says above about open tombs, and the like, and the invisible nature of Jesus and the saints.

1. Jesus knew what was in man, not only those present before him, but in the Sodomites, Ninevites and all the dead. They do not have to be raised up to testify to what they would have done if they could have had opportunity; neither Tyre nor Sidon will be raised up to be given a chance, for Jesus says they would have repented in sackcloth and ashes. He knew them, then, perfectly.

2. Every man will be judged, with righteous judgment. The Judge of all the earth will do right. That does not mean all will be saved.

Dawnists make light of the fact that "ignorance" is a weakness often rather than a crime, or sin; and think it could not be a factor in the judgment. Why did Saul obtain mercy? Because what he did he did ignorantly. (I Tim. 1:13). Why did the merciful Lord pray, "Father forgive them; for they know not what they do?" (Luke 23:24). Ignorance helped out in these cases. See also (Acts 3:17). "Jesus said unto them, if ye were blind, ye should have no sin; but now ye say, we see; therefore your sin remaineth." (Jno. 9:41). Blindness, (not willful), seemed to be in the favor of men, when a just God dealt with them.

"But all these things will they do unto you for my name's sake, because they know not him that sent me. If I had not come and spoken unto them, they had not had sin; but now they have no cloak for their sin." (Jno. 15:22-23). "Therefore to him that knoweth to do good and doeth it not, to him it is sin. (Jas. 4:17). "And that servant that knew his lord's will, and prepared not himself, neither did according to his will, shall be beaten with many stripes. But he that knew not, and did commit things worthy of stripes, shall be beaten with few stripes. For unto whomsoever much is given of him much shall be required; and to whom men have committed much, of him they will ask the more." (Luke 12:47-48). Here is a distinction between ignorance of, and contempt for, law, and is an element in all righteous judgments. It runs throughout the Mosaic law, as well as the gospel. Under the law they were called sins of ignorance and of presumption, respectively; a sacrifice was appointed for one but not always for the other. The Philistines could with safety build a cart and haul the sacred Ark upon it, but David and thirty thousand men of Judah could not— one had no law on the subject; the other had. (II Sam'l 6).

Peter used this language, to teach just the opposite of their theory. If the Millennium is a part of the restoration or restitution, then, says Peter, it is to come and go before Jesus leaves heaven. The heavens must retain Jesus. It was expedient that he go away, or the Comforter would not come.

He ascended to the right hand of power. He sent his truth forth on its mission of mercy. And the heaven must retain him till all things spoken by the prophets are restored. This cannot mean that all men are restored to sinless perfection; that Edenic conditions are restored to the whole human family living and dead; that the earth shall be restored to the fertility of its primitive state. It is a moral and spiritual restoration unto God. Jesus will not come to change the message or supplant it. When men repent and turn to God their sins are blotted out, the refreshing from the presence of the Lord comes to them, and, ultimately, when the whole work predicted shall close; (all that the *prophets have spoken*, not all that Millennialists have speculated), then Jesus comes the *second* time without sin (offering) unto salvation. So, to the Jew, (who thought Messiah would abide on earth forever (Jno. 12:34). Peter made it plain that he would RULE FROM HEAVEN, and to reject him was to be destroyed as Moses predicted. This over-worked text is wrested as all others, of necessity, to make it mean that all things will be restored to their former state. I say wrested because:

1. "While the earth remains seed time and harvest,

and summer and winter and cold and heat and day and night shall not cease." (Gen. 8:22).

2.   To restore all things as they were would be to blot out the human race, all but Adam and Eve. If we should allow Millennialists to include the resurrection of the righteous and change of the living, they would be in immortal bodies, not subject to death, which Adam was not.

3.   If we should say it is the earth restored to Edenic conditions, that is different from what it was when man was created, and that requires the fire of (II Pet. 3) BEFORE THE MILLENNIUM, and I prove that is literal five as the water of the Flood was literal.

4.   All theories of the Millennium have some wicked men living on earth, and this is not the condition of primitive man.

5.   But, granting that the prophets foretold the coming of Christ, how he must suffer and enter into his glory; and that he now has the glory which he had with his Father before the world was, we may then consider that the heavens must retain him, and he must rule till he has put all enemies under his feet. The last enemy that shall be destroyed is death. For he hath put all things under his feet. But when he saith all things are put under him [Christ] it is manifest that he [God] is excepted, who did put all things under him. And when all things shall be subdued unto him, then shall the Son also himself be subject unto him that put all things under him, that God may be all in all." (I Cor. 15:24-28).

CHAPTER XLI.

LITTLE FLOCK.

"Fear not little flock, for it is your Father's good pleasure to give you the Kingdom." (Luke 12:32).

One should always observe the speaker, person spoken to and the time or dispensation when spoken, in reading the Bible. One can "prove" almost anything by neglecting this rule. Let us try it. "Thou must not muzzle the ox that treadeth out the corn; for of such is the kingdom of God." This is all scripture, but in detached fragments. "Judas went and hanged himself, go thou and do likewise; what thou doest do quickly." In the first instance we "prove" there are oxen in the kingdom of God. In the second that suicide by hanging is commanded, both of which are absurd. Before the kingdom of heaven was set up Jesus taught his disciples to pray, "Thy Kingdom come." That prayer, after the kingdom came, was like hoping for something one already has. "Hope that is seen is not hope; what a man seeth, why doth he yet hope for?" Now to the Colossians Paul wrote: "Who hath delivered us from the power of darkness, and hath translated us into the kingdom of his dear Son." (Col. 1:13). So, manifestly, Paul could not pray and hope for the kingdom to come when he was in the kingdom. I have shown that we enter the kingdom of Christ on earth and if faithful to him we pass at death into paradise, and that Jesus rules there; (Rev. 1:18), and at the resurrection and judgment we enter into the everlasting kingdom of our Lord and Savior, Jesus Christ. (Matt. 25:34; II Pet. 1:10-11). This completes the subject as outlined by our Savior. We pass at death to be with the Lord, (Phil 1:23-26); (Luke 23:43). But when one gets it into his mind that Jesus meant for the disciples to pray for a reign with Christ on earth personally for (1000) years over the wicked, he readily wrests the whole body of Scripture relative to the kingdom. For instance, in "The Time Is At Hand", "Elijah must first come" p. 249. We are gravely informed:

1. John the Baptist and Christ *did not* fulfill (Mal. 4:5-6); "The reference of the prophecy is evidently to the second advent; to the Messenger of the Covenant in glory and power; and to the testing and great trouble of the Day of the Lord at that time."

Who then is Elijah? Mr. Russell says:

2. "It is thus seen that the *Church in the flesh* (the Christ in the flesh, head and body) is the Elijah or forerunner of the *church in glory*, Jehovah's anointed. Not the nominal church, but the really consecrated Church, which on the other side of the tomb will be the great Anointed Deliverer,—these constitute the Elijah. Their mission is to reprove error and sin, and to *point to the coming kingdom of glory.* Our Lord Jesus and the Apostles, and all the faithful in Christ Jesus since *are* of the antitypical Elijah, prophet or teacher—the same class (head and body) which shall shortly compose the King in Glory. The work in which the church is now engaged is merely preliminary to its future work, so far as the reforming of the world is concerned. In its kingly office the church shall accomplish for the world what it fails to do as the Elijah, teacher."

This Elijah *teacher*, for eighteen centuries has been *attempting* the conversion of the world to Christ, doomed to failure from the start, and soon, what?

1. Well, you see, Elijah is a collective, not an individual, Elijah, and is made up of all the true saints from the days of Christ till his second coming, (in the above teaching).

2. Then the Christ instead of being an individual, will be a collective Christ, or cease to be collective Elijah and become the collective Christ. What becomes of *Elijah*, then? As Elijah is not one but many, the class, or Little Flock, (Head, Christ: Body, his people); when by the so-called birth of the spirit at the so-called resurrection (1878); when the bodies were not raised from the dead; when the spirits began to be again which had been extinct (some of them for ages) but not now as perfect *human* beings but as *divine* beings, the Christ (Head and Body) WAS NO LONGER ELIJAH—I wish to know what became of Elijah?

3. Furthermore, the same class, the bride class, (Head and Body) shall shortly compose the King of Glory.

This little flock is a strange assortment of human beings. First, till Christ comes (1874), they are Elijah; when resurrected (1878) they are Christ; and when the kingdom begins, they are the King of Glory. They become *divine* because they lived before the second advent, helped to visit the Gentiles, and tried to do what the Lord knew they could not do, convert the world; but succeed only in forming the "little flock."

The apostles of Christ were full of notions of a temporal kingdom such as the Jews then held and the Millennialists now seek. Jesus sought by degrees to undeceive them, and explain the spiritual nature of his kingdom, up till his crucifixion. The apostles, being selected from the other disciples, naturally cherished hopes of superiority over others. They wished to sit on the right and left hand of Christ, who to them at that time, was a prospective temporal King. Jesus rebuked these rising ambitions, from time to time, but sought to replace them with true conceptions of himself and of his kingdom. The companion to this text is found in (Matt. 19:16-30; 20:1-16). There the whole subject is plainly unfolded in the closing days of our Savior's earthly ministry.

No doubt that fixed the matter satisfactorily, for the then present, with the apostles. The vision of *twelve thrones* was agreeable. I do not say that they knew the meaning of the regeneration, or the nature of the dominion, or the spiritual as contrasted with the nature of the King, they expected. But to mention thrones, twelve only, assured them of their pre-eminence, and that was enough. Later they lost this hope, buried it in the tomb of Christ, and were "begotten again to a living hope by his resurrection from the dead, to an inheritance incorruptible, and undefiled and that fadeth not away, reserved in heaven for you who are kept by the power of God through faith unto salvation ready to be reaveled in the last time." (I Pet. 1:3-5).

There is no hope here not common to all faithful disciples. There is not a line that ever fell from the pens of the apostles that betrays that old carnal, Jewish hope of pre-eminence after Jsus inspired them with the Holy Spirit on Pentecost. They are the heaven-ordained rulers in the kingdom of God, the ambassadors for Christ in this regenerative period. Paul confidently expected a crown—but it was of righteousness and belongs to all that love his appearing. The apostles entertained no hope of constituting a bride class in a Millennial age, with thrones on earth. Hope of heaven was their all-sufficient motive to make them the most tireless and efficient servants of Christ. If any were the original bride class and little flock, these were. The hope they had we should have, and should not go back of the *new* hope for which they exchanged the *dead* hope which they had held of the traditionary, temporal reign of the Messiah, and of their pre-eminence in office and earthly riches. There were but *twelve thrones*, yet this numeral has no forbidding aspect to Millennialists; but they appropriate the thrones to themselves, for the use of the little flock, the bride class, to be used, when? In the Millennium. We *are* the collective Elijah; *shall* be the collective Christ; and the collective King of Glory and need the thrones, not now, but in the regeneration, is the theory. They ignore the regeneration now in progress and thus misapply the Scripture to a kingdom which they think Christ will set up when he comes; and multiply the twelve thrones, that they may have "one apiece."

The "little flock" was the apostles. Everything at Christ's death, viewed from the human standpoint, was hopeless. The Kings of the earth and the rulers set themselves against the Lord and his Christ. Terrible indeed it must have been to have one's prospective king humilated to the death on a Roman cross. Black as the midnight darkness hovering over the scene, were the propspects of the apostles to realize their cherished hope to be men of eminence in their contemplated kingdom. Little, indeed, was there to relieve the despondency of their hearts, when the superscription, "This is the King of the Jews," was elevated above the rough instrument of death, upon which the beloved Jesus suffered and died. Swords were sheathed as useless, and the "little flock" of scattered sheep had no lingering hope of seeing their dreams realized. How crushed! How helpless and lonely! How overwhelmingly disappointed!

"But he that sitteth in the heavens shall laugh; the Lord shall have them in derision. Then shall he speak to them in his wrath and vex them in his sore displeasure.

Yet have I set my King upon my holy hill of Zion. I will declare the decree; the Lord hath said unto me, thou art my Son; this day have I begotten thee. Ask of me and I shall give thee the heathen for thine inheritance, and the uttermost parts of the earth for thy possession. Thou shalt break them in pieces as a potter's vessel." (Ps. 2).

In fulfillment of these great predictions and others, Jesus arose from the dead. He was with the apostles forty days and spake of the things pertaining to the Kingdom. His disciples were *yet in confusion*; and he opened their understanding, that they might understand the Scriptures. They asked him if he would at this time restore again the Kingdom to Israel. On this passage Calvin remarks:

"There are as many errors as words. They dream of an earthly Kingdom; they assign the *time*, THIS *time*— they shut out the Gentiles restraining the Kingdom of God to Israel. They were not content with what was revealed, and the Savior promised them power after the Holy Spirit came upon them and they should be his witnesses in Jerusalem and in all Judea and in Samaria and to the uttermost parts of the earth. But of the times or seasons, which were not for them to know, but which the Father hath put in his own power of course he would not speak."

It was not for the apostles to know; he did not say, "NOT NOW, YOU SHALL KNOW LATER"; but, it is not FOR YOU TO KNOW. Man is curious. Moses wished to see God; Philip requested to see the Father; the disciples wished to know things that were not for them to know. Peter wished to know what John was to have. Many wish to know what the heathen shall have. Jesus said to Peter, "What is that to thee, follow thou me." To these disciples he made no reply that either corrected or sanctioned their idea of Israel having the kingdom restored to them. But on the memorable Pentecost, when the Holy Spirit guided them, they preached Jesus as David's Lord and the predicted Messiah. They received the Kingdom. They were elevated higher than any body of senators, governors or kings that ever sat in legislative assembly. They proclaimed a divine law, and enforced obedience thereto by the most wonderful promises of rewards, or most terrible threatenings of punishment, ever spoken by men. The Holy Spirit guided them day by day into the truth, everything pertaining to life and godliness. They were the inspired law makers for the Kingdom. Thus they received the Kingdom; and it exists today nineteen centuries thereafter, without any proposed change to the end of time.

How, strange that men today, with dreams of a Kingdom not yet set up, should apply this consolation to themselves—"Fear not little flock it is your Father's good pleasure to give YOU the Kingdom"! Jesus did not give the apostles what *they expected*; but he gave them RULE and AUTHORITY. He made them the great legislators of the New Covenant, the spiritual rulers in the Kingdom of heaven. As officials, they are upon the twelve thrones in this regenerative period. The so-called "little flock," of our day, are subject to these rulers in heaven's sight, and must obey Christ by obeying his apostles. "We are of God; he that knoweth God heareth us; he that is not of God heareth not us. Hereby know we the Spirit of truth, and the spirit of error. (I Jno. 4:6).

SONS AND SERVANTS.

The Dawnists elevate their bride class to sonship and thrones; and these are now "Elijah" (or were till Christ came in 1874, when the special Kingdom honors were withdrawn); and the Old Testament saints are to be the servants. David, Moses, Abraham, Ezekiel, Daniel and their class, are to constitute the earthly phase of the Kingdom, or be the servants; while Paul, Peter, James, John, the martyrs and the Dawnists are the Elijah class, and are to be the upper class, the sons, have a divine nature, be the Christ and the King, and the invisible but proper rulers and sovereigns of the earth. Who would have thought this little innocent looking text contained so much? Not I, for one. The idea that one class of human beings will be *divine*, while Christians of the Golden Age, or Millennium, will only be *human*, although, according to the theory, living a PERFECTLY SINLESS LIFE, is so gross and highly destructive of Biblical teaching as to merit the rejection of all lovers of heaven's saving truth. Some make the earth to be the eternal residence of man, his only heaven. All these vagaries grow up around this word Restitution. The whole thought in it is that all that was predicted to be done in restoring man back to God, in accomplishing the prophecies, must be done while the heavens retain our Savior. He does not return in the midst of earthly probation to close the Gospel age and to start another age. The Jews, to whom Peter addressed this language, expected an earthly ruler as their Messiah. See how repeatedly and plainly Jesus rebuked this idea in his apostles. They were blinded to his exalted spiritual rule up to the very day he ascended to heaven. It required his going away, and the guidance of the Holy Spirit to get this carnal view out of their minds. Hence it was levelling this notion to the very dust, right in the beginning, for Peter to say the heaven must retain him. This idea had to take the place of the other, (so long cherished by the Jews), before they could obey the Messiah. As long as they held to the view that Messiah was an earthly ruler, they would not accept the spiritual rule of Christ and walk by faith in ultimate salvation. It was to refute their erroneous idea on this very subject that Peter said that heaven must retain him, as they thought earth must retain him. Strange, indeed, it is, that Gentiles should adopt the Jewish hope, and tell us Jesus must come back to make the restitution, or accomplish the prophecies, when Peter said heaven must retain him till they are accomplished. Millennialists would have him return to make the restoration predicted, and the apostle says the restoration is accomplished with him in heaven. Thus they side with the Jews against the apostle, and belittle the Kingdom he did establish, preach one he did not establish, and, instead of hoping for the things the apostles hoped for, (in the later period of their lives after they learned the gospel), THEY HOPE FOR WHAT THE APOSTLES HOPED FOR BEFORE THE GOSPEL WAS GIVEN. They are thus reviving the *Jewish* hope, which the *apostles gave up*, but which the blind Jews entertain to this day. They strengthen the Jew in his rebellion against the true Messiah and hope for another Messiah and weaken the motives of men to serve Christ in his Kingdom. You can not think of a grace or virtue that is not already given. You can live as pure and heavenly as any human being is called upon to live, and aid in doing all the work the Lord intends to be accomplished before the resurrection and eternal estate, or while the heaven retains him.

"God is no respecter of persons, but in every nation, he that feareth him, and worketh righteousness is accepted with him." "And I say unto you, that many shall come from the east and west, and shall sit down with Abraham, and Isaac and Jacob in the Kingdom of heaven." (Matt. 8:12).

"There shall be weeping and gnashing of teeth when ye shall see Abraham, and Isaac and Jacob in the Kingdom of God, and you, yourselves thrust out. And they shall come from the east and west, and from the north and from the south and shall sit down in the Kingdom of God." (Luke 13:28-29).

Thus our Savior teaches that Gentiles sit down *with* Jews in the Kingdom of God. There is no distinction as to nationality. He does not say they shall be *over* Abraham, Isaac and Jacob, but *with* them. Abraham and all the ancient worthies died in faith. To die in faith is to be looking forward. They did not die in disappointment, in despair; they died in faith. In faith or belief of what? Returning to Palestine to serve the bride-class, the little flock for a thousand years? "These all died not having received the PROMISES; but having seen them afar off, and were persuaded of them and embraced them, and confessed that they were strangers and pilgrims on the earth. For they that say such things declare plainly that they *seek a country*. And truly if they had been mindful of that country from whence they came out, they might have had opportunity to have returned. BUT NOW THEY DESIRE A BETTER COUNTRY, THAT IS AN HEAVENLY; wherefore God is not ashamed to be called their God; for he hath prepared for them a city." (Heb. 11:13-16). Is Palestine heaven? After all, are Enoch and Elijah, (two glorified specimens of our humanity), to be *servants* to the *little flock*, which in our day, is assumed to be composed in the "feet members" of Milennial Dawnists? Are Dawnists to be made DIVINE? To be RULERS over Moses, Aaron, all the holy prophets, dead and translated, reaching from the martyred Abel to the last devoted saint of God, who lived before the gospel age? Is John the Baptist to be as inferior *forever* to C. T. Russell, as a *servant* is to a *son*? a *subject* is to a *ruler*? and a *human* is to a *divine* being? The sons shall shine as the sun, and the servants as the stars. This distinction is not in the Bible. This distinction is as arbitrary and fanciful as any fable of Aesop. It is the hallucination of a man who is laboring to destroy the idea of punishment after death. But let the sinner know that Russell's doctrine fails to convert Gog and Magog. Let him know that his teaching is subversive of the Bible, and is untried, untested, unreal, and as impractical as perpetual motion in mechanics, or the Fountain of Perpetual Youth, in nature. Remember he added one hundred years to (I Ks. 6:1) to make it plausible that Jesus would come during (1874); he left out all the time between Caleb's receiving his inheritance and the rule of the first Judge; he rejected what John said, "The rest of the dead lived not till the thousand years were finished," although retained and edited by the scholarship of the world. He asks, "Where are the dead?" and replies, they do not exist. They have become extinct. He says the man Christ Jesus became extinct at death. He joins Hymaneus and Philetus in saying "the resurrection is passed." He says God has not been with any of the churches in "Christendom" since (1881). He divided the saints into three clases, put himself and the "little flock" as rulers over all the Old Testament saints, divine in nature, and with spirit-bodies. He makes all other saints to be eternally inferior, only perfected human beings. He splits the Christian age, or age of probation, into two parts; the first from Christ to his second coming; the latter a miraculous age, lasting (1000) years. He gets rid of all the apostles, prophets, heroes and heroines of all ages, just as turning a gas jet puts out *that* light forever; if it is ever ignited again, it is a *new* light—hence the Christians become divine beings. He misapplies the new birth to this event. He says the church is Elijah. The kingdom of God was not set up in apostolic days. That Jesus will never come literally in the clouds of heaven with a shout and great glory. That the earth shall never be destroyed. That sinners do not need to fear the Judgment, for it is a great blessing; and thus he patches together Universalism, Restoration, Unitarianism, Annihilationism, Second Chanceism and destroys New Testamentism.

CHAPTER XLII.

THE JUDGMENT.

"Do you not know that the saints shall judge the world? and if the world shall be judged by you, are ye unworthy to judge the smallest matters? Know ye not that we shall judge angels? How much more things that pertain to this life?" (I Cor. 6:2-3).

Millennialists would make the Judgment day (1000) years long. It is preceded by the resurrection of the just. Mr. Russell's theory would bring all the wicked back to earth to have a chance for eternal life during the thousand years. These are favorite texts. To rule over somebody seems to be the height of their ambition. You will remember reading of the apostles entertaining such a Jewish view of the Bible, too before Jesus' death and resurrection. They tell us that the Judges under the law Judged Israel, and that meant delivered them, ruled them. Very, well! The word "judged" like many other words is not restricted to one meaning.

What is meant by the following:

"Therefore thou are inexcusable, O man, whosoever thou are that *judgest*; for wherein thou judgest another, thou condemnest thyself; for thou that judgest doest the same things. But we are sure that the judgment of God is according to truth against them which commit such things. But after thy hardness and impenitent heart treasurest up unto thyself wrath against the day of wrath and revelation of the righteous judgment of God. Who will render to every man according to his deeds. "And shall not uncircumcision which is by nature, if it fulfill the law, Judge thee, who by the letter and circumcision dost transgress the law?" (Rom. 2).

"For the time is come that judgment must begin at the house of God; and if it first begin at us, what shall the end be of them that obey not the gospel of God?" (I Pet. 4:17).

"Judgment" has to be considered in the connection in which it is found to ascertain its meaning. These texts can not mean rule or sovereignty. It is evident that we shall judge the world (condemn it) by living faithfully the Christian life. Noah's righteous life condemned, or (judged) the world, (Heb. 11:7). The Gentiles, by living a pure life, without a written Revelation; and the Sodomites, Ninevites and other heathen cities, will rise in Judgment with the unrepentant Jews of Christ's day, among whom so many of his mighty works were done, and condemn or (Judge) them. It will be more tolerable for Sodom, Nineveh, the Queen of the south, Tyre and Sidon, than for those wicked Jewish cities. (Matt. 11:20-24; 12:41).

This can not mean that Sodom will rule over Capernaum; Ninevites will reign over Israelites; Tyrians and Sidonians will reign over the cities of Chorazin and Bethsaida; or the Queen of the south, will rule over the unrepentant Jews of Christ's generation; and all for a thousand year Millennium. This "judgment" or condemnation of the world, and of angels who kept not their first estate, is not a sovereignty or rule over them; but rather that sinners turned, repented of their sins, while other sinners did not, although enjoying equal or greater opportunities and abilities. The angels forsook holiness and fell, while the church is made up of those who did just the opposite, forsook sin and obeyed God.

ACCOUNTABILITY.

Another way of stating this matter is that man has certain abilities. For these he is responsible and will ultimately be accountable—in the Judgment day. (II Cor. 5:10). No one escapes judgment. It is plain also that God holds one accountable for the use or abuse of what he has, and not for what he has not. (II Cor. 8: 12). "But Jesus did not commit himself unto them, because he knew all men, and needed not that any should testify of man; for he knew what was in man. (Jno. 2: 24-25). He knew what was in the Ninevites, Sodomites, Tyrians and Sidonians, and all men. Paul said, "In the day when God shall judge the secrets of men by Jesus Christ, according to my gospel." (Rom. 2:16). Not that the whole world will be judged by the *requirements* of the gospel; but, rather, it is Paul's gospel that all men shall be judged by Jesus Christ. To be Judged by Jesus Christ, and to be judged and condemned by the gospel, who were never gospel subjects is another and far different thing. Jesus has been appointed the judge of the living and the dead, (that is all mankind), of all time.

The law given through Moses made a distinction between sins of "ignorance" and presumptuous sin;" and the penalties were in corespondence with the sins committed. The cities of Refuge proclaimed aloud the fact of degrees of guilt among man-slayers. (Num. 35). The thieves were classified. (Ex. 22). Jesus showed this discrimination in the cases of these cities, which reveals the principles on which he determines the degrees of guilt. On the one hand it was contempt for divine authority, on the other hand, ignorance. Willful ignorance and unavoidable ignorance are both considered also, in forming Judgment and sentence.

"And that servant, who knew his Lord's will, and made not ready, nor did according to his will, shall be beaten with many stripes; but he that knew not, and did things worthy of stripes, shall be beaten with few stripes. And to whomsoever much is given of him shall much be required; and to whom they commit much, of him will they ask the more. (Luke 12:47-48).

This was a human landlord and servants; but Jesus cited the facts, approved the course, and thus illustrated his method of dealing with sinners according to ability and opportunity. He holds men responsible for the use they make of their abilities and opportunities, is the thought.

"And Jesus said: For Judgment I come into this world, that they that see not might see; and that they that see may become blind. Those of the Pharisees who were with him heard these things, and said unto him, are we also blind? Jesus said unto them: If ye were blind, ye would have no sin; but now ye say, we see, therefore your sin remaineth." (Jno. 9:39-40). "But all these things will they do unto you for my name's sake, because they know not him that sent me. If I had not come and spoken unto them, they had not had sin; but now they have no excuse for their sin. He that hateth me hateth my Father also. If I had not done among them the works which none other did, they had not had sin; but now have they both seen and hated both me and my Father." (Jno. 15:21-24).

Paul, who was a persecutor, a blasphemer and injurious, obtained mercy because he acted in ignorance and unbelief. (I Tim. 1:12-13). Jesus prayed upon the cross, "Father, forgive them for they know not what they do." These citations and quotations are ample on this subject. Jesus knew what was in man; hence "God shall bring every work into Judgment, with every secret thing, whether it be good, or whether it be evil." (Eccl. 12:14).

Is all this preparatory for the (1000) years' reign on earth of the righteous over the one hundred and forty-two billions of those who have never been gospel subjects, who are to be given a chance? and for what? To partake of the divine nature like the *collective* Christ into which the saints have been changed, (rather exchanged, for their bodies do not rise, their souls were human, ceased to exist at death, and at resurrection whatever that is, were divine)? No, these one hundred and forty-two billions of the wicked, according to Mr. Russell are simply to be on trial for *eternal life.* Their first sojourn on earth had nothing to do with that, so they come back, when the devil is in the pit, the saints, the collective Christ, is reigning, to be tried for *eternal life.*

But when all the machinery seems to be ready to convert these billions, and Mr. Russell looks around for them, they are not there. His Millennium has been running now for thirty-six years, and the sleeping billions are in the graves, none of the wicked yet raised. And when we read John to learn the prospects, he says "THE REST OF THE DEAD *lived not again till the thousand years were finished.* So Mr. Russell's fine-spun theory, worked at so persistently for the last half century, (to make gospel subjects of the countless dead who in their life-time, were not gospel subjects, that is died without obedience to Christ), breaks down hopelessly.

I see no way to make gospel subjects of them now, unless Mr. Russell can throw out (Rev. 20:5) that holds them in the embrace of death till the thousand years are finished, and substitute here what he wants as he did in (I Ks. 6:1) where he makes four hundred and eighty

years read five hundred and eighty.   Then he can fix it
as follows:

*"But the rest of the dead lived not till the thousand
years were finished"* are spurious.   They are not found in
the earliest and most reliable Greek MSS, the Siniatic,
Vatican, Nos:. 1219 and 1160, nor the Syriac MS.   We
must remember that many passages found in the modern
copies are additions which do not properly belong to the
Bible.   However, the repudiation of this clause is not
essential to the "Plan" as herein set forth; for the rest
of the dead—the world at large—will not *live* again in
the full sense, in the perfect sense that Adam *lived* before
he sinned and came under the sentence, *dying* thou shalt
die.

The process of resurrection will be a gradual one,
requiring the entire age for its full accomplishment;
though the mere awakening to a measure of life and
consciousness, as at present enjoyed, will of course, be
a momentary work."   "The Divine Plan, etc. pp. 288-
289."

I was expecting Mr. Russell to throw these words
out.   Wescott and Hort's critical New Testament has
them.   Every critical Greek editor known to me retains
the sentence.   All the versions have them.   Every *uncial*
save the Siniatic preserves them.   The omission, (for
such it was), can be placed at the door of a copyist.   The
words are in the great plan of God, and this overthrows
Millennial Dawnism with all students of the inspired
Word.   One might read the voluminous jargon and spe--
ulative theories of the Dawnists till his faith in God's
eternal purpose and eternal Word would grow so weak that
he would dare with impious hand to strike out the imperishable truth, but it will not change the reality.   Jesus
said: "He that rejecteth me, and receiveth not my words,
hath one that Judgeth him; the word that I have spoken,
the same shall *judge* him in the last day."   (Jno. 12:48).
Does this mean rule him for (1000) years?

I notice King James retained it, likewise the American Revisionists (1881); Robert Young, LLD's Edition;
Bible Union; Dr. Doddridge; Dr. Adam Clark; Dr. Bloom-
field; Campbell Doddridge and MacKnight; Bishop
Lowth; Thomas Scott; and Comprehensive Commentary
have it.   On the whole, how do you like Mr. Russell's
explanation "rest of the dead live not again in the *full
sense*"—with John, they live not again in *any* sense;

during the 1000 years. "Though the *mere* awakening to a *measure* of life and consciousness, *as at present enjoyed, will of course be a momentary work.*"

He seems determined to contradict John who says: "They lived not again till the thousand years were finished." Mr. Russell in effect says: John is wrong, they do live, have life and consciousness AS AT PRESENT ENJOYED, receive it in a MOMENT." MR. RUSSELL HAS TO HAVE THEM AWAKEN, OR HIS THEORY IS GONE. But at what moment, please, during the 1000 years? I bring you face to face with the facts, so that you may choose between the inspired apostle and Mr. Russell. He has to have these one hundred and forty-two billions of people ALL RAISED FROM THE DEAD IN COURSE OF THE MILLENNIUM; ALL ON TRIAL FOR ETERNAL LIFE; OR HIS WHOLE SYSTEM IS GONE. So he has them slip back to earth, RESURRECT BY DEGREES; but, mark you! they are ENTIRELY RESURRECTED, HAVE ALL TH*A*T RESURRECTION CAN EVER MEAN TO THEM, BEFORE THE 1000 YEARS END, in his theory.

This squarely contradicts John. Come to think of it, Mr. Russell is representing these great matters as all done under cover, a sort of *secret* work *throughout*.

1. Jesus comes in (1874) no one sees him, not even the Dawnists. Jesus warns us to beware of those prophets who say he is in the secret chamber.

2. The saints are all resurrected in (1878), no one sees, hears or senses their presence, not even the International Bible Students Association, or its founder.

3. The door of hope closes against all churches in (1881). Notwitstanding some of the strongest, purest, holiest men and women have lived, and labored during this "Harvest" without discovering that Mr. Russell was the Servant mentioned in (Luke 12:42), giving them "meat in due season."

One word on (Rev. 20). Who are Gog and Magog? Who are as numerous as the sand of the sea and are gathered together to battle against the people of God *after* the (1000) years are finished? (This slipping back and resurrecting gradually during the thousand years, UTTERLY FAILS ON THEM). So, Mr. Russell will have to cut out another text, and make still another to suit him, or his *restitution is gone.*

On Scriptural principles, all is plain. The revival of Christianity, in spirit and power, her emancipation from Babylon, is a resurrection. It was so in the case of fleshly Israel, the typical people, (Ezek. 37), when they were released from Babylon; why not of spiritual Israel here? It was the souls of the martyrs that lived. This is not the manner of speaking of a literal resurrection. The church had been depressed, trodden down, robbed, spoiled and "killed all the day long." The wild beast and the false prophet devastated the church. Their cause lived, while the cause of truth and righteousness was humiliated into the dust of death. But by the power of the ever-living Christ in his deathless Word, he quickened the church, made her alive, to truth and holiness, so that she that had been dead, like Sardis, was awakened from sleep; they obey the call to life as did Lazarus, only he physically, these spiritually, *Awake thou that sleepest, and arise from the dead,* and Christ shall give thee light." (Eph. 5:14). From this state the church comes forth as the Beast is slain and popery is destroyed. These people awake to righteousness, arise from death, and Christ gives them light. On the other hand, idolatry, priestcraft, tyranny which prevailed for ages and destroyed the church, are destroyed. The devil is restrained that he can no longer deceive the nations into these false, iniquitous systems of idolatry and despotism; he is bound, or his power thrwarted, for (1000) years.

The *contrast* is between the *two Rulers,* and their *followings.* The devil had reigned *invisibly* and wholly *impersonally,* through the sovereigns of the earth, for ages. He never vacated *his* throne to *Christ*; and it is by keeping this fact before us that we see the tremendous, far-reaching revolution, described under these symbols.

The picture is of one chief and his under rulers, being conquered and dethroned by another Chief and his under rulers. It was the old Serpent, the devil and Satan cast out of heaven in (Ch. 12); the same names are used here, but this time he is cast down to hell or the Abyss. His under rulers could not hold the field; the beast was taken; also the false prophet, by the symbolic Rider and

THE JUDGMENT.

his followers on white horses as the battle went against
them; and, as their energy and direction came from beneath, they are represented as going to the Abyss.   So
the Beast, the false prophet, and, lastly, their leader,
the devil, all go to the pit; on the other hand the white-
robed victors, with Jesus at their head, take the dominion.
This is beautifully set forth by resurrection and elevation
to sovereignty for (1000) years.   But as the devil has
not occupied a literal throne on earth, or been visible,
so Jesus does not literally ride a white horse and wear
many crowns.   But he triumphs.   His truth is vindicated.
His martyred saints live in the person of others as John
the Baptist was Elijah.   As the lives of primitive Christians shine forth in the lives of their faithful sucessors.
As the Jews, when converted to God, will be received as
alive from the dead.   They are now blind, in unbelief,
in bondage, and in death.   But even from this state of
death they can awaken, as the nation arose from the
valley of dry bones when Ezra, Nehemiah, Zechariah,
Haggai, Malachi and the spiritual hosts returned to God.
It seems to me that, this nation, sleeping in death today,
in enmity against our Savior, is to share in this first
resurrection, by arising from this death and Christ will
give them light.

But despotism is dying; Catholicism is receiving her
mortal wounds—slain by the sword of him who sat upon
the white horse, which sword proceedeth out of his
mouth; state churches are doomed to extinction.   Militarism must die.   The toiling, struggling, oppressed, misguided, misgoverned millions are tired of the Giant Man
and the "Beastly" Governments.

CHAPTER XLIII.

THE SYMBOLS TRACED OUT.

The virtues of the seven churches grouped together constitute the true church; the vices constitute the apostate church; and the blessings of all the overcomers combined make up the reward of the faithful disciples of Christ. Just as we apply the exceeding great and precious promises of all the letters to Christians of all ages, and not simply to Corinth or Rome or Ephesus, so do we apply these promises and threatenings, in the seven letters. Otherwise, there would be no seven-fold promise of "blessing" or seven-fold warning of "cursing" to apply to any churches after those seven passed away.

THE SECOND DEATH.

Freedom from the second death was promised to the "overcomers" at Smyrna, (2:11). But this was not a promise *limited* to Smyrna. It is of universal application. Jesus said, "And *whosoever* liveth and believeth in me shall never die. Believest thou this?" (Jno. 11:26. See the references). That promise is the same and applies to all the saints living and dead; and not simply to Smyrna and a little company (20:6). In (6:8-11) John saw the souls of the martyrs, under the altar and heard their cry,

"How long, O Lord, holy and true, dost thou not *judge* and *avenge* our blood on them that dwell on the earth? And *white* robes were given unto every one of them; and it was said unto them, that they should rest yet for a little season, until their fellow servants also and their brethren, that should be killed as they were, should be fulfilled."

Here is a "little season," like (20:3); but it has covered many ages. James, Paul, Peter, Stephen and many others, whom John had known, and loved personally, were in that company. The chief questions are, *when* is their blood avenged on them that dwell on the earth? And, *how* is it avenged? The persecutors and the persecuted have all passed from the scenes of earth. Unless Nero, Caligula, Domitian and other heathen Emperors who slew these martyrs are raised from the dead, THEY can not be judged ON EARTH. Unless the popes and their inquisitors are brought back to earth, they can not be punished on earth for their crimes. It seems to me that nothing is plainer than the oft-repeated facts stated in (II Thess: 1). The *actual* murderers and persecutors will receive punishment, and the martyred and persecuted be rewarded, WHEN THE LORD. COMES. That is the final doom of the persecutors. But these martyrs are JUDGED and AVENGED on them that DWELL ON THE EARTH BEFORE THAT. If we understand the "first resurrection," it is the fulfillment of this promise. My contention is that if James, (who was beheaded by Herod), or Stephen, (who was stoned to death), have to come to earth TO GET the JUDGMENT and VENGEANCE of this text against their enemies, then their ENEMIES WHO COMMITED THE CRIMES WILL HAVE TO BE HERE TO RECEIVE THE JUDGMENTS. Judgment and vengeance twenty centuries after a man is dead, (and visited upon somebody else), is making the justice of God to be misdirected. The fact is, that the seals were symbolic, and these symbols, traced out, show us that the persecuted disciples would be vindicated on earth, their enemies condemned, and their entire system of tyranny and oppression overthrown. The *persons* are not to come back to earth and swarm over Asia and Europe; but their *cause* is to be judged and their blood avenged.

LOCAL JUDGMENT.

Jesus said to the Jews, "That upon you may come all the righteous blood shed upon the earth, from the blood of righteous Abel unto the blood of Zechariah, son of Barachias, whom ye slew between the temple and the altar," (Matt. 23:35). Then, was Cain excused? Were the actual murderers passed by? Nay, verily. But the Jews slew apostles and prophets, and by such acts endorsed the murderous policy of their predecessors. Their fathers killed the prophets, and they built their sepulchers, thus testifying that they killed holy men. And they killed the Lord Jesus and his followers of whom these prophets spake, showing they were of the same murderous race. But none of the prophets of the Old Testament came back and none of their assassins.

I. The Judgment here, is not prophetic of the last day, (Rev. 6:8-11); but is the judgment of the Anti-Christian powers. It is at the Judgment of the "little horn," (Dan'l 7); "But the Judgment shall sit, and they shall take away his dominion to consume and to destroy it unto the end." Then the saints possess the kingdom.

II. The time for the dead that they should be Judged, and that God should reward his servants the prophets, and to the saints and to them that fear his name small and great, and SHOULDEST DESTROY THEM THAT DESTROY THE EARTH. (Rev. 11:15-18). The same time is set forth here for "the kingdom of the world has become the kingdom of the Lord and of his Christ, and he shall reign forever and ever."

III. The Judgment of Babylon, (not the Judgment of the whole world), is described at length beginning with (ch. 16) and in (18:20) it is said,

"Rejoice over her thou heaven, and ye saints, and ye apostles, and ye prophets; FOR GOD HATH JUDG-ED YOUR JUDGMENT ON HER." And in (Ver. 24) "And in her was found the blood of prophets and of saints, and of ALL THAT HAVE BEEN SLAIN UPON THE EARTH." Their Judgment, (righteous Judgment), was given against Babylon—"For her sins have reached unto heaven, and God hath remembered her iniquities. Reward her even as she rewarded you, and double unto her double according to her works; in the cup which she hath filled, fill to her double." (18:5-6). "Come hither, I will show thee the JUDGMENT OF THE GREAT HAR-LOT that sitteth upon many waters." (17:2).

When BABYLON IS OVERTHROWN, he says, "For true and righteous are his Judgments: for he HATH JUDGED the GREAT HARLOT, her that corrupted the earth with her fornication, and he HATH AVENGED THE BLOOD of his servants at HER HANDS. (19:2).

Are these the end of the world? the end of time? No.   These are the end of Babylon. In (ch. 6) the souls cried for vengeance; in these chapters they get it. John saw the souls in (ch. 6), and also in (ch. 20), although the events were ages apart.

THE SOULS CRIED TO HAVE THEIR BLOOD

AVENGED ON THEM THAT DWELL ON THE EARTH (ch.6); THEIR BLOOD WAS AVENGED IN THE OVER-THROW OF BABYLON (19:2) ON EARTH, AND IN TIME, NOT ETERNITY.

Were their actual murderers present on earth in the last use of the symbols? Unless a literal resurrection of the persecuted takes place it is not the Judgment day. Nero, Domitian, Dioclesian and Galerius, slew multi-tudes. Why insist that the murdered come back, but not the murderers? Strange judgment that, when God "HATH JUDGED—HATH AVENGED THE BLOOD OF HIS SERVANTS and NONE of the actual MURDERERS were PRESENT! The literal martyrs and their literal persecutors do not need to return to earth for *this judg-ment*, any more than Abel, Zecharias and all between, and their murderers, needed to be present at the destruc-tion of Jerusalem for their blood to be avenged. That certainly is a strange rule of interpretation that would bring all the martyrs back, who are strewn along the ages, but leave their persecutors and murderers to be tried a thousand years or so later! Mr. Russell comes with the bold assumption that these martyrs, all the saints and holy angels are here now; but, none of the Pharaohs, Caesars, or popes have arrived yet. The fact is, the whole theory is false and makes John's sym-bols to be realities; or the THINGS *he used to make* A PREDICTION *and the things* PREDICTED *to be the* SAME THINGS. It is to make the Judgment against the Beast, false prophet and dragon, (symbols used in his book), to be the universal judgment of all the *righteous* dead; and *leaves* the *wicked*, the very *ones* against whom the JUDGMENT IS PREDICTED not to be JUDGED at all, for the (1000) YEARS AND MORE, LATER.

THE BOTTOMLESS PIT.

The Bottomless pit was opened (ch. 9:1); closed (20:3). The infernal powers that produced the Anti-Christian governments came out in the first; and were restrained in the last. It was open during the life-time of the symbols, that foretold the rise, exploits and car-nage of the dragon, the beast and false prophet; it was closed when *their* mission ended. It was neither opened, nor closed by miracle. To say that it was, is to affirm that miracles were performed by the Beast and False Prophet. The devil was ACTIVE on earth from the garden of Eden till the pit was opened; and, evidently, will be after its close; but not in deceiving the nations as he did while the pit was open, as he acted through the *beast* and *false prophet*. These three, in an unholy combination, constitute Babylon. When separated (the city divided into three parts 16:19), Babylon is fallen. There is no *literal* city of Babylon on earth today. It is "Mystery Babylon" that we are studying.

Was there no devil in the days of the Flood? Of Babylon? of Medo-Persia? of Greece? and Rome? until the opening of the seventh seal and the pit was opened? or till early in the seventh century?

Who tempted Christ? Who worked in the children of disobedience? Who plotted the murder of Jesus in his infancy and put it into the heart of Judas Iscariot to betray him? Who compassed his death on Calvary? Who hatched up the "mystery of iniquity" in Paul's day? To whom did the Gentiles offer sacrifices in idolatrous fashion? Who controlled the ten fiendish, bloody persecutions before Constantine's day? The devil claimed to own all the kingdoms of this world in Christ's day. Yet in (Rev. 9) he gets out of the Pit; in (ch. 20) he is put back. Do you not see that this was not a literal transaction in either case? Did not John *see* the whole transaction related in both chapters, and did it not take place, therefore, eighteen hundred years ago? Was not this a symbolic prophecy? Did not John in (ch. 12) see A SIGN *in* HEAVEN, *a great*, *red* DRAGON, having seven heads and ten horns, and crowns upon his heads? Did not he say this was a *sign*? Did he not say the great dragon was cast out, that old serpent called the Devil and Satan, which DECEIVETH the whole world; he was cast out into the earth and his angels were cast out with him? Have you observed that he has the same names in (ch. 20:2) where he is put back into the pit as in (ch. 12) where HE IS A SIGN?

In (11:7) the beast *ascends* out of the bottomless pit—his end is *perdition*.

In (17:7-11) the beast has seven heads, ten horns,

and the eighth head (little horn of Dan'l 7) and *goeth to perdition.*

In (11:7) the beast comes out of the pit for (1260) prophetic days. In (20:3) he returns.

In (ch. 12) the same period is covered under the imagery of the dragon persecuting the woman the same prophetic period. The great red dragon was a SIGN.

In (ch. 13) the composite beast received a mortal wound, *was healed,* and survived FORTY-TWO MONTHS. The wounded beast is photographed in (ch. 17). There we see the Roman Empire ridden by a church—a beast ridden by a scarlet-clad woman. No doubt the Roman Empire existed, but in ten parts, while the Roman Catholic church controlled the government and was supported by it, as a woman rides a beast and is upheld by it. The ten horns of the beast, (the ten governments that supported popery so long), hated the rider, stripped her naked and desolate, (took her dominion from her and deserted her); and shall burn her with fire. This reads like modern history in Europe since the ten Governments of Europe got tired of popery, hated her, took away her dominion (A. D. 1870) and all forsook her, one by one, from that day to the present.

In (chs. 19 and 20) the beast, false prophet and dragon, (the triple alliance of these symbols), are grouped together in defeat. They worked together and their combined power was overcome. As their origin was Satanic, their doom is perdition. You do not conceive that such a Beast, or such a Harlot, ever existed in reality as horses, cattle and humanity exist. But in (ch. 12:3), John saw the dragon, as a SIGN. This was the same as saying, "As I was to SIGNIFY in this prophecy (ch. 1:1), I give you another great symbol. Then for us to ignore the SIGN whenever the dragon appears, is to fail to grasp his meaning. For instance, (ch. 11:7): Did an animal literally come from hell? No. He *signified* what some government would be and do. When we are looking along the pathway of history for such a government, we are doing what the *symbols* demand. So of the opening and the closing of the Abyss. It is not to give the origin of the devil, or the beginning of his work on earth in the one instance; nor the close

of his work on earth, (even for a thousand years), in the
other.   The fact is plain that the devil is a spirit, now
rules in the hearts of the disobedient; but his masterpiece of sorcery and iniquity, by which he deceived the
nations, is to go down; the Beast and the false prophet
are to lose the battle of centuries to Christ.   But the
imagery does not indicate that the devil will cease to
work at all, or that God will bind and imprison him
literally with a chain in a pit.   He can deceive the
NATIONS no more for a very definite period, one thousand years.   The symbols are connected with his tyranny, but ultimate defeat.

THE LAMB.

The signs(or symbols) are in groups at the opening
and in the close of the book.   To follow them is to see
the logical structure of the volume.   What is shown by
the agents, actions, and results in symbols, must have
corresponding agents, actions and results in the history
of the things symbolized.

1.   The slain and resurrected Lamb is seen all
through the book after (ch. 5:6).   He has seven horns
and seven eyes, (perfect power and perfect wisdom),
He is NEXT TO THE THRONE, angels and saints worship him, (vs. 8, 9, 12, 13).   That is his place in the
believer's heart and praises forever.   Next are the four
living ones; next the twenty-four enthroned elders; these
are surrounded by the multitude of redeemed men; and
the outer circle is composed of the angelic hosts.   This
grouping of symbols is carried in this order through the
book.

2.   The Lamb is worshipped after the victory over
pagan Rome in (chs. 6 and 7; 9-11).   Here are the
throne, Lamb, angels, four living creatures, the multitude
worshipping God, the nations, kindreds and tongues
clothed in white robes, with palms in their hands.

3.   The four and twenty elders worship God and
praise his name for victory in (11:16-18).

4.   The Lamb stands with his victorious, rapturous
throng on Mt. Zion (14:1-13), contrasted with the two-
horned Lamb (ch. 13).

5.   At the marriage of the Lamb to his church, the

bride, *immediately after* the Harlot, (false church), is
judged, the same elders, living creatures and the multitude, worship God and the Lamb. This picture is of the
counterfeit bride, the Harlot, who had mixed religion
with carnal things, was rejected, and the true church was
exalted to her rightful place in fealty to Christ; as the
Corinthians were espoused, as a congregation, (or a
chaste virgin), to Christ. The church should not question this consolation as it is an old illustration, (Eph.
5:25). You observe the marriage of the Lamb takes
place AS SOON as the Harlot is JUDGED. As Babylon
was that Harlot, as soon as Babylon falls, the marriage
of the Lamb *follows*, (ch. 19). Babylon is pictured as a
Harlot; the true church as a Virgin; hence when the Harlot is destroyed (chs. 17 and 18) the Virgin is joined to
the Lamb, (ch. 19). The seven-fold virtues of the seven
churches constitute the Virgin; the seven-fold vices, constitute the Harlot, *in this world*.

The elders and four living creatures are not seen in
the vision after the marriage of the Lamb (19:4), unless
it be in (20:4). In (6:9-10) was the prediction that
they should reign on the earth; but not exclusively, as
(11:15; 12:10) show, and these *reign*, as here, *after the
defeat* of the Beast and dragon respectively.

CHAPTER XLIV.

MYSTERY BABYLON DESTROYED.

1. The white horse and Rider appear (6:2); disappear after the signal victory (19:11-21).

2. The martyr scene opens under the fifth seal
(6:9-11); closes after the judgment against the combined antagonists (chs. 16 to 20:4).

3. The Bottomless pit opens (ch. 9); closes (ch.
20), after the victory over Babylon, the Beast, False
Prophet, and Dragon.

4. Spiritual harlotry is presented in the person of

the scarlet clad woman, drunken and making the nations drunk (ch. 17); after a long career of crime, she is made desolate, naked, her flesh eaten and she burned with fire, (17:16). Under the name "MYSTERY BABYLON, fire, (17:16). Under the name "MYSTERY BABYLON THE GREAT, MOTHER OF HARLOTS AND ABOMINA-ished in (ch. 18) with plagues, death, mourning, famine; and is burned with fire.

John gives several striking illustrations of the over-throw of these aged enemies of the church and of the triumph of the gospel. These all relate to this life, and are in the nature of parables or figures of the tremen-dous realities.

HARVEST SCENE.

In (ch. 14:14-20) the vine of the earth is harvested. This scene *follows* the overthrow of Babylon, same chap-ter. It is plain that these scenes are of closing events, illustrated or SIGNIFIED. I do not analyze here this scene further than to say, the harvest is put into the winepress of the WRATH OF GOD. The wrath of God is contrasted in the book with the wrath of the Harlot, who terrorized the nations into the acceptance of her abominations. It is reported that Pope Pius X when dying said, "The time was when the pope could have stopped this conflict with a word, but now he is impo-tent." His word is not regarded by the nations now at war, whereas at one time, he crowned or uncrowned kings at pleasure. How long would the popes leave Protest-ant churches in the city of Rome if they could either start or stop wars among the ten governments? He is now an antiquated sovereign, stripped of his temporal dominion, with all the governments that upheld him, for the predicted (42 months), hating him and despising his assumption of temporal authority.

MARRIAGE SCENE.

This woman appeared in (ch. 12) all glorious in heaven's sight; but persecuted by the monster dragon for the oft-repeated (1260) prophetic days. In (ch. 19: 7-10) she appears, all radiant and beautiful, clothed in white, amid an Alleluiah chorus at her marriage to the Lamb. A Harlot, yea, the mother of harlots, has been

prominent in the period between her disappearance in
the wilderness, (moral and spiritual wilderness); but
when the spurious Harlot Queen, exulting in her pride,
is deposed (18:8-24; 19:1-3) the heavenly Queen is
married. The Harlot's false, counterfeit reign was not
begun or ended by miracle; and the marriage of the true
church is no more *miraculous here* than in (II Cor. 11:2, 3;
or Eph. 5:25). One needs but slight acquaintance with
the prophets to know that marriage was one of their common figures to illustrate the relationship between God
and Israel.—(Ezek. 16 and 23 chs) show us God as
the Husband of Aholah and Aholibah, sisters, (that is
Israel and Judah, or Samaria and Jerusalem). Their
unfaithfulness to the covenant branded them as fornica-
tors. When did God come down to earth to *marry* fleshly
Israel? The question needs no reply. As the illustration in Revelation is *borrowed* from *these* prophets, (see
Hosea Chs. 1-3) IT IS NECESSARY TO INTERPRET
THE ILLUSTRATION HERE AS WE DO THERE. Jesus
does not need to *come to earth* to *marry* the *bride*, the *church*,
even as God did not come to earth, formerly. It is just
as appropriate to say that the *church* proved to be a
Harlot and untrue to *her* husband, Christ, as to say that
Israel and *Judah* were unfaithful in wedlock. In both
cases idolatry is fornication. Furthermore, when Judah
repented and returned to her husband, she illustrated
what the true church does in (Rev. 19:1-10). It seems
to me that this is too plain to need argument. As God
remained in heaven ALL THE TIME OF THE ILLUSTRA-
TIONS, throughout the whole history of Aholah and
Aholibah, so does Christ throughout the history of the
Harlot and the Bride. But the Millennialists say, "Did
not the marriage take place when the Bridegroom came
in (Matt. 25:1-12)?" Certainly. And did not the
fisherman, put real *fish* in vessels at the *same* time?
And did not the husbandman put *wheat* in the barn, at
the *same time*? And did not the Nobleman set one man
over ten cities, another over five cities, at the *same
time*? These are all holy *illustrations*. We are not fish,
wheat, or dealing in real estate. But these illustrate
our position as servants of God. The man with the ten
talents received money, a talent; as the man with ten

pounds, received another pound. THESE WERE ALL HUMAN TRANSACTIONS, chosen by our Lord, not to teach us there is a WEDDING, A FISHING PARTY, A REAL ESTATE TRANSACTION, or A FARMING INDUSTRY, ACTUALLY IN PROGRESS; but these things bring home to us the reality of our service to Christ; and we are to be watchful as virgins; diligent with our talents and pounds; careful to grow wheat (or children of God, not children of the wicked one); and to be choice fish in the gospel net. For, in all these illustrations, it is evident we make *choice* for one or the other result; and we are "blessed" or "cursed" for our decision and conduct. So Paul taught the Corinthians concerning being chaste virgins. This wedding in (Rev. 19) is not some local affair, any more than God's marriage to typical Israel was a local, earthly affair. But in all lands and both sexes, the true followers of the Lamb constitute the wife (in the figures of former prophets). The Harlots in both cases were rejected, and the women who were acknowldged as the brides were faithful in obdience to God.

THE WAR SCENE.

The wedding scene is shifted for a thrilling war scene. (19:11-21). Here are the white horse, the Rider, wearing many crowns, or diadems; his vesture dipped in blood; his sword, (a spiritual sword as it comes out of his mouth); and his name is the Word of God. This Rider is followed by the ARMIES in HEAVEN all riding WHITE HORSES, themselves clothed in fine linen white and pure. The whole scene is a war picture, even to birds eating the carcasses of the slain. But, at the close, the beast and the false prophet were taken and cast alive into the lake of fire. The kings of the earth and their armies "were killed with the sword of him, that sat upon the horse, even the sword which came forth out of his mouth; and all the birds were filled with their flesh." (Ignoring the chapter division, we should read on down to verse ten, but I reserve this to the next chapter of this book).

You will see that this is not a single battle. The "Little horn," (Dan'l 7:21) "made *war* with the saints and prevailed against them" in the symbols; "Wears out the saints of the Most High," in the interpretation. "But the Judgment shall sit, and they shall take away his dominion, to consume and to destroy it unto the end." (ver. 26). So, here, the age-long battle is over; the warriors dressed in white win the victory.   Of course the battle is not pitched in heaven, for the beast ascendeth out of the pit, (11:7).   The *time* of this RESURRECTION SCENE (20:4) is the *same* as the others, at the end of the (1260 prophetic days). ˙So we have:

1.   The Harvest Scene.   2.   The Marriage Scene. 3.   The War Scene. These illustrations, like so many parables of our Lord, bring before us the whole thrilling history. To these is added, 4.   The Resurrection and Reigning Scene.   All of them point out the victory of the King of Kings and Lord of Lords, over all the forces of darkness, the Kings of the earth, the Beast, the False Prophet and the Dragon.   People who understand the gospel, do not expect to be kings and priests as popes were kings and priests, that is reigning on earth as rulers in earthly governments.   That is the old Jewish notion that Christ rebuked while on earth.   Popery usurped the offices of Christ and reigned over all as kings and priests, and when that power is taken away, the disciples return to their long lost rights as kings and priests.   We are now kings and priests; so were the martyrs; and so were the disciples in the apostolic age.   The clergy, or heritage of God, is not the lordly priests of our day; but each disciple of Christ is a king and priest in his own right.   John predicted that self-appointed kings and priests would usurp these functions and tyrannize over the church for (1260) years; and they certainly did.   But as one class goes down, or dies, the other class revives, or lives; and this is a resurrection, (in the figurative style of this book). Not that any one man has to live here again after he has once lived and died a martyr; but that such people live, as Elijah lived again in the person of John the Baptist; and as the Jewish nation came up out of their graves, when they returned from their captivity in Babylon.   It was not necessary for Daniel, Ezekiel, and the very same people to return for the nation to be resurrected; in fact, that would have changed the whole system of faith. So the true kings and priests of God, after the long night

of tyranny and misrule, exercised over them by the Babylon of Revelation, shall unseat the counterfeit priesthood and unlawful rulers; then they shall reign, not alone, but with God and Christ. Neither God nor Christ come to earth; but the saints recover their rights; and, in obedience to God and Christ, they exercise their long-forfeited priesthood as they did in the apostolic age, (I Pet. 2:5-9). As John the Baptist was the Elijah who was for to come, (not the very man; but came in the spirit and power of Elijah); after this manner the old saints live again, in the figurative language of John. He saw the souls or spirits of the martyrs and faithful ones living and reigning with Christ. John the Baptist taught and lived in the spirit and power of Elijah; this was done in the close of the Jewish age; and a revival of the apostolic church in spirit and power is all that is needed or promised for this earth to win mankind to God. Elijah did not give John his body, nor his spirit; he was not reincarnated in John; so, the saints do not return literally under the gospel age. It is as plain as day, however, that one can be Paul, or Peter, or John, or any other saint, as John was Elijah. As I have shown that Christ is the David of the prophets; the church is the temple; Christians are the Levites; the ordinary priests and kings in the kingdom of heaven; and that Zion, Jerusalem, the sacrifices and feasts of the law are all reproduced in the spiritual realities of the gospel; just so the disciples are to revive the dead, who have long since quit this mortal scene. The SOULS were, literally, never dead; but their priesthood and spiritual royalty were dead, when the "mystery Babylon" ruled. In the sense of recovering their heritage and exercising their functions as they did while on earth, John saw the souls or spirits of the departed live again. They lived in a multitude of disciples, who lived and taught the same as they did when alive among men; and they resurrected their cause, by reproducing their lives of faith, power, holiness, and courage; and were blessed and made happy in the service of God in this life, and shall live forever with the Lord, (as the second death has no power over a Christian). Elijah did not die; yet he lived again in the life and labors of John the Baptist; and our Savior said, "He that hath ears to hear let him hear." Just so the martyrs and faithful Christians who would not worship the "Beast" neither his "Image," served their day and generation as Elijah did his and passed to their reward; and their souls or spirits lived in others, not literally, but in the sense that John the Baptist was Elijah.

THE SEVEN BOWLS.

The Harvest scene is in the close of (ch. 14). The "vine" is reaped and cast into the great wine-press of the wrath of God. The wine-press was without the city, and the profusion of blood was very great. The contrasts between the faithful and the unfaithful are preserved. This vine was of the earth. It was not planted by the Lord, and must be plucked up. Similar teaching was given concerning fleshly Israel, (Is. 5; also Ps. 80:8-19). The (15 and 16 chs) are a great summary of the Judgment against Babylon. The "Sign" was the seven last plagues. You observe the "Temple" was opened and the ark of the covenant was seen (chs. 11:19; 14:17; 16:10); this, evidently, is like the Lord's announcement to Moses at the burning bush, (Ex. 3:1-10). God had seen the affliction of Israel and had remembered his covenant, and had come down to deliver them. He sent Moses with a series of plagues against the Egyptians, and brought Israel out, having overthrown their oppressors. God's faithfulness to spiritual Israel is suggested here by bringing to view the ARK OF HIS TESTIMONY. He promised to deliver our Israel from Babylon, and these terrifying plagues, seven in number, do the work. A few facts connected with the introduction of the "Sign" throw much light on the whole story. (Ch. 15:1-4) shows us the "Beast," the "Image" and the "Mark" are still to be considered. The sea of glass mingled with fire and redeemed Israel standing upon it show us the contest has not ceased that has been in progress ever since the Beast arose as a persecutor of the people of God. The Beast was composed of people; so was the Image; and these people are contrasted with the other class. The false church was not the Roman Government at any time; but was upheld by that government, and patterned her rule after it; and was thus the "Image" of it. Here the

saints are true overcomers, and are cleansed by the sea
and the fiery trials through which they pass.

(Ver. 7), "And one of the four living creatures gave
unto the seven angels seven golden bowls full of the
wrath of God, who liveth forever and ever." The living
creatures are representatives of redeemed humanity, and
this one, therefore, was a standard bearer, so to speak, of
the grand encampment of Israel. This indicated the
work would be a Judgment from God, but advanced by his
people, the soldiers of the cross. The voice of authority
came from the "Temple" (16:1). It was the temple,
the altar, and the worshippers that were measured in
(11:1-2); and the court and holy city were trodden
under foot for forty and two months. When these
months pass, (in these symbols), the temple and furniture
come into view again, for the church is to be seen in
another relation—somebody else is to be trodden under
foot, without the city, that is not the church, but her
age-long persecutors.

Each of the "bowls" contained one of the seven
last plagues, (that is the seven fill up the full measure
of Judgment that was prayed for by the souls under
the altar, that was then promised and is here visited, in
the symbols). The first vial, or bowl, produced a noi-
some and grievous sore upon "the men who had the
mark of the beast and worshipped his Image" You see
that it was time to "Judge" them. The first plague here
is like the sixth inflicted by Moses on Egypt. There it
was against Jannes and Jambres, counterfeit priests, or
magicians, and sorcerers; here it is against sorcery and
lying wonders. The second plague was poured upon the
sea, and it became as the blood of a dead man. (17:1-
15). If this sea was humanity, then the lesson is that,
the waters upon which the Harlot sat were deadly, that is
the peoples, multitudes, nations and tongues deal out
death to the Harlot, ultimately, and destroy such a tyrannous government. They destroyed "the man of sin."
The third plague was that the rivers and fountains of
water were turned into blood. Moses did this literally as
a judgment against Pharaoh and the Egyptians. I
think we may safely say, however, that the rivers and
fountains of water are symbols of people here, as John

has used and continues to use them that way. The desolation of despotism is by bloody war. "All they that take the sword shall perish by the sword."

In (16:5-7) the reader is informed that this was a merited judgment. Many expositors attempt to apply these plagues to individual events. This is an error. Mahometanism, Catholicism, and Despotism are being destroyed piecemeal. The great sea of humanity is swallowing them up politically. But the rivers and fountains, (the nations, peoples, and tongues), one by one, are turned into blood. One by one they pay the price of liberty in the sacrifice of life and treasure, and free themselves from tyranny and oppression. It is more fanciful than wise to attempt to fit one vial to one revolution; the next to another; and thus limit these plagues to a few events. The fourth bowl was poured upon the sun. The ninth plague in Egypt was darkness. This plague was the opposite, as it was light. Light shines behind the ramparts of sin. Closed doors and barred windows cannot keep it out. As the Sun of glory rises into the noon-day heavens, the fogs of superstition, priest-craft and king-craft are destroyed before it. That was a "cloudy and dark day" when God's sheep were scattered. Yet these men scorched with great heat do not repent to give God glory. These Vials like the trumpets in (ch. 8) are destructive. There they overthrew pagan Rome; here they are a new set of symbols used to picture the overthrow of Babylon. I would love to see the Sun with which the woman was clothed pour life and health into the darkest recesses of earth. Under the full-orbed light of heaven's truth, the last shadow of the "Dark Ages" should pass away. All of those plants that grew up in that midnight should wilt, droop and die under the power of the unobstructed light of the Sun of Righteousness.

The fifth vial was poured on the throne, or sovereignty, of the "Beast." This is getting down to the very roots of despotism. The whole territory, ruled for ages by despots, is full of darkness. Pharaoh was about ready to yield when darkness hung above his throne and kingdom. So, here, earthly tyrants find that their sun has set to rise no more. The plagues are continuous. These governments, like Israel of old, are incurable. "From the sole of the feet even unto the head there is no soundness in it; but wounds and bruises and putrefying sores; they have not been closed, neither bound, neither mollified with ointments," (Is. 1:6). The disease was fatal. So these unrepentant sinners fail to see the impending doom written over all these thrones of despotism; and, in this symbolism, over the "Beast" that does not repent to give God glory. The sixth vial dried up the symbolic river Euphrates, preparatory to the entrance of our Cyrus into Babylon, who will release the captives. This is "MYSTERY BABYLON" (17:5), as literal Babylon perished from the earth ages ago. The fleshly Israel was at one time captives in literal Babylon; so, here, spiritual Israel were captives in this "mystery Babylon." As the river Euphrates that flowed through literal Babylon was turned into another channel, and the city fell; so, here, the river of humanity (17:1-15) is turned into a new channel, deserts the old city and it falls. As Cyrus released the typical Israel and they rebuilt their temple, so now, the people of God restore his temple.

THREE UNCLEAN SPIRITS.

But we see there are three unclean spirits at work in these times. When the masses turn from despotism, Catholicism and Mahometanism, they are dangerous to civil and religious liberty. The dragon sends forth his spirit of infidelity; and anarchy, of every shade and grade, is the fruit of it. All lands are cursed today with this spirit. The "beast" has corrupted millions. The spirit of the money lords, the trusts, and unholy combines, is out of the mouth of the beast of 'Despotism'. It is the same foul spirit that governed all the kings and tyrants of past ages. The autocracy of wealth is wielding its iron scepter in all lands. The trusts and merciless combines among the men of fabulous fortune, impoverish and practically enslave the masses, to the greed and plunder of the few. These men would be the Caesars and Czars of the whole earth. The spirit comes from the mouth of the Old World Despotisms that have crushed and robbed their millions from time immemorial, especially during the days of the four governments symbolized by the Metallic Man and the four Wild Beasts, and since the ten-horned beast arose into power.

Lastly, the spirit of the false prophet works in the hearts of the disobedient. I have said there are more popes than the one on the Tiber. What moral distinction can be drawn between lordly bishops and lawmakers in one church and the same class of men in another church? Is the Roman church alone in her assumption to change times and laws? Is she alone guilty of desecrating the Lord's day? Does not the same spirit that animated her sway multitudes? The spirit of worldliness, of pride, of vain show in religion, of irreverence for sacred things, and of ungodliness in general pervades our modern society. The masses live for pelf and self, in all the rounds of carnality and grossness of heart from which it is the chief mission of the gospel in this world to deliver them. This spirit of carnality, and formalism, is deadly. Why condemn Tetzel for selling indulgences to sin and then say we may indulge our lusts without scruple? This spirit is not from above but is earthly, sensual, devilish; and it is swaying multitudes. Here is an open field and a fair fight. The battalions of hell come up from beneath; and the army from heaven, on white horses, and clothed in linen white and clean, engage in this fight. This is Armageddon, the great Battle from which none are exempt. Jesus says, "Behold I come as a thief. Blessed is he that watcheth and keepeth his garments, lest he walk naked and they see his shame." Millennialists say, "There it is! Jesus is coming invisibly and at this time." Some say, he has been here since (1874). But this phase of our subject needs no further explanation in this connection, having been shown to be false from so many standpoints. Men assume this is an earthly, carnal battle. Some say it is the present war in Europe. They have selected most of the great national upheavals in the past five centuries with the same degree of confidence. But you are scarcely done reading that it is "Spirits" that gather men together for this Armageddon. The whole earth is engaged in this battle. It is a moral and spiritual conflict. The "dragon," the "beast" and the "false" prophet" are the "Triple Alliance" that is waging war against the armies of heaven.

It has been thus in all the symbols. It is not a single battle in a mortal combat, in Palestine, or elsewhere. If we keep our garments clean and white we may fight and help to win the victory in this mighty conflict. The seven-headed, ten-horned dragon is in these symbols; but here, as elsewhere, as the agent of that old dragon, the devil and Satan.

What happened when the seventh Bowl was poured out? Victory for truth and righteousness. The same as the victory of the Little Stone; the same as the Man-child; and all the other symbols of that time indicate, as I have shown in The Symbols traced out,

"There were voices, and thunders and lightnings; and there was a great earthquake, such as was not since men were upon the earth, so mighty an earthquake and so great. And the great city was divided into three parts, and the cities of the nations fell: and great Babylon came in remembrance before God, to give unto her the cup of the wine of the fierceness of his wrath, and every Island fled away, and the mountains were not found."

Then the Triple Alliance was dissolved. The unholy combination, composed of the Beast, the Dragon and the False Prophet, so strikingly styled "Babylon," falls into her three component parts, in the religious and political revolution or earthquake. "It is done." The (18th ch.) gives an explanation of this Judgment, so long and so ardently hoped and prayed for by martyrs and saints of God. Babylon goes down to rise no more. Just as the metallic man was ground up and swept away; and the fourth beast was consumed by fire, horns and all. So, in the symbols that follow, we learn that the Harlot is cast off and the true woman, or church, comes to her own, as worthy of eternal honor and glory. The three unclean spirits are active and vigilant, and they make day and night hideous with their croaking. Into this conflict we may go, sustained by the promise of Christ that, "To him that overcometh will I grant to sit with me in my throne, even as I overcame and am set down with my Father in His throne. He that hath ears to hear let him hear what the Spirit says unto the churches," (Rev. 3:21,22). We may rest assured that, these plagues are against this "Mystery Babylon." The bloody rivers and fountains of water, the great hail, and the terrifying symbols, should arouse all indifferent ones, that they would hasten to "Come out of her, my people, that ye be not partakers of her sins and that ye receive not of her plagues," (18:4).

In (ch. 6:12-17) there was a great earthquake, when Pagan Rome went down; and mountains and islands fled. In (ch. 11:13) there was a great earthquake, and one-tenth of this figurative city of Babylon fell. Here (ch. 16:18-21) is earth's mightiest earth-quake, for the whole "mystery Babylon" falls. She is divided into the three elements that all along have composed her, a union without which there can be no Babylon—confusion. The church (false prophet) is separated from the Beast, and this dismemberment destroys mystery Babylon. The mountains and islands, or great and small governments, disappear also, and the long night of despotism is ended. Men wish to know which will prevail, the tyrannous governments, or the free; and the symbols testify in trumpet tones, it is the stone, the man-child, and the saints of God that win the victory.

CHAPTER XLV.

THE FIRST RESURRECTION.

From (Rev. 19:11; 20:1-10) is a section that should not be separated by a chapter heading. You notice that the long battle ends in victory for the Rider on the white horse, and the beast and false prophet were disposed of, and the kings of the earth and their armies were killed, by the sword of the Rider on the white horse in the (19th ch.), and the disposition of the dragon follows. He was bound, imprisoned in the bottomless pit for a thousand years. Now the field is clear, like when the Metallic Man was crushed by the stone; but there the stone had a constructive work before it, and became a great *mountain* and filled the whole earth. With the fourth wild beast, and the judgment against the "little horn" the *result* was the same, they 'took away his dominion to consume and destroy it to the end; but the kingdom and dominion and the greatness of the kingdom under the whole heaven, shall be given to the people of the saints of the most High, whose kingdom is an everlasting kingdom, and all dominions shall serve and obey him." (Dan. 7:26-27). The same resurrection scene and universal rule for Christ are set forth in (Rev. 11:11-18).

There is no statement that Christ is on earth. He was riding a white horse in heaven in the last symbol. Is this all literal? or all figurative? You have anticipated my answer. John was to SIGNIFY in the twentieth chapter as well as in the rest of the book. The preceding prophecies demand that this should be figurative. The two witnesses prophesied in sackcloth for (1260) days. Not even Methusaleh lived that long, if these days are prophetic of years. Their death was not the death of men or individuals; hence their resurrection was not individual. The devil is a spirit, and mind operates on mind. A chain, a pit, a seal, and a thousand year sentence, are appropriate symbols of his defeat, temporarily, in governments. Just as the battle or war scene is a good illustration of the defeat of Anti-Christ. I give some reasons why I believe this is a figurative resurrection.

1. Because it is in the most figurative book in the Bible, in a book wherein we are plainly told in the first verse that the realities were SIGNIFIED.

2. The beast that had a deadly wound and was healed, was like these resurrected ones, in that the beast signified a government, destroyed, then revived. As the government of Christ was first destroyed, his priesthood and Lordship usurped by the pope, so to revive his religion was to give it life from the dead, in a similar manner to the revival of the beast. Death and revival for the Beast; here death and revival of the church.

3. Paul said "Awake thou that sleepest and arise from the dead and Christ shall give thee light." Death is often applied to a *cause*, as well as to *individuals*, (always, of course), in a figurative sense. The church at

Sardis had a name to live but was dead. (Rev. 3:1). It could arise from the dead.

4.   Paul in (Rom. 11:15) says of the Jews, "For if the casting away of them be the reconciling of the world, what shall the receiving of them be but *life* from the *dead*?" He did not mean to say that portion of the nation that is actually dead will arise from their graves, but they are a spiritually dead nation, and for them to turn to God would be a national, spiritual resurrection.

5.   John was following closely the teaching of (Ezek. 37) where he predicted the return of fleshly Israel from *literal* Babylon under the *symbol* of *resurrection*. The likeness is indeed striking in (Ezek. 37) and (Rev. 20). One fleshly Israel, the other spiritual Israel; the first was delivered from Babylon as a nation, and this was pictured as a resurrection; the latter was delivered from "Mystery Babylon," and exalted, and this is a resurrection:—One is as justly and beautifully pictured as a resurrection as the other.

If Ezekiel (37) is an appropriate use of resurrection from *graves* of *bodies that were dismembered*, all simply to illustrate the revival of the *typical* kingdom of Israel from Babylon, is it not an appropriate use of such a metaphor to speak of the revival of the *spiritual* kingdom of God under the *same* figure? No one can deny that inspired men used the figure of rising from the dead as applied to men whose literal resurrection was not meant. It is not that we are forcing a new meaning to a word, thus to apply it; the only question is as to which of the meanings belongs here. In (Eek. 37) the figurative meaning is now plain, because the event is so remote. But I seek to show that figurative resurrection is the only possible view that fits all the Scriptures cited, for there is a time coming when all the figurative resurrections are past and only the literal is possible; but death is the *last* enemy destroyed, and certainly there were enemies after this First resurrection. I cite the facts revealed that we may see that literalism breaks down here. John *saw* the angel, the chain, the binding of the Dragon, the sealed pit and so on. Did he see these things in fact? or in figure? If in fact, then that is the way the devil will be caught, chained and sealed up, for a literal thousand years; there will be a literal resurrection of the wicked, a literal gathering of the wicked against a literal camp of saints and a literal city. If figurative, these agents, actions and results are symbols of agents, actions and results, which I think is shown to a demonstration.

6. Ezekiel even saw the *bones* of Israel in a *valley*; and the *bones* had to come together, be clothed with flesh and skin and have life from God breathed into them. So, in fact, he entered into details of a bodily resurrection, all the time using the transaction figuratively. John says nothing of bodies being raised, but even if he did, his language would be no stronger than Ezekiel's, because he brings Israel out of their graves; when in fact, the actually dead have never been subject to any such marvellous change. He believed in a literal resurrection. and chose that great event to explain to Israel their revival as a nation. Strange, too, that John used his figure of women representing the faithful and unfaithful wives; God married to fleshly Israel; Jesus married to spiritual Israel, both illustrative but not literal in either case. The women represented governments in their relationship to God.

A CRITICAL VIEW.

There is a resurrection that precedes that thousand years; another suceeds it; and still another comes after Satan has been loosed a "little season." There are two births, two marriages, two circumcisions and two resurrections, one literal, the other figurative in the Bible. There were two Elijahs, one the literal man, the other foretold under his name. There were two Babylons, one literal, the other figurative. There were two Egypts; two Sodoms; two Jerusalems; two Israels; two Davids, one to rule fleshly Israel; one to rule spiritual Israel in the spiritual Jerusalem, from the spiritual Mount Zion. There were two covenants, one sanctified by animal sacrifice, the other by the blood of the Lamb of God. There are two Canaans. The reader should remember that only Millennialists, who mix the law and the gospel, the types and anti-types, feel any need of a literal resurrection here. Their carnal system demands it. They wish to have all the countless righteous dead to return to earth to carry forward the Millennium. I have shown that the temple is *legislated* away, with its priesthood, its animal sacrifices, its feasts, fasts, and old order entire, never to be revived. You have not forgotten, that I showed the moral and spiritual impossibility of Christ coming to begin the Millennium, as follows:

1. The types are, by divine authority, set aside forever by the things which they typified, among these the literal throne of David, for the spiritual throne of Christ. Can you conceive how Christ could be a local Ruler in Jerusalem as David was and not have exchanged heaven for earth? Did not David reign with God, over Israel, while God was in heaven? Can not we reign with Christ as a kingdom of priests, without either God or Christ on earth? Did not Jesus ascend to heaven to reign? He is upon a throne. Do not Paul, and the martyred apostles, rule the church of God today? Is there not a kingdom over which Jesus is king, and did not they preach this kingdom of God? When that rule was set aside by false apostles, false priests, during the dark ages, their rule was ignored. But upon the death of these organized beasts or persecuting governments, is it not plain that, when John saw thrones he saw the truth of heaven triumphant? The chain and pit represent degredation, for one class; the thrones represent exaltation for the other class; but one a thousand years before the other, and the latter a "little season" before the resurrection.

I insist that the resurrection that opens the thousand years is of the *same nature* as the one that closes the (1000) years. And, bear in mind that, the last is followed by a "little season" which may be centuries, and this "little season" is closed by the resurrection which can not be other than the one literal resurrection of all the dead as *death* and *hades* give up their dead, also the sea and they that are in it and each is judged and sentenced. If death and hades had given up the righteous dead at the opening and the wicked at the close of the (1000) years, they could not have them to give up at the close of the "little season." As these (death and *hades*) were destroyed we are sure it was the coming of Christ and the end of the world, for death is the last enemy to be destroyed.

2. The annual Feasts of the Law, two of them, The Passover and Pentecost, typified Christ's death and resurrection, (that is his resurrection was typified by the wave-sheaf), and Pentecost typified the *opening*, formally, of the gospel age; the Feast of Tabernacles its close. There is not even a remote hint of a resurrection of saints and a Millennium in them.

3. I showed that the Jubilee year, like the day of Pentecost, was the fiftieth, not the forty-ninth, and began an eighth week and did *not* conclude *a seventh*. So Mr. Russell's theory is (1000) years too early for either Pentecost or Jubilee to typify it. But Jubilee is on the *eighth* week, after seven complete, and can not fit any theory that makes the *seventh* day, or seventh week of days, or seventh week of years, a Millennium.

4. I dropped down to the New Testament and showed conclusively that the theory contradicts every one of our Lord's parables, and is, therefore, false. The net was cast into the sea but *once*; there was *one* sowing of the field; but *one* harvest of the wheat and tares; but *one* reckoning with the servants who had the talents and pounds; but *one* marriage of the king's son; but *one* separation of the virgins, and so on. It is positively impossible to have any probation in any parable, after Jesus comes. The parables were made by the King of the Kingdom of heaven to teach us *what the kingdom is like*. It certainly is not like Millennialism—that has Jesus come soon and begin a different kind of a kingdom, from that these parables have illustrated for nineteen centuries; and which Jesus said was "at hand," and which began formally on Pentecost (Acts 2) *according to the type* and the *prophecies* (Is. 2; Micah 4). Jesus illustrated but *one* kingdom.

5. One might hesitate, at least, in deciding whether the "first resurrection" were literal or figurative, if shut up to this passage alone. But when one sees that Jesus knew whether he would return to raise the dead and reign with them on earth (1000 years) or not; and God knew when he gave the types, and we go to these types and search these parables, and find the doctrine *contradicted*, we know to a moral certainty, the figurative interpretation is correct.

ANOTHER CLASS OF EXPOSITORS.

Some few expositors say, yes you are correct that Jesus does not come to earth to reign, but he raises the righteous dead, at least the martyrs, and they reign with him in heaven for (1000) years. I will show that this contradicts the Bible. Any interpretation that has the dead literally raised before the end of the world contradicts the Bible.

"But man dieth and wasteth away; yea, man giveth up the ghost and where is he? As the waters fail from the sea, and the flood decayeth and drieth up: *So man lieth down, and riseth not: till the heavens be no more, they shall not awake nor be raised out of sleep,*" (Job 14:10-12).

There is the millstone around the neck of Millennialism that drowns it in the deep. Where is Mr. Russell's theory that says the dead *have been raised out of sleep thirty-six years?* Where is the theory that says *part* of the dead shall rise at the Millennium and reign somewhere for a thousand years? James says *Job was a prophet* (Jas. 5:10-11). Job says *"man,"* (not most men, or all but the martyrs), but *"man lieth down, and riseth not; till the heavens be no more, they shall not awake nor be raised out of sleep."* Do you believe the prophet? There is positively no room for "Pastor Russell's" bride class, feet or head members, to *rise out of sleep or be awakened* in either the spring or fall of (A. D. 1878), or at any other time till the heavens *be no more.* When is that?

John tells us (Rev. 20:11-15). This is the resurrection and Judgment. Peter tells us "the heavens shall pass away with a great noise," (II Pet. 3:10).

"Blessed and holy is he that hath part in the first resurrection; over these the second death hath no power; but they shall be priests of God and Christ and shall reign with him a thousand years." They are priests of God as well as of Christ. God does not come to earth, to reign with them in this or any other text. Does Jesus? Ancient Israel was a kingdom of priests and an holy nation" (Ex. 19:6). Peter said the church was an holy priesthood to offer up spiritual sacrifices acceptable to God by Jesus Christ. He said further the church was in his days "a royal priesthood, an holy nation"—not that in some far away Millennium they might be both kings and priests, (I Pet. 2:5-9). John said Christ "hath made us kings and priests unto God and his Father; to him be glory and dominion forever and ever. Amen." In (chap. 5:10), "And hast made us unto our God kings and priests; and we shall reign on the earth," (Or Revised V), "And madest them to be unto our God a kingdom and priests; and they reign upon the earth." So to be a kingdom and priests and reign with Christ is no greater honor after the "first resurrection," than was enjoyed by the church in Peter's day, before the "first resurrection," according to these plain Scriptures. I have showed the second death hath no power over any true disciple of Christ, *who lives in any age of the church* (Jno. 6:49-50), as well as the |whole discourse. But it was a blessed privilege to revive the cause of Christ on earth, when the beast, false prophet and dragon had slain the witnesses, or killed the institution, as it were, and it required the zeal, heroism, faith, self-denial, or in a word, holiness, without which no man shall see the Lord, to revive the church of God. It demanded the martyr spirit, and many martyrs fell in the holy attempt. But, they had the assurance that death only affected their bodies, and could not reach the soul. (Matt. 10:28).

THE RESURRECTIONS.

There is one resurrection at the beginning, another at the close, of the (1000) years. The first included no wicked; the second included no righteous. If the first is literal; so is the second. But I have showed that the resurrection is *when the heavens are no more.* So resurrection is used here in both cases figuratively. The two **resurrections** are (1000) years apart. The devil is **bound** (1000) years. He is sealed up in the abyss the same (1000) years. He can not *deceive* the *nations* for (1000) **years.** The *nations* are still here; and at the expiration of the (1000) years the nations are still in the four quarters of the earth. This spoils the whole theory in another feature, (especially Dawnism), that the nations are to be annihilated and the kingdom of Christ alone survives. The facts in (ch. 19) of the *taking* of the beast and false prophet, and *killing with the sword that came out of the mouth of the Rider on the white horse,* the kings of the **earth** and their armies, are related, as cause and effect, to the events in the opening of (ch. 20), or the binding and imprisonment of the dragon. What *sort of death* will the word of God produce? The kings and armies were *killed by it.* It has been killing kingcraft and priest-craft, and destroying the armies of these once triumphant despotisms. Kings are all virtually dead now. The present war is confidently predicted by many statesman to be the death of despotic rule. I am not so sanguine as this exact date would demand. I believe the *Time*-prophecies have a very narrow margin to be filled yet, and rejoice in the consoling fact. But this seems plain to me; when king-craft and priest-craft are slain, and the dragon can no more deceive the nations, there is a long period, wherein the devil is bound, no longer rules as of yore, in idolatrous, persecuting nations and Christ and his people are loosed, so to speak, and reign. The nations through whom the beast, the false prophet and the dragon ruled, are slain, and these leaders in crime are helpless. The governments die to that order of things; the truth concerning civil and religious liberty slays them. Their existence is not disturbed, but their ignorance, superstitions, veneration for kings ruling by divine right, and slavish fear of pope and priests, have been killed by the Word of God. This we know to be the present day facts, and the sentiment is growing more and more intense, and, I believe it to be the sentiment of these verses. Hence the saints take the kingdom, not by violence, or bloodshed, not by a series of miracles the most wonderful in all earth's long history; neither by *giving up* the church, the Bible, the present kingdom; and by Christ and the holy dead returning to earth, either visibly or invisibly, either in spirit-bodies or spiritual bodies, to inaugurate and conduct a Millennial Kingdom; but the *word of God* in its present form wins the victory. Strange indeed, when Jesus has popery, Mahometanism and despotism so nearly destroyed, and has the Bible today printed and sown broadcast winning its silent way to the very innermost thoughts of millions of our race, and working the mightiest changes in men and nations, if Jesus should call a halt, and come down to earth himself, with all the holy angels, and countless righteous dead, to give the church what is all but achieved, or the indirect control of nations.

You have not forgotten the symbols in (ch. 12) where the woman gives birth to a man-child who rules all nations with a rod of iron. It is not the church, but it is through the ministry of the church, that this sovereignty comes. The church gives birth to the man-child, and he, not she, rules the nations. There is no fifth monarchy features in the symbols, or the church alone or kingdom alone, ruling. Hence to read into (Rev. 20) what contradicts (Rev. 12), is like contradicting (Job 14:10-12); except one is symbolic, the other, literal. Again I remind you that the symbols in (Dan. 7) of the Son of Man in the clouds of heaven represent him as *coming to God* and not coming *from God* to receive his kingdom. The fact that man does not rise, and is not awakened out of sleep till the heavens be no more, is proof that this is not the second coming of Christ, for at his coming:

1. All the saints are with him. (I Thess. 3:13); them that sleep in Jesus will God bring with him; (not a part of them that sleep in Jesus, but all of them) (I Thess. 4:14). "For as in Adam *all* die, *even so* in Christ shall *all* be made alive. But every man in his own order: Christ the first fruits; then they that are Christ's at his coming. Then cometh the end, when he shall have delivered up the kingdom to God, even the Father; when he shall have put down all rule and all authority and power. For he must reign till he hath put all enemies under his feet. The last enemy that shall be destroyed is death." (I Cor. 15:22-26). Briefly, at present, it is plain that:

Jesus is the first fruits; The harvest is at his coming. But Millennialists say Yes, harvest of the righteous, then, (1000) years later, the end, and the wicked raised. This will not do for the following reasons:

(Is. 25:8; Hosea 13:14) are quoted by the apostle, at the conclusion of his argument (vs. 54-57), and he tells us *"death is* swallowed up in victory," *at the time* the *righteous* become immortal and incorruptible. *The last enemy is destroyed then.* Jesus must reign, (not in some new kingdom yet to be inaugurated), but as he has reigned, until the resurrection, until our enemies are destroyed, and the last one is death; and this is fulfilled *when our mortality puts on immortality.* Thus Paul groups *three inspired witnesses* (Isaiah, Hosea and himself) on this point, and informs us *when death is destroyed,* (See Rev. 20:12-14).

2. The living righteous are all to be changed at the same time, in a moment. (I Cor. 15:51-52; I Thess. 4:17). The apostle shows in the latter passage the order of the change; resurrection first, change of the living righteous last. The Millennialists tell us the saints shall rise first, at his coming; the wicked at the end of the (1000) years; and apply the word "first" to resurrections. I request the reader to notice the context, and read (I Thess. 4:11-18; 5:4-11) and see the day of the Lord cometh as a thief in the night, (finding the wicked unprepared); the righteous, children of light, prepared. The wicked are involved in destruction. Then turn to his next letter to these brethren (as part of this teaching was not understood then, and is not now, without this teaching). "Seeing it is a righteous thing with God to recompense tribulation, to them that trouble you; and to you who are troubled, rest with us, WHEN THE LORD JESUS SHALL BE REVEALED FROM HEAVEN WITH HIS MIGHTY ANGELS, in flaming fire taking vengeance on them that know not God, and that obey not the gospel of our Lord Jesus Christ; who shall be punished with everlasting destruction from the presence of the Lord, and from the glory of his power; *when he shall come* to be *glorified in his saints, and to be admired in* ALL *them that believe,* (because our testimony among you was believed), in that day, (II Thess. 1:6-10).

This text throws light back on the preceding letter. Put the two passages together, both written by the same inspired man to the same congregation, and they show that Jesus will be revealed from heaven with his mighty angels, with all his resurrected saints, and changed living saints; that the day will find the wicked unprepared, that the destruction comes *suddenly,* (as in the Flood and the destruction of Sodom which the Lord cites as like it, (Luke 17:24-30); *then* the wicked and disobedient shall be punished, the righteous admire him; (and while they are *forever with* the Lord, the wicked are punished with *everlasting* destruction *from* the *presence* of his power). "For the Son of Man shall come in the glory of his Father with the holy angels; and *then* he shall reward *every* man according to his works." (Matt. 16:27). So of (II Cor. 5:10; Rom. 14:10; Matt. 25:31; Rev. 20:11-15).

Jesus said "My kingdom is not of this world," (Jno. 18:36). "The kingdom of God cometh not with observation; neither shall they say, lo, here! or lo, there! for behold, the kingdom of God is within you." (Luke 17:20-21). In (Mark 9:1) Jesus said some that stood with him should not taste of death till they had seen the kingdom of God come with power. I believe it came with power on Pentecost. It came with power during the life-time of the apostles, and it is shocking to hear men affirm that the kingdom is not yet set up. It was *kingdom, kingdom, kingdom*, with Jesus and the apostles. It was kingdom in all the parables. It was "the kingdom of heaven is *at hand*" with the Baptist, Jesus, the twelve and the seventy. The *church* was never mentioned by either Mark, Luke or *John* in their histories of Christ's teaching. Mathew mentions the church three times, (16:18; 18:17). And yet Millennialists tell us, "The Kingdom has not come." This makes the Baptist, Jesus, the twelve and the seventy to preach "The Kingdom of heaven is at hand," when it was *nineteen centuries* distant. It makes the promise to the apostles of receiving the power "to bind" and " to loose" like this;—"Some two thousand years from now, I will return in my kingdom, which I will then set up, and *then* you shall bind and loose." "Ye are they which have continued with me in my temptations; and I appoint unto you a kingdom, as my Father hath appointed unto me; that ye may eat and drink at my table in my kingdom and sit upon thrones Judging the twelve tribes of Israel, (Luke 22: 28-30). Did you never sit at the Lord's table in his kingdom. (I Cor. 10:21)? Do you eat the Lord's supper, (ch. 11:17-34)?

The Colossians were in the kingdom of God, (Col. 1:13). John was in the kingdom of God, (Rev. 1:9). Was all the teaching of Christ, all his promises of the kingdom, repeated by the apostles, preached and advocated by a multitude, who never saw the kingdom? which is not even now in being? Was it all a kingdom to be reigned over by some saints who have to rise from the dead to begin it at the Millennium? How does Jesus "sup" with his disciples *now*? (Rev. 3:20). Jesus says four times in one speech to his disciples, "I will raise him up at the *last day*," (Jno. 6:39, 40, 44, 54).

THE MILLENNIUM IS NOT THE LAST DAY, EVEN CONCEDING ALL MILLENNIALISTS ASK AS TO ITS LENGTH, (1000 YEARS), FOR IT IS FOLLOWED BY A "LITTLE SEASON." AS IT CAN NOT BE THE LAST DAY, IT IS NOT THE RESURRECTION DAY, THE DAY WHEN JESUS WILL RAISE HIS DISCIPLES—ALL OF WHICH SHOWS THE FIRST RESURRECTION IS FIGURATIVE AND NOT THE RESURRECTION JESUS PROMISED FOUR TIMES IN ONE SPEECH.

"Marvel not at this: for the hour is coming in the which all that are in the graves shall hear his voice and come forth they that have done good to the resurrection of life; and they that have done evil unto the resurrection of damnation," (Jno. 5:28-29). How long is that *hour*? Millennialists say (1000) years. The voice is linked with a trumpet-blast (I Cor. 15:52; I Thess. 4:16). Quite a protracted shout and blast! Seems the wicked heard it at the *end* of the (1000) years; but it ceased before the "little season" began, and before the heaven fled away. Their theory demands two shouts and two blasts of the trumpet. If this hour is (1000) years long, how long is the moment (I Cor. 15:52)? The shout begins the (1000) years with the resurrection of the Just. (Luke 14:14; Acts 24:15); ends with the unjust at its close. God sends rain on the just and upon the unjust, *at the same hour*. That is, it rains on just and unjust, but the same rain; it does not rain on the just then, later, on the unjust. The *event* is *one*.

In (Heb. 11:35; Luke 20:36; Acts 24:15; Phil 3: 11) it is the *nature* of the resurrection, not the *time* of it, that is insisted upon. There is nothing distinctive in *time* in (Phil. 3:11). The resurrection of the just has great distinction of *nature*, but not in *time*. The *"from the dead"* statement Millennialists apply to the righteous and *"of the dead,"* (1000) years later. A resurrection *of* the dead, is *from* the dead; and the expression *"of the dead"* is used (I Cor. 15:21, 42) *and applied to the saints.* This, therefore, is a distinction without a difference. They would have the *saints raised* from *among* the dead; and, (1000) years later, these *wicked* raised but only a resurrection *"of* the dead." But these texts show that the distinction is not there, because the resurrection *of the saints* to *immortality* is expressed by the phrase they depend on to *postpone* the resurrection of the wicked another (1000) years. Whereas the glory of the resurrection is to have our vile bodies changed, (not exchanged), and fashioned like unto his glorious body, (Phil. 3:21). (Eph. 1:15-23) shows what the distinction is in the resurrection; it is not to be before others in *time*, but in the *nature* and glory of the *event* to the righteous.

A MORAL DEMONSTRATION.

1. Job says man is not raised nor awaked out of sleep till the heavens be no more, (Job. 14:12). John says earth and heaven fled away *at the resurrection*, (which Millennialists have to admit is literal and final after the thousand years, and after the "little season" following the thousand years); therefore, man does not arise, (resurrect) or awake out of sleep, (the sleep of death), at the "First resurrection," (Rev. 20:11-15).

2. The righteous dead are all raised, the living saints all changed, *at Jesus' coming*; (Zech. 14:5; I Thess. 4:8; I Cor. 15:51; I Thess. 3:13; Jude 14, 15; Matt. 16:27).

3. The wicked are all raised and judged at the same time, as the righteous. This is shown in all the literal predictions of the events, (Jno. 5:28, 29; II Thess. 1:6-10; Jude 14, 15; Rev. 20:11-15; Matt. 25:31-46). It is shown in each of the Parables where the reckoning is made with *all* at the *same time*. To stretch that reckoning over a thousand years, in order to make it a *trial* and not a *sentence*, destroys the sense of every parable, because the *trial ends* and sentence is given when *separation takes place* which is *at the coming of Christ*.

4. The (1000) years opens and closes with a resurrection, each of which is figurative, because, further, the wicked dead lived *before* the "little season" of Satan's

release. As the First resurrection was before the (1000) years, the second *at its close*, and before the "little season"; and the "little season" is *followed* by a *literal* resurrection at the consummation of the ages, or end of the world, it is demonstrably true that the *first* and *second* were figurative, as the parables do not end with them, and the earth and heaven do not pass away, as they are to do when men arise and are awaked out of sleep.

5. The *nations* were in the four quarters of the earth, the wicked as numerous as the sands of the sea, at the *close* of the (1000) years, when the dragon is released for a 'little season." How long is that? The "little while" (Hag. 2:6) was five centuries; the little season (Rev. 6:11) was many centuries. The rising of the righteous at the opening of the (1000 years); and the rising of the wicked at its close, as numerous as the sand of the sea, indicate success of their respective causes; the church for (1000) years, the wicked for "a little season," how long not defined; and closing in widespread wickedness and opposition to the church, (as all the literal prophecies foretell), as when the Lord comes, the resurrection and judgment follow, he finds wickedness as in the days of Noah and of Sodom.

Ezekiel used this figure to illustrate the revival of his nation from Babylon five centuries before Christ came; Paul used the figure to represent the conversion of the same nation; John used it to show the suppression and later exaltation of the witnesses; he also pictured the beast, (government), as mortally wounded, and lived; the saints are finally shown as killed and resurrected; and the wicked dead as killed, and, (1000) years later, resurrected; then *follows all this* with the *literal* resurrection, right where Job, Paul, Christ and all the inspired writers place it, at the end of the world, when the heaven and earth pass away; where the ordinances all end; and where probation ends.

As Ezekiel's figurative resurrection of the nation from captivity in Babylon was five centuries before the first coming of Christ; John's figurative resurrection is (1000) years, plus the "little season," before Christ's second coming to immortalize his saints and punish the wicked. This leaves out all the mysterious, stupendous changes demanded by Millennialists; harmonizes all the scriptures on the subject; and leaves the church as the pillar and support of the truth, and the gospel the power of God unto salvation to every one that believeth.

The Parables were all given by the King of the Kingdom, now in power, to illustrate its nature, progress, growth, maturity and close on earth; and not an imagined Millennial kingdom not yet in being. The Jews rejected him because his kingdom did not have the literal David, Temple, Priest-hood, sacrifices and temporal rewards of their then existing kingdom. The Millennialists are Judaizers in hoping for a restoration of these things which were set aside by divine legislation. Take the Judaism out of their theory and they have nothing left but the kingdom of God as it is and will continue to be in law and ordinances to the end of time.

CHAPTER XLVI.

THE MILLENNIUM.

In John's symbols, after the two-horned, dragon-lamb was introduced, (13:11) you notice "the Beast, his Image and the mark of the beast" are associated together. They constitute Babylon—confusion—and as the Beast, Image and Mark were SIGNS, not realities in nature, we should learn what they signify. See the grouping in (13:14-17; 14:9-11; 15:2; 16:2; 19:20; 20:4). It is the "Overcomers" who are blessed. In the last instance, the federation is dissolved and the saints are victorious. I have said much concerning "the rest of the dead living not again until the thousand years are finished." I did this, not because I believe the first resurrection is literal, or this one at the end of the (1000) years is literal; but rather to show, to the humblest understanding, that second chanceism is wrong. Thus, after one has assumed the first resurrection is *literal* at the opening of the thousand years, it necessarily follows that the living again of the rest of the dead at the close of the thousand years is literal (in such theory) and this forever nullifies second chanceism, because the latter dead were *not living again during the thousand years.*

But it is just as evident that the first and second resurrections are figurative because they are alike, one of the righteous, the other of the wicked, and they a (1000) years apart and the one at the close of the (1000) years is *before* the "little season," and this little season *ends* with the one and only literal resurrection predicted by Christ and his apostles, and includes all classes. We might notice briefly, in this concluding chapter, that the threatened *fire* to consume the earth and elements, when the Lord comes, makes it impossible to have this Judaistic Millennium.

In (I Pet. 3) the apostle closed his inspired warnings against sin. He cited the Flood in Noah's day. It *destroyed* the world. Peter says the fire is stored up to *destroy* it again. It is not a mild, metaphorical, gospel fire, but it destroys the earth and consumes the elements at the *perdition,* (not the salvation) of ungodly men. Our Savior gave the same warning (Luke 17:26-27). Paul cited this case and says Noah condemned the world (Heb. 11:7). Surely these holy writers did not cite a case of damnation to predict salvation. Noah and the Flood were the nearest parallel to the universal destruction by fire impending over our world, to be executed when the Lord is revealed. These warnings will be unheeded, as the former were, but *destruction,* not salvation, follows. Fire is sometimes used as a metaphor; so is water. But Noah's Ark was not a metaphor. The billows of death that rolled twenty-two and a half feet deep over the summits of the mountains were not waves of salvation to impenitent sinners; and it is plain to the mind of any one (except one seeking to bolster up a theory at any hazard) that Jesus, Paul and Peter were not alluding to the doom of the old world to foretell that Millennial fire will purify society. "Do not live as they did in Noah's day, and knew not till the flood came and swept them all away; for if you do, the Son of man will come upon you unawares, and so deluge the earth with Millennial fire that none of you can possibly escape, but all will be converted;" this makes mockery out of the most terrible realities of Judgment. In one case is the historic flood; in the other the prophetic doom of an impenitent, sinful world. The reader sees how the Millennial theory wrests this text. 1. It makes it a metaphorical, saving fire. 2. It is all at the end of the gospel age *leaving absolutely* no destruction foretold for the *end of time*. This is the way Millennialists *picture* a Millennium. They fulfill *all* the promises of resurrection of the Just at the opening of the Millennium, leaving not one for the close. They make the Parables to end, as well as the gospel age and all the commands and ordinances peculiar to it. They unhinge creation and revelation, and have everything made over. The earth becomes a garden of Eden physically; the beasts are changed; the wicked are practically all converted; the righteous dead come back to earth; the Lord returns in person; and miracles are the everyday rule for a (1000) years. As so much has been said about this (1000) years, and Millennialists who find metaphorical fire in (I Pet. 3) find the proof of the "day of Jehovah" being (1000) years long, we may consider it, also, and learn there is no proof of that (but the opposite) in this text.

A THOUSAND YEARS.

"But beloved, be not ignorant of this one thing, that one day is with the Lord as a thousand years and a thousand years as one day." (ver. 8). "For a thousand years in thy sight are but as yesterday when it is past, and as a watch in the night." (Ps. 90:4). You observe the similarity in these texts. Neither text says God's days are (1000) years in length. The Psalmist was showing God is from everlasting to everlasting. He considers him as the eternal One, contrasted with man whose days are three score years and ten. So one thousand years taken from God's eternity of being is as yesterday, or less, even "a watch in the night," some three hours. What yesterday, or a watch in the night, is to man's lifetime, one thousand years are to God—a very short time. They certainly did not mean to teach that each creative day was either historically or prophetically one thousand years long. When Peter used the language he was not predicting the length of time the *Judgment* would last, or a Millennium; but rather, that the long slumbering wrath of God would overtake sinners. The scoffers doubted and denied it. They saw no signs of it.

"But the day of the Lord will come as a thief in the night; in the which the heavens shall pass away with a great noise, and the elements shall melt with fervent heat, the earth also and the works that are therein shall be burned up."

So what appears to men a long time, and as slackness (because God is long-suffering to usward, not willing that any should perish but that all should come to repentance) is misunderstood and abused to their final destruction. It seems to you as though it were a long time back to Christ; and, measured by your life-time on earth, it is; but, measured by God's life-time in heaven, it is as a day is to you or shorter still, a watch in the night. I hope you notice the reason Christ does not come sooner, he is not anxious to destroy men; he is long-suffering, not willing that any should perish, but that all should come to repentance. If he was to come to institute a thousand year millennium, one might think, How long, O Lord, how long!

He was cautioning men not to think the Lord had delayed his coming because it was long to us after he promised it; but to live in view of it and all its blessings to the righteous, and terrors for the wicked; and to *count God's time*, of a thousand years, as you would man's by a day or a watch in the night, a brief time. For he exists on and on, from Adam to Abraham; thence to Moses; to David; to Christ; to the end of time, and of the earth and all things therein. As the Psalmist looked *backward* to the eternity before ever God had formed the earth and the world, so the apostle looked forward to when they shall all pass away, and both say one day is with the Lord as a thousand years, and the Psalmist adds, "as a watch in the night." This shows us he was not *giving a rule to measure God's days* and call his day (1000) years long, because a watch in the night is not a measure for God's day of equal length. I have as much right to say "a watch in the night" is a literal thousand years, as to say, one day is a thousand years. Neither writer says a day is a thousand years with the Lord, but both say,

"*As* a thousand years." It is God's continued Being and our scenes of time contrasted with it. We are but for a moment; He is the Ancient of days. It is a strange and vain conceit that would make "one day is with the Lord a thousand years," when neither writer says that. It is to lose what they *did* say to give the texts that meaning. It was to impress us with his vastness, his unending Being, how brief were a thousand years to him, so that we should not be impatient after centuries upon centuries for Christ to come; or should profanely conclude he was not coming, because generation after generation of men came and went. Remember God's eternity of Being, that he is from everlasting to everlasting God; that a *thousand* years are in His sight but *as yesterday*, when it is passed, *as a watch in the night*. This statement, "As a watch in the night," shows that the inspired writer was not giving a rule to measure God's days, for that would make three hours the measure of a thousand years.

OUR SAVIOR'S RESURRECTION.

Reference has been made heretofore to the fact that the Shakers' and Mr. Russell's teaching concerning our Lord's resurrection are similar. In "The Time is at Hand," the writer devotes (70) pages to "The manner of our Lord's return and appearing." He, like Mrs. Ann Lee (who professed to be the female Christ returned to earth in (A. D. 1770) tries to explain away all literalities in our Lord's resurrection; makes his coming as a thief an invisible presence; the clouds in which he comes; his visibility to the natural eye; the lightning; and the great shout; all this is passed or is passing daily. Mrs. Lee wished to represent Jesus as a spirit, so she could be Christ; Mr. Russell would have Jesus and the saints here in spirit-bodies, but invisible, so as to carry out his Millennial program. But, one hour in the New Testament, ought to show any one that Jesus arose and was identified in his pierced body. He showed his hands and side as *testimony* to the apostles, on the day he arose from the dead, also eight days later. He had said destroy this temple and in three days I will raise it up. He spake of his body. He ate and drank in that wounded and mangled body after death was conquered. His flesh saw no corruption. He had flesh and bones; a spirit has not. The fact is all was normal and natural, as much so as was Lazarus who ate with the disciples, or as was the Ruler's daughter. Mary did not recognize him, for it was dark. The disciples at Lake Galilee did not recognize him at once in the dawn, as they were in their boats out on the lake. The two disciples did not recognize him for *their eyes* were *holden*. But Jesus walking upon the water, or escaping from the mob at Nazareth, or Transfigured, was just as much a *mystery* as he was *after* his *resurrection*. His entrance into the room where the doors were shut, was like Peter's going out of a prison when the doors were shut, or the other apostles whom an angel delivered, and the officers found the doors shut with all safety; or like Paul and Silas in the Philippian Jail. Jesus in a flesh and bones body did not go through a material door. This would have made the identification of his pierced body impossible. It was as easy for him to open the locked door in the evening, as to open the sealed tomb in the morning, of that glorious day. He did not go through the walls of the sepulcher, but opened the door, just as the doors were opened on the other occasions. It was not natural; but was a surprise and the wonderful fact of his resurrection that made the disciples think he was a spirit, just as they thought later when Peter was delivered from prison, or before when Jesus walked on the water. He arose from the dead—all of him that was dead, his body and it *was not* invisible. It was not invisible when he ascended to heaven. The disciples *watched him*, as he went up; they gazed on him; and a *cloud* received *him* out of their *sight*. So he is to come again. The cloud, the angels, the shout, the voice of the archangel, the resurrected family of man, the glorious son of man in the plenitude of power, the final judgment and eternal destiny of the human race are before us. These things did not all pass by invisibly and inaudibly in the fanaticism of Mrs. Ann Lee and her followers in (A. D. 1770). Neither have any of them passed in the days of Mr. C. T. Russell and his desperate attempts to explain them all away. These writers were aware their theories are lifeless without they can explain away the literal, bodily resurrection of Christ; the bodily resurrection of the saints at the Lord's coming; and could explain away the literal fire in (II Pet 3) which consumes the earth and the works therein at the Lord's coming; and, hence, the wild dreams that all is past, or passing. I have shown that the Bible uses figures and symbols and have sought to show *why* they are used. The *Types* were not typical of themselves; but of the gospel, hence we now have the fulfillment of the Types and, necessarily of the Type-Prophecies. But there is an end for all these things, too, and Jesus has promised to come again, at the end of time, end of the world, end of probation, and then the redeemed of earth shall awaken in his likeness, and the fearful and unbelieving and reprobate of earth shall be cast off forever. The exhortation and warning are, "Blessed are they that do his commandments, that they may have right to the tree of life, and may enter in through the gates into the city. For without are dogs and sorcerers, and whoremongers, and murderers, and idolaters, and whosover loveth and maketh a lie. I, Jesus, have sent mine angel to testify unto you these things in the churches. I am the root and the offspring of David, and the bright and morning star." (Rev. 22:14-16).

CHAPTER XLVII.

BRIEF REVIEW OF J. A. BATTENFIELD.

Mr. Battenfield of the Christian Church, has written a series of articles for the Christian Standard, (since published in book form), running from (Oct. 18, 1913, to Sep. 1914). My quotations and citations are chiefly by reference to the pages of that Journal. He holds to the year-day theory; counts (2520) years from Jehoiakim's captivity (607 B. C.) to (Oct. 10, 1914), as the end of the symbolic week; just as Mr. Russell does. Another great defect of his, (in common with Mr. Russell and many other Millennialists), is that he attempts to set the exact year and day of events. This one fact alone stamps all such productions as speculations pure and simple. He sets the exact day when the (2520) years expired (Oct. 10, 1913; and April 14, or Passover, 1914). It is just the same with the Millennium date, counting (2300) years from (328 B. C. to 1972). My space is limited and I can only examine Mr. B's production in some of its fundamental errors to show how dangerous it is to follow such speculators. If either his or Mr. Russell's theory was correct we could know the exact day when all the martyrs are to be resurrected and the Millennium begin. One has Millennial fever bad enough when he can assume to know to a year, month and a day, when Paul, Peter, Daniel and all the martyrs are to return to this earth; or when he can tell, (58) years beforehand, not only when the martyrs will come back to begin their thousand year term of office in the governments of the world; but also can tell what is to take place in every year from (Oct. 11, 1913) till (1972).

Mr. Russell grouped his guesses around (1874); Mr. B. groups his romance around (1972); Mr. Miller thought (1844) was the proper date; and others have selected other dates with the same degree of confidence only to be defeated in the end. All such calculations grow out of the notion that there is one certain date to begin the Millennium. Mr. Battenfield's production is given the name "The Great Demonstration." For brevity, I shall sometimes call it the Demonstration; and allude to the author as Mr. B. You will learn as we proceed that neither the name nor the contents of these articles is inspired, although they are quite pretentious. What I have to say will be given under seven headings, and is to suggest the visionary nature of the work. 1. Battenfield's assumptions. 2. Battenfield a prophet. 3. Battenfield's violation of Ezekiel's year-day rule. 4. The Three Couplets in Daniel. 5. Ezekiel rescued from his perverters. 6. Reasoning by analogy. 7. Revelation versus imagination.

BATTENFIELD'S ASSUMPTIONS.

The Demonstration is erected on three assumptions:

1.   That the (7000th) year of the world is to be a Millennium of righteousness.

2.   That the Kingdom of Christ is to be the only Kingdom on earth during that period, and that the resurrected martyrs are to conduct it.

3.   That (1973) is the first year of the (1000) years of peace.

It is sufficient, at present, to cite the diagrams, pages 408-409; 456-7; 552-3; 600-1).

If the reader is familiar with the arguments of this volume he will detect at once the folly of such theorizing. Mr. Russell says (6000) years from creation ended (Oct. 10, 1874). Mr. Battenfield says they end (Oct. 10, 1972). Can both be right? If Mr. B. is right, then Mr. R's. whole scheme is wrong; and *vice-versa*. All the arguments used heretofore, to show how unreliable other Millennialists have been, in setting *one particular date* for the beginning of the Millennium, apply to the Demonstration. Bengel and Wesley failed in (1836); Miller, Cunninghame and Habershon failed in (1843); Joseph Wolff failed in (1847); J. C. Shimeall failed in (1868); C. T. Russell failed in (1874); and now J. A. Battenfield would rally the forces around (1972). He gets at it very nicely, by assuming it was (4028) years from creation to Christ; and (4028 plus 1972 equals 6000) to the Millennium. Simple is it not? A child ought to see that! But his *first* problem is to show that the prophets of God foretold a Millennium to begin the (6001st) year from creation; and he must follow this with positive proof that it was (4028) years from creation to Christ; neither of which things he could prove if his life depended upon his doing so. If (1972) is first proven beyond doubt to be the (6000th) year of the world; then he will have to prove that it was *predicted* that the Millennium was to begin at that date.   THERE IS NO SUCH PROOF IN THE BIBLE. You have not forgotten the two "missing links" in the Old Testament chain, and can see, at a glance, that Mr. Russell and Mr. Battenfield vary (98) years in giving their lengths, one saying (6000) years ended (1874); the other that they end (1972); but as neither of them know, we may set them down as speculators who seek to be wise above what is written.

ERROR AS TO THE KINGDOM.

A fundamental error is that the Kingdom of God is to be the only kingdom on earth for (1000) years. This can not be true, for the following reasons, among many.

1. Jesus' Kingdom was "at hand" from the time John began to preach (Matt. 3). It was to be set up during the life-time of the apostles (Mark 9:1). Peter had the "keys of the kingdom of heaven," (not exclusively), but as an apostle, (Matt. 16:17; 18:18). The disciples used these keys on Pentecost and during their ministry, (Acts 2; Col. 1:13; Rev. 1:9).

2. The Parables all illustrate this kingdom and no other, and all end not *in a trial*, (or 1000-year Judgment), but *end the trial* of all parties engaged. The Virgins were not put on trial when the bridegroom came; the man with the talents, and the men with the pounds were not put on trial when the landlord came; but their trial ended with his coming. Just so with all the parables, they end trial or probation. We know these were all human transactions, and these became sacred to us as illustrations of divine realities. It is a false and mischievous theory that would make the kingdom of God such a rule among men that the teaching of Christ will not fit it. It is amazing to see how sectarian theories warp the judgment of men concerning the kingdom. I was especially surprised, in reviewing the Demonstration, to find that old Jewish notion that the kingdom of Christ or of Messiah is an earthly kingdom to begin, more than nineteen centuries after Christ. (pp. 457, 458, also April 18). On page (548) he tells us the kingdom of God is to be set up in (1972). He does not tell us how the kingdom of God can be set up (as he explains that Christ remains in heaven till the end of time), and the martyrs are not raised till (1973). But he wishes to make (1927) a critical year for Catholics, unconverted Gentiles and Jews, in his self-confident way, so he informs us the kingdom will be set up at that date. In the last reference the rulers are said to be the resurrected martyrs to commence (1973), their 1000 year term of office. This according to the Battenfield program.

THE MAN-CHILD RULE.

I have showed, at length, on the compound symbol

of the Woman and Man-child that the woman (or church) does not rule the world directly, but gives birth to a man-child who does. The fact that the woman does not give birth to a woman (or church), but to a man-child, FOREVER SETS ASIDE THE THEORY THAT THE CHURCH IS TO RULE THE WORLD. The glory is to be given to God "in the church, by Christ Jesus, throughout all ages, world without end. Amen," (Eph. 3:21), and this shows that the church is to continue to the end. If "throughout all ages" that includes the Millennial age, evidently;, and, "world without end," is the eternal world. So the church is not to be displaced half way between the first and second coming of Christ as the Battenfield program would demand, that a kingdom may be set up; or, as Mr. Russell would have it, with Christ here in person. If the people of God are a sheepfold, Christ is the Shepherd; if they are an army, he is the Captain; if they are servants, he is the Master; if they are a kingdom, he is the king; if they are a church, he is the Head of it; if we are the redeemed, he is the Redeemer. He is all these all the time, from the first to the last; and these but illustrate and enforce the relationship we sustain to him. If you are in the church, you are in the kingdom, in the sheepfold, in the army, and in the household, now.

When Constantine changed the form of church government and modeled it after the corrupt state, he polluted the church. Catholicism was the masterpiece of human folly in uniting the functions of church and state. The old Mother and her daughters, (the state churches), are condemned in the Bible. The complete separation of church and state is what is contemplated in the symbols of the woman and her son (Rev. 12); and it is this very separation that destroys the Babylon of Revelation. It betrays confusion of thought, and failure to grasp the meaning of the prophets, to argue that the church should ever unite the separate functions of CIVIL and RELIGIOUS rule in the SAME OFFICIALS.

Notice a few dates. America was discovered in (1492). The Reformation began in Germany in (1517), or twenty-seven years later. The French Revolution began in France (1774). The Declaration of Independence of these United States was signed in (1776). There was a close affinity between our country and France through the labors of Lafayette and others, and what proved to be the greatest upheaval in Old World Govern- ments, overturning the power of popery, from (1774 to 1815) when Napoleon fell, were years of crisis in this new-born Republic. Napoleon's earthquake will never be forgotten. "The French Revolution" by Thiers or others shows this to have been the dawn of a new Era. Napoleon was crowned Emperor of France in (1804). The year (1809) marked a forward movement of the hosts of Zion in demanding a return to apostolic Christianity in the United States. This is the year when the cele- brated Declaration and Address were given by Thomas Campbell and others and a plea was made for a return of all the people of God to the New Testament as their in- spired and all-sufficient rule of faith and practice. As the United States was the first nation of the world to recog- nize the equality before the law of the Jew, and write in the great constitution (1776) the sovereign rights of all men, so here was a declaration of religious freedom from priest-craft worthy of the man who formulated and promoted it.

Napoleon overthrew the temporal dominion of the pope, took him prisoner, plundered the Vatican, opened the monasteries, and destroyed the assumptions of the popes to *temporal* dominion, from which they never re- covered. Before and while his wars were devastating Europe and propstrating the papacy, our war for inde- pendence, and the war of (1812) were emphasizing, on a national scale, the principles of civil and religious liberty. As the protest went up against the authority of pope and priest to rule *in the church*, the people of God raised their voices in thunderous, deafening tones against the *rule of popes in the state*. From that crucial Era sprang forth new nations. Thus the church foiled the dragon, defeat- ed his hopes, and taught mankind that the pope is a usurper in church and state. When in (1860 to 1870) another war in Europe shook the temporal throne of popery into the dust and made Victor Immanuel King of Italy, America passed through a crisis in her life as a nation and liberated four millions of men, in one of the greatest civil wars in all history. The reconstruction of the Government was so wisely conducted as to unite and solidify the North and South, and present to the nations of the world the young and fearless government, which pledged her all but boundless resources to the welfare of the human race. From the shores of Europe and Asia have poured in upon us a large part of our present population. The vices as well as the virtues of alien populations have been imported from across the seas. Our problems are complex. Not least among these is how to purify the minds and hearts of Communists, Anarchists and Infidels, whose sole education has been acquired in foreign despotisms, where the wrongs inflicted by the state are fastened upon them by the assumption of "divine authority" by the priests. The present war in Europe may give vent to the pent-up fury of men against intolerant aggression in church and state. The principles of Republicanism are everywhere. The church can no longer rule the state. It is no longer possible to maintain the old regime. Catholicism is but the lingering shadow of its former self; all because despotism is dying. When despotism is dead, the church, however, does not take its place; but the *church* has despots to be dethroned. Papacy is the concrete expression of the foul spirit of tyranny that must be cast out. Sectarianism is sinful. The voice of Christ alone must rule the church. Then the church, by precept and example and holy zeal, can not only free men nominally from beastly tyranny in church and state, but can so influence legislation as to secure the overthrow of the entrenched privileged class. These barnacles on the old ship of state must be scraped off. We may put down the manufacture and sale of intoxicants, and suppress the whole business. The white slave trade; the enforced child labor question; prison reforms; the tenement house problem; pool halls and gambling dens; and all the elements of social evil are amenable to intelligent effort on the part of the forces of righteousness. The church should not become an institutional church; but the people of God should learn that the church must be the example to all mankind. The church must influence legislation, but can never legislate. By sovereignty of example she wields the scepter that moves the world. She is capable of illustrating in life freedom from the gambling spirit, in the parlor or in the stock exchange. She should be free from a desire to patronize vulgarity in picture shows and theaters. She may cultivate that tenderness of conscience that will shrink from the polluting touch of vice, and rear her sons and daughters into all the elements of true nobility of purpose and of life. But her mission is religious, not civil, till the end of time.

THE GIANT TREE.

Mr. B. has vitiated his whole system making the government of Christ, beginning in (1973), the only government on earth. He has the giant tree (Dan. 4) to illustrate human governments cut down to the stump, and later the stump dug up by the roots, (1972). But the stump and roots were preserved by a band of brass and iron and wet with the dews of heaven. The church does not grow out of the roots of civil government; neither does the government of Christ in (1972), or at any other time, grow out of the roots of civil government. But that tree represented *despotic* government, (such as Nebuchadnezzar the great, tyrrannous ruler then exercised), and not righteous, civil government. *That* was cut down. But the dews of heaven, or the blessing of God watered the roots of that tree, and new life grew out of it. "For there is hope of a tree, if it be cut down, that it will sprout again, and that the tender branch thereof, will not cease. Though the root thereof wax old in the earth, and the stock thereof die in the ground; yet through the scent of water, it will bud, and bring forth boughs like a plant." (Job. 14:7-9). The tree (despotism) being severed from the roots, *died*. But the roots, being blessed of heaven, *lived*. This was true of Nebuchadnezzar. His Kingdom was taken from him only till he learned *that the heavens do rule*, then civil government was safe in his hands, and his speech that followed his restoration has this lesson as its dominant note. If this was, in type, what was to be done in the governments of the world, then, manifestly, despotism is to go down, and civil governments are to continue; but the rulers are such as administer the governments in fear of God. THAT IS

THE WHOLE LESSON. That *stump* and its *roots* never disappear in the vision; but the old *tree* does.

The people of God, like Daniel of old, advise and counsel, teach and influence, the rulers for their own safety, and for the proptection and happiness of man. The tree represented the king of Babylon, then head of civil government. Nebuchadnezzar lived through the "seven times," (2520) days; his *heart* was changed, then his government was restored to him. IF THE GOVERN-MENT HAD BEEN TAKEN FROM HIM AND GIVEN TO DANIEL (in the type), then, indeed, the symbols might appear to demand that Daniel and other saints, return to earth at the end of "seven times," or (2520) years, to rule the whole world in anti-type, as Mr. B, along with other "fifth monarchy" folks, contends. But the *same king ruled after* the "seven times" that *ruled before* and his kingdom was held in reversion for him during the years of his insanity, showing that the change was a *moral change in him.* That is all that governments need today. We are not anarchists, wishing to do away with all government. Indirectly, the church rules, for the government is given "to the people of the saints of the most High God." As certainly as the tree was the King, and the whole change the King underwent was symbol-ized by the change in the tree; we see that the same tree, at root, survived for the King was restored to his king-dom, *but a changed man or ruler.* If what took place in the "seven times" was typical, that is, if the days were typical days, (2520) days typified (2520) years; and the change of heart experienced by the king was typical of the universal reformation among despotic rulers, then we may see the dream fulfilling before our eyes. The despotisms of ages are being swept away, and, in their stead, are rulers with new principles, new laws, humane consideration for the oppressed masses, and the gospel of Jesus Christ, (like Daniel of old), stands forth as the rebuker of all tyranny, and the faithful counsellor in all that ministers to the peace and happiness of man. The cry for such governments is all but universal. Failure to study these symbols carefully makes our Millennialist expositors to look for miracles and to expect literal Daniel and Paul and millions of other dead saints to return to earth to overthrow all civil government.

A QUOTATION AND COMMENT.

"Telabib means the hill or pinnacle of Abib, which is the first month of the Jewish religious year. The pinnacle of this month was of course the passover. They were Israelites of the captivity, so we have here a cryptographic date. Ezekiel came to prophesy or opens his prophetic vision at passover of the first year of the captivity or B. C. 606. He does this among the people by the river Chebar, which means "extent of time," "a great while," "hitherto," "formerly," "already," "now"; in other words a great extent of time at last reaching the present. He was overwhelmed or silent among them seven days. These days represent years. They are shortened to days out of mercy to the prophet (comp. Ezek. 4:12-15). That they are years is apparent from the name Chebar which accompanies them, and also from the kindred vision, given to Nebuchadnezzar, who was not spared, but bore the full seven times, or (2520) days, in madness as a punishment for his presumptuous sin. That this is a parallel vision to that of Nebuchadnezzar cannot be doubted. The visions came the same year, related the same facts, were set in the same number seven, were given by the same God, one to the King, and the other to the priestly prophet of the same Jewish people, and were messages to that people. These were like the dreams of the butler and baker, which came at the same time and were related to the same period, but came to different individuals (Gen. 40:1-23). So we have here the time limit of the vision. It began in April, 606, and runs (2520) years to the passover of this April, 1914, or from "a great while ago to this now." It marks the present enlargement of "The Demonstration" just as Nebuchadnezzar's kindred limit of 2520 years, began in October, 607, and marked the beginning of "the demonstration," which was on time, "Oct. 10, 1913, as indicated." (p. 829).

This is a fair sample of Mr. B's home-made prophecy and fanciful interpretation of prophecy. He certainly produced nothing reliable.

1. A *town*, or place of residence, "Telabib," he says, means the Passover, or dates the prophecy (Apr. 14, 606 B. C.)

2. "Chebar," the name of a river, means "extent of time," "now," or from Ezekiel to Battenfield; that is from (Apr. 14, 607 B. C. to Apr. 14, 1914), when Mr.

B. enlarged the Demonstration by a few more lengthy articles in the Christian Standard.

3. He says Ezekiel's "seven days" *meant* seven years (and not seven days at all); that they were prophetic, and that it was mercy that shortened the dumbness of the prophet to days instead of years, (or reduced 2520 years to seven days). That was such a great reduction of time that one should KNOW why it was made, (if it was), and not *guess it off*. But it is this method of *guessing off* things that makes it possible for men to write such speculations.

4. Nebuchadnezzar had a dream of a giant tree and of its being cut down, a band of brass and iron fastened around the roots, and it was wet with the dews of heaven. Mr. B. tells us this dream and Ezekiel's vision came the same year, (although the Bible does not say so), and we are left to his inference for proof; (Ezek. 1:2) says it was the *fifth year of the captivity*! Mr. B. says it was the *first*. And, pray, what likeness is there between Ezekiel being amazed seven days, and Nebuchadnezzar being driven to herd with the beasts of the field for seven years (at the least), three hundred and sixty times as long? And how comes it that Mr. B. is so anxious to have us think there is an analogy? Well! he says, the king sent a message to the nations after his seven *years* expired; Ezekiel sent a message to the Jews after his seven *days* expired; so, if he can persuade you that these messages were typical of the Demonstration, then he will have us think that the king's message was (2520) years before the *beginning* of the Demonstration; and the Ezekiel message was (2520) years before the *enlargement* of the Demonstration. Great! is it not? That would certainly be quite a certificate of honor for the author of the articles in the *Christian Standard*, (after he has gone a step farther and informed us how we may know that the Lord had the Demonstration in contemplation, when He gave the king his dream and Ezekiel his vision; so that Mr. B. could get in with his Clay City, Ill., articles on time to announce the impending doom of nations far and near, the next day after the (2520) years expired). I do not believe that Mr. B. or his message is related to either Ezekiel's seven

days, or to the king's twenty-five hundred and twenty days. I do not think the Lord had Mr. B. in mind, when either the king or Ezekiel had their revelations and gave their messages or that they typify the Demonstration, either as to its *origin*, (Oct. 10, 1913) or its *enlargement*, (Apr. 14, 1914). First of all, it takes more than assumption to establish the claims of being a subject of prophecy! If Mr. B's claim could be *established*, it would make him the most marvellous man now living.... indeed, the greatest since we had *inspired* men. The fact is, (as one can see by only a hasty glance at his production), that he feels competent to the task of revealing the future to all the nations of the earth; and he has sent his message forth as a "Challenge from God," to these nations.

AN IMPORTANT QUERY.

Why did Mr. B. select Jehoiakim's captivity (B. C. 607), rather than Zedekiah's captivity (587), twenty years later, from which to measure the (2520) years? The last date was the final captivity of the nation; and not the former. Was it because it would fit the Demonstration dates better than the time when the last king was removed to Babylon, the temple burnt, and the cities and land desolated?

It is a fine turn he took on the names "Telabib" and "Chebar" also. Is it not fine to have the very names given to towns and rivers to proclaim that one is a special servant of the Lord sent, "after so long a time," to recover Ezekiel's voice? I recall just here that, he alluded to the possible, (though not definitely stated fact), that John the Baptist began preaching six months before Christ, as though that, too, was related to the fact that Mr. B. began the Demonstration in (Oct. 11, 1913, and enlarged it in Apr., 1914)! My Book says "Honor to whom honor is due;" but it also says, "Let no man think of himself more highly than he ought to think." If Mr. B. is not *deserving* of the high honor of being Ezekiel's mouthpiece, (after his silence of (2520) years), then we should not tolerate his assumption.

Remember that Ezekiel tells us (12:21-28) that, it was a *false* sentiment, that the people of his day enter-

tained that, "The vision that he seeth is for many days
to come, and he prophesieth of the times that are afar
off;" then how could it be a *true* sentiment now?   Inspiration is not decreased by time; and, on the other
hand, time does not exalt a human production into the
rank of inspiration.   Mr. B. tells us "The present voicefulness of Ezekiel is PREDICTED in the words, But
when I speak with thee, I will open thy mouth," etc.
(Page 829).   I think it is a case of mistaken identity, as
I shall try to make evident to the reader.   The task is
not difficult.   Mr. B. professes to know the *day*, when
(2520) years from Nebuchadnezzar ended; the *day* when
Ezekiel's voice should be recovered.   If this is not speculation, then there can be none.   Such romancing is beneath the dignity of sober exegesis.   It is as impossible
to tell even the exact year when Nebuchadnezzar had his
dream as it is to tell what month and day of the month
John the Baptist was born.   *It is not revealed.*

CHAPTER XLVIII.

BATTENFIELD A PROPHET.

"The Great Demonstration is in itself one of the
signs of our Times.   It comes on time Oct. 11, 1913, at
the end of the times of the Gentiles, and the seven times
of Nebuchadnezzar."

"It makes no pretentions to human skill or earthly
wisdom. *The work is plainly not an invention of the human
mind*; it simply grasps the divine.   The author seeks
neither worldly honor nor advantage by its publication."

"*It delivers this message in the name and by the authority
of God* and applies his words of challenge to the great
nations and false religions of the world."   (pp. 406-7).

I think it easy to show the Demonstration is an invention of the human mind, and a very clumsy invention
at that.   As to the message, "being delivered in the name
and by the authority of God," one would naturally expect something conclusive.   I do not go outside the
Demonstration to disprove that egotistic statement. After

informing us that God sealed up the vision and the prophecy in the last or seventieth week of Daniel (A. D. 34) and that Paul was as one born out of due time, although within the week, he informs us that this rules out false prophets. I think he intended this chiefly to shut out Catholics, Mahomet and Mormons, but it is a fine rule to use on some other folks when they feel the prophetic impulse as Mr. B. does so often. Judged by his own rule God's prophets ceased in the apostolic age. Then what apology can be offered for Mr. Battenfield's predictions in the Demonstration? I give a few out of many at hand.

ILLUSTRATIONS OF HUMAN PROPHECY.

"THAT PART OF THE WORLD WHICH IS CONVERTED TO CHRIST MUST BE CONVERTED BY 1927. AT THAT TIME CHRIST WILL CLAIM HIS BRIDE, AND PROTECT HER THROUGH THE SEVEN LAST PLAGUES, EVEN AS ISRAEL WAS PROTECTED THROUGH THE SEVEN LAST PLAGUES OF EGYPT." P. 457.

Is it not humiliating to the servants of God to have an uninspired man to put forth such a mess of guesses and imaginations? Note again. "Thus Israel comes first in the forty-five years of war, and between (1927-1934) all Jews who do not accept the Christ shall be destroyed." p. 551.

"Now, in the first seven years of judgment, viz., 1927-1934—wherein the Jew goes out, he falls at the hand of Mahomet, the son of Ishmael, his nearest national, and nearest religious kin.

So in this second seven years (1935-1941) it is brother against brother—Turk against Mahommedan—the Turk being wiped out. So in the third seven (1942-1948) it will be Mohammedan against Mohammedan; and in the fourth seven (1949-1955) it will be politician against politician, people against their rulers; and in the fifth seven (1956-1961) it will be Protestant sectarian against Protestant sectarian, and in the sixth seven (1962-1969) it will be pagan against pagan. Then, in the last seven, the schedule changes, and it will be God against sinners." (p. 554).

SPECULATIONS FOUNDED ON NAMES.

"Daniel saw the river of Jewish Life, called Hiddekel, flowing out of the land of captivity, guarded by angels, and brooded over by the Lord himself (Dan. 12: 5-7). That river, according to Daniel's time limits, began to enter the Holy Land in 1897, and will be completely returned, for the purposes of prophecy, by 1927.

In April B. C. 606, Ezekiel sees the river of Jewish

life under the name of "Chebar," or "a great extent of time reaching to the present," and now, after his dumbness, or silence, of (2520) years are passed, as indicated by his seven days dumbness, he opens his mouth this April, 1914, to tell us about it, (it is April, 1914, as we write his words). He tells of the river as belonging to the distant past, and it becomes *a present* river in his prophecy at about the middle of that portion of it indicated by Daniel." (1897-1914-1927).

"At the end of the seven years, or 2520 years,—i. e., in April, 1914—Ezekiel becomes the watchman to Israel. If he warns of the impending judgment, he is free of the blood of his people. If, knowing the will of God and the counsel of God, he nevertheless, forbears to warn, the blood of those who perish for lack of warning, will be required at his hand. Ezekiel, being dead, has no responsibility, but each man who understands his prophecy bears the burden of the prophet's responsibility. Those who know that Israel shall pass through the fires of judgment 1927-1934, and forbear to give warning, will be held guilty of their blood before God.   Read Ezek. 3:16-21."

THE SIGN THRICE GIVEN.

"In verses 22-27 of the third chapter we have the sign of the 2520 years wherein the prophet was not understood. The certainty of this silence is emphasized in a three-fold manner: (1) Ezekiel is shut up in his own house; (2) the people lay bands on him; (3) The Lord himself strikes him dumb. It is the will of the prophet, the will of the people and the will of God that Ezekiel's message be not understood till the 2520 years have passed."

"The present voicefulness of Ezekiel is predicted in the words: "But when I speak with thee, I will open thy mouth," etc., p. 829.

Thus Mr. Battenfield would modestly inform us that Ezekiel has found his voice in the person of a resident of Clay City, Ill. If this would not make J. A. Battenfield as much a subject of prophecy as John the Baptist, then I am deceived. It was *not the will* of the *prophet,* of the *people,* or of *God* that the message be *understood,* till (April 1914); and, the writer of this Demonstration, "delivers the message in the name and by the authority of God." THEN HE WAS ORDAINED TO "BRING IT FORTH!" The disposition of the writer to foretell the years when Catholicism, Judaism, the Turks, and the Mahometans perish from the earth; when the people overthrow their rulers; the Protestants destroy each other; the pagans destroy pagans; and God destroys them all, shows that he entertains very exalted views of his mission as a preacher. One who can tell when all unconverted Jews will die; the year when all Catholics will be dead; the years when there will be wars, and the years when there will be no wars; the time when (144,000) Jews will be converted, and the year when no unconverted men can be converted, must be some several degrees above the *average* gospel preacher. But, added to all these things, for one to know the year and day when Paul, Peter, Daniel and some one hundred millions of martyred dead are to be resurrected, SO THAT HE CAN DELIVER THE MESSAGE FIFTY-EIGHT YEARS BEFOREHAND, is surely not anything short of miraculous. I doubt if there is more than one man on earth who *absolutely knows these things* and that is the author of "The Great Demoistration"!

Mr. B. has left the ranks of common mortals and has joined the ranks of the prophets, (whether true or false prophets, however, remains to be seen). That you may have something to consider as to his ability to foretell (58) years of history, try the following:

Mr. Battenfield predicted in a (Mar, 1914) number that, "The Jews were gathered into the new covenant in three and one-half years (A. D. 30-34). Will not the same time suffice for them now? Thus the *political arena*, threatening as it *may seem*, will be *noticeably quiescent for the next fourteen years*, save for the *downfall of Catholicism*. This last is not the rising up of a *new* kingdom, but the casting down of an old one, and therefore is not a matter included in the restrained province of the winds." p. 455. (I italicize a few words in quoting him).

He tries to make it appear that (144,000) Jewish converts are to be made, and that (Rev. 7), (where the four winds were restrained), was a prophecy of these years, beginning (April, 1914) and occupying three and one-half years. "DURING THIS TIME THERE SHOULD BE NO INTERNATIONAL WAR OR OTHER GREAT COMMOTION TO FRUSTRATE THEIR SEALING." Mar. 28. p .546. Most likely he has heard of the European war that is destroying, What? HIS PREDICTION!

It is, indeed, humiliating to have men compromise our holy religion, and load its sacred evidences with the incubus of their imaginations. Think of the state of mind necessary in a man, to embolden him to write what will be done by the Jews in the next (3½) years from (April, 1914), and to answer questions as follows:

"Will all the Jews who do not accept Jesus Christ meet death before 1972?" "Yes by 1934. See proof in Demonstration."

"Will all unbelieving Gentiles also meet death before that time?" "Yes." p. 783. The prophetic impulse ran away with him in these replies.

THINGS UNPROVED.

1. That the times of the Gentiles ended, (Oct. 10, 1913).

2. That "The Great Demonstration" speaks by the authority of God, or even in harmony with his Word.

3. That the sealing of the Jews began (Oct. 10, 1913), or since; or that it is a fulfillment of (Rev. 7th and 14th chs.) to be expected by the church, now or hereafter.

4. That the ten federated churches will ever go to war in carnal battle with the Catholics; or that they are the ten horns of the beast (Rev. 17:12), or are foretold in symbols or verbal prophecies.

5. That all Catholics will be killed by (1927).

6. That all who are converted from the world are to be converted by (1927). Prophetic fever ran high here!

7. That all Jews will be killed who do not accept Christ by (1934). A Clay City prophecy only!

8. That the Turks perish in the next seven years war, (1935-1941). Who told Mr. B. there will be so many seven year wars?

9. That Mahommedanism destroys itself in the next period, (1942-1948). Another section of home-made prophecy!

10. That the people overthrow their rulers (1949-1955).

11. That Protestantism will destroy Protestantism in the next seven years (1956-1961). (Prophetic, but not inspired!)

12. That pagan destroys pagan in the closing war of the last seven, (1962-1969). How definite! But not a word of proof!

13.   That the gospel age will close with (3½) years of God against sinners (1969-1972). Another wild guess!

Until mankind are ready to resign their faith to the leadership of men, who have no fear of imposing their *guesses* upon them for the veritable Word of God, such "Demonstration" will only be a demonstration of conceit and baseless assumption.   The whole theory is a clumsy attempt to fasten the old Jewish tradition of (1000) years' Millennium upon us, and to set the time for it to *begin, to a day*, when Mr. B. can not prove the age of the world within *several years*, not to say *months, weeks* and *days*.   He denounces tradition as the father of Mahometanism and Catholicism, THEN ADOPTS A JEWISH TRADITION AND BUILDS HIS WEAK AND UNPROVABLE THEORY UPON IT.   What a pity he could not see how far he was wandering from the path of the interpreter into the province of an inspired prophet of God, who alone could foretell the future which he has foolishly attempted to do.   There are several reasons why one should put no confidence in these predictions.

1.   A mathematical error by him would upset the system from end to end.

2.   The seven bowls and the seven trumpets in Revelation are specialized to fit this scheme.   This is purely fanciful and not defensible.

3.   Mr. B. had not time to get his articles into Book form until one of the most desolating, international wars of all history was raging.

4.   The Jews are not heeding Ezekiel, Battenfield, or Christ, and no change whatever is apparent among them.

5.   His carnal wars, that he schedules as due in seven year periods, are purely imaginary, and wholly improbable throughout.

6.   He would exalt the Demonstration, and, incidentally, its author, to the rank of prophecy or a prophet, and subjects of prophecy.

7.   He confuses types and anti-types, and uses incidents of history as predictions of similar things, when no inspired writer said they were prophetic.

8.   There is not a single thing predicted in his

catalogue of which any conservative teacher can say, this is a true prediction in the Word of God.

9. The scheme is not true historically, placing the origin of Mahometanism before Catholicism.

10. The author ignores the Lunar count; infers that (2300) years should lead to the end of (6000) years; assumes that they end (1972); and then accepts the Jewish tradition that the (7000th) year begins the Millennium.

THREE COUPLETS IN DANIEL.

The Demonstration has three couplets in full page or double page diagrams and as outlines of the whole system. It is reassuring to note that it is dawning upon men that the prophecies are a system. I rejoice to see this. When the fact is fully realized and acted upon then the mists will roll away, and we may hope to see harmony and beauty in the great symbols, and literal prophecies, and that the prophecies are all related to each other as members of one great family, or system, as sun, moon, stars and comets are all related, or the members of an animal body are related. I find it necessary, however, to point out some grievous errors in these so-called couplets. They are grouped as follows:

1. Nebuchadnezzar's dream of the Image and Stone.
   Nebuchadnezzar's dream of the giant tree.

2. Daniel's interpretation of the dream of the Image.
   Daniel's vision of the four Wild Beasts.

3. Daniel's vision of the Ram and He-Goat.
   Daniel's Seventy Weeks.

All this supplemented and explained in the open vision. (chs. 10 to 12). The King's dream of the Image and the Stone, and Daniel's interpretation, constitute one prophecy, and as there is but one set of symbols, it is using one prophecy twice to make the King's dream, and Daniel's interpretation, *two prophecies*. The case is not parallel to Pharaoh's two dreams, or the Butler's and the Baker's dreams, because Pharaoh dreamed in two sets of symbols; and the Butler dreamed one set of symbols, and the Baker a different set. Daniel did not

dream a different set of symbols; but simply recovered
the King's dream and gave the interpretation. Pharaoh's
dream was a prophecy in two sets of symbols; the Butler's dream was an independent prophecy, without any
connection whatever with the Baker's, only as to time,—
three days. One could make a couplet out of the two
sets of symbols given to Pharaoh in one night, concerning seven years of plenty followed by seven years of
famine; but one is not justified in making a couplet out
of one set of symbols, such as the Image and the stone.
It betrays one's eagerness for couplets to do so. Then
the giant tree was not given as a prophecy, primarily, of
the universal empires, but simply a prophecy concerning
the King of Babylon, and was limited to the "seven
times," (most likely years), that were to pass over him.
This transaction was as literal as Abraham's sacrifice
of Isaac. If the sacrifice of Isaac was to be a typical
transaction, that was another matter altogether. So if
the King's debasement and recovery after "seven times"
was to be used as a figure of the beastly nature of all
Gentile rule for (2520) prophetic days, or (2520) years,
the tree, first so stately and great, cut down, but the
roots made secure and wet with the dews of heaven,
must have *their* fulfillment in the *history of Nebuchadnezzar*. If there was any prophecy concerning the long
debasement, but final recovery of Gentile dominion to
the favor of God (and evidently there was), it was founded upon the literal history of the King. The King literally fulfilled the *tree prophecy*; and in so doing became a
TYPE OF GENTILE DOMINION through (2520) years.
Mr. B. seems to discover no difference between making
couplets out of Joseph's two dreams at different times
in different symbols; Pharaoh's two dreams in different
symbols, but the same night and on the same subject;
the Butler's and Baker's dreams in different symbols, but
the same night, and with entirely different issues; and
Nebuchadnezzar's dream and Daniel's interpretation of it.
So he makes the King's *dream* a member of his *first*
couplet; and Daniel's *interpretation* a member of the *second*
couplet. This is like making the Parable of the Sower
one prophecy; and the divine interpretation another pro-

phecy. But it is in the third couplet where the Demonstration throws aside sober exegesis and violates,

EZEKIEL'S YEAR DAY RULE.

I think it scarcely possible to find a more bunglesome piece of work than we have in this part of the Demonstration. Of course (1972) is the objective point. Mr. B. set out to make the Millennium due at that date, and he does so, seemingly to his own satisfaction; but, after what manner, we shall now inquire. This, you should know, is the GREAT POINT in his system. I cite the figures as given in the Diagrams. First, let us remember that he ASSUMES (4028 B. C.) was the beginning of time; secondly, that (6000) years lead to the Millennium. Then (4028 plus 1972 equals 6000). But it is necessary *to prove* that his (4028) years .are correct, A THING ASSUMED THROUGHOUT, AND THIS THE FUNDAMENTAL FACT AND BASIS OF HIS WHOLE SYSTEM OF DATES.

Next he ASSUMES, contrary to historic proof, that Mahometanism arose (A. D. 637); and Catholicism thirty years later, (666). I have cited the historic fact that Catholicism was a "mystery of iniquity" at work in the church in Paul's day; but was hindered till the Roman Emperor was taken out of the way, which was done (A. D. 476), when Romulus Augustulus was removed, as the last Emperor, over the Western Roman Empire, and the government was partitioned into the ten toes, and the ten horns, of the symbols. Popery sprang up at once, into power.

A. D. 533 was the Justinian decree, making the first pope.

A. D. 590 was the reign of Gregory the Great.

A. D. 606-7 Phocas made Boniface III the pope.

A. D. 663-6 The Vitellian decree, (that all services should be in Latin, in the Catholic church). MR. B. USES THIS DATE ALONE, as the origin of popery.

Are we ready to say there was no popery before (666)? The whole world knows the bishop of Rome was pope in all these dates, and that (606) found him in supreme authority not only in the Western Roman Empire, but in the Eastern as well, by decree of theEmperor. Why does Mr. B. ignore the FORMER dates here as he did the LATTER in Zedekiah's reign?

Mr. B.'s *figures* demand that Mahometanism be thirty years older than popery; but is it? No; for there were popes in Rome more than half a century before Mahomet was born! Again he begins his (1335) years of Mahometan rule (A. D. 637), when Jerusalem fell into their hands. But shall we accommodate Mr. B. by permitting him to date the Mahometan Empire FIFTEEN YEARS after the Mahometans began it, (A. D. 622); and FIVE YEARS AFTER MAHOMET DIED, (632)? The fact is that popery was fully installed in office, with sanction and support of the Emperor of the East, the very year that Mahomet retired to the cave to devise his imposture. Through the next twenty-six years, till his death, popery was in full blast. It is not possible to wrest the facts of history to make Mahometanism first. The system of popery in the church was being matured from the days of Constantine the Great, who united church and state in the early part of the fourth century, and popes were reigning throughout Mahomet's history. It is to contradict the entire history of both to make the religion and empire first, which originated with a man who was born after the system of popery had been in power half a century, and was in full blast in (606) when he contemplated his religion and empire, but had not a single follower. It is just as foolish to begin the religion and empire five years after the originator of one, and founder of the other, was dead, as he does Mahometanism. Mr. B will have to revise the histories and induce the Mahometans to change the date from which they count, or (A. D. 622) to (637), to give even plausibility to his scheme. (2300) years after the rise of the Goat Empire (328 B. C.) lands one at (A. D. 1972). And (1335) years after (637 A. D.) brings one to the same date. (4028 plus 1972 equals 6000 years) or the Millennium. (B. C. 328 plus 2300 equals 1972 A. D.) (A. D. 637 plus 1335 equals 1972 A. D.)

All beautiful and a demonstration! The only trouble with it is:

1. He does not *know* how long (1972 A. D.) is after creation. This is the rubber date that can be stretched

to any desired length by our Millennialist folks, for they purport to give the time from creation—an impossibility.

2. He does not know that the Goat Empire began in (B. C. 328) nor that the (2300) years are to begin there.

3. (637 A. D.) WAS NOT THE BEGINNING OF THE POLITICO-RELIGIOUS EMPIRE OF MAHOMET, AS IT WAS FIVE YEARS AFTER THE FALSE PROPHET'S DEATH; FIFTEEN YEARS AFTER THE DATE UNIVER-SALLY KNOWN AS THE CALENDAR OF MAHOMETANS; TWENTY-FIVE YEARS AFTER HIS FIRST WAR; AND TWENTY-EIGHT YEARS AFTER HE PROCLAIMED HIM-SELF THE PROPHET OF GOD.

SACRED HISTORY DESPISED.

Ezekiel gives a rule to measure symbolic prophecy, (4:4-6), known as the Year-day theory. He lay (390) days on his left side for Israel; followed by (40) days on his right side, for Judah. He thus worked out in figure, what was being done in fact in Israel and Judah, only he could not lie (390) years, or (40) years, on his side, and the Lord gave him a day for a year, like he did Israel when he condemned them to wander forty years in the wilderness, a year for each day they searched the land, (Num. 14:33, 34). It was (390) years from the time Jeroboam divided the nation till the captivity of Zede-kiah, (B. C. 976 to 587). It was some forty years from Josiah's covenant with Judah, to keep God's law, until the same judgment. It is evident that both prophecies had an exact, historic fulfillment, (as nearly as we can approximate any of these remote dates). The reader should note that this establishes two points; first that in the *symbolic* prophecies the NUMBERS are *typical* as well as the EVENTS; as *illustrated* by these two *fulfill-ments*, on the year-day theory, of Ezekiel's *typical* actions; and, secondly, that HIS FIGURES were concerning HIS people AT THAT TIME, and not some centuries later, as the Demonstration would have it. By what authority can one use the year-day theory if he ignores the (390) years and the (40) years' applications to Israel and Judah in Ezekiel's days?

I refresh your memory, at this point, concerning Mr. B.s claims, quoted in the preceding chapter, that neither the prophet, the people nor the Lord wished the message of Ezekiel understood for (2520) years; and, then, with the courage of a Crusader, he opens the message on time in (April, 1914), in Clay City, Ill. Let us see about this. In (Ezek. 3:16-22) Ezekiel sat *astonished* among his brethren at the river "Chebar" *seven days*; then the word of the Lord came to him. The theory of interpretation, set forth by the Demonstration, is that as Ezekiel was silent seven days and afterwards a watchman to Israel; and it was a matter of life or death with him to warn the sinner, and a matter of life or death to those warned, so after (2520) years from the year (606 B. C.), or (A. D. 1914), it would be a question of life or death with *preachers* and *teachers* to make known the doom of Israel (1927 to 1934), as set forth in the Demonstration from Clay City, Ill., *on time*, (April, 1914). Let us try the year-day theory out here and see how empty all this great claim is of Scriptural authority. (pp. 866-867).

1.   (390) days represented (390) years to Israel, the *ten* tribes.

2.   (40) days represented (40) years to Judah, the *two* tribes.

3.   "Seven times," (regarded as years), are (360x7 equals 2520) days of symbolic prophecy, (while Nebuchadnezzar was herding with beasts), which, being enlarged on the year-day theory, is a (2520) years' lease for the Gentiles in idolatrous, cruel governments; or the life-time of the Metallic Man and the symbols of the four wild beasts.

4.   Ezekiel was silent or amazed seven days. Enlarging these into a prophecy, ACCORDING TO THE RULE, A YEAR FOR A DAY, he was not to be understood for *seven years only*, not the (2520) years Mr. B. would make him dumb.

Mr. B. IGNORES EZEKIEL'S OWN RULE, A DAY FOR A YEAR, and instead of enlarging THE WEEK by THAT rule, he MULTIPLIES IT BY (360) to bring it down in history (2513) years further, and *incidently*, APPOINT THE AUTHOR OF THE DEMONSTRATION as the man to give VOICE to Ezekiel. How clever!

5.   Mr. B. tells us, (p. 457) that *one hour* in (Rev. 17:12) *means fifteen years* on the year day theory; that *seven years* (Dan. 4:23) mean (2520) years; and then

informs us that (7) *days* (Ezek. 3:16) *mean* (2520) *years*.

He was needing this last twenty-five centuries very much, indeed, to cause him to trample under foot (Ezek. 4:4-6), (which every expositor on the year-day theory must use, and which he uses), and MAKE A RULE OF MEASUREMENT THREE HUNDRED AND SIXTY TIMES AS LONG AS THE INSPIRED PROPHET DESIGNATED. After this shameful disregard of the time, he vaults across the intervening centuries to (Oct. 11, 1913); and the TIME FOR EZEKIEL'S PROPHETIC DUMBNESS TO CEASE, (APRIL, 1914)!

EZEKIEL RESCUED FROM HIS PERVERTERS.

The fact that Ezekiel's predictions are thus removed twenty-five centuries from their historic setting, introduces a NET-WORK OF SPECULATIONS into Mr. B.'s Demonstration. He must land at (1972) for Millennial day, so he dates the captivity of the ten tribes at (B. C. 718); adds the (390) years to bring him to the Goat or Grecian Empire, (B. C. 328), where he hooks on to his (2300) year period to the Millennium. This is misleading, for three reasons:

1. In (Isaiah 7:8) it *was* predicted that within sixty-five years Ephraim should *cease to be a nation*. It was some forty-five years from the first captivity of the ten tribes (723-21 B. C.) to Esar-Haddan (678 B. C.), *who fulfilled this prophecy* and brake Ephraim till they ceased to be a people, (II Ks. 17:25; Ezra 4:2). Mr. B. ignores the fulfillment of this prophecy, and begins his (390) year count forty-five years before they ceased to be a people, and lands nicely at (1972), after (2690) YEARS! Is that giving voice to Ezekiel?

2. This (390) years had a *historic fulfillment*, beginning with Jeroboam and ending with Zedekiah, when all the remnant of the ten tribes, (remaining with Judah in the land), were carried to Babylon. THIS IS ITS ONLY TRUE FULFILLMENT, (it seems to me), and it does not give a forced interpretation, AND ADD (170) YEARS TO THE "LONG WEEK," (TO MAKE IT COME OUT RIGHT).

3. To preface the (2300) years with the (390) years makes the Gentile rule (2690) years long, instead of the long week of (2520) years, predicted, (in figure),

in the person of Nebuchadnezzar and the giant tree; and *leaves out* its fulfillment *after Jeroboam,* where it belongs.

All this to bring the fulfillment of Ezekiel down to the twentieth century! Job's three friends "sat down with him upon the ground seven days and seven nights. and none spake a word unto him; for they saw that his grief was very great." (Job 2:13). That did not mean Job would not be understood for (2520) years after (606 B. C.); but it could as consistently be interpreted that way as Ezekiel's sitting amazed seven days among his people, could be wrested to mean what Mr. B. injects into it. Both are statements of what the men did, *without any reference to prophecy.* One could as well say that Joseph's mourning seven days for his father, was prophetic of the (2520) years his descendants would be abased, *and dead,* after (606 B. C.) There is as much authority for using one as a prophecy as there is for using the other; that is absolutely none. If Ezekiel's seven days' amazement were typical THEN HIS PRO-PHECIES WOULD HAVE BEEN UNDERSTOOD IN SEVEN YEARS AFTER THEY WERE UTTERED, NOT (2520) YEARS LATER, TO PLEASE MR. BATTENFIELD. WHAT CONFIDENCE CAN ONE HAVE IN A MAN'S SCHEME OF PROPHECY PUT TOGETHER AFTER SUCH A FASHION ? IT WAS FULFILLED (2500) YEARS AGO!

But let us notice the forty years. This is lifted up bodily from Ezekiel's day and fitted into the middle of the last of Daniel's Seventy Weeks from (A. D. 30 to 70); and made to apply to the destruction of Jerusalem by the Romans, nearly *seven centuries after the prediction was fulfilled* by Nebuchadnezzar and his army. By what rule can one dissect a passage of Scripture like that! First he applies the (390) years to Israel, (the ten tribes), from the captivity under Shalmaneser, (which I have shown was forty-five years before (Is. 7:8) was fulfilled and Ephraim ceased to be a people). But as Mr. B. goes *backward* one hundred years to a captivity date, (not the first nor the last of Israel's captivity dates), to begin his (390) years' count; by what authority does he go *forward* six centuries to begin the (40) years' count for Judah? This must be by the simple and convenient law of "Do it."

CAPTIVITY ERA.

It has been shown, on the Time-Prophecies, that there were three methods of counting, Solar (365) days; Lunar (354) days; and Calendar (360) days to the year. It was also *demonstrated* that each of these counts may be used to measure the long week, or (2520) years, from the Captivity Era to modern times. It is evident that it was a century and a half, from the first captivity of the ten tribes, to the last captivity of Judah; or from (745-7) to (587-8 B. C.) There are corresponding dates, marking the decline of the combinations of apostasy and cruelty, and especially the wasting away of popery, Mahometanism and the life of the Image and the fourth wild beast, represented in the toes of the Image and the horns of the Beast. Such expositors ignore the GRADUAL CAPTIVITY of ISRAEL AND OF JUDAH, in course of more than A CENTURY AND A HALF; select some ONE DATE OF CRISIS in the process, and make all their measurements from that, reaching (1843) with Miller; (1874) with Russell; (1972) with Battenfield; and so on. There is an element of truth, usually, in these calculations; but it is like a thimble full cf wheat in a bushel of chaff. The dates are fixed; but the measure is to be applied to various beginning dates and ends at as many closing dates. The Catholic church did not come up in one year, and it does not go down in one year. It has a closing era; so has Mahometanism. Of course, Mr. B. can say God began to count time on Catholicism (A. D. 666); and (1260) years later, (1926), there will be *no* Catholics left; and then *prophesy* that the ten federated churches, (Quakers included), WILL KILL THEM ALL OFF BY THAT DATE! But how does he reach that conclusion? Simply by adding the half week, 1260) years, to a date he ASSUMES CATHOLICISM BECAME A POWER, and the saints were given into her hand. He can tell you exactly when Mahometanism will go down; and, how? BY ASSUMING IT BEGAN (637 A. D.) and then applying the last date in Daniel, (1335) years, to it. But there was a Catholic church and a pope one hundred and thirty-three years before (666); and, a pope over the whole apostate church, sixty years before (666). Ma-

hometanism was established many years before Mr. B.
begins the count, according to all historians of the times,
and the Calendar of the Mahometans. Bishop Newton
would make (A. D. 774) the year when Catholicism
reached the zenith of her power; and, hence, the year
from which to measure her predicted life of (1260) years.
There is some truth in all these counts; and, grouping
them all together, you get the whole truth. We learn
that such powers came up, as they were predicted; they
flourished for more than twelve centuries; and are being
consumed in our day. We live in an ERA OF PRO-
PHETIC FULFILLMENT; and, as events follow events,
the prophecies are being verified before our eyes. When
we shall have gotten rid of this mystical, dreamy Millennium of the days of heaven on earth TO BEGIN AT
SOME SET DATE; and shall see that(as measures fill
in sin, God measures out Judgment to nations and
churches), then we may know that Mahometan, Catholic,
Jewish and pagan measures are all about full.   The
measure of pride; the measure of idolatry; and the measure of time, alloted to them, are about full. Judaism,
Catholicism, Mahometanism, Paganism and Sectarianism
are doctrines. We do not need TO KILL ALL THE
PEOPLE TO KILL THESE SYSTEMS! Mr. B's. programme of mutual slaughter is only a conceit of his,
without solid merit. The killing business is not the
Lord's method of saving the nations from themselves.
It is impossible to say how many *Catholics were killed by
the gospel* in the days of Luther, for Luther himself was
a former priest. But "peace hath her victories no less
renowned than war," and her heroes and heroines are
multiplying. Mr. Battenfield tells us to detect his errors.
I have detected a few fatal to his whole scheme as
shown by the following:

ASSUMPTIONS.

1.   His assumption that time began (B. C. 4028).

2.   That the Millennium is an event to begin (Oct.
11,1973) by the resurrection of the martyrs, at the end
of (6000) years from creation.

3.   That the Kingdom of Christ will be the sole
kingdom on earth for (1000) years, (contrary to the
compound symbol of the woman and man-child), as well

as contrary to all the Parables, the *nature* of the kingdom, and its *conquests* thus far. If the governments, already changed and undergoing change, shall succeed as well as others have done in the past, how long is it, think ye, till not a vestige of the old despotism remains?

4. I have touched upon the point that Battenfield is a prophet; and his first year has proved him to be a false prophet; as the Jews were to begin to be sealed, (converted), in large numbers, and no international wars disturb the earth for fourteen years. Europe is his humiliation.

5. He makes Mahometanism to have arisen thirty years before Catholicism, when history shows that Catholicism was in power when Mahomet was born, and continued in power throughout his whole history as false prophet, and the founder of an Empire. This discredits his interpretation that Mahomet revived the Beast that was wounded to death (Rev. 13); and that popery was only the Image of Mahometanism, or of the Beast.

6. He makes seven *common days* in (Ezek. 3:16) to predict (2520) *years*, in order to have Ezekiel dumb till the twentieth century. THIS IGNORES THE TRUE HISTORIC FULFILLMENT OF EZEKIEL IN HIS DAYS, AND INVESTS MR. B. WITH THE HONOR OF BEING THE MODERN EZEKIEL, IN THE DEMONSTRATION. If the Lord had intended Ezekiel's Message not to be understood for (2520) years or to span the ages from Ezekiel to the Demonstration, Ezekiel would have been dumb seven years or (2520) days each prophetic of a year just as he lay (390) days on his left side for Israel, and (40) days on his right side for Judah; but as he was dumb, or marvelled, *but seven days*, Mr. B. and his Demonstration are not contemplated in the transaction, being some (2513) years too late. This is a hard knock on the Demonstration, but it is the plain truth.

CHAPTER XLIX.

REASONING BY ANALOGY.

The reader is anxious to know how one can prophesy with the confidence of Mr. Battenfield. He reasons by analogy. For instace: John the Baptist preached the Kingdom of God six months, then Jesus was baptized. Jesus labored three and one-half years to convert the Jews and was crucified; special gospel favor was shown three and one half years longer, then the Gentiles were called. Forty years from the crucifixion of Christ, many Jews were crucified and the nation destroyed. Now, such speculators seek to parallel these events. Having selected a possible date, they turn the imagination loose and are soon predicting what is *due to happen now*. To illustrate this, I quote a sample of such home-made prophecy from (Mar. 28th number). (p. 546).

"FIRST ANGEL SOUNDS NOW, (Rev. 14:6, 7)."

"The first of these angels sounds out his message right now. He does so from mid-heaven, or from that point where all beneath the heaven, i. e., all the earth, can best hear him. His voice occupies the ears of all for three and a half years."

"PERIODS OF TIME JUST AHEAD OF US."

Let us say right here that the fourteen years between Oct. 10, 1913, and the full year 1926, is divided into periods as follows: One-half year for the sounding out of the message to the Jews, three and a half years for the conversion of the Jews; an additional three and a half years for the conversion of the Gentiles, three and a half years of warning to all in the Babylonian confusion: and, finally, two years for the Judgment upon the unconverted Catholic. We will give our reasons for this division of the time later.

"PAST PERIODS SHOW LENGTH OF PRESENT PERIODS."

We have already, in this fourteenth chapter, heard about the conversion of the Jews, which occupies three and one-half years. The ministry of Jesus lasted that long, among his people, and was preceded by six months of preparatory message on the part of John the Baptist, making, in all, four years. After the death and resurrection, the Holy Spirit ministered to the Jewish people for another three and a half years before their special privileges were taken away. Thus three and a half is the normal time established by precedent for the conversion of the Jewish people. Moreover, three and a half is the normal division of fourteen years into four parts, and such a division is indicated here by the account of the conversion of the Jews followed by *three* angels," etc.

"EMPHASIS IS ON DIVISION OF FOURTEEN YEARS JUST BEFORE US."

And in this connection we wish to recur to our statement that we believe Israel will be gathered in four years from Oct. 10, 1913, or THREE AND A HALF YEARS from this coming spring. This date, Oct. 10, 1913, is the one fixed, BY THE RECOVERY OF NEBUCHADNEZZAR'S REASON, for the recovery of sanity by the nations, by reason of a message sent, LIKE *Nebuchadnezzar's*, to the end of the earth. In a consecrated EFFORT TO FULFILL THIS PROPHECY, this message of "The Great Demonstration," began to go forth ON THAT DATE. Heeded or unheeded, it is a message to the whole earth, and, in as far as its interpretation of prophecy is correct, it is a message from Jehovah, and will call the people to sanity. Between this date and 1926 and 1927 the destruction of the Catholic and the conversion of the first-fruits of Israel, and of the Gentiles, MUST TAKE PLACE. But how are the fourteen years to be divided? No man can answer dogmatically, BUT REASONING BY ANALOGY DRAWN FROM PRECEDENT, the Jewish conversion ought to take place in half a week, for Jesus labored with them personally from his thirtieth to his thirty-third year, or half of the last of the Seventy weeks."

"Again, as the Catholic has until 1926 to quit the stage of action, and as the restraining angel of (Rev. 7) shows that the sealing of the Jews will not take place *in wartime*, it seems *reasonable to suppose* that the conversion of the Jews will be the first thing on the program, for there is much to be done in the balance of the fourteen years, for the harvest of the Gentiles, the completion of the *Salvation harvest*, must be all gathered before 1927, for the grape harvest of Judgment will be fully meted out on Catholic and Protestant warriors in 1926."

Mr. B. thus delivers himself on a variety of topics. His trouble is, primarily, that he selected one date (606 B. C.) from which to measure the "times of the Gentiles." Then (B. C. 607 plus 2520 equals 1913 A. D.), as you subtract. Of course that ends the "long week." But lo! it did not come out right, for he had set (A. D. 666) for the rise of Catholicism; (and, as its life-time is measured by the half-week), he has (666 plus 1260 equals 1926) as the end of Catholicism. So he has from (Oct. 10, 1913 to 1927) or these fourteen years on his hands, and devises the ingenious method of dividing them into four parts of (3½) years, each. Then he thinks of John the Baptist preaching six months before Jesus began his ministry, and modestly announces "The Great Demonstration" as anti-type of that work! also of Nebuchadnezzar's message! But, you have observed that, one year of the program is now ended without Jewish converts; and the "war of the ages" is raging in Europe. HE SET THE WRONG DATE FOR THE RISE OF CATHOLICISM. The fourteen year period is purely imaginary.

Israel was not entirely deported from their land, the capital destroyed and the temple burned, till (B. C. 587. I do not use one captivity date to the exclusion of others; but cite this one to remind the reader of the *necessity* of using *all* of them. (B. C. 587 plus 2520 years equals A. D. 1933). So we can push ahead the date from (1913), where Mr. B. anchored, to (1933), as another measurement of the long week from Captivity Era to Restoration Era. As the systems of tyranny are going down in this Era, reaching from the Reformation to the present, and this measure is among the last possible measures of the long week, we are full of hope for the Israel of God. But to divide and sub-divide the periods, and assume to know *what must be* for the next *fifty-eight years* is to become prophet without authority or inspiration, and insures one inglorious defeat. It is reasoning by analogy, or assuming that history repeats itself, in fulfilling revelation, and events must come on the dates he has chosen, to correspond to events that were necessary in giving the revelation; a wholly gratuitous assumption.

A GROUP OF ERRORS.

Before Mr. B. could begin his interpretation of Ezekiel and Daniel, he had to make the *seven days* in (Ezek. 3:16) equal in length to the *seven years* of the tree (Dan. 4), (granting that "seven times" signify seven years). Next, he had to pick out ONE captivity date and EXCLUDE ALL THE REST, and he chose (606-7 B. C.) Then he had to fix the date for the rise of Popery and Mahometanism and seized upon (666 A. D.) and (637 A. D.), respectively. Then he had to assume that the half week, measured from these dates, would bring one to the time of the end (1926-7), covering forty-five years to the Millennium. Then he has all things ready and he puts the measuring reed down as follows:

(B. C. 607 plus 2520 equals 1913), time for the Demonstration Message, the John the Baptist or Harbinger mesasge; the Nebuchadnezzar anti-typical message, at the end of the "times of the Gentiles;" the time for Ezekiel to recover his voice—hence the foolish and sinful claims set up for the Demonstration, as a consecrated effort to *fulfill* the *prophecy*, (Oct. 11, 1913), to a day!

Had Mr. B. simply measured the (2520) years from the FINAL captivity date of Judah, (587 B. C.; II Ks. 25), he would have seen that he had at least an even twenty years more to work on his Nebuchadnezzar,—Ezekiel—John the Baptist message, *before it was due.* This score of years would have enabled him to counsel prudence and not make a day mean a year in (Dan. 4: 23; Rev. 17:12; Ezek. 4:4-6); and a day to mean (360) years in (Ezek. 3:16). This fact having dawned upon him, it would have freed him from the necessity to trying to recover Ezekiel's voice after a (2520) years' dumbness, for he could have known that it *was not* predicted. He might then have felt no necessity to contradict the plain facts of history as to the time when Catholicism and Mahometanism arose; and would not have fought the inevitable by trying to make the latter thirty years earlier in history than the former. It might have dawned upon him, eventually, that the Mahometans did not revive the wounded beast of the Roman Empire; but Catholicism did, through ages of intrigue, cunning, and political strategem, and ruled from the old capital, Rome, for some thirteen centuries.

He would have had time and opportunity during these twenty years to discover that "reasoning by analogy" is dangerous business, especially when comparing the labors of inspired men with whom God dealt, such as Ezekiel, Nebuchadnezzar and John the Baptist, with plain every day folks, like the author of the Demonstration. I have never read more arrogant assumption than is set forth in the Demonstration. It is as follows:

1. Nebuchadnezzar was insane for (2520) days, predictive of Gentile rule; this predicted period ended, after (2520) years, (Oct. 10, 1913). As Nebuchadnezzar issued a message "to all people, nations, and languages, that dwell in all the earth," at the end of his seven times," so Mr. Battenfield, *In a consecrated effort* to fulfill this prophecy, this message of The Great Demonstration began to go forth on that date." Where is the *prophecy* that such a message should go forth? It is not in the Bible, for that date or for any other conceivable date.

2. He assumes that Ezekiel was to be dumb till the (2520) *years* were passed, then his mouth was to be opened; and Mr. B. makes *seven days* predictive of *twenty-five hundred and twenty years*, and lands at (Apr. 1914), again, and begins to send forth his message to the Jews, six months later than (Oct. 1913). Ezekiel's seven days dumbness could not predict more than seven years, if predictive at all. We have all learned this.

3. As John the Baptist preached six months before Christ was baptized and began to preach, so Mr. B. sends forth the modern John the Baptist, Nebuchadnezzar— Ezekiel's message six months before the time for the great ingathering of the Jews from (April, 1914 to 1917). All this depends upon whether he should measure from (606 B. C. or from 587 B. C.) which was the final captivity date; AND WHETHER THE PROPHECIES CAN BE INTERPRETED SAFELY BY ANALOGY.

Did ever mortal man, (disclaiming inspiration), intrude his scheme of prophecy upon the world with more lofty pretentions? But all this romancing comes from Clay City, Ill., published in a great denominational Journal, and is advertised to the four winds as "God's Message to this age is Revealed in The Great Demonstration." Solemn regret runs through every word of my pen as I point out the errors of this production, because of the injury it is destined to work in the minds of the unstable and the unlearned. Pity for Mr. B. would be somewhat out of place, for his advertised book is likely to bring him financial compensation. But the great God who tells us to "beware of false prophets," and that we "shall know them by their fruits," will know what to do with men who assume to speak in his name.   If God were the Author of the Demonstration it would not contradict the facts of history as to the rise of Catholicism and Mahometanism; it would not make (7) days mean seven years in one verse, and (7 years or 2520 days) mean the same length of time in another verse.   It would not ignore the fact that Ezekiel's prophecies were fulfilled in the history of Aholah and Aholibah, and in the literal nations mentioned in (chs. 26 to 32) and were confined, by the year-day theory, to that period of the world.   No one should brush aside prophecy and fulfillment as plain as the Bible gives of Aholah and Aholibah and seek to vault over the ages, and reasoning *by analogy*, make the modern nations of the earth to be the nations whose fortunes and destinies were predicted.   Only plenary inspiration of God could enable any man to predict as follows:

"The ten horns of the beast (Rev. 17:12) is federated Protestantism.   They received their crowns in 1912; they will wear them one hour, or fifteen years, and will destroy the harlot—the Roman Catholic church — by 1926.   Then they will be in full flower, and, with the Episcopalian Church in the lead, they will be known as the English or Anglican Catholic Church.   They will give their Kingdom to the beast, and rule from Rome—the old seat of the beast—till the fifth plague (Rev. 9:1-11; 16:10-11) is ushered in, twenty-nine years after their conquest of 1926.   For a period of seven years (from 1955-1961 inclusive) they will be rent by internal dissension, and will finally use the sword on each other as in the day of Midian; and when the plague is over they will be strewn out over the battle-field, and the earth will be rid of all traditionalism and division." p. 457.

A man who is competent to write in such matter of fact style, naming dates and events future to the human race, is so far gone from the plain functions of a sober interpreter of FULFILLED PROPHECY, and is so unwarrantably invading the exclusive province of an inspired prophet of God, that he is not easily convinced of his folly.   But I cherish the hope that his brethren, of more sober mind, may detect at once his costly and dangerous experiment as a prophet, and his assumed role as a subject of prophecy, and not be partaker of his sins by bidding him God-speed in his enterprise.

THE BATTENFIELD DIAGRAMS.

Some one wrote. "I want your charts in sizes large enough for church use and made in colors. Can you have these made for me, and if so, what would they cost me?"

"Large charts (10x14 feet) in colors, such as I now use, would cost $100 to $200. It is an immense advantage to have the painted visions of the prophets before the eyes of those who would learn the meaning of the Book wherein these visions are recorded, that the world may be informed of the impending doom of all corruption." p. 782.

FALSE PROPHETS DEFINED.

"But the prophet which shall presume to speak a word in my name, which I have not commanded him to speak or that shall speak in the name of other gods, even that prophet shall die. And if thou shalt say in thine heart, how shall we know the word which the Lord hath spoken? When a prophet speaketh in the name of the Lord, if the thing follow not, nor come to pass, that is the thing which the Lord hath not spoken, but the prophet hath spoken it presumptuously: thou shalt not be afraid of him," (Deut. 18:20-22). Judged by this rule, all false prophets are detected. If the conversion of (144,-000) Jews was to begin in (April, 1914); and the winds were to be restrained that there be no international war for three years and a half, according to the Demonstration, then, pray, where is the evidence of fulfillment, when all the furies of war are raging in Europe? If the "long week" is to date from Judah's final overthrow, and will end in (1934), then what becomes of the Battenfield diagrams and prophecies for these next twenty years? If one should concede that his articulation of the prophecies is correct, (which it is not), then his whole program is advanced twenty years; and the details, so liberally submitted in the Demonstration, as to what is to happen to Jews, Catholics, and Gentiles generally from now till (1934) are false in whole and in part. It remains to be seen, whether preachers and teachers will swing his elaborate diagrams upon their chapel walls, and, pointer in hand, solemnly drill the children into the hopes outlined therein. My old Book says, "Preach the Word." Shall we hear from the pulpits and through the press, and in the class room, the prophecies of A. J. Battenfield? If the preachers and teachers are induced, (by momentary excitement), to do so, will they preach that all Jews are to be converted or killed by (1934)? and that (144,000) are to be converted by (1917)? Will they point to (1926) as the last date for Gentile converts to Christ, before the predicted overthrow? Will they storm the forts of Catholicism with the sorrowful message that their probation ends (1926), because it began (A. D. 666)? Will they carry their charts to their County, State and National Conventions and inform the entranced delegates and awe-stricken brethren that the federated churches must kill off all the Catholics by (1927), for this is predicted? Will the children, (now in their receptive and retentive years), have the seven last plagues of Revelation, and the woes of the trumpets, drilled into their young hearts, as outlined in Mr. Battenfield's diagrams and writings? Will the teachers first *prove* that from (1914 to 1972) is a period God divided? or will they preach the Battenfield division and subdivisions? Shall the Sunday School children be drilled so faithfully that they can tell their companions at play, "The times of the Gentiles ended (Oct. 10, 1913); and J. A. Battenfield came in next day with, 'The Great Demonstration' "? Shall solemn assemblies be held, and intelligent Catholics told that, their doom is fixed and scheduled to end in their death by (1926), because God began to count time against them (A. D. 666)? Will not some historian cite the fact that, they had a line of popes reaching back sixty years, before that, and that (666) is one of the minor dates in the history of the papacy? When the colored charts are unrolled before a Mahometan audience, locating the origin of the Politico-Religious Empire in (637 A. D.), will not the learned Moslem laugh in derision, and point out the fact that, the founder of the Empire had been dead five years, and that they have uniformly dated their empire from (622

A. D.), when Mahomet was accepted as a prophet of God at the Hegira or Flight to Medina? (July 16, 622), is the date from which the Mahometan Calendar began nearly thirteen centuries ago. From this time the Mahometans date their conquest of nearly one-half the then known world. To ignore this fact, in order to substitute a system of dates, is too broad a challenge to the intelligence of men to pass unrebuked.

When the Jewish Rabbi glances at the diagrams, and hears Mr. B. contend that because Ezekiel was silent at the river Chebar that he was DUMB IN TYPE, and that *seven days* were predictive of (2520) *years*, will he not disover a discrepancy of twenty-five hundred and thirteen years in the time seven days would predict, and what Mr. B. *assumes* they predict, to have Ezekiel's dumbness end (April 14, 1914)?

I have seen the Photo-Drama of Creation and heard the lectures; but I had not expected to see a preacher, of the Christian Church, diagram the next fifty-eight years, and write a prophecy, page after page, revealing the future, year by year, of Jews, Catholics, ten federated churches, the Turks, the Mahometans, Great Britain, Germany, France, Russia, Egypt, the yellow race and the whole earth, from (1913 to 1972), so that one can make a Pocket Memorandum and tell what is coming next. I will say more; if Mr. B's. program is to be carried out, as he has detailed it in his elaborate charts and wordy predictions, he would justly be ranked with Moses, Ezekiel, Daniel, Paul and John, as inspired prophet. Otherwise he ranks with false prophets.

REVELATION VERSUS IMAGINATION.

Mr. B. makes much of his base line of (2300) years, and measures from the rise of the "Goat Empire" (328 B. C. to 1972 A. D.) The reader is aware that this measure is (220) years shorter than the Great week, (2520) years. Expositors are undecided where to begin it; whether to count Solar, Lunar or Calendar years; whether it should include the Seventy Weeks of Daniel and begin with them (B. C. 457); and, on many points. Page after page, volume after volume, has been written around these points, with no general agreement being reached. Mr. B. says they have (58) years to run yet and end in (Oct. 10, 1972). That is longer than I expect to be here; and, not being blessed with pre-vision, I can not follow him, when he *predicts the last days*, or time of the end. The people living at that time may *see* things *differently*. I have stripped his base line of all its limbs and leave the naked trunk for time and events to discredit. One single fact, however, may be mentioned: If Mr. B. is correct here then the world, from this day forward, SHOULD KNOW THE VERY DAY THAT ALL THE MARTYRS ARE TO ARISE FROM THE DEAD AND ASSUME THE GOVERNMENT. He has not been explicit as to the day of the week, but it will be (Oct. 11, 1972).

That is ciphering things out a little too well for me, especially when his PREDECESSORS have strewn the date OVER ONE HUNDRED AND FIFTY YEARS. It is enough to know that the Mahometans have dated their empire from (July 16, 622) for the last thirteen centuries, lacking some eight years—twelve years *before* Mahomet's death, and then they had overrun half the world: while Mr. B. dates it at (637) FIVE YEARS AFTER THE FALSE PROPHET AND FOUNDER OF THE RELIGION AND EMPIRE WAS DEAD, (in order to make some dates fit). The prophecy that all Catholics will perish by (1927) is a wild guess of Mr. B's, founded on the easily disproved assumption that, the Catholic church began (A. D. 666) and, *therefore*, all Catholics must *die*, (1260) years later! His prediction that the Jews must be converted in (3½) years from (April, 1914), rests on two colossal assumptions; first that the "long week" should be counted from (607 B. C.), Jehoiachin's captivity; and not from the final captivity and overthrow of the nation under Zedekiah, twenty years later, (587 B. C.), which ends the week (A. D. 1934); and, secondly, his assumption of the Demonstration being in time to answer as WATCHMAN in Ezekiel, the MESSAGE of Nebuchadnezzar, and the John the Baptist HARBINGER periods. This is frivolous romancing.

His ten toes of the Image, and ten horns of the beast, and ten roots of the tree, should be exposed by those who have time and space. The proper fulfillment of the symbols of the Image and Beast is set forth in this volume.   It is evident that Germany, France, Italy, Spain, and Great Britain are not the whole of Europe, or of the Western Empire.   The Pope of Rome ruled over the whole Empire sixty years before Mr. B's. count begins.   Mahomet carved his empire out of the Eastern half of the Empire, both politcically and religiously; and there it is to this day, only as it has been cut short in this restoration period.   If these five governments are five horns, and Persia, Syria, Egypt, Macedonia and Russia are the other five horns, then the "little horn" of (Dan.7) did not rule over the ten kingdoms for (1260) years.   The fact that Mr. B. makes ten federated churches the ten horns of the beast (Rev. 17:12) shows how far one's prejudice against religious movements, in his generation, will sway him to find prophecy to fit them.   He names every horn; makes the Christian Church last to come in, (1912); gives the Catholics (15) years till this federation will kill them; and tells us they will have a pope and that the combination will be called the Anglican Catholic Church.   I knew there was a good deal of opposition to the Federation in some quarters, but had not hoped to see all PROTESTANTISM labeled, and her destiny revealed in quite such definite manner.   I have not consulted the Congregationalists, the Dunkards, the New Lights, or various other religious bodies left out of this enumeration, as to its correctness, and whether it includes all Protestants; but think it will fall short about as much as the five toes do in covering the territory of the Western Empire.

Beginning with (May 9, 1914), Mr. B. romances to the close of his series of articles on the book of Ezekiel.   As Ammon, Moab, Edom, Tyre and other peoples against which Ezekiel uttered his prophecies have perished from the earth, Mr. B. has to revive them to be subjects of the judgments he tells us are now impending over the nations.   So he assumes that Great Britain is the Modern Tyre, and proceeds to tell us, (in his prophetic style), that she is to go down in (1927), and informs us what power will destroy her.   But I hold that, types *never* typify *themselves*.   Under the law of Moses the *animals* burned on the brazen altar did not typify the same sort of sacrifices to be offered under the gospel of

Christ. Aaron did not typify another weak and fallible priest. The temple did not typify another material temple. The bondage in Egypt and deliverance therefrom did not typify a similar national bondage and deliverance for Israel; and this, in turn, to become a duplicate type; (or the Babylonian captivity, destruction of the nation, burning of the temple, and the like, a type of the destruction by Titus and the Roman army six centuries later). And, just now, all these types are to be fulfilled again, and after the same literal manner, this is to fail to distinguish things that differ.

When the types were given, there were higher realities to come later, of which these were only shadows. For instance, the paschal lamb was a type of Christ; the high-priest typified Christ; and the king was a type of Christ, as a spiritual Ruler over all the people of God. The tabernacle was a type of the church. Egyptian or Babylonian captivity or deliverance typified the captivity of the church in sin, or a spiritual deliverance of men. It is evident that ancient, temporal Babylon was only a type used, (with a temporal typical people), of bondage and ultimate deliverance from "Mystery Babylon."

Mr. B. makes one human government typify another human government; Nebuchadnezzar and his carnal war typical of Titus and his carnal war; fleshly Israel, destroyed by the Babyolnians, a type of fleshly Israel destroyed six centuries later by the Romans; and (1927-1935) by the Turks. He hunts for analogies, and gets nowhere as an interpreter. There is not a single prediction made by him concerning the Jews, the Catholics, the federated churches, the Turks, and others that is worthy of serious thought. The predictions of death, (physical death by physical means), is all founded on *supposed analogies* that do not exist. To make Ezekiel's spiritual message a type of the Demonstration; John the Baptist's spiritual message the type of another spiritual message, even the Demonstration; to make Tyre, one marine people, a type of a modern marine people, and apply the predictions of judgment against the former to the latter, is wholly wrong. This is to stammer over the a, b, c, of typology. To say that the tower and idol in the plain of Dura was a type of ten modern federated churches; Nebuchadnezzar a type of an Episcopal pope, (predicted by Mr. B. yet to arise); the three Hebrews in the fiery furnace typical of church members from (1920-1926), that this imagined pope over ten federated church-es will issue his self-exalting decree to last thirty years, (1927-1955), because Darius gave a decree that was in effect for thirty days; and all of such like predictions (for they certainly are human prophecies), is to "reason by analogy." This method of *prophesying* is the ruination not only of the author of the romance as a religious guide; but of all who are mislead by him; "If the blind lead the blind both shall fall into the ditch."

These home-made types and anti-types are all of the same nature. He reasons by analogy, paying no heed to the fact, that he makes one supreme pontiff, Nebuchad-nezzar, the type of another supreme pontiff; Darius, (one supreme earthly ruler), the type of the pope, (yet to be), over ten federated churches; or one earthly affair, the type of another earthly affair of the *same kind*. In fact, the more analogies one can find between ancient and modern men, and ancient and modern nations, the stron-ger is his assertion that they are in the nature of type and anti-type. To illustrate from Mr. B's. pen see the following:

He says, for instance, on Ezekiel (14:21, 22, 23):
"The first thing we should note is that the judg-ments which are about to come have a four-fold nature— famine, evil beasts, the sword and the pestilence. In the Catholic-Protestant strife, which is to end in 1926, many lands will be visited with judgment because of sin; but none of these lands are to be called upon to bear all four of these judgments at the same time. Such an infliction of the united force of the four-fold judgment is reserved for the succeeding war which centers around Jerusalem (1927-1934). Then the famine, the bestial brutality of unrestrained soldiers, the carnage of battle, the gangrene of incurable wounds, and the ashen paleness of pestilence will join forces to work havoc on a *land* and *city* which are to be thoroughly sifted of its people, and the good only spared, with not a rebel left." page 996.

This is Literalism, straight and simple. Note that such a war *was predicted* and *came* against *fleshly* Israel in Ezekiel's days, *when they were carried to Babylon*. Now, Mr. B. would have us believe that, this *fulfilled prediction* is to be *repeated* against *fleshy* Israel, for *rejecting the Lord Jesus Christ*. Not a rebel will be left among the Jews by (1934)! This is to make *one carnal* war a type of *another carnal* war. It makes one *temporal judgment,,* a type of *another temporal judgment.* This is a conceit of Mr. B's and makes temporal rewards and punishments, under the gospel, like the temporal rewards, and punishments under the law. It betrays dense confusion of thought as to the manner of God's dealing with the Jews under the gospel age; and it is this disposition to Judaize that I have been exposing in this whole volume.

When Mr. B. learns that temporal bondage and temporal deliverance under the Mosaic law were not types of the same sort of things under the gospel, he will need to revise his Demonstration from end to end. He will discover that a series of prophecies in Ezekiel concerning "famine, evil beasts, the sword and pestilence" were fulfilled against unhappy Israel, and were in harmony with the law under which they were then living; but that each and all are withdrawn under the gospel, or as *punishments* for *rejecting Christ,* or *disobeying* the *gospel.* Then his so-called ANALOGIES will disappear. He can not then affirm, so confidently, that like experiences await cities, nations, prophets, priests, kings, prophetesses, and all classes, today, to those who lived in Ezekiel's time, and were the subjects of his prophecies. THE CASES ARE NOT PARALLEL. Hence, his pet theory that, the nations and peoples are to be mutually hostile to and will slaughter each other, "As in the day of Midian," will be seen to be simply a conceit of his founded upon supposed analogy that does not exist; and, hence, THE WHOLE SCHEME IS A ROMANCE.

His schedule of the seven last wars, in which Catholics, who do not repent, are all literally killed by (1927); all Jews, who do not accept Christ, are killed by (1935), with not a rebel left; and, on and on, till (1972), when the whole race has become extinct on earth, (except the saints); is only possible to a romancer who makes *famine* a *type* of *famine*; evil *beasts* a *type* of *evil beasts*; the *sword* a *type* of the *sword*; *pestilence* a *type* of *pestilence*; and the *temporal* a *type* of the *temporal*, throughout. As I have showed at length, that all types of Christ and the church were simply shadows of good things yet to come, when they were given, and they were, in their very nature and use, only for a limited time, the reader can detect at once the weakness of all such productions as Mr. B's.

As these types passed away with the introduction of the gospel, and the Jews are in rebellion against Christ, their lawful King, it should be evident that the rebellious people are now condemned by the *gospel* and *its* penalties.

So I regard Mr. B's. long, verbose statement of analogies as simply a romance. It is not possible to conclude that blood and famine, evil beasts and pestilence are at the door of the impenitent for their rejection of Christ.

There were judgments *predicted*, and faithfully *meted out* to the *Jews* under the *former* dispensation, or the law of Moses. A good way to test the strength of this romance is this: If the Jews would accept Christ, would the Lord bless them, temporally, as he did under the law of Moses? This is decided at once by learning whether He gave the apostles and early Jewish converts land, houses, and plenteous fruits and crops in Palestine *when they obeyed the gospel.* You are aware that the Jewish converts, "took joyfully the spoiling of their goods," knowing in themselves they had a better, an enduring substance. We can not mix the law and the gospel, and affirm that a temporal reward or a temporal punishment will fall upon a people, *in our days, because* it *was promised* or *threatened* against a people living under *another law,* and was *fulfilled* to *that* people. As well assume that we should offer our children as Abraham offered Isaac, that we may show our faith!

It is not for mortal men to say how many wars are yet ahead of the race; what year they will come, the issues involved; how many Catholics will be killed; or when the Jews go out by the Turks; when the nations are all destroyed; and tell us when the Millennium begins over the graves of the slaughtered race. Of one thing I am sure: Mr. B. has no helpful message for anybody. His wild speculations, (founded upon supposed ANAL-OGIES), are only dreams, not interpretations. His disposition to make literal the very wars, famines, sword, and bloodshed of ancient Israel, contending with other temporal nations, as God's method of punishing the Jews who reject Christ now, and to set the *very year* when there will not be *a rebel left,* is certainly pitiable in one who seeks to expound prophecy. One should see that Israel, under Joshua, entered and conquered Palestine by a series of miracles. There is no Joshua to lead

Israel into Palestine now; but a Lord Jesus to take them to their *anti-typical home* if they obey HIM.   To affirm so confidently that, the nations of earth are *all* to be destroyed by (1972), and send such *speculations* broadcast as GOD'S CHALLENGE TO THE NATIONS, beggars description.   I think we may safely say that, there is not a single war predicted by the Demonstration, *that is predicted in the Bible*; and not one which it is reasonable to conclude will ever take place.   The result of all such speculation is to discredit the Bible with a certain class, especially its prophecies.   I could heartily wish Mr. B. had never indulged his imagination in the production of such a manifestly erroneous exposition of the holy prophecies.

Mr. B. has a reason for every calamity he predicts. Jesus preached three and a half years; *therefore* the Jews now have three and a half years to gather in the (144,-000).   The apostles went to the Gentiles later; *therefore* the Gentiles are to yield the great harvest later.   Darius issued a decree that no man should make any request of God or man for thirty days; and, if he did, should be cast into the lion's den; *therefore* the pope, yet to arise, will issue a decree good for thirty years, (1927-1955). Daniel was preserved one night in the lion's den; *therefore*, the faithful will be preserved (30) years.   The king of Babylon built a tower, erected an idol, and made proclamation that all his subjects must worship that idol or be cast into a fiery furnace; *therefore*, ten federated churches (including the peaceful Quakers) are to persecute all who do not bow to federation, and these are to be in the fiery furnace (1920-1926); and this same federation is to kill off all Catholics by (1927).   Nebuchadnezzar was driven from men to herd with beasts till seven times passed over him; then he issued a message to the nations; *therefore*, the Demonstration should begin, and did begin, (2520) years later to a day.   Ezekiel sat amazed *seven days* then gave the Jews a message; *therefore*, after *nine hundred and seven thousand two hundred days*, Mr. B. should enlarge his Demonstration!   The Lord, through his inspired prophets, challenged the idolaters to produce a true prophecy; *therefore* the Demonstration should challenge the Catholics, Jews, and all classes.   As all of Mr. B's. predictions of war and vio-

lence, famine, pestilence and death are based upon supposed analogies, and the analogies do not exist, because
we are living under another law, and famine, pestilence,
the sword and evil beasts are not threatened judgments
for the violation of it. I need not elaborate this phase
of the subject further. Please see the chapters on "Literalism and Israel;" "A Two-Fold Error;" and "Age
of the Human Race."

Mr. B. should know that God designed *seven* days
to predict a silence for Ezekiel of nine hundred seven
thousand two hundred days; and that God designed the
Demonstration to be as positively a warning of physical
death to the human race as Mr. B. has pictured, or he
should not hazard such a group of predictions. To me
they are, mildly speaking, a romance. But their terrifying message may startle the unlearned. I can not hope
to make plainer the reasons I hold for so characterizing
his writing. The Types settle the whole issue. I apprehend that we shall all be made wiser as the years
roll by freighted with their blessings and fulfillments of
divine prophecy. I have sought to remain wholly within
the rules of interpretation set forth by Christ and the
apostles. I know the types in temporal Israel foretold
spiritual realities, for the whole New Testament is my
book of evidence. I know these types did not typify
themselves; and I lay down my pen with the sincere
prayer that the readers of this imperfect volume, may
fear to offend God by endorsing or advancing any theory
of prophecy that ignores the fundamental fact that, prophecy is a divine system, and the typical features being
legislated away forever, can never be revived or repeated.